PREHISTORIC SETTLEMENT PATTERNS IN THE TEXCOCO REGION, MEXICO

MEMOIRS OF THE MUSEUM OF ANTHROPOLOGY
UNIVERSITY OF MICHIGAN
NUMBER 3

PREHISTORIC SETTLEMENT PATTERNS IN THE TEXCOCO REGION, MEXICO

By

JEFFREY R. PARSONS

Contributions by Richard E. Blanton and Mary H. Parsons

ANN ARBOR

1971

CONTENTS

TABLES

MAPS

FIGURES

PLATES

ACKNOWLEDGEMENTS

This project has grown out of a long period of association with the personnel of the Teotihuacan Valley Project (Sanders, 1965) beginning in 1961. As far as I can determine, the realization of the value and utility of intensive regional archaeological surveys over the whole Valley of Mexico originated with William T. Sanders, the director of the Teotihuacan Valley Project between 1960 and 1964. It was through Sanders that my own interests became focused on central Mexico, and much of my own methodological and theoretical orientation has developed directly from my involvement with his work during my graduate student years.

The resources and facilities of the University of Michigan Museum of Anthropology have permitted me to devote large blocks of time over the past two years to both the fieldwork and report-writing phases of this present project. The bulk of our financial support was provided by the National Science Foundation (Grant GS 1617). A National Science Foundation grant for undergraduate research participation (GY 4639) also provided support for two undergraduate field assistants. In Mexico our fieldwork was greatly facilitated by the courteous cooperation of the Instituto Nacional de Antropolgía e Historia, whose directors and personnel supplied us with necessary permits for survey and export papers for our ceramic type collections. The office of the Presidente Municipal at Chimalhuacan, Estado de Mexico, was most helpful in sanctioning our investigations in the Chimalhuacan area and in granting us access to the large collection of prehispanic artifacts in the Municipio's museum.

Sr. Benito Hernández of Texcoco very kindly assisted us in hiring four local workmen, and placed a section of his own house at our disposal for use as a ceramic laboratory. He and his large and amiable family often went far out of their way to aid us in a great variety of ways.

I am much indebted to Dr. Rene Millon and his associates of the Teotihuacan Mapping Project for allowing us to examine in detail their ceramic type collections at San Juan Teotihuacan. In particular I thank Mrs. Evelyn Rattray for her interest and patience in examing several of our surface collections whose chronological placements were not wholly clear to our own less practiced eyes.

Sincere thanks are due Dr. Angel Palerm and several of his students at the Universidad Iberoamericana and the Escuela de Antropología in Mexico City. They participated in some parts of our fieldwork, and expressed strong interest in the project throughout its course.

My student assistants deserve the highest commendation for their unflagging fortitude and high spirits in the face of several months of taxing physical exertion, poor food, cultural isolation, and Moctezuma's revenge:

Survey supervisors:	Richard Blanton, Robert Hirning, Mary Hrones, Theron Price
Field Assistants:	Susan Caswell, Rosemary Cross, E. William Jowdy, JoAn Moran
Lab Supervisor:	Nancy Ryanen

I am also grateful to a number of people who have assisted in the tedious and time-consuming tasks of preparing descriptions and illustrations of artifacts and sites. Virginia Currath very diligently tabulated masses of climatic data and prepared most of the sherd profiles used in this report. Richard Blanton did the tracing of our 1:25,000 topographic base map, and was responsible for measuring the surface areas of modern communities and tabulating population figures from maps and census lists. He also prepared most of the ceramic descriptions which appear in Appendix I. George Stuber and Chris Moser very generously contributed their time and skills to the preparation of several photographic plates. To my wife Mary has fallen a wide variety of miscellaneous tasks. She has contributed substantially to the section on site descriptions (Chapter 2 and Appendix II), and prepared most of the site maps and floor plans. It would be difficult to fully express my appreciation for her patience and devotion throughout the entire course of preparing this report for final publication.

Finally, I express my sincere thanks to several colleagues whose comments and criticisms on several sections of this report in manuscript form have contributed significantly to my interpretations and general orientation. In particular, William T. Sanders and Kent V. Flannery have both been highly generous of their time. I have not always followed their advice, but have often been considerably enlightened by their suggestions. Pedro Armillas, James B. Griffin, Robert McC. Adams, and Peter Tscholl have also provided me with a variety of insightful observations. I accept full responsibility for whatever uses (or misuses) I have made of their commentary.

I am most grateful to the University of Michigan Horace H. Rackham School of Graduate Studies for providing financial assistance toward the publication of this monograph from the Horace H. Rackham Endowment.

J. R. Parsons

I

INTRODUCTION

GENERAL BACKGROUND

For over 2000 years the Valley of Mexico has been a key nuclear area in Mesoamerica. In prehispanic times this region was the locus of major Classic and Postclassic power centers whose influences were pan-Mesoamerican. The Valley of Mexico has retained this cultural dominance throughout the colonial and republican eras, and up to the present day.

In 1960 a symposium of anthropologists sought to formally direct and stimulate the attention of social science research to the Valley of Mexico. At that time the conference chairman (E. R. Wolf) drew up a listing of 13 specific research objectives to which interest could profitably be directed (Sanders n.d.):

1) Changes in the natural and man-made environment of the Valley of Mexico over time and the possible correlation of these changes with cultural factors.

2) The antiquity, development, and relative importance of major and minor patterns of land use over time.

3) The characteristics of settlement in the Valley and changes in settlement patterns over time and related population problems.

4) The nature of the relationships between hamlets, villages, towns, cities, and similar units at various periods including a discussion of relations between specific sites.

5) Problems of urbanization.

6) The characteristics of symbiotic regions in the Valley in various periods of time and their social consequences.

7) The relevance of environment to agriculture and settlement patterns, and to the problems of social controls at various levels.

8) Patterns of ceremonial control at various time levels.

9) Patterns of political control at various time levels.

10) Patterns of warfare in the prehispanic period.

11) Effects of the Spanish conquest and colonization on social and cultural groups in the Valley of Mexico.

12) Cultural persistence or change in major patterns throughout all known time periods within the Valley.

13) Causal or functional relationships between various cultural patterns at different time levels.

This same year (1960) also saw the inception of the Teotihuacan Valley Project, directed by W. T. Sanders. Modelled after the pioneering Virú Valley Project, Sanders' research design was directed toward several specific objectives (Sanders, n.d. 1):

1) To trace the origin and history of developments in prehistoric agriculture such as irrigation, terracing, chinampas, the colonization of marginal lands, and maguey cultivation.

2) The definition and history of rural and small urban community types during the prehistoric periods.

3) The demographic history of the Valley from the earliest human occupation to the period of the Spanish Conquest.

However, Sanders and his co-workers viewed this work as the initiation of a long-term program of systematic archaeological survey and excavation which would eventually incorporate the entire Valley of Mexico. The ultimate goal was to contribute to an evaluation of the Valley of Mexico's key role in the prehispanic cultural development of Mesoamerica.

The Texcoco Region Project is the second major field program to be undertaken within the framework of the broader program envisioned for the Valley of Mexico as a whole. Several factors predicated its selection as the immediate follow-up to the Teotihuacan Valley Project. First, its proximity to the previously-studied area, thereby reducing to a minimum spatial variations in ceramic types and assemblages defined in the Teotihuacan Valley. Second, it represented a discrete, well-defined topographic unit, whose significant geographical features had been outlined, and for which there had been some antecedent archaeological investigation (e.g., Wolf and Palerm, 1955; Palerm and Wolf, 1954-55; Dixon 1963, 1966; Hicks and Nicholson, 1964; Noguera, 1943; Apenes, 1943).

Third, the principal investigator was personally better acquainted with the Texcoco Region than with other sectors of the Valley of Mexico aside from the Teotihuacan Valley.

PURPOSE AND SCOPE

The Texcoco Region Project represents a direct outgrowth in orientation, objectives, and methodology of the antecedent Teotihuacan Valley Project. Its organization, however, is somewhat different. Instead of proceeding from start to finish as a single five-year program, we have preferred to operate in terms of a series of one- or two-year projects, each of these a complete and independent program, whose specific objectives, procedures, and research designs are structured and determined by results of preceding work. Thus, we envision a highly flexible program, to proceed at several different and logically related levels. Separate field programs can be spaced in quick succession, or can be delayed for a period of time in accordance with a wide variety of considerations.

The 1967 segment of the Texcoco Region Project was the pilot phase of our fieldwork program in this area. During the six-month period between late May and the end of November, our aim was to carry out intensive surface surveys over as much territory as could be feasibly examined. Our main objective was to delineate the main configurations of prehispanic settlement for all major periods from Formative through Postclassic times. It was expected that the results of this work would serve as the base from which to structure the designs of a variety of future research projects aimed at testing and evaluating a specific set of problems and hypotheses defined in the course of our initial survey program. Our data would be additionally meaningful in view of the antecedent body of comparable information accumulated from the adjacent Teotihuacan Valley (Sanders, 1965).

Thus this report is by no means intended to present a complete analysis of all information and sources of data bearing on prehispanic occupation in the Texcoco Region. We have not yet carried out specific geographic, ecological, geomorphological, palynological, ethnographic, or archival studies—all of which will one day be required to explain a wide variety of settlement features. Neither have we attempted an exhaustive search of potentially relevant published documentary sources. Rather, up to this point, we have relied on the most easily available of the limited published studies of environment and modern land use, together with the best known and most accessible documentary sources. One of the major functions of our investigation should be to stimulate and orient specific research programs which could be undertaken by geographers, geologists, paleobotanists, ethnographers, and ethnohistorians interested in an interdisciplinary approach to archaeological problems in the Texcoco Region and the Valley of Mexico.

In structuring the content of the interpretative and comparative sections of this report, we have attempted to restrict ourselves to problems and data that have a fairly direct bearing on the character and configuration of prehispanic occupation in the Texcoco Region. Nevertheless, at several points the implications of our own findings, and the ramifications of a variety of related phenomena have tempted (and required) us to go somewhat farther afield. However, we are making no attempt to construct a general synthesis or overview of Mesoamerican cultural development. Our major concern has been to present a body of data in such a way that it will have a permanent and enduring value for Mesoamericanists.

NATURAL ENVIRONMENT

For purposes of the survey, the Texcoco Region is defined as that area extending from the eastern edge of Lake Texcoco eastward to the foothills of the Sierra Madre Oriental (a distance of about 25 km). Its northern and southern borders are respectively fixed by the Patlachique Range (a rugged westward-trending spur of the Sierra Madre Oriental), and a line of high hills including Cerro Chimalhuacan and Cerro Texolotl. This region comprises about 700 square km, and forms a well-defined natural topographic unit situated immediately south of the Teotihuacan Valley in the eastern Valley of Mexico (Pl. 1; Map 2).

The Valley of Mexico—General Environmental Characteristics

The Valley of Mexico is a large internal drainage basin whose lowest point lies somewhat below 2240 meters above sea level. Situated near the southern end of the central

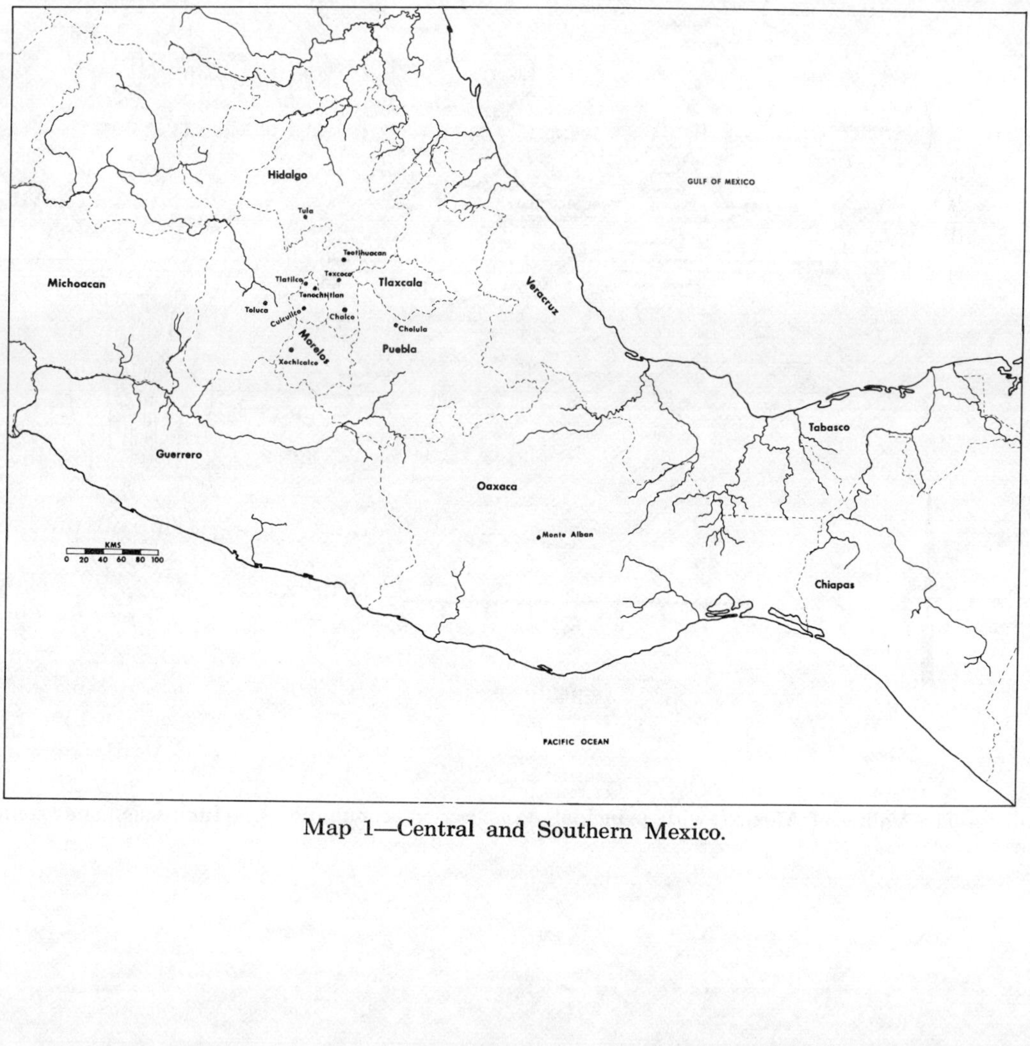

Map 1—Central and Southern Mexico.

Map 2—The Valley of Mexico, with principal Aztec-period communities. (Impressionistic contour lines.)

Mexican *altiplano* (Map 1), it measures roughly 130 km north-south and 60 km east-west. This irregular elliptical depression is rimmed on the west, south, and east by high rugged mountain ranges of volcanic origin, whose highest peaks approach 4300 meters above sea level. A number of extinct volcanic peaks and ranges within the Valley of Mexico itself set off several distinct subregions of varying size. At the time of the Spanish conquest a large, continuous lake system occupied roughly 1000 square km of the central basin.

As a whole the area fits into Palerm and Wolf's (1960: 13) Central Highland Type I, Variant B ecological type, characterized as "Cold. Dry for the better part of the year, with abundant rain in summer." Nevertheless, the region is one of great natural diversity, with a series of closely juxtaposed environmental zones as one proceeds upward in altitude from the lake, to the low-lying lakeshore plain, across a gently sloping piedmont, over gentle slopes onto steeper slopes, and ultimately into the rugged mountains themselves. Although the volcanically derived soils seem to be of about equal fertility over the whole of the Valley, those of lower, flatter areas are deeper and capable of retaining moisture over longer periods of time. Moving upslope in any direction one encounters progressively shallower soil cover, greater surface erosion, and an increasingly deep water table. Rainfall tends to increase at higher elevations. Lower areas are more subject to frost damage than hillslopes. The higher hillslopes rimming the basin sustain a heavy oak-conifer vegetation. At lower elevations natural vegetation has been completely altered through several millennia of intensive agriculture.

Annual rainfall averages about 700 to 800 mm, falling almost wholly within the summer months, but varies from a high of about 1500 mm on the southeastern slopes of the basin to 1000 mm on the Chalco plain in the southeast, to 500 or 600 mm in the drier northern third of the basin (Sanders, 1965: 20). In any particular local area precipitation tends to be erratic and nonuniform both at a single point in time (i.e., rain may fall heavily in one locality, while only a short distance away no rain occurs), and from one year to the next. Rains may also begin as early as April, or be delayed until mid June. A similar situation exists with respect to the onset and cessation of frosts in the spring and fall.

The central segment of the lake system (Lake Texcoco), into which the northern and southern lakes drained, was salty; the northern segment (Lakes Zumpango-Xaltocan) was somewhat less so; while the southern segment (Lakes Chalco-Xochimilco) was fresh. Thus, *chinampa* cultivation (West and Armillas, 1950; M. Coe, 1964; Sanders, 1965: 22) was most feasible in Lake Chalco-Xochimilco, less so in the Lake Zumpango-Xaltocan Region, and of very limited utility in the Lake Texcoco area.

In addition to its great utility as an artery of transportation and communication, the lake system offered a variety of important resources. Probably most significant were the great numbers of waterfowl, both permanent and migratory, which nested in large expanses of marshland around the edges of the lake. Fishing, together with the collection of aquatic plants and insect larvae, were of some importance in late prehispanic and historic times. (Linne, 1948). The only source of salt in the Valley of Mexico was the salt-saturated soil around the shoreline of Lake Texcoco. A fair amount of documentary data (Mendizabal, 1946: 277-85; Anglerius, 1628: 188) indicate that salt production was of some importance in this area at the time of the Spanish conquest and in the Colonial period.

Limestone, an important item in prehispanic and historic times, is unavailable throughout most of the basin where volcanic activity has been recent and rock outcrops are exclusively volcanic in origin. Only along the northern edge of the basin, in the vicinity of Zumpango, Hueypoxtla, and Tequixquiac does limestone outcrop in any abundance. Here the quarrying and burning of limestone were important commercial activities in the early Colonial period (Gibson, 1964: 36).

Rock suitable for building material and grinding tools is abundantly distributed throughout the Valley of Mexico. Cutting and scraping tools were manufactured primarily from flint and obsidian. Little or nothing is known concerning the source of flint or other siliceous stone. The only known obsidian sources in the basin are the relatively small outcrops near Otumba in the southeastern corner of the Teotihuacan Valley. Huge obsidian quarries are known from southern Hidalgo (Holmes, 1900; Spence and Parsons, 1967) at the northeastern edge of the Valley of Mexico.

The repertoire of aboriginal food crops in the central Mexican *altiplano* is quite diverse. Principal items include several varieties of maize and amaranth, beans, and squashes—all of which grow best on well-watered, deep soils. Maguey, important as the source of the mildly alcoholic, nutritious beverage pulque, and for fibers, thrives readily on badly eroded slopes with thin soil cover where little else will grow. Nopal cactus, whose edible leaf and sugary fruit are important foods in this area today, occupies a similar marginal niche.

The Texcoco Region—General Environmental Characteristics

Tables 1, 2, and 3 present monthly precipitation averages, maximum-minimum temperature averages, and occurrences of frosts over a five-year period (1962 through 1966). These figures were compiled by us from records in the meteorological station at Chapingo Agricultural College. This station, the only one in the Texcoco Region, is situated just south of the modern town of Texcoco. Generally speaking, the intensity of rainfall increases at higher eleva-

TABLE 1

PRECIPITATION

Monthly Averages (mm)

Month	1962	1963	1964	1965	1966	5-yr. Average
Jan.	0.0	0.9	7.7	3.0	10.3	4.4
Feb.	3.4	0.2	0.0	26.5	6.5	7.3
March	6.7	25.2	10.0	0.0	57.7	19.9
April	82.6	27.1	11.8	18.2	31.5	34.2
May	22.7	47.2	98.5	43.4	7.4	43.8
June	95.7	99.1	189.9	82.3	55.2	104.4
July	42.9	178.8	97.4	105.6	173.9	119.7
Aug.	105.8	114.0	66.0	164.0	116.9	113.3
Sept.	85.3	106.1	105.2	117.8	53.9	93.7
Oct.	92.5	25.3	32.2	48.6	49.2	49.6
Nov.	4.7	1.5	5.0	0.0	0.0	2.2
Dec.	8.1	11.9	6.7	22.3	4.8	10.8
TOTAL	550.4	637.3	630.4	631.7	567.3	603.3

TABLE 2
MAXIMUM-MINIMUM TEMPERATURES (°C)
Monthly Averages

Month	1962		1963		1964		1965		1966		5-yr. Average	
	Max.	Min.	Max.	Min.	Max.	Min.	Max.	Min.	Max.	Min.	Max.	Min.
Jan.	24.2	0.8	24.3	0.3	22.7	2.6	22.0	--0.9	22.2	2.5	23.1	1.1
Feb.	26.4	1.7	23.8	0.4	25.7	2.7	23.2	2.0	23.6	4.7	24.5	2.3
March	27.8	4.6	27.1	5.5	27.4	4.1	27.4	3.8	24.8	3.6	26.9	4.3
April	25.2	6.4	29.7	6.7	29.6	6.7	27.3	5.5	25.9	6.1	27.5	6.3
May	28.0	7.7	27.3	8.4	27.3	8.5	28.6	7.9	27.7	5.9	27.8	7.7
June	27.1	8.5	25.7	10.4	24.5	10.0	29.0	9.5	26.2	9.6	26.5	9.6
July	25.6	8.8	23.6	9.5	24.7	8.7	24.1	9.5	24.5	9.5	24.5	9.2
Aug.	25.7	9.0	24.2	9.1	25.3	7.7	23.0	10.3	24.0	9.4	24.4	9.1
Sept.	24.0	10.1	22.9	8.9	24.8	9.1	24.3	8.6	23.4	9.1	23.9	9.2
Oct.	24.4	7.0	21.6	7.5	23.2	4.3	22.8	6.3	23.0	6.8	23.0	6.4
Nov.	24.0	0.9	23.4	3.1	23.7	3.3	24.9	2.0	22.9	0.8	23.8	2.0
Dec.	22.7	3.3	22.6	2.2	22.1	1.8	23.8	1.9	21.8	0.3	22.6	1.9

TABLE 3
NUMBER OF DAYS WITH FROST

Year	March	April	May	June	Oct.	Nov.
1962	10	3	4	3	5	23
1963	7	7	0	0	5	8
1964	0	0	2	0	8	2
1965	4	2	0	0	3	15
1966	2	0	3	0	1	15

tions to the east and south. Furthermore, the severity of frost activity tends to be somewhat reduced on the piedmont slopes relative to the main alluvial plain where the meteorological station is located.

The critical relationship between rainfall, frost, and agricultural productivity and dependability in the central highlands of Mexico has been discussed and elaborated at some length (e.g., Sanders, 1956; 1965, 1968; Palerm, 1960). We wish to re-emphasize here the basic importance of artificial humidity control in achieving high, dependable agricultural productivity in this region. Table 1 shows that the cultivation of maize, beans, and squash is restricted to the rainy summer season between late May and early October. The successful germination of seeds and maturation of plants during other parts of the annual cycle are severely restricted by inadequate rainfall and even more so by severe winter frosts. Killing frosts occur practically every day in December, January, and February. Table 3 indicates that frosts are also common in November and March, and occur with some frequency in October. Frosts are also recorded for April and May, and even for June in 1962. Only July, August, and September were completely frost free during the five-year period for which we have records.

When the behavior of frost is correlated with that of rainfall, we find that the timing of planting and harvesting becomes particularly critical. The onset of the full rainy season may occasionally be delayed until well into June. However, if planting is also delayed to this point, there is serious danger of having the immature crop partially or wholly destroyed by killing frosts in October. On the other hand, if planting is done in mid-May, or earlier, thus giving adequate time for full crop maturation before any possible danger from frost in October, there is a good possibility that seeds dependent upon rainfall for moisture will not germinate because of the delayed onset of the rains. Thus, except in a few restricted locations where a natural high water table permits early planting, there is strong selectivity for the development of artificial mechanisms for supplying water to plants during the critical planting stage in May or early June. Rainfall is normally adequate throughout July and August, and there is much less need for artificial watering devices during these months.

The Texcoco Region—Natural Zones and Modern Occupation

The Texcoco Region includes four principal natural zones (Wolf and Palerm, 1955: 266-68) which occur as roughly parallel bands between the lakeshore on the west and the high crest of the Sierra Madre Oriental on the east (Map 3).

1) The *Sierra zone* forms the rugged eastern division of the Texcoco Region, rising rapidly from the 2750 meter contour line to well over 4000 meters along the continental divide to the east. This is a rugged, precipitous area, today devoid of any permanent habitation. Along its lowermost western flanks, agricultural fields have been cleared in small valley bottoms and along the tops of long, gently sloping ridges and spurs. Here maize is raised up to about 2800 meters, and the last wheat and barley fields disappear at roughly 3000 meters. The hillsides and narrow valley floors are heavily forested, with oaks and conifers the dominant species. As one moves upward, conifers gradually replace oaks, and the tops of the highest peaks (Cerro Tlaloc and Cerro Tolapan) rise just above the treeline. The soft needle-carpeted pathways, tiny sparkling rivulets, and quiet cool fragrance of this isolated wooded zone provide a welcome and striking contrast to the sun baked, erosion scarred, and densely populated areas below.

Despite its lack of permanent occupation, the Sierra plays an important role in the exploitative pattern of numerous communities situated in the piedmont flanks below. Herds of cattle, mules, and horses graze on the lush grassy cover that extends over much of the Sierra. Timber for construction, fuel, and charcoal burning is continuously carried and dragged down from the mountain slopes. A number of isolated permanent springs strung out along the lower western flanks provide water for household uses and some garden terrace irrigation at several piedmont villages. A few deer and smaller mammals are occasionally hunted.

2) The *Upper Piedmont zone* (100 square km) (the "Arid Zone" of Wolf and Palerm, 1955) extends westward from the foot of the Sierra at 2750 meters to approximately the 2500-meter contour where a noticeable flattening and lowering of the terrain marks the uppermost limit of the Lower Piedmont. Modern settlement in this area is limited to a half dozen dispersed villages strung out along the juncture of the Sierra and the Upper Piedmont (Map 4) (Pl. 11, 12). These communities have been characterized by Wolf and Palerm (1955: 266):

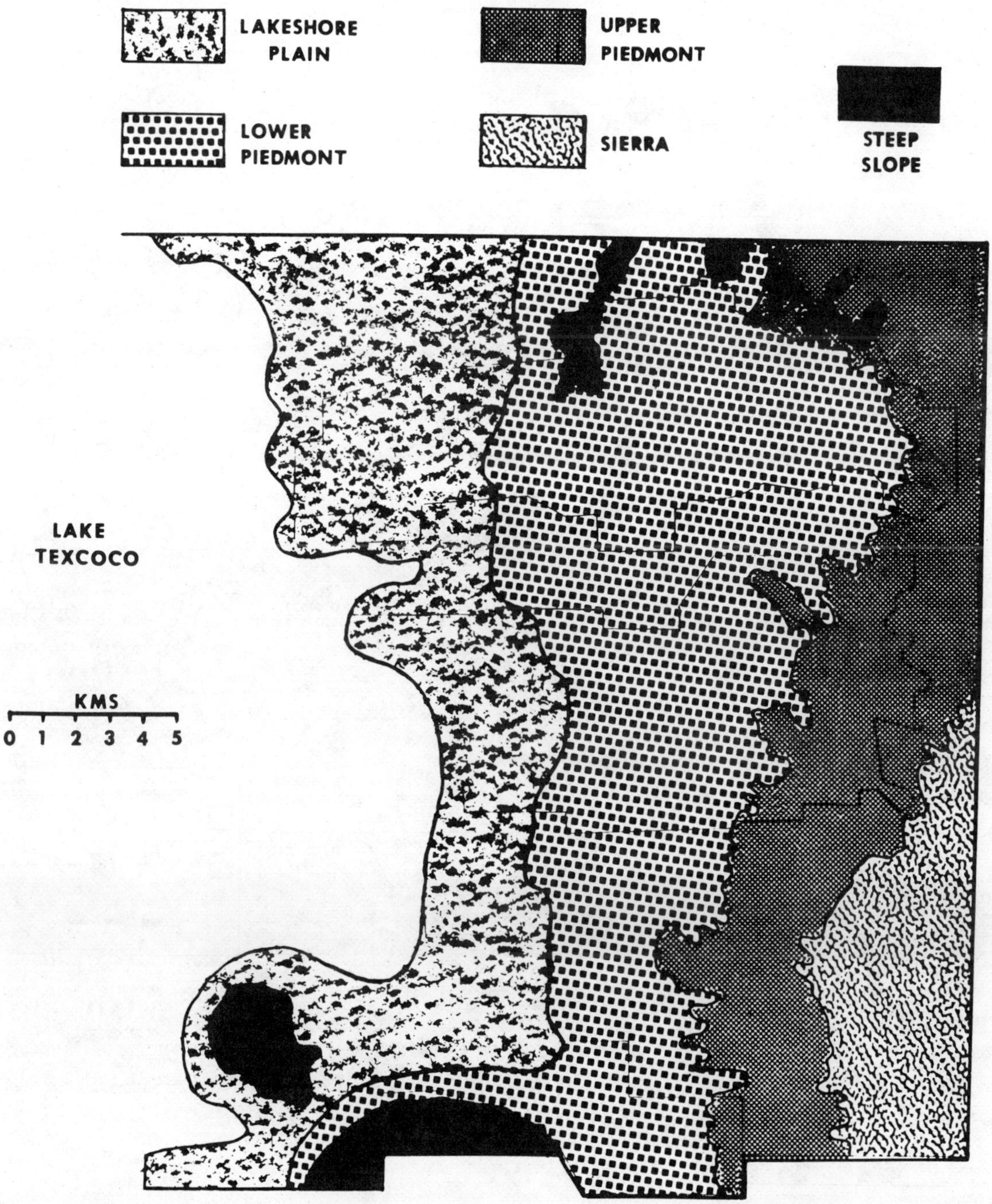

Map 3—Texcoco Region: principal natural zones.

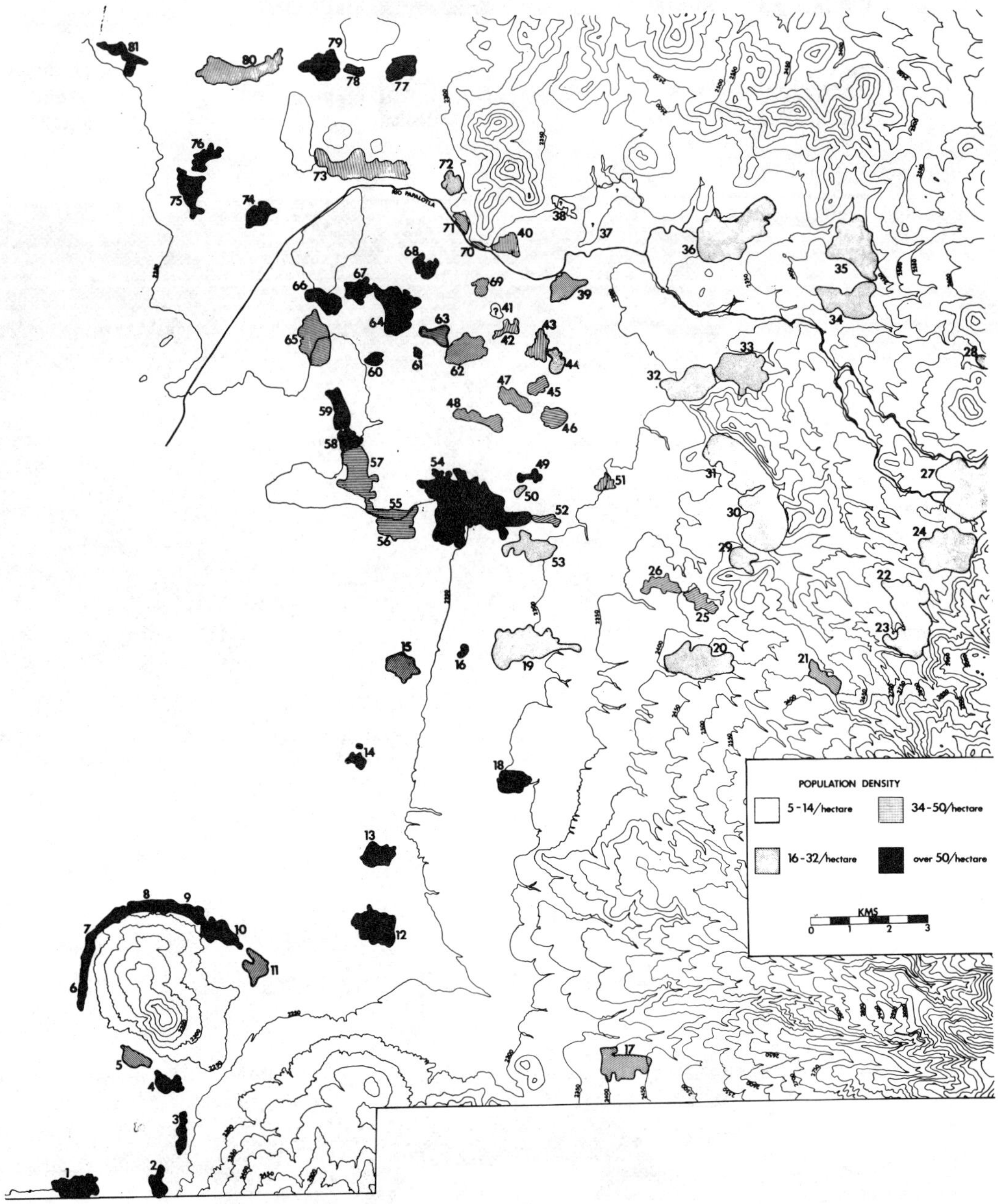

Map 4—Modern Occupation of the Texcoco Region. Contour interval 50 meters.

Each of these . . . communities has a church and a small plaza, but dwelling units are widely scattered, each house with its own garden, vasiform granary, and sweatbath standing apart from the others. Crops are grown on levelled plots of uneven dimension, hedged about by maguey plants. The main food crops are wheat and corn, both of which are grown primarily for subsistence. Barley and rye are also grown. Wheat is preferred since it resists frosts and is thus more secure than corn. A few flowers are grown for sale in Valley towns, but *pulque*—produced from the maguey—and wood burned to charcoal are the main products sold for cash in the lower piedmont and flatland communities. Some hunting is carried on for both food and pleasure.

The remaining, lower, section of the Texcocan Upper Piedmont consists of empty, barren, though occasionally spectacular, badland country. Numerous deep, narrow barrancas have gouged themselves 15 to 30 meters into the sloping surface, and wholesale sheet erosion has completely removed practically all topsoil (Pl. 3, 4). Scattered erosional remnants reveal that even the underlying hardpan subsoil (*tepatate*) has been stripped off over huge areas for depths of two to four meters. Each new rainfall wears away the loose edges of surviving soil patches, and watercourses fill with incredible speed during heavy storms when even the deepest barrancas are choked with rushing red-brown water cutting ever deeper into the scarred land surface.

Along some barranca bottoms there has been sufficient preservation to suggest something of the former character of soil and vegetation in the Upper Piedmont. Here, in narrow linear bands along the watercourses, there are topsoil deposits up to one meter deep, supporting a thick mixed oak-conifer vegetation (Pl. 4*b*, 13). Over the rest of the land, except for scattered erosional remnants where small patches of maize and beans dependent upon rainfall cultivation are grown, only an occasional hardy scrub bush or tuft of long grass breaks the bleak monotony of the sterile tan-brown landscape (Pl. 11, 12, 13).

3) The *Lower Piedmont zone* (197 square km) consists of the gently sloping terrain below 2500 meters, which merges into the flat Lakeshore Plain at approximately 2275 meters (Pl. 2, 6, 8, 9, 10). The transition from the Upper to the Lower Piedmont is marked by lower slope angle, deeper soils, greatly reduced sheet erosion, and abrupt shift in character of barrancas. These latter features are shallow and narrow relative to their rampaging and deeply downcut antecedents in the Upper Piedmont. Most of these barranca systems carry significant quantities of water only during the rainy season (May through September). Only the Rio Papalotla and Rio Jalopango, running between Texcoco and Tepetlaoxtoc in the north, have year-round flows of any consequence. In addition to the unique quality of these permanent watercourses, the floodplain of the Rio Papalotla-Jalopango drainage system forms a larger expanse of low-lying, gently sloping ground than occurs elsewhere in the Lower Piedmont of the Texcoco Region. Relative to the southern two-thirds of the Texcoco Region, the Lower Piedmont is considerably more extensive in the northern segment of our survey area (Map 3).

Modern population in the Lower Piedmont is clustered in two distinct bands (Map 4):

a) A series of dispersed and seminucleated villages stretching across the upper end, including Coatepec in the far south; Tequesquinahuac, San Dieguito, Nativitas, San Nicolas Tlaminca, San Miguel Tlaixpan, Purificacion, San Joaquin Ixtlilxochitl, and San Juan Tezontla in the center; San Bernardino Tlamimilolpa, San Pedro Chiautzingo, and Tepetlaoxtoc in the north.

Wolf and Palerm (1955: 267) have observed that

These piedmont villages grow corn for subsistence and flowers for sale in Mexico City flower markets. Fruit trees are cultivated, and fruit is sometimes sold, sometimes bartered for such lake products as moth eggs collected by the people on the lake shore. San Joaquin Ixtlilxochitl resembles the flat land communities in possessing an artisan speciality, the production of powder for fireworks.

Cultivation seems to be much more intensive in the [Lower] Piedmont than in the Sierra [our Upper Piedmont], and agricultural methods show greater care. Especially at San Miguel Tlaixpan and San Nicolas Tlaminca, agriculture is carried on on irrigated terraces, carefully built of adobe and stone. Plants are allowed to mature in seedbeds before transplanting. Flowers raised for the market are covered to protect them against frost. Animal fertilizer is collected and in general use. Water distribution is handled by a communal body of water commissioners (*regidores de agua*), and each landowner receives water once every Mesoamerican month of twenty days. The amount of water distributed to each person depends on the size of the terraces owned by him. Small storage tanks, situated on the terraces are used to conserve water for household use. . . .

In comparison with the Sierra [our Upper Piedmont] villages, dwelling units in the piedmont communities tend to cluster around the church and plaza, but the settlement pattern in general still shows more dispersion than in the flat land below. At San Miguel Tlaixpan and San Nicolas Tlaminca, houses are usually located on or near agricultural terraces [Plate 7].

b) The broad gentle slopes below this band of Lower Piedmont communities are mainly devoted to intensive rainfall cultivation of maize, beans, barley, and alfalfa (usually irrigated), and are largely empty of modern settlement. At the very base of the Lower Piedmont, at the abrupt juncture of the gentle slope and the flat shoreland, is a second band of larger and more nucleated communities, including Coatlinchan, Huexotla, and the eastern half of Texcoco (Map 4).

Along the northern and southern margins of the Texcoco Region the Lower Piedmont does not grade gradually into the Upper Piedmont zone as is the case over the remainder of this area. Instead, there is a rather abrupt juxtaposition of steep hillslope with the gently sloping piedmont surface where massive hill spurs (the Patlachique Range in the north, and, to the south, the chain formed by Cerro Texolotl and Cerro Chimalhuacan) extend westward from the base of the main Sierra (Map 3).

4) The *Lakeshore Plain zone* (127 square km) extends from its upper limit at about 2275 meters westward to the shoreline of old Lake Texcoco at about 2240 meters. This comprises a broad, flat, fertile agricultural zone, the largest expanse of such land in the eastern Valley of Mexico (Pl. 7*a*). As Wolf and Palerm (1955: 268) have observed, there are two types of communities in this zone today: *a*) tightly nucleated villages and towns, including Texcoco, the region's only true urban center; and *b*) large commercial ranchos and haciendas, primarily engaged in dairy and alfalfa production. A huge market is held weekly in Texcoco. Smaller markets occur at periodic intervals in several other large communities in the Lakeshore Plain and Lower Piedmont zones. Craft specializations tend to be well developed in nucleated communities in both the Lakeshore Plain and the Lower Piedmont. This is particularly true at San Miguel Chiconcuac where the manufacture of woolen textiles supports a large segment of the population.

The Lakeshore Plain is the most densely populated and intensively utilized zone within the Texcoco Region today (Table 4). The chief attraction for modern agriculture is its wide, level expanse of deep soil, whose natural fertility can be greatly augmented by means of large irrigation systems based on deep wells and expensive gasoline or diesel powered pumping machinery. Such humidity control is limited to the large commercial dairy-alfalfa enterprises, which control much of the agricultural land in this zone. Subsistence agriculture here remains largely dependent upon the vagaries of natural rainfall, except for limited increments of floodwater withdrawn from the several major canalized barrancas that cross the flat Lakeshore Plain from the western edge of the Lower Piedmont.

Drainage is a crucial aspect of agriculture in the Lakeshore Plain zone today.

TABLE 4

MODERN DEMOGRAPHIC DATA FOR THE TEXCOCO REGION

No.	Name	Population	Hectares	Persons/Hectare	Comments
1	Los Reyes	3851	53	73	Not within borders of Texcoco Region
2	Tecamachalco	884	19	46	Not within borders of Texcoco Region
3	La Magdalena	1331	21	64	
4	San Sebastian Chimalpa	951	23	41	
5	San Augustín Atlapulco	560	25	22	
6	San Lorenzo Chimalco				
7	Guadalupe Xochioca				
8	Xochitenco	9373	159	59	Calculated as a single unit since individual borders could not be distinguished on map
9	San Juan				
10	Chimalhuacan				
11	Barrio Sta. María Natívitas	542	29	19	
12	San Vincente Chicoloapan	3670	77	48	
13	Santiago Cuatlalpan	1498	40	38	
14	Montecillo	469	16	29	
15	San Bernardino	1053	38	28	
16	San Mateo Huexotla	201	6	34	
17	Coatepec	1239	64	20	
18	Coatlinchan	2195	36	61	
19	San Luis Huexotla	1262	116	11	
20	Tequesquinahuac	1156	88	13	
21	San Pablo Ixayoc	617	28	22	
22	San Miguel	1372	137	10	Calculated as a single unit since individual borders could not be distinguished on map
23	Sta. Catarina del Monte				
24	Sta. María Tecuanulco	854	115	7	
25	San Dieguito	721	23	31	
26	Natívitas	620	28	22	
27	San Gregorio Amanalco	841	*ca.* 150	*ca.* 6	Surface area could not be completely measured on map available to us.
28	St. Tomás Apipilhuasco	Not calculated since most of this community is outside our map			
29	San Nicolás Tlaminca	332	24	14	
30	San Miguel Tlaixpan	1439	131	11	
31	La Purificación	785	129	6	

No.	Name	Population	Hectares	Persons/Hectare	Comments
32	San Joaquín	556	69	8	
33	San Juan Tezontla	607	89	7	
34	San Bernardino Tlamililopa	392	78	5	
35	San Pedro Chiautzingo	575	110	5	
36	Tepetlaoxtoc	1360	163	8	
37	San Francisco Olalpa	est. 600 ?	98	?	No population statistics in 1960 Census
38	Barrio San Pablo	est. 150 ?	13	?	No population statistics in 1960 Census
39	Papalotla	738	37	20	
40	Tepetitlan	582	22	26	
41	Amajac	est. 100 ?	8	?	No population statistics in 1960 Census
42	Barrio Nonoalco	274	11	25	
43	Barrio Pentecostes	490	23	21	
44	Barrio Los Reyes	113	14	8	
45	Barrio Texepa	333	14	24	
46	Resurección	718	24	30	
47	San Simón	598	28	21	
48	Tulantongo	652	27	24	
49	Barrio Sta. Cruz de Arriba	529	9	59	
50	Barrio Sta. Cruz	38	4	10	
51	Xocotlan	353	14	25	
52	Barrio San Sebastián	191	9	21	
53	Barrio La Trinidad	308	50	6	
54	Texcoco	11,215	241	47	
55 56	Barria Sta. Cruz de Abajo Barria San Felipe	1054	65	16	Calculated as a single unit since individual borders could not be distinguished on map
57	San Miguel Tocuila	1936	68	28	
58	San Andrés Riva Palacio	967	21	46	
59	La Magdalena Panoaya	1480	33	45	
60	Barrio Zapotlan	542	9	60	
61	Barrio Sta. Catarina	196	4	49	
62	San Andrés Chiautla	845	52	16	
63	Barrio Huiznahuac	374	19	20	
64	San Miguel Chiconcuac	3050	81	38	
65	San Salvador Atenco	1958	70	28	
66	San Francisco Acuexcomac	1764	30	59	
67	Barrio San Pablo Cuahuimilolco	1930	24	80	

No.	Name	Population	Hectares	Persons/Hectare	Comments
68	Barrio Chimalpa	806	21	38	
69	Barrio Atenguillo	251	13	19	
70	Barrio Ixquitlan	59	3	20	
71	Tlaltecahuacan	249	11	23	
72	San Lucas	153	14	11	
73	Tezoyuca	2256	108	21	Not within borders of Texcoco Region
74	San Cristobal Nexquipayac	1310	23	57	
75	San Isabel Ixtapan	1767	33	54	Not within borders of Texcoco Region
76	Tequisistlan	1168	18	65	Not within borders of Texcoco Region
77	San Matéo Chipiltepec	1157	33	35	Not within borders of Texcoco Region
78	Barrio Zocango	332	9	37	Not within borders of Texcoco Region
79	Cuanalan	1541	45	34	Not within borders of Texcoco Region
80	Tepexpan	2619	94	28	Not within borders of Texcoco Region
81	San Miguel Totolsingo	850	24	35	Not within borders of Texcoco Region
Total for Texcoco Region		73,476	3219		

Note:—Site numbers refer to Map 4. Population figures are taken from *VIII Censo General de Población, 1960,* published by the Secretaria de Indústria y Comercio, Dirección General de Estadistica, México, D.F. Community surface area measurements were obtained, using a planimeter, from 1: 25,000 topographic maps published in 1959 by the Departamento Cartográfico Militar, Secretaria de la Defensa Nacional, México, D.F. (Hojas 14Q-h (57), 14Q-h (58), 14Q-h (73), 14Q-h (74)).

Virtually every field is bordered by large ditches of a meter or more in width, and between one and two meters deep. In addition, all major barrancas extending onto the Lakeshore Plain from the higher ground to the east have been canalized. Thus, all floodwater from the Sierra and Piedmont zones is contained within a series of large, generally straight ditches, built up to heights of two or three meters above ground level. Except for some secondary usage of this water for floodwater irrigation, practically all this moisture feeds directly into the main lake bed, and is not allowed to spread out over the Lakeshore Plain.

West of the Lakeshore Plain the dried up, salt incrusted bottom of former Lake Texcoco (now largely drained) is slowly being reclaimed for agriculture. However, even today most of the former lake bed (about 134 square km) remains a wasteland of barren mud flats, with a broad band of pastureland along its eastern edge where herds of cattle and sheep graze over the flat expanses on which only tough, wiry grass will grow (Pl. 16). Here, also, the last remnants of aboriginal salt-making linger on at a small community near Nezquipaya, where water is drained through salty earth and then boiled to recover its salt content (Apenes, 1944; Parsons, In Press) (Pl. 5*a*). Today the former lake bed and its shoreland in the Texcoco Region are without utility apart from limited salt-making and some grazing.

For a more detailed discussion of modern agricultural practices and land use in the eastern Valley of Mexico, the reader is referred to Sanders' extensive treatment of this subject (1965: 32-58).

PREVIOUS ARCHAEOLOGICAL INVESTIGATIONS IN THE TEXCOCO REGION

Published archaeological reports relevant to the Texcoco Region are not abundant, and, with a few exceptions, provide only fragmentary data on ceramic artifacts and architectural features. The most substantial sources have been Dixon's (1963, 1966) preliminary reports on his excavations of ceremonial-civic architecture at the Temesco Terminal Formative site (our Tx-TF-51). In 1956 substantial excavations were undertaken at the large Portezuelo Classic-Toltec-Aztec site (our Tx-EC-32, Tx-LC-18, Tx-ET-18, Tx-LT-53, Tx-A-103) by Brainerd. This work was continued by Hicks and Nicholson, who have reported their findings in preliminary form (1964). Noguera (1943) and Apenes (1943) carried out excavations at the Terminal Formative lake bed site of El Tepalcate (our Tx-TF-46) near Chimalhuacan. Noguera's report described the ceramic material in some detail, and Apenes' dealt with the general appearance of the site as a whole.

These comprise the most systematic and detailed reports available for the Texcoco Region. All three sites—Temesco, Portezuelo, and El Tepalcate—are situated along the southern edge of our survey area. Moving further north, there is much less useful information. In the early part of this century Batres (1904) undertook extensive reconstructions and excavations at some of the impressive architectural remnants in the Aztec center of Huexotla. In 1925 Blom and La Farge briefly described and photographed some of these features at Huexotla and another large mound in Texcoco (1926: 12-14). During the 1930s Vaillant carried out excavations at the Los Melones group of pyramids in Aztec Texcoco, but, apart from a brief mention in his *Aztecs of Mexico* (1941), this work was not published. In the 1950s Piña Chan (1956-57) carried out several small excavations at Toltec-Aztec sites in the vicinity of Tepetlaoxtoc in the northern part of the Texcoco Region. This latter report is principally devoted to the description of ceramics.

From documentary sources (e.g., Alva Ixtlilxochitl, 1965 *a* and *b*; Pomar, 1941; Diaz del Castillo, 1960), we know that at the time of the Spanish Conquest there was a major urban community at Texcoco, and secondary centers at Huexotla, Coatlinchan, Coatepec, Chimalhuacan, and Tepetlaoxtoc. The elaborate stone sculpture and remarkable hydraulic features of the Aztec royal retreat at Tetzcotzingo have been noted and described in the past (e.g., Coy, 1966).

METHODOLOGY

A variety of natural, cultural, and historical conditions and factors have been important in determining the methodology and productivity of surface survey in the Texcoco Region:

1) Airphoto coverage for the entire area is available at scales of 1: 10,000 and 1: 25,000.

2) Except in the Sierra, natural vegetation is not generally a problem either in obscuring prehispanic remains on the ground surface, or in obliterating cultural features on the airphoto. Likewise, except at and near the lakeshore zone, deposition and alluviation are not significant problems in covering traces of prehispanic occupation. Soil cover is predominately shallow (seldom exceeding 50 cm in depth), and there are sizable stretches where surface erosion has left little more than sherds and rock rubble atop bare bedrock—i.e., many

sites have been effectively "excavated," although all vertical control and architectural detail have been lost.

3) Large sections of ground have been divided into distinctly bordered fields which appear clearly on the airphoto and make ideal survey units.

4) Sizable areas inhabited during the prehispanic past have been totally or nearly deserted for centuries.

5) At least the main outlines of the entire prehispanic ceramic sequence have now been established.

In interpreting the significance of our findings, we have accepted as valid the following set of basic assumptions:

1) Visible mounds indicate the presence of buried structures, and substantial *in situ* concentrations of surface pottery indicate the former presence of residential structures and/or activities.

2) The location and distribution of sites systematically reflect basic exploitative activities, i.e., there will be a general tendency for residential sites to be situated so as to facilitate access to strategic resources.

3) At any one point in time, the range and variability of site size, character, location, and distribution systematically reflect inter community political, economic, and ceremonial relationships.

The main problem facing us in the initial stages of formulating a research design for the 1967 Texcoco Region survey was that of sampling procedure. We did not feel that complete coverage of the entire Texcoco Region was either possible or necessary for a one-season pilot investigation of the scope and character we had in mind. Furthermore, our understanding of the natural environment of the area was limited to a very generalized level. We were unaware of any of the significant internal variations in soil, hydrography, climate, and topography within each of the four broad zones delineated above which might have conditioned prehispanic settlement. Our knowledge of previously located and described archaeological sites was also quite superficial.

The strategy we decided to employ was simple, yet one that seemed most capable of taking into account all the significant known features of the Texcoco Region that might affect the character of prehispanic settlement. This plan was to carefully examine the ground surface contained in three wide bands extending from the bed of Lake Texcoco eastward across the broad Lakeshore Plain, into the slopes of the Lower and Upper Piedmonts, as far as the rugged foothills at the western base of the main Sierra. Two principal considerations guided our placement of these survey strips: (*a*) the need to transect large representative segments of as many different microenvironments as possible; and (*b*) the need to utilize our existing knowledge of archaeological site locations as far as feasible and useful. Our aim, of course, was to delineate a pattern of regional settlement configuration that we could, with reasonable confidence, extrapolate as generally valid for the Texcoco Region as a whole.

Our original intention was to run one northern survey strip (*ca.* three to four km wide) along the southern flanks of the Patlachique Range, extending from Nezquipaya on the lakeshore eastward through Tepetlaoxtoc, and into the foothills of the Sierra. A wider (*ca.* six to seven km) central strip was to pass through both the Aztec centers of Texcoco and Huexotla, running west-to-east from the lakeshore to the base of the Sierra. In the south, a third strip (*ca.* three or four km wide) was to incorporate the area between the lake bed around Cerro Chimalhuacan on the west, and the edge of the Sierra above Coatepec to the east. This coverage would incorporate all major archaeological sites known to exist in the Texcoco Region (except the Aztec centers of Coatlinchan and Chiautla), and would probably maximize the number of microenvironmental zones that could be incorporated into our survey area.

A variety of conditions and considerations somewhat modified these original intentions, but our actual survey activity did not depart significantly from that outlined above. Because we were able to cover more ground than originally expected, all three strips were substantially widened, especially the central and northern. The southern strip actually turned out to be roughly triangular, with a western base about eight to 10 km wide, and narrowing steadily eastward. This modification of the form of our southern survey band was predicated primarily upon an in-the-field realization that this sector contained the only close juxtaposition of hillslope and lakeshore in the Texcoco Region. We therefore greatly expanded our coverage of the Lakeshore Plain and Lower Piedmont around the base of Cerro Chimalhuacan.

In most cases our intensive survey stopped at or just below the western base of the Sierra. Except at San Pablo Ixayoc, the suspicion and distrust manifested toward us by the residents of villages at the base of the Sierra precluded any effective survey within the borders of these communities (Santa Catarina del Monte, Santa María Tecuanulco, and San Gregorio Amanalco). In the northern third of the Texcoco Region our eastern survey limit was more determined by the termination of airphoto coverage than by any topographic factor. Here we advanced only part way into the Upper Piedmont zone, and where we reached the eastern limits of our airphotos (which also corresponded to the eastern edge of our topographic base map), we were still a few kilometers west of the base of the Sierra.

The irregular rectilinear areas outlined in black on our maps (Maps 5 to 13) delineate the areas covered by our intensive surveys. In these strips we worked on a field-by-field basis, using 1: 5000 airphotos as base maps upon which to locate and plot archaeological features. The general procedure was to work in teams of two or three persons (occasionally one or four persons). One individual was responsible for carrying the airphoto (mounted on a plywood board roughly 75 cm square), keeping the team oriented and located, and plotting the features he and the others observed. The other team members walked parallel to the mapper at intervals of 15 to 100 meters. This interval varied according to the nature of the terrain, character of surface vegetation, and abundance of archaeological remains.

Each team member noted mounds, concentrations of surface pottery and rock rubble, gross ceramic chronology, and general features of modern land use. These were called out to the mapper who plotted them on the airphoto. Preserved architectural features (mounds, terraces, canals, room patterns, floors, etc.) were measured and described, and (where necessary) drawn and photographed. The mapper also recorded impressionistic contour lines, with roughly a five-meter interval. When sufficiently large areas had been mapped in this manner, the plotted features on the airphotos were traced onto large rolls of paper. At this stage, sites were defined, site numbers assigned, and descriptive reports prepared for each designated site.

For purposes of evaluating and refining our initial impressions of occupational chronology, systematic collections of surface pottery were made at periodic intervals. It should be emphasized that in this pilot survey we were not concerned with using differential frequencies and distributions of ceramic or lithic artifacts as a means of inferring site function or delineating differential status and functionally specific locations within and between communities. Neither were we particularly interested in plotting the areal distributions of specific stylistic variants of ceramic forms or decorative motifs. Thus, our surface collecting was very much oriented toward obtaining a representative body of between 100 and 200 diagnostic sherds whose chronological placement could be properly evaluated (see Appendix I for a description of the most important ceramic types used for this purpose). To achieve this we collected all rim sherds and decorated body sherds from within a specific locality. The size and placement of the localities from which such collections were made, as well as the frequency with which we sampled particular sites, were dependent upon two main factors: (*a*) the chronological complexity of occupation—one-component sites were not sampled as frequently as those with multi-component occupations because of the far greater reliability of the simple "eye-balling" means of evaluating ceramic chronology; (*b*) the density of surface pottery— where sherd concentrations were higher, collections were taken from over smaller areas than in cases where surface pottery was spread more thinly.

In areas where mounds were preserved, the sherds on and immediately around such features usually comprised the sampling unit. Where sherds were distributed continuously over the ground surface and mounds were absent, a specific area (usually in the vicinity of 10 meters square where sherd densities were high, but up to 50 meters square where there were few sherds) was marked off for collection purposes. When only a single occupational component was present, no more than one sample was generally taken from a site less than five hectares in area. On larger sites of this type approximately one field in ten was sampled. Where occupational history was more complex, we made an effort to sample every field. Sherd samples were placed in cloth bags, and transported to our lab in Texcoco where they were washed and tabulated.

In theory, then, our coverage within the three survey strips was completed. In actuality, we probably missed a few mounds and other occupational remnants, and occasionally failed to properly evaluate the full range of ceramic indicators on sites of long-term or mixed-period occupation. The quality of our control dropped off considerably within the borders of modern communities where detailed examinations were either impossible or quite difficult. There has very likely been some covering up of archaeological remains, particularly along the western margin of the survey area where alluvial deposits have built up in and along the lake. We do not feel, however, that these limitations and possibilities for error have seriously marred the basic validity of the general patterns of settlement configuration that we have defined.

We also systematically walked over the eastern two-thirds of the broad area between the central and southern survey strips. This region was not examined on a field-by-field basis, but we could not have missed any large sites, and probably recorded every occupational locality of more than five hectares in surface area. We did not examine the area lying between the central and northern survey strips. The main highway to Tlaxcala, however, runs through the middle of this region. Although we drove along this route practically every day, we failed to detect any large sites.

The total surface area included within our three intensive survey strips amounts to about 301 square km:

North Strip—99 square km
Central Strip—119 square km
South Strip—85 square km

The less intensively examined area between the central and southern strips measures roughly 76 square km in surface area.

Thus we have good to excellent control over the general outlines of prehispanic settlement distribution over a total area of about 377 square km. This amounts to about 68 per cent of the total Texcoco Region surface area of some 558 square km (not including the Sierra zone).

FIELDWORK TIMETABLE

We arrived in Texcoco in mid-May. The first week was spent in arranging residential and laboratory facilities, and in acquiring the necessary permits from the Instituto Nacional de Antropología e História. Fieldwork was initiated on May 22. During the first week the principal investigator and student assistants worked together as a single group for purposes of general orientation in survey methodology. In early June three separate survey teams were formed. These operated as independent units in different sections of the Texcoco Region through the end of the third week in August. At the beginning of July a fourth survey team was formed to assist in the wide central strip.

On August 24 the bulk of the field party returned to Ann Arbor. The principal investigator and one student assistant remained in Texcoco until November 27. During the period between late August and the end of November, a few stretches of intensive survey were completed, ceramic collections were analyzed, and extensive survey was carried out in the broad area between the central and southern survey strips.

II

SITE DESCRIPTIONS

Jeffrey R. Parsons
and
Mary H. Parsons

INTRODUCTION

We now proceed to a systematic description of the archaeological sites located during the course of our 1967 survey. In defining sites and drawing site borders our main purpose has been to delineate areas of occupation on the ground which correspond to prehistoric social communities. This task has often proved to be far from a straight forward one. At this stage in our investigations we have been guided by Sanders' (1965: 12-13) definition of an archaeological site as

> ". . . any localized area that shows signs of alteration by man as observable by archaeological method. This would include anything from an isolated home . . . or ceremonial structure, dams, canals, terrace systems, to a city of 100,000 inhabitants. The important point is that a site is 'a spatially isolatable unit.' A spatially isolatable unit should have some cultural significance to the prehistoric population and not be simply an archaeological abstraction if such units are to be used conveniently in settlement pattern analysis.

For most time periods we have had relatively little difficulty in distinguishing "spatially isolatable units" which can reasonably be regarded as various types of residential communities, temporary camps, isolated ceremonial structures or ceremonial-civic precincts. In these situations, occupation is so distributed that spatially isolatable units are readily apparent when one examines a regional map upon which this occupation has been plotted. While we are sometimes completely ignorant of the functions of such units, they do stand out as distinct entities about which certain conclusions can be drawn.

For the Aztec period, however, and most particularly the Late Aztec, we are sometimes faced with the problem of having to deal with nearly continuous distributions of dispersed occupation over wide areas. It is often extremely awkward to distinguish such an area as a single site. But, on the other hand, at our present level of observational intensity there is seldom any clearly apparent and objective means for breaking up such large areas into separate site units of a more manageable and meaningful size. In such cases we have fallen back upon a "fudging" process whereby site borders are drawn where natural features (barrancas or hills) appear to reinforce an actual fade-out in occupational density. In at least one case (Tx-A-72) however, we have dispaired of any reasonable success with even this procedure, and so have lumped this entire huge area of Upper Piedmont as a single "site."

In classifying sites we have considered the composite configuration of the following variables as our main criteria:

a) Site size (i.e., surface area in hectares)

b) Occupational density (primarily density of surface pottery)

d) Architectural complexity

c) Population, as calculated from *a* and *b*

e) Location of a site with respect to other contemporary sites

On this basis, we have set up the following site typology:

1) *Primary Regional Center*—A large, densely occupied, architecturally complex community, with an estimated population of several thousand or more.

2) *Secondary Regional Center*—Similar to Primary Regional Center, but with a population of many hundred to a few thousand.

3) *Segregated Elite District* (applicable only for the Terminal Formative period)—An isolated residential area, situated in a topographically prominent location, in which is concentrated a high proportion of ceremonial-civic architecture.

4) *Nucleated Village*—A densely occupied community, with relatively little architectural complexity, and a maximum population of roughly 1500 people. Following Sanders (1965) we have arbitrarily selected a minimum population level of 100 people. We have also used the arbitrary figure of 500 people for the division between Large Nucleated Villages (over 500 people) and Small Nucleated Villages (between 100 and 400 people).

5) *Dispersed Village*—Similar to Nucleated Village, but featuring a much more scattered occupation. Small and Large Dispersed Villages are distinguished on the same basis as Small and Large Nucleated Villages.

6) *Hamlet*—A residential community of fewer than 100 people.

7) *Camp*—A small area of scattered occupation and presumably temporary or seasonal residence.

8) *Isolated Ceremonial-Civic Precinct*—A concentration of obviously ceremonial-civic architecture, and very limited occupational debris.

In determining surface area we have used a compensating polar planimeter (Keuffel and Esser, Model 620015). Most sites of less than 30 to 40 hectares in size were measured from a 1: 5000 base map traced from airphotos. Larger sites were measured from our 1: 25,000 base map after the full extent of occupational debris had been plotted. For several very small sites of one hectare or less, no attempt was made to accurately determine the site area. Such sites are merely designated as "less than one hectare." It should be emphasized that no site measurements were made on the ground, and that our surface areas are to be regarded as rough approximations, probably maximal in most cases. We have usually drawn site borders at the break between light and very light occupation (see below for definitions of these terms), except on Aztec sites where the break between light-to-moderate and light sherd concentrations has been generally used for this purpose. Undoubtedly, erosion, plowing, and a variety of other mechanisms have served to spread surface pottery over a wider area than it originally occupied in many localities. Alternatively, alluviation in the Lakeshore Plain sector has probably partially obscured or even wholly obliterated sites, and very likely we have tended to underestimate the limits of some sites in this part of the survey area.

Our calculations of population have been based upon the more subjective process of extrapolating from the density of occupational debris (in which the most important element is surface pottery) to numbers of people per hectare. In designating occupational density in the field, we have employed a generalized, subjective visual scale of estimation: very light, light, light-to-moderate, moderate, and heavy:

1) *Very light*—A wide scattering of surface pottery, with single sherds visible only at

intervals of several meters. If no effort is made to search for sherds, one may expect that surface pottery is absent.

2) *Light*—Sherds distributed continuously, with single sherds at intervals of several cm, but no significant build up of sherd density beyond this point.

3) *Light-to-moderate*—A marked build up of sherd density to a point where sherds are clearly visible everywhere, and there are very few gaps in the distribution of surface pottery. Some one-meter squares selected at random might produce very few surface sherds, while others might yield up to 100, or so, pieces of pottery.

4) *Moderate*—A continuous layer of sherds in a situation where any randomly placed one-meter square would produce a count of roughly 100 to 200 pieces of pottery.

5) *Heavy*—A continuous layer of sherds in a situation where any randomly-placed one-meter square would produce a count of several hundred pieces of pottery.

This system obviously contains a number of shortcomings and limitations. Probably most serious are (*a*) the probability that any two observers will have somewhat different impression of sherd densities; and (*b*) the great decrease in reliability of eyeball observations on multi-component sites, especially where one component is greatly predominant. Our practice of making numerous systematic surface collections on multi-component sites has hopefully alleviated these problems to some extent. There are at least two areas, however, where occupational complexity warranted more intensive surface sampling than that which was actually carried out: (*a*) The Classic-Toltec-Aztec site (Tx-EC-32, Tx-LC-18, Tx-ET-18, Tx-LT-53, Tx-A-103) at the northern base of Cerro Portezuelo at the southern edge of our survey area; and (*b*) the Formative-Classic-Toltec-Aztec site within and around the modern village of Chimalhuacan (Tx-MF-13, Tx-LF-27, Tx-TF-50, Tx-EC-34, Tx-LC-20, Tx-ET-19, Tx-LT-54, Tx-A-109) in the southwestern corner of our survey area. The reader should regard our surface areas and population estimates for these sites as somewhat less reliable than for most other settlements.

In making population estimates we have used Sanders' (1965: 50) figures for population densities of modern settlement types characteristic of highland Mesoamerica. At sites where sherd densities are consistently in the light-to-moderate, moderate, and heavy ranges, we have used Sanders' figures of 2500 to 5000 people per square km (or, 25 to 50 per hectare) which characterize his "High-Density Compact Village." For sites where sherds are consistently in the light and light-to-moderate range, we have been guided by his density figures for "Compact Low-Density Village" (1000 to 2500 per square km; or, 10 to 25 per hectare), "Scattered Village" (500 to 1000 per square km; or, 5 to 10 per hectare), and "Compact Rancheria" (200 to 300 per square km; or, 2 to 3 per hectare).

Generally we have given an estimated population range with a maximum figure approximately double that of the minimum. However, in cases where occupational features have been obscured, and we are less certain of the demographic implications of surface remains, we have increased the maximum: minimum ratio up to 5: 1.

Our site typology is obviously intended to be a very generalized one. At this stage, we are unable to specify site function beyond a very general level. At certain places in our discussion of individual sites we present a variety of possibilities for specific types of extractive or exploitative activities, or for the political and religious roles to which particular sites may have been dedicated. We believe, however, that any attempt to incorporate these hypothetical functions into our general classification scheme would be unwarranted at this point. A much more rigorous methodology and whole new fieldwork programs will be required for this purpose.

In classifying mounds we have utilized a simple domestic vs. ceremonial-civic dichotomy. The basis for designating a mound as ceremonial-civic is principally a matter of relative height: that is, most mounds that are unusually high (generally two meters or more) are presumed to be something other than domestic residences.

With respect to our chronological control (see Appendix I for description of ceramic markers), the reader should be aware of our inability to resolve the distribution of settlement beyond the level of 200- to 300-year periods (Table 5). Complete or partial site abandonment, the reoccupation of abandoned localities, and other types of population movements are usually completely invisible within these temporal units. Each of our settlement pattern maps thus represents a composite configuration representing the cumulative sum total of the occupational activities of eight to ten human generations.

Despite the limitations inherent in our techniques of observation and analysis, we feel our data are adequate for the purposes of this pilot survey. Any attempt to be more rigorous and refined would have slowed the progress of our survey immensely. As it now stands, we have been able to draw generalized site borders and offer reasonable population estimates for eight major time periods over a span of roughly 2500 years. These provisional estimates and generalized patterns of settlement provide a basis for developing a wide variety of specific hypotheses which can be used to structure the designs of new research programs aimed at testing the problems that our pilot survey has defined.

In numbering sites, we have utilized a three-unit system. The first unit for each site is Tx (indicating that the site is located in the Texcoco Region). The second unit indicates the time period to which the site belongs (Table 5; Appendix 1): MF = Middle Formative; LF = Late Formative; TF = Terminal Formative; EC = Early Classic; LC = Late Classic; ET = Early Toltec; LT = Late Toltec; A = Aztec. The third unit is an Arabic numeral which is the specific number of each site within a time period. Thus, a complete site designation would be Tx-MF-1, etc. On most of our maps, we have simply indicated the numerical component of the full site designation.

We have lumped the two Aztec periods (Early and Late) together for demographic purposes. The reader should be aware that the figures we have provided for Aztec population, numbers of sites, hectares of occupied ground, etc., are actually Late Aztec. We have not attempted to make specific calculations for the Early Aztec period because this material is so mixed with, and overwhelmed by, Late Aztec occupational debris. Map 12 presents our general impressions of Early Aztec settlement.

MIDDLE FORMATIVE

TX-MF-1

Natural setting: 2290 m, in Lower Piedmont. In level area of deep soil near the Rio Papalotla.

Modern utilization: Intensive rainfall cultivation. Site area on northern edge of modern town of Papalotla.

Archaeological remains: Light concentration of surface pottery over an area of less than one hectare. No structural remains. Mixed with heavier Early Toltec (Tx-ET-4), Late Toltec (Tx-LT-12) and Aztec (Tx-A-16) material.

Classification: Hamlet; fewer than 50 people.

Tx-MF-2

Natural setting: 2330 m, in Lower Piedmont. On low, relatively level hilltop, near the Rio Papalotla, some 30 m above the level of the main Lower Piedmont Plain. Moderate erosion; shallow soil cover.

Modern utilization: Grazing.

Archaeological remains: Light concentrations of surface pottery over an area of less than one

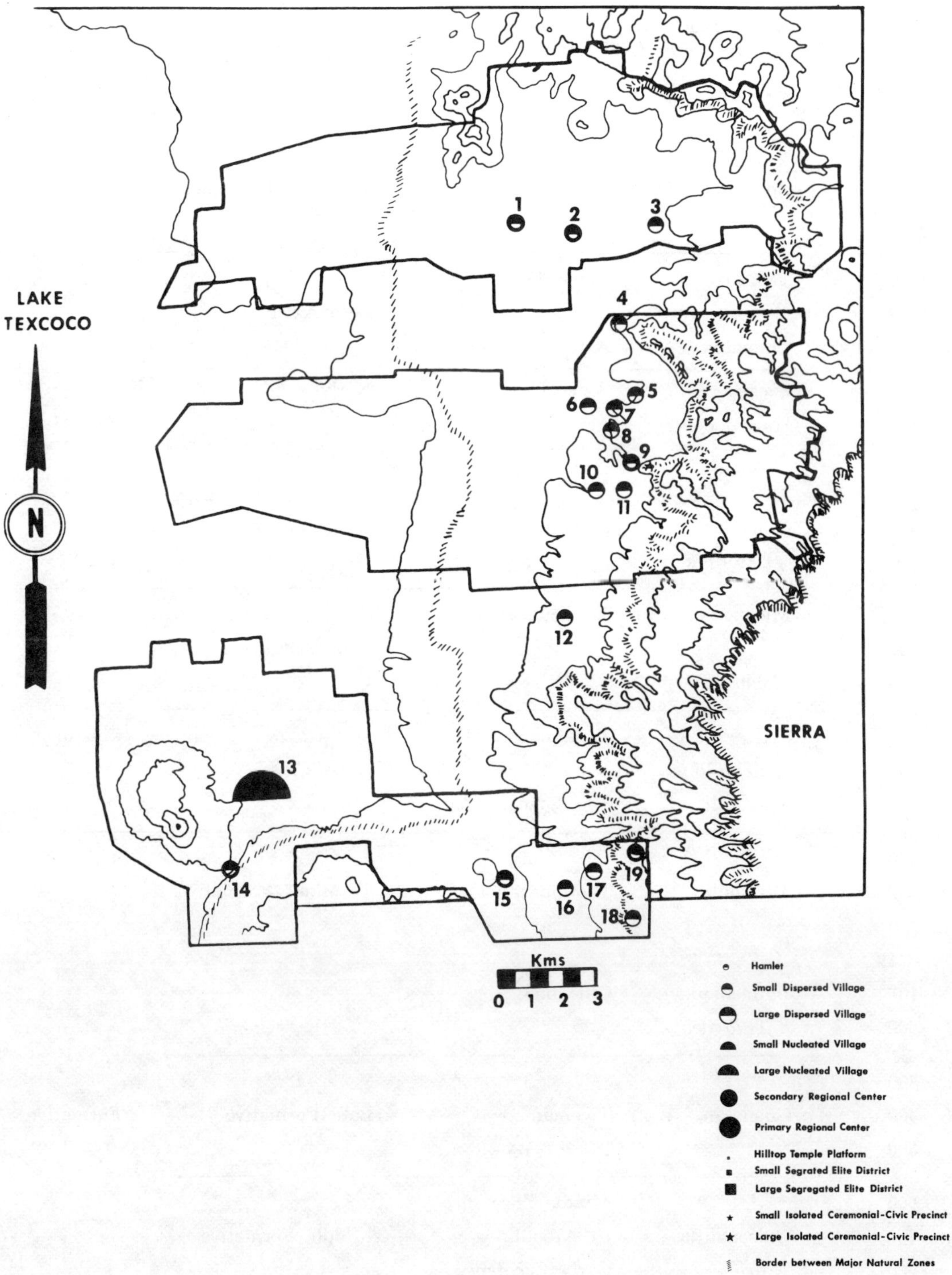

Map 5—Texcoco Region: Middle Formative settlement (schematic). Contour interval 100 meters. Key to schematic settlement pattern maps (Maps 5-13).

hectare. No structural remains can be assigned to this period. Mixed with much heavier Terminal Formative (Tx-TF-10) and some Late Formative (Tx-LF-5) material.

Classification: Hamlet; fewer than 50 people.

TABLE 5

CHRONOLOGY

Estimated Absolute Chronology	Teotihuacan Valley Phases	Valley of Mexico Phases	Chronological Periods for Texcoco Survey	Major Periods
1500	Teacalco	Aztec IV		
1400			Late Aztec	
1300	Chimalpa	Aztec III		
1200	Zocango	Aztec II	Early Aztec	
1100	Hueoxtoc	Aztec I		Post classic
1000	Mazpan	Mazapan	Late Toltec	
900	Xometla	Coyotlatelco	Early Toltec	
800	Oxtotipac			
700	Metepec	Teotihuacan IV		
600			Late Classic	
500	Xolalpan			
400		Teotihuacan III		Classic
300	Tlamimilolpa		Early Classic	
200	Miccaotli	Teotihuacan II		
100				
AD	Tzacualli	Teotihuacan I	Terminal Formative	
0				
BC				
100	Patlachique	Cuicuilco		
200	Tezoyuca			
300				
400	Cuanalan	Ticoman	Late Formative	Formative
500				
600		Middle Zacatenco		
700	Chiconautla	El Arbolillo	Middle Formative	
800	Altica	Early Zacatenco		
		Tlatilco		

Note:—Modified from Sanders, 1965: 16.

Tx-MF-3

Natural setting: 2335 m, in Lower Piedmont. In gently sloping saddle between two large hills. Moderate to severe erosion, with generally shallow soil cover. Site area adjacent to a major barranca.

Modern utilization: Grazing; plus some cultivated maguey.

Archaeological remains: Light concentrations of surface pottery over an area of about five hectares. No structural remains. Mixed with much heavier Late and Terminal Formative material (Tx-LF-8; Tx-TF-11).

Classification: Hamlet; fewer than 50 people.

TX-MF-4

Natural setting: 2310 m, in Lower Piedmont. Occupies a gently sloping, deep-soil zone adjacent to the shallow Río Jalapango. Site area situated at the base of the steep northern slope of Cerro Purificación.

Modern utilization: Occupied by village of San Joaquín, with garden plots and small cultivated fields interspersed among the houses. Lower hillslopes above the village are intensively terraced and cultivated. The hillslopes to the south of San Joaquín are honeycombed with small tezontle-gravel quarries, both operative and abandoned.

Archaeological remains: Light concentrations of surface pottery scattered through fields and gardens over an area of less than one hectare. Mixed with much heavier Late Formative material (Tx-LF-9). No structural remains.

Classification: Hamlet; fewer than 50 people. Modern houses may cover some occupational debris.

Tx-MF-5

Natural setting: 2335 m, in the Lower Piedmont. Badly dissected, relatively level zone, with numerous relicts of deep soil. Located next to a major barranca. A steep hill rises just to the north, across the barranca (Pl. 14,*b*).

Modern utilization: Immediate site area is marginal pasture. The surrounding fields are devoted to intensive rainfall cultivation. Lower hillslopes to the north have been extensively terraced, although many terraces are presently abandoned and uncultivated.

Archaeological remains: Light and moderate concentrations of surface pottery over an area of about four hectares. No structural remains. Mixed with some lighter Terminal Formative material (Tx-TF-17).

Classification: Hamlet; fewer than 100 people.

Tx-MF-6

Natural setting: 2335 m, in Lower Piedmont. In gently sloping area of shallow soil cover, lying between two major barrancas. High western spur of Cerro Purificación rises some 750 m to the northwest.

Modern utilization: Site area located at the west edge of an intensively cultivated (rainfall agriculture) zone. Soil cover thins to the west, where land is used only for grazing.

Archaeological remains: Light concentrations of surface pottery scattered over an area of roughly one hectare. No structural remains. Mixed with Terminal Formative (Ex-TF-17) and Classic (Tx-EC-12; Tx-LC-11) material.

Classification: Hamlet; fewer than 50 people.

Tx-MF-7

Natural setting: 2350 m, in Lower Piedmont. In gently sloping area of shallow soil, adjacent to a major barranca. Steep slopes of the western spur of Cerro Purificación rise about 600 m to the north.

Modern utilization: Grazing. Located near the southwestern corner of an intensively cultivated zone.

Archaeological remains: Variable light and light-to-moderate concentrations of surface pottery over an area of roughly four hectares. Great bulk of material is concentrated on and around a definite mound near the eastern end of this area. This feature measures about 20 m in diameter, and roughly 75 cm above the present ground level, with heavy rock rubble and moderate to heavy surface pottery over its entire surface. The dominant component of this ceramic material is Middle Formative, but some Terminal Formative (Tx-TF-17), and traces of Late Formative pottery are also present. No structural remains throughout rest of site area.

Classification: Hamlet; fewer than 50 people.

Tx-MF-8

Natural setting: 2335, in Lower Piedmont. In gently sloping, badly eroded area of shallow soil cover, immediately adjacent to a major barranca.

Modern utilization: Grazing.

Archaeological remains: Light concentrations of surface pottery over an area of about two hectares along the edge of a major barranca. A moderate concentration of sherds over an area approximately 50 m in diameter at the southern end of the site is the most significant occupational remnant. Mixed with roughly equal amounts of Late and Terminal Formative material (Tx-LF-11; TX-TF-17).

Classification: Hamlet; fewer than 50 people.

Tx-MF-9

Natural setting: 2375 m, in Lower Piedmont. Located in a pocket of deep soil on level ground at the base of steeply sloping Cerro Tetzcotzingo, immediately adjacent to a major barranca (Pl. 15,*a*).

Modern utilization: The hillslopes east and south of the site are intricately terraced and intensively cultivated. Many of the lower terraces are irrigated, with water brought from Sierra springs through several kilometers of canal networks. The immediate site area is used only for grazing.

Archaeological remains: Light concentrations of surface pottery over an area of less than one hectare. Mixed with much heavier Late Formative material (Tx-LF-12). A well defined tlatel is probably of Late Formative date, although its lower levels may contain Middle Formative construction.

Classification: Hamlet; fewer than 50 people. Probably only a single household unit.

Tx-MF-10

Natural Setting: 2405 m, in Lower Piedmont. In gently sloping, badly eroded area near the edge of a major barranca. Soil cover very thin to absent, with patches of bare tepetate.

Modern utilization: Marginal grazing land. The hillslopes to the northwest of the site area are intensively terraced and cultivated.

Archaeological remains: Light concentrations of surface pottery and abundant rock rubble over an area of less than one hectare. In some cases this occupational debris rests on bare tepetate. Mixed with large quantities of Late Formative and Terminal Formative pottery (Tx-LF-12; Tx-TF-21). No structural remains. The original configuration of the site has been badly obscured by severe erosion.

Classification: Hamlet; fewer than 50 people.

Tx-MF-11

Natural setting: 2425 m, in Lower Piedmont. In gently sloping area of shallow soil and moderate erosion, near the edge of a large barranca.

Modern utilization: Site area sits at southern edge of an intensively cultivated zone (rainfall and irrigation agriculture) just south of the dispersed village of San Dieguito. The hillslopes to the north of San Dieguito are intensively terraced and cultivated. The severely eroded land south of the site area is devoted to marginal grazing only.

Archaeological remains: Light concentrations of surface pottery and abundant rock rubble over an area of roughly one hectare. No structural remains. Mixed with larger quantities of Late Formative material (Tx-LF-12).

Classification: Hamlet; fewer than 50 people.

Tx-MF-12

Natural setting: 2390 m, in Lower Piedmont. In gently sloping, severely eroded area, near the edge of a major barranca.

Modern utilization: Marginal grazing. Intensively cultivated fields are found below the western end of the site area.

Archaeological remains: Light concentrations of surface pottery and abundant rock rubble over an area of less than one hectare. Sherds and rock rubble rest on bare tepetate or on small patches of very shallow soil. No structural remains. Mixed with greater quantities of Late Formative (Tx-LF-18) and a little Terminal Formative material (Tx-TF-32).

Classification: Hamlet; fewer than 50 people.

Tx-MF-13

Natural setting: 2240 m, on the Lakeshore Plain. In level, deep-soil zone at eastern base of Cerro Chimalhuacan (Pl. 14*a*).

Modern utilization: Most of the site area is intensively cultivated (rainfall agriculture). Sections of the site are covered by the residential structures of the Colonia de Guadelupe, and outlying barrio of Chimalhuacan. Small basalt quarries, both operative and abandoned, are found on the lower hillslopes west of the site.

Archaeological remains: Variable light, moderate, and heavy concentrations of surface pottery over an area of about 45 hectares. No definite Middle Formative structural remains are present, but the site area contains several large Aztec tlateles (Tx-A-109). Concentrations of Late Formative and Terminal Formative material also occur here (Tx-LF-27; Tx-TF-50). Formative sherds are found to a depth of about one meter in several pit profiles throughout the site area.

Classifications: Large nucleated village; 600 to 1200 people. This is by far the largest Middle Formative community in the Texcoco Region.

Tx-MF-14

Natural setting: 2270 m, in shallow soil zone on low bluff at juncture of the Lakeshore Plain and the Lower Piedmont, on the western flanks of Cerro Portezuelo.

Modern utilization: Grazing, plus a few maguey. The flat plain below the bluff is intensively cultivated, and is partly covered by a series of modern residential and industrial complexes.

Archaeological remains: Light concentrations of surface pottery over an area of less than one hectare. Prehispanic occupational debris is heavily dominated by Terminal Formative ceramics and architecture (Tx-TF-51). Excavations in two of the principal Terminal Formative mounds have revealed small quantities of Middle Formative pottery in the fill (Dixon, 1963, 1966).

Classification: Hamlet; fewer than 50 people.

Tx-MF-15

Natural setting: 2345 m, in Lower Piedmont. A gently sloping area of shallow to moderately deep soil and moderate erosion. Located at the base of a steep hill which rises to an altitude of 2440 m. Near the head of a shallow barranca.

Modern utilization: Fields below the hill base are intensively cultivated. The steeper slopes above the site are predominately pasture, with some maguey.

Archaeological remains: Light concentrations of surface pottery over an area of less than one hectare (only a few hundred square meters). Mixed with much heavier quantities of Late and Terminal Formative material (Tx-LF-25; Tx-TF-43). No structural remains.

Classification: Hamlet; fewer than 50 people. May represent only a single household group.

Tx-MF-16

Natural setting: 2430 m, in Lower Piedmont. In gently sloping area of moderately deep soil and slight to moderate erosion. Situated along the south edge of the modern nucleated village of Coatepec. About 750 m south of a major barranca, in the middle of a broad piedmont plain.

Modern utilization: Maintenance of terraces and other erosion controls has prevented severe erosion. Site area is cultivated, with maguey as a dominant crop due to the importance of the pulque industry in Coatepec. North edge of site borders on the south edge of Coatepec.

Archaeological remains: Variable very light and light concentrations of surface pottery over an area of roughly one hectare. Parts of the Middle Formative community may be covered by modern houses in Coatepec. No structural remains. Mixed with heavier quantities of Late Formative (Tx-LF-22). Terminal Formative (Tx-TF-41), and Aztec (Tx-A-99) material.

Classification: Hamlet; fewer than 50 people.

Tx-MF-17

Natural setting: 2450 m, in Lower Piedmont. Situated on a broad gentle slope, with moderate soil depth and relatively slight erosion. Soil becomes predominately shallower up slope to the east of site area. Located about 500 m south of a major barranca.

Modern utilization: The general area is principally devoted to maguey cultivation, with intervening patches of maize, beans, and barley. The immediate site area is in an adobe-making locality where large quantities of clayey earth have been removed in the manufacture of bricks. Modern nucleated village of Coatepec is located some 100 m east of the site area.

Archaeological remains: Light concentrations of surface pottery over an area of roughly one hectare. No structural remains. Mixed with much heavier Late Formative material (Tx-LF-22).

Classification: Hamlet; fewer than 50 people.

Tx-MF-18

Natural setting: 2500 m, at juncture of Upper and Lower Piedmonts. A gently sloping area with shallow soil cover. Erosion has been moderate to severe, and there are some patches of bare tepetate. Located near a small barranca.

Modern utilization: Most of site area devoted to intensive rainfall cultivation. The more severely eroded areas serve only for grazing.

Archaeological remains: Variable very light and light concentrations of surface pottery over an area of roughly one hectare. No structural remains. Mixed with much heavier Late Formative material (Tx-LF-23), and some Terminal Formative ceramics (Tx-TF-42).

Classification: Hamlet; fewer than 50 people.

Tx-MF-19

Natural setting: 2560 m, at lower end of Upper Piedmont. Situated in an area of moderate slope, on a hillspur immediately adjacent to a major barranca. Whole area is severely eroded, with large patches of bare tepetate and very little soil cover.

Modern utilization: Marginal grazing

Archaeological remains: Light concentrations of surface pottery over an area of less than one hectare. No structural remains. Sherds are badly weathered, and the sample is not particularly diagnostic, although Middle Formative material is probably present. Main occupational component is Terminal Formative (Tx-TF-39); a few Late Formative sherds may also be present

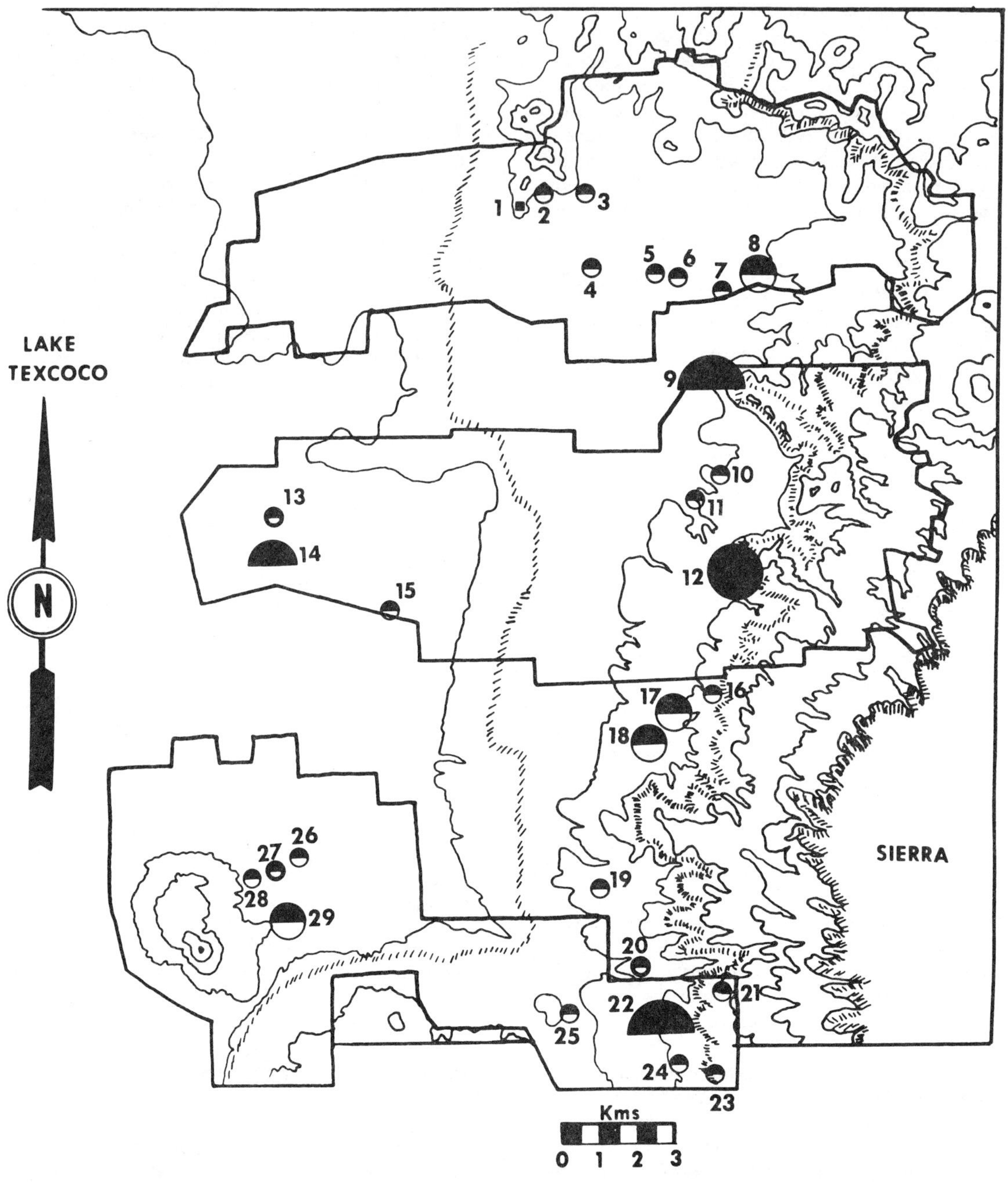

Map 6—Texcoco Region: Late Formative settlement (schematic). Contour interval 100 meters. For Key see map 5 p. 25.

(Tx-LF-21). Pottery is characteristically found washing from sides of erosional remnants.

Classification: Hamlet; fewer than 50 people.

LATE FORMATIVE

Tx-LF-1

Natural setting: 2430 m, on the level top of a long ridge extending southward from the main block of Cerro Azteca. Situated some 120 m above the level of the Lower Piedmont plain to the south and east, and the Lakeshore Plain to the west. Irregular ground surface throughout site area, with generally shallow soil cover and some rock outcroppings. Erosion has been moderate to severe. Río Papalotla flows at base of hill, south of the site.

Modern utilization: Grazing.

Archaeological remains: Very light concentrations of surface pottery over an area of roughly one-quarter hectare on the ridge top. Mixed with heavier Early Toltec pottery (Tx-ET-5). Very light Early Classic material is also present (Tx-EC-2). No structural remains, although large Early Toltec pyramid may contain earlier constructions within its core.

Classification: Hilltop ceremonial precinct. Probably no permanent occupation.

Tx-LF-2

Natural setting: 2350 m, in Lower Piedmont. Situated in gently sloping area at base of Cerro Azteca. Serious erosion has been prevented by the presence of a series of broad, low terraces over much of the lower hillslopes. Soil cover is generally moderately deep, becoming more shallow up slope.

Modern utilization: Grazing.

Archaeological remains: Variable very light and light concentrations of surface pottery over an area of less than one hectare. No structural remains. Mixed with much heavier Terminal Formative material (Tx-TF-1). Some Early Toltec (Tx-ET-4) and Aztec (Tx-A-17) pottery also occurs. The wide, stone-faced terraces which cover the low hill flanks in this region are probably prehispanic, and most likely relate to the Terminal Formative occupation of the site area.

Classification: Hamlet; fewer than 50 people.

Tx-LF-3

Natural setting: 2310 m, in Lower Piedmont. Situated on gently sloping ground at base of Cerro Azteca. Erosion has been moderate to severe; soil cover generally shallow.

Modern utilization: Grazing, plus some cultivated maguey.

Archaeological remains: Variable very light and light concentrations of surface pottery and heavy rock rubble over an area of less than one hectare. Mixed with much heavier Terminal Formative pottery (Tx-TF-1). No structural remains can be assigned to the Late Formative.

Classification: Hamlet; fewer than 50 people.

Tx-LF-4

Natural setting: 2290 m, in Lower Piedmont. Situated on level plain adjacent to the Río Papalotla, in zone of deep soil and little erosion.

Modern utilization: The site area is located at the northern edge of the modern town of Papalotla. Most of area is devoted to intensive rainfall cultivation.

Archaeological remains: Light concentrations of surface pottery over an area of less than one hectare. No structural remains. Mixed with Middle Formative (Tx-MF-1), Early Toltec (Tx-ET-4), and Late Toltec (Tx-LT-12) material.

Classification: Hamlet; fewer than 50 people.

Tx-LF-5

Natural setting: 2330 m, in Lower Piedmont. On low, relatively level hilltop, near the Río Papalotla, some 30 m above the level of the main Lower Piedmont Plain. Moderate erosion; shallow soil cover.

Modern utilization: Grazing.

Archaeological remains: Light concentrations of surface pottery over an area of less than one hectare. No structural remains can be assigned to this period. Mixed with much heavier Terminal Formative (Tx-TF-10), and some Middle Formative (Tx-MF-2) material.

Classification: Hamlet; fewer than 50 people.

Tx-LF-6

Natural setting: 2310 m, in Lower Piedmont. Situated in a gently sloping area adjacent to the Río Papalotla. Soil cover shallow to moderately deep; erosion has been moderate to severe.

Modern utilization: Immediate site area is uncultivated, and used as a picnic spot. Surrounding fields are intensively cultivated (rainfall agriculture).

Archaeological remains: Light concentrations of surface pottery over an area of less than one hectare. Mixed with Terminal Formative (Tx-TF-10), Early Classic (Tx-EC-6), Late Classic (Tx-LC-5), Early Toltec (Tx-ET-13), Late Toltec (Tx-LT-27), and Aztec (Tx-A-40) material. A single mound, about one meter high, is the only structural remnant. Its age is exceedingly questionable, but it may contain several occupational levels.

Classification: Hamlet; fewer than 50 people.

Tx-LF-7

Natural setting: 2320 m, in Lower Piedmont. Situated on a gently sloping hill flank adjacent to the Río Papalotla. Erosion has been moderate to severe; generally shallow soil cover.

Modern utilization: Grazing, with a few cultivated maguey.

Archaeological remains: Variable very light and light concentrations of surface pottery over an area of about two hectares. No structural remains. Mixed with much heavier Early and Late Toltec material (Tx-ET-13; Tx-LT-28).

Classification: Hamlet; fewer than 50 people.

Tx-LF-8

Natural setting: 2320 m, in Lower Piedmont. Situated in a gently sloping saddle area between two hills, just above the Río Papalotla. Erosion has been severe; soil cover scanty to absent, with patches of bare tepetate.

Modern utilization: Grazing, plus a few cultivated maguey.

Archaeological remains: Variable light, light-to-moderate, and moderate concentrations of surface pottery over an area of about 20 hectares. Mixed with lighter quantities of Middle and Terminal Formative material (Tx-MF-3; Tx-TF-11). The single structural remnant is a mound measuring about 1 meter high and some 40 meters in diameter, with moderate concentrations of Late Formative ceramics over its surface.

Classification: Small dispersed village; 250 to 500 people.

Tx-LF-9

Natural setting: 2310 to 2350 m in Lower Piedmont. Situated at the base of Cerro Purificación in a gently sloping-to-level zone of medium to deep soil cover. Soil thins progressively upslope. Northern border of site area is defined by the Río Jalapongo.

Modern utilization: Most of site area is devoted to intensive cultivation, including some alfalfa irrigated with water supplied from wells by gasoline pumps. Lower northern hillslopes of Cerro Purificación are intricately terraced and intensively cultivated; slopes to the south are predominantly pasture. The eastern arm of the site occurs beneath the garden plots and houses of the modern village of San Joaquín. Numerous tezontle-gravel quarries, both operative and abandoned, are found on the steeper slopes above the site.

Archaeological remains: Variable light, light-to-moderate, and moderate concentrations of surface pottery over an area of about 33 hectares. The site may be somewhat larger if the modern village of San Joaquín obscures some occupational debris to the northeast. No structural remains. A small amount of Middle Formative material appears at the north edge of the Late Formative site area (Tx-MF-4).

Classification: Large nucleated village; 650 to 1300 people.

Tx-LF-10

Natural setting: 2350 m, in Lower Piedmont. Situated on a broad, gentle slope, with shallow soil and moderate to severe erosion. Adjacent to a major barranca.

Modern utilization: Intensive rainfall cultivation, with intermittent fallowed fields and grazing land.

Archaeological remains: Light concentrations of surface pottery over an area of roughly one hectare. One definite tlatel, which is probably mainly Middle Formative (Tx-MF-7). Also mixed with heavier Terminal Formative material (Tx-TF-17).

Classification: Hamlet; fewer than 50 people.

Tx-LF-11

Natural setting: 2335 m, in Lower Piedmont. Located on a narrow tongue of level land immediately adjacent to a major barranca, at the base of a gentle slope extending down from the main piedmont surface. Moderate to severe erosion, with shallow soil cover.

Modern utilization: The immediate site area is used only for grazing. Adjacent fields on the main piedmont slope to north and east are devoted to intensive rainfall cultivation.

Archaeological remains: Light-to-moderate concentrations of surface pottery over an area of roughly one hectare. No structural remains. Mixed with approximately equal amounts of Middle and Terminal Formative material (Tx-MF-8; Tx-TF-17).

Classification: Hamlet; fewer than 50 people.

Tx-LF-12

Natural setting: 2350 to 2510 m, predominately in the Lower Piedmont, with some spill over onto the lower edge of the Upper Piedmont. The heaviest occupation is concentrated on the moderate-to-steeply-sloping western flank of Cerro

Tetzcotzingo-Metecatl, with arms of lighter occupation extending over the gentle piedmont slopes to the north, southwest, and southeast. The soil is generally of moderate depth due to maintenance of the intricate terracing which covers most hill slopes throughout the general region. The site area is cut through by a major barranca (Pl. 15,*b*).

Modern utilization: Most of the site area is intricately terraced and intensively cultivated in subsistence and orchard crops. The lower terraces are partially irrigated with water derived from springs in the Sierra, carried to this point over many kilometers of small canals. The modern village of San Nicolás Tlaminca borders the site on the north; the community of San Dieguito extends over part of the southwestern arm of the site.

Archaeological remains: Moderate to heavy concentrations of surface pottery and rock rubble throughout the core area on the terraced flanks of Cerro Tetzcotzingo-Metecatl. Light-to-moderate occupational debris over the remainder of the site area. There are a few vague mounded areas on the slope of Cerro Tetzcotzingo which may represent structural remnants. The total occupational zone is about 86 hectares. The Late Formative community has undergone considerable expansion from the three small hamlets located here in Middle Formative times (Tx-MF-9, Tx-MF-10, Tx-MF-11). Lighter quantities of Terminal Formative material are also present (Tx-TF-20, Tx-TF-21, Tx-TF-23),

Classification: Secondary regional center; 1700 to 3,500 people. This is the largest Late Formative community in the Texcoco Region.

Tx-LF-13

Natural setting: Below 2240 m, on flat Lakeshore Plain. Situated in zone of deep alluvial soil, in the general vicinity of the Conquest-period shoreline of Lake Texcoco. The ground surface is irregular, with many small grass-covered hillocks and intervening depressions.

Modern utilization: Grazing only. The salt content of the soil is apparently too high for effective cultivation. Only sharp, tough grass grows here today.

Archaeological remains: Light concentrations of surface pottery over an area of less than one hectare. No structural remains. Mixed with much heavier Late Toltec material (Tx-LT-35).

Classification: Hamlet; fewer than 50 people.

Tx-LF-14

Natural setting: Below 2240 m, on flat Lakeshore Plain, probably well within the borders of Conquest-period Lake Texcoco. Site area situated about 300 m north of the western terminus of a large canalized barranca, in a zone of deep alluvial soil (Pl. 16,*a*).

Modern utilization: Grazing only. The salt concentration in the soil is apparently too high for effective cultivation. Only sharp, tough grass grows here today.

Archaeological remains: Two large intersecting drainage ditches, roughly one meter deep, have exposed moderate to heavy concentrations of sherds for distances of about 250 m east-west and north-south along the ditches. Only a very light scattering of sherds appears on the ground surface between the ditches. Estimated site size is about four to five hectares, assuming a diameter of some 250 m. No structural remains.

Classification: Small nucleated village; 100 to 200 people. However, excavation here might reveal a drastically different community type.

Tx-LF-15

Natural setting: Below 2240 m, in flat Lakeshore Plain. Probably at or near the eastern edge of Conquest-period Lake Texcoco. Situated about 200 m south of a large canalized barranca, in zone of deep alluvial soil (Pl. 16,*b*).

Modern utilization: Immediate site area is grazing land. Apparently salt content of soil here is too high for effective cultivation. Sections of adjacent areas have recently been reclaimed for intensive cultivation by large-scale flushing and drainage projects. Two small modern residential complexes occur at the eastern and southern margins of the site area.

Archaeological remains: Variable light and light-to-moderate concentrations of surface pottery over a low mounded area roughly two hectares in size. No structural remains. Mixed with approximately equal quantities of Late Toltec pottery (Tx-LT-38), and traces of Terminal Formative (Tx-TF-32) material.

Classification: Hamlet; fewer than 50 people.

Tx-LF-16

Natural setting: 2480 m, near upper end of the Lower Piedmont. Situated on a gently sloping, broad ridge top, lying between two major barrancas. A severely eroded area, with very little soil cover, and large stretches of bare tepetate.

Modern utilization: Very marginal grazing land.

Archaeological remains: Very light surface pottery over an area of about six hectares. No structural remains. Sherds rest directly on bare tepetate in most cases.

Classification: Hamlet; fewer than 50 people.

Tx-LF-17

Natural setting: 2390 to 2410 m, in Lower Piedmont. Located along the lower, western end of a broad ridge top, lying between two major barrancas. A gently sloping area of severe erosion, with little soil cover and large stretches of bare tepetate.

Modern utilization: Marginal grazing land. Lower area, several hundred m to the west, is intensively cultivated.

Archaeological remains: Variable light and light-to-moderate concentrations of surface pottery over an area of about 8 hectares. The occupational debris generally rests on bare tepetate. No structural remains. Sizable quantities of Terminal Formative and some Early Classic material occur slightly upslope (Tx-TF-31; Tx-EC-21), with some overlap onto the eastern end of Tx-LF-17.

Classification: Small dispersed village, roughly 100 to 200 people.

Tx-LF-18

Natural setting: 2375 to 2410 m, in Lower Piedmont. Located along the top of a broad, gently sloping ridge, lying between two major barrancas. Severely eroded, with little soil cover, and large stretches of bare tepetate.

Modern utilization: Marginal grazing land. Lower area, several hundred meters to the west, is intensively cultivated.

Archaeological remains: Variable light and light-to-moderate concentrations of surface pottery over an area of about 9 hectares. Occupational debris is resting on bare tepetate. No structural remains. The site has expanded considerably from the small hamlet situated here in Middle Formative times (Tx-MF-12). Lighter quantities of Terminal Formative material are also found (Tx-TF-32).

Classification: Small dispersed village; 100 to 200 people.

Tx-LF-19

Natural setting: 2395 m, in Lower Piedmont. On gently sloping, broad ridge top, lying between two major barrancas. A severely eroded area, with very little soil cover and large stretches of bare tepetate.

Modern utilization: Marginal grazing land.

Archaeological remains: Light concentrations of surface pottery scattered over an area of about two hectares. No structural remains. Occupational debris generally rests on bare tepetate.

Classification: Hamlet; fewer than 50 people.

Tx-LF-20

Natural setting: 2405 m, at upper end of Lower Piedmont. Situated on a broad, gently sloping ridge top, lying between two major barrancas. A severely eroded area, largely consisting of bare tepetate and virtually no soil cover.

Modern utilization: Wasteland.

Archaeological remains: Light concentrations of surface pottery over an area of less than one hectare. No structural remains. Mixed with larger amounts of Terminal Formative material (Tx-TF-38). All occupational debris rests on bare tepetate.

Classification: Hamlet; fewer than 50 people.

Tx-LF-21

Natural setting: 2570 m, in Upper Piedmont. In area of moderate slope on a hillspur immediately adjacent to a major barranca. A severely eroded area, with large patches of bare tepetate and very little soil cover.

Modern utilization: Marginal grazing

Archaeological remains: Light concentrations of surface pottery over an area of less than one hectare. No structural remains. Surface pottery is badly weathered, and the sample is not particularly diagnostic. Dominant occupational component is Terminal Formative (Tx-TF-39); a few Middle Formative sherds are also probably present (Tx-MF-19). Pottery is characteristically found washing from the sides of erosional remnants.

Classification: Hamlet; fewer than 50 people.

Tx-LF-22

Natural setting: 2410 to 2490 m, at upper edge of the Lower Piedmont. Situated on a broad, gentle slope between two major barrancas. The soil cover is shallow to moderately deep and generally well preserved due to the maintenance of terrace and bancal systems. Soil depth thins upslope to the east, and there are some patches of bare tepetate in this latter zone.

Modern utilization: Much of the western half of the site is covered by the modern dispersed village of Coatepec. The area around Coatepec is intensively cultivated (all rainfall agriculture), with maguey for pulque production, a principal crop. There is some adobe manufacture in pockets of deep soil at the eastern end of the site area. A large commercial gravel quarry is located in the barranca to the north of the site.

Archaeological remains: The heaviest occupation occurs in the western sector of the site, under and around Coatepec, where light-to-moderate and moderate concentrations of surface pottery are distributed fairly evenly and continuously. The eastern half of the site area shows more dispersed settlement, with variable light and light-to-moderate sherd cover. There are no obvious structural remains. The occupational debris is mixed with abundant Aztec material in the western part of the site (Tx-A-99). The total surface area is roughly 40 hectares, but the original site may have encompassed as much as 50 hectares or more if Late Formative occupation extends beneath modern Coatepec.

Classification: Large nucleated village; 600 to 1800 people. Next to Tx-LF-12, this is the largest Late Formative site in the Texcoco Region.

Tx-LF-23

Natural setting: 2505 m, at the lowermost end of the Upper Piedmont. Situated on a broad, gentle slope lying between two major barrancas. Moderate to severe erosion, with thin soil cover and some patches of bare tepetate. The maintenance of few bancals has prevented wholesale sheet erosion on the site.

Modern utilization: Intensive cultivation of maize, beans, and maguey on noneroded areas. Badly eroded land useful only for marginal grazing.

Archaeological remains: Variable light and light-to-moderate concentrations of surface pottery distributed over an area of about six hectares. No structural remains. Sherds characteristically occur washing out of the walls of erosional remnants. Light Middle Formative material is also found here (Tx-MF-18).

Classification: Hamlet; fewer than 100 people.

Tx-LF-24

Natural setting: 2450 m, near the upper limits of the Lower Piedmont. Situated on a broad, gentle slope, adjacent to a major barranca. Moderate erosion, with shallow soil and some patches of bare tepetate.

Modern utilization: Intensive rainfall cultivation, with some areas of pasture where soil cover is very thin or absent.

Archaeological remains: Light-to-moderate concentrations of surface pottery over an area of roughly three hectares. No structural remains.

Classification: Hamlet; fewer than 50 people.

Tx-LF-25

Natural setting: 2340 to 2350 m, in Lower Piedmont. Located on gently sloping ground at the eastern base of Cerro Tonaltepec. The site area lies near the head of a small barranca. Area is only slightly eroded, with moderately deep soil.

Modern utilization: Intensive rainfall cultivation, with maguey as a dominant crop. The higher slopes above the site are grazing land.

Archaeological remains: Variable light and light-to-moderate concentrations of surface pottery over an area of roughly three hectares. No structural remains. Mixed with smaller amounts of Middle Formative (Tx-MF-15) and Terminal Formative (Tx-TF-43) material, together with Early Classic (Tx-EC-28) and Aztec (Tx-A-100) sherds.

Classification: Hamlet; fewer than 50 people.

Tx-LF-26

Natural setting: Below 2240 m, on the flat Lakeshore Plain. Located roughly at or near the Conquest-period shoreline of Lake Texcoco. In a zone of deep alluvial soil. Cerro Chimalhuacan rises steeply about one km to the west.

Modern utilization: Intensive rainfall cultivation, with some recently-built residential complexes in the area.

Archaeological remains: Variable light and light-to-moderate concentrations of surface pottery over an area of about one hectare. No structural remains. Mixed with traces of Terminal Formative occupation (Tx-TF-50).

Classification: Hamlet; fewer than 50 people.

Tx-LF-27

Natural setting: Below 2240 m, on flat Lakeshore Plain. Situated at or near the Conquest-period shoreline of Lake Texcoco. In a zone of deep alluvial soil Cerro Chimalhuacan rises steeply about 700 m to the west.

Modern utilization: Intensive rainfall cultivation, except in a few localities where Aztec salt tlateles occur and land is used only for grazing.

Archaeological remains: Variable light and light-to-moderate concentrations of surface pottery over an area of about one hectare. No structural remains can be assigned to this period. Mixed with heavier amounts of Middle Formative (Tx-MF-13) and Aztec (Tx-A-109) material.

Classification: Hamlet; fewer than 50 people.

Tx-LF-28

Natural setting: 2250 m, at northeastern base of Cerro Chimalhuacan, on a low bluff just above the main Lakeshore Plain. Situated in a gently sloping region of shallow to moderately deep soil. Terracing and bancal systems have prevented severe erosion.

Modern utilization: Some rainfall cultivation. Part of the area is a cemetery today. Higher slopes to the west are covered with abandoned terraces. The densely-packed houses of present-day Chimalhuacan extend up to the base of the bluff. Several small basalt quarries, both operative and abandoned, are found on the nearby hillslopes.

Archaeological remains: Very light concentrations of surface pottery over an area of less than one hectare. No structural remains. Mixed with much heavier Early Toltec (Tx-ET-19) and light Terminal Formative material (Tx-TF-49).

Classification: Hamlet; fewer than 50 people. These sherds may represent debris associated with working of the basalt quarry rather than with permanent residential areas.

Tx-LF-29

Natural setting: 2240 m, on flat Lakeshore Plain, at western base of Cerro Chimalhuacan. In zone of deep alluvial soil. Situated near the Conquest-period shoreline of Lake Texcoco.

Modern utilization: Intensive rainfall cultivation. Some basalt quarrying on a low bluff immediately adjacent to the site on the west. Site area is situated between the modern nucleated communities of Chimalhuacan to the west and Santa María Natívitas to the east.

Archaeological remains: Variable light and light-to-moderate concentrations of surface pottery over an area of about 12 hectares. No structural remains of this period. Mixed with larger quantities of Middle Formative (Tx-MF-13), Terminal Formative (Tx-TF-50), and Aztec (Tx-A-109) material. Some occupational debris may be obscured by the thick alfalfa growth in fields to the east of the site.

Classification: Small dispersed village; 150 to 250 people.

TERMINAL FORMATIVE

Tx-TF-1

Natural setting: 2300 to 2340 m, in the Lower Piedmont. Some scattered occupation up to 2410 m. Situated on the gently sloping southern flank of Cerro Azteca, with some spill over onto the adjacent Lower Piedmont plain. The site area is cut through by three major barrancas. Erosion has been severe; soil cover is thin, and there are numerous patches of bare tepetate.

Modern utilization: Most of the site area is suited only for grazing and scattered maguey. The piedmont plain to the south is intensively cultivated in subsistence crops (rainfall agriculture).

Archaeological remains: Variable light-to-moderate and moderate concentrations of surface pottery and rock rubble over an area of about 74 hectares. Several distinct mounds occur throughout the western half of the site area (Appendix 2). These are built on a series of six to eight broad terraces (*ca.* 10 m wide and 0.5 to 1 m high) which follow the contours of the lower hillslope (Pl. 17,*a*, 18,*a*). Such mounds are of two distinct types: (*a*) structures measuring 0.5 to 1.5 m high, covered with moderate concentrations of surface pottery and rock rubble, occasionally with small remnants of stone wall bases preserved on their upper surfaces; (*b*) larger structures, up to 8 m high, constructed in 2 or more tiers or platforms, also covered with abundant surface pottery (Pl. 17,*b*). Structures of the second category always occur in higher, steeper sections of the site area, above the hill base where mounds of the first group are clustered. The eastern half of the site lacks recognizable mounds, although sherds and rock rubble are abundant. Occupational debris from Early Toltec and Aztec times also occurs in this area (Tx-ET-4; Tx-A-17).

Classification: Secondary regional center; 1200 to 2500 people.

Tx-TF-2

Natural setting: 2480 to 2500 m, along top of a narrow ridge extending south from the main body of Cerro Azteca, some 100 m above the level of the main Lower Piedmont plain to the south and east. Ground surface is irregular, with generally shallow soil and numerous rock outcrops. Erosion has been moderate to severe.

Modern utilization: Grazing, plus some cultivated maguey.

Archaeological remains: Variable light and light-to-moderate concentrations of surface pottery over an area of about 8 hectares. Three tlateles can be distinguished (Appendix 2). Several stone wall bases can be distinguished at several points on the ridge top, including several in association with tlatel 867 (Fig. 1). Steep slopes below and above the site area have been partially terraced in the past, but these are presently in a badly deteriorated condition.

Classification: Small segregated elite district; 100 to 150 people.

Tx-TF-3

Natural setting: 2620 m, at top of Cerro Az-

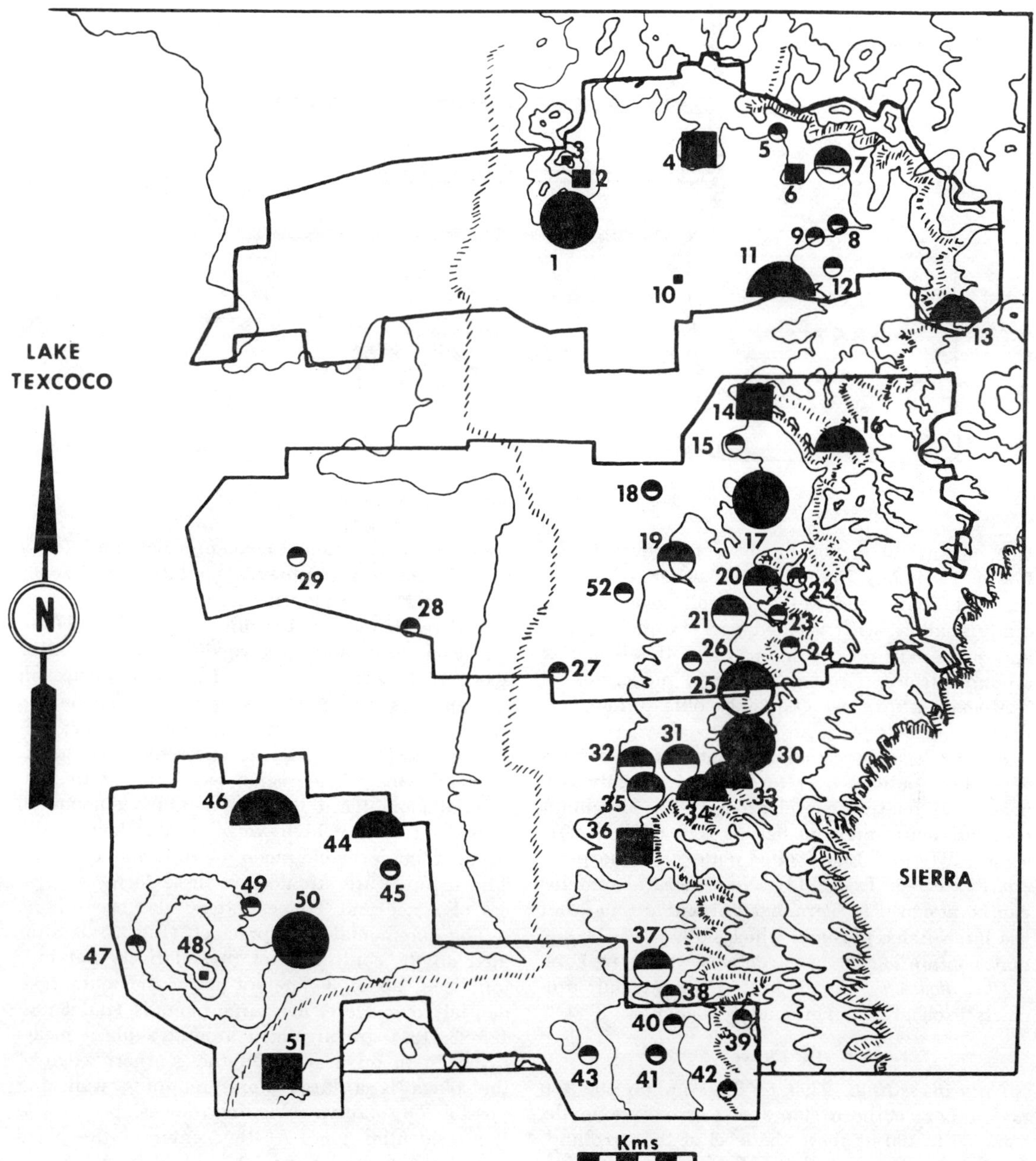

Map 7—Texcoco Region: Terminal Formative settlement (schematic). Contour interval 100 meters. For key see map p. 25.

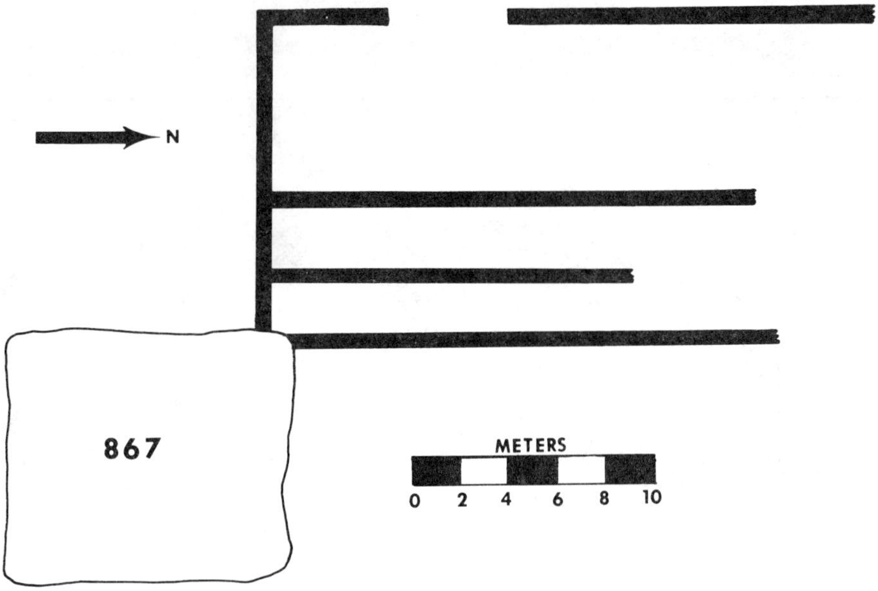

Fig. 1—Tlatel 867 complex, Tx-TF-2.

teca, about 250 to 300 m above the level of the Lower Piedmont Plain and Lakeshore Plain to the east, south, and west. The soil cover is generally shallow, with isolated pockets of deep soil and numerous rock outcrops over the irregular ground surface. Erosion has been moderate.

Modern utilization: Grazing, plus a few cultivated maguey.

Archaeological remains: Light concentrations of surface pottery over an area of roughly one hectare of relatively level ground. The dominant occupational component here is Aztec (Tx-A-20); some Early and Late Toltec pottery is also present (Tx-ET-6; Tx-LT-14). No structural remains can be assigned to Terminal Formative times, but the large Aztec pyramid which dominates the site may contain earlier constructions within its core.

Classification: Small hilltop ceremonial precinct; probably no permanent residents.

Tx-TF-4

Natural setting: 2390 to 2450 m, on the top and upper southern slopes of Cerro Teponaxtle, some 50 to 100 m above the level of the surrounding Lower Piedmont plain. Main part of site situated at 2420 m on a broad natural terrace. Ground surface is irregular, with shallow soil cover and some rock outcrops.

Modern utilization: Grazing, plus a few cultivated maguey.

Archaeological remains: The site may be divided into three distinct zones: (*a*) a residential area; (*b*) a ceremonial-civic precinct; and (*c*) a possible fortress complex. The latter two zones lack traces of permanent occupation.

The residential area contains light-to-moderate surface pottery and rock rubble over an area of about 15 hectares on a broad natural terrace on the upper southern slopes of Cerro Teponaxtle. Within this area at least 15 mounds (Fig. 2; Appendix II; Pl. 19, 20) can presently be distinguished. This whole region is covered with substantial stone-faced terraces measuring about 10 m wide, 1 to 2 m high, with variable lengths depending on local character of hillslope (Pl. 21). The mounds are situated on these terraces. Traces of Aztec and Toltec pottery also occur here.

The ceremonial-civic precinct (Fig. 3) is situated on the south side of the relatively flat hilltop itself, about 30 meters above the main residential zone. Here, five large mounds (tlatel nos. 185-88, 191) are arranged around a plaza measuring 24 m on a side. On the southern edge of the plaza is a large stone retaining wall and possibly a stairway leading downslope toward the residential zone. At the center of the plaza is a small mound some 50 cm high and 3 m on a side. This feature may represent a small altar. Surface pottery is very light throughout the ceremonial-civic precinct.

The "fortress" complex occupies the highest point on the hilltop, some 5 to 6 meters above the level of the ceremonial-civic precinct, to the southeast. The outstanding feature of the "fort-

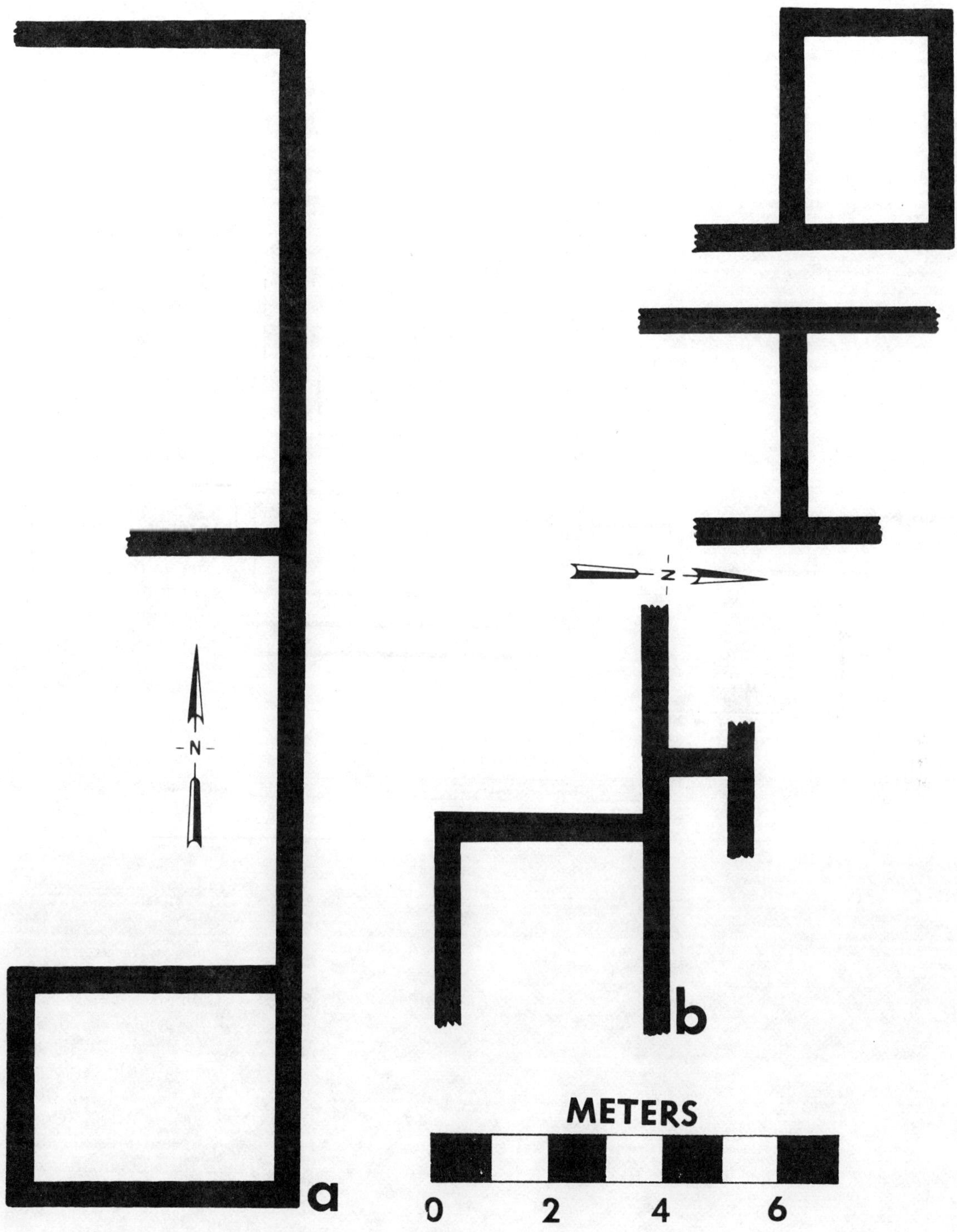

Fig. 2—*a*) Tlatel 148, Tx-TF-4; *b*) Tlatel 144, Tx-TF-4.

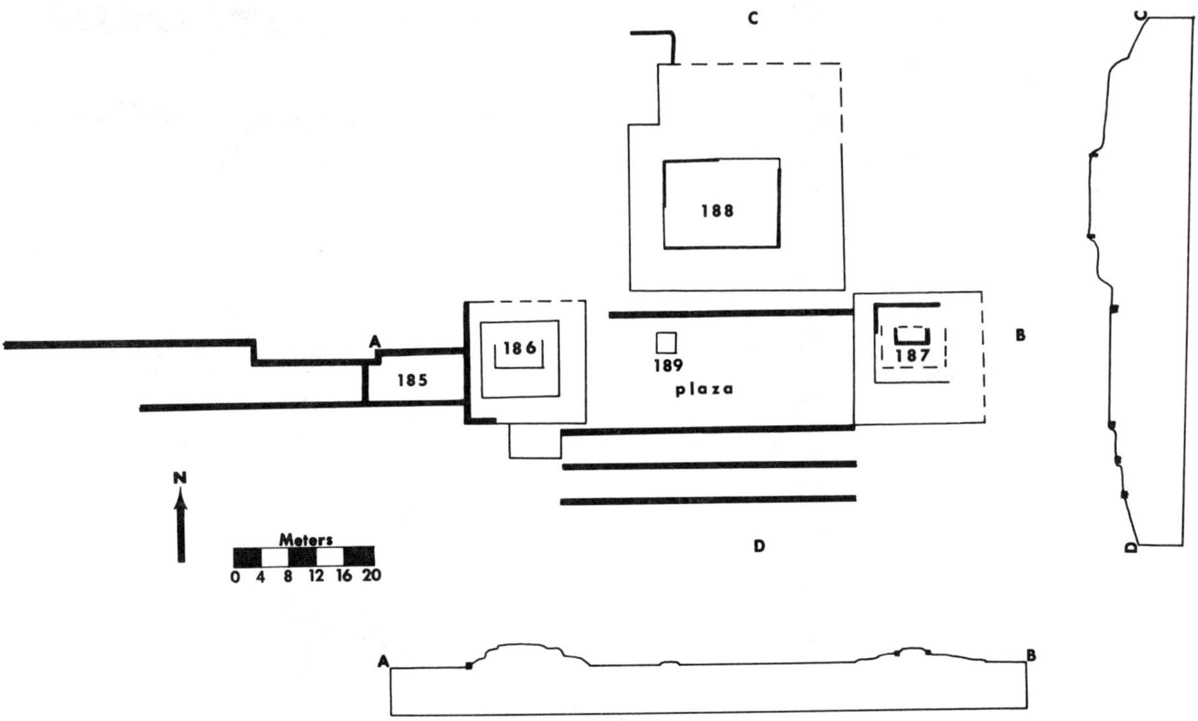

Fig. 3—Tlatel 185-189 complex, Tx-TF-4.

Fig. 4—Tlatel 317 complex, Tx-TF-4.

ress" zone is the large series of preserved stone wall bases which delineate a complex series of room and terrace patterns (Fig. 4). These walls are generally over 50 cm thick, and measure up to 64 m long. The fact that these walls are so solid and extensive, and that they appear to form long narrow passageways with few doorways, superficially suggests a fortress or defensive function. Very little surface pottery appears in this area.

The steep slopes north of the "fortress" are extensively terraced. All these terraces appear ancient, and all are presently in advanced stages of deterioration.

A large rock carving (Pl. 36,*b*) was discovered in an area of little occupational debris at the western base of Cerro Teponaxtle. This is probably Aztec, but could date to Terminal Formative times.

Classification: Large segregated elite district; 300 to 600 people.

Tx-TF-5

Natural setting: 2340 m, in Lower Piedmont. Situated on gently sloping ground at the southern base of Cerro Tepetlaoxtoc, near a major barranca. Severe erosion, with shallow soil cover and patches of bare tepetate.

Modern utilization: Grazing, with some cultivated maguey.

Archaeological remains: Light concentrations of surface pottery over an area of less than one hectare. Dominant occupational component is Aztec (Tx-A-24). No structural remains can be assigned to Terminal Formative times, although there are several Aztec mounds which may contain earlier construction levels. Slopes are covered with abandoned terraces, whose age is questionable.

Classification: Hamlet; fewer than 50 people.

Tx-TF-6

Natural setting: 2420 m, along the top of a narrow ridge extending southward from the main body of Cerro Teptelaoxtoc. Irregular ground surface, with shallow soil cover and numerous rock outcrops. The site is situated some 60 m above the level of the main Lower Piedmont Plain.

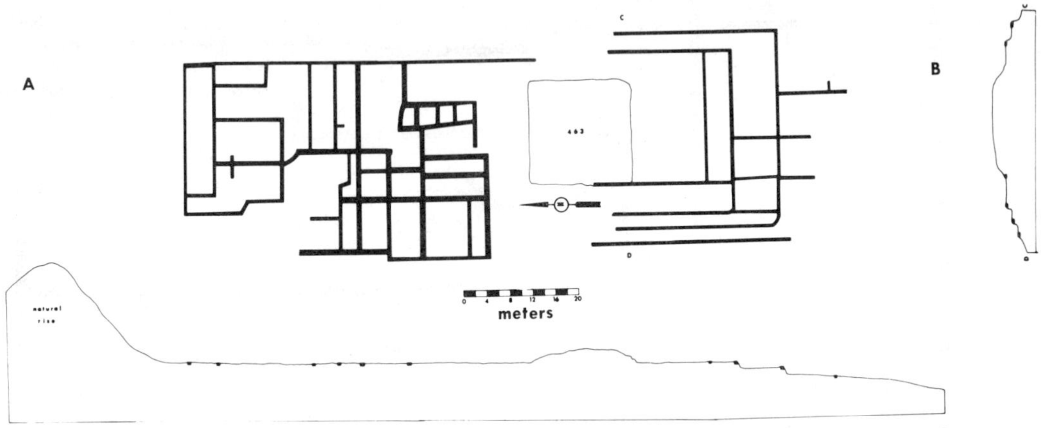

Fig. 5—Tlatel 462 complex, Tx-TF-6.

Modern utilization: Grazing, with some cultivated maguey.

Archaeological remains: Light-to-moderate concentrations of surface pottery and moderate rock rubble over an area of about two hectares. Much of the ridgetop is covered with a complicated series of wall bases which appear to define a complex of rooms, passageways, and platforms (Fig. 5). A pyramidal mound, some 2.5 m tall and 18 m on a side, rises from the center of the complex of walls and platforms. This mound rests on two tiers of broad platforms, each measuring about one meter high at the downslope face. In addition to the light-to-moderate Terminal Formative surface pottery on and around this structure, a trace of Aztec ceramics was also noted.

Classification: Small segregated elite district; 50 to 100 people.

Tx-TF-7

Natural setting: 2380 m, in Lower Piedmont. Situated on gently sloping ground at the southern base of Cerro Tepetlaoxtoc. The eastern end of the site area has been cut through by a large barranca, and several small barrancas and numerous washes have severely eroded the entire site. Soil cover is shallow or lacking, and there are large stretches of badly scarred bare tepetate.

Modern utilization: Intensive maguey cultivation and grazing. Site area was extensively terraced, but the terraces have now fallen into disrepair.

Archaeological remains: Light-to-moderate surface pottery over an area of about six hectares. Mixed with Aztec material in some parts of the site area (Tx-A-25). One mound can be distinguished. This measures 20 cm high, 7 m in diameter, and probably represents a Terminal Formative residential structure. Terminal Formative pottery is predominately Tzacualli (one of the few instances in which this material can be definitely identified in the Texcoco Region). The age of the abandoned terracing in the site area is unclear.

Classification: Small seminucleated village; 100 to 150 people.

Tx-TF-8

Natural setting: 2330 m, in the Lower Piedmont. Situated on a broad, gentle slope, near the Río Papalotla. The steep slopes of Cerro Xochihuatl rise abruptly a few hundred meters north of the site, across the river. Erosion has been moderate; soil is shallow to moderately deep.

Modern utilization: Intensive rainfall cultivation.

Archaeological remains: Variable light and light-to-moderate concentrations of surface pottery over an area of less than one hectare. No structural remains.

Classification: Hamlet; fewer than 50 people. May represent a single household unit.

Tx-TF-9

Natural setting: 2330 m, in Lower Piedmont. On broad, gently sloping area east of modern town of Tepetlaoxtoc. Slight to moderate erosion, with moderately deep soil cover.

Modern utilization: Intensive maguey cultivation, and grazing.

Archaeological remains: Variable light and light-to-moderate concentrations of surface pottery and rock rubble over an area of less than one hectare. No structural remains.

Classification: Hamlet; fewer than 50 people.

Tx-TF-10

Natural setting: 2310 to 2330 m, in Lower Piedmont. Situated on the top and eastern flanks of a small, low hill, adjacent to the Río Papalotla. Erosion has been moderate to severe. Soil cover is shallow to moderately deep, with some rock outcrops.

Modern utilization: Grazing and maguey cultivation. The lower fields to the east of the hill are intensively cultivated in subsistence crops.

Archaeological remains: Two distinct zones can be distinguished: a ceremonial-civic precinct on the hilltop; and a residential zone on the eastern flank and base of the hill. The ceremonial-civic precinct (Fig. 6) features a large plaza (50 by 40 m) bordered by large pyramidal mounds on its east and west sides (tlateles 119 and 123; see Appendix II). The main plaza is built up roughly two m above the level of the main hilltop. The western half of the plaza is about 1.5 m higher than the eastern half. Surface pottery is quite light throughout the ceremonial-civic precinct, though somewhat heavier on tlatel 119. This latter structure may have some Tzacualli sherds on its surface, but weathering has been too severe to be certain.

In the residential zone, variable light and light-to-moderate concentrations of surface pottery are found over an area of less than one hectare. No structural remains.

Classification: Small segregated elite district; fewer than 50 people.

Tx-TF-11

Natural setting: 2320 to 2350 m, in the Lower Piedmont. Situated on hilltop and gentle eastern flanks of Cerro Tepetlosco, about 500 m north of the Río Papalotla. Erosion has been severe. Soil cover generally shallow, with some patches of bare tepetate.

Modern utilization: Predominately grazing, with minor maguey cultivation. A small tezontle-gravel quarry is located in the central site area.

Archaeological remains: Variable light, light-to-moderate, and moderate concentrations of surface pottery over an area of about 25 hectares. Mixed with abundant Late Formative pottery in the eastern half of the site (Tx-LF-8). Some Early Toltec material also occurs (Tx-ET-13). A single mound can be distinguished. This measures about 60 cm high and 18 m in diameter, and is covered with light-to-moderate concentrations of Terminal Formative pottery. This feature probably represents a domestic residential structure that can be assigned to the Terminal Formative period. Light Late Formative and a trace of Aztec and Late Toltec material also occur on this feature.

Classification: Large nucleated village; 400 to 800 people.

Tx-TF-12

Natural setting: 2390 m, in the Lower Piedmont. Situated on a broad, gently sloping land surface. Erosion has been moderate. Soil cover

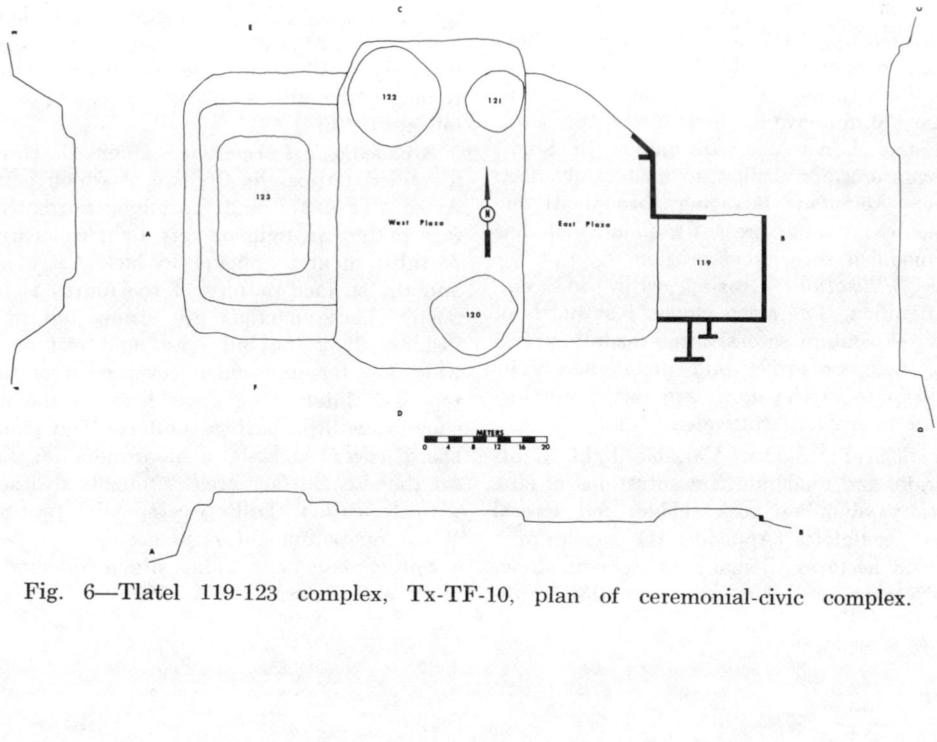

Fig. 6—Tlatel 119-123 complex, Tx-TF-10, plan of ceremonial-civic complex.

varies from shallow to moderately deep.

Modern utilization: Predominately devoted to maguey cultivation, with some minor production of maize and beans.

Archaeological remains: Variable light and light-to-moderate concentrations of surface pottery over an area of less than one hectare. No structural remains. Mixed with some Aztec material (Tx-A-38).

Classification: Hamlet; fewer than 50 people.

Tx-TF-13

Natural setting: 2560 to 2570 m, in Upper Piedmont. Situated on a broad gently sloping ridge top between two major barrancas. Erosion has been severe. Soil cover is thin to absent, and there are large stretches of bare tepetate and some outcrops of bedrock.

Modern utilization: Predominately grazing and some maguey cultivation. Small amounts of maize are also grown here (rainfall agriculture).

Archaeological remains: Variable light, light-to-moderate, and moderate concentrations of badly weathered surface pottery over an area of about 10 hectares. Only one structure can be distinguished: a large pyramidal mound measuring 2.5 m high and 20 m in diameter. Considerable pitting indicates that this is a solid rock rubble construction. There is very little surface pottery on the mound itself.

Classification: Small nucleated village; 150 to 300 people. This community apparently contained ceremonial-civic structure.

Tx-TF-14

Natural setting: 2460 to 2510 m, on a high level to gently-sloping saddle at the northern end of Cerro Purificación (Pl. 22). The site is situated some 170 m above the level of the surrounding piedmont plain to the west and north. Slight to moderate erosion; shallow to moderately deep soil cover. Abundant terracing throughout the site area, even though presently abandoned, has greatly modified severity of erosion.

Modern utilization: Grazing, with some maguey cultivation. The steep slopes just north of the site area contain several large tezontle-gravel quarries, both operative and abandoned. The lower hillslopes to the north are intricately terraced and intensively cultivated.

Archaeological remains: Variable light, light-to-moderate, and moderate concentrations of surface pottery, abundant rock rubble, and several fairly distinct tlateles (Appendix II) over an area of about 18 hectares. Remains of ancient stone-faced terracing are abundant over the southwestern sector of the site, and on some of the adjacent steep slopes above and below the site area. Terraces within the site measure 15 to 20 m wide, and roughly 100 m long. Surface pottery is scarce in this terraced zone, suggesting that the function of these features may have been agricultural (if they date to Terminal Formative times and are contemporary with the occupational debris). Terraces on the adjacent steep slopes are considerably narrower, shorter, less well defined, and were probably intended for agricultural purposes, or simply as erosion checks, since they lack occupational refuse.

The site consists of two major subunits: (a) a residential complex, which accounts for most of the archaeological remains, and (b) a ceremonial-civic precinct atop a low knoll at the northwest corner of the occupied zone. This latter area contains a large solid rock rubble pyramid mound (tlatel 413) (Pl. 22,*a*) situated at one end of a small plaza (15 by 25 m in area). Sherd cover throughout the entire ceremonial-civic precinct is quite light relative to the rest of the site area.

Classification: Large segregated elite district; 300 to 500 people.

Tx-TF-15

Natural setting: 2415 m, atop an isolated hill-spur extending off the northwest end of Cerro Purificación. Situated some 90 m above the level of the surrounding piedmont plain. Shallow soil cover, with some rock outcrops.

Modern utilization: Grazing, plus a few cultivated maguey. The lower eastern hill flanks below the site area are intricately terraced and intensively cultivated. The piedmont plain surrounding the hill is intensively cultivated (rainfall agriculture).

Archaeological remains: Four tlateles were identified (Appendix 2), two of which have both Aztec (Tx-A-67) and Terminal Formative surface pottery in light or very light concentrations. A third mound appears to lack Aztec pottery, and the surface pottery of the fourth is undiagnostic. These mounds are strung out in linear fashion along the hill crest, and rest on vague, wide, low terraces which cover most of the hilltop. The intervening areas between the mounds show very little surface pottery. The paucity of sherd cover suggests a nonresidential function for the site. Surface area is roughly five hectares.

Classification: Hilltop ceremonial precinct; little or no permanent residence.

Special comment: This site is referred to by Wolf and Palerm (1955: 269).

Tx-TF-16

Natural setting: 2505 m, at lower edge of the Upper Piedmont. Located on a high, flat bluff at the edge of a deep barranca, just to the northeast of the main pass between Cerro Purificación and Cerro San Miguel. Moderate to severe erosion, with shallow soil cover and some patches of bare tepetate. Wholesale sheet erosion over the whole site area has been prevented by the presence of stone and maguey terracing around the edges of the bluff.

Modern utilization: Grazing, with a few cultivated maguey.

Archaeological remains: Variable light, light-to-moderate, and moderate concentrations of surface pottery over an area of about six hectares. No structural remains. Pottery is extremely weathered, but looks predominately Tzacualli (one of the few sites where ceramics of this complex can be identified with any certainty).

Classification: Small nucleated village; 100 to 150 people.

Tx-TF-17

Natural setting: 2330 to 2360 m, in Lower Piedmont. On broad gentle slope between two major barrancas (Pl. 18,*b*). Generally moderate erosion and shallow soil cover, with smaller sections of severely eroded land. Pockets of deeper soil occur in low areas immediately adjacent to the barranca bed.

Modern utilization: Intensive rainfall cultivation over most of the site area, with some grazing land where erosion has been most severe.

Archaeological remains: Variable light-to-moderate and moderate concentrations of surface pottery and rock rubble over an area of about 118 hectares. The ceramic material is badly weathered, and no systematic attempt was made to distinguish Tzacualli from Tezoyuca-Patlachique sherds. Most pottery appears to be Tezoyuca-Patlachique, but some fairly definite Tzacualli material was noted, particularly in the northern third of the site area. There are no obvious structural remains. The Terminal Formative is mixed with Middle Formative (Tx-MF-6, Tx-MF-7, Tx-MF-8), Late Formative (Tx-LF-10, Tx-LF-11), Early Classic (Tx-EC-11, Tx-EC-12), Late Classic (Tx-LC-11), and Aztec (Tx-A-65) material. This should be a crucial area for testing problems related to the Formative-Classic transition.

Classification: Secondary regional center; 1800 to 3500 people.

Tx-TF-18

Natural setting: 2305 m, in Lower Piedmont. On broad, gentle slope, near a major barranca. Moderate to severe erosion in the immediate site area, with shallow soil and patches of bare tepetate.

Modern utilization: Grazing land, at eastern edge of an intensively cultivated zone.

Archaeological remains: Light concentrations of surface pottery over an area of less than one hectare. No structural remains. Mixed with larger quantities of Aztec material (Tx-A-64).

Classification: Hamlet; fewer than 50 people.

Tx-TF-19

Natural setting: 2330 to 2350 m, in Lower Piedmont. Located on broad, gentle slope, along both sides of a major barranca. Moderate to severe erosion, with generally shallow soil cover and some patches of bare tepetate.

Modern utilization: Most of site area is intensively cultivated (rainfall agriculture), except for the most severely eroded land which is now useful only for grazing.

Archaeological remains: Variable light and light-to-moderate concentrations of surface pottery over an area of roughly 11 hectares. No structural remains. Mixed with some Early Classic (Tx-EC-15) and Aztec (Tx-A-57) material.

Classification: Small dispersed village; 100 to 150 people.

Tx-TF-20

Natural setting: 2400 to 2460 m, in Lower Piedmont. Situated on the southwestern flank of Cerro Tetzcotzingo, just above a major barranca. Intricate terracing over the entire hillslope has maintained moderately deep soil cover, and erosion has been slight.

Modern utilization: An intricately terraced area, nearly all of which is intensively cultivated. The lower terraces are partially irrigated. Some of the higher terraces are presently uncultivated, and serve only as erosion checks on grazing land.

Archaeological remains: Variable light and light-to-moderate surface pottery over an area of about 24 hectares. No structural remains. Mixed with heavier quantities of Late Formative ceramics (Tx-LF-12).

Classification: Dispersed village; 200 to 350 people.

Tx-TF-21

Natural setting: 2380 to 2440 m, in Lower

Piedmont. Situated on a broad, gentle slope lying between two major barrancas. Generally shallow soil cover, with some patches of bare tepetate, except in and around village of San Dieguito where terrace and bancal systems have prevented severe erosion.

Modern utilization: The area in and around the village of San Dieguito is intensively cultivated, especially the intricately terraced barranca walls to the north of the site. The severely eroded land in the western part of the site area is used only as marginal pasture. The modern village of San Dieguito borders the site on the north, and probably covers some Terminal Formative occupation.

Archaeological remains: Variable light and very light concentrations of surface pottery widely scattered throughout an area of about 40 hectares. No structural remains. Mixed with heavier quantities of Late Formative (Tx-LF-12) and Aztec (Tx-A-58) material.

Classification: Small dispersed village; 100 to 200 people.

Tx-TF-22

Natural setting: 2575 m, on level ridge near top of Cerro Metecatl. Situated some 150 m above the level of the gentle piedmont slopes surrounding the hill. Shallow soil, with abundant rock outcroppings.

Modern utilization: Grazing, plus a few cultivated maguey. The terraced hillslopes to the north, west, and south are intensively cultivated.

Archaeological remains: Light concentrations of surface pottery over an area of about one hectare. No structural remains. Mixed with heavier quantities of Aztec (Tx-A-61) and some Late Toltec (Tx-LT-44) material.

Classification: Hamlet; fewer than 50 people.

Tx-TF-23

Natural setting: 2460 to 2500 m, at uppermost edge of Lower Piedmont. Situated on a broad, gentle slope between two major barrancas. Severely eroded, with little soil cover and large stretches of bare tepetate.

Modern utilization: Light concentrations of surface pottery over an area of about four hectares. No structural remains. Mixed with heavier quantities of Late Formative (Tx-LF-12) and Aztec (Tx-A-60) material. Occupational debris is usually resting on bare tepetate.

Classification: Hamlet; fewer than 50 people.

Tx-TF-24

Natural setting: 2480 m, at the upper end of the Lower Piedmont. Situated on a broad, gentle slope adjacent to a deeply entrenched major barranca. Severely eroded, with little soil cover and large stretches of bare tepetate. Only on the terraced slopes of the barranca at the north edge of the site area does any significant soil cover remain.

Modern utilization: Marginal grazing land, with some cultivation on the terraced slopes to the north.

Archaeological remains: Variable light to very light concentrations of surface pottery over an area of less than one hectare. No structural remains. Mixed with much more abundant Aztec material (Tx-A-86). The occupational debris is resting on bare tepetate.

Classification: Hamlet; fewer than 50 people.

Tx-TF-25

Natural setting: 2460 to 2510 m, at juncture of Upper and Lower Piedmonts. Situated on a broad, gentle slope lying between two major barrancas. The whole area is severely eroded, with very little or no soil cover and large stretches of badly scarred bare tepetate.

Modern utilization: Marginal grazing and wasteland, with isolated pockets of cultivated land where small terraces and erosional remnants exist.

Archaeological remains: Varible light and light-to-moderate concentrations of surface pottery over an area of about 50 hectares. No structural remains. Mixed with somewhat more abundant Aztec pottery (Tx-A-87), and a small amount of Late Formative material (Tx-LF-16).

Classification. Large dispersed village; 500 to 750 people.

Tx-TF-26

Natural setting: 2400 m, in Lower Piedmont. Situated on a broad, gentle slope to a major barranca. Severely eroded, with little soil cover and large streches of bare tepetate.

Modern utilization: Marginal grazing, with isolated patches of cultivation on erosional remnants and soil pockets.

Archaeological remains: Light concentrations of surface pottery over an area of roughly one hectare. No structural remains. Mixed with much more abundant Aztec material (Tx-A-87). Occupational debris rests on bare tepetate.

Classification: Hamlet; fewer than 50 people.

Tx-TF-27

Natural setting: 2290 m, in Lower Piedmont near edge of Lakeshore Plain. Situated on a broad, gentle slope near a major barranca. Erosion has been slight to moderate. Soil cover is moderately deep.

Modern utilization: Intensive rainfall cultivation.

Archaeological remains: Light concentrations of surface pottery over an area of less than one hectare. No structural remains. Mixed with much more abundant Aztec material (Tx-A-87), and light Early Classic pottery (Tx-EC-21).

Classification: Hamlet; fewer than 50 people.

Tx-TF-28

Natural setting: Below 2240 m, on Lakeshore Plain. Located in general vicinity of Conquest-period shoreline of Lake Texcoco. In area of deep alluvial soil.

Modern utilization: Immediate site area is grazing land. Apparently the salt content of the soil is too high for effective cultivation. Adjacent areas have recently been reclaimed for agriculture by means of large-scale flushing and drainage projects. Two small modern residential households occur at the eastern and southern edges of the site area.

Archaeological remains: Very light concentrations of surface pottery scattered over an area of about one hectare on a large irregular-mounded locality which rises roughly 2 m above the level of surrounding plain. No structural remains. Mixed with more abundant quantities of Late Formative (Tx-LF-15) and Late Toltec (Tx-LT-38) material.

Classification: Hamlet; fewer than 50 people.

Tx-TF-29

Natural setting: Below 2240 m, on Lakeshore Plain. Situated in a zone of deep alluvial soil, in the general vicinity of the Conquest-period shoreline of Lake Texcoco. Ground surface is irregular, with many grass-covered hillocks and intervening depressions.

Modern utilization: Grazing. The salt content of the soil apparently will not permit effective cultivation. Only sharp, tough grass grows here today.

Archaeological remains: Variable light concentrations of surface pottery over an area of roughly one hectare. No structural remains. Mixed with Late Formative (Tx-LF-13), Late Toltec (Tx-LT-36), and Aztec (Tx-A-44) material. All pottery is badly corroded and salt incrusted.

Classification: Hamlet; fewer than 50 people.

Tx-TF-30

Natural setting: 2430 to 2560 m, at juncture of Upper and Lower Piedmonts. Situated on a gently sloping, broad ridge top, lying between two major barrancas. There has been severe erosion over the whole site area, with little or no soil cover remaining. Even the upper layers of the tepetate subsoil have been stripped away to depths of 2 and 3 m over much of the site area.

Modern utilization: Marginal grazing and wasteland. There have been some recent attempts at reforestation in the eastern half of the site.

Archaeological remains: Variable light-to-moderate to moderate-to-heavy surface pottery and heavy rock rubble over an area of about 50 hectares. The original aspect of the site has been badly obscured by the severe erosion. Numerous badly destroyed mounds can be seen throughout the site area, including several pyramidal structures up to 5 m high. Occupational debris is mixed with less abundant Aztec material (Tx-A-89). Surface pottery rests on bare tepetate or is found washing from the sides of erosional remnants.

Classification: Secondary regional center; 1000 to 2000 people,

Tx-TF-31

Natural setting: 2410 to 2450 m, at upper end of the Lower Piedmont. Situated on a gently sloping, broad ridge top, lying between two major barrancas. The entire site area has been severely eroded, and is now predominately badly scarred bare tepetate with little or no soil cover.

Modern utilization: Marginal grazing and wasteland. The lower, flatter land to the west is intensively cultivated (rainfall agriculture).

Archaeological remains: Variable light and light-to-moderate concentrations of surface pottery and rock rubble over an area of roughly 19 hectares. No structural remains. Ceramics are very predominately Tezoyuca-Patlachique, but some Tzacualli material is present in the central site area. In this latter region there is also some Early Classic pottery (Tx-EC-21). The original aspect of the site is badly obscured by severe erosion. Most occupational debris rests on bare tepetate.

Classification: Small dispersed village; 200 to 400 people.

Tx-TF-32

Natural setting: 2380 to 2400 m, near upper edge of the Lower Piedmont. Situated on a gently sloping, broad ridge top, between two major barrancas. Site area has been severely eroded, leaving badly scarred bare tepetate and very little soil cover.

Modern utilization: Marginal grazing and wasteland. Lower, flatter region to the west is intensively cultivated.

Archaeological remains: Variable light and light-to-moderate concentrations of surface pottery over an area of roughly 12 hectares. No structural remains. Mixed with heavier quantities of Late Formative (Tx-LF-18) material. A small Middle Formative hamlet (Tx-MF-12) is also located here. The original aspect of the site has been badly obscured by severe erosion. Occupational debris rests on bare tepetate.

Classification: Small dispersed village; 100 to 200 people.

Tx-TF-33

Natural setting: 2440 to 2490 m, at the upper edge of the Lower Piedmont. Situated on a gently sloping, broad ridge top, between two major barrancas. Severe erosion has produced a ground surface of badly scarred bare tepetate, with little or no soil cover.

Modern utilization: Marginal grazing and wasteland.

Archaeological remains: Variable light-to-moderate concentrations of surface pottery and rock rubble over an area of about 15 hectares. No structural remains. Some Aztec material (Tx-A-90) occurs over most of the site area. At the eastern end of the site Early Classic sherds (Tx-EC-22) are mixed with the Formative pottery (with no definite Tzacualli admixture). The original aspect of the site has been badly obscured by severe erosion. Occupational debris is resting on bare tepetate or washing from the walls of erosional remnants.

Classification: Small nucleated village; 250 to 500 people.

Tx-TF-34

Natural setting: 2400 to 2430 m, in Lower Piedmont. On a gently sloping, broad ridge top lying between two major barrancas. Severe erosion throughout the site area has removed most of the soil cover, leaving little more than badly scarred bare tepetate.

Modern utilization: Marginal grazing and wasteland.

Archaeological remains: Variable light-to-moderate and moderate concentrations of surface pottery and rock rubble over an area of about 9 hectares. No structural remains. The original aspect of the site has been badly obscured by severe erosion. Occupational debris rests on bare tepetate.

Classification: Small nucleated village; 150 to 300 people.

Tx-TF-35

Natural setting: 2390 to 2410 m, in Lower Piedmont. Situated on a broad, gentle slope adjacent to a major barranca. Severe erosion, with shallow soil cover and large stretches of bare tepetate.

Modern utilization: Grazing. Lower land to the west is intensively cultivated.

Archaeological remains: Light concentrations of surface pottery over an area of about 16 hectares. No structural remains.

Classification: Small dispersed village; 100 to 200 people.

Tx-TF-36

Natural setting: 2390 to 2460 m, along the gently sloping top of a narrow ridge which juts out into the broad Lower Piedmont Plain (Pl. 23,*a*). The site area is situated some 50 to 75 m above the level of the surrounding piedmont plain to the north, west, and south. A broad, gently sloping ridge of higher ground connects the site area to the Sierra foothills. Moderate erosion, with shallow to moderately deep soil cover.

Modern utilization: The western end of the site area is used only for pasture and some maguey. The eastern half is intensively cultivated in subsistence crops (rainfall agriculture). Most of the lower ground on the adjacent piedmont plain is intensively cultivated.

Archaeological remains: Variable light-to-moderate and moderate concentrations of surface pottery and rock rubble over an area of about 35 hectares. Structural remains are found only at the western end of the site, where several sizable mounds are present. These include one pyramidal structure about 4 meters high and 15 m in diameter. The western end of the site probably contains the community's ceremonial-civic precinct where all substantial architecture was concentrated.

Classification: Large segregated elite district; 600 to 1200 people.

Tx-TF-37

Natural setting: 2420 to 2460 m, near the upper edge of the Lower Piedmont. Situated on a broad, gentle slope between two major barrancas. Erosion has been slight to moderate. Shallow soil and thick grass cover over most of the site area.

Modern utilization: Grazing, plus some cultivated maguey.

Archaeological remains: Variable very light,

light, and light-to-moderate concentrations of surface pottery over an area of about 10 hectares. No structural remains. Occupational debris mixed with some Early Classic material (Tx-EC-24) at the eastern end of the site.

Classification: Small dispersed village; 100 to 150 people.

Tx-TF-38

Natural setting: 2410 to 2420, near upper edge of the Lower Piedmont. Situated on a broad, gentle slope adjacent to a major barranca. Severe erosion has removed all soil cover, leaving only badly scarred bare tepetate.

Modern utilization: Wasteland.

Archaeological remains: Variable light and light-to-moderate concentrations of surface pottery over an area of about four hectares. No structural remains. Mixed with heavier Aztec material (Tx-A-97). Severe erosion has badly obscured the original aspect of the site. Occupational debris rests on bare tepetate.

Classification: Hamlet; fewer than 50 people.

Tx-TF-39

Natural setting: 2500 to 2580 m, at lower end of the Upper Piedmont. Situated in a moderately sloping area along the top and sides of a ridge spur extending westward from the main Sierra. Severe erosion has removed most of the soil cover, leaving a badly scarred surface of bare tepetate and a few isolated erosional remnants.

Modern utilization: Marginal grazing and wasteland.

Archaeological remains: Variable light and light-to-moderate concentrations of surface pottery scattered over an area of roughly 10 hectares. No structural remains. Most of the Terminal Formative pottery is Tezoyuca-Patlachique, but there are some Tzacualli sherds at the western end of the site area. Pottery is characteristically washing from the sides of erosional remnants. Severe erosion has badly obscured the original aspect of the site.

Classification: Hamlet; 50 to 150 people.

Tx-TF-40

Natural setting: 2430 to 2440 m, in Lower Piedmont. Situated on a broad, gentle slope adjacent to a major barranca. The moderately deep soil cover has been generally well preserved due to the maintenance of terrace and bancal systems in this area.

Modern utilization: Residential structures of the modern village of Coatepec border the site on the south. Most of the immediate site area is intensively cultivated (rainfall agriculture).

Archaeological remains: Variable light and light-to-moderate concentrations of surface pottery over an area of about four hectares. No structural remains. The modern community of Coatepec may cover part of the Terminal Formative residential area. This site could well extend into Tx-TF-41 if it underlies most or all of Coatepec. Occupational debris is mixed with Late Formative (Tx-LF-22) and a little Middle Formative (Tx-MF-17) material.

Classification: Hamlet; fewer than 100 people. Possibly somewhat larger if modern Coatepc covers a part of the site area.

Tx-TF-41

Natural setting: 2430 m, near the upper edge of the Lower Piedmont. Situated on a broad, gentle slope at the south edge of the modern nucleated village of Coatepec. The moderately deep soil cover is generally well preserved due to the maintenance of terrace and bancal systems in this area.

Modern utilization: The immediate site area is intensively cultivated (rainfall agriculture). The northern border of the site is covered with residential structures of Coatepec.

Archaeological remains: Light concentrations of surface pottery over an area of roughly one hectare. No structural remains. This may represent the south edge of a single Terminal Formative residential zone that extends north to Tx-TF-40. Mixed with more abundant Late Formative material (Tx-LF-22).

Classification: Hamlet; less than 50 people. Possibly larger if modern Coatepec covers part of the site.

Tx-TF-42

Natural setting: 2480 m, at the upper edge of the Lower Piedmont. Situated on a broad, gentle slope near a major barranca. Erosion has been most severe at the eastern end of the site area where little soil cover remains. Further west bancal and terrace systems have preserved a greater proportion of the topsoil.

Modern utilization: Rainfall agriculture where soil cover has been maintained. The more severely eroded areas are used only for grazing.

Archaeological remains: Variable light and light-to-moderate concentrations of badly weathered surface pottery over an area of roughly one hectare. No structural remains. The Terminal Formative ceramics seem to be predominately Tzacualli (one of the few locations where this is the case). Mixed with some Late Formative

(Tx-LF-23) and a trace of Middle Formative (Tx-MF-18) material.

Classification: Hamlet; fewer than 50 people.

Tx-TF-43

Natural setting: 2350 m, in the Lower Piedmont. Situated on gently sloping ground at the eastern base of Cerro Tonaltepec. The site area is near the head of a small barranca. Area is only slightly eroded, with moderately deep soil cover.

Modern utilization: Intensively cultivated (rainfall agriculture) with maguey as the dominant crop. The higher slopes above the site are used only for grazing.

Archaeological remains: Variable light and light-to-moderate surface pottery over an area of roughly one hectare. No structural remains. The occupational debris is mixed with light Middle Formative (Tx-MF-15), somewhat heavier Late Formative (Tx-LF-25) and Aztec (Tx-A-100) material.

Classification: Hamlet; fewer than 50 people.

Tx-TF-44

Natural setting: Below 2240 m, on the Lakeshore Plain. Situated in a zone of deep alluvial soil, at or near the Conquest-period shoreline of Lake Texcoco.

Modern utilization: Intensive cultivation, including some irrigated land, with water obtained from wells using gasoline pumps. The immediate site area is planted in maize; the surrounding fields are in alfalfa. The thick alfalfa growth may well obscure some Terminal Formative occupational debris.

Archaeological remains: Variable light, light-to-moderate, and moderate concentrations of surface pottery over an area of about 11 hectares. No structural remains. Mixed with Aztec material (Tx-A-110). Deep alluvial soil may obscure some of site area.

Classification: Small nucleated village; 150 to 300 people.

Tx-TF-45

Natural setting: 2240 m, on the Lakeshore Plain. Situated in a zone of deep alluvial soil, at or near the Conquest-period shoreline of Lake Texcoco.

Modern utilization: The site is located in uncultivated grazing land next to a railroad track, immediately adjacent to irrigated alfalfa fields to the west. There are several modern residential units and commercial poultry farms scattered around the peripheries of the site area.

Archaeological remains: Light-to-moderate concentrations of surface pottery and rock rubble over an area of roughly one hectare. No structural remains. Mixed with more abundant Aztec material (Tx-A-110). The alfalfa fields at the western edge of the site, and the deep alluvial soil, may obscure some Terminal Formative occupational debris.

Classification: Hamlet; fewer than 50 people. May represent one or more outlying households of Tx-TF-44.

Tx-TF-46

Natural setting: Below 2240 m, on the flat Lakeshore Plain. Situated in a zone of deep alluvial soil, probably well within the borders of Conquest-period Lake Texcoco. The site area was completely above water throughout our 1967 season, but twenty-five years ago Apenes (1943: 32) stated that "in the rainy season it is accessible only by canoe through a long canal running from the mainland."

Modern utilization: Grazing on the short thick grass which covers the southern third of the site area. The northern two-thirds of the site is dried up lake bottom, a barren wasteland lacking vegetation of any kind, and apparently too salty for effective agriculture (Pl. 24).

Archaeological remains: Moderate to heavy concentrations of surface pottery and rock rubble over an area of about 19 hectares. Apenes (1943: 32) has described the site as follows:

> It consists of two parts: a long, narrow grass-covered elevation . . . which contains well-defined layers of sherds; and a wide belt sloping slightly from the elevation to the water edge. It has so recently been under water—it is, in fact, still partly flooded in the rainy season—that practically no vegetation has yet gained a foothold on the salty and nitric soil. It is covered mainly by hundreds of peculiar round heaps of stones mixed with broken sherds and stone artifacts. In diameter, the heaps vary from 0.5 to about 4 meters. There are also rows of larger unworked stones forming straight lines across the field. The stone material has evidently been brought to the site from the mainland. In the center of the field are traces of some nearly rectangular structures.

Apenes' "long, narrow grass-covered elevation" runs along the entire southern side of the site area, rising about 1.5 m above the level of the surrounding lake bed. Sherds are not common on its grassy upper surface, but several small pits penetrating to depths of up to 50 cm have brought some pottery to the surface. The lake bed south of this elevation contains only light concentrations of surface pottery and rock rubble, and shows no indications of structural remains.

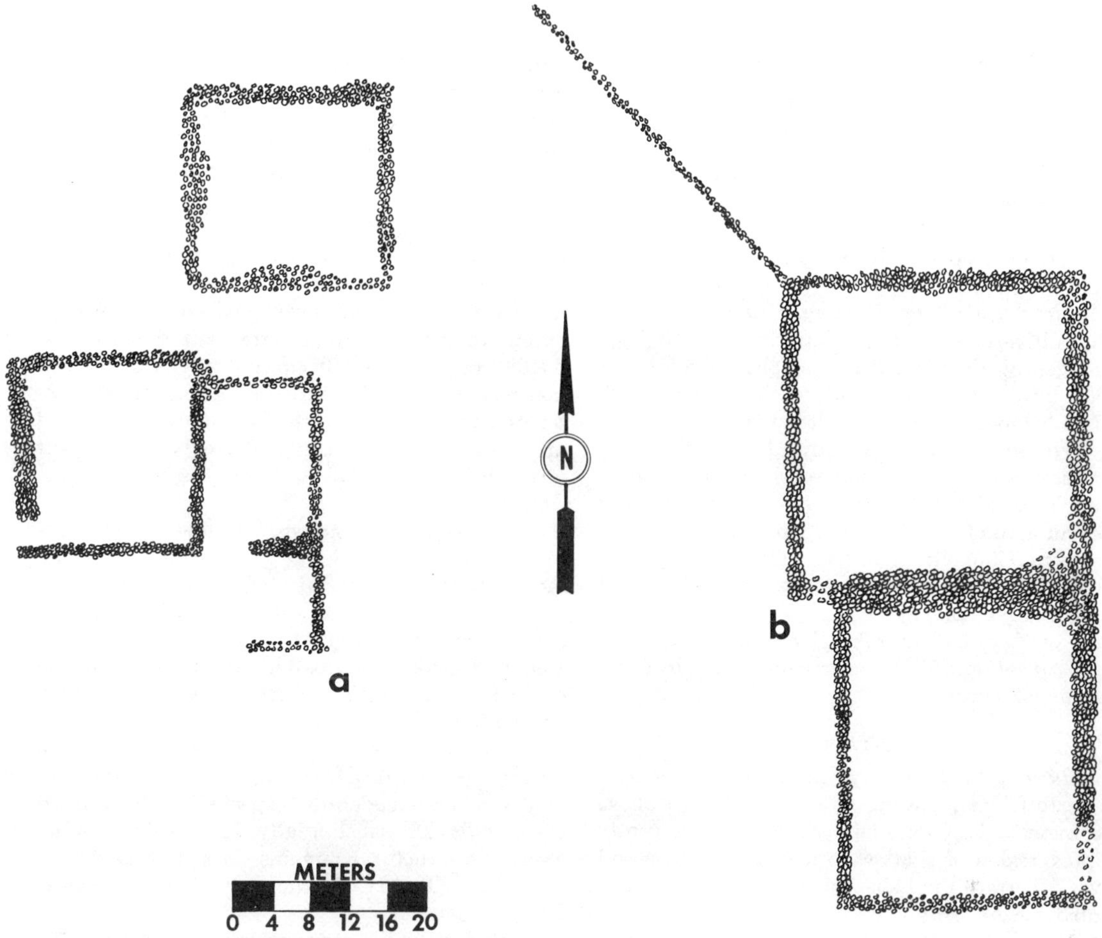

Fig. 7—Room patterns, Tx-TF-46.

North of the grassy rise occupational debris is much heavier, and wall bases of several large rectangular stone-walled compounds and/or rooms of variable size can be distinctly seen (Pl. 25, 26; Fig. 7), in addition to the other smaller features mentioned by Apenes. The function of architectural features is not at all clear. Construction material is basaltic rock, probably derived from Cerro Chimalhuacan some 2.5 km to the south where small basalt quarries, both operative and abandoned, are now abundant.

Classification: Large nucleated village; 400 to 800 people.

Tx-TF-47

Natural setting: 2250 m, at western base of Cerro Chimalhuacan, just above the level of the main Lakeshore Plain. The terrace systems in the area have maintained a moderately deep soil cover.

Modern utilization: The nucleated village of Chimalco borders the site area on the west, and may cover some of the Terminal Formative occupational debris in this area. Much of the immediate site area is covered with stone-faced terraces, only the lower of which are presently cultivated. Several basalt quarries, both operative and abandoned, are found in the area. The quarrying and finishing of this building stone are important activities in this area today.

Archaeological remains: Very light concentrations of surface pottery over an area of about five hectares. No structural remains. Mixed with much heavier quantities of Early Toltec material (Tx-ET-21).

Classification: Questionable. This material may represent the edge of a larger settlement now wholly obscured by the densely packed houses of modern Chimalco. Obviously the few sherds presently observable represent very little in the way of permanent residence. This material could be debris related to the use of the basalt quarries during Terminal Formative times.

Tx-TF-48

Natural setting: 2520 m, at the top of Cerro Chimalhuacan, some 280 m above the level of the surrounding Lakeshore Plain. Shallow to moderately deep soil cover, with abundant rock outcrops. Slight erosion.

Modern utilization: Grazing, plus limited rainfall cultivation on the relatively level hilltop. The gently sloping surface of the broad lower ridge top to the north is intensively cultivated. The hillslopes north of the site area are intricately terraced, but these features have fallen into disrepair and support only pasture land today.

Archaeological remains: A few sherds scattered over an area of about 20 by 20 meters at the peak of Cerro Chimalhuacan. No structural remains can definitely be assigned to this period. Mixed with more abundant Aztec (Tx-A-108), and a trace of Late Toltec (Tx-LT-55) material.

Classification: Hilltop ceremonial precinct; no permanent occupation.

Tx-TF-49

Natural setting: 2250 m, at northeastern base of Cerro Chimalhuacan, on a low bluff just above the main Lakeshore Plain. Situated in a gently sloping region of shallow to moderately deep soil cover. Terrace and bancal systems have prevented severe erosion.

Modern utilization: Some rainfall cultivation. Part of the area is a modern cemetery. The slopes to the west are covered with abandoned terraces. The densely packed houses of modern Chimalhuacan extend up to the base of the bluff. Basalt is presently being quarried in several places on the nearby hillslopes.

Archaeological remains: Light concentrations of surface pottery over an area of less than one hectare. No structural remains. Mixed with somewhat lighter Late Formative (Tx-LF-28) and heavier Early Toltec material (Tx-ET-19). Some occupational debris may be obscured by the residential structures of Chimalhuacan at the north edge of the site.

Classification: Hamlet; fewer than 50 people. These sherds may represent debris associated with working of basalt quarries rather than with permanent residence.

Tx-TF-50

Natural setting: 2240 m, on the flat Lakeshore Plain at the western base of Cerro Chimalhuacan. The southwestern corner of the site extends onto the end of a low ridge up to an elevation of 2260 m. Situated in a zone of deep alluvial soil, near the Conquest-period shoreline of Lake Texcoco.

Modern utilization: The northern and southeastern sections of the site are partially covered by residential units of the present-day nucleated communities of Chimalhuacan and Santa María Natívitas. The remainder of the site area is intensively cultivated over most of its surface, except in the vicinity of Aztec salt tlateles (Tx-A-109) where high salt concentrations in the soil make effective agriculture impossible. These latter areas are covered with short, tough grass, and are used only for grazing. There is some basalt quarrying on the hillslopes to the west of the site.

Archaeological remains: Variable light, light-to-moderate, and moderate concentrations of surface pottery over an area of about 52 hectares. The original aspect of the Terminal Formative site is somewhat obscured by heavy Aztec (Tx-A-109) and modern occupation, and by thick alfalfa cover in some places. There appear to be three occupational nodes: in the northern, southwestern, and eastern section of the site area. Surface pottery concentration is light-to-moderate and moderate and moderate respectively. This sherd cover falls off substantially in the intervening areas. No structural remains. Mixed with Middle Formative (Tx-MF-13) and Late Formative (Tx-LF-29) material.

Classification: Secondary regional center; 750 to 1500 people. May well be somewhat larger if modern and Aztec debris are obscuring some Terminal Formative material.

Tx-TF-51

Natural setting: 2270 to 2350 m, on and alongside a low bluff overlooking the main Lakeshore Plain at the western base of Cerro Portezuelo. The site area is situated at the east side of the main pass into the Texcoco Region from the southwest. An extensive terrace system (now abandoned and deteriorating) on the slopes in the western section of the site area has prevented severe erosion (Pl. 23,*b*). Soil depth ranges from shallow to moderately deep over the site area. There are some patches of bare tepetate. A major barranca runs along the southern edge of the site.

Modern utilization: The main part of the site area is grazing land, with some cultivated maguey. The numerous stone-faced terraces in the western section of the site are not presently cultivated, though they may once have been. The lower ground along the western edge of the site is now occupied by a paper factory, a commercial pig farm, and some cultivated fields. The construction of large commercial building complexes is proceeding rapidly in this low area to the west and southwest of the site area. Along the site's southern margin are two recently-abandoned tezontle-gravel quarries (Pl. 47,*b*).

Archaeological remains: Variable light, light-to-moderate and moderate concentrations of surface pottery and rock rubble extend over an area of about 40 hectares on the bluff and along its base. The only clearly defined structures are a series of five large pyramidal mounds (Pl. 27; Appendix 2) arranged along and on either side of a slight ridge, over a total east-west distance of about 150 m in the south-central section of the site area.

The site has been archaeologically tested by Dixon (1963, 1966) during a short field season in 1963, and a two-month excavation in 1965. In 1963, seventeen 1 m by 1 m, and 2 m by 2 m test pits were dug in the general vicinity of the four main mounds. These pits produced abundant sherd refuse in the upper 50 cm, but revealed no indications of floors or walls. In 1965 Mounds 3 and 4 (our tlateles 103 and 102, respectively) were partially excavated (1966: 9-10):

> In brief, each mound contained a stone-faced temple sub-structure that was later enlarged in three successive major building periods. (In Mound 4, there is evidence of another earlier platform which may have had a perishable structure on top that was destroyed by fire, but it cannot yet be connected to the sequence discussed below since no further details concerning it are known).
>
> In each mound, the rectangular mass of the first structure was built up with a sandy soil that was relatively free of trash and stone. In order to give the building architectural form and help prevent rapid erosion, the exterior surfaces were faced with an approximately 50^{0} angle sloping or battered wall (*talud*) made of stones set in mud mortar.
>
> The stone talud, or building profile, was divided into two segments or terraces by a narrow offset. The whole structure was probably topped with a horizontal platform upon which stood an altar or some kind of simple room built of perishable materials.
>
> In both mounds, each successive structure was of basically similar profile and was also faced with a stone talud, to give the structure form and hold in the added fill of the enlargement. However, the profiles of the successive structures, as well as the techniques and materials used to build the taluds, all differed from each other in detail to various degrees, and they were also different in the two mounds . . . even though each of the four successive stone-faced structures in one mound was not necessarily built simultaneously with any of the ones in the other mound, it is still likely that the total span of construction and use of the two mounds was about the same.
>
> Basically, the facing taluds of the structures were built of 1) unshaped small boulders laid against the fill, 2) large, rudely shaped stone blocks, 3) large, rudely shaped tepetate blocks, 4) small water-worn stone cobbles, 5) small tepetate *lajas* (small, thin, flat slabs), 6) small basalt *lajas,* or 7) various mixtures of these several materials. The basal course of many taluds, both upper and lower segments, was frequently a row of unusually large and heavy stones.
>
> The talud stones were always set in mud mortar, the amount varying considerably in the different building periods. And despite the non-uniform, shoddy appearance of most of the exterior surfaces, there was no evidence of a plaster covering (except a coat of mud plaster on a stairway and ballustrade of the earliest structure in Mound 3).
>
> The outer facing taluds of each period were sometimes made thicker by backings of two or three supporting walls.

The age of the numerous rough, stone-faced terraces on the slopes immediately west of the site's ceremonial-civic core is unclear. However, there are indications that these features postdate the construction of the pyramidal mounds: most important, a long, straight, low stone wall, clearly contemporary with the terraces (many terraces abut directly on this wall) extends over the top and sides of Mounds 2 and 4 (our tlateles 104 and 102). This same wall runs all the way from the eastern slopes of Cerro Chimalhuacan, across the low pass, and up the western slopes of Cerro Portezuelo, terminating in the vicinity of Mound 2 (tlatel 104). This feature is likely to be an ejido boundary of the early twentieth century, or a hacienda border of the last century or the colonial era.

Dixon (1963: 6) has described this terracing and wall system:

> [The terraces] appear to consist of rough walls built of boulders to a height which varies from 50 to 100 cm, the earth filling in behind to form a relatively flat surface. The terraces follow the contours roughly, with divisor walls of the same construction at angles to the slope. The major terraces in the southern part of the site seem to be limited by the northern wall which crosses the mounds. In the northern half of the mapped area, the terrace remnants seem to be mostly in slight incipient gullies and may have served simply as erosion checks. About 80 m northeast of Mound 1 is a large platform with all the appearances of an agricultural terrace wall on its west side, but it is about 2 m high [this is our tlatel 106]. Whether this in reality served some other function and had a different type of con-

struction not now exposed is a problem that must await excavation.

Classification: Large segregated elite district; 600 to 1200 people.

Tx-TF-52

Natural setting: 2310 meters, in the Lower Piedmont. Situated on a broad, gentle slope, over one km from the closest major barranca. Moderate erosion; shallow to moderately deep soil cover.

Modern utilization: Intensive rainfall cultivation.

Archaeological remains: Light concentrations of surface pottery over an area of less than one hectare. No structural remains. Mixed with somewhat heavier Classic material (Tx-EC-17; Tx-LC-15).

Classification: Hamlet; fewer than 50 people.

EARLY CLASSIC

Tx-EC-1

Natural setting: 2250 m, on the flat Lakeshore Plain. Situated on a large, low elevation, rising slightly above the level of the surrounding plain. Deep alluvial soil. A nearby well contains water at a depth of about 6 m.

Modern utilization: The site area is an island of uncultivated land in a region of intensive mechanized irrigation and rainfall agriculture. Short, tough grass covers most of the site area today, and permits some grazing over its surface. Soil for the manufacture of adobe bricks has recently been removed in large quantities. The main asphalt highway cuts through the central part of the site.

Archaeological remains: The site consists of an irregular earth mound, extending over an area of about 0.7 hectares, rising to a maximum elevation of about one meter. Light concentrations of surface pottery occur over most of this area, most of it having been exposed in the course of the large-scale pitting that has occurred on the mound's upper surface (for adobe manufacture). The dominant occupational component is Aztec (Tx-A-9). Light Late Classic and Late Toltec material is also present (Tx-LC-1; Tx-LT-5). There are no distinct structural remains.

Classification: Hamlet; fewer than 50 people. The abundance of Texcoco Fabric Marked, an Aztec ware presumably associated with salt-making, suggests that this location functioned to produce salt in Classic times as well.

Tx-EC-2

Natural setting: 2430 m, on the level top of a long ridge extending southward from the main block of Cerro Azteca. Situated some 120 m above the level of the Lower Piedmont Plain to the south and east, and the Lakeshore Plain to the west. Irregular ground surface throughout the site area, with generally shallow soil cover and some rock outcroppings. Erosion has been moderate to severe. The Río Papalotla flows at the base of the hill, to the south of the site.

Modern utilization: Grazing.

Archaeological remains: Very light to light concentrations of surface pottery over an area of roughly one-quarter hectare on the ridge top. Mixed with heavier Early Toltec pottery (Tx-ET-5). Very light Late Formative material is also present (Tx-LF-1). There are no structural remains, although a large Early Toltec pyramid may contain earlier constructions within its core.

Classification: Hilltop ceremonial precinct. Probably no permanent occupation.

Tx-EC-3

Natural setting: 2295 m, at the lower edge of the Lower Piedmont. Situated in a nearly level zone, of deep soil cover, about 150 m west of the Río Papalotla.

Modern utilization: Intensive rainfall cultivation.

Archaeological remains: Variable very light and light concentrations of surface pottery over an area of about 10 hectares. The dominant occupational component is Early Toltec (Tx-ET-4). The most abundant Early Classic material occurs on and around the numerous large mounds which are most likely of Early Toltec construction. Light Late Classic (Tx-LC-2) and Late Toltec (Tx-Lt-12) pottery are also present.

Classification: Hamlet; fewer than 100 people. Site may be somewhat large and more complex if the heavy Early Toltec overlay has obscured some Early Classic occupational debris.

Tx-EC-4

Natural setting: 2320 m, in the Lower Piedmont. Situated on a broad, gentle slope, near a major barranca. Much of the site area is severely eroded, with shallow soil cover and large patches of bare tepetate.

Modern utilization: Grazing.

Archaeological remains: Light concentrations of surface pottery over an area of roughly one hectare. More abundant quantities of Early Toltec (Tx-ET-8) and Aztec (Tx-A-24) material are also present. No structural remains.

Classification: Hamlet; fewer than 50 people.

Tx-EC-5

Natural setting: 2330 m, in the Lower Piedmont. Situated on the gently sloping southwestern flanks of Cerro Tepetlosco, about 500 m north of the Río Papalotla. Moderate erosion, with shallow to moderately deep soil cover.

Modern utilization: Grazing, plus some cultivated maguey.

Archaeological remains: Light concentrations of surface pottery over an area of less than one hectare. Mixed with heavier Early and Late Toltec material (Tx-ET-13; Tx-LT-28). Light Late

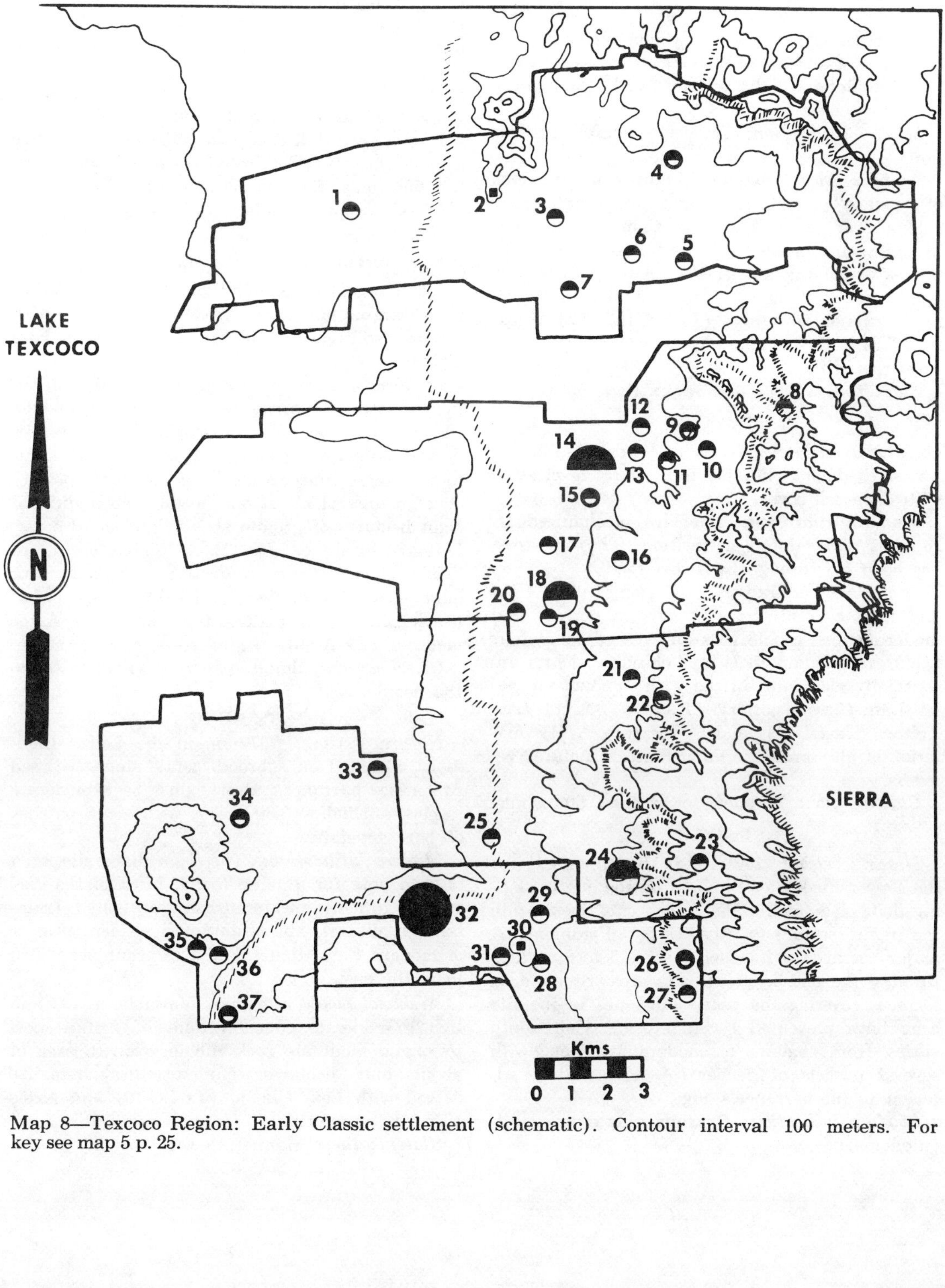

Map 8—Texcoco Region: Early Classic settlement (schematic). Contour interval 100 meters. For key see map 5 p. 25.

Classic (Tx-LC-6), Late Formative (Tx-LF-7), and Terminal Formative (Tx-TF-11) pottery is also present. No structural remains that can be assigned to Early Classic times.

Classification: Hamlet; fewer than 50 people.

Tx-EC-6

Natural setting: 2320 m, in the Lower Piedmont. Situated on the gently sloping southeastern flank of a small hill, about 500 m west of the Río Papalotla. Slight erosion, with moderately deep soil cover.

Modern utilization: Intensive rainfall cultivation.

Archaeological remains: Light concentrations of surface pottery and light-to-moderate rock rubble over an area of less than one hectare. Mixed with heavier Early and Late Toltec pottery (Tx-ET-13; Tx-LT-27). Also present are light concentrations of Late Formative (Tx-LF-6), Terminal Formative (Tx-TF-10), Late Classic (Tx-LC-5), and some Aztec pottery. No structural remains.

Classification: Hamlet; fewer than 50 people.

Tx-EC-7

Natural setting: 2290 m, at lower edge of the Lower Piedmont. Situated in a nearly level zone, with deep soil cover.

Modern utilization: Intensive mechanized irrigation and rainfall cultivation. The site area has been cut through by a dirt road.

Archaeological remains: Variable very light and light concentrations of surface pottery and moderate rock rubble over an area of about four hectares. Obsidian tools and chipping debris are especially abundant. Mixed with somewhat heavier Late Classic pottery (Tx-LC-7). Light Late Toltec (Tx-LT-11) and Aztec (Tx-A-14) material is also present. No definite structural remains.

Classification: Hamlet; fewer than 50 people.

Tx-EC-8

Natural setting: 2465 m, at the upper edge of the Lower Piedmont. Situated on the gently sloping floor of a small valley which cuts deeply into the main surface of the Upper Piedmont. A major barranca is intrenched some 5 to 8 m deep through the middle of the site area. Stone-faced terraces covering the gentle hillslopes in the site area have prevented severe erosion. Soil depth varies from shallow to moderately deep, with several pockets of deeper soil immediately adjacent to the barranca's edge.

Modern utilization: Grazing, plus a few cultivated maguey.

Archaeological remains: Variable light and light-to-moderate concentrations of surface pottery and heavy rock rubble over an area of about 2.5 hectares. Mixed with Late Classic material of about equal abundance (Tx-LC-8). No structural remains. The barranca has apparently cut into the occupational zone, as sherds are washing out of both its steep walls. The age of the numerous stone-faced terraces which cover much of the site area on the west side of the barranca is uncertain. These features measure roughly 25 to 50 cm high, and 8 to 10 m wide, with the down-hill face consisting of one or two tiers of loosely piled rough stones. Today they function only for erosion control.

Classification: Hamlet; fewer than 50 people.

Tx-EC-9

Natural setting: 2340 m, in the Lower Piedmont. Situated on a broad, gentle slope, adjacent to a major barranca. Moderate erosion, with shallow soil cover and some patches of bare tepetate.

Modern utilization: Intensive rainfall cultivation, except in areas of most severe erosion which now serve only for grazing.

Archaeological remains: Moderate and light-to-moderate concentrations of surface pottery over an area of about one hectare; an additional eight hectares of ground shows light sherd cover. No structural remains. Rock rubble occurs in light-to-moderate concentrations. Mixed with light Late Formative (Tx-LF-10), somewhat heavier Late Classic (Tx-LC-8), and some Aztec material (Tx-A-66).

Classification: Small dispersed village; 100 to 150 people.

Tx-EC-10

Natural setting: 2370 m, in the Lower Piedmont. Situated on a broad, gentle slope, between two major barrancas. Erosion has been moderate to severe. Shallow soil cover, with some patches of bare tepetate.

Modern utilization: The immediate site area is used only for grazing today. Most of the surrounding fields are intensively cultivated (rainfall agriculture). The westernmost residential units of modern San Miguel Tlaixpan occur about 500 m to the east.

Archaeological remains: Variable light and light-to-moderate concentrations of surface pottery, and moderate rock rubble, over an area of about four hectares. No structural remains. Mixed with Late Classic (Tx-LC-10) and Aztec (Tx-A-66) material.

Classification: Hamlet; fewer than 50 people.

Tx-EC-11

Natural setting: 2340 m, in the Lower Piedmont. Situated on a broad, gentle slope, between two major barrancas. Moderate to severe erosion, with generally shallow soil cover and some patches of bare tepetate.

Modern utilization: Grazing.

Archaeological remains: Very light concentrations of surface pottery and heavy rock rubble over an area of less than one hectare. No structural remains. The dominant occupational components are Terminal Formative (Tx-TF-17) and Aztec (Tx-A-65).

Classification: Hamlet; fewer than 50 people. This may represent only a single household.

Tx-EC-12

Natural setting: 2340 m, in the Lower Piedmont. Situated on a broad, gentle slope between two major barrancas. Moderate erosion, with shallow soil cover. Bancal systems have prevented severe erosion over much of the site area.

Modern utilization: The site area is located at the western edge of an intensively cultivated zone (rainfall agriculture). The areas to the west, north, and south are predominately grazing land, as are some parts of the site itself where erosion has been most severe and rock rubble is heaviest.

Archaeological remains: Variable light and light-to-moderate concentrations of surface pottery and moderate rock rubble over an area of roughly five hectares. No structural remains. Mixed with substantial Terminal Formative (Tx-TF-17) and Late Classic (Tx-LC-11) material, plus light Middle Formative (Tx-MF-6) and Late Toltec (Tx-LT-43).

Classification: Hamlet; fewer than 100 people.

Tx-EC-13

Natural setting: 2310 to 2320 m, in the Lower Piedmont. Situated on a broad, gentle slope, near a major barranca. The site occupies the edge of a low bluff and the adjacent lower ground. Moderate to severe erosion, with shallow soil cover and some patches of bare tepetate.

Modern utilization: Grazing. The lower part of the site is presently in use as a picnic area in the Molino de Flores park. The adjacent fields to the west and south are intensively cultivated (rainfall agriculture).

Archaeological remains: Variable light and light-to-moderate concentrations of surface pottery over an area of roughly six hectares. No structural remains. Mixed with lighter Late Classic pottery (Tx-LC-11), and with Aztec material in the western end of the site area (Tx-A-64).

Classification: Hamlet; fewer than 100 people.

Tx-EC-14

Natural setting: 2310 m, in the Lower Piedmont. Situated on a broad, gentle slope, next to a major barranca. Slight erosion; moderately deep soil cover.

Modern utilization: Intensive rainfall cultivation in the immediate site area. Land to the west and north is irrigated with water drawn from wells with gasoline pumps, and is primarily devoted to alfalfa.

Archaeological remains: Variable light-to-moderate and moderate concentrations of surface pottery over an area of about six hectares. No structural remains. Mixed with somewhat lighter Late Classic (Tx-LC-12), and light Late Toltec (Tx-LT-42) material.

Classification: Small nucleated village; 100 to 200 people.

Tx-EC-15

Natural setting: 2320 m, in the Lower Piedmont. Situated on a broad, gentle slope adjacent to a major barranca. Slight to moderate erosion, with moderately deep soil cover.

Modern utilization: Intensive rainfall cultivation, although the immediate site area is presently fallow.

Archaeological remains: Light concentrations of surface pottery over an area of less than one hectare. No structural remains. Mixed with more abundant Terminal Formative (Tx-TF-19) and Aztec (Tx-A-57) material.

Classification: Hamlet; fewer than 50 people.

Tx-EC-16

Natural setting: 2360 m, in the Lower Piedmont. Situated on a broad, gentle slope between two major barrancas. Moderate erosion, with shallow to moderately deep soil cover.

Modern utilization: Intensive rainfall cultivation.

Archaeological remains: Variable light and very light concentrations of surface pottery over an area of less than one hectare. No structural remains. Mixed with Late Classic (?) material (Tx-LC-14).

Classification: Hamlet; fewer than 50 people. May only represent a single household unit.

Tx-EC-17

Natural setting: 2310 m, in the Lower Piedmont. Situated on a broad, gentle slope, over one km from the closest major barranca. Moderate erosion; shallow to moderately deep soil cover.

Modern utilization: Intensive rainfall cultivation.

Archaeological remains: Variable light and light-to-moderate concentrations of surface pottery over an area of less than one hectare. No structural remains. Mixed with somewhat lighter Terminal Formative (Tx-TF-52) and Late Classic (Tx-LC-15) material.

Classification: Hamlet; fewer than 50 people.

Tx-EC-18

Natural setting: 2310 to 2320 m, in the Lower Piedmont. Situated on a broad, gently sloping ridge top lying between top major barrancas. Moderate erosion, with variable shallow to moderately deep soil cover.

Modern utilization: The western two-thirds of the site area is now planted in commercial fruit trees and some maguey. The barranca slopes at the north edge of the site are partially terraced, and some rainfall cultivation of maize and beans occurs there. The eastern third of the site is grazing land. The lower ground to the west is intensively cultivated (rainfall agriculture). There is a large commercial sand and gravel quarry about 250 m south of the site, across the barranca. The eastern edge of the modern town of Huexotla extends to within 200 m of the site's western border.

Archaeological remains: Variable light-to-moderate and moderate concentrations of surface pottery and rock rubble over an area of about two hectares. An additional 23 hectares of ground is covered with variable light and light-to-moderate surface pottery. No structural remains. Mixed with light Late Classic (Tx-LC-16), and some Aztec material (Tx-A-87) in the southern half of the site.

Classification: Small dispersed village; 250 to 500 people. This is the second largest Early Classic site in the Texcoco Region, exceeded in size only by Tx-EC-32.

Tx-EC-19

Natural setting: 2310 m, in the Lower Piedmont. Situated on a broad, gentle slope adjacent to a major barranca, near the intersection point of two major barrancas. Erosion has been slight to moderate, and soil cover is generally shallow to moderately deep.

Modern utilization: The site area is presently used only for grazing, but appears to have been plowed in the recent past. The lower ground to the west is intensively cultivated; the higher land to the east is all devoted to grazing. A large commercial sand and gravel quarry borders the site on the west, and may have obliterated some occupational debris.

Archaeological remains: Variable light-to-moderate and moderate concentrations of surface pottery over an area of about six hectares. No structural remains. Mixed with some Aztec material (Tx-A-87).

Classification: Small nucleated village; 100 to 200 people.

Tx-EC-20

Natural setting: 2290 m, at the lower edge of the Lower Piedmont. Situated on a broad, gentle slope near a major barranca. Erosion has been slight to moderate; soil cover is generally shallow to moderately deep.

Modern utilization: Intensive rainfall cultivation. The south edge of the modern town of Huexotla is situated about 1 km to the north.

Archaeological remains: Light concentrations of surface pottery over an area of less than one hectare. No structural remains. Mixed with much heavier Aztec material (Tx-A-87), plus light Terminal Formative pottery (Tx-TF-27).

Classification: Hamlet; fewer than 50 people. May represent a single household.

Tx-EC-21

Natural setting: 2430 to 2440 m, near the upper edge of the Lower Piedmont. Situated on a gently sloping, broad ridge top, lying between two major barrancas. The entire site is severely eroded, with a surface of badly scarred tepetate and little or no soil cover.

Modern utilization: Marginal grazing and wasteland. The lower flatter land to the west is intensively cultivated (rainfall agriculture).

Archaeological remains: Variable light and light-to-moderate concentrations of surface pottery and rock rubble over an area of about five hectares. No structural remains. Mixed with Terminal Formative (including some Tzacualli) (Tx-TF-31). The original aspect of the site has been badly obscured by severe erosion; the occupational debris rests on bare tepetate in most cases.

Classification: Hamlet; fewer than 100 people.

Tx-EC-22

Natural setting: 2490 m, at the upper edge of the Lower Piedmont. Situated on a gently sloping, broad ridge top, lying between two major barrancas. Severely eroded, with a surface of badly scarred bare tepetate and little or no soil cover.

Modern utilization: Marginal grazing and wasteland.

Archaeological remains: Variable light and

light-to-moderate concentrations of surface pottery over an area of about two hectares. No definite structural remains. Mixed with Terminal Formative (Tx-TF-23) and Aztec (Tx-A-90) material. The original aspect of the site has been badly obscured by severe erosion; occupational debris is resting on bare tepetate or washing from the sides of isolated erosional remnants.

Classification: Hamlet; fewer than 50 people.

Tx-EC-23

Natural setting: 2600 m, in the Upper Piedmont. Situated on a broad, gently sloping ridge top, lying between two major barrancas. In a badly eroded area, with irregular ground surface featuring large patches of bare tepetate and isolated pockets of soil and erosional remnants.

Modern utilization: Grazing. The lowermost limits of the thick oak-confier forest covering the Sierra begins roughly 1 km to the east. Charcoal and construction timber are presently taken from this wooded zone.

Archaeological remains: Discontinuous light concentrations of badly weathered surface pottery over an area of less than one hectare. No structural remains.

Classification: Hamlet; fewer than 50 people.

Tx-EC-24

Natural setting: 2470 to 2510 m, at the juncture of the Upper and Lower Piedmonts. Situated on a wide, gentle slope, adjacent to a major barranca. Except at the edge of the barranca, erosion has been slight over the site area. Soil cover, though shallow, is continuous, and held in place by a relatively thick grass cover.

Modern utilization: Grazing: The lower land to the west is intensively cultivated (rainfall agriculture).

Archaeological remains: Variable light and light-to-moderate concentrations of surface pottery and moderate rock rubble over an area of about 13 hectares. There are no definite structural remains, but several large, vague, low mounded areas may contain architectural features. The eastern edge of a Terminal Formative community (Tx-TF-37) overlaps the western end of the site area.

Classification: Small dispersed village; 125 to 250 people.

Tx-EC-25

Natural setting: 2260 m, at the juncture of the Lakeshore Plain and the Lower Piedmont. Situated on a broad, gentle slope, with occupational debris resting on the upper side of an abrupt low rise where the Lower Piedmont meets the flat Lakeshore Plain. Slight to moderate erosion, with shallow soil cover.

Modern utilization: The immediate site area is presently used for grazing. The lower, flat land to the west is intensively cultivated, with some mechanical irrigation. The adjacent sections of the Lower Piedmont plain are used for rainfall cultivation.

Archaeological remains: Light concentrations of surface pottery over an area of less than one hectare. No structural remains.

Classification: Hamlet; fewer than 50 people.

Tx-EC-26

Natural setting: 2520 to 2530 m, at the lower edge of the Upper Piedmont. Situated on a broad, gentle slope adjacent to a major barranca. The site area is a large remnant of relatively uneroded ground with shallow to moderately deep soil cover, surrounded by severely eroded land where most of the soil has been stripped away. Bancal and terrace systems have maintained soil cover in the site area.

Modern utilization: Mixed grazing and rainfall cultivation. The severely eroded areas adjacent to the site are largely wasteland. The recently settled hamlet of Pueblo Nuevo is situated at the south edge of the site area. Water for household purposes in Pueblo Nuevo is derived from a small canal cut into tepetate, or built up of earth and stone, which taps the barranca flow upstream and brings water down the slope into the modern community (Pl. 55*c*).

Archaeological remains: Variable light and light-to-moderate concentrations of surface pottery over an area of about four hectares. The only definite structure is a stone rubble platform mound, roughly 20 m in diameter and 2 m tall, with light-to-moderate surface pottery around its base (including relatively abundant Thin Orange pottery). A considerable amount of pitting has revealed the structure's solid rock rubble construction. Its function is presumably ceremonial-civic.

Classification: Hamlet; fewer than 100 people.

Tx-EC-27

Natural setting: 2530 m, at the lower edge of the Upper Piedmont. Situated on a severely eroded gentle hillslope. Soil cover exists only in isolated pockets and erosional remnants; the ground surface is very predominately badly scarred bare tepetate.

Modern utilization: Grazing; some rainfall cultivation in adjacent areas. The recently settled hamlet of Pueblo Nuevo is situated some 250 m north of the site.

Archaeological remains: Variable light and light-to-moderate concentrations of surface pottery over an area of about three hectares. No structural remains. The original aspect of the site has been badly obscured by severe erosion; the occupational debris occurs on bare tepetate, and is found washing from the sides of erosional remnants.

Classification: Hamlet; fewer than 50 people.

Tx-EC-28

Natural setting: 2340 m, in the Lower Piedmont. Situated on gently sloping ground at the eastern base of Cerro Tonaltepec, which rises steeply to a height of 2430 m. The site area lies near a small barranca. The land is only slightly eroded, with moderately deep soil cover.

Modern utilization: Intensive rainfall cultivation, with maguey a dominant crop. The higher slopes above the site are grazing land. A few small, recently worked tezontle-gravel quarries are located at the hill base near the site.

Archaeological remains: Variable light and very light concentrations of surface pottery over an area of roughly one hectare. No structural remains. Mixed with larger quantities of Late Formative (Tx-LF-25), Terminal Formative (Tx-TF-43), and Aztec (Tx-A-100) material, plus light Middle Formative pottery (Tx-MF-15).

Classification: Hamlet; fewer than 50 people.

Tx-EC-29

Natural setting: 2310 m, in the Lower Piedmont. Situated on a broad, gentle slope, near a small barranca. In zone of deep soil cover, with only slight erosion.

Modern utilization: Intensive rainfall cultivation.

Archaeological remains: Variable light and light-to-moderate concentrations of surface pottery over an area of less than one hectare. No structural remains. Mixed with lighter Late Toltec material (Tx-LT-51).

Classification: Hamlet; fewer than 50 people. May represent a single household.

Tx-EC-30

Natural setting: 2420 m, at the relatively level top of Cerro Tonaltepec. The site rests on a broken, irregular ground surface, some 50 m above the level of the surrounding Lower Piedmont plain. Erosion ranges from moderate to severe; variable soil cover, with some patches of bare tepetate.

Modern utilization: Grazing. The hillslopes below the site area have been extensively terraced in the past, but these structures have deteriorated badly, and the slopes are now badly eroded, and fit only for marginal grazing.

Archaeological remains: Variable light and very light concentrations of surface pottery over an area of less than one hectare. No structural remains can be assigned to the Early Classic, but a large Aztec mound (Tx-A-101) may contain earlier structures within its interior. Some Early Toltec material is also present (Tx-ET-24).

Classification: Hilltop ceremonial precinct; probably no permanent occupation.

Tx-EC-31

Natural setting: 2300 m, at the western base of Cerro Tonaltepec near the edge of the main Lower Piedmont plain. Slight to moderate erosion, with moderately deep soil cover over most of the site area.

Modern utilization: Intensive rainfall cultivation. The higher slopes above the site are now grazing land, although there are badly deteriorated remains of extensive terracing there.

Archaeological remains: Variable light and very light concentrations of surface pottery over an area of roughly five hectares. Occupational debris is mixed with much heavier Early Toltec material (Tx-ET-17) and some light Late Classic pottery (Tx-LC-17). There are abundant structural remains, but all would appear to be Early Toltec in age, although some could contain earlier constructions within their interiors. The age of the abandoned terracing on the slopes above the site area is unclear.

Classification: Hamlet; fewer than 100 people. Probably an outlying unit of Tx-EC-32.

Tx-EC-32

Natural setting: 2250 to 2300 m, on the northern lowermost flanks of Cerro Portezuelo at the edge of the Lower Piedmont plain. Deep alluvial soil is found in the lower part of the site area, with soil cover thinning to moderate and shallow depths upslope. The entire site area is cut through by numerous barrancas of varying size. Most of these barrancas are relatively narrow and deep, often cutting through prehispanic occupational zones.

Modern utilization: Most of the site area is devoted to intensive rainfall cultivation. Some fields are presently fallow and used for grazing only. The higher slopes above the site area are predominately grazing land. The level plain north of the site is intensively cultivated.

Archaeological remains: Variable very light, light, and light-to-moderate concentrations of surface pottery over an area of about 60 hectares. The character of the Early Classic site may be badly obscured by heavy Early Toltec occupation (Tx-ET-18) over this entire area. There are many structural remains throughout the site area, but none can definitely be associated with the Classic period. Late Classic (Tx-LC-18), Late Toltec (Tx-LT-53), and Aztec (Tx-A-103) material is also present.

Classification: The true extent and complexity of the site may be difficult to assess because of the heavy Early Toltec overlay. Apparently, Early Classic occupation represents a regional center, with a dispersed population of roughly 300 to 900 people. This is by far the largest Early Classic occupational loci in the Texcoco Region.

Tx-EC-33

Natural setting: 2240 m, on the flat Lakeshore Plain. Probably situated at or near the Conquest-period shoreline of Lake Texcoco. In a zone of deep alluvial soil.

Modern utilization: Intensive rainfall cultivation, with scattered residential households at the southwest edge of the modern village of Cuatlalpan.

Archaeological remains: Variable light and light-to-moderate concentrations of surface pottery over an area of roughly one hectare. No structural remains. Some occupational debris may be obscured by the deep alluvial soil, modern buildings, major asphalt highway (at the west edge of the site), and thick alfalfa vegetation in adjacent fields. Mixed with much lighter Late Classic (Tx-LC-19) and a trace of Late Formative pottery.

Classification: Hamlet; fewer than 50 people.

Tx-EC-34

Natural setting: 2240 m, on gently sloping land at the northeastern base of Cerro Chimalhuacan, near the Conquest-period shoreline of Lake Texcoco. Situated in a zone of deep to moderately deep soil cover, and slight erosion.

Modern utilization: The site area is spread out over several cultivated fields in the heart of the present-day nucleated community of Chimalhuacan.

Archaeological remains: Variable light and very light concentrations of surface pottery scattered over an area of roughly three hectares. The densely packed modern structures and heavy Aztec occupation (Tx-A-109) have badly obscured the original extent and character of the Early Classic site. Early Classic sherds can occasionally be picked up in fields to the east and south of the Tx-EC-34 site area, but never in large enough quantities to warrant a site designation. No structural remains. Very light Late Classic (Tx-LC-20), and some Early and Late Toltec (Tx-ET-19; Tx-LT-54) material also occur in this area.

Classification: Hamlet; fewer than 50 people. May be a somewhat larger community if significant quantities of occupational debris are covered by modern and Aztec structures.

Tx-EC-35

Natural setting: 2240 m, on gently sloping ground at the southern base of Cerro Chimalhuacan, just above the flat Lakeshore Plain. Moderate to severe erosion, with generally thin soil cover. The site area is cut through by several small barrancas.

Modern utilization: The site is situated between the eastern edge of the modern village of Atlapulco and the western end of present-day Chimalpa. Most of the site area is used only as grazing land today. The steeper slopes above the site have been extensively terraced in the past, but only a few of these fields are now cultivated, and all terraces are in a bad state of disrepair. Some cultivated maguey occurs throughout the area.

Archaeological remains: Variable light, light-to-moderate, and moderate concentrations of surface pottery and rock rubble over an area of roughly four hectares. No structural remains. Some occupational debris may be obscured by modern buildings in Atlapulco and Chimalpa. Mixed with much lighter Late Classic material (Tx-LC-21).

Classification: Hamlet; fewer than 100 people.

Tx-EC-36

Natural setting: 2240 m, on gently sloping ground at the southern base of Cerro Chimalhuacan, just above the flat Lakeshore Plain. Moderate to severe erosion, with generally shallow soil cover. The site area is adjacent to a major barranca, and is cut through by several small ones.

Modern utilization: Grazing. The steep slopes above the site have been extensively terraced in the past, but only a few of these fields are now cultivated, and all terraces are in a bad state of disrepair. Some cultivated maguey occurs throughout the site area.

Archaeological remains: Variable light, light-to-moderate, and moderate concentrations of surface pottery and rock rubble over an area of roughly three hectares. No structural remains. Mixed with much lighter Late Classic material (Tx-LC-22).

Classification: Hamlet; fewer than 50 people.

Tx-EC-37

Natural setting: 2270 m, on gently sloping ground near the western base of Cerro Portezuelo, some 30 m above the level of the Lakeshore Plain to the west. The site is situated between two major barrancas in an area of irregular ground surface and thin soil cover. Erosion has been moderate to severe.

Modern utilization: Grazing and scattered maguey cultivation. The steeper slopes above the site area have been extensively terraced in the past, but these structures are presently badly deteriorated and serve only as indifferent erosion checks. Numerous basalt quarries (both operative and abandoned) are found in the hillslopes above and to either side of the site area. The lower, level land immediately below the site, on either side of the main highway, is largely covered with a variety of very recently built industrial and residential complexes. The nucleated village of La Magdalena is located about 600 m west of the site area.

Archaeological remains: Variable light and very light concentrations of surface pottery over an area of roughly one hectare. No structural remains. Mixed with much heavier Early Toltec (Tx-ET-23), and lighter Late Classic (Tx-LC-23) material. A few sherds of Early Classic Pottery can also be found scattered over the adjacent hillslopes, never in sufficient quantity to warrant designation as a site. The heavy cover of modern construction in the area immediately below the site may be obscuring some prehispanic occupational debris.

Classification: Hamlet; fewer than 50 people.

LATE CLASSIC

Tx-LC-1

Natural setting: 2250 m, on the flat Lakeshore Plain. Situated on a large, low elevation, rising slightly above the level of the surrounding plain. Deep alluvial soil. A nearby well contains water at a depth of about 6 m.

Modern utilization: The site area is an island of uncultivated land in a region of intensive rainfall and mechanized irrigation agriculture. Short, tough grass covers most of the site area today, and permits some grazing over its surface. Soil for the manufacture of adobe bricks has recently been removed in large quantities. The main asphalt highway cuts through the central part of the site.

Archaeological remains: The site consists of an irregular earth mound, extending over an area of about 0.7 hectare, rising to a maximum elevation of about 1 m. Light concentrations of surface pottery occur over most of this area, most of it having been exposed in the course of the large scale pitting that has occurred on the mound's upper surface (for adobe-making). The dominant occupational component is Aztec (Tx-A-9). Light Early Classic (Tx-EC-1; somewhat less abundant than Late Classic material), and light Late Toltec (Tx-LT-5) pottery is also present. There are no distinct structural remains.

Classification: Hamlet; fewer than 50 people. The abundance of Texcoco Fabric Marked, an Aztec ceramic ware presumably associated with salt-making, suggests that this location functioned to produce salt in Classic times as well.

Tx-LC-2

Natural setting: 2295 m, at the lower edge of the Lower Piedmont. Situated in a nearly level zone of deep soil cover, about 150 m west of the Río Papalotla.

Modern utilization: Intensive rainfall cultivation.

Archaeological remains: Variable very light and light concentrations of surface pottery over an area of about 10 hectares. The dominant occupational component is Early Toltec (Tx-ET-4). The most abundant Late Classic material occurs on and around the numerous large mounds which are most likely of Early Toltec construction (although they may contain earlier constructions within their interiors). Light Early Classic (Tx-EC-3) and Late Toltec (Tx-LT-12) pottery are also present.

Classification: Hamlet; fewer than 100 people. Site may be somewhat larger and more complex if the heavy Early Toltec overlay has obscured some Late Classic occupational debris.

Tx-LC-3

Natural setting: 2340 m, in the Lower Piedmont. Situated on gently sloping ground at the eastern base of Cerro Azteca. Moderate erosion, with moderately deep soil cover.

Modern utilization: Intensive rainfall cultivation.

Archaeological remains: Light concentrations of surface pottery over an area of less than one hectare. Mixed with much heavier Aztec material (Tx-A-21). No structural remains.

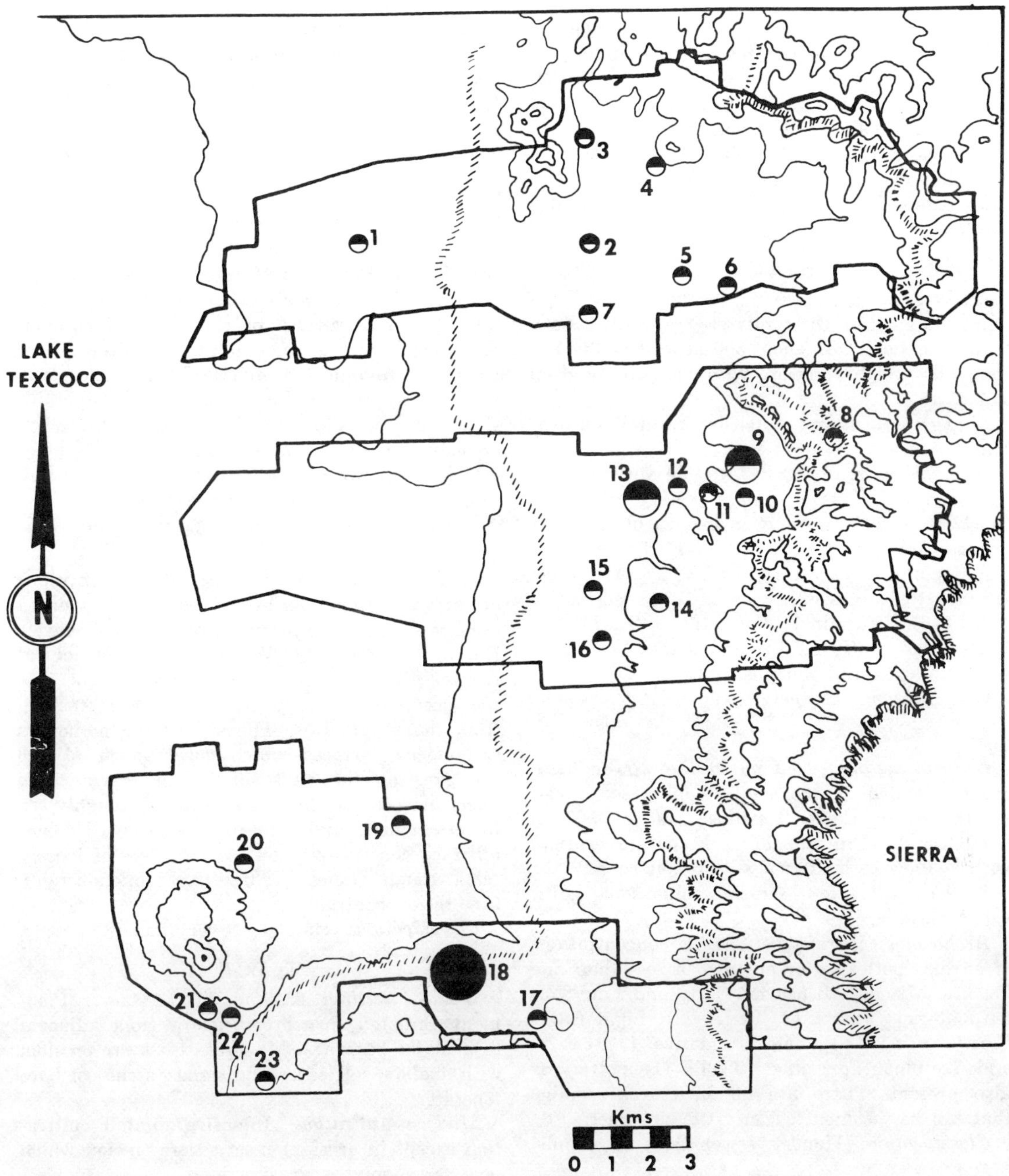

Map 9—Texcoco Region: Late Classic settlement (schematic). Contour interval 100 meters. For key see map 5 p. 25.

Classification: Hamlet; fewer than 50 people. May represent only a single household unit.

Tx-LC-4

Natural setting: 2320 to 2340 m, in the Lower Piedmont. Situated on gently sloping ground at the southern base of Cerro Teponaxtle. Moderate to severe erosion, with generally shallow soil cover and some patches of bare tepetate.

Modern utilization: Intensive rainfall cultivation.

Archaeological remains: Variable very light to

light concentrations of surface pottery over an area of about three hectares. The dominant occupational component is Early Toltec (Tx-ET-7), and the numerous mounds undoubtedly date largely or wholly to that period.

Classification: Hamlet; fewer than 50 people. The character of the Late Classic site may be to some extent obscured by the heavy Early Toltec overlay.

Tx-LC-5

Natural setting: 2320 m, in the Lower Piedmont. Situated on the gently sloping southeastern flank of a small hill, about 500 m west of the Río Papalotla. Slight erosion, with moderately deep soil cover.

Modern utilization: Intensive rainfall cultivation.

Archaeological remains: Variable very light to light concentrations of surface pottery and light-to-moderate rock rubble over an area of less than one hectare. Mixed with heavier Early and Late Toltec pottery (Tx-ET-13; Tx-LT-27). Also present are light concentrations of Late Formative (Tx-LF-6), Terminal Formative (Tx-TF-10), Early Classic (Tx-EC-6), and some Aztec pottery. No structural remains.

Classification: Hamlet; fewer than 50 people.

Tx-LC-6

Natural setting: 2330 m, in the Lower Piedmont. Situated on the gently sloping southwestern flanks of Cerro Tepetlosco, about 500 m north of the Río Papalotla. Moderate erosion, with shallow to moderately deep soil cover.

Modern utilization: Grazing, plus some cultivated maguey.

Archaeological remains: Light concentrations of surface pottery over an area of less than one hectare. Mixed with heavier Early and Late Toltec material (Tx-ET-13; Tx-LT-28). Light Early Classic (Tx-EC-5), Late Formative (Tx-LF-7), and Terminal Formative (Tx-TF-11) pottery is also present. There are no structural remains that can be assigned to Early Classic times.

Classification: Hamlet; fewer than 50 people.

Tx-LC-7

Natural setting: 2290 m, at the lower edge of the Lower Piedmont. Situated in a nearly level zone, with deep soil cover.

Modern utilization: Intensive mechanized irrigation and rainfall cultivation. The site area has been cut through by a dirt road.

Archaeological remains: Variable very light concentrations of surface pottery and moderate rock rubble over an area of about four hectares. Obsidian tools and chipping debris are especially abundant. Mixed with somewhat lighter Early Classic pottery (Tx-EC-7). Light Late Toltec (Tx-LT-11) and Aztec (Tx-A-14) material is also present. No definite structural remains.

Classification: Hamlet; fewer than 50 people.

Tx-LC-8

Natural setting: 2465 m, at the upper edge of the Lower Piedmont. Situated on the gently sloping floor of a small valley which cuts deeply into the main surface of the Upper Piedmont. A major barranca some 5 to 8 m deep is intrenched through the middle of the site area. Stone-faced terraces covering the gentle hillslopes in the site area have prevented severe erosion. Soil depth varies from shallow to moderately deep, with several pockets of deeper soil immediately adjacent to the barranca.

Modern utilization: Grazing, plus a few cultivated maguey.

Archaeological remains: Light concentrations of surface pottery and heavy rock rubble over an area of roughly two hectares. Mixed with heavier Early Classic (Tx-EC-8) material. No structural remains. The barranca has apparently cut into the occupational zone as sherds are washing from the steep walls. The age of the numerous stone-faced terraces which cover much of the site area on the west side of the barranca is uncertain. These features measure roughly 25 to 50 cm high, and 8 to 10 m wide, with downhill face consisting of one or two tiers of loosely piled rough stones. Today they function only for erosion control.

Classification: Hamlet; fewer than 50 people.

Tx-LC-9

Natural setting: 2340 m, in the Lower Piedmont. Situated on a broad, gentle slope adjacent to a major barranca. Moderate to severe erosion, with shallow soil cover and some patches of bare tepetate.

Modern utilization: Intensive rainfall cultivation except in areas of most severe erosion which now serve only as grazing land.

Archaeological remains: Moderate and light-to-moderate surface pottery over an area of about one hectare. An additional eight hectares have light sherd cover. No structural remains. Mixed with light Late Formative (Tx-LF-10), somewhat lighter Early Classic (Tx-EC-9), and some Aztec material (Tx-A-66).

Classification: Small dispersed village; 125 to 175 people.

Tx-LC-10

Natural setting: 2370 m, in the Lower Piedmont. Situated on a broad, gentle slope, between two major barrancas. Moderate to severe erosion, with shallow soil cover and some patches of bare tepetate.

Modern utilization: The immediate site area is used only for grazing today. Most of the surrounding fields are intensively cultivated (rainfall agriculture). The westernmost residential units of modern San Miguel Tlaixpan occur about 500 m to the east.

Archaeological remains: Light concentrations of surface pottery and moderate rock rubble over an area of about two hectares. No structural remains. Mixed with heavier Early Classic (Tx-EC-10) and some Aztec material (Tx-A-66).

Classification: Hamlet; fewer than 50 people.

Tx-LC-11

Natural setting: 2240 m, in the Lower Piedmont. Situated on a broad, gentle slope between two major barrancas. Moderate erosion, with shallow soil cover. Bancal systems have prevented severe erosion over much of the site area.

Modern utilization: The site area is located at the western edge of an intensively cultivated zone (rainfall agriculture). Areas to the west, north, and south are predominately grazing land, as are some parts of the site area itself where erosion has been most severe and rock rubble is heaviest.

Archaeological remains: Variable light and light-to-moderate concentrations of surface pottery and moderate rock rubble over an area of about 5 hectares. No structural remains. Mixed with substantial Terminal Formative (Tx-TF-17) and Early Classic (Tx-EC-12) material, plus light Middle Formative (Tx-MF-6) and Late Toltec (Tx-LT-43) pottery.

Classification: Hamlet; fewer than 100 people.

Tx-LC-12

Natural setting: 2310 to 2320 m, in the Lower Piedmont. Situated on a broad, gentle slope, near a major barranca. The site occupies the edge of a low bluff and the adjacent lower ground. Moderate to severe erosion, with shallow soil cover and some patches of bare tepetate.

Modern utilization: Grazing. The lower part of the site is presently in use as a picnic area in the Molino de Flores park. Adjacent fields to the west and south are intensively cultivated.

Archaeological remains: Light concentrations of surface pottery over an area of about three hectares. No structural remains. Mixed with heavier Early Classic (Tx-EC-13) material.

Classification: Hamlet; fewer than 50 people.

Tx-LC-13

Natural setting: 2310 m, in the Lower Piedmont. Situated on a broad, gentle slope next to a major barranca. Slight erosion; moderately deep soil cover.

Modern utilization: Intensive rainfall cultivation in the immediate site area. The land to the west is irrigated from wells using gasoline pumps, and is devoted primarily to alfalfa.

Archaeological remains: Light-to-moderate concentrations of surface pottery over an area of about six hectares. No structural remains. Mixed with somewhat heavier Early Classic (Tx-EC-14), and light Late Toltec material (Tx-LT-42).

Classification: Small nucleated village; 100 to 150 people.

Tx-LC-14

Natural setting: 2360 m, in the Lower Piedmont. Situated on a broad, gentle slope between two major barrancas. In zone of moderate erosion, with shallow to moderately deep soil.

Modern utilization: Intensive rainfall cultivation.

Archaeological remains: Variable light and very light concentrations of surface pottery over an area of less than one hectare. No structural remains. Mixed with Early Classic material (Tx-EC-16).

Classification: Hamlet; fewer than 50 people. May represent only a single household unit.

Tx-LC-15

Natural setting: 2310 m, in the Lower Piedmont. Situated on a broad, gentle slope, over 1 km from the nearest major barranca. Moderate erosion; shallow to moderately deep soil cover.

Modern utilization: Intensive rainfall cultivation.

Archaeological remains: Light concentrations of surface pottery over an area of less than one hectare. No structural remains. Mixed with light Terminal Formative (Tx-TF-52) material, and somewhat more abundant Early Classic pottery (Tx-EC-17).

Classification: Hamlet; fewer than 50 people.

Tx-LC-16

Natural setting: 2310 to 2320 m, in the Lower Piedmont. Situated on a broad, gently sloping ridge top lying between two major barrancas. Moderate erosion, with variable shallow to moderately deep soil cover.

Modern utilization: The immediate site area is now devoted to commercial fruit trees and some maguey. The slopes to the north of the site are partially terraced, and some rainfall cultivation of maize and beans occurs there. The land east of the site is used for grazing only. The lower region to the west is intensively cultivated (rainfall agriculture). A large commercial sand and gravel quarry is located south of the site area.

Archaeological remains: Variable light and very light concentrations of surface pottery over an area of about four hectares. No structural remains. Mixed with much heavier Early Classic material (Tx-EC-18), and with some Aztec pottery (Tx-A-87).

Classification: Hamlet; fewer than 50 people.

Tx-LC-17

Natural setting: 2300 m, at the western base of Cerro Tonaltepec, near the edge of the main Lower Piedmont plain. Slight to moderate erosion, with moderately deep soil cover.

Modern utilization: Intensive rainfall cultivation. The higher slopes above the site are now grazing land, although there are badly deteriorated remains of extensive terracing.

Archaeological remains: Variable light and very light concentrations of surface pottery over an area of about four hectares. Occupational debris is mixed with much heavier Early Toltec material (Tx-ET-17) and some Early Classic pottery (Tx-EC-31). There are abundant structural remains, but all appear to be Early Toltec in age. The age of the abandoned terracing above the site area is unclear.

Classification: Hamlet; fewer than 100 people. Probably an outlying unit of Tx-LC-18.

Tx-LC-18

Natural setting: 2250 to 2300 m, on the northern lowermost flanks of Cerro Portezuelo, at the edge of the main Lower Piedmont plain. Deep soil is found in the lower part of the site, with soil cover thinning to moderate and shallow depths upslope. The entire site area is cut through by numerous barrancas of varying sizes. Most of the barrancas are relatively narrow and deep, often cutting through prehispanic occupational zones.

Modern utilization: Most of the site area is devoted to intensive rainfall cultivation. Some fields are presently fallow, and used for grazing only. The higher slopes above the site area are predominately grazing land. The level plain north of the site is intensively cultivated.

Archaeological remains: Variable very light, light, and light-to-moderate concentrations of surface pottery over an area of roughly 80 hectares. The character of the Classic site may be badly obscured by the heavy Early Toltec occupation (Tx-ET-18) over the site area. There are many structural remains, but none can definitely be associated with the Late Classic. Early Classic (Tx-EC-32), Late Toltec (Tx-LT-53), and Aztec (Tx-A-103) material is also present.

Classification: The extent and complexity of the Late Classic site here may well be badly obscured by the heavy Early Toltec overlay. Apparently, the Late Classic occupation represents a regional center with a dispersed population of roughly 400 to 1200 people. This is by far the largest Late Classic occupational locus in the Texcoco Region.

Tx-LC-19

Natural setting: 2240 m, on the flat Lakeshore Plain. Probably at or near the Conquest-period shoreline of Lake Texcoco. In a zone of deep alluvial soil.

Modern utilization: Intensive rainfall and irrigation cultivation, with scattered residential households at the southwest edge of the modern village of Cuatlalpan.

Archaeological remains: Very light concentrations of surface pottery over an area of less than one hectare. No structural remains. Some occupational debris may be obscured by deep alluvial soil, modern buildings, a major asphalt highway (at the west edge of the site), and thick alfalfa vegetation in the adjacent fields. Mixed with much heavier Early Classic material (Tx-EC-33).

Classification: Hamlet; fewer than 50 people. May represent a single household or set of transient individuals.

Tx-LC-20

Natural setting: 2240 m, on gently sloping land at the northeastern base of Cerro Chimalhuacan, near the Conquest-period shoreline of Lake Texcoco. In zone of deep to moderately deep soil cover, and slight erosion.

Modern utilization: The site area is spread out over several cultivated fields in the heart of present-day Chimalhuacan. There is abundant terracing on the higher slopes above the site, but most terraces are now abandoned and in disrepair.

Archaeological remains: Very light concentrations of surface pottery over an area of roughly one hectare. The densely-packed modern structures and heavy Aztec occupation (Tx-A-109) have badly obscured the original character of the Late Classic site. The occupational debris is mixed with somewhat heavier Early Classic material (Tx-EC-34). Some Early and Late Toltec sherds are also present (Tx-ET-19; Tx-LT-54).

Classification: Hamlet; fewer than 50 people. May represent a single household, or a small transient group.

Tx-LC-21

Natural setting: 2240 m, on gently sloping ground at the southern base of Cerro Chimalhuacan, just above the flat Lakeshore Plain. Moderate to severe erosion, with shallow soil cover. The site area has been cut through by several small barrancas.

Modern utilization: The site is situated between the eastern edge of the modern village of Atlapulco and the western end of present-day Chimalpa. Most of the site area is used only as grazing land today. The steeper slopes above the site have been extensively terraced in the past, but only a few of these fields are now cultivated, and all terraces are in a bad state of disrepair. Some cultivated maguey occurs throughout the site area.

Archaeological remains: Light concentrations of surface pottery and moderate rock rubble over an area of roughly two hectares. No structural remains. Some occupational debris may be obscured by modern buildings in Atlapulco and Chimalpa. Mixed with much heavier Early Classic material (Tx-EC-35).

Classification: Hamlet; fewer than 50 people.

Tx-LC-22

Natural setting: 2240 m, on gently sloping ground at the southern base of Cerro Chimalhuacan, just above the flat Lakeshore Plain. Moderate to severe erosion, with shallow soil cover. The site area is adjacent to a major barranca, and is cut through by several small ones.

Modern utilization: Grazing. The steep slopes above the site have been extensively terraced in the past, but only a few of these fields are now cultivated, and all terraces are in a bad state of disrepair. Some cultivated maguey throughout the site area.

Archaeological remains: Light concentrations of surface pottery and moderate rock rubble over an area of roughly one hectare. No structural remains. Mixed with much heavier Early Classic material (Tx-EC-36).

Classification: Hamlet; fewer than 50 people.

Tx-LC-23

Natural setting: 2270 m, on gently sloping ground near the western base of Cerro Portezuelo, some 30 m above the level of the Lakeshore Plain to the west. The site is situated between two large barrancas in an area of irregular ground surface and thin soil cover. Erosion has been moderate to severe.

Modern utilization: Grazing and scattered cultivated maguey. The steeper slopes above the site have been extensively terraced in the past, but these structures are presently badly deteriorated and serve only as indifferent erosion checks. Numerous basalt quarries (both operative and abandoned) are found in the hillslopes above and to either side of the site area. The lower, level land immediately below the site, on either side of the main highway, is largely covered with a variety of very recently built industrial and residential complexes. The nucleated village of La Magdalena is located about 600 m west of the site area.

Archaeological remains: Very light concentrations of surface pottery over an area of less than one hectare. No structural remains. Mixed with more abundant Early Classic material (Tx-EC-37), and much heavier Early Toltec pottery (Tx-ET-23). The heavy cover of modern constructions in the area below the site may be obscuring some prehispanic occupational debris.

Classification: Hamlet; fewer than 50 people.

EARLY TOLTEC

Tx-ET-1

Natural setting: 2250 m, on the Lakeshore Plain. Situated at the edge of a low island of higher ground on the broad, level plain. Deep alluvial soil cover. Probably at or near the Conquest-period shoreline of Lake Texcoco.

Modern utilization: The northern half of the site is intensively cultivated (rainfall agriculture). The southern half, on top of the low island, is now a part of a Federal park (Parque El Contador), heavily covered with large ahuehuete trees and utilized as a picnic ground.

Archaeological remains: Variable very light and light concentrations of surface pottery over an area of about two hectares. Mixed with light Late Toltec material (Tx-LT-4). The dominant occupational component is Aztec (Tx-A-6). There are no structural remains that can be assigned to Early Toltec times.

Classification: Hamlet; fewer than 50 people.

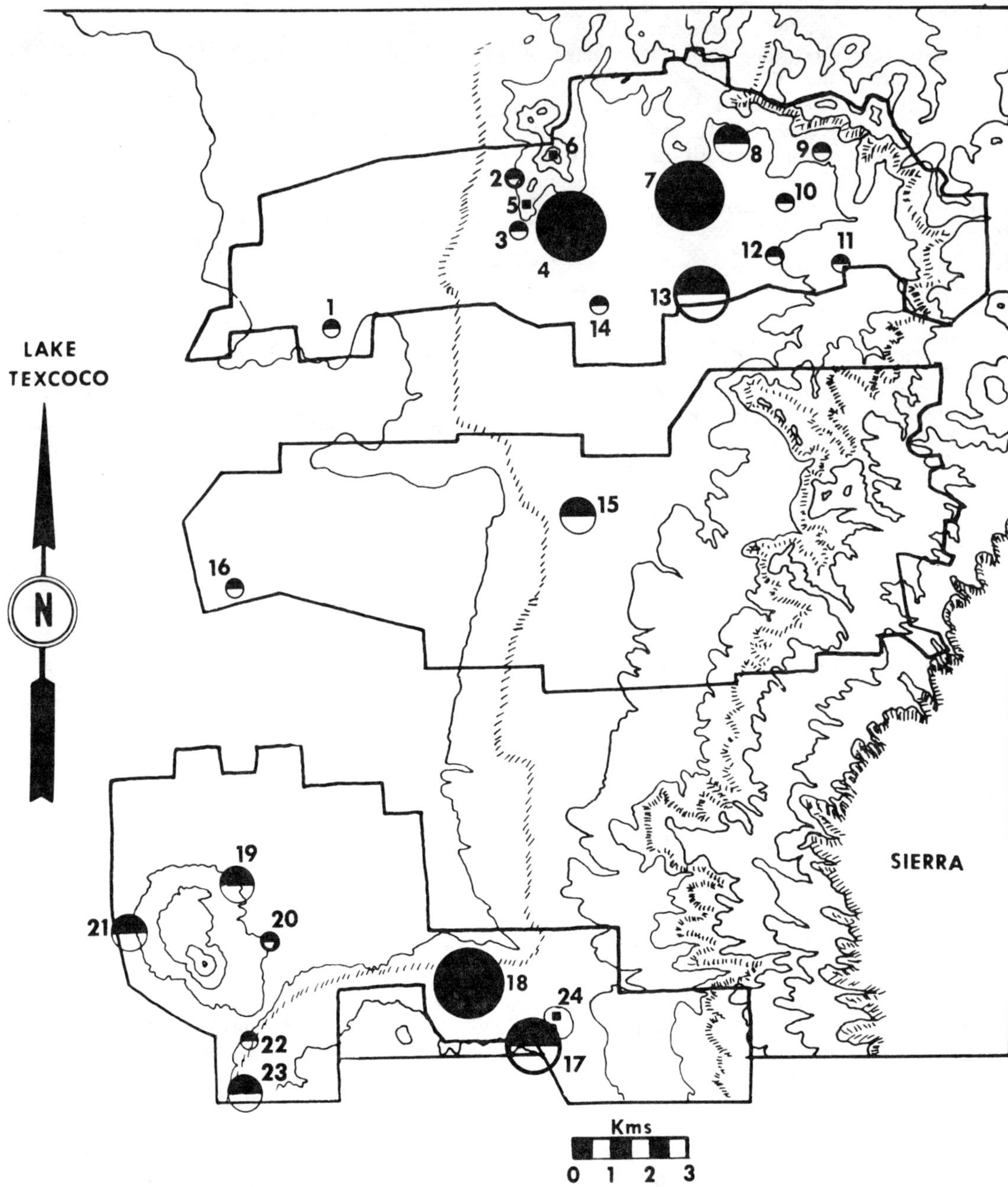

Map 10—Texcoco Region: Early Toltec settlement (schematic). Contour interval 100 meters. For key see map 5, p. 25.

Tx-ET-2

Natural setting: 2330 to 2340 m, on the gently sloping lower western flanks of Cerro Azteca. Severe erosion, with very shallow soil cover and large stretches of bare tepetate.

Modern utilization: Marginal grazing land, plus a few cultivated maguey.

Archaeological remains: Variable light and light-to-moderate concentrations of surface pottery and moderate rock rubble over an area of about three hectares. Mixed with somewhat more abundant Aztec material (Tx-A-18). The steep slopes above the site are covered with extensive ancient terracing of indeterminate age.

Classification: Hamlet; fewer than 50 people.

Tx-ET-3

Natural setting: 2290 to 2330 m, on gently sloping ground at the southern base and lowermost flanks of Cerro Azteca at the edge of the main Lower Piedmont plain. Situated in a zone of moderate to severe erosion and variable soil cover (shallow upslope, to moderately deep at the hill base), adjacent to Río Papalotla.

Modern utilization: The immediate site area lies at one edge of the modern village of Tepetitlan, and some prehispanic occupational debris extends underneath the residential units of the modern community. Some rainfall cultivation is practiced. The higher slopes serve as grazing land, and support some cultivated maguey. There are several basalt quarries on the adjacent slopes. The main Lower Piedmont plain to the south is intensively cultivated.

Archaeological remains: Variable light, light-to-moderate, and moderate concentrations of surface pottery over an area of about two hectares. No structural remains. The heaviest occupation occurs at the base of the hill, with progressively less surface pottery upslope.

Classification: Hamlet; fewer than 50 people. Probably an outlier of Tx-ET-4 to the east.

Tx-ET-4

Natural setting: 2290 to 2350 m, on the level Lower Piedmont plain and adjacent gently sloping southern flanks of Cerro Azteca, next to the Río Papalotla. (Pl. 28). Soil cover throughout the lower section of the site area is deep; moving up the gentle hillslopes to the north this soil cover thins progressively and erosion becomes increasingly severe. Shallow soil and large patches of bare tepetate are characteristic of the higher, northern sections of the site.

Modern utilization: The lower ground on the main piedmont plain is intensively cultivated (rainfall agriculture). The hillslopes are used predominately for grazing land and maguey cultivation.

Archaeological remains: Variable light, light-to-moderate, and moderate concentrations of surface pottery over an area of about 180 hectares (Fig. 8). The northern and southern sections of the site are separated by a strip of ground about 200 m wide which contains light surface pottery. Definite structural remains occur only in the southern part of the site, where several large pyramidal mounds and a number of domestic residences can be distinguished (Appendix 2; Pl, 28,*b*). The concentration of obvious and abundant ceremonial-civic architecture in the southern site area strongly suggests that Tx-ET-4 is an important regional center. The occupational debris in the northern sector of the site is mixed with somewhat heavier Terminal Formative pottery (Tx-TF-1), in addition to light Aztec material (Tx-A-17). The extensive terracing in this northern area has been described under the Tx-TF-1 site description, but its age is unclear. Light amounts of Early Classic, Late Classic, Late Toltec, and Aztec pottery occur over the southern site area (Tx-EC-3; Tx-LC-2; Tx-LT-11; Tx-A-16).

Classification: Primary regional center; 3600 to 7200 people.

Tx-ET-5

Natural setting: 2430 m, on the level top of a long ridge extending southward from the main block of Cerro Azteca (Pl. 49; Fig. 8). Situated some 120 m above the level of the Lower Piedmont plain to the south and east, and the Lakeshore Plain to the west. Irregular ground surface throughout the site area, with generally shallow soil cover and some rock outcroppings. Erosion has been moderate to severe. The Río Papalotla flows at the base of the hill, south of the site.

Modern utilization: Grazing.

Archaeological remains: Variable very light and light concentrations of surface pottery over an area of about two hectares on the ridge top and immediately adjacent slopes. The length of the ridge top is terraced in three broad steps, each with a downslope height of about 2 m. A total of four large rock rubble mounds has been constructed on these terraces (Appendix 2). Light Late Formative (Tx-LF-1) and Early Classic (Tx-EC-2) material is also present.

Classification: Hilltop ceremonial precinct. Probably lacking any permanent occupation.

Tx-ET-6

Natural setting: 2620 m, at the top of Cerro Azteca, about 250 to 300 m above the level of the Lower Piedmont plain and the Lakeshore Plain to the east, south, and west. The soil cover is generally shallow, with isolated pockets of deep soil and numerous rock outcrops over the irregular ground surface. Erosion has been moderate.

Modern utilization: Grazing, plus some cultivated maguey.

Fig. 8—Site plan, Tx-ET-4 (impressionistic contours).

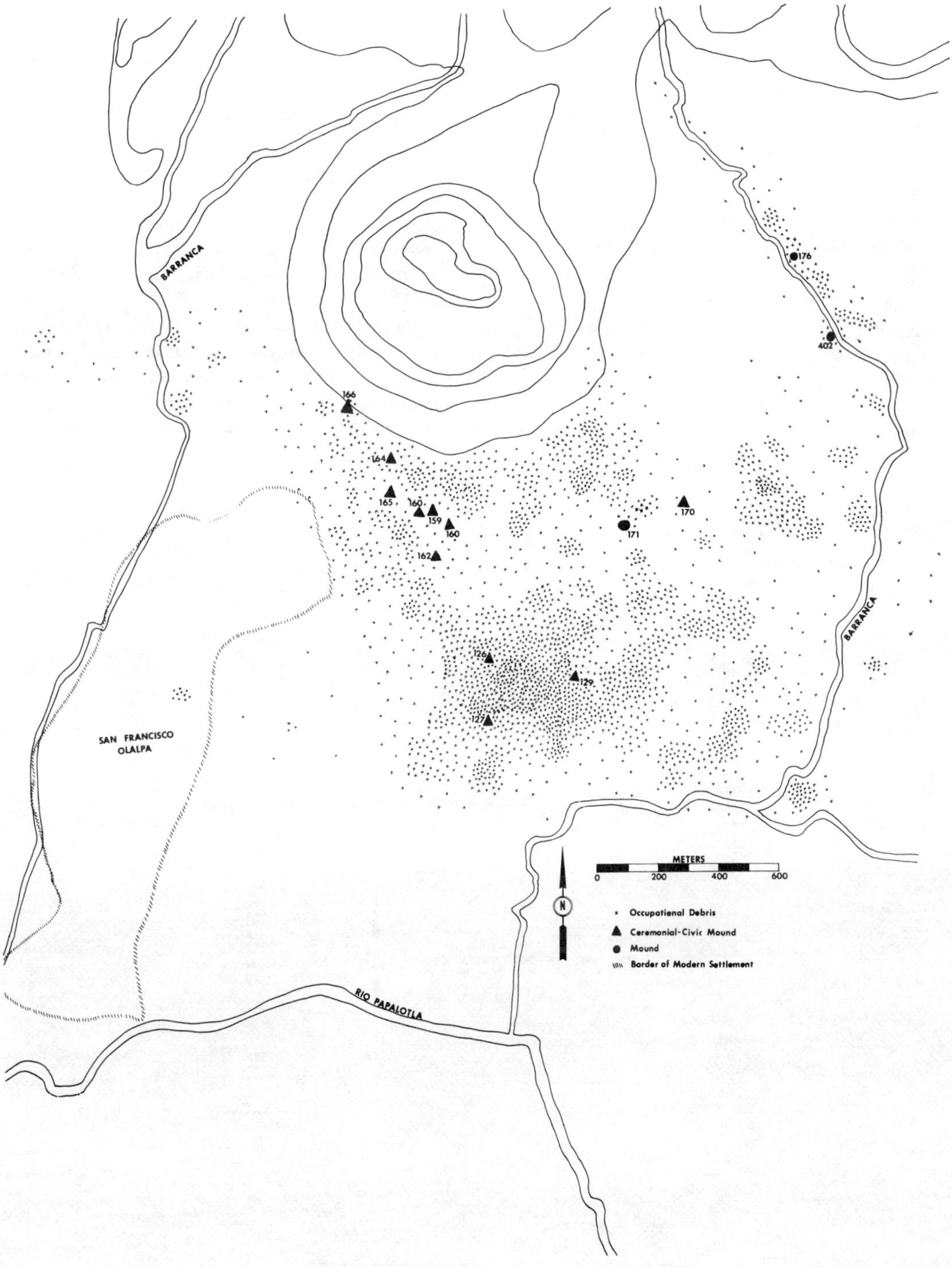

Fig. 9—Site plan, Tx-ET-7 (impressionistic contours).

Archaeological remains: Variable very light and light concentrations of surface pottery over an area of roughly one hectare of relatively level ground. The dominant occupational component here is Aztec (Tx-A-20); some Terminal Formative and Late Toltec pottery is also present (Tx-TF-3; Tx-LF-14). No structural remains can be assigned to Early Toltec times, but the large Aztec pyramid which dominates the site may contain earlier constructions within its core.

Classification: Small hilltop ceremonial precinct; probably lacking any permanent occupation.

Tx-ET-7

Natural setting: 2300 to 2350 m, on the gently sloping southern flank of Cerro Teponaxtle, extending southward onto the edge of the main Lower Piedmont plain to the edge of the Río Papalotla. Soil depth varies from deep at the plain's edge in the south, to shallow in the northern half of the site area. Erosion has been slight or nonexistent on the piedmont plain, and moderate to severe on the hill flanks, with some stretches of badly scarred bare tepetate. The eastern and western limits of the site are marked by two major barrancas, and several smaller barrancas cut through the site area at various points.

Modern utilization: Intensive rainfall cultivation over much of the site area, except at some points on the hill flanks where erosion has been severe. Part of the western half of the site extends beneath the modern village of San Francisco Olalpa.

Archaeological remains: Variable light-to-moderate and moderate concentrations of surface pottery and rock rubble over an area of about 200 hectares (Fig. 9). A number of very distinct structural remains are distributed throughout the

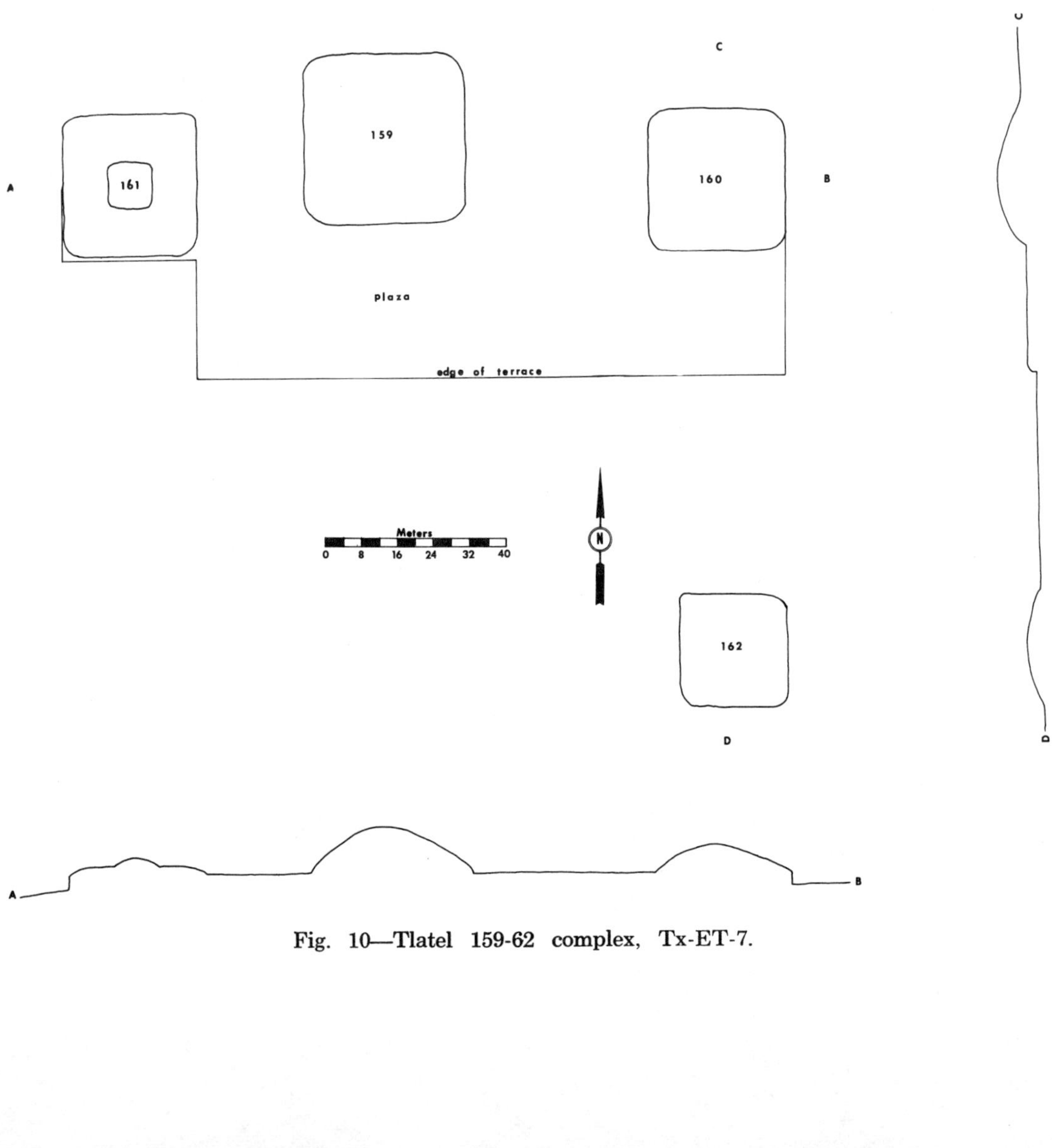

Fig. 10—Tlatel 159-62 complex, Tx-ET-7.

site area, including several large pyramidal constructions concentrated on the western side of the site (Appendix II). The site's ceremonial-civic precinct focuses on three large pyramids (tlateles 159-161) arranged around a large plaza, which is in turn built up some 2.5 m above the general ground surface (Pl. 29, 34*a*; Fig. 10). Light Early Classic (Tx-EC-4), Late Classic (Tx-LC-4), and Aztec (Tx-A-24) pottery is also found at various points within the site area.

Classification: Primary regional center; 4000 to 8000 people.

Tx-ET-8

Natural setting: 2300 to 2330 m, on gently sloping ground on the eastern flanks of Cerro Teponaxtle. Situated along either side of a major barranca which has apparently cut through sections of the site area as it has widened and deepened. Entire area is badly eroded, with very little soil cover and large stretches of bare tepetate.

Modern utilization: Immediate site area serves only as marginal grazing land. Less severely eroded land to the east and west is presently devoted to rainfall cultivation of subsistence crops.

Archaeological remains: Variable light and light-to-moderate concentrations of surface pottery and rock rubble over an area of about 19 hectares. Severe erosion has badly obscured the original aspect of the site, and there are no distinguishable structural remnants apart from two small mounds (Appendix II).

Classification: Small dispersed village; 200 to 300 people. This may represent an outlier of the Tx-ET-7 community.

Tx-ET-9

Natural setting: 2380 m, in the Lower Piedmont. Situated on the gently sloping lower southern flanks of Cerro Tepetlaoxtoc, near a major barranca. Severe erosion, with very shallow soil cover, and large stretches of bare tepetate.

Modern utilization: Grazing and maguey cultivation.

Archaeological remains: Light concentrations of surface pottery and moderate rock rubble over an area of less than one hectare. Mixed with more abundant Terminal Formative (Tx-TF-7) and Aztec (Tx-A-25) material. No structural remains.

Classification: Hamlet; fewer than 50 people.

Tx-ET-10

Natural setting: 2300 m, in the Lower Piedmont. Situated on gently sloping ground, along either side of the Río Papalotla, at the edge of the main Lower Piedmont plain.

Modern utilization: A section of the site is partially covered by the northeastern edge of the modern town of Tepetlaoxtoc. Land not occupied by residential structures is devoted to intensive rainfall cultivation of subsistence crops.

Archaeological remains: Variable very light, light, and light-to-moderate concentrations of surface pottery over an area of about nine hectares. No structural remains. Mixed with somewhat heavier Aztec material (Tx-A-25).

Classification: Hamlet; fewer than 100 people.

Tx-ET-11

Natural setting: 2420 m, in the Lower Piedmont. Situated on nearly level ground, near the top of a very broad ridge top. Slight erosion, with moderately deep soil cover.

Modern utilization: Grazing and maguey cultivation. The site area is just north of the modern village of San Bernardino Tlamimilolpa.

Archaeological remains: Variable light and light-to-moderate concentrations of surface pottery and rock rubble over an area of about two hectares. No structural remains. Mixed with some Aztec material (Tx-A-37).

Classification: Hamlet; fewer than 50 people.

Tx-ET-12

Natural setting: 2340 to 2350 m, in the Lower Piedmont. Situated on a broad, gentle slope just east of the modern town of Tepetlaoxtoc. Severe erosion, with very shallow soil cover, and large stretches of badly scarred bare tepetate.

Modern utilization: Marginal grazing, plus some cultivated maguey.

Archaeological remains: Four low mounds (Appendix II) covered with moderate concentrations of surface pottery, over an area of about three hectares. The intervening areas between the mounds contain very little surface pottery.

Classification: Hamlet; fewer than 50 people.

Tx-ET-13

Natural setting: 2300 to 2330 m, in the Lower Piedmont. Situated on the gently sloping lower flanks of two adjacent low hills, and in the intervening saddle along the Río Papalotla. Erosion has been moderate over most of the site area, and severe along sections of the southern margin. Soil cover is generally shallow to moderately deep, with some patches of bare tepetate in the most severely eroded sections. Several small barrancas cut through the site area.

Modern utilization: Rainfall cultivation of subsistence crops, except in the most severely eroded portions which are useful only for grazing.

Archaeological remains: Variable light and light-to-moderate concentrations of surface pottery over an area of about 80 hectares. There are several well defined mounds, but most of them probably date from the Aztec occupation of this same area (Tx-A-40), although some or all may contain levels dating to Early Toltec times. Light Terminal Formative (Tx-TF-11) and Late Toltec (Tx-LT-26, Tx-LT-27, Tx-LT-28) also occur. The hillslopes on both sides of the river have been extensively terraced—these structures are presently abandoned and badly deteriorated. The age of terracing here is uncertain. The site area actually continues somewhat to the south of where our survey terminated.

Classification: Large dispersed village; 800 to 1600 people.

Tx-ET-14

Natural setting: 2290 m, on the main Lower Piedmont plain near its juncture with the Lakeshore Plain. Deep alluvial soil.

Modern utilization: Intensive cultivation (both rainfall and mechanized irrigation).

Archaeological remains: Variable very light and light concentrations of surface pottery over an area of roughly one hectare. Mixed with more abundant Early Classic (Tx-EC-7), Late Classic (Tx-LC-7), Late Toltec (Tx-LT-11), and Aztec (Tx-A-14) material. Obsidian debris is especially abundant over the site area. No definite structural remains.

Classification: Hamlet; fewer than 50 people.

Tx-ET-15

Natural setting: 2280 to 2290 m, in the Lower Piedmont, near its juncture with the Lakeshore Plain. Slight erosion, with moderately deep soil cover over most of the site. Situated on a broad, gentle slope adjacent to a major canalized barranca.

Modern utilization: Roughly half the site area lies within the modern village of San Diego (an outlying barrio of Texcoco). The remainder of the site is devoted to intensive rainfall and canal-irrigation cultivation. All irrigation is completely mechanized, based on wells and gasoline pumps.

Archaeological remains: Variable light and light-to-moderate concentrations of surface pottery over an area of about 23 hectares. No structural remains can be attributed to the Early Toltec period. However, a large Aztec pyramidal mound in the southwest quadrant of the site may be superimposed over one or more earlier structures. Mixed with heavier Aztec material (Tx-A-56).

Classification: Small dispersed village; 200 to 300 people.

Tx-ET-16

Natural setting: Below 2240 m, on the Lakeshore Plain, well within the borders of Conquest-period Lake Texcoco. Situated in an area of small sand dunes which rise about 2 m above the general level of the old lake bed. In a zone of deep alluvial soil.

Modern utilization: Wasteland. The salt content of the soil and poor drainage of the area prohibits effective cultivation. The region is even unfit for grazing as vegetation of any kind is absent.

Archaeological remains: A light scattering of surface pottery over an area of less than one hectare. The sherds occur within a slightly elevated, localized cluster of small sand dunes, and are generally found in the low intervening areas between individual dunes. No structural remains. Mixed with some Late Toltec (Tx-LT-37) and more abundant Aztec pottery (Tx-A-43).

Classification: Questionable. It is doubtful if these few sherds represent permanent residence of any kind. More probably we are dealing with a temporary camp on a small island or directly in the lakeshore marsh for hunting water fowl and/or gathering lake resources.

Tx-ET-17

Natural setting: 2290 to 2350 m, in the Lower Piedmont. Situated along a shallow barranca on the gentle slopes of a narrow pass between Cerro Tonaltepec and Cerro Portezuelo. Erosion has generally been slight, and soil cover is moderately deep over most of the site area.

Modern utilization: Intensive rainfall cultivation. The higher slopes to the northeast and southwest have been extensively terraced in the past, but these structures are presently abandoned and the higher ground serves only for grazing.

Archaeological remains: Variable light and light-to-moderate concentrations of surface pottery and light-to-moderate rock rubble over an area of about 35 hectares. Four distinct large pyramidal structures are clustered in the northern half of the site area (Appendix II). These quite clearly represent ceremonial-civic buildings. No overall architectural planning or ordering can be observed in any part of the site area. Much lighter Early and Late Classic material (Tx-EC-31; Tx-LC-17) also occur here.

Classification: Large dispersed village; 350 to 700 people. The site is a detached eastern segment of a primary regional center, whose central area is included under Tx-ET-18. The population density of this eastern segment is somewhat more dispersed than for Tx-ET-18.

Tx-ET-18

Natural setting: 2250 to 2300 m, on the gently sloping northern flanks of Cerro Portezuelo, at the edge of the main Lower Piedmont plain (Pl. 30). Deep alluvial soil occurs over the lower part of the site area. Upslope the soil cover thins progressively to moderate and shallow depths. The entire site area is cut through by numerous barrancas of varying size. Most of these barrancas are relatively narrow and deep, often cutting through prehispanic occupational zones.

Modern utilization: Intensive rainfall cultivation over most of the site area. Some fields are presently fallow, and used for grazing only. A number of archaeological mounds are plowed over and planted in maize and beans. The higher slopes above the site are predominately grazing land. The level piedmont plain north of the site is intensively cultivated.

Archaeological remains: Variable light, light-to-moderate, and moderate concentrations of surface pottery over an area of about 400 hectares (Fig. 11). At least 22 distinct structural units can be delineated, all of which seem to be pyramidal mounds with a ceremonial-civic function (Pl. 31, 32, 33, Appendix II). Remains of domestic architecture are also present, but generally appear as vague, low mounded areas, with a relatively heavy cover of rock rubble and sherd debris. Figure 11 indicates the arrangement of distinct structures and the distribution of occupational debris. There is no apparent overall planning for the site as a whole, but there are a number of distinct clusters of several ceremonial-civic structures grouped around small plazas, which might represent barrio- or calpulli-like socio-political divisions within the community: for example, mounds 116 to 120, and 128; mounds 122 to 124; mounds 135 to 138; mounds 130 and 131; mounds 145 and 146; mounds 147 to 149. A similar function may also be served by single large structures (e.g., 151, 152, 133, 129, 127, 112).

The occupational debris is mixed with much lighter Early and Late Classic (Tx-EC-32; Tx-LC-18), Late Toltec (Tx-LT-53), and Aztec (Tx-A-103) material.

Classification: Primary regional center; 6000 to 12,000 people.

Tx-ET-19

Natural setting: 2240 to 2260 m, at the northeastern base of Cerro Chimalhuacan. The site occupies a gently sloping area on a low bluff overlooking the flat Lakeshore Plain, with some occupation extending down onto the edges of the plain itself. Erosion has been moderate to severe, and the site area has been cut through by several small barrancas. The soil cover is variable, ranging from shallow to moderately deep, with some patches of bare tepetate.

Modern utilization: Marginal rainfall cultivation and grazing in the immediate site area. The lower area immediately below the site is largely occupied by the densely packed residential structures of modern Chimalhuacan. The higher slopes above the site have been extensively terraced in the past, but little of this area is now cultivated (except for a few maguey), and terraces are rapidly falling into disrepair. Several small basalt quarries (both operative and abandoned) are located on the adjacent hillslopes. A modern cemetery occupies a section of the central site area.

Archaeological remains: Variable light and light-to-moderate concentrations of surface pottery over an area of about 30 hectares. Some occupational debris may be obscured by heavy Aztec (Tx-A-109) and modern overlays along the northern edge of the Early Toltec site. No structural remains can be assigned to this period, but the large Aztec ceremonial-civic complex at the northeast corner of the site may overlie earlier structures. The occupational debris is mixed with light Early Classic (Tx-EC-34), very light Late Classic (Tx-LC-20), and light Late Toltec (Tx-LT-54), in addition to the more abundant Aztec material.

Early Toltec sherds also occur scattered widely over the terraced northern flanks of Cerro Chimalhuacan, above the Tx-ET-19 site area. Nowhere are these traces found in such concentrations as to warrant a site designation. They may indicate cultivation of the upper slopes by agriculturalists resident in Tx-ET-19.

Classification: Small dispersed village; 300 to 600 people. May be somewhat larger if some occupational debris has been obscured by modern and Aztec overlays.

Tx-ET-20

Natural setting: 2260 m, on the end of a low, flat-topped hillspur projecting out from the west-

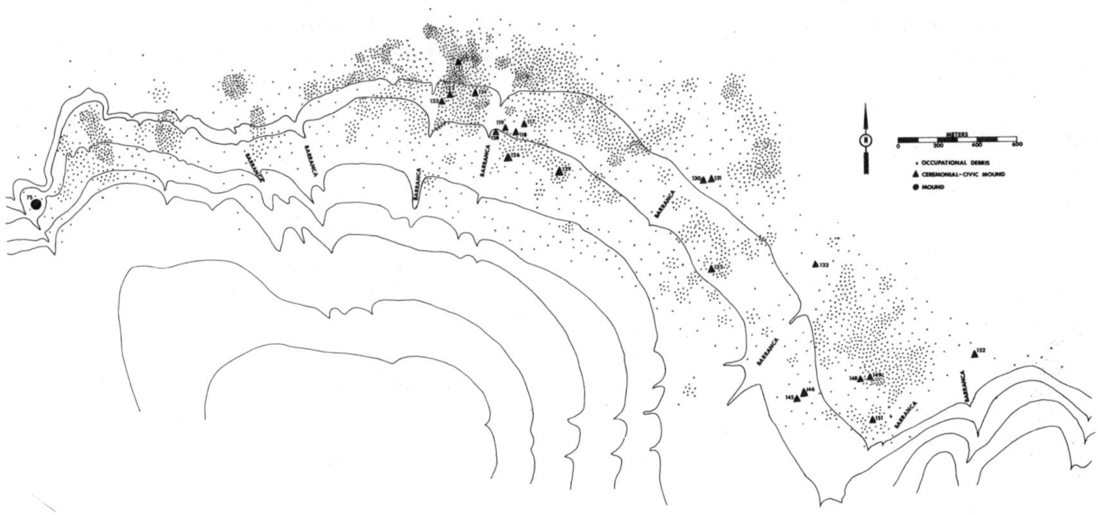

Fig. 11—Site plan, Tx-ET-18 (impressionistic contours).

ern side of Cerro Chimalhuacan. Moderate erosion, with relatively shallow soil cover and some rock outcrops.

Modern utilization: Rainfall agriculture and grazing. There are abundant small basalt quarries (both operative and abandoned) on the hillslopes in and around the site area.

Archaeological remains: Light concentrations of surface pottery over an area of about one hectare. No structural remains.

Classification: Hamlet; fewer than 50 people. May represent quarrying, rather than permanent residence.

Tx-ET-21

Natural setting: 2240 to 2250 m, along the western base of Cerro Chimalhuacan, at the edge of the Lakeshore Plain. Probably at or near the Conquest-period shoreline of Lake Texcoco. The site occupies a gently-sloping to fairly level area, where terracing has maintained a relatively deep soil cover.

Modern utilization: The nucleated village of Chimalco borders the site area on the west. The flat land west of the village is now used only for grazing. Much of the sloping area immediately east of the site has been extensively terraced in the past. At present, however, only the lowermost terraces support cultivation, and the higher slopes serve as pasture. Several basalt quarries (both operative and abandoned) are found in the area. The quarrying and finishing of this building stone are important activities in Chimalco and Xochioca today.

Archaeological remains: Variable very light, light, and light-to-moderate concentrations of surface pottery over an area of roughly 20 hectares. No definite structural remains. Mixed with Late Toltec (Tx-LT-56) pottery throughout the site, and with heavier Aztec material (Tx-A-107) in the southern half. A scattering of Terminal Formative sherds (Tx-TF-47) also occurs.

Classification: Small dispersed village; 100 to 200 people. May be somewhat larger if modern and Aztec overlays have obscured significant quantities of Early Toltec occupational debris.

Tx-ET-22

Natural setting: 2250 m, on the lowermost western flank of Cerro Portezuelo, at the edge of the main pass into the Texcoco Region from the southwest. Situated in a gently sloping to nearly level zone, with deep alluvial soil cover and very little erosion.

Modern utilization: Intensive rainfall and canal-irrigation cultivation. The site area lies between the nucleated village of Chimalpa to the west and a rapidly growing industrial-residential complex along the main highway which cuts through the center of the site.

Archaeological remains: Variable light and light-to-moderate concentrations of surface pottery over an area of about eight hectares. No structural remains. Mixed with some Late Toltec material (Tx-LT-58).

Classification: Hamlet; fewer than 100 people. May be somewhat larger if significant quantities of Early Toltec occupational debris have been obscured by modern construction.

Tx-ET-23

Natural setting: 2250 to 2270 m, at the western base of Cerro Portezuelo, adjacent to the main floor of the Lakeshore Plain to the west. The site is located on a low bluff where the main hillslope terminates, and extends over a section of the lower flat land immediately below the bluff along both sides of the modern highway (Pl. 34,*b*). The site area is cut through by three major barrancas. Numerous smaller barrancas and their tributaries also pass through the site. Erosion has been moderate to severe in the upper part of the site, and soil cover there is shallow. Deep alluvial soil covers much of the site area below the bluff.

Modern utilization: Grazing and some maguey cultivation along the bluff top; intensive cultivation in the lower land to the west. The steeper slopes above the site area have been extensively terraced in the past, but these structures are now abandoned and badly deteriorated. Much of the level ground immediately below the bluff is occupied by a rapidly expanding complex of residential and industrial buildings. Small basalt quarries, both operative and abandoned, are abundant on the adjacent hillslopes.

Archaeological remains: Variable very light, light, and light-to-moderate surface pottery over an area of roughly 35 hectares. This area includes some 10 hectares of land covered by a modern industrial complex, where all prehispanic occupational debris has been completely obliterated. Other details of prehispanic occupation may have been obscured by other modern buildings and the asphalt highway. Structural remains are lacking except for one definite small ceremonial-civic complex situated at the edge of the bluff in the upper part of the site area. This complex features four rock rubble pyramidal or platform mounds on the bluff's nearly level upper surface (Fig. 12; Appendix II). The flat bluff top contains only light concentrations of surface pottery, although rock rubble is relatively abundant. A series of distinct stone wall bases (50 cm wide) may represent explicit demarcations of the ceremonial-civic zone.

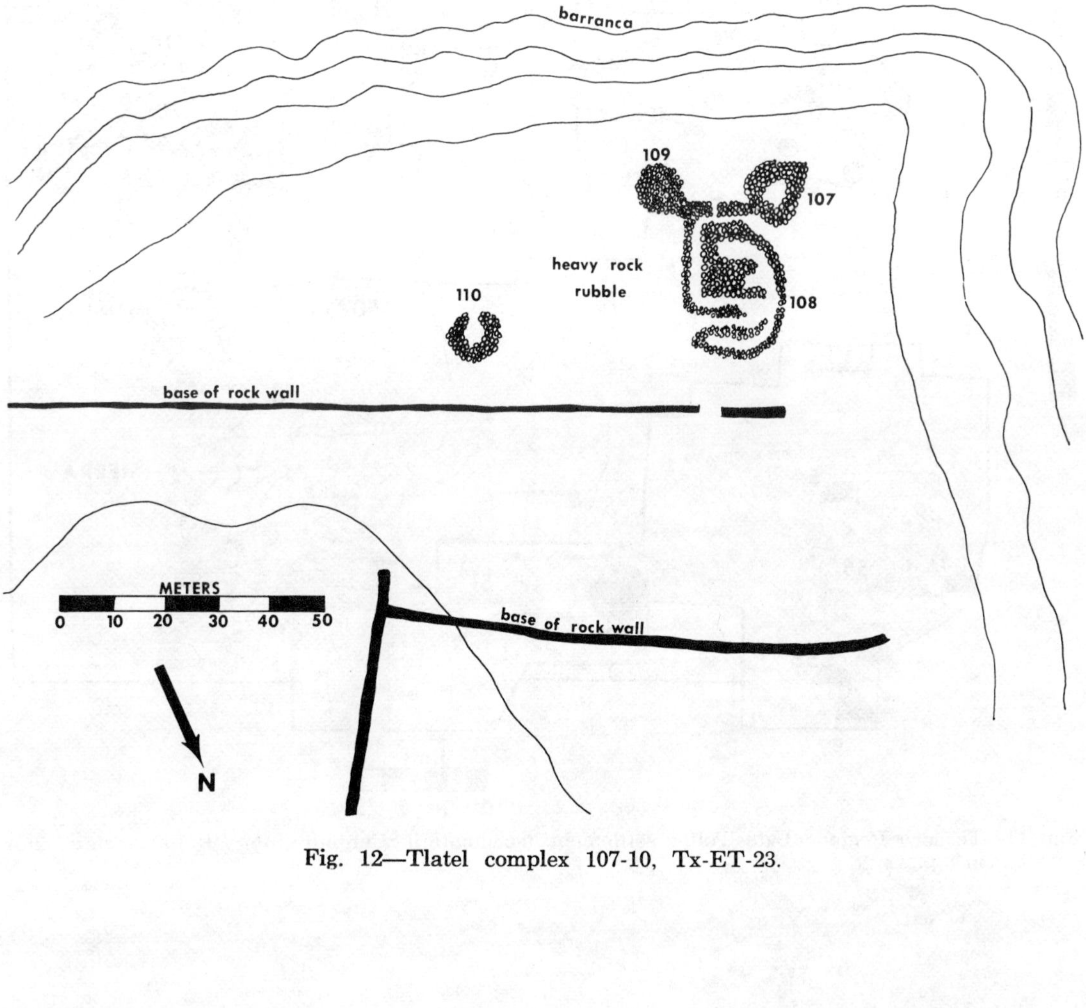

Fig. 12—Tlatel complex 107-10, Tx-ET-23.

Occupational debris is mixed with light Classic (Tx-EC-37; Tx-LC-23) and Aztec pottery, together with substantial Late Toltec material (Tx-LT-59).

Classification: Small dispersed village; 150 to 400 people.

Tx-ET-24

Natural setting: 2420 m, at the relatively level top of Cerro Tonaltepec. The site rests on a broken, irregular ground surface, some 50 m above the level of the surrounding Lower Piedmont plain. Erosion ranges from moderate to severe;

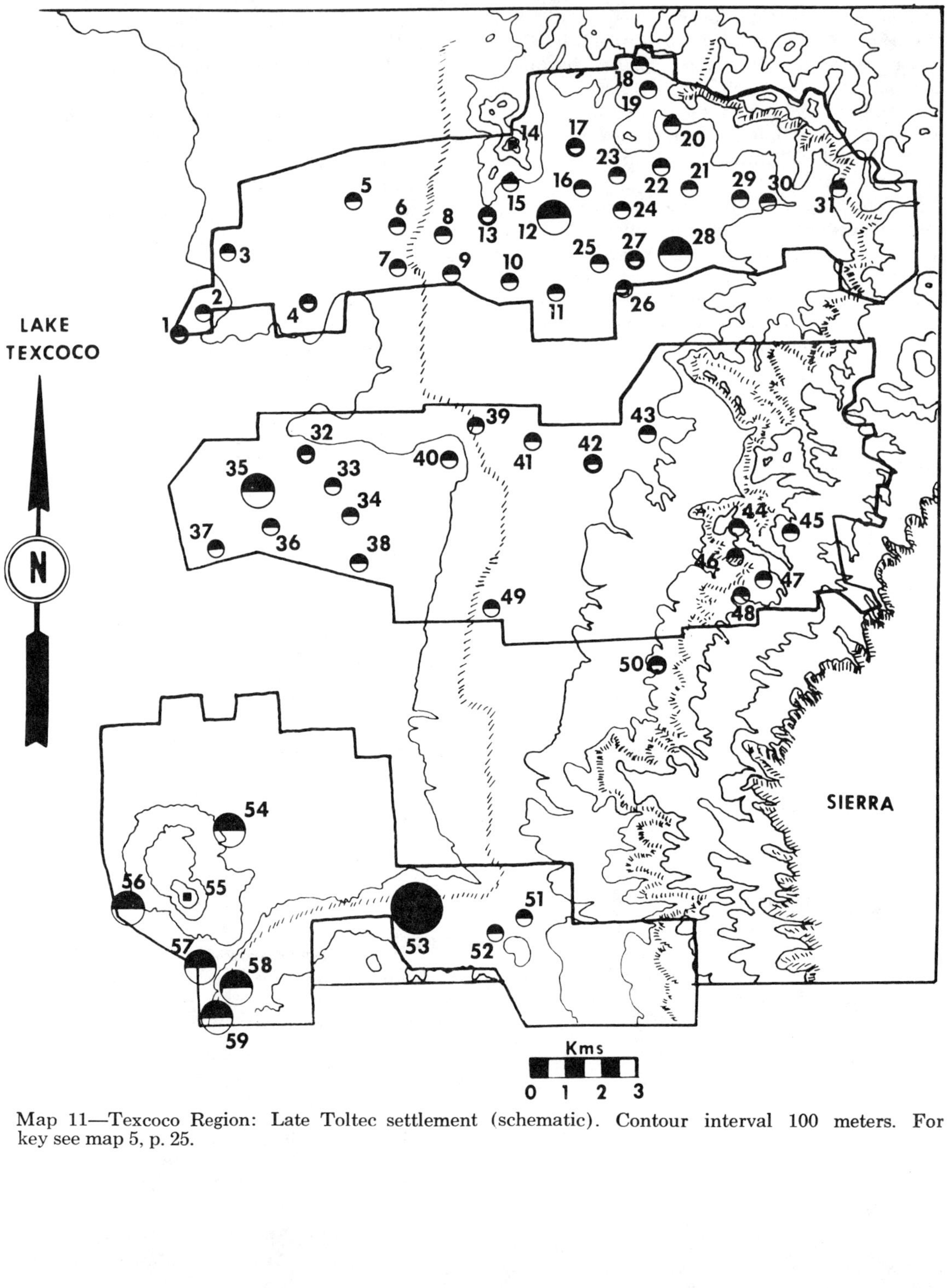

Map 11—Texcoco Region: Late Toltec settlement (schematic). Contour interval 100 meters. For key see map 5, p. 25.

variable soil cover, with some patches of bare tepetate.

Modern utilization: Grazing. The hillslopes below the site area have been extensively terraced in the past, but these structures have deteriorated badly, and the slopes are now badly eroded, and fit only for marginal grazing.

Archaeological remains: Variable light and very light concentrations of surface pottery over an area of less than one hectare. No structural remains can be definitely assigned to Early Toltec times, but a large mound, which we presume to be Aztec (Tx-A-101) may contain earlier structures within its interior, or may actually date from the Early Toltec period. Some Early Classic material is also present (Tx-EC-24),

Classification: Hilltop ceremonial precinct; probably no permanent occupation.

LATE TOLTEC

Tx-LT-1

Natural setting: 2250 m, on a low island rising about 10 m above the level of the surrounding main floor of the Lakeshore Plain. Situated at or near the Conquest-period shoreline of Lake Texcoco, probably within the borders of the old lake. Erosion over the island's surface has been moderate to severe; soil cover is generally shallow, and there are patches of bare tepetate and rock outcrops. Surrounding land is covered with deep alluvial soil.

Modern utilization: Grazing. Salt content of soil in this area apparently prohibits effective cultivation.

Archaeological remains: Variable light and light-to-moderate concentrations of surface pottery over an area of about three hectares (most of the island's surface). Mixed with somewhat heavier Aztec pottery (Tx-A-1). No structural remains.

Classification: Hamlet; fewer than 50 people.

Tx-LT-2

Natural setting: 2240 m, on a broad elevation rising some 2 m above the level of the surrounding main Lakeshore Plain. Deep alluvial soil cover. Situated at or near the shoreline of Conquest-period Lake Texcoco.

Modern utilization: Grazing. Salt content of the soil is apparently too high for effective cultivation. Entire site area covered with short tough grass.

Archaeological remains: Light-to-moderate and moderate concentrations of surface pottery over an area of roughly one hectare. No structural remains. Mixed with somewhat lighter Aztec material (Tx-A-2).

Classification: Hamlet; fewer than 50 people.

Tx-LT-3

Natural setting: 2250 m, on the Lakeshore Plain. Deep alluvial soil cover. Located at or near the Conquest-period shoreline of Lake Texcoco.

Modern utilization: Intensive rainfall cultivation. This area has only recently been reclaimed for agriculture through flushing and drainage projects.

Archaeological remains: The site consists of a mounded area measuring about 30 by 20 m in area and rising roughly 1 m above the level of the surrounding plain. There are light concentrations of Late Toltec surface pottery over this area. Somewhat more abundant Aztec material is also present (Tx-A-4). The surface of the mound has a distinct gray-white coloration which sets it clearly apart from the surrounding land surface (Pl. 35,*b*).

Classification: Hamlet; fewer than 50 people. Probably a single household unit.

Tx-LT-4

Natural setting: 2250 m, on the Lakeshore Plain. Situated at the edge of a low island of higher ground on the broad, level plain. Deep alluvial soil cover. Probably located at or near the Conquest-period shoreline of Lake Texcoco.

Modern utilization: The northern half of the site is intensively cultivated (rainfall agriculture). The southern half, on top of the low island, is now a part of a federal park (Parque El Contador), and is heavily covered with large ahuehuete trees and utilized as a picnic ground.

Archaeological remains: Variable very light and light concentrations of surface pottery over an area of about two hectares. Mixed with light Early Toltec material (Tx-ET-1). The dominant occupational component is Aztec (Tx-A-6). There are no structural remains that can be assigned to Late Toltec times.

Classification: Hamlet; fewer than 50 people.

Tx-LT-5

Natural setting: 2250 m, on the flat Lakeshore Plain. Situated on a large, low elevation, rising slightly above the level of the surrounding plain. Deep alluvial soil cover. A nearby well contains water at a depth of about 6 m.

Modern utilization: The site area is an island of uncultivated land in a region of intensive rainfall and mechanized irrigation agriculture. Short, tough grass covers most of the site today, and permits some grazing over its surface. Soil for the manufacture of adobe bricks has recently been removed in large quantities. The main asphalt highway cuts through the central part of the site.

Archaeological remains: The site consists of an irregular earth mound extending over an area of about 0.7 hectares, rising to a maximum elevation of about 1 m. Light concentrations of Late Toltec surface pottery occur over most of this area, most of it having been exposed in the course of the large scale pitting that has occurred on the mound's upper surface (for adobe-making). The dominant occupational component here is Aztec (Tx-A-9). Light Early Classic (Tx-EC-1) and Late Classic (Tx-LC-1) material are also found. There are no distinct structural remains.

Classification: Hamlet: fewer than 50 people. The abundance of Texcoco Fabric Marked, an Aztec ceramic ware presumably associated with salt-making, suggests that this location functioned to produce salt in Late Toltec times as well.

Tx-LT-6

Natural setting: 2260 m, on the Lakeshore Plain. Deep alluvial soil cover.

Modern utilization: Intensive rainfall cultivation.

Archaeological remains: The site consists of three tlateles (Appendix II) distributed over an area of about five hectares. These tlateles are areas of gray-white soil discoloration, strikingly distinct from the surrounding normally-colored brown soil. These areas of soil discoloration contain some rock rubble and light-to-moderate concentrations of Late Toltec surface pottery, mixed with somewhat lighter Aztec material (Tx-A-10). A drainage ditch cutting through one of these tlateles has exposed layers of ceramic debris from 40 to 100 cm thick beneath the ground surface. One plaster floor was also exposed in the ditch profile. The intervening ground between these tlateles contains little or no surface pottery or rock rubble.

Classification: Hamlet; fewer than 50 people. Probably three household units.

Tx-LT-7

Natural setting: 2260 m, on the Lakeshore Plain. Deep alluvial soil cover.

Modern utilization: Intensive rainfall and mechanized irrigation agriculture.

Archaeological remains: Variable light and light-to-moderate concentrations of surface pottery over an area of about seven hectares. There are no definite structural remains. Mixed with an equal amount of Aztec material (Tx-A-11).

Classification: Hamlet; 50 to 100 people.

Tx-LT-8

Natural setting: 2270 m, at the juncture of the Lakeshore Plain and the Lower Piedmont. Deep alluvial soil cover.

Modern utilization: Intensive rainfall cultivation. Modern village of Santiago Chimalpa borders the site area on the north.

Archaeological remains: Light concentrations of surface pottery over an area of about two hectares. The single structural remnant is a mound standing about 75 cm high and measuring about 20 m in diameter, which is presently plowed over and planted in maize and beans.

Classification: Hamlet; fewer than 50 people.

Tx-LT-9

Natural setting: 2270 m, at the juncture of the Lakeshore Plain and the Lower Piedmont. Deep alluvial soil cover.

Modern utilization: Part of the site is located within the borders of the modern village of Huitznahuac. The remaining area is devoted to intensive rainfall and mechanized irrigation agriculture.

Archaeological remains: Variable light and light-to-moderate concentrations of surface pottery over an area of roughly one hectare. The site consists of two occupational foci separated by about 500 m of nearly empty ground. The southern component of the site centers on an area of discolored gray-white soil measuring about 20 m in diameter. This feature may represent a discrete living unit.

Classification: Hamlet; fewer than 50 people.

Tx-LT-10

Natural setting: 2280 m, at the juncture of the Lakeshore Plain and the Lower Piedmont. Deep alluvial soil cover.

Modern utilization: Intensive rainfall cultivation. South edge of the site area extends into the modern village of Nonoalco.

Archaeological remains: Light concentrations of surface pottery over an area of about six hectares. No structural remains. Mixed with somewhat more abundant Aztec material (Tx-A-13).

Classification: Hamlet; fewer than 100 people.

Tx-LT-11

Natural setting: 2290 m, at the juncture of the Lakeshore Plain and the Lower Piedmont. Deep alluvial soil cover,

Modern utilization: Intensive rainfall and mechanized irrigation arriculture.

Archaeological remains: Light concentrations of surface pottery over an area of about two hectares. Mixed with heavier Classic (Tx-EC-7; Tx-LC-7). and Aztec (Tx-A-14) material. Some Early Toltec pottery also occurs (Tx-ET-14). Obsidian debris is especially heavy over the site area. No definite structural remains.

Classification: Hamlet; fewer than 50 people.

Tx-LT-12

Natural setting: 2290 m, at the juncture of the Lower Piedmont and the Lakeshore Plain. Situated in a zone of deep soil at the northern edge of the Río Papalotla.

Modern utilization: Intensive rainfall cultivation.

Archaeological remains: Light concentrations of surface pottery over an area of about 50 hectares. Mixed with much heavier Early Toltec material (Tx-ET-4). There are numerous structural remains, most of which probably date to Early Toltec times, although some probably continued to be used through the Late Toltec period. Late Toltec occupation concentrates around the ceremonial-civic core of the Early Toltec community (Fig. 8). Light Classic (Tx-EC-3; Tx-LC-2) and some Aztec (Tx-A-17) material is also present here.

Classification: Large dispersed village; 500 to 750 people.

Tx-LT-13

Natural setting: 2280 m, at the edge of the Río Papalotla in the Lower Piedmont. Situated on gently sloping ground at the base of a southern extension of Cerro Azteca. Moderate erosion; shallow to moderately deep soil cover.

Modern utilization: Grazing and maguey cultivation. There is a small basalt quarry north of the site. The modern village of Tepetitlan is situated just east of the site area.

Archaeological remains: Site consists of a single tlatel measuring about 10 m in diameter (partially destroyed by a modern dirt road) and 30 cm high. Light-to-moderate concentrations of Late Toltec surface pottery occur on the mound's surface.

Classification: Hamlet, probably a single household unit; 5 to 15 people.

Tx-LT-14

Natural setting: 2620 m, at the top of Cerro Azteca, about 250 to 300 m above the level of the Lower Piedmont plain and the Lakeshore Plain to the east, south, and west. The soil cover is generally shallow, with isolated pockets of deep soil and numerous rock outcrops over the irregular ground surface. Erosion has been moderate.

Modern utlization: Grazing, plus some cultivated maguey.

Archaeological remains: Variable very light and light concentrations of surface pottery over an area of roughly one hectare of relatively level ground. The dominant occupational component here is Aztec (Tx-A-20). Some Terminal Formative and Early Toltec pottery is also present (Tx-TF-3; Tx-ET-6). No structural remains can be dated to Late Toltec times, but the large Aztec pyramid which dominates the site may contain earlier constructions within its core.

Classification: Small hilltop ceremonial precinct; probably lacking any permanent occupation.

Tx-LT-15

Natural setting: 2310 to 2320 m, in the Lower Piedmont. Situated on gently sloping ground on the lowermost southern flanks of Cerro Azteca. Severe erosion, with shallow soil cover and patches of bare tepetate.

Modern utilization: Grazing, plus some cultivated maguey.

Archaeological remains: Variable very light and light concentrations of surface pottery over an area of roughly one hectare. The dominant occupational components here are Terminal Formative (Tx-TF-1) and Early Toltec (Tx-ET-4). Some Aztec material is also present (Tx-A-17). No structural remnants can be assigned to Late Toltec times.

Classification: Hamlet; fewer than 50 people.

Tx-LT-16

Natural setting: 2300 m, on a broad, gently sloping surface in the Lower Piedmont. Situated between two large barrancas, in a zone of deep soil cover.

Modern utilization: Intensive rainfall cultivation.

Archaeological remains: Light concentrations of surface pottery and moderate rock rubble over an area of less than one hectare. Mixed with light Early Toltec (Tx-ET-7) and somewhat heavier Aztec (Tx-A-22) material. No structural remains.

Classification: Hamlet; fewer than 50 people. Probably a single household unit.

Tx-LT-17

Natural setting: 2310 m, in the Lower Piedmont. Situated on a broad, gentle slope adjacent to a major barranca. Moderate to severe erosion, with shallow to moderately deep soil cover.

Modern utilization: Eastern end of the site extends into the modern village of San Francisco Olalpa. Mixed rainfall cultivation and grazing over rest of site area.

Archaeological remains: Variable light and light-to-moderate concentrations of surface pottery over an area of less than one hectare. Sherds also are found washing from the banks of the large barranca at the east edge of the site. Somewhat heavier concentrations of Aztec material (Tx-A-24), are also present.

Classification: Hamlet; fewer than 50 people.

Tx-LT-18

Natural setting: 2450 m, in the Lower Piedmont. Situated on gently sloping ground on the southern flanks of Cerro Cuajio. Severe erosion, with shallow soil cover and large stretches of bare tepetate.

Modern utilization: Marginal grazing, with a few cultivated maguey.

Archaeological remains: Variable light and light-to-moderate concentrations of surface pottery over an area of about two hectares. The only structural remnants are two mounds, both apparently domestic residences. One measures 15 m in diameter and 1 m high. The second is about 25 m in diameter and 1 m high. Both structures show higher concentrations of both surface pottery and rock rubble than is general for the site area as a whole.

Classification: Hamlet; fewer than 50 people.

Tx-LT-19

Natural setting: 2410 m, in the Lower Piedmont. Situated on a broad, gentle slope near a major barranca. Severe erosion; shallow soil cover with large stretches of bare tepetate.

Modern utilization: Marginal grazing and wasteland.

Archaeological remains: Very light and light concentrations of surface pottery over an area of less than one hectare. Mixed with much heavier Aztec material (Tx-A-24). No structural remnants can be assigned to Late Toltec times.

Classification: Hamlet; fewer than 50 people. Probably a transient campsite.

Tx-LT-20

Natural setting: 2330 m, in the Lower Piedmont. Situated on gently sloping ground at the edge of a major barranca. Severe erosion, with little soil cover and large stretches of bare tepetate.

Modern utilization: Marginal grazing and wasteland.

Archaeological remains: Very light concentrations of surface pottery over an area of less than one hectare. Mixed with light Early Toltec (Tx-ET-8), and much heavier Aztec material (Tx-A-24). No structural remains.

Classification: Hamlet; fewer than 50 people.

Tx-LT-21

Natural setting: 2300 m, in the Lower Piedmont. Situated on gently sloping ground adjacent to a large barranca. Moderate erosion, with shallow soil cover.

Modern utilization: Grazing and maguey cultivation. Adjacent fields are devoted to rainfall cultivation.

Archaeological remains: Moderate concentration of surface pottery over an area about 30 m in diameter. Mixed with somewhat lighter Aztec material (Tx-A-24). No structural remains.

Classification: Hamlet; fewer than 50 people. Probably a single household or camp unit.

Tx-LT-22

Natural setting: 2325 m, in the Lower Piedmont. Situated on a broad, gentle slope, in a zone of moderate erosion and shallow soil cover.

Modern utilization: Grazing and maguey cultivation.

Archaeological remains: Light concentrations of surface pottery over an area of about two hectares. Mixed with heavier Early Toltec (Tx-ET-7) and Aztec (Tx-A-24) material.

Classification: Hamlet; fewer than 50 people.

Tx-LT-23

Natural setting: 2300 m, in the Lower Piedmont. Situated on the nearly level floor of the main piedmont plain, in a zone of slight erosion and deep soil cover.

Modern utilization: Intensive rainfall cultivation.

Archaeological remains: Light concentrations of surface pottery over an area of less than one hectare. Mixed with considerably heavier Early Toltec material (Tx-ET-7). No structural remains.

Classification: Hamlet; fewer than 50 people. Probably a single household unit.

Tx-LT-24

Natural setting: 2290 m, in the Lower Piedmont. Situated on level ground at the edge of the Río Papalotla. Slight erosion and deep soil cover except at the banks of the river itself.

Modern utilization: River banks are used for grazing only. Adjacent fields are devoted to intensive rainfall cultivation.

Archaeological remains: Variable very light, light, and light-to-moderate concentrations of surface pottery over an area of about three hectares. Mixed with Aztec material of about the same density (Tx-A-41). No structural remains.

Classification: Hamlet; fewer than 50 people.

Tx-LT-25

Natural setting: 2320 m, in the Lower Piedmont. Situated on gently sloping ground on the eastern flanks of a low isolated hill, just south of the Río Papalotla. Moderate to severe erosion, with shallow soil cover and some rock outcrops.

Modern utilization: Extensive quarrying for tezontle-gravel. Since the time this locality was surveyed (June, 1967) the entire surface of the hillside has been stripped off in the course of mining operations, with a complete obliteration of the archaeological materials described here.

Archaeological remains: The site consists of a thick lens (about 2 m of ceramic debris running continuously for a distance of about 15 m in the profile of a steep quarry cut about midway up the hillslope (Pl. 35,*a*). The ceramic material is almost wholly Late Toltec, with only traces of Early Toltec and Early Aztec. No rock rubble was present in the lens, but obsidian debris was abundant. Recent quarrying operations have so disturbed the site context that it is impossible to determine the original aspect of the site situation. We may be dealing with material associated with prehispanic quarrying or cave occupation. At the base of the hillslope to the east of the site are a series of intact caves dug into the tezontle-gravel. These features penetrate to depths of 10 or 20 m, and the lower interior walls of some have been partially plastered and show beam holes at roughly 2 m above floor level. This probably represents colonial or recent use of these caves as stables or kitchens.

Classification: Questionable. May represent cave occupation associated with quarrying, or small groups occupying old quarries in preference to constructing residences on open ground.

Tx-LT-26

Natural setting: 2300 m, in the Lower Piedmont. Situated on a broad, gentle slope in a zone of slight erosion and moderately deep soil cover.

Modern utilization: Intensive rainfall cultivation.

Archaeological remains: Light concentrations of surface pottery over an area of about three hectares (southern limit of site may extend beyond the edge of our survey area at this point). Mixed with light Early Toltec (Tx-ET-13) and more abundant Aztec material (Tx-A-40). No structural remains can be assigned to Late Toltec times.

Classification: Hamlet; fewer than 50 people.

Tx-LT-27

Natural setting: 2310 m, in the Lower Piedmont. Situated on gently sloping ground at the base of a low, isolated hill, about 300 m west of the Río Papalotla in a zone of slight erosion and deep soil cover.

Modern utilization: Intensive rainfall cultivation.

Archaeological remains: Variable very light and light concentrations of surface pottery over an area of less than one hectare. Light Late Formative (Tx-LF-6), Terminal Formative (Tx-TF-10), Early Classic (Tx-EC-6), and Late Classic (Tx-LC-5) are also present. The two dominant occupational components are Early Toltec (Tx-ET-13) and Aztec (Tx-A-40). No structural remnants. The abandoned terracing on the higher hillslopes to the west may be prehispanic.

Classification: Hamlet; fewer than 50 people. Probably a single household unit.

Tx-LT-28

Natural setting: 2300 to 2330 m, in the Lower Piedmont. Situated on the gently sloping lower western flanks of Cerro Tepetlosco near the Río Papalotla. Moderate erosion, with shallow to moderately deep soil cover.

Modern utilization: Intensive rainfall cultivation.

Archaeological remains: Variable light and light-to-moderate concentrations of surface pottery over an area of about 14 hectares. No structural remains. Mixed with Terminal Formative (Tx-TF-11) and Early Toltec (Tx-ET-13) material. Abandoned terracing on the hillslopes above the site may be prehispanic.

Classification: Small dispersed village; 100 to 150 people.

Tx-LT-29

Natural setting: 2310 m in the Lower Piedmont. Situated in a level zone of deep soil cover and slight erosion at the edge of the Río Papalotla.

Modern Utilization: Intensive rainfall cultivation.

Archaeological remains: Variable very light and light concentrations of surface pottery over an area of about four hectares. Mixed with heavier Early Toltec material (Tx-ET-10). No structural remains.

Classification: Hamlet; fewer than 50 people.

Tx-LT-30

Natural setting: 2320 m, in the Lower Piedmont. Situated in a gently sloping area, along the banks of the Río Papalotla. Moderate erosion, with moderately deep soil cover.

Modern utilization: Intensive rainfall cultivation, except the higher banks themselves which are used for grazing only.

Archaeological remains: Light concentrations of surface pottery over an area of about two hectares. Mixed with somewhat heavier Aztec material (Tx-A-25). No structural remains.

Classification: Hamlet; fewer than 50 people.

Tx-LT-31

Natural setting: 2400 m, in the Lower Piedmont. Situated on a broad, gentle slope near a major barranca. Severely eroded, with a surface of badly scarred bare tepetate and very little soil cover.

Modern utilization: Marginal grazing and wasteland.

Archaeological remains: The site consists of four distinct tlateles (Appendix II) containing light-to-moderate and moderate concentrations of Late Toltec surface pottery. These mounds are distributed over an area of about two hectares, and are separated by ground containing much lighter sherd and rock rubble cover. Two of these mounds also have substantial Aztec surface pottery (Tx-A-27).

Classification: Hamlet; fewer than 50 people.

Tx-LT-32

Natural setting: 2245 m, on the Lakeshore Plain, at or near the Conquest-period shoreline of Lake Texcoco. Situated in a level zone of deep alluvial soil. A large canalized barranca runs east-west several hundred meters to the south. A nearby well indicates that the water table at this point is about 2 m below the ground surface.

Modern utilization: Most of the immediate site area is grazing land, but the immediately adjacent fields to the east are cultivated in maize and alfalfa (partly irrigated from wells using gasoline pumps).

Archaeological remains: Light-to-moderate concentrations of surface pottery over an area of about four hectares. No structural remains. Mixed with somewhat less abundant Aztec material (Tx-A-47).

Classification: Hamlet; fewer than 100 people.

Tx-LT-33

Natural setting: 2240 m, on the Lakeshore Plain. Situated in a level zone of deep alluvial soil just south of a large canalized barranca. Located at or near the Conquest-period shoreline of Lake Texcoco.

Modern utilization: Intensive cultivation of maize and alfalfa. Predominately rainfall agriculture, with some mechanized irrigation.

Archaeological remains: Variable very light, light, and light-to-moderate concentrations of surface pottery over an area of about five hectares. No structural remains.

Classification: Hamlet; fewer than 100 people.

Tx-LT-34

Natural setting: 2240 m, on the Lakeshore Plain. Situated in a level zone of deep alluvial soil, 500 m south of a large canalized barranca. Located at or near the Conquest-period shoreline of Lake Texcoco.

Modern utilization: Intensive cultivation of maize and alfalfa. Both rainfall agriculture and mechanized irrigation are practiced.

Archaeological remains: Variable very light, light, and light-to-moderate concentrations of surface pottery over an area of about 12 hectares. A single definite structure was noted: a mound measuring 50 to 75 cm high, 15 m in diameter, covered with light-to-moderate concentrations of Late Toltec pottery and a few Aztec sherds.

Classification: Hamlet; roughly 100 people.

Tx-LT-35

Natural setting: Below 2240 m, on the Lakeshore Plain. Situated in a level zone of deep soil, 400 m south of a large canalized barranca. Located at or near the Conquest-period shoreline of Lake Texcoco.

Modern utilization: Intensive maize cultivation. Mostly rainfall agriculture, with the exception of a small area east of the site where water is carried to the plants by hand from a nearby shallow well (water level at about 2.5 m below ground surface). During the time of our survey (late May), the maize plants in nonirrigated fields were badly withered. A local farmer informed us that rainfall was decidedly scanty relative to its usual behavior for that time of year.

Archaeological remains: Variable light, light-to-moderate, and moderate concentrations of surface pottery over an area of about 20 hectares. No definite structural remains are present, but several vague mounded areas suggest the presence of buried constructions. Drainage ditches cut at several localities throughout the site area reveal layers of sherd refuse at 20 to 30 cm below ground level. Such sherd concentrations are often much heavier than those on the ground surface immediately above.

Classification: Small dispersed village; 150 to 300 people.

Tx-LT-36

Natural setting: Below 2240 m, on the Lakeshore Plain. Situated in a zone of deep alluvial soil, in the general vicinity of the Conquest-period shoreline of Lake Texcoco. The ground surface is irregular, with many small grass-covered hillocks and intervening depressions.

Modern utilization: Grazing. The salt content of the soil is apparently too high for effective cultivation. Only sharp, tough grass grows here today.

Archaeological remains: Variable light and light-to-moderate concentrations of surface pottery over an area of about two hectares. All sherds are badly corroded and salt incrusted. No structural remains. Mixed with light Late Formative (Tx-LF-3), light Terminal Formative (Tx-TF-29), and light-to-moderate Aztec (Tx-A-44) material.

Classification: Hamlet; fewer than 50 people.

Tx-LT-37

Natural setting: Below 2240 m, on the Lakeshore Plain, well within the borders of Conquest-period Lake Texcoco. Situated in an area of small sand dunes which rise about 2 m above the general level of the old lake bed. In a zone of deep alluvial soil.

Modern utilization: Wasteland. The salt content of the soil apparently prohibits effective cultivation. This region is even unfit for grazing because vegetation of any kind is lacking.

Archaeological remains: A light scattering of surface pottery over an area of less than one hectare. The sherds occur within a slightly elevated, localized cluster of small sand dunes, and are generally found in the low intervening areas between the dunes. No structural remains. Mixed with some Early Toltec (Tx-ET-16), and more abundant Aztec pottery (Tx-A-43).

Classification: Questionable. It is doubtful whether these few sherds represent a permanent residence. More probably we are dealing with a temporary marsh camp for hunting water fowl and/or gathering lake resources.

Tx-LT-38

Natural setting: Below 2240 m, on the Lakeshore Plain. Located in the general vicinity of the Conquest-period shoreline of Lake Texcoco. In an area of deep alluvial soil.

Modern utilization: The immediate site area is grazing land. Apparently the salt content of the soil is too high for effective cultivation. Adjacent areas have recently been reclaimed for agriculture by means of large-scale flushing and drainage projects. Two small modern residential households occur at the eastern and southern edges of the site area.

Archaeological remains: Moderate concentrations of surface pottery over an area of about three hectares on a large irregular-mounded locality which rises about 2 m above the general level of the surrounding plain. No structural remains. Mixed with light Late Formative (Tx-LF-15) and Terminal Formative (Tx-TF-28) material.

Classification: Hamlet; fewer than 100 people.

Tx-LT-39

Natural setting: 2270 m, at the juncture of the Lakeshore Plain and the Lower Piedmont. Situated in a level zone of deep alluvial soil.

Modern utilization: The site area is located at the north edge of the modern town of Texcoco. The fields immediately to the north are intensively cultivated in maize and alfalfa. The alfalfa is irrigated with water derived from wells using gasoline pumps. The immediate site area is presently used for rainfall cultivation of maize.

Archaeological remains: Light concentrations of surface pottery over an area of about three hectares. Mixed with light Aztec ceramics (Tx-A-56). Modern buildings in Texcoco and the main highway just west of the site may obscure some occupational debris.

Classification: Hamlet; fewer than 50 people.

Tx-LT-40

Natural setting: 2245 m, on the Lakeshore Plain. In a zone of deep alluvial soil on the western side of the modern town of Texcoco.

Modern utilization: Intensive rainfall cultivation of subsistence crops. The site area is surrounded by modern residential structures and scattered agricultural fields.

Archaeological remains: A few sherds scattered over an area of less than one hectare, on and around a large Aztec ceremonial-civic structure. Mixed with much heavier Aztec material (Tx-A-56). No structural remains can be assigned to Late Toltec times, although the interior of the large Aztec mound may contain earlier structures.

Classification: Questionable. Perhaps a small hamlet of fewer than 50 people.

Tx-LT-41

Natural setting: 2285 m, at the juncture of the Lower Piedmont and the Lakeshore Plain. In a zone of deep soil about 300 m north of a large canalized barranca.

Modern utilization: Intensive rainfall cultivation. The eastern edge of modern Texcoco lies about 400 m west of the site area.

Archaeological remains: Variable light and

very light concentrations of surface pottery over an area of less than one hectare. No structural remains.

Classification: Hamlet; fewer than 50 people.

Tx-LT-42

Natural setting: 2310 m, in the Lower Piedmont. Situated on a broad, gentle slope near a major barranca. Erosion has been slight. Moderately deep soil cover.

Modern utilization: Intensive rainfall cultivation in the immediate site area. The land to the west and north is irrigated with water drawn from wells with gasoline pumps, and is devoted primarily to alfalfa production.

Archaeological remains: Light concentrations of surface pottery over an area of about one hectare. No structural remains. Mixed with more abundant Early and Late Classic pottery (Tx-EC-14; Tx-LC-12).

Classification: Hamlet; fewer than 50 people.

Tx-LT-43

Natural setting: 2340 m, in the Lower Piedmont. Situated on a broad, gentle slope between two major barrancas. Moderate erosion, with shallow soil cover. Bancal systems have prevented severe erosion over much of the site area.

Modern utilization: The site area is located at the western edge of an intensively cultivated zone (rainfall agriculture). The areas to the west, north, and south are predominately grazing land, as are some parts of the site itself where erosion has been most severe and rock rubble is heaviest.

Archaeological remains: Variable light and light-to-moderate concentrations of surface pottery and moderate rock rubble over an area of roughly one hectare. No structural remains. Mixed with more abundant Terminal Formative (Tx-TF-17), Early Classic (Tx-EC-12), and Late Classic (Tx-LC-11) material. Light concentrations of Middle Formative (Tx-MF-6) also occur.

Classification: Hamlet; fewer than 50 people.

Tx-LT-44

Natural setting: 2575 m, on a level ridge top near the peak of Cerro Metecatl. Situated some 150 m above the level of the gentle piedmont slopes surrounding the hill. Shallow soil cover, with abundant rock outcroppings.

Modern utilization: Grazing, plus a few cultivated maguey. The terraced hillslopes to the north, west, and south are intensively cultivated.

Archaeological remains: Light concentrations of surface pottery over an area of roughly one hectare. No structural remains. Mixed with some Terminal Formative pottery (Tx-TF-22) and more abundant Aztec material (Tx-A-61).

Classification: Hamlet; fewer than 50 people.

Tx-LT-45

Natural setting: 2560 m, near the lower edge of the Upper Piedmont. Situated in a gently sloping area at the base of a steep ridge, immediately adjacent to a major barranca. Severe erosion has produced a surface of badly scarred bare tepetate, with little or no soil cover.

Modern utilization: The immediate site area is largely wasteland or very poor pasture. The lower land to the west is cultivated (rainfall agriculture) where erosion has not been too severe. Terrace remnants are found over the adjacent hillslopes, but are now abandoned and badly deteriorated.

Archaeological remains: Variable very light and light concentrations of surface pottery over an area of roughly one hectare along the edge of the barranca. Mixed with much heavier Aztec material (Tx-A-78). The original aspect of the site has been badly obscured by the severe erosion.

Classification: Hamlet; fewer than 50 people.

Tx-LT-46

Natural setting: 2520 m, at the lower edge of the Upper Piedmont. Situated on a broad, gentle slope, adjacent to a major barranca. Severe erosion has produced a surface of badly scarred bare tepetate throughout the site area, with no soil cover apart from isolated erosional remnants.

Modern utilization: Wasteland and marginal grazing. Adjacent hillslopes often contain remnants of badly deteriorated terraces. The hillslopes to the northeast (southern flanks of Cerro Tetzcotzingo-Metecatl) are intricately terraced and intensively cultivated.

Archaeological remains: Light concentrations of surface pottery over an area of roughly one hectare. No structural remains. Mixed with much more abundant Aztec material (Tx-A-59). The original aspect of the site has been badly obscured by severe erosion. The occupational debris rests on bare tepetate or is found washing from the sides of erosional remnants.

Classification: Hamlet; fewer than 50 people.

Tx-LT-47

Natural setting: 2510 m, at the lower edge of the Upper Piedmont. Situated on a broad, gentle slope near a major barranca. Severe erosion has removed practically all soil cover, leaving a surface of badly scarred bare tepetate and a few isolated erosional remnants.

Modern utilization: Predominately marginal grazing and wasteland, except where a few terraces, on the slopes north of the site, have preserved sufficient soil cover to permit rainfall cultivation of subsistence crops.

Archaeological remains: Variable light and very light concentrations of surface pottery over an area of about one hectare. No structural remains. Mixed with much heavier Aztec material (Tx-A-60). Occupational debris rests on bare tepetate, or is found washing from the sides of erosional remnants.

Classification: Hamlet; fewer than 50 people.

Tx-LT-48

Natural setting: 2560 m, in the Upper Piedmont. Situated on a broad, gentle slope adjacent to a major barranca. Severe erosion has removed most of the soil cover, leaving a surface of badly scarred bare tepetate and a few scattered erosional remnants.

Modern utilization: Predominately marginal grazing and wasteland. Several of the erosional remnants in the area contain sufficient soil to permit limited maize cultivation (rainfall agriculture).

Archaeological remains: Light concentrations of surface pottery over an area of roughly one hectare. There are no structural remains that can be assigned to Late Toltec times. Mixed with much more abundant Aztec material (Tx-A-86). Occupational debris rests on bare tepetate, or is found washing from the sides of erosional remnants.

Classification: Hamlet; fewer than 50 people.

Tx-LT-49

Natural setting: 2275 m, at juncture of the Lower Piedmont and the Lakeshore Plain. Situated on a broad, gentle slope, about 150 m south of a major barranca. Erosion has been moderate. Soil cover is moderately deep.

Modern utilization: Intensive rainfall cultivation. The site area is located some 200 m south of the southwestern corner of modern Huexotla. The Lakeshore Plain to the west is intensively cultivated, predominately in mechanically-irrigated alfalfa.

Archaeological remains: Light concentrations of surface pottery over an area of roughly one hectare. Mixed with much heavier Aztec material (Tx-A-87). There are no structural remains.

Classification: Hamlet; fewer than 50 people.

Tx-LT-50

Natural setting: 2450 m, near the upper edge of the Lower Piedmont. Situated on a broad, gently sloping ridge top between two major barrancas. Severe erosion has produced a surface of badly scarred bare tepetate and small isolated erosional remnants where shallow pockets of soil support scattered grass cover.

Modern utilization: Marginal pasture.

Archaeological remains: Two badly destroyed mounds separated by about 100 m of empty terrain. Both mounds measure roughly 10 m in diameter, and reach up to 50 cm high in a few spots where they have not been reduced to rock rubble and sherds resting on bare tepetate.

Classification: Hamlet; fewer than 50 people.

Tx-LT-51

Natural setting: 2305 m, in the Lower Piedmont. Situated on a broad, gentle slope adjacent to a small barranca. Moderately deep soil cover, with slight to moderate erosion.

Modern utilization: Intensive rainfall cultivation.

Archaeological remains: Very light concentrations of surface pottery over an area of about one hectare. No structural remains. Mixed with much heavier Early Classic material (Tx-EC-29).

Classification: Hamlet; fewer than 50 people.

Tx-LT-52

Natural setting: 2290 m, at the lower edge of the Lower Piedmont. Situated in a gently sloping area near the northwestern base of Cerro Tonaltepec. Deep soil cover; slight erosion.

Modern utilization: Intensive rainfall cultivation.

Archaeological remains: Variable light and light-to-moderate concentrations of surface pottery over an area of about four hectares. No structural remains.

Classification: Hamlet; fewer than 100 people.

Tx-LT-53

Natural setting: 2250 to 2280 m, on the gently sloping northern flanks of Cerro Portezuelo at the edge of the main Lower Piedmont plain. Deep alluvial soil is found in the lower part of the site area; upslope the soil cover thins to moderate and shallow depths. The entire site area is cut through by numerous barrancas of varying size. Most of these barrancas are relatively narrow and deep, often cutting through prehispanic occupational zones.

Modern utilization: Intensive rainfall cultivation over most of the site area. Some fields are presently fallow, and used for grazing only. A number of archaeological mounds are plowed over and planted in maize and beans. The higher slopes above the site are predominately grazing land. The level piedmont plain north of the site is intensively cultivated.

Archaeological remains: Variable light and light-to-moderate concentrations of surface pottery over an area of about 125 hectares. This occupational debris is mixed throughout with heavier Early Toltec material (Tx-ET-18). Some lighter amounts of Early and Late Classic pottery also occur (Tx-EC-32; Tx-LC-18). Aztec pottery is present in light quantities (Tx-A-103). Thus, the problem of the relative dating of construction and utilization of the numerous structural remnants throughout the site area becomes exceedingly difficult on the basis of surface remains alone. Since the site's dominant occupational component is Early Toltec, and since virtually all mounds have Early Toltec surface pottery, we have assumed that all such mounds were constructed in Early Toltec times. The interiors of mounds that also have Classic surface pottery may contain smaller Classic structures; mounds with Late Toltec surface pottery probably continued to be used, or may even have been partially rebuilt or added to, during Late Toltec times. Tlateles 122, 124, 152 (Appendix II Fig. 11) all have significant amounts of Late Toltec surface pottery. Several others have traces of this material (Appendix II).

Classification: Secondary regional center; 750 to 1500 people.

Tx-LT-54

Natural setting: 2240 to 2260 m, at the northeastern base of Cerro Chimalhuacan. The site occupies a gently sloping area on a low bluff overlooking the Lakeshore Plain, with some occupation extending down onto the edges of the plain itself. Erosion has been moderate to severe, and the site area has been cut through by several small barrancas. The soil cover is irregular, ranging from shallow to moderately deep, with some patches of bare tepetate.

Modern utilization: Marginal rainfall cultivation and grazing in the immediate site area. The lower area just below the site is largely occupied by the densely packed residential structures of modern Chimalhuacan. The higher slopes above the site have been extensively terraced in the past, but little of this area is now cultivated (apart from a few maguey), and the terraces themselves are rapidly falling into disrepair. Several small basalt quarries (both operative and abandoned) are located on adjacent hillslopes. A modern cemetery occupies a section of the central site area.

Archaeological remains: Light concentrations of surface pottery over an area of about 25 hectares. Some occupational debris may be obscured by the heavy Aztec and modern overlays along the north edge of the Late Toltec site. No structural remains can be assigned to this period, but the large Aztec ceremonial-civic complex at the northeast corner of the site may overlie earlier structures. The occupational debris is mixed with light Early Classic (Tx-EC-34), very light Late Classic (Tx-LC-20), and light-to-moderate Early Toltec (Tx-ET-19), in addition to the more abundant Aztec (Tx-A-109) material.

Late Toltec sherds also occur scattered widely over the northern flanks of Cerro Chimalhuacan, above the Tx-LT-54 site area. Nowhere are these fragments found in such concentrations as to warrant a site designation. They may indicate cultivation of the slopes by agriculturalists resident in Tx-LT-54.

Classification: Small dispersed village; 125 to 250 people. May be somewhat larger if some occupational debris is obscured by Aztec and modern overlays.

Tx-LT-55

Natural setting: 2520 m, at the top of Cerro Chimalhuacan, some 280 m above the level of the surrounding Lakeshore Plain. Shallow to moderately deep soil cover, with abundant rock outcrops over an irregular ground surface.

Modern utilization: Grazing, plus limited rainfall cultivation on the relatively level hilltop. The gently sloping surface of the broad lower ridge to the north is intensively cultivated. The hillslopes north of the site are intricately terraced, but the terraces have fallen into disrepair and support only grazing land today.

Archaeological remains: A few sherds scattered over an area of about 20 by 20 m, at the peak of Cerro Chimalhuacan. No structural remains can definitely be assigned to Late Toltec times. Mixed with more abundant Aztec (Tx-A-108), and a trace of Terminal Formative (Tx-TF- 48) material.

Classification: Hilltop ceremonial precinct; no permanent occupation.

Tx-LT-56

Natural setting: 2240 to 2250 m, along the western base of Cerro Chimalhuacan, at the edge of the Lakeshore Plain. Probably at or near the Conquest-period shoreline of Lake Texcoco. The site occupies a very gently sloping to relatively level area where terracing and alluviation have maintained a deep soil cover.

Modern utilization: The nucleated village of Chimalco borders the site on the northwest. The flat land west of the village is now used only for grazing. Much of the sloping area immediately east of the site has been extensively terraced. At present, however, only the lowermost terraces support cultivation, while the higher slopes serve as pasture land. Several basalt quarries (both operative and abandoned) are found in the area. The quarrying and finishing of this building stone are important activities in Chimalco today.

Archaeological remains: Variable very light, light, and light-to-moderate concentrations of surface pottery over an area of roughly 40 hectares. No definite structural remains. Mixed with Early Toltec material (Tx-ET-21) in the northern half of the site, and with substantial Aztec pottery throughout the site area (Tx-A-107). A scattering of Terminal Formative also occurs in the northern part of the site (Tx-TF-47).

Classification: Small dispersed village; 200 to 400 people. May be somewhat larger if the modern and Aztec overlays have obscured significant quantities of Late Toltec occupational debris.

Tx-LT-57

Natural setting: 2240 m, on gently sloping to level ground along the southern base of Cerro Chimalhuacan. Situated in a zone of deep soil on the Lakeshore Plain near the southern end of the major pass leading into the Texcoco Region from the southwest.

Modern utilization: Predominately intensive rainfall cultivation, with some mechanized canal irrigation. The modern village of Chimalpa borders the site on the south.

Archaeological remains: Variable light and light-to-moderate concentrations of surface pottery over an area of about 30 hectares. No structural remains. Mixed with some Aztec material at the eastern end of the site (Tx-A-106), and light Early Toltec pottery at the site's western edge (Tx-ET-22).

Classification: Small dispersed village; 150 to 300 people.

Tx-LT-58

Natural setting: 2250 m, on level ground with deep soil cover at the western base of Cerro Portezuelo. Situated along the eastern edge of the main pass into the Texcoco Region from the southwest.

Modern utilization: The main asphalt highway and railroad tracks run through the center of the site area from north to south. Modern industrial and residential complexes are strung out along the highway throughout the site area. Empty land to either side of the highway is devoted to rainfall cultivation.

Archaeological remains: Variable very light, light, and light-to-moderate concentrations of surface pottery over an area of about 17 hectares. No structural remains. The heavy overlay of modern construction may obscure some prehispanic occupational debris. Mixed with some Early Toltec material (Tx-ET-23).

Classification: Small dispersed village; 100 to 200 people.

Tx-LT-59

Natural setting: 2260 to 2270 m, on a low bluff overlooking the main Lakeshore Plain, at the western base of Cerro Portezuelo. The site area is cut through by three major barrancas. Numerous smaller barrancas and their tributaries also pass through the site. Erosion has been moderate to severe. Soil cover is shallow.

Modern utilization: Predominately grazing, plus a few cultivated maguey. The steeper slopes above the site area have been extensively terraced in the past, but these structures are now abandoned and badly deteriorated. Much of the level ground immediately below the site area is occupied by a rapidly expanding industrial and residential complex. Small basalt quarries (both operative and abandoned) are abundant on the adjacent hillslopes.

Archaeological remains: Variable very light, light, and light-to-moderate surface pottery over an area of roughly 15 hectares. The small ceremonial-civic complex which dominates the site's archaeological remains has been described under Tx-ET-23. Late Toltec surface pottery is about equally abundant here relative to Early Toltec, and these structures were probably built and rebuilt and utilized during both periods. No other structural remains are present. Some light Classic material is present in the northern half of the site (Tx-EC-37; Tx-LC-23).

Classification: Small dispersed village; 100 to 150 people.

AZTEC

Writing in 1582, Pomar (1941: 50) offers an interesting general depiction of Late Aztec occupation of the Texcoco Region relative to that of the late sixteenth century:

At about the time of the Spanish Conquest

> . . . era sinumero la gente que había y parece bien claro que debía ser así por la mucha tierra que labraban y cultivaban, que hoy dia parece acamellonada generalmente en todas partes, la mayor parte de la cual está desierta y eriaza, y con tres pestilencias generales que han tenido desde que los ganaron se han consumido y menguado de tal suerte, que dicen los indios viejos y antiguos con quien esta relacion se hace, que pueblos y lugares pequeños sujetos é esta ciu-

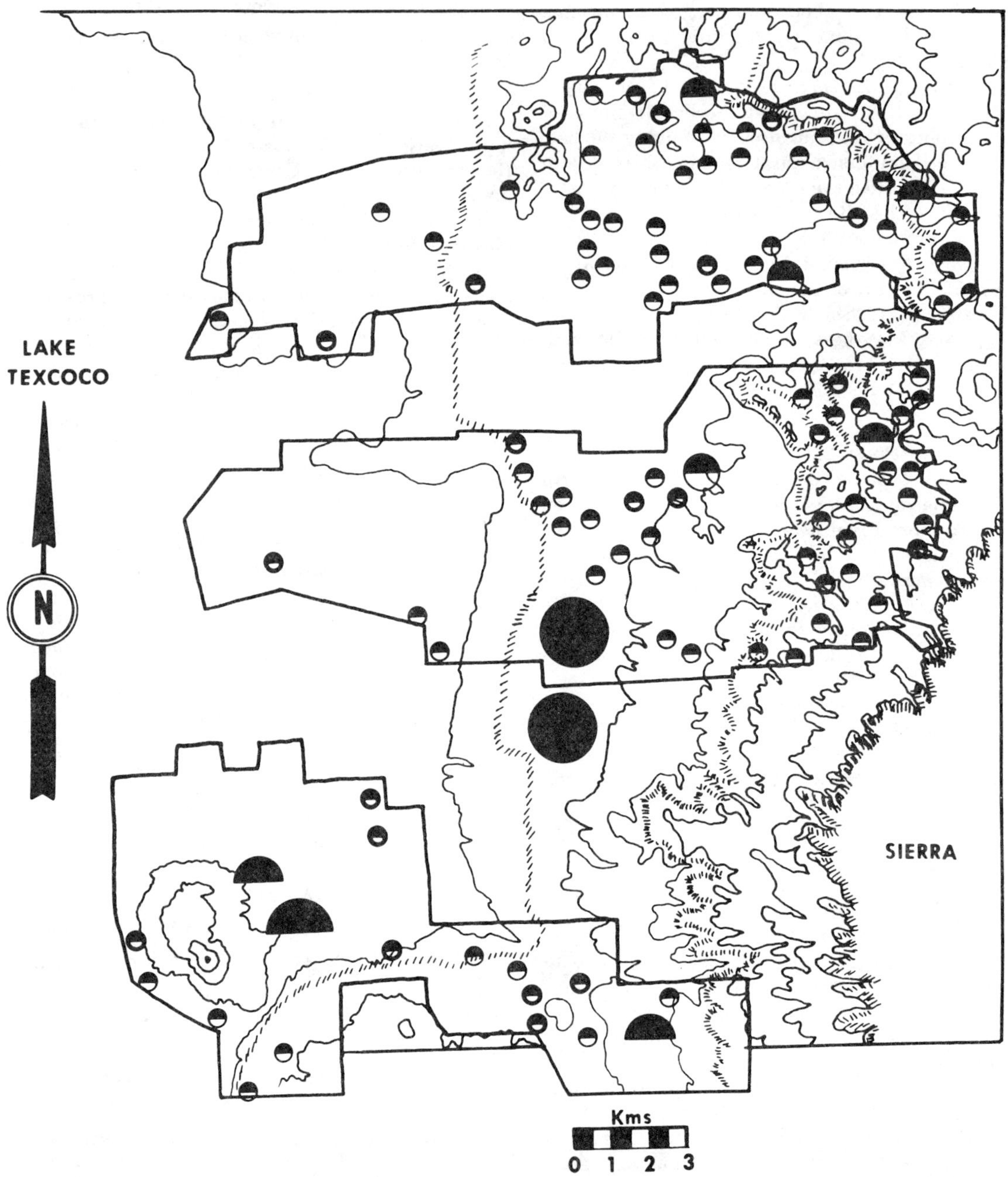

Map 12—Texcoco Region: Early Aztec settlement (schematic). Contour interval 100 meters. For key see map 5, p. 25.

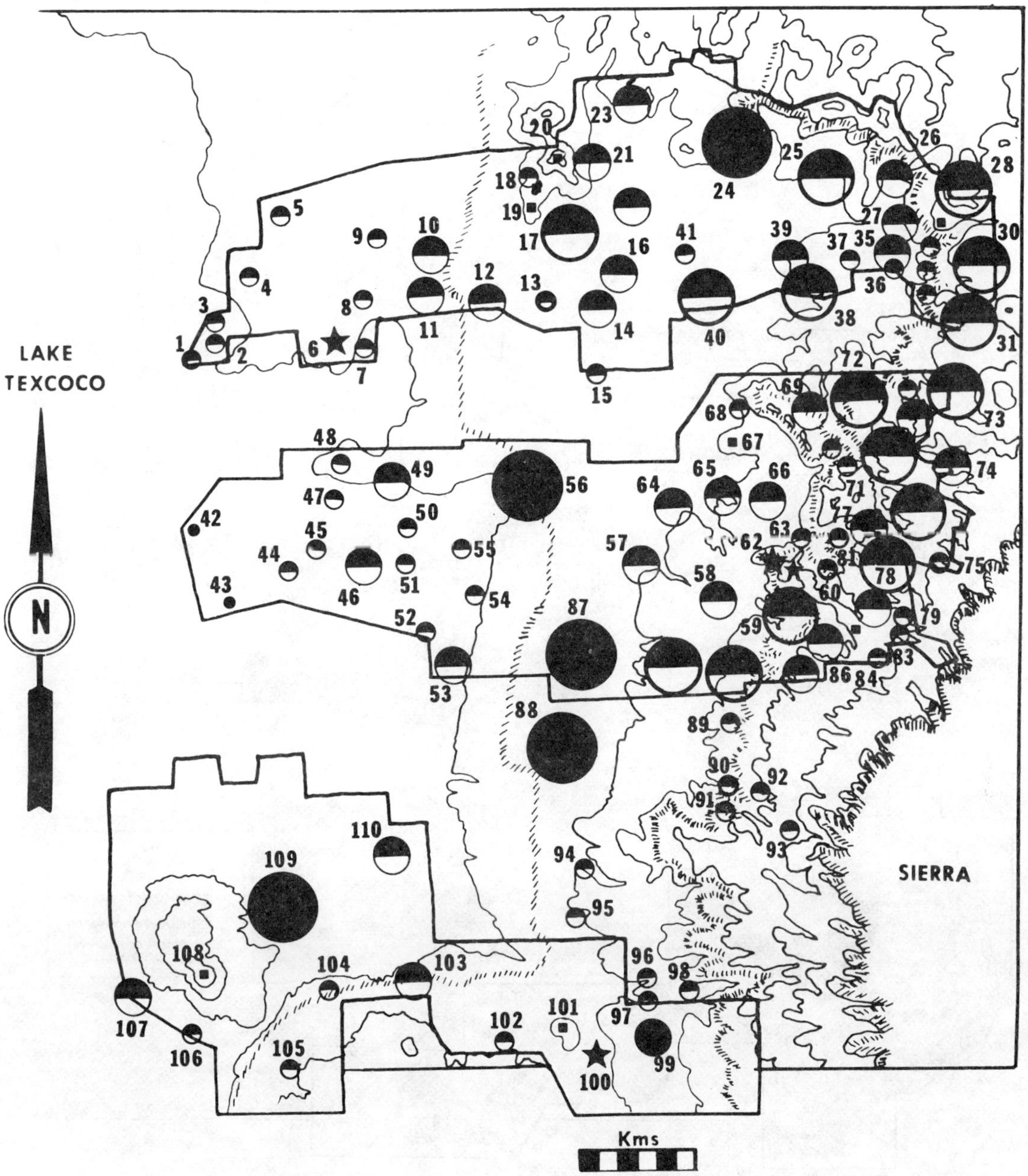

Map 13—Texcoco Region: Late Aztec settlement (schematic). Contour interval 100 meters. For key see map 5, p. 25.

Map 14—The Texcoco Region: Aztec settlement. Contour interval 50 meters.

dad [Texcoco] que tenían en su infidelidad más de a quince mil vecinos, no tienen al presente a seiscientos; y otros que no eran tan grandes están del todo despoblados y desiertos; y es cosa notoria que en la pestilencia general que hubo desde el año pasado de setenta y seis hasta el de ochenta se llevó de tres partes de la gente las dos, a lo menos en esta ciudad [Texcoco] y de la de sus sujetos, que se sabe por el numero y copia que de ella antes había, y por la cuenta que despues aca se ha hecho de su cantidad por mandado de la Real Audiencia para hacer las tasaciones de su tributo; y en otras que hubo a casi cuarenta años hizo otro tanto estrago, sin la primera de las viruelas al tiempo que estaban los conquistadores en la conquista de la ciudad de México, que se entiende por cosa averiguada haber hecho mayor daño que en las que después acá han tenido, sin otras muchas pestilencias que han tenido de menos furia.

Tx-A-1

Natural setting: 2250 m, on the Lakeshore Plain, probably within the borders of Conquest-period Lake Texcoco. Situated on a small island, standing about five meters above the main plain surface. The island has an irregular ground surface, with a shallow soil cover and numerous exposures of bedrock and bare tepetate. The surrounding plain is covered with deep alluvium.

Modern Utilization: Predominately grazing, with some cultivated maguey. The surrounding plain is presently used only for pasture, but large-scale flushing and drainage projects are underway to reclaim the area for agriculture. Several small rock quarries, now abandoned, are scattered over the island's surface.

Archaeological remains: Variable light and light-to-moderate concentrations of surface pottery over most of the island's surface, an area of about four hectares. Texcoco Fabric Marked pottery is abundant. No recognizable structural remains. A distinct earth causeway, 3 m wide and 2 m high, runs northwest from the island a distance of about 750 m to a second, larger island (Tx-A-3). There are light concentrations of surface pottery scattered along the length of the causeway. The ceramic material on the island is predominately Late Aztec, but a few Early Aztec sherds are present. Light Late Toltec material (Tx-LT-1) is also present.

Classification: Hamlet; fewer than 50 people. Salt-making was probably an important activity.

Tx-A-2

Natural setting: 2240 m, on the Lakeshore Plain. In an area of deep alluvial soil, at or near the Conquest-period shoreline of Lake Texcoco. Situated on a slight elevation, rising about 2 m above the level of the main plain surface.

Modern utilization: Grazing only. Salt content of soil prohibits effective agriculture. Only short, tough grass grows here today.

Archaeological remains: Variable light and light-to-moderate concentrations of surface pottery over a slightly mounded area of about one hectare. No structural remains. Aztec ceramics are predominately Late. Somewhat heavier Late Toltec material (Tx-LT-2) is also present. Texcoco Fabric Marked pottery is present, but not in substantial quantities.

Classification: Hamlet; fewer than 50 people.

Tx-A-3

Natural setting: 2250 to 2260 m, on the Lakeshore Plain. Situated on an island, rising some 10 m above the level of the main plain. The island has an irregular ground surface, with a shallow soil cover and numerous exposures of bedrock and bare tepetate.

Modern utilization: Grazing, plus some cultivated maguey. The remains of an abandoned salt-making station (probably 19th century, or early 20th century) are found along the eastern base of the island (this information from an elderly resident of nearby Nexquipaya). The surrounding plain is presently used for grazing only, although large-scale flushing and drainage projects are now underway to reclaim the area for agriculture.

Archaeological remains: Variable light and light-to-moderate concentrations of surface pottery over the entire island, an area of about 8 hectares. This ceramic material is predominately Late Aztec, although a few sherds of Early Aztec pottery are present. The site area consists of two distinct subregions: (1). An area of irregular hillocks and intervening depressions along the eastern edge of the island, extending slightly onto the main plain. These earth hillocks range from one to 2.5 m high, with diameters of six to 15 m, and are generally covered with light-to-moderate concentrations of Aztec surface pottery, including substantial quantities of Texcoco Fabric Marked pottery. This is also the area of the modern salt works, and modern (i.e., glazed) pottery is somewhat more abundant than the prehispanic. (2). The slopes and level top surface of the island, showing considerable rock rubble and light and light-to-moderate concentrations of surface pottery, including some Texcoco Fabric Marked. Two badly destroyed housemounds can be delineated: each measuring about 15 m in diameter and one m high, with light surface pottery. An earth causeway (described under Tx-A-1) extends from the southwest corner of the island, southwestward to the small island upon which Tx-A-1 occurs.

Classification: Hamlet; fewer than 100 people, Salt-making was apparently of some importance here.

Tx-A-4

Natural setting: 2250 m, on the Lakeshore Plain, at or near the Conquest-period shoreline of Lake Texcoco. Situated in a zone of deep alluvial soil.

Modern utilization: Intensive cultivation. The area has recently been reclaimed for agriculture by means of large-scale flushing and drainage projects.

Archaeological remains: Light-to-moderate concentrations of surface pottery over an area of about 20 by 30 m in area. The location is elevated about 1 m above the general level of the surrounding plain, and is colored a distinct gray-white which stands out in marked contrast to the brown color of the rest of the field (Pl. 35,*b*). This probably represents a single isolated household residential unit. The ceramic material is predominately Late Aztec.

Classification: Hamlet; fewer than 50 people. Probably a single household unit of 10 to 20 people.

Tx-A-5

Natural setting: 2260 m, on the Lakeshore Plain, at or near the Conquest-period shoreline of Lake Texcoco. Situated in a zone of deep alluvial soil.

Modern utilization: Intensive cultivation, partially by means of mechanized irrigation. This region has recently been reclaimed for agriculture through large-scale flushing and drainage projects. Salt continues to be produced by traditional, primitive processes in a small community some 200 meters northeast of the site are (Apenes, 1944). There are several adobe-making localities in the area, where soil removal has produced large pits.

Archaeological remains: The site consists of a single, isolated mound, about 30 m in diameter and 1.5 m high. This feature is covered with moderate to heavy surface pottery, which is almost wholly Texcoco Fabric Marked. A drainage ditch cutting through the mound reveals only uniform earth fill and sherd debris.

Classification: Salt-making locality; probably no permanent residence.

Tx-A-6

Natural setting: 2260 m on the Lakeshore Plain, at or near the Conquest-period shoreline of Lake Texcoco. Most of the site is situated on a large island rising about 10 m above the general level of the broad plain. Soil cover on the island is shallow to moderately deep. The surrounding plain is covered with several meters of alluvium.

Modern utilization: The area surrounding the island is presently under intensive rainfall cultivation. The island itself is now a federal park (El Contador), and is covered with large ahuehuete trees and used as a picnic ground.

Documentary descriptions: Alva de Ixtlilxochitl (1965*b*: 209, 265) states that the Late Aztec rulers of Texcoco had two pleasure gardens, or retreats, (Acatetelco and Tepetzinco) at the edge of Lake Texcoco, "en donde tenía muy insignes laberintos, jardines, baños fuentes, estanques, lagunas y acequias de agua, que corrían debajo tierra y en partes ocultas, que sin ser vistas se comunicaban con la laguna grande. . . ."

Pomar (1941: 54) notes that Acatetelco was situated about one-fourth of a league from Texcoco, and was supplied with water from the springs at Teotihuacan:

> Y otro río que nace de las fuentes de Teotihuacan . . . que es tres leguas de aqui [Texcoco] a la parte del Norte, que asimismo Nezahualcoyotzin sacó de su vía y trujó a unas casas de placer como a un cuarto de legua de esta ciudad [Texcoco], que llaman Acatetelco, aunque ahora no llega a ellas por estar en muchas partes rompido y correr por diferentes vías, porque después que se acabó el poder que tenían los sucesores de estos señores, se han caído y venido en gran diminución y ruina todas sus cosas, y una de ellas es ésta.

A map of the Valley of Mexico prepared in the mid 16th century (Linne, 1948) shows an area at the lakeshore containing large trees, into which three main canals are feeding from the north and east (Fig. 13). One of these canals comes from the Teotihuacan Valley; the second is obviously feeding off the Rio Papalotla, just south of Tepetlaoxtoc, and the third derives from the western edge of the Sierra east of Texcoco. This area is situated precisely at the location of Tx-A-6, and may undoubtedly be identified with the Acatetelco pleasure garden mentioned by Pomar.

Archaeological remains: The site covers the entire island, and extends north and east onto lower ground, over a total area of about 30 hectares. Variable very light, light, and light-to-moderate concentrations of surface pottery are found over this area, mainly restricted to the surfaces and profiles of several distinct structures. The ceramic material is predominately Late Aztec, but some Early Aztec sherds are present. Four distinct structures were delineated (Appendix II), at least two of which (tlateles 78 and 79) are definite ceremonial-civic constructions.

The largest pyramid (tlatel 79) consists of a

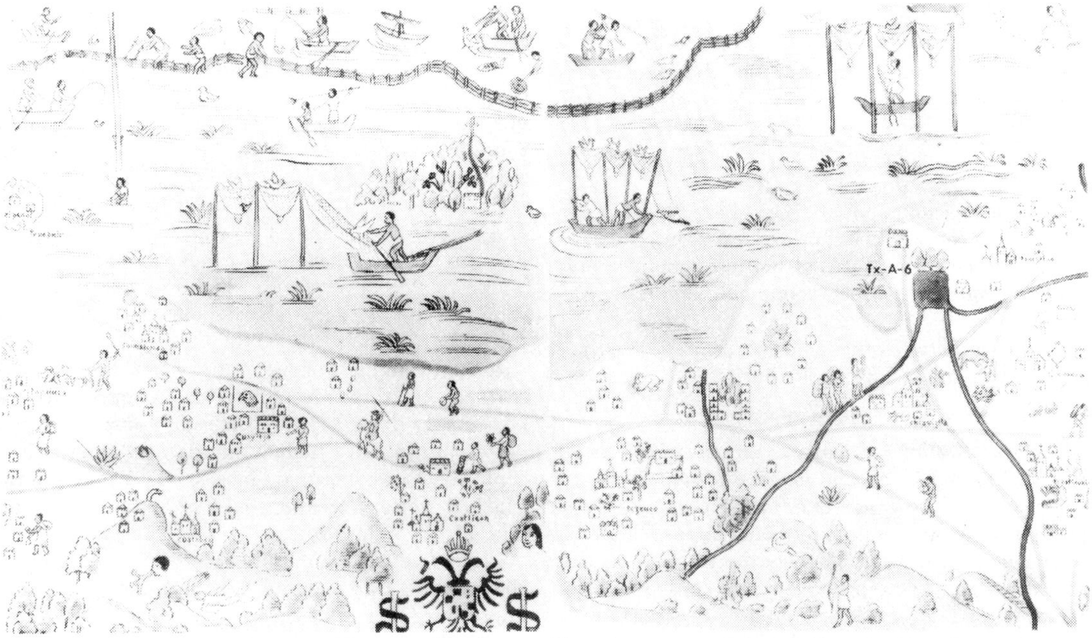

Fig. 13—Map of Texcoco Region, mid-16th century, from Linne (1948).

series of three superimposed platforms: the lowermost measuring 140 m square, the middle 120 m square, and the top 100 m square. A large pit in the southwest corner of the mound has exposed three superimposed plaster floors in the uppermost platforms. There is about 20 cm of fill above the lowermost floors, and about 15 cm of fill between the two upper surfaces. The inter-floor fill consists of chunks of old plaster and rock rubble. Beneath the lowermost floor some Texcoco Fabric Marked sherds were found, in addition to a small amount of Late Toltec material (Tx-LT-4). Several pits in the large mound indicate that substantial concentrations of sherd debris extend down to depths of at least 1 m in the structure.

Extending east from tlatel 79, for some 400 m before it fades away in the alluvium of the main Lakeshore Plain, is a linear structure measuring about seven m wide and 2 m high. Cuts at several points have exposed an interior construction of earth and tepetate rubble. There are light concentrations of surface pottery scattered along the length of this feature. This construction appears to have been a causeway connecting the island to the mainland over the shallow water at the eastern edge of Lake Texcoco. Since the characteristics of the site, and its lakeshore location, strongly suggest that Tx-A-6 is the remains of Netzahualcoyotl's Acatetelco pleasure garden, this causeway very likely carried water from the Teotihuacan springs for the benefit of the exotic vegetation once contained within the site area.

Classification: Ceremonial-civic precinct, or secular pleasure garden for ruling elite of Texcoco. Probably little or no permanent occupation.

Tx-A-7

Natural setting: 2250 m, on the Lakeshore Plain, at or near the Conquest-period shoreline of Lake Texcoco. Situated in a zone of deep alluvial soil.

Modern utilization: Intensive rainfall cultivation.

Archaeological remains: The site consists of two distinct light-to-moderate concentrations of surface pottery separated by an interval of about 350 m in which surface pottery is very light to absent. One of the concentrations, measuring 45 by 30 meters in surface area, has been cut through by a drainage ditch which has exposed a section of an earth-stone wall in addition to fragments of plaster. Despite its lack of elevation, this feature probably represents a living structure, now completely levelled through alluviation and plowing. The second sherd concentration may represent a similar structure, but only a vague scattering of sherds over an area of about 50 m in diameter is now visible. The total site area is roughly two hectares. The ceramic material is very predominately Late Aztec.

Classification: Hamlet; less than 50 people. Probably two household units.

Tx-A-8

Natural setting: 2250 m, on the Lakeshore Plain. Situated in a zone of deep alluvial soil cover.

Modern utilization: Intensive rainfall cultivation.

Archaeological remains: Light-to-moderate concentrations of surface pottery over an area of less than one hectare. No structural remains. The ceramic material is very predominately Late Aztec.

Classification: Hamlet; fewer than 50 people. Probably a single household unit.

Tx-A-9

Natural setting: 2250 m, on the Lakeshore Plain. Situated in a zone of deep alluvial soil.

Modern utilization: The immediate site area is an island of uncultivated land in a region of intensive agriculture. The southern part of the site area has been pitted in the course of soil removal for adobe brick-making. The site area is cut by the modern paved highway.

Archaeological remains: The site consists of two irregular mounded areas separated by a level interval of about 30 m containing very little ceramic material. One mound measures about 35 m in diameter, and roughly 1 m high. Its eastern end has been extensively pitted (in the course of adobe brick-making). The pitting has exposed a section of a stone wall, and has thrown up moderate concentrations of ceramics, almost all of which is Texcoco Fabric Marked. The western two-thirds of the mound's surface shows light-to-moderate concentrations of Classic pottery (Tx-EC-1; Tx-LC-1), and light Aztec material (also predominately Texcoco Fabric Marked). The second tlatel, measuring 15 by 10 m in area, with very little elevation, is covered with moderate concentrations of Late Aztec pottery, very largely comprised of Texcoco Fabric Marked sherds. The total site area is about 1 hectare.

Classification: Hamlet; fewer than 50 people. Probably a salt-making locality, with only seasonal or temporary occupation.

Tx-A-10

Natural setting: 2260 m, on the Lakeshore Plain. In a zone of deep alluvial soil, just north of the modern village of San Pablo Cuahuimilolco.

Modern utilization: Intensive cultivation. Some adobe brick-making has been carried out on the site area.

Archaeological remains: Light concentrations of surface pottery over an area of about 36 hectares. Three localities within this area have moderate concentrations of surface pottery, and show up as zones of gray-white coloration which stand out distinctly from the brown soil of the surrounding agricultlral fields (Appendix II). The surface pottery on these localities is mixed Aztec (predominately Late, with light Early material) and Late Toltec (Tx-LT-6). These three features are probably household residential complexes. Three of the several pits dug into the site area show lenses of dense sherd debris, up to 1.5 m thick, buried beneath 50 to 75 cm of alluvium, with only light surface pottery on the ground surface. In these instances, the ceramic debris is comprised largely of Texcoco Fabric Marked pottery, and Late Toltec sherds are absent. Except for these buried lenses, Texcoco Fabric Marked pottery is very light or absent over the rest of the site area.

Classification: Small dispersed village; 150 to 300 people. Salt-making was obviously of some importance here.

Tx-A-11

Natural setting: 2260 m, on the Lakeshore Plain. Situated in a zone of deep alluvial soil.

Modern utilization: The northern and eastern edges of the site extend into the modern town of Chiconcuac. The densely packed structures of this community may well obscure some Aztec occupational debris. The remainder of the site area is devoted to intensive cultivation, including some mechanized irrigation of alfalfa and maize.

Archaeological remains: Variable light and light-to-moderate concentrations of surface pottery over an area of about 24 hectares. There are no definite structural remains, although there is some correlation of gray-white soil with areas of heaviest sherd densities. Equivalent concentrations of Late Toltec material are also present, over a somewhat smaller area (Tx-LT-7).

Classification: Small dispersed village; 150 to 250 people. May be somewhat larger if significant amounts of occupational debris are obliterated by modern Chiconcuac.

Tx-A-12

Natural setting: 2270 m, at the juncture of the Lakeshore Plain and the Lower Piedmont. Situated in a zone of deep alluvial soil cover.

Modern utilization: Aztec surface pottery occurs at the northern and southern edges of the Barrio Huiznahuac, a detached segment of San Andres Chiautla, and can also be found within the borders of this community. The surrounding fields are devoted to intensive cultivation, including some mechanized irrigation of maize and alfalfa.

Archaeological remains: Variable light and light-to-moderate concentrations of surface pottery over an area of roughly 12 hectares. The dense modern occupation of the Barrio Huiznahuac may obscure some Aztec occupational debris. The ceramic material is mixed Early and Late Aztec. There are two locations of distinctive gray-white soil coloration, both about 20 m in diameter, which may be vestiges of domestic residential structures. One of these also contains light Late Toltec material (Tx-LT-9). A thick lens of dense Aztec sherd refuse buried below 75 cm of alluvium, was noted in the profile of a small well in an area where only light concentrations of pottery appeared on the surface.

Classification: Estimates of size and occupational density are somewhat difficult due to possibilities of obliteration of surface pottery by heavy modern overlay and alluviation. This is apparently a small dispersed village, with 100 to 150 people.

Tx-A-13

Natural setting: 2280 m, at the juncture of the Lakeshore Plain and the Lower Piedmont. Situated in a zone of deep alluvial soil.

Modern utilization: Intensive cultivation. The southern and western edges of the site extend into the modern village of Amajac.

Archaeological remains: Light concentrations of surface pottery over an area about five hectares, with a single recognizable mound containing light-to-moderate sherd debris. This structure is about 1 m high, and roughly 8 m in diameter, although its correct diameter is difficult to ascertain due to alluviation in this region. The ceramic material is very predominately Late Aztec, with some light Late Toltec pottery also present (Tx-LT-10).

Classification: Hamlet; fewer than 50 people. May be slightly larger if modern Amajac obscures some occupational debris.

Tx-A-14

Natural setting: 2290 m, in the Lower Piedmont. In a level area of deep alluvial soil.

Modern utilization: Intensive cultivation, including some mechanized irrigation of alfalfa and maize.

Archaeological remains: Variable light and light-to-moderate concentrations of surface pottery over an area of about 15 hectares. Both Early and Late Aztec ceramics were present in roughly equal proportions. A single mound was located. This feature measured about 20 m in diameter, and about 1 m high. Surface pottery occurred in moderate quantities over the mounded area, and obsidian debris was especially heavy. Light Classic (Tx-EC-7; Tx-LC-7) and Toltec (Tx-ET-14; Tx-LT-11) material was also present on and immediately around this mound.

Classification: Small dispersed village; 75 to 150 people.

Tx-A-15

Natural setting: 2290 m, in the Lower Piedmont. Situated on flat ground, at the banks of the Rio Jalapango, in a zone of deep alluvial soil.

Modern utilization: Intensive cultivation.

Archaeological remains: Variable light and light-to-moderate concentrations of surface pottery over an area of about two hectares. No structural remains. Ceramics are very predominately Late Aztec.

Classification: Hamlet; fewer than 50 people.

Tx-A-16

Natural setting: 2290 m, in the Lower Piedmont. Situated on level ground, in a zone of deep alluvial soil, near the Rio Jalapango.

Modern utilization: Site borders the northeastern edge of modern Papalotla, and some Aztec occupational debris may extend below the nucleated structures of the modern town where intensive survey could not be carried out. The site area lies in a region of intensive cultivation, including some mechanized irrigation of alfalfa.

Archaeological remains: Light-to-moderate concentrations of surface pottery over an area of six hectares. The site may be considerably larger if modern Papalotla covers significant quantities of Aztec occupational debris. Both Early and Late Aztec pottery are present, with Early predominant. Traces of Early Toltec material (Tx-ET-4) also occur. There are no structural remains.

Classification: Small dispersed village; 100 to 200 people.

Tx-A-17

Natural setting: 2290 to 2360 m, in the Lower Piedmont. The site occupies the flat plain north of the Rio Jalapango, and extends northward onto the gently sloping lowermost southern flanks of Cerro Azteca. The southern two-thirds of the site lies in a zone of deep alluvial soil. The soil cover thins progressively to the north, where some patches of bare tepetate are found.

Modern utilization: The southern two-thirds of the site is devoted to intensive cultivation. The northern third is used for grazing and maguey cultivation.

Archaeological remains: The site covers an area of about 115 hectares, but only along the base of Cerro Azteca does Aztec surface pottery occur in greater than light concentrations. In this latter zone, the concentration of surface pottery is generally light-to-moderate, and three tlateles were sufficiently preserved to be recognizable as such (Appendix II). The Aztec pottery is predominately Late, but some Early Aztec material is present. Terminal Formative (Tx-TF-1) and Early Toltec (Tx-ET-4) pottery is found here in much heavier concentrations. Small quantities of Middle Formative (Tx-MF-1), Classic (Tx-EC-3; Tx-LC-2) and Late Toltec (Tx-LT-12; Tx-LT-15) material is also present. Several additional structural remnants occur, but we have assigned these to Terminal Formative and Early Toltec times.

Classification: Large dispersed village; 300 to 600 people.

Tx-A-18

Natural setting: 2330 to 2340 m, in the Lower Piedmont. The site occupies a broad natural terrace of gently sloping ground on the western flank of Cerro Azteca. Erosion has been severe. Soil cover is shallow, with large patches of bare tepetate.

Modern utilization: Grazing, plus a few cultivated maguey.

Archaeological remains: Variable light and light-to-moderate concentrations of surface pottery and moderate rock rubble over an area of about three hectares. Both Early and Late Aztec sherds occur. No structural remains. Mixed with somewhat lighter Early Toltec material (Tx-ET-1). The steep slopes above the site are covered with badly deteriorated terraces, of indeterminate age.

Classification: Hamlet; fewer than 50 people.

Tx-A-19

Natural setting: 2470 m, at the top of a long, high ridge extending south from the main body of Cerro Azteca. Irregular ground surface, with shallow soil cover and numerous outcrops of bedrock.

Modern utilization: Marginal grazing.

Archaeological remains: The site consists of a single large irregular mound, measuring about 35 m in diameter, and standing about 3 m high. This appears to be predominately composed of solid rock, loosely piled in large, irregular fragments, with no bonding material. A number of circular depressions around the outer edges may indicate the former existence of rooms or chambers. These depressions vary from 3 to 4 m in diameter, and are usually about one to 1.5 m deep. About midway along the south edge of the main mound there is a level, rock-free area, about 10 m square, standing about 1.5 m above the general ground level. This plaza-like feature has been artificially built up and levelled by means of stone terrace faces and rock fill. Several remnants of stone wall bases are found on the upper surface of this plaza. Surface pottery is very light Aztec over the whole site area.

Classification: Hilltop ceremonial precinct; no permanent occupation.

Tx-A-20

Natural setting: 2620 m, at the top of Cerro Azteca, about 250 to 300 m above the level of the Lower Piedmont plain and the Lakeshore Plain to the east, south, and west. The soil cover is generally shallow, with isolated pockets of deep soil and numerous rock outcrops over the irregular ground surface. Erosion has been moderate.

Modern utilization: Grazing, plus some cultivated maguey. Several small stone quarries occur at the west end of the hilltop.

Archaeological remains: Variable light and light-to-moderate concentrations of surface pottery over an area of roughly one hectare. The site consists of three main features (Fig. 14): (1) a large temple platform of solid earth and rock rubble construction, built in two stages. The lower stage is a basal platform, about 30 by 40 m in area, standing about 1 m high. The second stage is a pyramidal mound about 35 by 25 m in area and standing about 3 m high. A small modern stone chapel presently rests atop the ancient mound. (2) The temple platform sits at the east end of a level area, measuring some 30 by 50 m, which appears to have been a plaza. (3) South of the plaza, slightly downslope, is a large stone platform or terrace, about 20 m wide and 50 m long. Sherd debris, composed largely of crude ceremonial vessels, was especially abundant along the south edge of the plaza, just above the lower stone terrace.

The ceramic material over the site is predominately Late Aztec, but smaller quantities of Early Aztec sherds are also present. Small amounts of Terminal Formative (Tx-TF-3), Early Toltec (Tx-ET-6), and Late Toltec (Tx-LT-14) pottery also occur here.

Classification: Hilltop ceremonial precinct; probably no permanent occupation.

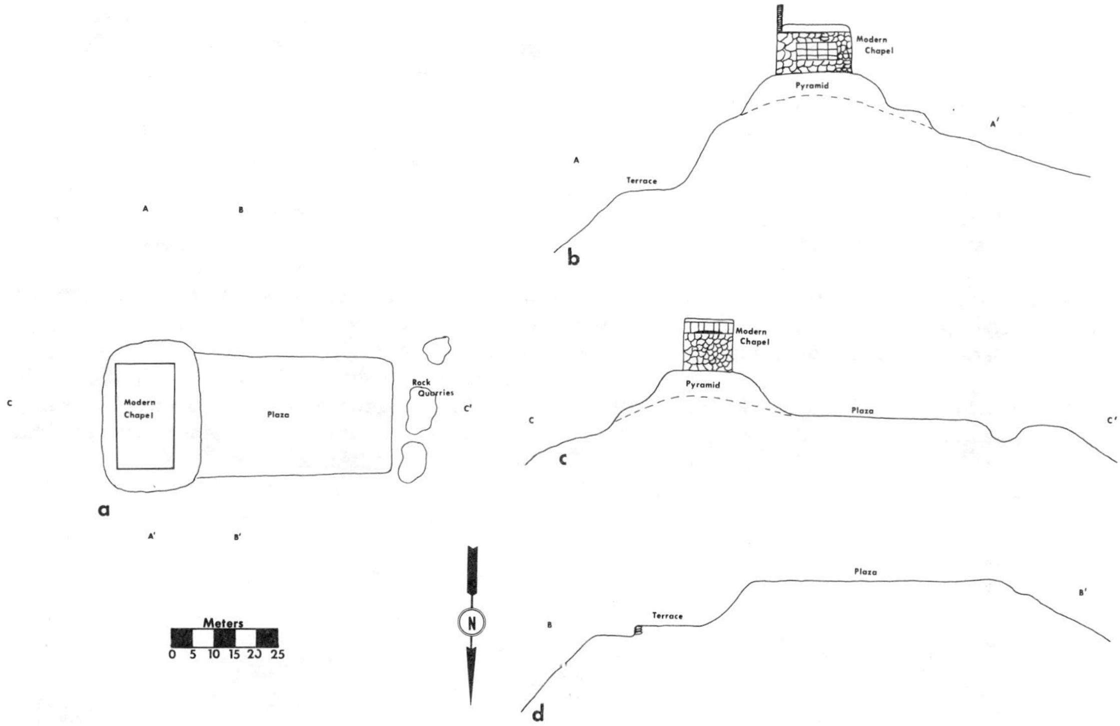

Fig. 14—Site plan and cross sections, Tx-A-20 (not to scale).

Tx-A-21

Natural setting: 2320 to 2400 m, in the Lower Piedmont. Situated on gently sloping ground at the eastern base of Cerro Azteca. The site area is cut through by two major barrancas. Erosion has been severe, and soil cover is very shallow, with large patches of bare tepetate.

Modern utilization: Predominately grazing, with some maize cultivation along the southern edge of the site area.

Archaeological remains: Variable light and light-to-moderate concentrations of surface pottery over an area of about 55 hectares. The ceramic material is predominately Late Aztec, but some Early Aztec sherds are present. No structural remains.

Classification: Small dispersed village; 250 to 500 people.

Tx-A-22

Natural setting: 2290 m, in the Lower Piedmont. Situated on level ground, in a zone of deep alluvial soil, just north of the Río Papalotla.

Modern utilization: Most of the site is covered by the modern village of San Francisco Olalpa. Surrounding fields are devoted to intensive rainfall cultivation.

Archaeological remains: Variable light and light-to-moderate concentrations of surface pottery at the eastern and western edges of San Francisco Olalpa, and scattered throughout the modern village in those few empty areas where survey could be conducted. At the western edge of the village pottery does not occur on the ground surface, but rather is found washing from the walls of a deep barranca cut, at depths of 25 cm to 3 m below ground level, over a horizontal distance of about 50 m. Very little pottery actually occurs on the ground surface adjacent to the cut. There are no structural remains. Total site area is not known, but amounts to at least 13 hectares.

Classification: Size, density, and extent of site remain unknown due to the heavy modern overlay, plus substantial alluviation. The occupational debris located here may well be continuous with that of Tx-A-17 to the west and south. At the very least, we are dealing with a small dispersed village of 75 to 150 people.

Tx-A-23

Natural setting: 2360 m, in the Lower Piedmont. Situated on gently sloping ground at the southern base of Cerro Coyochimo, lying between two major barrancas. Erosion has been moderate. Soil cover is shallow to moderately deep.

Modern utilization: Grazing and maguey cultivation. There is a small rock quarry on the slopes above the site area.

Archaeological remains: Variable very light, light, and light-to-moderate concentrations of surface pottery and rock rubble over an area of about 18 hectares. Both Early and Late Aztec materials are present. There are no structural remains. The steeper slopes above the site contain badly deteriorated stone terracing of indeterminate age.

Classification: Small dispersed village; 100 to 150 people.

Tx-A-24 (Aztec Tepetlaoxtoc)

Natural setting: 2300 to 2500 m, in the Lower Piedmont. The site occupies a broad stretch of gently sloping, severely eroded land along the lower southern flanks of the Patlaichique range, north of the broad floodplain of the Río Papalotla. The site area is cut through by several major barrancas, and the surface of the northern half of the site now consists predominately of badly scarred bare tepetate, with little or no soil cover except in occasional pockets and isolated erosional remnants. Soil cover is somewhat more continuous to the south, but never exceeds shallow depth, and patches of bare tepetate are common everywhere.

Modern utilization: Northern half of the site is useful only for marginal grazing. The southern section is devoted to intensive rainfall cultivation of subsistence crops.

Archaeological remains: Variable very light,

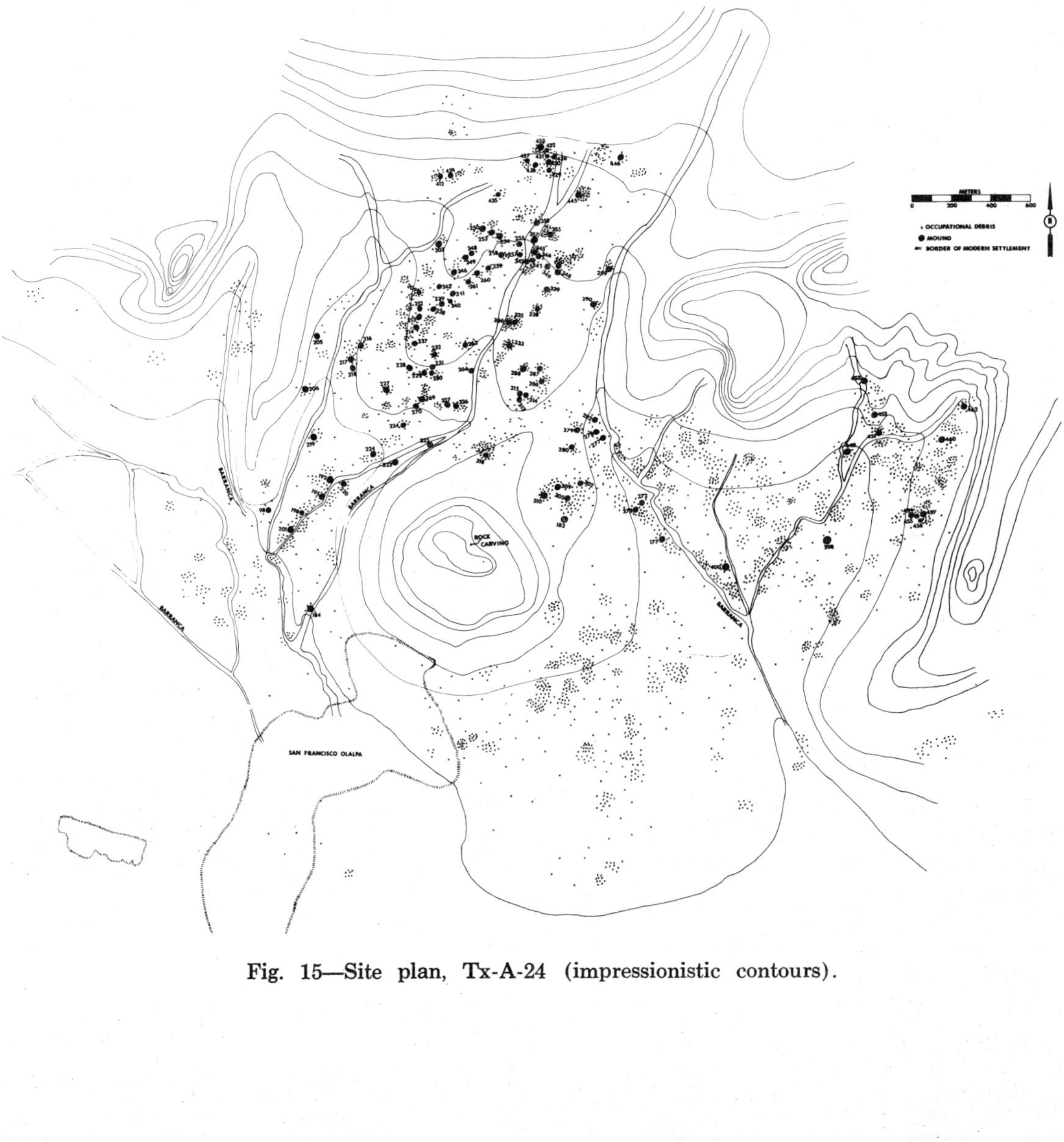

Fig. 15—Site plan, Tx-A-24 (impressionistic contours).

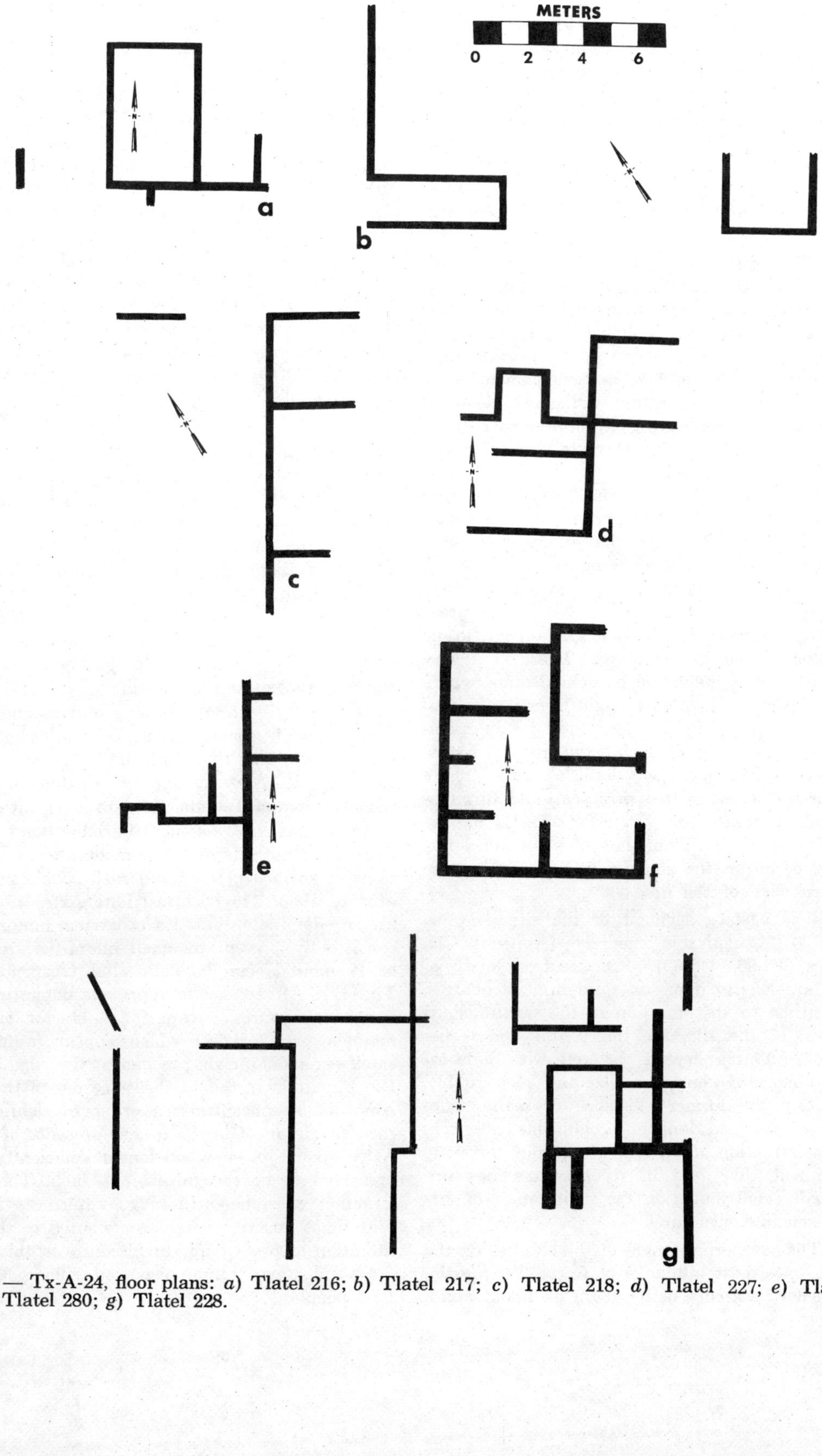

Fig. 16 — Tx-A-24, floor plans: *a*) Tlatel 216; *b*) Tlatel 217; *c*) Tlatel 218; *d*) Tlatel 227; *e*) Tlatel 326; *f*) Tlatel 280; *g*) Tlatel 228.

light, light-to-moderate, and moderate concentrations of surface pottery over an area of about 450 hectares (Fig. 15). Late Aztec pottery is predominate, but Early Aztec sherds are present in smaller quantities. Because of the size of the site, it is convenient to discuss it in three separate sections: (1) a northwestern segment, comprising about 60 per cent of the total site area; (2) an eastern segment; and (3) a southern segment.

1) The northwestern segment is the most eroded part of the site. Despite the great havoc wrought on the archaeological materials, some 216 mounds could be delineated, 112 of which were sufficiently well preserved to provide data on household size and room arrangement (Appendix; Fig. 16). The stone walls and plastered floors of the Aztec living structures have functioned as erosion checks. Discrete structures can usually be recognized as very distinct mounds containing practically the only soil cover and vegetation in an otherwise barren tepetate wasteland (Pl. 36,*a*). The fact that many wall bases and house floors rest directly on, or very close to, bare tepetate, indicates that soil cover has always been relatively shallow in this area. The great majority of recognizable mounds appear to be domestic residential structures. There is a very clear pattern of individual household units, where surface pottery is found in light-to-moderate and moderate concentrations, separated by intervening stretches of bare tepetate where sherd concentrations are only very light to light. There are several small Toltec sites scattered throughout this general area (Tx-ET-7, Tx-ET-8; Tx-LT-16, Tx-LT-18). Remnants of stone-faced terracing occur on the steeper hillslopes along the western edge of the area.

2) The eastern segment of the site contains only 20 recognizable mounds (Appendix II, tlateles 396-66, 448-62). The great majority of these are clearly domestic residential structures. In contrast to the situation in the northwestern segment of the site, the intervening spaces between structures here is littered with light-to-moderate sherd concentrations and rock rubble, indicating the former existence of many more mounds, now no longer recognizable as such. The construction of earth-stone maguey terracing throughout this area in recent times has undoubtedly contributed to the obliteration of Aztec residential structures.

3) The southern segment of the site lies on the broad, lowermost hillflanks of Cerro Teponaztla, at the northern edge of the main piedmont plain. Here is the deepest soil cover and the least severe erosion of the entire Tx-A-24 site area. Early Toltec is the dominant occupational component in this area (Tx-ET-7), and light Late Toltec pottery is also present (Tx-LT-21, Tx-LT-23). Aztec occupation here is generally light, with a few light-to-moderate concentrations of surface pottery. There are no structural remains that can definitely be assigned to Aztec times.

A large flat-sided stone boulder, on the upper northern slope of Cerro Teponaxtla, has been elaborately carved (Pl. 36,*b*). This feature may be Aztec, or could be associated with the large Terminal Formative site on Cerro Teponaxtle (Tx-TF-4).

Classification: Primary regional center; 6750 to 13,500 people.

Tx-A-25

Natural setting: 2300 to 2390 m, in the Lower Piedmont. Situated on the gently sloping southern flanks of the Patlachique range, extending southward onto the edge of the broad, level floodplain of the Río Papalotla. Erosion has been severe throughout the northern two-thirds of the site area, and soil cover is shallow with large stretches of bare tepetate. Soil cover is uniformly shallow to moderately deep over the southern end of the site. A major barranca cuts through the site's eastern edge.

Modern utilization: Grazing and maguey cultivation, with some rainfall cultivation of subsistence crops at the southeastern corner of the site. The site does not appear to extend into the modern town of Tepetlaoxtoc to the southwest.

Archaeological remains: Variable very light, light, light-to-moderate, and moderate concentrations of surface pottery and rock rubble over an area of about 115 hectares. Late Aztec ceramics are predominate, but Early Aztec material is consistently present in small quantities. A total of 17 mounds can be delineated (Appendix II; Fig. 17). All appear to represent domestic residential structures, except for a cluster of four mounds (475-77, 479) which appear to form a small ceremonial-civic precinct at the edge of the Río Papalotla in the southeast corner of the site. Amorphous concentrations of sherd debris and rock rubble attest to the former presence of other Aztec structures, now no longer sufficiently well preserved to be recognizable as such. The construction of stone-earth maguey terraces in recent times has very likely contributed to the obliteration of prehispanic architecture in this area.

Classification: Large dispersed village; 600 to 1200 people.

Tx-A-26

Natural setting: 2420 to 2470 m, in the Lower Piedmont. Situated on gently sloping ground along the western base of a high ridge extending southward from the main body of the Patlachique Range. A major barranca cuts through the site area. Erosion has been severe throughout the site. Soil cover is shallow to absent, with large stretches of bare tepetate.

Modern utilization: Marginal grazing. Maguey

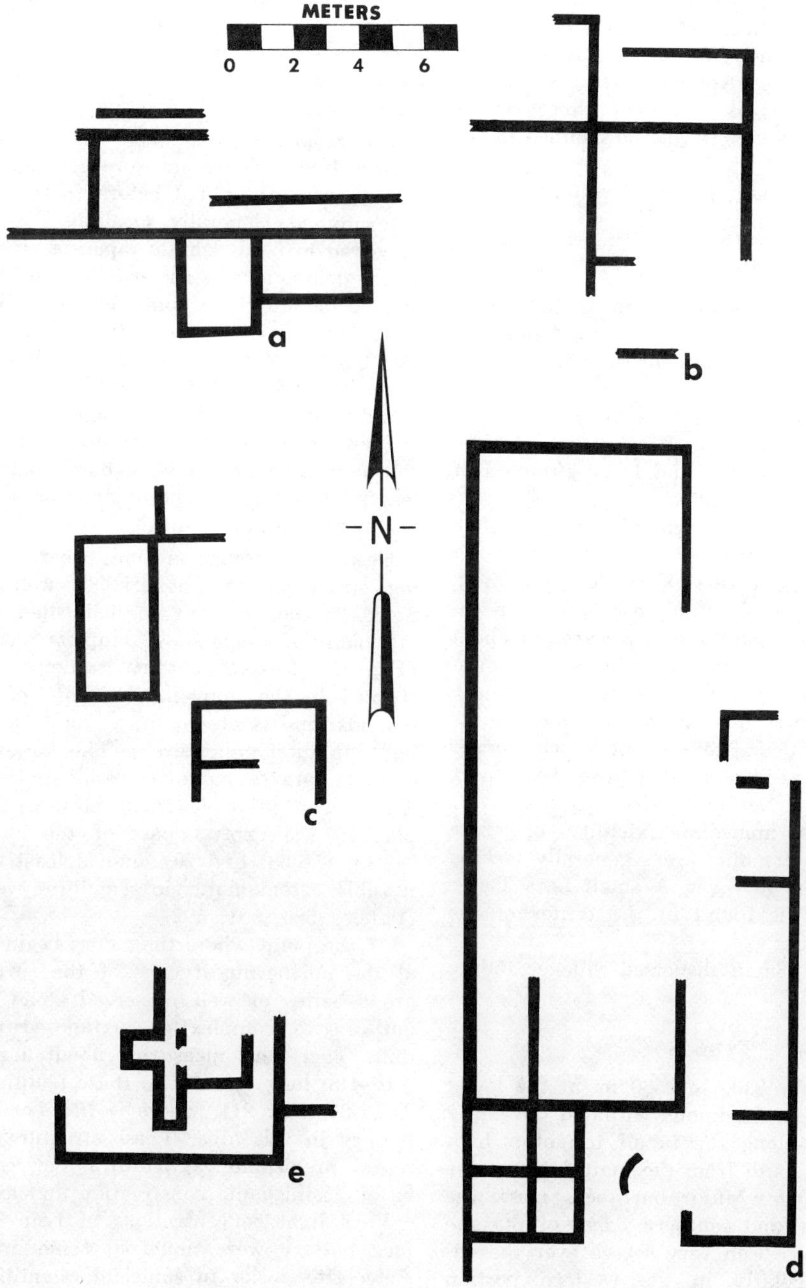

Fig. 17—Floor plans: *a*) Tx-A-25, Tlatel 472; *b*) Tx-A-26, Tlatel 615; *c*) Tx-A-26, Tlatel 617; *d*) Tx-A-27, Tlatel 566; *e*) Tx-A-27, Tlatel 561.

is being cultivated on the terraced steeper slopes above the site.

Archaeological remains: Variable very light, light, light-to-moderate, and moderate concentrations of surface pottery over an area of about 10 hectares. The ceramic material is predominately Late Aztec, but Early Aztec sherds are present in small quantities. Some 14 mounds can be delineated, all of which appear to be domestic residential structures (Appendix II; Fig. 17; Pl. 37). Surface pottery is restricted almost wholly to the immediate vicinity of the mounds themselves.

Classification: Small dispersed village; 75 to 150 people.

Tx-A-27

Natural setting: 2370 to 2420 m, in the Lower Piedmont. Situated on gently sloping ground at the western base of a high, broad range which extends southward from the main body of the Patlachique Range. A major barranca forms the western border of the site. Very severe erosion, with very little soil cover and large stretches of badly scarred bare tepetate.

Modern utilization: Marginal grazing, plus a few cultivated maguey.

Archaeological remains: Variable very light, light, light-to-moderate, and moderate concentrations of surface pottery over an area of about 17 hectares. The ceramic material is predominately Late Aztec, with Early Aztec consistently present in lighter quantities. A total of 28 mounds can be delineated, all of which appear to be domestic residential structures (Appendix II; Figs. 17, 18). Surface pottery is largely restricted to the immediate vicinity of these mounds, with intervening areas generally lacking any significant sherd cover. A small Late Toltec site (Tx-LT-31) is found in the center of the Aztec community.

Classification: Small dispersed village; 150 to 300 people.

Tx-A-28

Natural setting: 2500 to 2580 m, at the lower edge of the Upper Piedmont. Situated on gently sloping ground along the broad top of a high ridge extending south from the main body of the Patlachique Range. Major barrancas mark the western, eastern, and southern edges of the site area. Erosion has been very severe over the entire site, particularly in the western portion where narrow arroyos have cut deeply, leaving numerous isolated erosional remnants standing as much as 10 m above the general level of the badly scarred bare tepetate. There is some soil cover over the eastern half of the site, but large stretches of bare tepetate are also abundant there.

Modern utilization: The western half of the site is a barren tepetate wasteland, unfit even for marginal grazing. There is marginal grazing over the eastern half, and some minor rainfall cultivation of maize and maguey along the southeastern edge.

Archaeological remains: The northern and eastern limits of the site were not defined, as our survey was terminated before these areas could be examined. Generally speaking, however, there appeared to be a definite tapering off of occupational debris at the eastern limit of our survey area, although there continued to be indications of substantial Aztec occupation north of our survey borders. The surveyed portion of the site comprises about 75 hectares. Surface pottery is found in variable very light, light, light-to-moderate, and moderate concentrations over this area. The ceramic material is predominately Late Aztec, but Early Aztec sherds are consistently present in substantial quantities.

Despite the severe erosion, the remains of living structures are remarkably well preserved. Some 95 mounds can be delineated (Appendix II), many of which show complete room patterns (Fig. 19). Surface pottery is almost wholly restricted to the immediate vicinity of individual mounds, and is absent or, at most, very light to light, in intervening areas. The majority of the mounds are apparently residential structures. There is a probable small plaza-pyramid complex in the central part of the site (tlateles 845-48, 856-58; Fig. 20), and at least three other possible ceremonial-civic structures were located (tlateles 580, 581, 592).

At the point where the slopes begin to steepen at the northernmost edge of the surveyed area are a series of well preserved stone wall bases outlining a complex of juxtaposed rectangular units, each unit measuring about 3 m wide by 3 to 4 m long (similar to those features noted at Tx-A-30, Fig. 21). There is little or no surface pottery in this area. These structures may represent prehispanic agricultural devices, or could be of posthispanic construction and use.

Very light concentrations of Late Toltec surface pottery were noted in some areas of the Aztec site, never in sufficient quantities to warrant a site designation.

Classification: Large dispersed village; 600 to

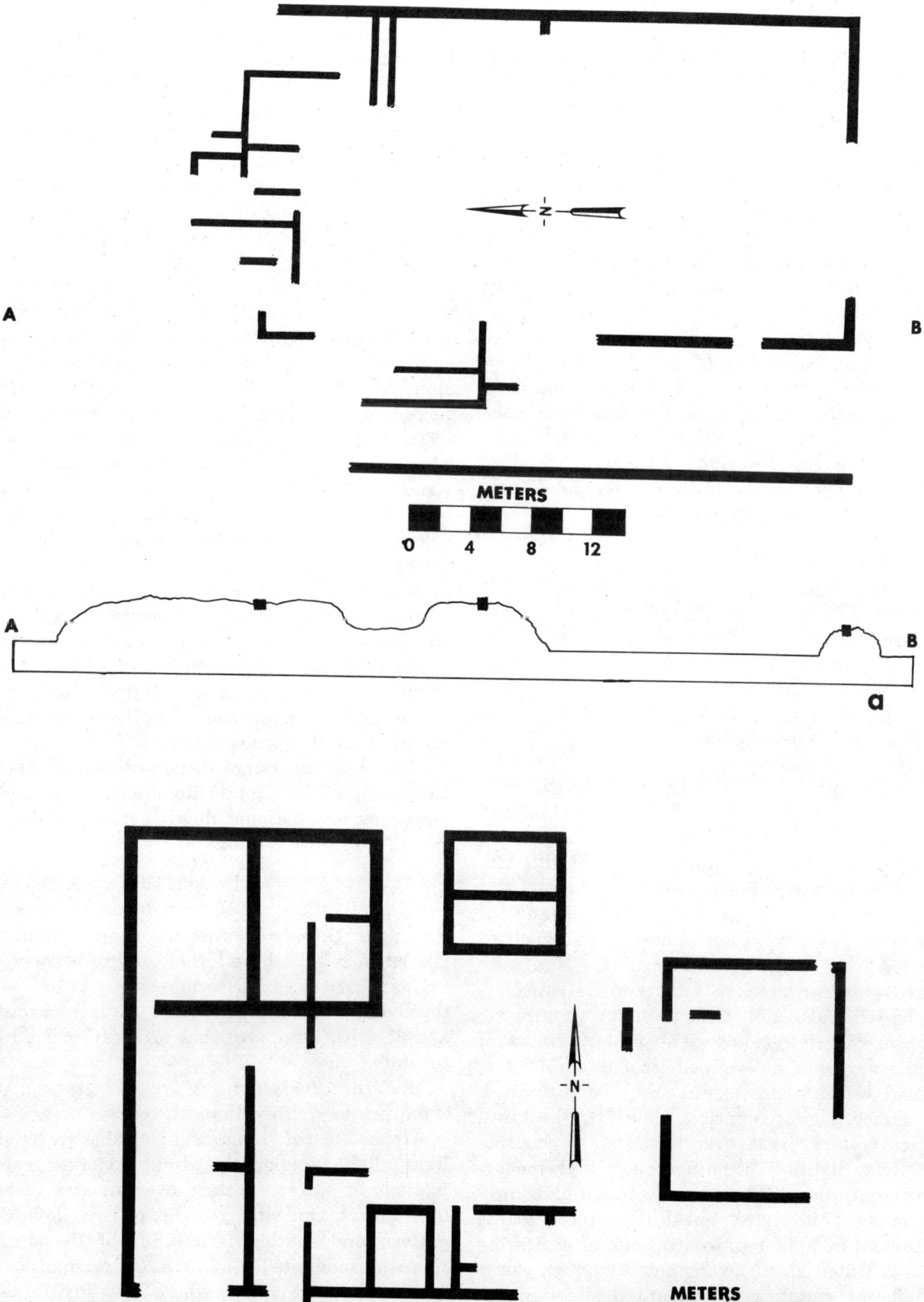

Fig. 18—Tx-A-27, floor plans: *a*) Tlatel 554; *b*) Tlatel 612.

1200 people. The total site area is substantially larger than this, as occupational debris continues well to the east and north of our survey limit.

Tx-A-29

Natural setting: 2610 m, at the top of Cerro Tezontepec, the highest peak in the area. The ground surface is irregular, with shallow soil cover and some outcroppings of bedrock.

Modern utilization: Grazing, plus some cultivated maguey.

Archaeological remains: The site consists of a single mound. Remnants of stone wall bases define a structure about 10 by 5 m in surface area, standing roughly 35 cm high. The enclosing walls are nearly a meter thick. Very light to light concentrations of Aztec surface pottery.

Classification: Small hilltop ceremonial precinct; no permanent occupation.

Tx-A-30

Natural setting: 2500 to 2610 m, in the Upper Piedmont. The site is situated on the gently sloping upper surface of a broad ridge top, lying between two major barrancas. A smaller barranca bisects the site. Very severe erosion, with little or no intact soil cover, and large stretches of badly scarred bare tepetate.

Modern utilization: A program of systematic land reclamation is being carried out in the eastern half of the site. Here, ditches are dug into the hard tepetate surface, perpendicular to the hillslope, following the contour lines of the hill. These ditches are lined with cut brush and maguey. In this way, erosion is checked, and intensive maguey cultivation is now being effectively carried out. The remainder of the site area is used only for grazing, and there is considerable barren wasteland, unfit even for pasture.

Archaeological remains: The eastern limits of the site were not determined, as our survey terminated before that region could be examined. The surveyed site comprises about 100 hectares. Surface pottery exists over this area in variable very light, light, light-to-moderate, and moderate concentrations. The ceramic material is predominately Late Aztec, but Early Aztec sherds are present in lighter concentrations. A scattering of Late Toltec sherds were noted, though never in sufficient quantity to warrant a site designation. Despite the severe erosion, some 105 mounds were sufficiently well preserved to be recognizable as such (Appendix II). Surface pottery was largely restricted to the immediate vicinity of these mounds, with only very light and light sherd concentrations in intervening areas. As in the case of other Aztec sites in this general area, the walls and floors of ancient structures have acted as erosion checks, and usually stand out clearly as islands of soil cover and vegetation in an otherwise barren tepetate wasteland. In many cases, Aztec structures occur atop erosional remnants, often as high as 2 to 5 m above the general level of the badly scarred tepetate surface.

Most of the preserved mounds appear to be domestic residential units, but at least two or three probable small ceremonial-civic structures were located (tlateles 722, 723, 752). At the southwestern edge of the site area, remnants of stone wall bases define a complex of juxtaposed rectangular enclosures on gently sloping ground (Fig. 21). This complex covers an area of about 30 by 75 m, and contains light concentrations of Aztec surface pottery. This may represent some form of prehispanic terracing, or could be of colonial or modern construction and use.

The occupational debris in the north-central portion of the site appears to be quite distinct relative to that observed elsewhere within the site area. Here there are a noticeably larger number of figurines, spindle whorls, and high proportions of decorated pottery. Most of the Aztec IV Black-on-Orange pottery on the site occurred in this same zone.

Classification: Large dispersed village; 1000 to 1500 people. The total site area is considerably larger, as occupational debris extends well to the east of our survey limits.

Tx-A-31

Natural setting: 2550 to 2610 m, in the Upper Piedmont. Situated across the gently sloping upper surface of a broad ridge, lying between two major barrancas. Erosion has been severe throughout the site area. Soil cover is scanty to absent, with large stretches of badly scarred bare tepetate.

Modern utilization: Marginal grazing, plus some maguey cultivation.

Archaeological remains: Variable very light, light, light-to-moderate, and moderate concentrations of surface pottery over an area of about 50 hectares. Our survey seems to have defined the eastern and southeastern limits of the site, but there is undoubtedly more Aztec occupation east of the large barranca where our survey terminated. The ceramic material is predominately Late Aztec, but Early Aztec sherds are also present in some localities. Despite the severe erosion, some 53 mounds can be defined (Appendix II; Fig. 22). Most of these seem to be badly de-

Fig. 19—Tx-A-28, floor plans: *a*) Tlatel 582; *b*) Tlatel 587; *c*) Tlatel 583; *d*) Tlatel 596; *e*) Tlatel 597.

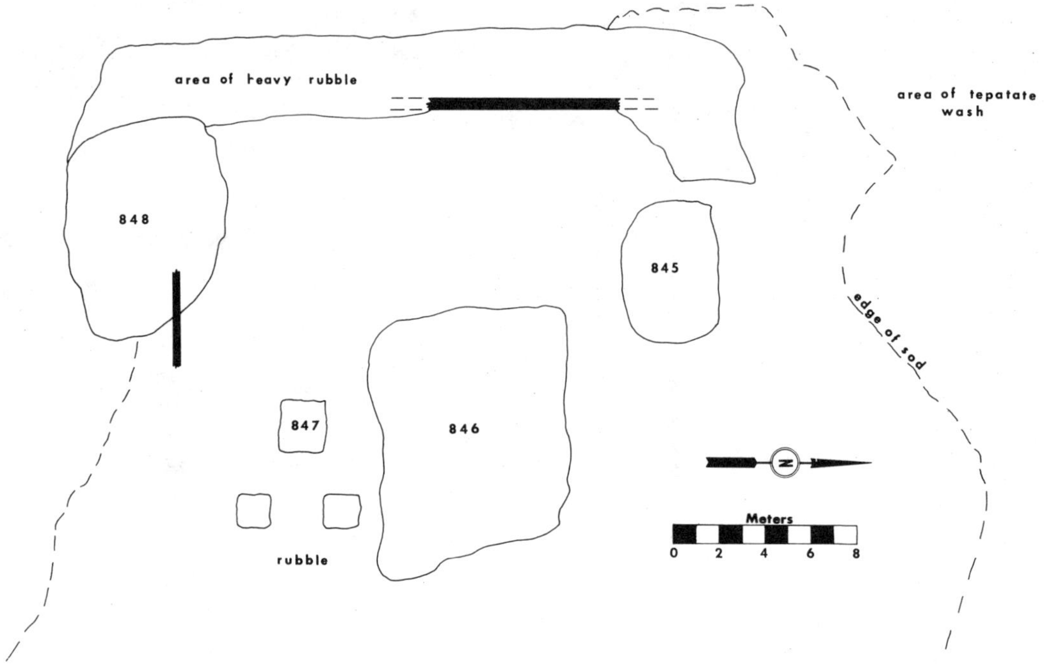

Fig. 20—Tlatel 845-48 complex, Tx-A-28.

stroyed domestic residences, but there is at least one probable small ceremonial-civic structure (tlatel 638). Another tlatel (673) is unusual in having much heavier concentrations of obsidian debris than were noted elsewhere in the site area. Surface pottery is largely restricted to the immediate vicinity of the mounds, with only very light and light sherd debris in intervening areas. Badly deteriorated terrace remnants are found on the steep slopes at the northwestern corner of the site. A few Late Toltec and Terminal Formative sherds occur scattered throughout the site area, never in sufficient quantities to warrant a site designation.

Classification: Large dispersed village; 350 to 700 people.

Tx-A-32

Natural setting: 2400 to 2440 m, in the Lower Piedmont. Situated near a major barranca on gently sloping ground, at the western base of a long, high ridge extending westward from the main Sierra. Erosion has been severe. Soil cover is scanty to absent, with large stretches of badly scarred bare tepetate.

Modern utilization: Marginal grazing.

Archaeological remains: Variable light, light-to-moderate, and moderate concentrations of surface pottery over an area of about four hectares. The ceramic material is predominately Early Aztec, with much lighter concentrations of Late Aztec sherds. The badly eroded remnants of eight structures can be delineated (Appendix II), most of which appear to be domestic residential units. One possible small ceremonial-civic structure (tlatel 535) was noted at the east end of the site. Surface pottery is largely restricted to the immediate vicinity of the mounds, with only light sherd cover in intervening areas. A few Late Toltec sherds are scattered over the site area, never in sufficient concentration to warrant a site designation.

Classification: Hamlet; fewer than 100 people.

Tx-A-33

Natural setting: 2400 m, in the Lower Piedmont. Situated on a tongue of relatively level land between two barrancas at the base of a high, broad ridge extending westward from the main Sierra. Moderate erosion. Generally shallow soil cover, with intermittent patches of bare tepetate.

Modern utilization: Grazing.

Archaeological remains: Variable light and light-to-moderate concentrations of surface pottery over an area of less than one hectare. Both Early and Late Aztec sherds are present in roughly equal proportions. A single structural remnant was noted: measuring about 6 by 4 m,

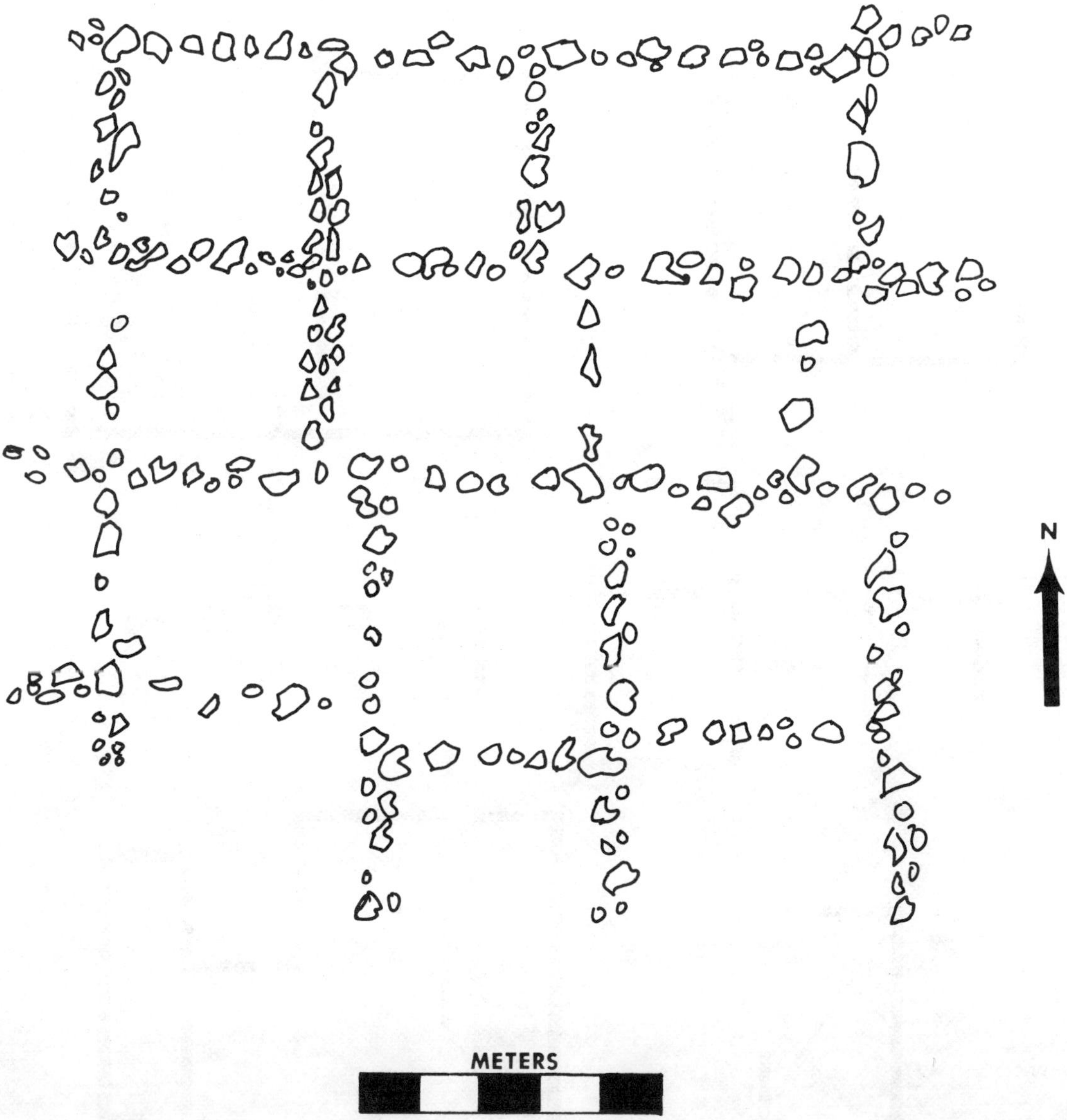

Fig. 21—Tx-A-30, possible terraces.

and standing about 25 cm high, with moderate rock rubble and light Aztec surface pottery.

Classification: Probably a single isolated household unit, of 5 to 15 people. Probably a part of the Tx-A-30 community.

Tx-A-34

Natural setting: 2400 to 2420 m, in the Lower Piedmont. Situated on gently sloping ground between two major barrancas, at the base of a high, broad ridge extending westward from the main Sierra. Erosion has been moderate to severe. Soil cover varies from moderately deep, to shallow, to absent, and there are large patches of bare tepetate over some of the site area.

Modern utilization: Grazing, with some maize cultivation in the southwestern corner where the soil cover is deepest. A gravel road has recently been built through the site area, and large piles of stone construction debris cover portions of the Aztec occupational zone.

Archaeological remains: Variable very light,

Fig. 22—Foor plans: *a*) Tx-A-31, Tlatel 654; *b*) Tx-A-31, Tlatel 675; *c*) Tx-A-39, Tlatel 486; *d*) Tx-A-69, Tlatel 257; *e*) Tx-A-69, Tlatel 249.

light, light-to-moderate, and moderate concentrations of surface pottery over an area of about six hectares. Both Early and Late Aztec sherds are present in roughly equal proportions. Nine tlateles can be defined, all of which appear to be domestic residential structures (Appendix II). Surface pottery is largely restricted to the immediate area of these mounds, with very little sherd cover in intervening areas.

Classification: Hamlet; fewer than 100 people.

Tx-A-35

Natural setting: 2360-2420 m, in the Lower Piedmont. Situated in a gently sloping zone at the upper end of the main piedmont plain, along the edges of a major barranca. Erosion has been slight to moderate. Moderately deep soil cover.

Modern utilization: Part of the town lies within the modern village of San Pedro Chiautzingo. The surrounding area is intensively cultivated in subsistence crops (rainfall agriculture).

Archaeological remains: Variable very light, light, light-to-moderate, and moderate concentrations of surface pottery over an area of about 30 hectares. The ceramic material is predominately Late Aztec, but some Early Aztec sherds are also present. There are no structural remains.

Classification: Small dispersed village; 200 to 400 people.

Tx-A-36

Natural setting: 2400 m, in the Lower Piedmont. Situated at the north edge of a broad, flat ridge top, in a zone of moderately deep soil cover and slight erosion.

Modern utilization: Intensive rainfall cultivation.

Archaeological remains: Variable very light, light, and light-to-moderate concentrations of surface pottery over an area of about one hectare. Both Early and Late Aztec ceramics are present, with Late predominate. There are no recognizable structural remains. The southern limits of the Aztec occupation were not determined.

Classification: The surveyed site is a hamlet of fewer than 50 people. This location may well be the northern end of a substantially larger community.

Tx-A-37

Natural setting: 2400 to 2420 m, in the Lower Piedmont. Situated on gently sloping ground along the upper surface of a broad ridge extending westward from the main Sierra. Erosion has been slight. Soil cover is moderately deep.

Modern utilization: Intensive rainfall cultivation.

Archaeological remains: Variable very light, light, light-to-moderate, and moderate concentrations of surface pottery over an area of about five hectares. The Aztec pottery is very predominately Late. A single structural remnant can be delineated: measuring about 12 m in diameter and 20 cm high, with moderate Aztec surface pottery and moderate rock rubble. Substantial quantities of Early Toltec material also occur on the mound's surface (Tx-ET-11). The southern limits of Aztec occupation were not precisely defined.

Classification: Hamlet; fewer than 100 people. The site may be considerably larger if there is substantial occupation south of our survey limit.

Tx-A-38

Natural setting: 2300 to 2390 m, in the Lower Piedmont. Situated on gently sloping ground across the western flanks of a broad ridge, and along the north edge of a major barranca (through which flows the Río Papalotla) which formed the southern limit of our survey area in this section of the Texcoco Region. Erosion has been severe over most of the site area. Soil cover is generally shallow, with large stretches of bare tepetate.

Modern utilization: Predominately grazing, with some cultivated maguey and scattered fields of maize in the southwest corner of the site where soil cover tends to be somewhat deeper.

Archaeological remains: Variable very light, light, light-to-moderate, and moderate concentrations of surface pottery cover an area of about 65 hectares. Both Early and Late Aztec pottery are present, with Late predominate. A total of 28 structures can be delineated (Appendix II; Fig. 23), most of which appear to be domestic residential units. A least one possible small ceremonial-civic structure was noted near the western end of the site area (tlatel 514). Surface pottery is largely restricted to the mounds, and intervening spaces contain only very light or light sherd concentrations. Late Formative pottery occurs in the southwest section of the Aztec site (Tx-LF-8), and some Terminal Formative material is present in the north (Tx-TF-12). Traces of Late Toltec pottery occur in some parts of the site, never in sufficient quantity to warrant a site designation.

Classification: Large dispersed village; 325 to 650 people. There may be substantial Aztec occupation immediately south of our survey limit.

Tx-A-39

Natural setting: 2340 to 2350 m, in the Lower

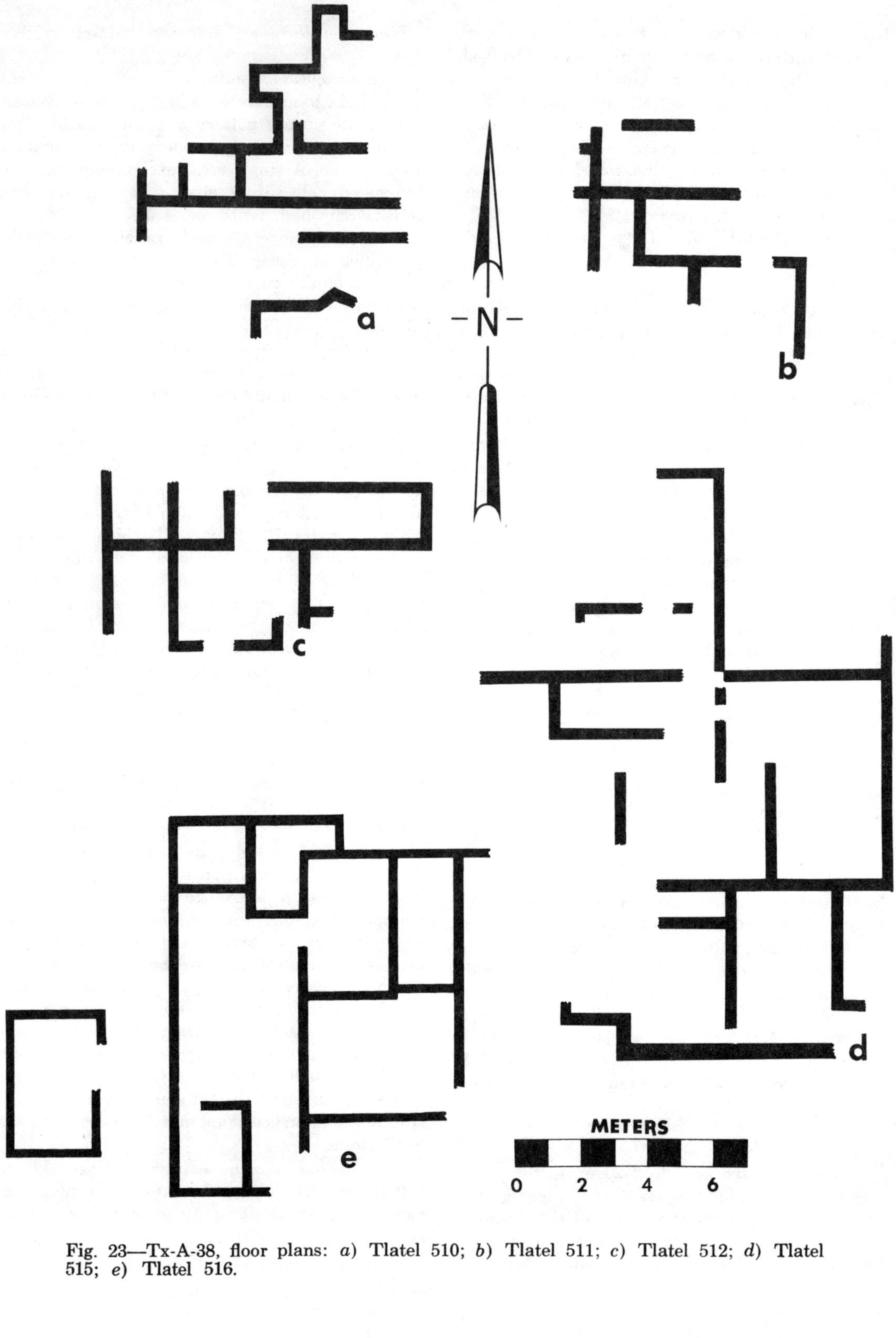

Fig. 23—Tx-A-38, floor plans: *a*) Tlatel 510; *b*) Tlatel 511; *c*) Tlatel 512; *d*) Tlatel 515; *e*) Tlatel 516.

Piedmont. Situated on gently sloping ground above the level of the main piedmont plain, in a zone of severe erosion. Scanty soil cover, with large stretches of badly scarred bare tepetate.

Modern utilization: Wasteland, at the southeast edge of the modern town of Tepetlaoxtoc.

Archaeological remains: Variable very light, light, light-to-moderate, and moderate concentrations of surface pottery over an area of about 10 hectares. Both Early and Late Aztec sherds are present, with Late predominate. A total of 15 mounds can be delineated, all of which appear to be remnants of domestic residential structures (Appendix II; Fig. 22). Surface pottery is largely restricted to the mounds themselves, with only very light and light sherd concentrations in intervening areas. Some Early Toltec material is also present (Tx-ET-12).

Classification: Small dispersed village; 75 to 150 people.

Tx-A-40

Natural setting: 2290 to 2340 m, in the Lower Piedmont. Situated on gently sloping to relatively level ground in the broad saddle between two low hills. The Papalotla River bisects the site area. Erosion has been moderate. Soil cover varies from shallow on the hillslopes to moderately deep in the saddle along the river banks.

Modern utilization: Intensive rainfall cultivation.

Archaeological remains: The southern limit of the Aztec occupation of this area was not defined. It extends well beyond the arbitrary southern limit of our survey area here. Within the surveyed area we noted variable very light, light, light-to-moderate, and moderate concentrations of surface pottery over an area of about 100 hectares. Some 18 definite mounds can be defined (Appendix II) and the former existence of several more is indicated by amorphous concentrations of surface pottery and rock rubble. Both Early and Late Aztec ceramics are present, with Late somewhat predominate. Most of the distinct mounds seem to represent domestic residential units, but some ceramic-civic architecture is apparent. Tlateles 369-73 form a small pyramid-plaza complex at the eastern end of the site. (Pl. 37,*a*). A very large pyramidal structure is located at the southwestern edge of the site (tlatel 103, locally known as El Gavilan [Piña Chan 1956-57]). Another large pyramid is found in the south-central site area, near the edge of the Río Papalotla (tlatel 378). Nine m south of this latter pyramid is a circular stone-lined basin, about 11 m in diameter and 3 m deep. Extending south from this basin is the vague outline of a rubble-choked canal, about 6 m wide and 3 m deep, which runs in a straight line for about 40 m to a point where it joins the Río Papalotla at about 1 m above the present river level. The age of construction and use of this basin-canal feature is not clear.

Substantial Early and Late Toltec pottery is also found over parts of the site area (Tx-ET-13; Tx-LT-26; Tx-LT-28).

Classification: Large dispersed village; 1000 to 1500 people. It is obvious that substantial Aztec occupation extends well beyond our southern survey limit.

Tx-A-41

Natural setting: 2290 m, in the Lower Piedmont. Situated on relatively level ground, at the edge of the Río Papalotla. Soil cover is moderately deep. Moderate erosion along the river's edge.

Modern utilization: River banks are used for grazing only. Adjacent fields are intensively cultivated in subsistence crops (rainfall agriculture).

Archaeological remains: Variable light, light-to-moderate, and moderate concentrations of surface pottery over an area of about three hectares. Both Early and Late Aztec sherds are present in roughly equal proportions. No structural remains. Substantial Late Toltec material also is present (Tx-LT-24).

Classification: Hamlet; fewer than 50 people.

Tx-A-42

Natural setting: Below 2240 m, on the Lakeshore Plain, well within the borders of Conquest-period Lake Texcoco. Situated in an area of small dunes which rise about 2 m above the general level of the old lake bed. In a zone of deep alluvial soil.

Modern utilization: Wasteland. The salt content of the soil and poor drainage of the area prohibit effective cultivation. The region is even unfit for grazing, as vegetation of any kind is lacking.

Archaeological remains: Light concentrations of surface pottery, including a number of whole vessels, scattered over an area of roughly two hectares. The pottery occurs within a slightly elevated, localized cluster of small sand dunes, and is generally found in the low intervening areas between the individual dunes or on the immediately adjacent lake bed. No structural remains. All diagnostic pottery is Late Aztec, but many sherds are badly corroded and salt incrusted.

Classification: Questionable. It is doubtful that these sherds represent a permanent residence of any kind. Most probably we are dealing with a temporary marsh camp for hunting water fowl and/or gathering lake vegetation and insect larvae.

Tx-A-43

Natural setting: Below 2240 m, on the Lakeshore Plain, well within the borders of Conquest-period Lake Texcoco. Situated in an area of small dunes which rise about 2 m above the general level of the old lake bed. In a zone of deep alluvial soil.

Modern utilization: Wasteland. The salt content of the soil and poor drainage of the area prohibit effective cultivation. The region is even unfit for grazing, as vegetation of any kind is lacking.

Archaeological remains: Variable light and light-to-moderate concentrations of badly corroded and salt-incrusted surface pottery, including several whole vessels, over an area of about three hectares. The pottery occurs within a slightly elevated, localized cluster of small dunes, and is generally found in the low intervening areas between the dunes or on the immediately adjacent lake bed. (Pl. 40,*a*). No structural remains. Mixed with a few sherds of Early and Late Toltec material (Tx-ET-16; Tx-LT-37).

Extending north-northwest for about 1650 meters from the north edge of the elevated dunes is a rather curious linear feature. This is a distinct strip of light soil, sometimes elevated a few cm above the main level of the lake bed, and sometimes running even with the ground surface, which measures slightly over 1 m wide along its entire length. A few Aztec sherds are scattered along its surface. At roughly 1370 m north of the Tx-A-43 site area, this "causeway" turns sharply eastward for another 280 m, at which point it intersects with a similar, wider "causeway." This latter feature measures 6 m wide, and can easily be traced for about 600 m north and 220 m south of its intersection point with the first "causeway." Scattered Late Aztec sherds also occur along this second "causeway."

Another possible interpretation of these linear features is that they are the remains of wiers, or dikes, similar to those illustrated on a map of the Valley of Mexico dating to the middle 16th century (Fig. 13 [Linne, 1948]). On this map, these wiers, or dikes, appear as long rows of stakes, between which was placed a tightly woven or closely packed mass of reedy or bushy vegetation. Particularly significant is the fact that these linear features divide Lake Texcoco into two segments: (1) an eastern segment, full of reedy lacustrine vegetation, and colored bluish-green; and (2) a western segment, lacking such vegetation, colored solid blue. The activities depicted within each segment are similar, except that waterfowl are being netted in large stationary traps in the eastern segment, but are being speared from canoes to the west.

Classification: Questionable. We are probably dealing with a marsh camp, occupied intermittently by persons engaged in the hunting and gathering of lacustrine resources.

Tx-A-44

Natural setting: Below 2240 m, on the Lakeshore Plain. Situated in a zone of deep alluvial soil, in the general vicinity of the Conquest-period shoreline of Lake Texcoco. The ground surface is irregular, with many small grass-covered hillocks and intervening depressions.

Modern utilization: Grazing. The salt content of the soil is apparently too high for effective cultivation. Only sharp, tough grass grows here today.

Archaeological remains: Variable light and light-to-moderate concentrations of surface pottery over an area of about two hectares. All sherds are badly corroded and salt incrusted. Both Early and Late Aztec material are present, and there are a few sherds of Texcoco Fabric Marked pottery. No structural remains. Mixed with light Late Formative (Tx-LF-14), light Terminal Formative (Tx-TF-29), and light-to-moderate Late Toltec (Tx-LT-36) pottery.

Classification: Hamlet; fewer than 50 people. The low frequency of Texcoco Fabric Marked pottery suggests that salt-making was not a significant activity at this locality.

Tx-A-45

Natural setting: Below 2240 m, on the Lakeshore Plain. Situated in a level zone of deep alluvial soil, 500 m south of a large canalized barranca. Located at or near the Conquest-period shoreline of Lake Texcoco.

Modern utilization: Intensive rainfall cultivation.

Archaeological remains: Variable light and light-to-moderate concentrations of surface pottery over an area of about five hectares. No definite structural remains are present, but several vague mounded areas suggest the presence of buried constructions. Mixed with substantial Late Toltec material (Tx-LT-35).

Classification: Hamlet; fewer than 50 people.

Tx-A-46

Natural setting: 2240 m, on the Lakeshore Plain. Situated in a level zone of deep alluvial soil, 500 m south of a large canalized barranca. Located at or near the Conquest-period shoreline of Lake Texcoco.

Modern utilization: Intensive cultivation of maize and alfalfa. Both rainfall agriculture and mechanized irrigation are practiced.

Archaeological remains: Variable light and light-to-moderate concentrations of surface pottery over an area of about 20 hectares. No definite structural remains are present, but several vague mounded areas suggest the presence of buried architecture. Mixed with some Late Toltec material ((Tx-LT-34).

Classification: Small dispersed village; 100 to 200 people.

Tx-A-47

Natural setting: 2240 m, on the Lakeshore Plain, at or near the Conquest-period shoreline of Lake Texcoco. Situated in a level zone of deep alluvial soil. A large canalized barranca runs east-west several hundred meters to the south. A nearby well indicates that the water table at this point is about 2 m below the ground surface.

Modern utilization: Most of the immediate site area is grazing land, but the immediately adjacent fields to the east are cultivated in maize and alfalfa (the latter cultivated by means of mechanized irrigation).

Archaeological remains: Light-to-moderate concentrations of salt-incrusted surface pottery over an area of about five hectares. There are no definite structural remains, but one or two vague mounded areas suggest the presence of buried construction. Mixed with substantial Late Toltec material (Tx-LT-32). Aztec pottery appears to be wholly or predominately Late. Only a few sherds of Texcoco Fabric Marked pottery are present.

Classification: Hamlet; fewer than 100 people. The low frequency of Texcoco Fabric Marked pottery suggests that this was not a salt-making locality.

Tx-A-48

Natural setting: 2250 m, on the Lakeshore Plain, near the Conquest-period shoreline of Lake Texcoco. In a zone of deep alluvial soil.

Modern utilization: Mixed rainfall cultivation of subsistence crops and mechanized irrigation of commercial alfalfa. This region has recently been reclaimed for agriculture through large-scale flushing and drainage projects.

Archaeological remains: Light-to-moderate concentrations of salt-incrusted surface pottery over an area about 30 m in diameter. No structural remains. There are only a few sherds of Texcoco Fabric Marked pottery.

Classification: Hamlet; probably a single household unit of 10 to 15 people. The low proportion of Texcoco Fabric Marked pottery suggests that this was not a salt-making locality.

Tx-A-49

Natural setting: 2250 m, on the Lakeshore Plain. Situated at or near the Conquest-period shoreline of Lake Texcoco in a zone of deep alluvial soil. Several shallow wells in the area contain water at depth of about 2 m. The site area is some 700 m north of a large canalized barranca.

Modern utilization: Intensive rainfall cultivation. The eastern edge of the site area is partially covered with modern residential structures belonging to an outlying barrio of Texcoco.

Archaeological remains: Variable light, light-to-moderate, and moderate concentrations of surface pottery over an area of roughly 25 hectares. The heaviest sherd densities occur on and around four distinct mounds (Appendix II) scattered over the site area. One of these (tlatel 1) is clearly a ceremonial-civic structure; the function of the others is not clear. All diagnostic pottery is Late Aztec. A substantial amount of Texcoco Fabric Marked pottery occurs throughout the site area.

Classification: Small dispersed village; 150 to 300 people. May represent a detached barrio of Aztec Texcoco (Tx-A-56), with a specialization in salt production and possibly other types of lacustrine exploitations.

Tx-A-50

Natural setting: 2240 m, on the Lakeshore Plain, near the Conquest-period shoreline of Lake Texcoco. Situated in a zone of deep alluvial soil just north of a large canalized barranca.

Modern utilization: Intensive cultivation of maize and alfalfa. The latter crop is mechanically irrigated.

Archaeological remains: Variable light and light-to-moderate concentrations of surface pottery over an area of about three hectares. Texcoco Fabric Marked sherds are highly predominate. No structural remains.

Classification: Hamlet; fewer than 50 people. May represent a salt-making locality, with perhaps only seasonal or intermittent occupation.

Tx-A-51

Natural setting: 2240 m, on the Lakeshore Plain, near the Conquest-period shoreline of Lake Texcoco. Situated in a zone of deep alluvial soil.

Modern utilization: The site is located in a vacant lot at the northwest corner of the Colonia Netzahualcoyotl, a recently established nucleated village. Fields to the north and west are intensively cultivated in maize and alfalfa (both rainfall agriculture and mechanized irrigation). Large quantities of soil have been removed from the immediate site area for the manufacture of adobe bricks.

Archaeological remains: The site consists of a single large mound measuring about 50 m in diameter and 2 m high (Pl. 5,*b*). Moderate concentrations of Late Aztec pottery occur over its surface, throughout its interior, and around its base. The ceramic assemblage is heavily dominated by Texcoco Fabric Marked pottery. Extensive pitting throughout the mound has revealed no traces of walls, floors, or any type of internal construction.

Classification: Hamlet; fewer than 50 people. Probably a salt-making locality, with intermittent or seasonal occupation by a few household units.

Tx-A-52

Natural setting: 2240 m, on the Lakeshore Plain, at or near the shoreline of Conquest-period Lake Texcoco. In a zone of deep alluvial soil, about 250 m south of a large canalized barranca.

Modern utilization: Intensive cultivation, predominately rainfall agriculture, with some mechanized irrigation of alfalfa and truck crops. The western edge of the modern village of San Bernardino lies about 150 m to the east. There are a few modern residential units scattered over the site area.

Archaeological remains: Variable light and light-to-moderate concentrations of surface pottery over an area of about three hectares. There are no structural remains, apart from a distinct mound on the west side of the site area. This feature measures 15 by 10 m in area, and 1.5 m high. Extensive pitting at one end has revealed a stucco floor overlying rock rubble fill near the base of the mound. The moderate concentrations of surface pottery over and around the mound are predominately Early Aztec, though Late Aztec material predominates throughout the rest of the site area. There is little or no Texcoco Fabric Marked pottery.

Classification: Hamlet; fewer than 50 people. The lack of Texcoco Fabric Marked pottery indicates that this was not a salt-making locality.

Tx-A-53

Natural setting: 2245 m, on the Lakeshore Plain, at or near the shoreline of Conquest-period Lake Texcoco. In a zone of deep alluvial soil.

Modern utilization: Intensive cultivation, both rainfall agriculture and mechanized irrigation. Only the surfaces of the larger mounds remain uncultivated. However, the area has only recently been reclaimed for agriculture by means of large-scale flushing and drainage projects to remove the soil's high salt content. The modern village of San Bernardino borders the site on the east. A considerable amount of soil has recently been removed from the site area for the manufacture of adobe bricks.

Archaeological remains: Variable light, light-to-moderate, moderate, and moderate-to-heavy concentrations of surface pottery (both Early and Late Aztec in about equal proportions) over an area of about 25 hectares. Sherd densities are highest on and around six distinct mounds distributed fairly evenly over the site area (Appendix II). Several pits in unmounded areas show layers of sherd refuse at depths of up to 1 m below the present ground surface. Despite considerable pitting, none of the mounds reveal traces of internal architecture. Texcoco Fabric Marked pottery is scarce throughout the site.

Classification: Small dispersed village; 250 to 500 people. The near absence of Texcoco Fabric Marked pottery indicates that this was not a salt-making locality.

Tx-A-54

Natural setting: 2250 m, on the Lakeshore Plain. In a zone of deep alluvial soil, about 240 m north of a large canalized barranca.

Modern utilization: The site area is situated on the grounds of the Chapingo Agricultural College, in an area devoted to experimental plots of wheat, barley, and maize.

Archaeological remains: Variable light and light-to-moderate concentrations of surface pottery over an area of about five hectares. No structural remains.

Classification: Hamlet; fewer than 50 people.

Tx-A-55

Natural setting: 2245 m, on the Lakeshore

Plain. In a zone of deep alluvial soil, about 500 m south of a large canalized barranca.

Modern utilization: Intensive cultivation, both rainfall agriculture and mechanized irrigation. A small isolated modern household is located at the south edge of the site.

Archaeological remains: Light-to-moderate concentrations of surface pottery over an area of less than one hectare. No structural remains. The site area has been partly cut through by a large drainage ditch which has thrown up additional sherd material. No Texcoco Fabric Marked pottery was noted.

Classification: A single household unit of 10 to 15 people. The lack of Texcoco Fabric Marked pottery indicates that this was not a salt-making locality.

Tx-A-56 (Aztec Texcoco)

Natural setting: 2250 to 2300 m, at the juncture of the flat Lakeshore Plain and the gently sloping Lower Piedmont. Except for the eastern edge, the site area is covered with deep alluvial soil. Erosion has been absent or very slight. A large canalized barranca runs through the southern edge of the site area.

Modern utilization: The urban complex of modern Texcoco covers much of the site area. The surrounding unoccupied fields are intensively cultivated, predominately in commercial alfalfa and maize by means of mechanized irrigation. A number of commercial dairy and poultry farms cluster around the edges of the modern town. Only to the southeast of the site area do subsistence crops predominate.

Documentary descriptions: According to Pomar (1941: 51): "El asiento de esta ciudad [Texcoco] y población de la mayor y más principal parte de ella es en un llano descubierto que se hace entre la laguna y la serranía y montaña grande de Tlaloc. . . ."

Both Pomar (ibid: 7) and Alva Ixtlilxochitl (1965*a*: 235) speak of six major wards or *barrios* in Texcoco during the rule of Netzahualcoyotl in the mid 15th century: Mexicayan, Colhuacan, Tluiznahuac, Tepan, Tlaylotacan, and Chimalpan. The population within each ward was responsible for the care of the principal ceremonial structures located within its territory.

Alva de Ixtlilxochitl (1965*b*: 173-86) has provided a detailed description of the main ceremonial-civic complex at Texcoco in the time of Netzahualcoyotl (*ca.* mid 15th century), together with a discussion of some of the functions and uses of these structures:

Tenían las casas de longitud que corrían de Oriente a Poniente, cuatrocientas y once medidas y media, que reducidas á nuestra medida, hacen mil doscientas treinta y cuarto varas y media, y de latitud que es de Norte á Sur, trescientas veintiseis medidas que hacen novecientas y setenta y ocho varas: por la cuadra que caía hacia la parte del Sur y Oriente era la cerca de una pared muy fuerte de adobes, y cimiento era de muy fuerte argamasa, que tenía de grueso dos varas, y de alto tres estados; y por la parte del Poniente (que era hacia la laguna) y la de Norte, estaba cercada de una muralla muy fuerte, que tenía cinco estados de alto, y esta muralla hasta el tercio de la altura iba disminuída á manera de estribo, y los dos tercios de allí para arriba á plomo cuadrada: en medio de toda esta cuadra estaban los cuartos de la vivienda del rey, las salas de los consejos, y los demás cumplimientos que se irán describiendo: tenían estas casas, para lo que era la vivienda y asistencia del rey dos patios principales, que el uno y más grande era el que servía de plaza y mercado, y aun el día de hoy lo es de la ciudad de Tetzcuco; y el otro, que era más interior (en donde estaban las salas de los consejos), tenía por la parte del Oriente la sala del consejo real, en la cual tenía el rey dos tribunales, y en medio de ella estaba un fogón grande, en donde de ordinario estaba el fuego sin que jamás se acabase; y por el lado derecho del fogón, estaba un tribunal, que era el supremo, á quien llamaban Teoicpalpan que es lo mismo que decir asiento y tribunal de Dios, demás de estar más alto y encumbrado que el otro, la silla y espalda era de oro engastado en piedras turquescas y otras piedras preciosas, delante de la cual estaba uno como á manera de sitial, y en él una rodela y macana y un arco con su aljaba y flechas, y encima de todo una calavera y sobre ella una esmeralda piramidal, en donde estaba incado un plumaje ó plumero que se llama Tecpilotl, que atrás queda referido, y unos montones de piedras preciosas; á los lados servían de alfombra unas pieles de tigres y leones y mantas hechas de plumas de águila real, en donde asimismo estaban por su orden cantidad de brazaletes y grebas de oro. Las paredes estaban entapizadas y adornadas de unos paños hechos de pelo de conejo, de todos colores, con figuras de diversas aves, animales y flores: tras de la silla estaba puesto de plumería rica uno á manera de dosel, y en medio de unos resplandores y rayos hechos de oro y pedrería. El otro tribunal que llamaban del rey, tenía su silla y asiento más llano, y asimismo otro dosel hecho de plumería con las insignias de escudo de armas que solían usar los reyes de Tetzcuco; en este tribunal de ordinario asistían los reyes, en donde hacían sus despachos y audiencias públicas; y cuando determinaban las causas graves y de entidad ó confirmaban algunas sentencias de muerte, se pasaban al tribunal que llamaban de Dios, poniendo la mano derecha sobre la calavera, y en la izquierda una flecha de oro que les servía de cetro, y entonces se ponían la tiara que usaban, que era como media mitra; asimismo estaban tres de estas tiaras en el sitial referido, la una era de pedrería engastada en oro, la otra de plumería, y la tercera tejida de algodón y pelo de conejo de color azul. En esta sala asistían los catorce grandes del reino por su orden y antigüedades; la cual salía hacía tres divisiones. La primera era donde estaba el rey. La segunda, en donde estaban seis de los grandes en sus asientos y estrados: el primero de la mano derecha era el señor de Teotihuacan, el segundo el de Acolman, el tercero el de Tepetlaoztoc; y por el lado izquierdo estaban, el primero el señor de Huexutla, el segundo el de Coatlichan, el tercero el de Chimalhuacan. La tercera división (que era la más exterior) estaban otros ocho señores por su orden y antigüedades: por el lado derecho, el primero era el señor de Otompan, el segundo el de Tolantzinco, el tercero el de Quauhchinanco, el cuarto el de Xicotepec; y por el lado izquierdo, el primero el de Tepechpan, el segundo el de Teyoyocan, el tercero el de Chicunauhtla y el cuarto el de Chiauhtla. Asimismo se seguía otra sala que estaba en par de ésta por la parte de Oriente, que se dividía en dos partes: en la una, que caía por la parte interior, había en lo más principal y en los primeros puestos ocho jueces, que eran nobles y caballeros; y los otros cuatro eran de los ciudadanos, y después de ellos se seguían otros quince jueces provincianos, que eran naturales de todas las ciudades y pueblos principales del reino de Tetzcuco, los cuales oían todos los pleitos así civiles como criminales. . . . En la otra parte de la sala, que caía á la parte exterior, estaba un tribunal en donde estaban cuatro jueces supremos, que eran los cuatro presidentes supremos de los consejos, y un postigo por donde entraban y salían á comunicar con el rey. Por la parte del Norte de este patio se seguía otra sala muy grande, que llamaban de ciencia y música, en donde estaban tres tribunales supremos: en el uno, que caía frontero del patio estaba el tribunal y asiento del rey de Tetzcuco; y por un lado á mano derecha estaba el otro tribunal, que era del rey de Mexico; y por el lado izquierdo estaba el del rey de Tlacopan: en donde estaban muchas insignias, como eran muchas rodelas, borlas, penachos y otras insignias de plumería rica, y cargas de mantas de mucho precio, y muchas joyas de oro y pedrería, en los cuales se sentaban y asistían los reyes cuando se juntaban. Allí en medio tenían un instrumento musical que llaman huehuetl, en donde de ordinario estaban y asistían los filósofos, poetas y algunos de los más famosos capitanes del reino, que de ordinario estaban cantando los cantos de sus historias, cosas de moralidad y sentencias. Tras de esta sala se subía á otra que estaba sobre la muralla fuerte, en donde estaban muchos capitanes y soldados valerosos, que eran los de la guarda del rey; y luego se seguía otra casi opuesta á la sala real, en donde asistían los embajadores de los reyes de Mexico y Tlacopan: después estaba un tránsito por donde se entraba á este patio del otro grande de la plaza, y en el otro lado de él estaba otra sala grande del consejo de guerra, en donde asistian en lo más principal de ella seis capitanes naturales de la ciudad de Tetzcuco, tres nobles y tres ciudadanos, y después de ellos se seguían otros quince capitanes naturales de las ciudades y pueblos más principales del reino de Tetzcuco, á quienes se despachaban todos los negocios pertenecientes al consejo de guerra. Por la parte de Mediodía se seguían otras dos salas, en donde estaban y asistían otros tantos jueces por la orden que está dicho, del consejo de hacienda. Tras de ella se seguía la segunda sala, en donde estaba cierta dignidad de hombres, que eran como jueces pesquisidores, que salían fuera de la ciudad á las provincias y cuidades á averiguar y castigar lo que el rey les mandaba. Después de esta sala se seguía otra que era el almacén de las armas; y por la parte interior estaban los cuartos de la reina y otros de las damas, las cocinas y los retretes en donde el rey dormía, con muchos patios y laberintos, con las paredes de diversas figuras y labores. Cada una de estas salas que eran casi cuadradas, eran de largo de cincuenta varas y ancho poco menos, y otras tenían á más y á menos. Por la parte de Mediodía y por la de Oriente de las salas y cuartos referidos estaban los jardines y recreaciones del rey, con muchas fuentes de agua, estanques y acequias con mucho pescado, y aves de volatería, lo cual estaba cercado de más de dos mil sabinos, que hoy está la mayor parte de ellos en pie; y asimismo había en estos jardines otros muchos laberintos, que estaban en los baños que el rey tenía, en donde estando los hombres no daban con la salida, con muchos torreones y chapiteles adornada la casa, y el otro patio, que era el mayor y servía de plaza, en medio del cual estaba el juego de la pelota; y hacia la entrada del segundo patio estaba un brasero muy grande sobre una peana, el que siempre ardía día y noche, sin que jamás se apagase. Esta plaza cercada de portales, y tenía asimismo por la parte del Poniente otra sala grande, y muchos cuartos á la redonda, que era la universidad, en donde asistían todos los poetas, históricos y filósofos de reino, divididos en sus clases y academias conforme era la facultad de cada uno; y asimismo estaban aquí los archivos reales: por un lado de estos cuartos era una de las entradas y puertas principales del palacio. Luego se seguían otros cuartos con su patio, salas y aposentos, en donde estaban aposentados los reyes de Mexico cuando iban á Tetzcuco; y después se seguían los cuartos en donde se recogían y guardaban los tributos de la provincia de Cuauhnahuac, y luego otros de la provincia de Chalco. Todos los Estados y provincias tenían sus cargos de tributos dentro de palacio, y todos los demás los tenían fuera en casas particulares que estaban dedicadas para este efecto. Por la parte del Norte junto á donde caían los templos, . . . y por la parte de afuera de la muralla, se seguían las casas en donde se aposentaban los reyes de Tlacopan cuando iban á esta ciudad; y más adelante frontero de los templos estaba la casa de aves, en donde el rey tenía todos cuantos géneros y diversidad había de aves y animales, sierpes y culebras traídas de diversas partes de esta Nueva España, y las que no podían ser habidas estaban sus figuras hechas de pedrería y oro, y lo mismo era de los peces, y así de los que hay y se crían en el mar como en los ríos y lagunas, de tal modo, que no faltaba allí ave, pez ni animal de toda esta tierra, que no estuviese vivo ó hecho figura y talla en piedras de oro y pedrería. Finalmente contenía toda la casa del rey, entre los grandes y medianos aposentos y retretes, más de trescientas piezas, todo ello edificado con mucha arte de arquitectura; y al tiempo que se cubrían algunas de las salas, queriendo cortar las maderas y planchas por los extremos, y quitar las maromas con que las habían arrastrado, que eran de incredible grandeza, les mandó el rey que las dejasen así, que tiempo vendría en que sirviesen á otros, y no trendrían trabajo de hacerles nuevos horados, ni ponerles nuevas maromas para arrastrarlas, y así se hizo; é yo los he visto dentro de los huecos de los pilares y portales sobre que cargaba; y se cumplió su profecía, pues lo han desbaratado y aprovechádose de la madera.

Estas casas que hemos ido describiendo no tenían más de tan solamente tres puertas y entradas principales, que la una caía por la parte de hacia la laguna que es al Poniente, y la otra hacia la montaña que es hacia el Oriente, y la otra hacia el Mediodía, y eran á manera de calles que tenían diez y ocho varas de ancho: otras entradas y portadas tenía la casa, que caían donde estaban los templos, los cuales tenían unas gradas, por donde en las entradas de ellas recibían y bajaban dentro de estos palacios. Por la parte del Poniente de los templos estaban otros cuartos con su patio, sala y aposentos, que se llamaba Tlacateo, en donde criaban y doctrinaban los hijos del rey, y allí asistían con ellos sus ayos y maestros, que les enseñaban toda la policía de su buen modo de vivir, y todas las ciencias y artes que sabían y alcanzaban, hasta las mecánicas de labrar oro, pedrería y plumería, y las demás; y asimismo el ejercicio militar, con tanto cuidado que no los dejaban un punto estar ociosos. En otros, que estaban divididos de estos, se doctrinaban y criaban las hijas del rey. . . .

Los templos eran más de cuarenta; pero el principal y mayor que era Huitzilopuchtli y Tlaloc, cuadrado y maciso, hechas de cal y canto las paredes de la parte de afuera, y lo de adentro terraplenado de barro y piedra: tenía en cada cuadro ochenta brazas largas, y de alto este terraplén ó cue veintisiete estados, y se subía por la parte de Poniente por unas gradas que eran ciento y sesenta: comenzaba su edificio por el cimiento ancho, y como iba levantándose, iba disminuyendo y estrechando de todas partes en forma piramidal con sus grandes relieves, que como iba subiendo, asimismo le iban disminuyendo, y de trecho en trecho las gradas hacían un descanso, y encima estaba edificado un templo con dos capillas, la una mayor que la otra: la mayor hacia la parte del Sur en donde estaba el ídolo Huitzilopochtli; y la menor que estaba á la parte del Norte, era del ídolo Tlaloc, y estas capillas y sus ídolos miraban hacia la parte del Poniente; y por delante de este templo había un patio prolongado de Norte á Sur en donde cabían muy bien quinientos hombres, y en medio de las puertas de las dos capillas estaba una piedra tumbada que llamaban techcatl, en donde sacrificaban los cautivos en guerra; y tenía cada una de estas capillas tres sobrados que se mandaban por la parte de adentro por unas escaleras de madera movediza, y los sobrados estaban llenos de todo género de armas, como eran macanas, rodelas, arcos, flechas, lanzas y guijarros, y todo género de bastimentos, arreos y adornos de guerra. Los demás templos casi todos eran á este talle; unos tenían dos, tres, y más capillas, y algunos que no tenían más de sólo una: había más de cuatrocientas salas y aposentos en donde estaban estos templos, para las viviendas de los sacerdotes y ministros del templo, y en donde se criaban y doctrinaban los muchachos de la ciudad, y en estos templos había uno en donde había muchas mujeres reclusas y encerradas, y asimismo se criaban algunas de las hijas de los señores y ciudadanos. Había un templo redondo que era de Quetzalcoatl, dios del aire, y asimismo un estanque que se decía Tetzapan, en donde se lavaban todos los basos de los sacrificios, y los que se sacaban sangre se iban á lavar allí. Asimismo había en un cercado cantidad de árboles y matas de todo género de espinas llamado Teotlapan, que significa tierra de dios. Tenía esta máquina de edificios más de cuarenta patios entre grandes y chicos, sin los jardines y laberintos.

Alva Ixtlilxochitl (1965*b*: 266) also reported a series of large grain storehouses to the north of the main architectural complex:

Por la parte que caía al Norte de las casas referidas y cerca de las cocinas, estaban unos graneros y trojes de admirable grandeza, en donde el rey tenía gran cantidad de maíz y otras semillas que se guardaban para los años estériles, y en cada una de ellas cabían cuatro ó cinco mil fanegas. . . .

Here, as elsewhere, we must allow for Alva Ixtlilxochitl's obvious penchant for extolling, and probably exaggerating, the glories and accomplishments of prehispanic Texcoco. The general outlines of his description, however, can probably be accepted as valid. Clearly, there was an elaborately constructed and exotically furnished ceremonial-civic complex associated with the ruling establishment of Late Aztec Texcoco. Included within this complex were a variety of elite residences, council chambers, meeting halls, warehouses, pleasure gardens, and principal religious temples.

Archaeological remains: Except for several large ceremonial-civic structures which are to be found within modern Texcoco and around its perimeter (Appendix II), there are few surface traces of this important Aztec center. The great majority of the empty fields and vacant lots around and within the borders of the modern town contain little or no Aztec surface pottery, although some vague mounds and concentrations of sherd debris are occasionally encountered. Only on the slightly higher ground to the southeast, in and around the detached *barrio* of San Diego, is surface pottery found in appreciable quantities. At least one deep pit near the center of modern Texcoco, however, shows a thick (*ca.* 30 cm) lens of Late Aztec sherd debris at a depth of 1.5 m below the present ground level, in a small cultivated field containing only light Aztec surface pottery.

With respect to the above-noted division of

Late Aztec Texcoco into six territorial wards or *barrios,* it may be significant that we identified six principal ceremonial-civic structures within the general Tx-A-56 site area: tlatel 1, which we placed in site Tx-A-49, west of the main Tx-A-56 site area; tlateles 17 (Pl. 38,*a*) and the 89-90-91 (Pl. 39,*a*) complex in the central part of Tx-A-56; tlatel 92 (Pl. 39,*b*), at the northern edge of Tx-A-56; and tlateles 18 (Pl, 38,*b*) and 65, at the eastern end of the Tx-A-56 site area. These features may represent the barrio divisions mentioned by Pomar and Alva de Ixtlilxochitl.

Most of the Aztec community is presumed to lie beneath the densely packed buildings and paved streets of the modern town. The deep alluvial soil is undoubtedly another major factor in obscuring prehispanic features: it is precisely at the relatively abrupt juncture between the Lower Piedmont and the Lakeshore Plain, where a gentle slope and flat plain meet, that the greatest alluviation would expectably occur in the severe erosion of post-Conquest times.

Our estimates of the extent and character of this important center are thus highly tentative. Assuming that all the modern town overlies the Late Aztec community, and including the areas of scattered sherd cover at the fringes of modern Texcoco, we calculate an area of roughly 450 hectares for Late Aztec Texcoco. A number of nearby sites, distinguished here under separate numbers, may represent detached barrios of the main Aztec community (e.g., Tx-A-44, -49, -50, -55, and -57).

Substantial Early Toltec material occurs at the southeast corner of the Aztec site (Tx-ET-15), and a few Late Toltec sherds are concentrated in the western sector (Tx-LT-39, -40). Apart from these localities, no obvious pre-Aztec surface pottery was found. Aztec material was very predominately Late, although Early Aztec pottery is consistently present in smaller quantities.

Classification: Primary regional center; 12,000 to 25,000 people.

Tx-A-57

Natural setting: 2330 to 2340 m, in the Lower Piedmont. Situated on gently sloping ground on both sides of a major barranca. Erosion has been moderate to severe. Soil cover is moderately deep to shallow, with some stretches of bare tepetate along the edges of the barranca.

Modern utilization: Predominately rainfall cultivation of subsistence crops. Some small-scale canal irrigation is practiced, with water derived from a large jaguey at the western edge of the site. A series of small, makeshift canals lead from the jaguey into nearby fields below the reservoir. Some areas, where erosion has been most severe, are presently used only as grazing land.

Archaeological remains: Variable very light, light, and light-to-moderate concentrations of surface pottery over an area of about 50 hectares. The pottery is predominately Late Aztec, but light Early Aztec material is consistently present. There are no distinct structural remains, but several vaguely defined mounded areas with relatively heavy concentrations of sherds and rock rubble, suggest the prior existence of domestic residential architecture. Mixed with a small amount of Early Classic material at the site's western edge (Tx-EC-15).

Classification: Small dispersed village; 200 to 400 people.

Tx-A-58

Natural setting: 2360 to 2410 m, in the Lower Piedmont. Situated on gently sloping ground along either side of a major barranca. Erosion has been severe except for the southwestern corner of the site area where moderately deep soil cover has been preserved. Throughout the rest of the site, soil is shallow to absent, and there are large stretches of bare tepetate.

Modern utilization: Predominately grazing, but with intensive rainfall cultivation in the site's southwestern corner and along its northern border at the southern edge of the modern dispersed villages of San Dieguito and Natívitas.

Archaeological remains: Variable very light, light, and light-to-moderate concentrations of surface pottery over an area of about 100 hectares. There are no distinct structural remains, but a number of discrete concentrations of heavy rock rubble and sherd debris, together with an occasional small remnant of a stone wall base, indicates the prior existence of several small residential structures. Severe erosion has greatly obscured the original aspect of the community, and much sherd and rock rubble debris now rests on bare tepetate. The ceramics are predominately Late Aztec, but small amounts of Early Aztec material are scattered throughout the site area. The Aztec occupational debris is mixed with light Late Formative (Tx-LF-12) and Terminal Formative (Tx-TF-21) material at the east end of the site area.

Classification: Small dispersed village; 250 to 500 people.

Tx-A-59

Natural setting: 2430 to 2560 m, at the juncture of the Upper and Lower Piedmont. The site occupies a zone of gently sloping ground along the top of a broad ridge lying between two major barrancas. The terrain at the eastern end of the site is somewhat steeper. The steep mass of Cerros Tetzcotzingo-Metecatl rises abruptly to the north and northwest of the site area. The entire area is severely eroded, with soil cover existing only on scattered erosional remnants.

Modern utilization: Predominately marginal grazing and wasteland. Rainfall cultivation of subsistence crops is restricted to small patches of relict soil at the tops of scattered erosional remnants. The steep slopes north of the site area have been extensively terraced in the past. All terracing is presently abandoned except for the south flank of Cerro Tetzcotzingo and the west side of Cerro Metecatl where intensive cultivation of subsistence crops is now carried out. Some of the lowermost of these terraces are partially irrigated with water brought from springs in the Sierra over several km of small canal networks. These same canals supply household water to the modern villages of San Dieguito, Natívitas, and Tequexquinahuac to the west and south of the site area. The eastern fringes of San Dieguito border the site on the west.

Archaeological remains: Variable very light, light, light-to-moderate, and moderate concentrations of surface pottery over an area of about 75 hectares. Most of the ceramic material is Late Aztec, but Early Aztec sherds are consistently present in lighter concentrations over much of the site area. Despite the severe erosion, the badly destroyed remnants of some 15 structures can be clearly recognized (Appendix II). All these are clustered within the eastern third of the site area. Amorphous concentrations of rock rubble and sherd debris indicate the prior existence of many more similar structures throughout the site. In many cases, the walls of the ancient buildings have functioned as erosion checks, and much of the scant soil cover still intact within the Aztec residential zone consists of that earth now held in place by the crumbling stone wall bases.

Sherd cover is always relatively heaviest on and immediately around the remains of former structures when these are recognizable as such. In the intervening areas between these mounds, sherds are markedly less abundant.

Substantial Terminal Formative material (Tx-TF-23) occurs throughout the western two-thirds of the site area.

Classification: Large dispersed village; 375 to 750 people.

Tx-A-60

Natural setting: 2490 to 2520 m, at the lower edge of the Upper Piedmont. Situated on gently sloping ground adjacent to a major barranca. Erosion has been moderate to severe; soil cover is generally shallow, with some patches of bare tepetate. Partial terracing of the hillslope has prevented wholesale sheet erosion of the site area.

Modern utilization: Predominately grazing, with some rainfall cultivation in the eastern sector of the site where fairly extensive terracing has maintained soil cover.

Archaeological remains: Variable very light, light, and light-to-moderate concentrations of surface pottery over an area of about 20 hectares. Late Aztec material is clearly predominate, but Early Aztec sherds occur consistently in lighter quantities. A total of five badly destroyed structures can be distinguished (Appendix II). These mounds occur scattered throughout the site area, and all seem to represent small domestic residential units.

Classification: Small dispersed village; 100 to 200 people.

Tx-A-61

Natural setting: 2570 to 2580 m. The site occupies the broad, level top of Cerro Metecatl, extending slightly downslope to the north along a narrow saddle leading to Cerro Cocotl. Steep slopes surround the site on the south, west, and north. Eastward, the broken surface of the severely eroded Upper Piedmont rises gradually from its juncture with Cerro Metecatl some 25 m below the site. Erosion has been moderate in the site area. A series of ancient stone walls have checked runoff to some extent, and a shallow soil cover is present over most of the site.

Modern utilization: Grazing, plus a few cultivated maguey. Some rainfall cultivation in a series of small fields downslope from the site on the east.

Archaeological remains: The site comprises two distinct subunits within an area of about five hectares: (1) A higher section focusing around a large rock rubble structure on the top of Cerro Metecatl; and (2) a walled compound containing a small pyramidal mound at one edge of a level plaza on the narrow saddle between Cerro Metecatl and Cerro Cocotl. The intervening area between these two units is devoid of structures and surface pottery.

The higher complex is dominated by a stone-walled enclosure, 40 by 36 m in size. Only the wall base, measuring roughly 2.5 m thick and up to 25 cm high, is now preserved. The enclosed area is empty, but slightly mounded to a maximum elevation of about 50 cm. Large amorphous quantities of loosely piled rock occur on the north, south, and east sides of the enclosure. These may represent collapsed walls, or merely attempts to clear the rocky hilltop for cultivation or pasture in relatively recent times. Surface pottery is very light on and around this structure. All diagnostic pottery is Late Aztec.

Traces of another large wall, about 3 m wide, extends due east from the midpoint of the main walled enclosure for a distance of about 50 m downslope where it makes a right angle bend and continues south for roughly 100 m.

Another possible structure within this first complex is located some 100 m north of the main walled enclosure. This feature is a mound of loosely piled rock rubble standing about 1.5 m high and measuring 15 m in diameter. Light surface pottery—all of which appears to be Late Aztec—occurs on and around this mound.

The second subunit of Tx-A-61 lies about 350 m north-northeast of the main walled enclosure described above. Here we find traces of a low wall enclosing an area of 200 by 100 m. This enclosing wall measures about 50 to 75 cm wide, and is generally preserved only to heights of 25 to 50 cm, except along the northern side where it is 2 m tall along the top edge of a steep cliff face. Near the center of the north wall is a distinct mound, about 20 m in diameter and 2 m high. A large pit in the mound's center indicates that it is a solid platform of rock rubble and earth construction throughout. This structure rests atop a low basal platform about 60 m in diameter and 50 cm high. Immediately west of this mound is a large, relatively flat area (70 by 30 m in size) which appears to have been artificially levelled with rock and earth fill. Surface pottery is very light over the mound itself, but occurs in light-to-moderate concentrations over the "plaza" area just west of the structure. Late Aztec pottery predominates, but light Late Toltec (Tx-LT-44) and Terminal Formative (Tx-TF-22) material is also present.

Just east of the main mound is a large outcrop of the tough volcanic lava which forms the hill. Here are found several intriguing stone sculptures which are apparently models of temples, carved into blocks and boulders of rock, each complete with steep stairway and indications of construction atop the main platform (Pl. 46,*b*). Cook de Leonard (1955) has illustrated one of these same models, and others from different sites in central Meixco.

Classification: Hilltop ceremonial precinct; with little or no permanent occupation.

Tx-A-62 (Tetzcotzingo)

Natural setting: 2560 to 2620 m, on the steep upper slopes and along the gently sloping top of Cerro Tetzcotzingo, about 60 to 100 m above the level of the Lower Piedmont plain to the north, west, and south. The ground surface is irregular, with abundant outcrops of bedrock. Erosion has been slight to moderate. Soil cover is generally shallow.

Modern utilization: The immediate site area now serves only for grazing, plus a few cultivated maguey. The lower hillslopes to the north, west, and south are intricately terraced and intensively cultivated. Some of the lower of these terraces are partially irrigated with water derived from springs in the Sierra, carried over several km of small canal networks. The modern village of San Nicolás Tlaminca occupies the lowermost slopes of Cerro Tetzcotzingo to the north of the site area.

Documentary descriptions: Alva de Ixtlilxochitl (1965*b*: 210-12) has described the Tetzcotzingo complex and its use in Late Aztec times:

> De los jardines, el más ameno y de curiosidades fué el bosque de Tetzcotzinco, porque demás de la cerca que tenía tan grande para subir á la cumbre de él y andarlo todo, tenía sus gradas, parte de ellas hecha de argamasa, parte labrada en la misma peña; y el agua que se traía para las fuentes, pilas, baños y caños que se repartían para el riego de las flores y arboledas de este bosque, para poderla traer desde su nacimiento, fué menester hacer fuertes y altísimas murallas de argamasa desde unas sierras á otras, de increíble grandeza, sobre la cual hizo una tarjea hasta venir á dar en lo más alto del bosque; y á las espaldas de la cumbre de él, en el primer estanque de agua, estaba una peña, esculpida en ella en circunferencia los años desde que había nacido el rey Nezahualcoyotzin hasta la edad de aquel tiempo, y por la parte de afuera los años, en fin de cada uno de ellos asimismo esculpidas las cosas más memorables que hizo; y por dentro de la rueda esculpidas sus armas que eran una casa que estaba ardiendo en llamas y deshaciéndose; otra que estaba muy ennoblecida de edificios, y en medio de las dos un pie de venado, estaba en él una piedra preciosa, y salían del pie unos penachos de plumas preciosas; y asimismo una cueva, y en ella un brazo asido de un arco con unas flechas, y como un hombre armado con su morrión y orejeras, cozelete, y dos tigres á los lados de cuya boca salían agua y fuego, y por orla doce cabezas de reyes y señores, y otras cosas que el primer arzobispo de Mexico D. Fr. Juan de Zumárraga mandó hacer pedazos, entendiendo ser algunos ídolos, y todo lo referido era la etimilogía de sus armas: y de allí se repartía esta agua en dos partes, que la una iba cercando y rodeando el bosque por la parte del Norte, y la otra por la del Sur [this

complex is very likely our Area D, described below]. En la cumbre de este bosque estaban edificadas unas casas á manera de torre, y por remate y chapitel estaba hecha de cantería una como á manera de maceta, y dentro de ella salían unos penachos de plumería, que era la etimología del nombre del bosque; y luego más abajo hecho de una peña un león de más de dos brazas de largo con sus alas y plumas: estaba echado y mirando á la parte del Oriente, en cuya boca asomaba un rostro que era el mismo retrato del rey, el cual león estaba de ordinario debajo de un palio hecho de oro y plumería; un poquito más abajo estaban tres albercas de agua, y en la del medio estaban en sus bordos tres ramas esculpidas y labradas en la misma peña, que significaban la gran laguna, y las ramas las cabezas del imperio; y por un lado (que era hacia la parte del Norte) otra alberca, y en una peña esculpido el nombre y escudo de armas de la ciudad de Tolan, que fué cabecera del imperio de los tultecas [this may be our Area H, described below]; y por el lado iquierdo que caía hacia la parte del Sur estaba la otra alberca, y en la peña esculpido el escudo de armas y nombre de la ciudad de Tenayocan que fué la cabecera del imperio de los chichimecas, y de esta alberca salía un caño de agua que saltando sobre de unas peñas salpicaba de agua, que iba á caer en un jardín de todas flores olorosas de tierra caliente, que parecía que llovía con la precipitación y golpe que daba el agua sobre la peña. Tras de este jardin se seguían los baños hechos y labrados de peña viva, que con dividirse en dos baños eran de una pieza; y por aqui se bajaba asimismo por una peña grandísima de unas gradas hechas de la misma peña, tan bien labradas y lisas que parecían espejos, y por el pretil de estas gradas estaba esculpido el día, mes, año y hora en que se le dió aviso al rey Nezahualcoyotzin de la muerte de un señor de Huexotzinco á quien quiso y amó notablemente, y el cogió esta nueva cuando se estaban haciendo estas gradas: luego consecutivamente estaban el alcázar y palacios que el rey tenía en el bosque, en los cuales había entre otras muchas salas, aposentos y retretes, una muy grandísima, y delante de ella un patio, en la cual recibía á los reyes de Mexico y Tlacopan, y á otros grandes señores cuando se iban á hogar con él, y en el patio se hacían las danzas y algunas representaciones de gusto y entretenimientos [this complex may be our Area C, described below]. Estaban estos alcázares con tan admirable y maravillosa hechura, y con tanta diversidad de piedras, que no parecían ser hechos de industria humana: el aposento en donde el rey dormía, era redondo: todo lo demás de este bosque, como dicha tengo, estaba plantado de diversidad de árboles y flores odoríferas; y en ellos diversidad de aves, sin las que el rey tenía en jaulas traídas de diversas partes, que hacían una armonía y canto que no se oían las gentes; fuera de las florestas, que las dividía una pared, entraba la montaña en que había muchos venados, conejos y liebres . . . .

This description brings out two principal features of the Cerro Tetzcotzingo complex: (1) the hydraulic works bringing water from the Sierra were intended largely, or wholly, for the benefit of the exotic vegetation of Netzahualcoyotl's rural retreat; and (2) there was little or no Aztec occupation of the site area apart from the Texcocan ruler's personal apartments and a series of associated baths, patios, stairways, and waterworks.

Archaeological remains: Figure 24 presents a general sketch plan of the archaeological complex. The total surface area is roughly 15 hectares, but Aztec surface pottery is present only in very light concentrations, suggesting a lack of permanent residence anywhere on the site area.

Clear traces of an ancient canal can be traced for several km from far back in the Upper Piedmont, around the upper southern and western flanks of Cerro Metecatl, to a stone-lined reservoir just above the east end of Cerro Tetzcotzingo (Pl. 41). From this point the canal leads directly into the Tx-A-62 complex passing over a causeway (Tyler's Causeway, Wolf and Palerm, 1955) built up some 7.5 m above the level of the saddle connecting Cerro Metecatl and Cerro Tetzcotzingo (Pl. 42,*a*). This causeway is about 160 m long, and measures about 2.5 m across at the top and roughly 10 m wide at the base. A large pit in its upper surface indicates solid rock-rubble construction. Traces of a small, stuccoed canal (15 cm wide) can still be seen running along the top. The causeway has smooth, sloping walls, with no indications of any subsidiary canals running at lower levels along its sides.

At the west end of the causeway the canal extends for some 500 m around the south side of Cerro Tetzcotzingo on the upper surface of a level, artificial roadway, some 2 to 3 m wide, which has been built onto (and sometimes, cut into) the steep slope of the hillside. For most of this distance the stuccoed interior base and lower walls of the canal are clearly visible. (Pl. 42,*b;* 43,*a*). A number of secondary canals, at nearly right angles to the main water flow, once diverted water onto the steep hill flanks below the roadway (Pl. 42,*b*).

A series of archaeological features appear along the roadway upon which the canal rests. These will be described in order, from east to west. Following this, we will proceed to the north side and top of the hill.

Area D.

At the west end of Tyler's Causeway an area of 8 by 10 m has been carved into the steep rocky hill slope (Pl. 45,*a*). The front (eastern) section has been built up somewhat with low

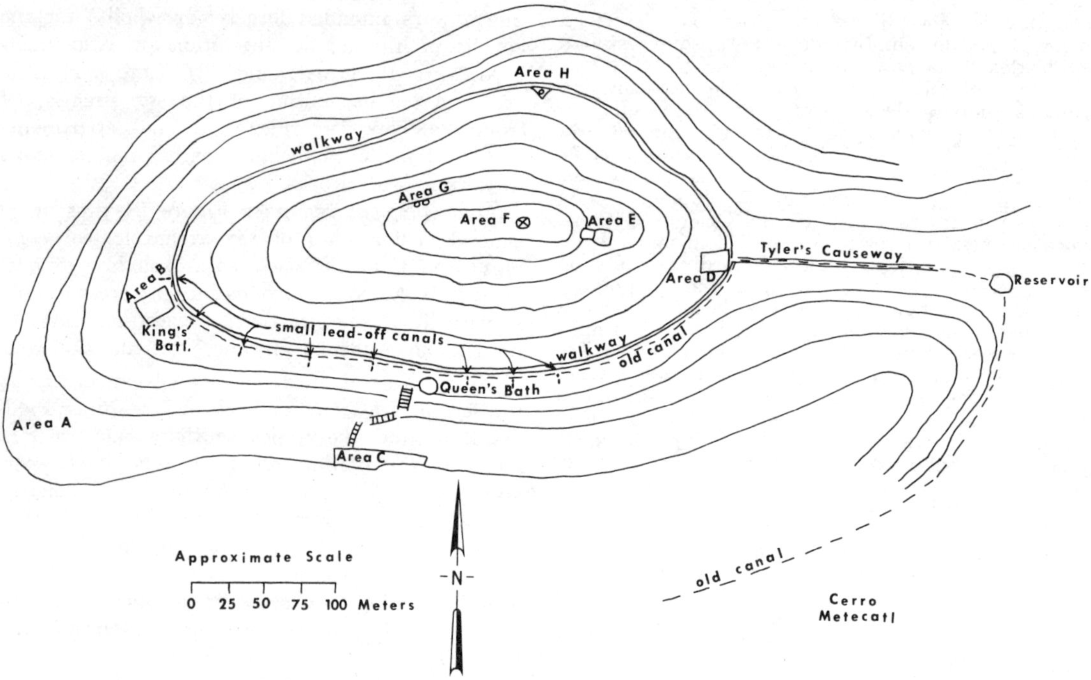

Fig. 24—Site plan, Tx-A-62 (not to scale). Contour interval approximately 5 meters.

stone terraces, which define a small stairway leading up into the main chamber. At the rear of the main chamber is a low altar (1.5 m square, and about 10 cm high), carved out of the solid rock floor. Behind this altar, against the rear wall, there seems to have once been a large statue carved in low relief into the wall's surface, but now totally obliterated. Near the front end of this complex there is a large natural basalt column, about 2.5 m long, and 50 cm thick.

"Queen's Bath."

This feature is found about 300 m west of Area D, a few meters below the level of the main canal and roadway to which it is connected by a small secondary canal and a series of stone steps. The "bath" itself (about 1.5 m in diameter, and 1 m deep) has been carved into a large block of rock, and features several small seat or foot- and arm-rest appurtenances (Pl. 44,*b*).

Area C.

A series of rather remarkable stairways cut into the solid rock of the steep hill face extend from the Queen's Bath downslope some 10 or 15 m to a walled enclosure resting on a broad terrace. The main section of this area is a compound measuring 24 by 12 m enclosed on three sides by a stone wall some 50 cm thick, still standing to a height of about 2 m in some spots (Pl. 43,*b*). Abutting on this compound is a second, less well-defined and narrower, covering an area of 40 by 10 m, with much lower stone walls lacking the precise construction and regularity of the first. No traces of interior rooms or partition walls were found in either compound, and sherd cover was very light over the whole complex.

Area B.

The main canal appears to terminate at the western end of the hill, at the spot popularly known as the "King's Bath" (Pl. 44,*a*). This feature is a magnified, and architecturally more complex, version of the Queen's Bath further east. Here we find a complex system of three broad, partially stuccoed stone-faced terraces, the lowermost of which contains a stuccoed, stone-walled, step-down depression about 3.5 m in diameter and 1.6 m deep, into which the main canal empties. Near the edge of this depression sits a badly battered large frog, carved into the top of a large stone boulder imbedded in the terrace surface.

Area A.

Roughly 200 m east, downslope from the King's Bath, and about 30 to 50 m below the level of the main canal, are a series of four broad artificial terraces, the lowermost and largest of which contains sufficient remnants of plaster to indicate that much of its entire surface (*ca.* 60 by 30 m) was once stuccoed. Only very light Aztec surface pottery occurs here, as opposed to light-to-moderate concentrations of Late and Terminal Formative material (Tx-LF-12; Tx-TF-20). Some 200 m north of this stuccoed terrace, and connected to it by a well-worn pathway along the modern irrigation canal, lies a small cave. This feature, measuring about 1.5 to 2 m in diameter, is said (by local informants) to penetrate a distance of 70 m into the hillside. No ceramic debris of any kind was noted.

Area G.

Moving up the steep slopes northeast of the King's Bath, several archaeological features are encountered as one moves along the gently sloping long crest of the hill. The first consists of the badly destroyed remnants of two large statues carved in high relief into the rock cliff face just below the crest on the hill's uppermost north flank (Pl. 46,*a*). Only portions of the feet and segments of the headdresses are still in position. Piled in front of the ruined carvings are large fragments of headdresses and other pieces of sculpture. Fronting on these carvings is a small stone-faced terrace, approached by a short stone stairway, measuring about 5 m wide and 15 m long.

Area F.

At the peak of the hill is a low, rather vague platform of rock rubble, about 15 m in diameter and 25-50 cm high. This now supports a small modern shrine. Very light Aztec surface pottery is scattered over the general area.

Area E.

This complex is situated on a broad natural terrace just below the hill crest to the west. Here a steep rocky cliff (into which a shallow cave about 2 m deep has been dug) overlooks a series of three broad, stone-faced terraces, or plazas, arranged in steplike fashion (Pl. 45,*b*). The surface of the uppermost plaza (10 by 15 m) has been stuccoed. The middle plaza measures 22 by 15 m. The lowermost plaza is vaguely defined and its dimensions are not wholly clear, but roughly measures 8 m wide, and contains a small stone structure at one end.

Area H.

The only distinct archaeological feature on the north side of the hill, apart from the roadway itself, is a two-sided cut into the rock face of the steep hillslope similar to that of Area D, but lacking its size and complexity. Each side of the cut measures 2.5 m, and its vertical walls are roughly 3 m high. A circular depression, 1 m in diameter and 25 cm deep, has been carved into the flat rock floor at the center of the cut.

Classification: The traditional identification of this location as Netzahualcoyotl's pleasure garden is probably essentially correct. It is quite apparent that this was a civic (or ceremonial-civic) complex, upon which a great deal of effort was lavished in the form of construction, architectural finesse, and water control. It is equally clear that there was little or no permanent residence here in Aztec times.

Tx-A-63

Natural setting: 2440 m, in the Lower Piedmont. Situated on gently sloping ground, at the northern base of Cerro Cocotl next to a mjaor barranca. The site sits at the edge of an intricately terraced area, and a number of terraces here have prevented severe erosion. Soil cover varies from shallow over the general surface, to moderately deep behind terrace walls.

Modern utilization: The immediate site area is used only for grazing. The intricately terraced hillslopes to the west and southwest are intensively cultivated in subsistence crops, orchard crops, and flowers. The lower terraces are partially irrigated with water brought from Sierra springs over several km of small canal networks. These same canals supply household water for the modern villages of San Miguel Tlaixpan to the north of the site, and San Nícolas Tlaminca to the west.

Archaeological remains: Variable light and light-to-moderate concentrations of surface pottery over an area of less than one hectare. There is one badly destroyed mound roughly 10 m in diameter and 50 cm high. The Aztec ceramics are undiagnostic as to being Early or Late.

Classification: A single isolated household unit; 10 to 15 people.

Tx-A-64

Natural setting: 2310 to 2370 m, in the Lower Piedmont. Situated at the edge of a broad, gentle slope, on a low bluff above a major barranca. Erosion has been moderate over most of the site area, and severe along the edge of the bluff. Soil cover is generally shallow, with some patches of bare tepetate.

Modern utilization: The site is located at the eastern edge of intensively cultivated piedmont plain (rainfall agriculture). Some sections of the site area are also cultivated, but a large proportion is used principally for grazing. The thin soil cover and heavy concentrations of stone rubble make the site marginal for agricultural purposes.

Archaeological remains: Variable very light, light, and light-to-moderate concentrations of surface pottery over an area of about 35 hectares. A total of seven structures can still be distinguished (Appendix II). Amorphous concentrations of rock rubble and sherds indicate the prior existence of several more, which are now no longer recognizable as such. The occupational debris occurs in the form of a thin linear strip extending along the barranca. Southeast of the main site are several isolated localities (totaling roughly one hectare in surface area) scattered along the barranca where surface pottery exists in light-to-moderate concentrations. These probably represent isolated household units belonging to the Tx-A-64 community.

Surface pottery is predominately Late Aztec, but Early Aztec material is consistently present in smaller quantities. Some Early and Late Classic material occurs toward the north end of the site (Tx-EC-13, Tx-LC-12).

Classification: Small dispersed village; 200 to 400 people.

Tx-A-65

Natural setting: 2320 to 2350 m, in the Lower Piedmont. Situated on a broad, gentle slope between two major barrancas. Erosion has been moderate to severe. Soil cover is generally shallow, with some patches of bare tepetate.

Modern utilization: The southern two-thirds of the site is used for grazing only. Intensive rainfall cultivation of subsistence crops is carried out in the northern third. Basalt is presently being removed at several small quarries on the barranca slopes at the south edge of the site.

Archaeological remains: Variable very light, light, and light-to-moderate concentrations of surface pottery and rock rubble over an area of about 25 hectares. This material is predominately Late Aztec, but Early Aztec sherds are consistently present in smaller quantities. There are no well preserved structural remains, but the badly destroyed outlines of about 10 domestic residential units can be discerned, and amorphous concentrations of rock rubble and sherds indicate the former existence of several more. The occupational debris is mixed with heavier Terminal Formative material (Tx-TF-17). Lighter concentrations of Middle Formative (Tx-MF-7) and Late Formative (Tx-LF-10, Tx-LF-11) are also present.

Classification: Small dispersed village; 150 to 300 people.

Tx-A-66

Natural setting: 2340 to 2380 m, in the Lower Piedmont. Situated on a broad, gentle slope between two major barrancas. Erosion has been moderate over most of the site area, and more severe along the barranca edges. Soil cover is generally shallow, with some patches of bare tepetate along barranca edges.

Modern utilization: Intensive rainfall cultivation except for the severely eroded barranca edges that now serve only for grazing. The eastern fringes of the site extend into the westernmost edges of the modern village of San Miguel Tlaixpan.

Archaeological remains: Variable very light, light, and light-to-moderate concentrations of surface pottery and rock rubble over an area of about 50 hectares. Most of this material is Late Aztec, but Early Aztec sherds are consistently present in smaller quantities. There are no definite structural remains, but several amorphous concentrations of rock rubble and sherds suggest the former presence of several residential structures, now no longer recognizable as such. The occupational debris is mixed with light Early and Late Classic material (Tx-EC-9, Tx-EC-10, Tx-LC-10 Tx-LC-11). The eastern edges of Tx-TF-17 slightly overlap the western borders of Tx-A-66.

Classification: Small dispersed village; 200 to 400 people.

Tx-A-67

Natural setting: 2415 m, atop an isolated hillspur extending off the northwest end of Cerro Purificación. Situated some 90 m above the level of the surrounding piedmont plain. Shallow soil cover, with some rock outcrops.

Modern utilization: Grazing, plus a few cultivated maguey. The lower hill flanks to the east are intricately terraced and intensively cultivated. The piedmont plain surrounding the hill is intensively cultivated (rainfall agriculture).

Archaeological remains: Four tlateles were identified (Appendix II), two of which have both Aztec and Terminal Formative (Tx-TF-15) surface pottery in light or very light concentrations. A third mound appears to lack Aztec pottery, and the surface pottery of the fourth is undiagnostic. These mounds are strung out in linear fashion along the hill crest, and rest on vague, wide, low terraces which cover most of the hilltop. The intervening areas between the mounds show very little surface pottery. The paucity of sherd cover suggests a nonresidential function for the site. The surface area of the hilltop complex is about five hectares. There is a small light-to-moderate concentration of Aztec surface pottery at the southwestern base of the hill which probably represents a single household residential unit.

Classification: Hilltop ceremonial precinct, with no permanent occupation. The small concentration of occupational debris at the base of the hill may represent a group associated with the maintenance of the ceremonial zone.

Tx-A-68

Natural setting: 2335 m, in the Lower Piedmont. Situated on gently sloping ground on the lowermost western flanks of Cerro Purificación, just above the level of the main piedmont plain. Erosion has been moderate to severe. Soil cover is generally shallow, with a few patches of bare tepetate.

Modern utilization: The northern third of the site area is used for grazing and some maguey cultivation. The southern two-thirds is devoted to intensive rainfall cultivation of subsistence crops. The northern fringes of the modern village of Purificación extend onto the southern edges of the site area.

Archaeological remains: Variable light and light-to-moderate concentrations of surface pottery and rock rubble over an area of about five hectares. No structural remains.

Classification: Hamlet; fewer than 50 people.

Tx-A-69

Natural setting: 2420 to 2490 m, at the upper edge of the Lower Piedmont. Situated on gently- to moderately-sloping ground on the lower eastern flank of Cerro Purificación, at the edge of a major barranca. A second large barranca cuts into the northern end of the site. Erosion has been severe. Soil cover, except in scattered pockets and erosional remnants, is shallow to absent, with large stretches of bare tepetate.

Modern utilization: Grazing and maguey cultivation. The hillslopes to the east of the site area are covered with extensive maguey terracing. There are several abandoned rock quarries on the steep slopes north of the site.

Archaeological remains: Variable very light, light, and light-to-moderate concentrations of surface pottery and moderate rock rubble over an area of about 30 hectares. A total of 13 distinct mounds are recognizable (Appendix II; Fig. 22), and amorphous concentrations of rock rubble and sherds suggest the former existence of several more, which are now no longer recognizable as such. The ceramics are very predominately Late Aztec, with a light scattering of Early Aztec sherds.

The higher, more sloping sections of the site contain a number of very badly deteriorated terraces, which may have been living surfaces in Aztec times.

Some of the abandoned rock quarries north of the site may be prehispanic.

Classification: Small dispersed village; 200 to 400 people.

Tx-A-70

Natural setting: 2500 to 2520 m, at the lower edge of the Upper Piedmont. Situated on a broad, gently sloping promontory on the lower southeastern flanks of Cerro Purificación, deeply cut into by large barrancas on the north and south. Erosion has been severe over the whole area. Soil cover is very shallow to absent, with large stretches of badly-scarred bare tepetate.

Modern utilization: Marginal grazing and a few cultivated maguey. The slopes just east of the site are covered with wide stone-faced terraces reinforced with maguey. The main canal carrying irrigation and household water from the Sierra springs to the modern village of Purificación runs through the southern edge of the site area immediately after passing over a large causeway (Causeway C).

Archaeological remains: Variable very light, light, and light-to-moderate concentrations of surface pottery and moderate rock rubble over an area of about seven hectares. This material is very predominately Late Aztec. Two definite mounds can be delineated (Appendix II), and amorphous concentrations of rock rubble and sherds indicate the former presence of several more residential structures now no longer recognizable as such. The north end of a large causeway (Causeway C) extends onto the southeastern edge of the site, and the traces of an abandoned canal leading off the causeway around the eastern flanks of Cerro Purificación pass through the length of the site.

Classification: Hamlet; fewer than 100 people.

Tx-A-71

Natural setting: 2500 to 2530 meters, at the lower edge of the Upper Piedmont. Situated on a broad, gently sloping promontory lying between major barrancas on the east and west. Erosion has been severe throughout the site. Soil cover is generally shallow, with large stretches of bare tepetate. Stone terraces on the slopes at the northern and southern margins of the site have preserved a moderately deep soil cover there. Maguey terracing has likewise maintained a shallow soil cover in portions of the central site area.

Modern utilization: Predominately grazing, with some rainfall cultivation of subsistence crops in the central site area where maguey terraces have held soil in place. The terraced slopes to the south are also cultivated. The main canal bringing irrigation and household water to the modern village of Purificación passes through the middle of the site.

Archaeological remains: Variable very light, light, and light-to-moderate concentrations of surface pottery and moderate rock rubble over an area of about nine hectares. Most of this ceramic material is Late Aztec, but lighter quantities of Early Aztec sherds are present. One definite mound was identified: a domestic residence about 15 m in diameter and 20 cm high, with moderate rock rubble and light-to-moderate surface pottery. Remnants of stone wall bases define a complex of at least four or five rooms in this structure. Amorphous concentrations of rock rubble and sherds indicate the former presence of several more residential structures, now no longer recognizable as such.

Classification: Hamlet; fewer than 100 people.

Tx-A-72

Natural setting: 2470 to 2650 meters, predominately in the Upper Piedmont. Most of the Aztec residential zone occupies the gently sloping top surfaces of two long, broad, parallel ridges defined by three deep, wide barrancas running southeast-northwest. These main ridges have been cut into at many points by numerous secondary barrancas tributary to the main channels. Some occupation spills over onto the upper sections of more steeply-sloping barranca walls, and down onto the narrow band of relatively flat land immediately adjacent to the barranca channel itself.

Erosion has been extremely severe throughout the entire region. Over the ridge-top surfaces topsoil occurs only on widely scattered, isolated erosional remnants. Here, even the upper layers of tepetate subsoil have been stripped away for depths of 1 to 3 m. Narrow strips of deeper soil occur at the bases of hillslopes, well below the ridge-top surfaces, immediately adjacent to the barranca beds. In these latter spots one finds small ribbons of thick oak-conifer forest, totally different from the barren wasteland on the ridge tops above.

Maguey terracing has preserved shallow soil cover on a few hillslopes.

Modern utilization: Predominately wasteland, with some marginal grazing, and a little maguey cultivation. A few large erosional remnants are partially cultivated (rainfall agriculture) in subsistence crops, but little effort is made to preserve even these last remnants of productive soil. The eastern margins of the site are marked by the terraced agricultural fields belonging to the modern villages of Santa Catarina, San Miguel, San Gregorio, and Santa María.

Archaeological remains: Variable very light, light, light-to-moderate, and moderate concentrations of surface pottery and rock rubble over an area of about 400 hectares. This large area has been designated a single site because no significant breaks in occupation could be detected anywhere within its borders. There are points where the density of occupational debris decreases markedly, but no large discontinuities exist. Late Aztec pottery is very predominate, but Early Aztec sherds are consistently present in lighter and less-continuous concentrations.

Despite severe erosion, the remains of 87 fairly distinct mounds (nearly all of which seem to be residential structures) can still be clearly delineated (Appendix II; Pl. 40,*b*; Fig. 25). The less distinct traces of another hundred, or so, possible mounds, now largely reduced to amorphous concentrations of rock rubble and sherd debris, can also be seen. The former existence of many more structures, now totally obliterated and unrecognizable as such, is suggested by sherd and rock rubble concentrations scattered throughout the site area.

The original aspect of the site has been badly obscured by the severe erosion. Most occupational debris now rests on bare tepetate, or atop isolated erosional remnants. No internal structuring or ordering of residential zones, apart from that dictated by topography, is apparent. The frequency of decorated pottery is generally low relative to that of Aztec sites on the Lower Piedmont. A handful of widely scattered Late Toltec sherds were noted over the site area, never in sufficient quantity or concentration to warrant a site designation.

Classification: Several large dispersed villages; total population between 4000 and 8000.

Tx-A-73

Natural setting: 2540 to 2600 m, in the Upper Piedmont. Situated on the gently sloping top surfaces of two broad, parallel ridges, separated by deep, wide barrancas. Erosion has been extremely severe throughout the site area. Over the ridge-top surfaces topsoil occurs mainly on widely scattered erosional remnants. Here, even the upper layers of tepetate subsoil have been stripped away to depths of up to 2 m. Narrow strips of deeper soil occur at the bases of hill-

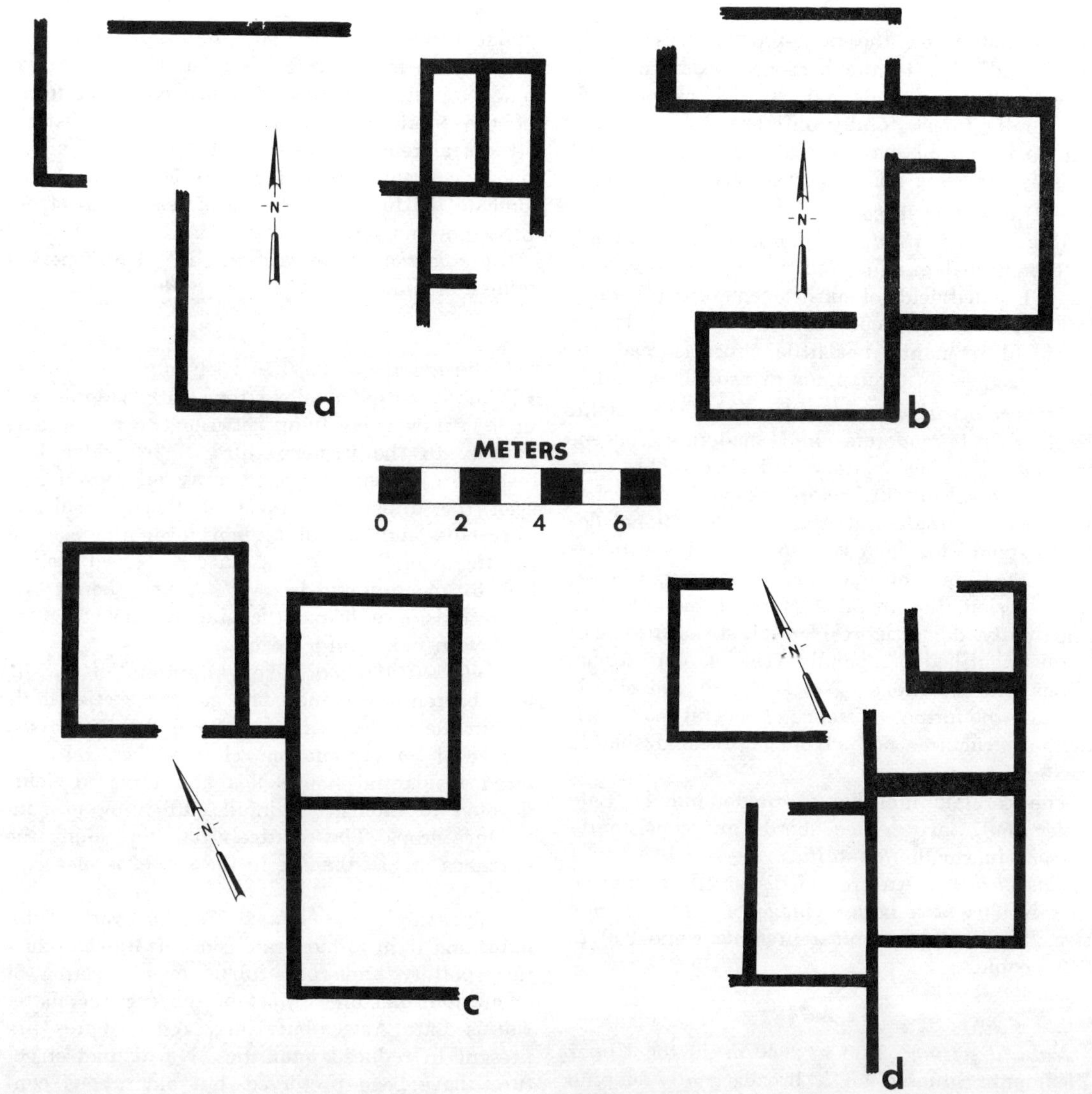

Fig. 25—Tx-A-72, floor plans: *a*) Tlatel 183; *b*) Tlatel 194; *c*) Tlatel 242; *d*) Tlatel 270; *e*) Tlatel 209; *f*) Tatel 274; *g*) Tlatel 283.

slopes, well below the ridge-top surfaces, immediately adjacent to the barranca beds. In these latter spots, one finds narrow ribbons of thick oak-conifer forest, totally different from the barren wasteland on the ridge tops above. Scattered maguey terracing has preserved shallow soil cover on some hillslopes.

Modern utilization: Predominately wasteland, with marginal grazing and some cultivated maguey. Isolated fields of subsistence crops (all rainfall agriculture) occur on a few of the larger erosional remnants, but little effort is made to preserve these last remnants of productive soil.

Archaeological remains: Variable very light, light, light-to-moderate, and moderate concentrations of surface pottery and rock rubble over an area of about 30 hectares. This is part of a much larger residential zone, as occupational debris extends to the east, north, and south beyond the limits of our survey. Despite the severe erosion, the remains of eight mounds (all apparently domestic residential structures) can be distinguished (Appendix II; Fig. 26). Amorphous concentrations of rock rubble and sherds indicate the former existence of several more residential structures now no longer recognizable as such.

The ceramic material is predominately Late Aztec, but Early Aztec sherds are consistently present in smaller quantities.

Classification: An area of dispersed occupation that is part of a larger village of undetermined size. The surveyed unit represents some 250 to 350 people.

Tx-A-74

Natural setting: 2630 to 2640 m, in the Upper Piedmont. Situated on a broad, gently sloping ridge-top, surrounded on three sides by deep, narrow barrancas. Severe erosion, with the uppermost 1 or 2 m of topsoil and tepetate subsoil stripped away, except on a few isolated erosional remnants. Some terracing and bancal systems have preserved shallow soil cover in a few localities.

Modern utilization: Grazing, plus some cultivated maguey. Some cultivation of subsistence crops (rainfall agriculture) in a few places where soil cover has been maintained. Just north of the site area are two small, isolated modern residences, the westernmost outposts of Santa Maria.

Archaeological remains: Variable very light, light, and light-to-moderate concentrations of surface pottery and rock rubble over an area of about three hectares. This represents only the corner of a much larger residential zone that extends an undetermined distance east and north of the limits of our survey here. No distinct structural remains are present, but several amorphous concentrations of rock rubble and sherds indicate the former existence of residential structures now no longer recognizable

Classification: The western edge of a dispersed village of unknown extent; 20 to 40 people.

Tx-A-75

Natural setting: 2650 to 2680 m, in the Upper Piedmont. Situated along the gently sloping top of a narrow ridge lying between two major barrancas. In the western third of the ridge top, severe erosion has stripped away all topsoil and even the uppermost levels of tepetate subsoil. Terracing and bancal systems over the eastern two-thirds of the ridge top have preserved a shallow to moderately deep soil cover there. The steep hillslopes below the site are heavily covered with oak-conifer vegetation.

Modern utilization: The western end of the site is a barren wasteland. The eastern section falls within the western edges of the modern dispersed village of Santa Catarina. Here are several scattered residential households and terraced fields devoted to intensive rainfall cultivation of subsistence crops. The relatively flat land along the barranca, below the site to the south, is also cultivated.

Archaeological remains: Variable very light, light, and light-to-moderate concentrations of surface pottery and rock rubble over an area of about four hectares. Most of the ceramic material is Late Aztec, but Early Aztec sherds are present in reduced quantities. No distinct structures have been preserved, but amorphous concentrations of rock rubble and sherds indicate the former presence of several residential units, now no longer recognizable. This location seems to be the easternmost Aztec residential community of any size or permanence in this general region.

Classification: Hamlet; fewer than 50 people.

Tx-A-76

Natural setting: 2570 to 2600 m, in the Upper Piedmont. Situated on a broad, gently sloping shelf on the lower eastern flanks of Cerro San Miguel. The site's eastern edge is defined by steep slopes falling away abruptly down to a deep, wide barranca running south-north along the site's length. Erosion has been severe. Except at the southwest corner of the site where

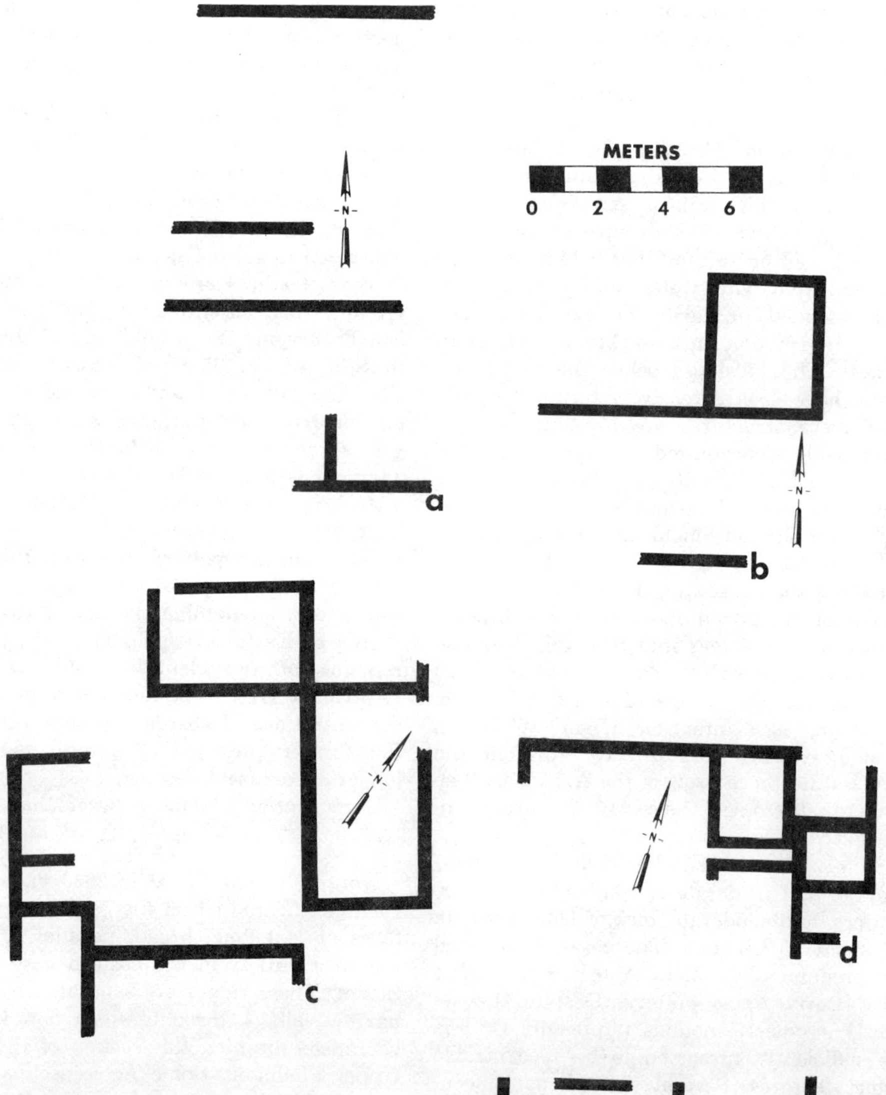

Fig. 26—Floor plans: *a*) Tx-A-73, Tlatel 393; *b*) Tx-A-73, Tlatel 399; *c*) Tx-A-76, Tlatel 134; *d*) Tx-A-76, Tlatel 149; *e*) Tx-A-78, Tlatel 179; *f*) Tx-A-78, Tlatel 157.

modern terrace and bancal systems have preserved a shallow to moderately deep soil cover, most of the ground surface consists of badly scarred bare tepetate and scattered erosional remnants.

Modern utilization: Grazing, plus a few cultivated maguey in the immediate site area. The terraced fields at the southeast corner of the site are intensively cultivated. This agriculture is predominately based on rainfall, but a few fields are partially irrigated with water stored in a large reservoir intended primarily for household use and terrace irrigation in San Miguel Tlaixpan to the west. The hillslopes below the south end of the site have been extensively terraced in the past, but these structures are presently abandoned and badly deteriorated.

Just southeast of the site is a large causeway (Causeway B), over which passes the main canal bringing water for household use and terrace irrigation from springs in the Sierra (Pl. 55,*a*,*b*). After crossing the causeway, the water enters the large reservoir mentioned above, from which point the canal system diverges into two branches, one leading north around the eastern flanks of Cerro San Miguel into the village of Purificación, the second leading east into San Miguel Tlaixpan. Both canal systems pass directly through the southern and northern arms of the Aztec site. The northern canal crosses Causeway C enroute to Purificación.

Archaeological remains: Variable light, light-to-moderate, and moderate concentrations of surface pottery and moderate rock rubble, over an area of about 15 hectares. The ceramic material is very predominately Late Aztec, with a few sherds of Early Aztec pottery. Despite the severe erosion, some 13 mounds (Appendix II; Fig. 26) are sufficiently preserved to be recognizable as distinct features. Several amorphous concentrations of rock rubble and sherds indicate the former presence of other structures, now no longer recognizable as such. The age of the extensive terracing below the south end of the site is uncertain. These structures average about 10 m wide, and up to 2 m high at the downhill face.

Classification: Small dispersed village; 125 to 250 people.

Tx-A-77

Natural setting: 2520 to 2550 m, in the Upper Piedmont. Situated on the gently sloping lower southern flanks of Cerro San Miguel, adjacent to a major barranca, just east of the main pass between Cerro Cocotl and Cerro San Miguel. Erosion has been severe throughout most of the site area, except on the higher slopes to the north, west, and east where extensive terracing has preserved a shallow to moderately deep soil cover.

Modern utilization: Most of the site area is presently used for grazing, plus a few scattered maguey. The higher slopes to the north, west, and east have been extensively terraced, and those to the north and west are now intensively cultivated in subsistence and orchard crops. Some of these terraces are partially irrigated with water derived from springs in the Sierra. The main canal carrying household and irrigation water to San Miguel Tlaixpan passes just above the site area (Pl. 55,*a*) and some moisture is drawn off for irrigation purposes along its length.

A large cemetery, belonging to San Miguel Tlaixpan, sits at the northwest corner of the site.

Archaeological remains: Variable very light, light, light-to-moderate, and moderate concentrations of surface pottery and rock rubble over an area of about seven hectares. The ceramic material is very predominately Late Aztec, but a few sherds of Early Aztec material are present. The remains of two definite residential structures (Appendix II) can be delineated, and amorphous concentrations of sherds and rock rubble indicate the former presence of several more, now no longer recognizable as such.

Classification: Hamlet; fewer than 100 people.

Tx-A-78

Natural setting: 2500 to 2630 m, in the Upper Piedmont. Situated on the gently sloping top surfaces of two long, broad, parallel ridges extending westward from the eastern base of the main Sierra. These ridges are separated by three deep, narrow valleys, through which flow the principal barrancas draining this section of the Sierra and Upper Piedmont. Some Aztec occupation extends onto the steep slopes above the barrancas, and down onto the narrow bands of fairly level land adjacent to the barranca beds.

In this area the severely eroded Upper Piedmont landscape attains its greatest spectacularity in the Texcoco Region. Generally speaking, topsoil and the uppermost 2 to 5 m of tepetate subsoil have everywhere been stripped away, leaving a highly dissected surface of badly scarred bare tepetate and scattered erosional remnants. The barranca channels themselves plunge vertically to depths of 50 m, or more, often with widths of less than 10 m. Only where terracing has been maintained, along the eastern margins of the site and on a few gentle hillslopes in the south central section of the site, has a shallow soil cover been preserved.

Modern utilization: Predominately a barren wasteland, with some very marginal grazing and a few cultivated maguey. The terraced fields and scattered westernmost houses of Santa Catarina extend onto the eastern end of the site. More systematic maguey cultivation occurs at several localities in the south-central site area, where hillslopes are covered with stone-faced maguey terraces.

Archaeological remains: Variable very light, light, light-to-moderate, and moderate concentrations of surface pottery and rock rubble over an area of about 100 hectares. The ceramic material is predominately Late Aztec, but Early Aztec sherds are consistently present in lighter and more restricted concentrations. Despite the severe erosion, the remains of 21 distinct mounds can still be delineated (all of which appear to be domestic residential structures, (Appendix II; Fig. 26). Amorphous concentrations of sherds and rock rubble indicate the former presence of many more, now no longer recognizable as such.

An examination of mounds in this area clearly indicates that the extremely severe erosion has been largely or wholly posthispanic. Aztec residential structures are frequently found perched atop erosional remnants standing up to 5 m above the present general ground surface.

Throughout the site area, one encounters badly deteriorated remnants of stone-faced terraces, whose age of construction and use is unclear (e.g., Pl. 47,*a*).

Classification: Large dispersed village; 750 to 1500 people.

Tx-A-79

Natural setting: 2580 to 2610 m, in the Upper Piedmont. Situated on gently sloping ground near the head of a major barranca. Erosion has been extremely severe throughout the site area. Much of the topsoil, and even the uppermost two to three meters of tepetate subsoil, has been stripped away, except for a few scattered erosional remnants, and some stretches of shallow soil cover. The main barranca, and its numerous tributaries, continue to cut deeply into the site area at many points.

Modern utilization: Predominately wasteland and some marginal grazing. Small patches of subsistence crops are now cultivated on erosional remnants and intermittent patches of shallow soil, and there has been a half-hearted attempt to construct a few small terrace walls to prevent continued erosion in a few places.

Archaeological remains: Variable very light, light, and light-to-moderate concentrations of surface pottery over an area of about 11 hectares. The ceramic material is very predominately Late Aztec, but a few sherds of Early Aztec are present. Decorated pottery is consistently scarce. Despite severe erosion, the remains of two former residential structures can still be recognized (Appendix II). Amorphous concentrations of sherds and rock rubble indicate the former presence of several more, now no longer recognizable as such.

Classification: Hamlet; fewer than 100 people.

Tx-A-80

Natural setting: 2560 to 2630 m, in the Upper Piedmont. Situated along the gently sloping top of a broad ridge, and down the flanks on either side, with some occupation spreading out over the relatively level floor of a small valley on both sides of a deep narrow barranca. Scattered oaks and conifiers dot the landscape, particularly along the crest of the ridge and on the narrow valley floor. Erosion has been severe throughout the site area. Intermittent terracing has maintained a shallow to moderately deep soil cover at several localities, but elsewhere all topsoil and up to 2 or 3 m of tepetate subsoil have been stripped away.

Modern utilization: Predominately grazing, with some maguey. Some maize is also cultivated on the partially terraced slopes.

Archaeological remains: Variable very light, light, and light-to-moderate concentrations of surface pottery and rock rubble over an area of about 30 hectares. The ceramic material is very predominately Late Aztec, although a few sherds of Early Aztec pottery are also present. The badly destroyed remnants of eight structures, all apparently small residential complexes, can still be delineated (Appendix II; Fig. 27). Amorphous concentrations of rock rubble and sherds indicate the former presence of a few other housemounds, now no longer recognizable as such.

The remnants of abandoned and badly deteriorated stone-faced terraces can be seen scattered throughout the site, often near or clearly associated with the remains of Aztec residential structures.

Classification: Small dispersed village; 100 to 150 people.

Tx-A-81

Natural setting: 2480 to 2530 m, at the juncture of the Upper and Lower Piedmonts. Situated on gently sloping ground on the lower eastern flanks of Cerro Cocotl, along either side of

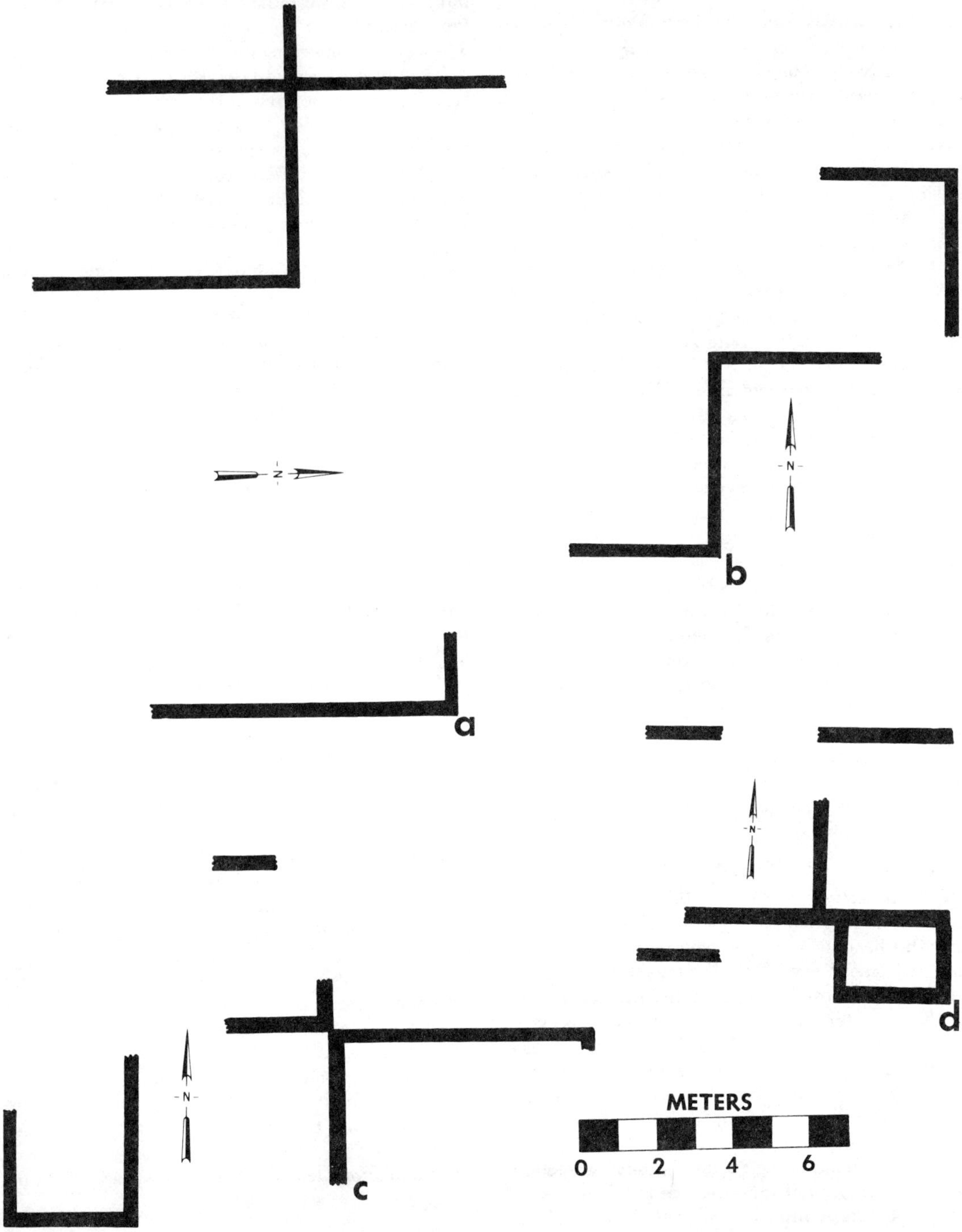

Fig. 27—Floor plans: *a*) Tx-A-80, Tlatel 60; *b*) Tx-A-80, Tlatel 64; *c*) Tx-A-87, Tlatel 36-C; *d*) Tx-A-87, Tlatel 52-C.

a major barranca. The site area is just east of the main pass between Cerro Cocotl and Cerro San Miguel. Erosion has been severe over most of the site area. Only where terraces and bancals have been built and maintained is there any significant soil cover apart from scattered erosional remnants.

Modern utilization: Predominately grazing, with some cultivation of subsistence crops (rainfall agriculture) in small fields where terracing and bancal systems have preserved adequate soil cover. Most of the site area has been extensively terraced in the past, but most terraces are now abandoned and badly deteriorated. The main canal bringing water for household use and terrace irrigation from the Sierra springs to San Miguel Tlaixpan, San Dieguito, and Natívitas passes through the center of the site. No water is drawn from the canal for irrigation in the immediate site area.

Archaeological remains: Variable very light, light, light-to-moderate, and moderate concentrations of surface pottery and rock rubble over an area of about 30 hectares. The ceramic material is very predominately Late Aztec, although a few Early Aztec sherds are also present. Three badly destroyed mounds, apparently representing domestic residential structures, can still be delineated (Appendix II). Amorphous concentrations of sherds and rock rubble indicate the former presence of several more, now no longer recognizable as such.

The date of construction and use of the numerous abandoned stone-faced terraces throughout the site area is not clear. A prehispanic date for terracing in this general area is strongly suggested by a recently uncovered terrace face—previously buried by a local pocket of deep alluvium—which shows a well-built stone-faced wall, totally different from modern terrace construction, about 1 m high in an area of moderate slope in the northeast corner of the site (Pl. 47,*b*). The immediate vicinity is barren of surface pottery, and this feature is probably not part of a residential structure.

Classification: Small dispersed village; 150 to 300 people.

Tx-A-82

Natural setting: 2570 m, in the Upper Piedmont. Located on the upper surface of a long, narrow ridge lying between two major barrancas. Severe erosion has stripped off most of the topsoil except where stone and maguey terraces have preserved a shallow soil cover on the lower hillslopes below the ridge top to the south. Scattered oak-conifer vegetation along the ridge top to the east has also maintained a spotty shallow soil cover.

Modern utilization: Grazing, with some maguey cultivation.

Archaeological remains: The badly destroyed remains of a single rock rubble platform, about 10 m square and 50 cm high, with fragmentary stone wall bases defining its outer edges. Remnants of stucco indicate the upper surface of the platform was formerly plastered. Surface pottery is lacking, except for a few scattered Aztec sherds. This structure lies above and just east of Causeway A (Pl. 56,*a*). This latter feature is part of the ancient hydraulic complex (described below) that once carried water from springs in the Sierra over several km of canal and aqueduct networks, to the Tetzcotzingo complex (Tx-A-62).

Classification: Isolated ceremonial-civic structure, perhaps associated with the operation of Causeway A. No residential occupation.

Tx-A-83

Natural setting: 2600 m, in the Upper Piedmont. Situated on gently sloping ground near a major barranca. The immediate site area is severely eroded, with scanty soil cover and large stretches of badly scarred bare tepetate. Terrace and bancal systems to the east have prevented such serious, large-scale sheet erosion in that area.

Modern utilization: Marginal grazing in the immediate site area. To the east are scattered fields where subsistence crops are cultivated (rainfall agriculture) by residents of Santa Catarina del Monte.

Archaeological remains: Variable light and light-to-moderate concentrations of surface pottery and rock rubble over an area of less than one hectare. No structural remains.

Classification: Hamlet; fewer than 50 people. Probably a single household unit of 5 to 15 people.

Tx-A-84

Natural setting: 2600 m, in the Upper Piedmont. Situated on gently sloping ground at the eastern end of a small valley at the foot of the main Sierra. Erosion has been severe in the immediate site area, leaving scanty soil cover and considerable bare tepetate. The higher slopes surrounding the site are forested (mixed oak-conifer) and not seriously eroded. Terraces and bancals in the land to the west have prevented severe sheet erosion there.

Modern utilization: Grazing, plus some cutting of trees for fuel and construction material. The modern dispersed village of San Pablo Ixayoc lies just southwest of the site. Cultivated fields and kitchen gardens are scattered throughout its residential zone.

Archaeological remains: Variable light and light-to-moderate concentrations of surface pottery and rock rubble over an area of less than one hetcare. Both Early and Late Aztec ceramics are present in about equal quantities.

Classification: Hamlet; fewer than 50 people. Probably a single household unit of 5 to 15 people.

Tx-A-85

Natural setting: 2525 m, in the Upper Piedmont. Situated on gently sloping ground near the edge of a major barranca. Erosion has been severe; but substantial, though spotty, soil cover is present because of fairly abundant oak-conifer vegetation. Terracing on the slopes just north of the site area has prevented serious erosion there.

Modern utilization: Grazing in the immediate site area. Subsistence crops are cultivated (rainfall agriculture) on the terraced slopes north and west of the site

Archaeological remains: Variable light and light-to-moderate concentrations of surface pottery over an area of less than one hectare. The ceramic material is predominately Early Aztec. No structural remains.

Classification: Hamlet; fewer than 50 people. Probably a single household unit of 5 to 15 people.

Tx-A-86

Natural setting: 2500 to 2540 m, in the Upper Piedmont. Situated on a broad, gentle slope between two major barrancas. Erosion has been very severe throughout the site area. Except for scattered erosional remnants, virtually all topsoil, and even the uppermost 1 or 2 m of tepetate subsoil, have been stripped away.

Modern utilization: The immediate site area is predominately marginal grazing land. Some of the larger erosional remnants are now being cultivated (all rainfall agriculture). The easternmost edges of the modern dispersed village of Tequexquinahuac extend nearly to the western edges of the site.

Archaeological remains: Variable very light, light, light-to-moderate, and moderate concentrations of surface pottery and rock rubble over an area of about 20 hectares. The remains of a single badly destroyed mound are still discernable. This structure measures about 30 cm high and 20 by 16 m in surface area, covered with moderate concentrations of surface pottery and rock rubble. Amorphous concentrations of sherds and rock rubble indicate the former existence of several more residential complexes, now no longer recognizable as such.

Classification: Small dispersed village; 150 to 300 people.

Tx-A-87 (Aztec Huexotla)

Natural setting: 2270 to 2590 m, from the edge of the Lakeshore Plain into the Upper Piedmont. The site area thus crosscuts a variety of environmental types. The western quarter is situated on the broad, gently-sloping surface of the main Lower Piedmont plain. Here erosion has been slight to moderate, and soil cover is generally deep to moderately deep. Moving upslope to the east, several changes are apparent: (1) The terrain becomes increasingly irregular, with major barrancas cutting deeply into the ground surface. The continuous broad sweep of the Lower Piedmont plain now gives way to a series of wide, roughly parallel ridges, separated by deep, narrow, steep-sided valleys formed by the rapidly down-cutting barrancas. (2) Soil cover becomes progressively shallower as the severity of erosion increases markedly, and large stretches of badly scarred bare tepetate are common. Within the eastern half of the site, except for isolated erosional remnants, most topsoil has been stripped away completely, and even the uppermost tepetate subsoil has been removed up to depths of 3 m. (3) The slope of the general land surface remains gentle, but becomes progressively steeper eastward.

Modern utilization: In very general terms, the western half of the site is intensively cultivated (rainfall agriculture), while the eastern half is predominately wasteland and grazing land. There is a considerable amount of pasture in the western site area, and some agriculture is practiced in the east, but these generalizations are basically valid. To the east, cultivation usually is associated with earth or stone terracing, reinforced with maguey, which occur scattered irregularly over the hillslopes. Throughout this eastern zone there are abundant traces of extensive, systematic terracing, now abandoned and badly deteriorated.

The modern town of Huexotla sits on the northwestern corner of the Aztec site, and isolated household units occur scattered through much of the western half of Tx-A-87 .

The level Lakeshore Plain west of the site is intensively cultivated in maize and alfalfa, much of it by means of mechanized irrigation.

Archaeological remains: The site consists of two distinct segments (Fig. 28): (1) A nucleated urban core, of roughly 300 hectares, at the lower, flatter western end of the site area; and (2) an area of dispersed settlement covering about 540 hectares at the northern and southern margins of the urban core, and extending more than 5 km upward and eastward along two major barranca networks. Modern Huexotla lies along the northern edge of the Aztec urban core. Our survey could not be carried into the modern town on an intensive basis, and our understanding of the extent and character of the prehispanic occupation lying within and beneath it are based only on our observations made from streets and main pathways. However, it seems evident that the modern town lies north of the main urban core of Aztec Huexotla, and overlaps only its northern fringes.

The urban core contains practically all the sites' definite ceremonial-civic architecture, and is covered with continuous concentrations of surface pottery which are predominately in the light-to-moderate, moderate, and heavy ranges. Only at a few places does the sherd cover diminish noticeably in density. Early and Late Aztec ceramics occur in approximately equal proportions throughout most of the urban core.

A total of 13 structures—all but one clearly ceremonial-civic in character—were defined within the urban core (Figs. 27-30; Pl. 48-50; Appendix II, tlateles 19-21, 26, 27, 31-37, 40, 41, 43). Only tlatel 40 seems to be a residential structure, an isolated housemound at the southern edge of the nucleated zone. Within the urban core itself, the dense surface pottery probably represents closely packed, contiguous residential wards, with little or no space intervening between structures.

The dispersed segment of Tx-A-87 contains a total of 26 recognizable structures (Appendix II, tlateles 22-24, 44, 49, 52, 53, 64, 85, 29-C, 31-C, 32-C, 34-C, 35-C, 36-C, 40-C, 41-C, 50-C, 52-C, 53-C, 54-C, 55-C, 56-C, and 57-C). All but four of these (52, 53, 64, 55-C) appear to be small domestic residences, and two (52, 53) of these exceptions are large pyramidal structures on the Huexotla-Coatlinchan (Tx-A-88) frontier, situated midway between the urban cores of these two major Aztec centers. Within the dispersed zone of Tx-A-87, surface pottery occurs in variable very light, light, light-to-moderate, and moderate concentrations. In contrast to the urban core, the ceramic material is predominately Late Aztec, with Early Aztec sherds present only in much lighter and more restricted concentrations.

The site's ceremonial-civic core consists of a large walled complex (partially restored by Ba-

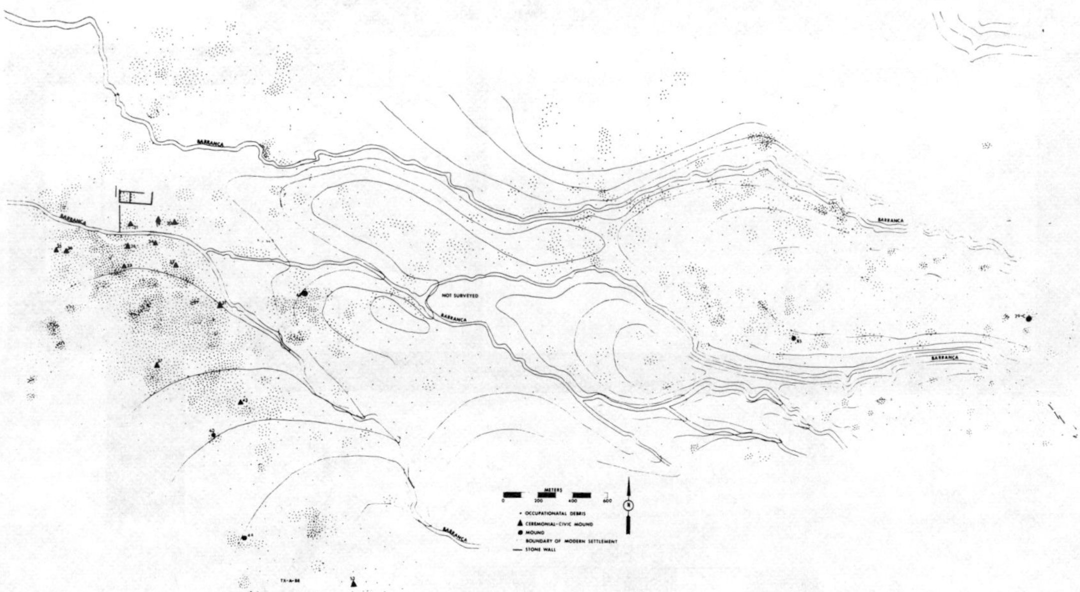

Fig. 28—Site plan, Tx-A-87 (impressionistic contours).

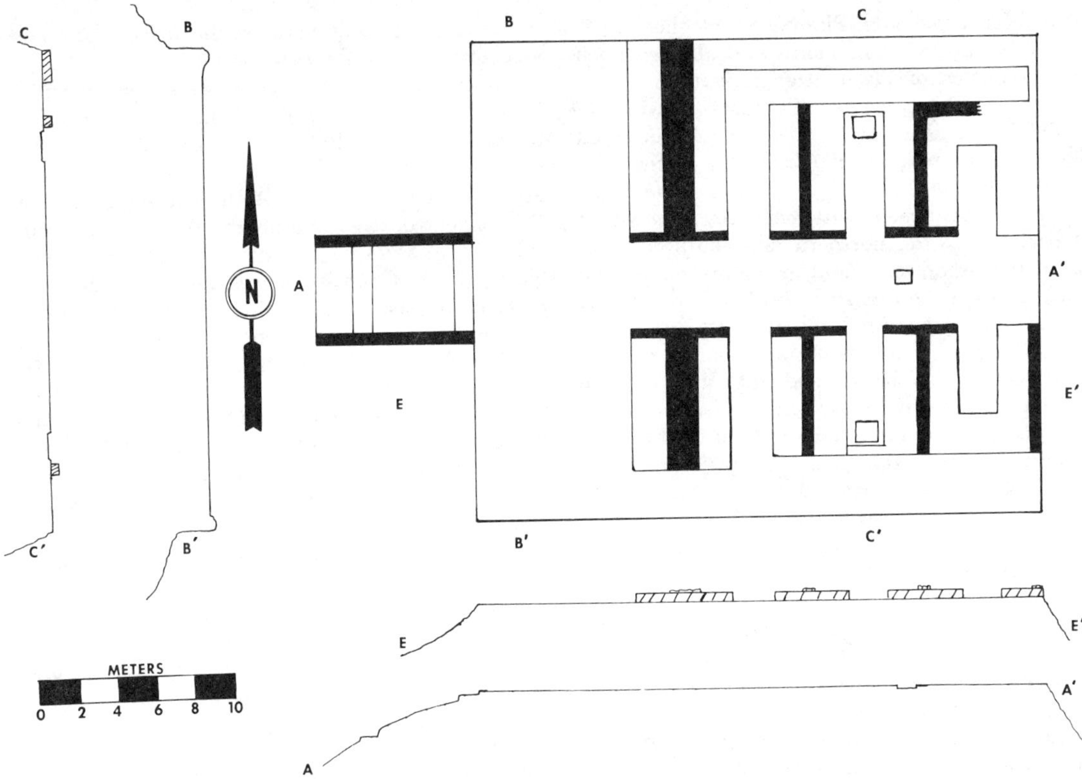

Fig. 29—Tlatel 20, plan and profiles, Tx-A-87.

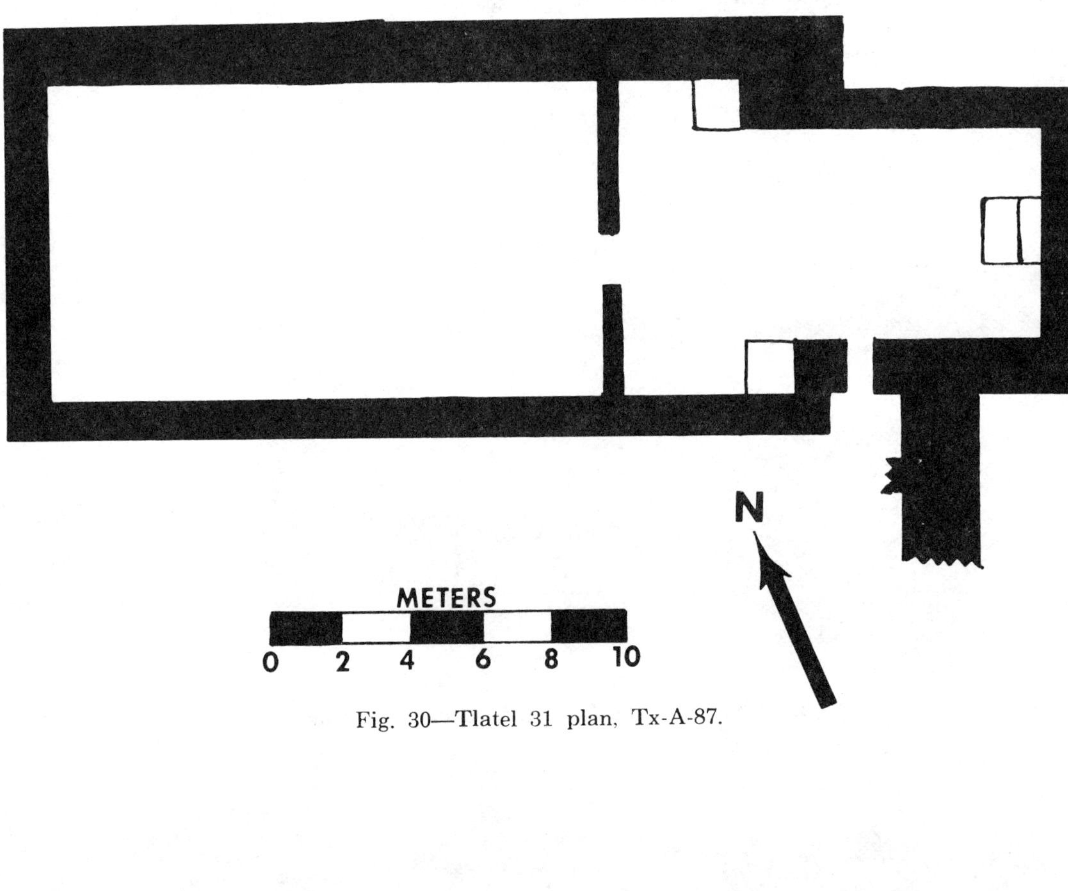

Fig. 30—Tlatel 31 plan, Tx-A-87.

tres in the early 20th century) covering about nine hectares at the south edge of present-day Huexotla, and extending slightly into the modern town (Fig. 28), about as far as the main church. The restored sections of the wall stand up to 6 m high, and measure between 2 and 3 m thick at the base (Pl. 50,*b*). The precise character and full extent of the walled enclosure has been badly obscured by modern occupation. It is clear, however, that there were formerly several internal divisions within the main walled enclosure.

Classification: Primary regional center. Population of the nucleated urban core: 7500 to 15,000; population of the dispersed sector: 4000 to 8000.

Tx-A-88 (Aztec Coatlinchan)

Natural setting: 2290 to 2350 m, in the Lower Piedmont. The western border of the site begins near the eastern edge of the Lakeshore Plain. Situated on a broad, gentle slope between two major barrancas. Slight to moderate erosion, with shallow to moderately deep soil cover.

Modern utilization: Intensive rainfall cultivation of subsistence crops, except for an area of 34 hectares in the south-central site area occupied by the modern nucleated village of Coatlinchan. The Lakeshore Plain to the west is intensively cultivated in maize and alfalfa, largely by means of mechanized irrigation.

Archaeological remains: Variable light-to-moderate, moderate, and heavy concentrations of surface pottery and rock rubble over an area of about 210 hectares. This includes modern Coatlinchan, although only limited observations could be made within the limits of the modern town. The density of occupational debris fades off quickly around the fringes of this area, except to the north where light and light-to-moderate sherd concentrations continue into the southern edge of Tx-A-87 (Aztec Huexotla). Early and Late Aztec ceramics occur in about equal proportions throughout this area.

At least 10 major ceremonial-civic structures were noted (the largest measuring 7 m high and about 30 m in diameter; Pl. 52,*b*). Badly obliterated and obscured traces of dense Aztec occupation, including superimposed stuccoed floors, stone walls, and heavy sherd and rock rubble debris occur within modern Coatlinchan, particularly along its western edge.

Classification: Primary regional center; 5500 to 11,000 people.

Tx-A-89

Natural setting: 2475 m, at the upper edge of the Lower Piedmont. Situated on a broad, gentle slope, near a major barranca. Severe erosion, with shallow soil cover and large stretches of badly scarred bare tepetate.

Modern utilization: Marginal grazing and wasteland. Scattered cultivation of subsistence crops on erosional remnants and in narrow bands of level ground immediately adjacent to barranca beds.

Archaeological remains: Variable light and light-to-moderate concentrations of surface pottery and rock rubble over an area of about four hectares. No definite structural remains. Ceramic material is predominately Late Aztec.

Classification: Hamlet; fewer than 50 people.

Tx-A-90

Natural setting: As Tx-A-89.

Modern utilization: As Tx-A-89.

Archaeological remains: As Tx-A-89.

Classification: Hamlet; fewer than 50 people.

Tx-A-91

Natural setting: 2470 to 2520 m, at the juncture of the Upper and Lower Piedmonts. Situated along the gently-sloping upper surface of a long, narrow ridge, lying between two major barrancas.

Modern utilization: As in Tx-A-89.

Archaeological remains: As in Tx-A-89, but over an area of 15 hectares.

Classification: Hamlet; fewer than 100 people.

Tx-A-92

Natural setting: 2530 to 2550 m, in the Upper Piedmont. Otherwise, as in Tx-A-89.

Modern utilization: As in Tx-A-89.

Archaeological remains: As in Tx-A-89, over an area of about seven hectares.

Classification: Hamlet; fewer than 50 people.

Tx-A-93

Natural setting: 2600 m, in the Upper Piedmont. Situated on the gently sloping top of a narrow ridge, lying between two major barrancas. Moderate erosion, with shallow soil and continuous grass cover. Heavily forested ridges extending off the main Sierra terminate just to the east.

Modern utilization: Grazing.

Archaeological remains: As in Tx-A-89, over an area of about two hectares.

Classification: Hamlet; fewer than 50 people.

Tx-A-94

Natural setting: 2330 to 2360 m, in the Lower Piedmont. Situated on a broad, gentle slope, at the edge of a major barranca. Moderate erosion, with shallow soil.

Modern utilization: Grazing and rainfall cultivation of subsistence crops.

Archaeological remains: As in Tx-A-89, over an area of about seven hectares.

Classification: Hamlet; fewer than 50 people.

Tx-A-95

Natural setting: 2320 to 2360 m, in the Lower Piedmont. Otherwise, as in Tx-A-94.

Modern utilization: As in Tx-A-94.

Archaeological remains: As in Tx-A-89, over an area of about 10 hectares.

Classification: Hamlet; fewer than 100 people.

Tx-A-96

Natural setting: 2400 m, in the Lower Piedmont. Otherwise, as in Tx-A-94.

Modern utilization: As in Tx-A-94.

Archaeological remains: As in Tx-A-89, over an area of about four hectares.

Classification: Hamlet; fewer than 50 people.

Tx-A-97

Natural setting: As in Tx-A-96.

Modern utilization: As in Tx-A-94.

Archaeological remains: As in Tx-A-89, over an area of about four hectares.

Classification: Hamlet; fewer than 50 people.

Tx-A-98

Natural setting: 2450 m, near the upper edge of the Lower Piedmont. Otherwise, as in Tx-A-89.

Modern utilization: As in Tx-A-89.

Archaeological remains: As in Tx-A-89, over an area of about four hectares.

Classification: Hamlet; fewer than 50 people.

Tx-A-99 (Aztec Coatepec)

Natural setting: 2390 to 2450 m, near the upper edge of the Lower Piedmont. Situated on a broad, gentle slope, near a major barranca. The soil cover is shallow to moderately deep, and generally well preserved due to the maintenance of terrace and bancal systems. Soil becomes progressively thinner upslope.

Modern utilization: Most of the site area is occupied by the modern dispersed village of Coatepec. The area surrounding this community is intensively cultivated (all rainfall agriculture), with maguey, for pulque production, a principal crop. The modern village of Coatepec is supplied with water for household use by a small canal from a spring in the Sierra foothills (Pl. 55,*c*).

Documentary descriptions: In the 1579 *Relación de Coatepec y su Partido* (Paso Y Troncoso, 1905: 39-65), Coatepec was described as a community of *cabecera* status, whose authority extended over five subordinate villages: Sanct Martyn Tlaylotlacan, Sanct Jhoan Tlachichco, Sanct Sebastian Xocoatlahco, Sancta Maria Magdalena Ameyalco, and Sancta Cathalina Ancapa. In 1579 Coatepec was also the principal *cabecera* within a local district that included four other *cabecera* communities together with their 11 dependent villages.

This same *Relación* describes the environmental setting and water resources of the 1579 community of Coatepec in the following manner (Paso y Troncoso, 1905: 44-45):

> El asiento deste pueblo es tierra descubierta, rrasa y sin monte ni arboleda: tiene pocas fuentes, no ay en el ny en su comarca rrio cabdaloso; solamente ay dos fuentes de agua manantiales, la vna procede desta sierra que de suso se haze myncion; y la otra de otro cerro montuoso y grande que esta hazia el sur—La primera fuente corre e viene derecho a este pueblo y, por estar su nacimiento en tierra alta, la an sacado y abierto vn ojo grande que tiene, e viene por sus caños de ocho o nueve años a esta parte, por que los tiempos de atras este pueblo y sus subjetos carescian de agua y era esteril, y los naturales bebian de aguas lluvias que rrecogian en vnos jagueyes hechos a mano que para este efeto tenian los yndios, y tienen el dia de oy en algunas estancias deste pueblo donde no participan desta agua ny la alcancan: esta fuente corre todo el año—La otra fuente corre todo el tiempo de las aguas y alcanca en algunos pueblos subjetos a esta cabecera, y en tiempo de secano corre y se sume en vn sumidero que tiene cerca de su nascimiento: son ynutiles para rregadios por que la vna fuente y la otra tienen muy poca agua.

In 1579 the total population of Coatepec and its subordinate villages amounted to some 700 "yndios tributarios enteros, y al pie de quatrocientos nyños y nyñas de poca edad. . . ." (ibid: 46). Old people still living in 1579 reported (ibid: 46-47) that in their youth there were

> en esta provincia de Coatepec, mas de diez mill yndios de guerra, sin otra gente menuda, y que en el tiempo de su ynfidelidad las lomas, laderas y valles deste pueblo estauan muy poblados y llenos de caserias y estancias de yndios, y en todas las quebradas, como paresce oy en dia por los paredones, cimyentos de casas y 'cues' que en aquel tiempo avia, y que ansi lo hallaron los españoles quando vinieron a la conquista; y despues de pacifica la tierra lo a estado ansi hasta que de quarenta años a esta parte poco mas o menos, por pestilencias grandes que a avido en diversos tiempos y años, se an dismynuydo en gran manera los naturales, y esta es la causa de que aya al presente tan poca gente en esta provincia, y ansi se cree que sera en las demas desta Nueva España.

Archaeological remains: Variable light, light-to-moderate, and moderate concentrations of surface pottery and rock rubble around the edges of modern Coatepec. Survey could not be effectively carried out within all of the modern village, but it appears that Aztec occupation underlies much of the present-day community. If this is the case, the Aztec site area would total about 85 hectares. Early and Late Aztec ceramics occur in roughly equal proportions. Culhuacan phase Black/Orange, while occuring in limited quantities, seems to be more abundant here than elsewhere in the Texcoco Region.

A single structure was delineated, at the southeast corner of modern Coatepec. This is a flat-topped, solid rock rubble platform, about 3 m high and 30 by 40 m in area, with light-to-moderate concentrations of Aztec surface pottery (Pl. 51,*a*). We have assigned this a ceremonial-civic function.

A prehispanic ballcourt goal marker has been set up at one edge of the main plaza of modern Coatepec. Its original provenience is not known.

Classification: Secondary regional center; 1250 to 2500 people.

Tx-A-100

Natural setting: 2330 to 2340 m, in the Lower Piedmont. Situated on gently sloping and nearly level ground below the eastern base of Cerro Tonaltepec. Slight erosion, with moderately deep to deep soil cover, except at the northeast end of Cerro Tonaltepec where the soil is shallow and there are patches of bare tepetate. A major barranca runs along the north edge of the site.

Modern utilization: Intensive rainfall cultivation, with abundant maguey. The more severely eroded areas at the northwestern corner of Cerro Tonaltepec now serve as grazing land.

Archaeological remains: A series of seven large structures (Appendix II; Pl. 53, 54), all of which appear to be ceremonial-civic in function, are scattered in a linear fashion over a distance of about 2.5 km. There is very little indication of permanent occupation in this area except perhaps at the northwest corner of Cerro Tonaltepec where there are variable light and light-to-moderate concentrations of surface pottery over an area of about two hectares. Otherwise, there is only very light sherd cover throughout the site area.

Classification: Ceremonial-civic precinct, with little or no permanent residence.

Tx-A-101

Natural setting: 2420 m, at the relatively level top of Cerro Tonaltepec. The site rests on a broken, irregular ground surface, some 50 m above the level of the surrounding Lower Piedmont plain. Erosion ranges from moderate to severe. Soil cover is generally shallow, with some patches of bare tepetate.

Modern utilization: Grazing. The hillslopes below the site area have been extensively terraced in the past, but these structures have deteriorated badly, and the slopes are now badly eroded and fit only for marginal grazing.

Documentary references: The *Relación de Coatepec y su Partido* (Paso y Troncoso, 1905: 46), dating from 1579, indicates that Cerro Tonaltepec had ritual significance for the population of Coatepec during Late Aztec times:

> . . . en este cerro, a vn lado del, esta vna cueva oscura, hondable y temerosa, en donde al tiempo que estos naturales comencaron a ydolatrar, por yndustria de los *mexicanos* que fueron los *culhuas* y *mecites*, adoravan al demonyo y se sacrificavan las orejas rronpiendoselas con puntas de nabajas de la tierra, y esta rresina le encendian con que le encensavan la parte donde el ydolo estaua, y le hazian otros sacrificios, y el demonio se rrevestia en el dicho ydolo de piedra y alli consultavan con el, y el rrespondia a los dichos *tlenamacaz* y les dezia lo que avian de hazer.

We did not locate this cave during the course of our survey.

Archaeological remains: Variable very light and light concentrations of surface pottery over an area of roughly one hectare. A single large mound, measuring roughly 20 m in diameter and about 4 m high, dominates the site. A large pit has revealed a solid rock rubble core, with at least four levels of stuccoed flooring within or atop the structure. This is apparently a ceremonial-civic structure. Much of the hilltop in the vicinity of the mound has been artificially levelled with stone walled terraces, which are now badly deteriorated. Early Classic (Tx-EC-30) and Early Toltec (Tx-ET-24) ceramics are also present in very light concentrations.

Classification: Small hilltop ceremonial precinct. No permanent occupation.

Tx-A-102

Natural setting: 2290 m, in the Lower Piedmont. Otherwise, as in Tx-ET-18.

Modern utilization: As in Tx-ET-18.

Archaeological remains: Variable very light, light, and light-to-moderate concentrations of surface pottery over an area of about 12 hectares. The Aztec ceramic material is very predominately Late, with a few sherds of Early Aztec. The dominant occupational component here is Early Toltec (Tx-ET-18). All the abundant structural remains are presumed to date from Early Toltec times, although some may have continued to be used in the Aztec period. Small amounts of Classic material (Tx-EC-32; Tx-LC-18) are also present.

Classification: Hamlet; fewer than 100 people. The extent and character of the Aztec site here are much obscured by the heavy Early Toltec admixture.

Tx-A-103

Natural setting: 2250 to 2260 m, at the edge of the Lakeshore Plain. Otherwise as in Tx-ET-18.

Modern utilization: As in Tx-ET-18.

Archaeological remains: As in Tx-A-102, over an area of roughly 45 hectares. Light Early Classic (Tx-EC-32), Late Classic (Tx-LC-18), and Late Toltec (Tx-LT-53) pottery is also present. The dominant occupational component is Early Toltec (Tx-ET-18).

Classification: Small dispersed village; 225 to 450 people. The extent and character of the Aztec site are obscured by the heavy Early Toltec admixture.

Tx-A-104

Natural setting: 2250 m, at the edge of the Lakeshore Plain. In a zone of deep alluvial soil, below the northern base of Cerro Portezuelo.

Modern utilization: Intensive rainfall cultivation.

Archaeological remains: Variable very light, light, and light-to-moderate concentrations of surface pottery over an area of about five hectares. No structural remains. Ceramics are predominately Late Aztec, with a few Early Aztec sherds.

Classification: Hamlet; fewer than 50 people.

Tx-A-105

Natural setting: 2310 m, otherwise, as Tx-TF-51.

Modern utilization: As Tx-TF-51.

Archaeological remains: Variable very light, light, and light-to-moderate concentrations of surface pottery over an area of about three hectares. No structural remains can be assigned to the Aztec period with any certainty. Aztec pottery is predominately Late, with small quantities of Early Aztec sherds. The dominant occupational component is Terminal Formative (Tx-TF-51), and all structural remains here are assumed to belong to that period.

Classification: Hamlet; fewer than 50 people.

Tx-A-106

Natural setting: 2240 m, at the southern base of Cerro Chimalhuacan, near the Conquest-period shoreline of Lake Texcoco. Situated in a zone of deep alluvial soil.

Modern utilization: The site area is located at the northern edge of the modern village of Chimalpa. The land to the north and east is devoted to intensive rainfall cultivation of subsistence crops. The old lake bed to the west is presently used for grazing only.

Archaeological remains: Variable light and light-to-moderate concentrations of surface pottery over an area of about one hectare. The ceramic material is predominately Late Aztec, but a few Early Aztec sherds occur. Mixed with somewhat heavier Late Toltec pottery (Tx-LT-57). No structural remains. Modern Chimalpa may overlie substantial quantities of Aztec occupational debris, but effective survey could not be carried out within this village.

Classification: Questionable. If modern Chimalpa covers most of the site, this may only be an edge of a large Aztec village. If Aztec occupation does not extend significantly beneath Chimalpa, we are probably dealing with an Aztec hamlet of fewer than 50 people.

Tx-A-107

Natural setting: 2240 m, along the southwestern base of Cerro Chimalhuacan, at or near the Conquest-period shoreline of Lake Texcoco. Situated in a zone of deep alluvial soil. The ground surface tends to be irregular, with numerous small hillocks and intervening depressions.

Modern utilization: The site occupies a stretch of vacant land between the nucleated village of Chimalco to the north and Atlapulco to the southeast. At present, the site area serves predominately as grazing land. Much of the sloping area immediately east and north of the site has been extensively terraced. Only a few of the lowermost terraces, however, now support cultivation, while the higher slopes serve only as pasture. Several small basalt quarries (both operative and abandoned) are found in the area. The quarrying and finishing of this building stone are important activities in Chimalco today.

Archaeological remains: Variable very light, light, light-to-moderate, and moderate concentrations of surface pottery over an area of about 32 hectares. The ceramic material is very predominately Late Aztec, but a scattering of Early Aztec sherds occurs. Substantial proportions of Texcoco Fabric Marked pottery at certain localities within the site suggest that salt-making was of some importance here during Aztec times. Only two structures are recognizable (Appendix

II). Concentrations of sherd debris, and vaguely mounded areas suggest the former existence of other structures now no longer recognizable as such. The irregular ground surface makes it even more difficult to distinguish and delineate prehispanic structures.

Substantial Late Toltec (Tx-LT-56) is also present throughout most of the Aztec site.

Classification: The size of the Aztec site is questionable, as substantial occupational debris could underlie the closely packed structures of modern Chimalco and Atlapulco where effective survey could not be carried out. The surveyed area, considered as an isolated unit, represents a small dispersed village of 200 to 400 people.

Tx-A-108

Natural setting: 2520 m, at the top of Cerro Chimalhuacan, some 280 m above the level of the surrounding Lakeshore Plain. Shallow to moderately deep soil cover, with numerous rock outcrops over an irregular ground surface. Slight erosion.

Modern utilization. Grazing, plus limited rainfall cultivation on the relatively level hilltop. The gently sloping surface of the broad lower ridge to the north is intensively cultivated. The hillslopes north of the site are intricately terraced, but these terraces have fallen into disrepair and support only grazing land and some maguey today.

Documentary descriptions: The 1579 *Relación de Chimalhuacan-Atenco* (Paso y Troncoso, 1905: 73) mentions that in addition to the religious temples within the Chimalhuacan center itself during Late Aztec times, there were also others "encima deste cerro Chimalhuacan." A variety of ceremonial and ritual activities were performed at these localities.

Archaeological remains: Variable very light and light concentrations of surface pottery over an area of about 20 by 20 m at the peak of Cerro Chimalhuacan. This ceramic material appears to be mixed Early and Late Aztec, but is not particularly diagnostic in this respect. There are no definite structural remains, but heavy concentrations of rock rubble and traces of stone wall bases, suggest the former existence of a small temple platform. An anomalous rock carving was found near this possible structure.

Traces of Late Toltec (Tx-LT-55) and Terminal Formative (Tx-TF-48) pottery are also present.

Classification: Hilltop ceremonial precinct; no permanent occupation.

Tx-A-109 (Aztec Chimalhuacan)

Natural setting: 2240 to 2250 m, with scattered occupational debris up to 2380 m. Situated on gently sloping to level ground at the northwestern base of Cerro Chimalhuacan, extending northward into the main Lakeshore Plain, at or near the Conquest-period shoreline of Lake Texcoco. In a zone of deep alluvial soil, with no significant erosion except where small parts of the site extend onto the lower hillslopes. The ground surface is characteristically irregular, with numerous small, dunelike hillocks separated by intervening depressions.

Modern utilization: The western end of the modern town of Chimalhuacan, and the nucleated village of Santa María Natívitas, are situated within the Aztec site. These modern communities appear to overlie substantial prehispanic occupation, but effective survey could not be carried out everywhere within their borders. The modern asphalt highway and railroad tracks cut through the eastern end of the site. The hillslopes south and west of the site have been extensively terraced in the past, but all terraces are now badly deteriorated, and only limited cultivation is carried out there today. A narrow band of flat land around the northern base of Cerro Chimalhuacan is intensively cultivated, and an intricate system of drainage ditches have given this area a distinctly chinampa-like appearance. The broad, gently sloping plain south of the site is devoted to intensive rainfall cultivation of subsistence crops. The old lake bed north of the site area is predominately grazing land, except to the east where large-scale drainage and flushing operations have reclaimed considerable land for agriculture. Small basalt quarries, both operative and abandoned, occur throughout the hillslopes above the modern town.

Documentary descriptions: The *Relación de Chimalhuacan-Atenco* (Paso y Troncoso, 1905: 65-79) describes Chimalhuacan as a community of *cabecera* status in 1579, under the local jurisdiction of Coatepec, with a tributary population of "trezientos yndios escasos y ciento y noventa nyños de nueve para diez años . . ." (ibid: 67). At that time

> este pueblo de Chimalhuacan esta fundado y asentado en tierra llana y descubierta, a la halda del dicho cerro que dizen *Chimalhuacan*, a la parte del poniente: los pueblos que le son sujetos estan poblados al rrededor del dicho cerro que esta dicho, y todos rrodean el dicho cerro Chimalhuacan, y poblados a la orilla de van laguna grande de agua que alcanca a Mexico, Texcuco

y otros pueblos; el asiento deste pueblo es tierra rrasa syn montes ny arboledas; tiene muchas fuentes de agua manantiales de muy buena agua que corren y entran en la dicha laguna: el agua destas fuentes, de noche y a la mañana, suele estar caliente y tibia, y entre dia fria: nascen todas estas fuentes del dicho cerro *Chimalhuacan*: en este pueblo ny su comarca no ay rrio cabdaloso; es tierra fertil de pastos para ganado menor; no hay nyngunas frutas de Castilla; de la tierra no hay otra sino las tunas blancas, coloradas y amarillas y leonadas; algunos años, como esta dicho, suelen ser esteriles de mantenimyentos de mayz, agi e frijoles y otras legumbres de la tierra; la tierra es salitral por cause de muchas lagunillas de agua que ay cerca del pueblo: probeense de bastimientos en las probincias de Chalco y Coatepec los naturales deste pueblo (ibid: 66-67).

Lake Texcoco was of considerable significance to the inhabitants of Chimalhuacan in early colonial times (ibid: 59):

. . . los naturales del dicho pueblo tienen sus canoas grandes y pequeñas de madera en que pasan la dicha laguna y van e vienen en ellas a la dicha cibdad e a otros pueblos comarcanos questan poblados dentro de la dicha laguna, a sus contrataciones y granjerias que tienen: en esta laguna se cria pescado poco mas de un palmo de largo y casi son como albures; y ansi mismo hay otro genero que dizen pescado blanco, sano, bueno y sabroso de comer, que algunos son de a palmo y otros mas grandes y mas pequeños; crianse ansi mismo pescadillos pequeños, rranas y camaroncillos y otros generos de chucherias, y marisco, que pescan los naturales para su sustento y contrataciones que tienen en los mercados y 'tianguez' que se hazen en cada semana en los pueblos comarcanos. . . .

In constructing their houses (ibid: 78), the natives of Chimalhuacan in 1579

sacan el cimiento de piedra, como lo hazen los españoles, las paredes son de adobes y la techumbre de azoteas: los caciques gouernadores y otros prencicipales, e yndios que tienen posible, labran sus casas del arte y manera que las labran los españoles; las paredes de cal y canto; los materiales son de cal, tierra y arena, todo mezclado, y con esto tiene gran fortaleza; hazenlas con sus altos y baxos, corredores, portadas y ventanas de piedra, con sus encalados y pinturas de colores; la cal que an menester la traen de doze leguas deste pueblo poqure en el no se haze; la madera para maderar y entablar las casas la compran los yndios en los pueblos de Coatepec e Iztapaluca; questan distantes deste pueblo a legua y legua y media, de donde se trae porque no alcancan montes; la piedra blanca que an menester para las portadas y ventanas se sacañ deste cerro Chimalhuacan, que ay cantidad. . . .

In 1579 there was no salt produced in the community of Chimalhuacan. All salt required for household purposes was obtained ". . . de la comarca de Mexico, donde se haze. . . ." (ibid: 77-78).

Cotton for clothing was brought in from the tierra caliente, and purchased in the weekly market held in Chimalhuacan each Monday (ibid: 78).

Chimalhuacan's pre-Conquest population is said to have been more than 8000 (ibid: 67).

Archaeological remains: Variable light, light-to-moderate, moderate, and heavy concentrations of surface pottery over an area of about 260 hectares. The heavy modern overlay undoubtedly obscures substantial Aztec occupational debris, and the site may extend considerably further to the west. Both Early and Late Aztec material is present in roughly equal proportions throughout most of the site area, with Late Aztec pottery distributed somewhat more widely and continuously. Texcoco Fabric Marked pottery is abundant at many localities throughout the eastern two-thirds of the site, and also at the western end.

Despite the large surface area and relatively dense sherd cover, recognizable structural remains are few, and only six (in addition to the large pyramid-plaza complex described below) could be delineated with any degree of certainty (Appendix II). The irregular ground surface and heavy modern overlay have undoubtedly obscured much Aztec architecture (e.g. Pl. 51,*b*). Alluviation has also been a factor in obliterating archaeological features: pits and road cuts throughout the site reveal thick lenses of sherd debris and plastered floors buried at depths of 1 to 2 m below the present ground surface.

The most impressive Aztec structure is a large pyramid-plaza complex in an island of empty ground surrounded on all sides by the densely-packed houses of modern Chimalhuacan. This complex, which has been partially restored in recent years, features a large pyramidal platform mound, built into the hillside, fronting on a level, empty plaza that measures about 50 m square (Pl. 52,*a*). The platform mound stands about 4 m high, is roughly 50 m square, and is constructed of solid rock rubble and earth fill, with plastered exterior stone walls and flat, stuccoed upper surface. A deep pit in its top surface has exposed a large stone sculpture of a coiled serpent, carved from dark basalt. Traces of several stone-walled rooms can be seen at the southern and northern edges of the pyramid, and there are several large, unexcavated mounds on the higher ground just above the west end of the main structure.

Classification: Primary regional center; 6000 to 12,000 people. The site may be somewhat larger if Aztec occupational debris extends significantly westward below modern Chimalhuacan.

Tx-A-110

Natural setting: 2240 m, on the Lakeshore Plain, at or near the Conquest-period shoreline of Lake Texcoco. In a zone of deep alluvial soil.

Modern utilization: The immediate site area is used only as pasture today. The modern railroad track cuts through the length of the site, and the main asphalt highway runs through the western end of the site area. The surrounding plain is intensively cultivated in alfalfa and maize, largely by means of mechanized irrigation. A number of residential households, and several industrial and commercial agricultural complexes are scattered over the general site area. The modern nucleated village of San Vincente Chicoloapan lies to the southeast of the site area.

Archaeological remains: Variable light, light-to-moderate, and moderate concentrations of surface pottery and rock rubble over an area of about 17 hectares. The surrounding alfalfa fields and modern construction may obscure some Aztec occupational debris. The ceramic material is predominately Late Aztec, with a few sherds of Early Aztec pottery. There is very little Texcoco Fabric Marked pottery. There are no distinct structural remains, but several large, vague mounded areas, which contain relatively higher concentrations of sherds and rock rubble, suggest the presence of buried residential complexes.

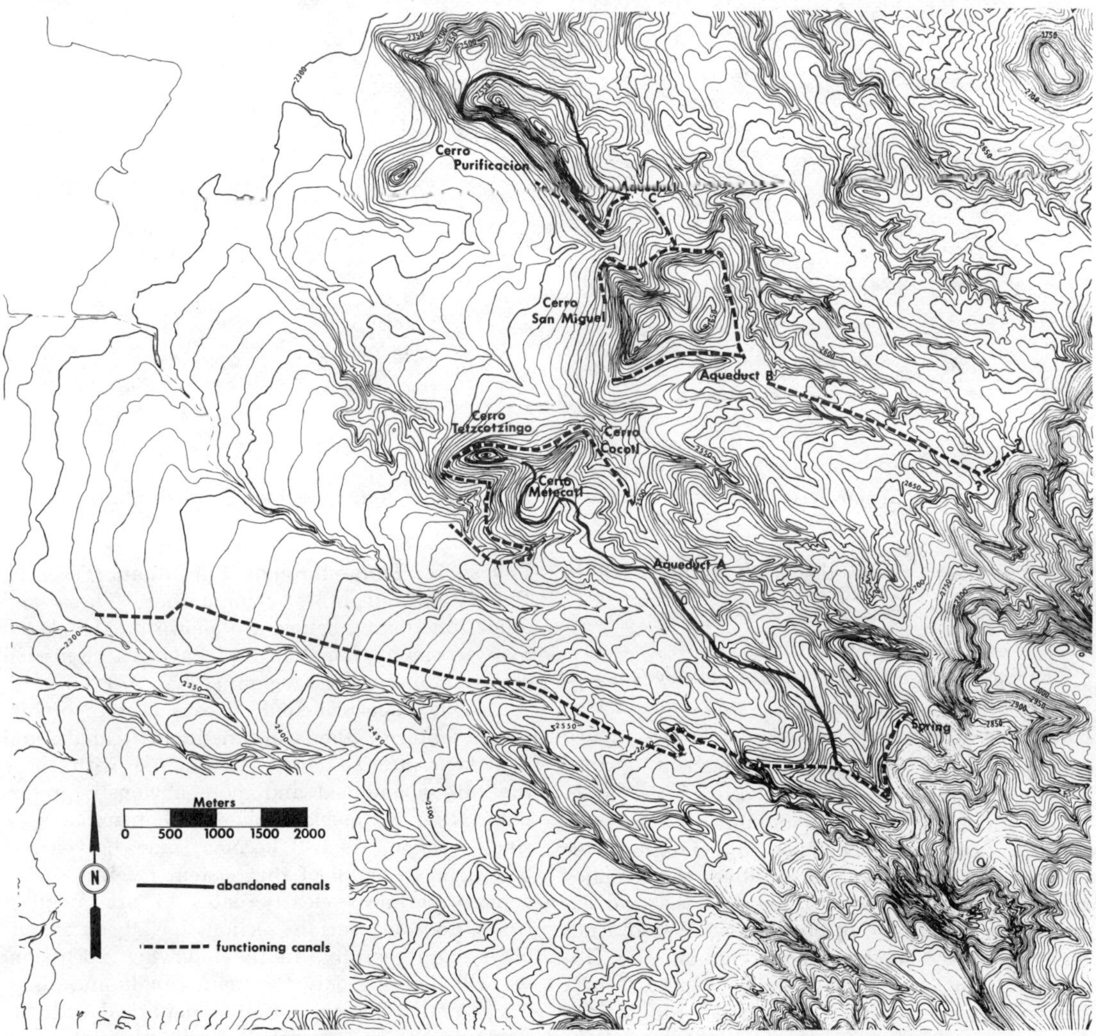

Fig. 31—Major irrigation canals examined, functioning and abandoned. Topographic map.

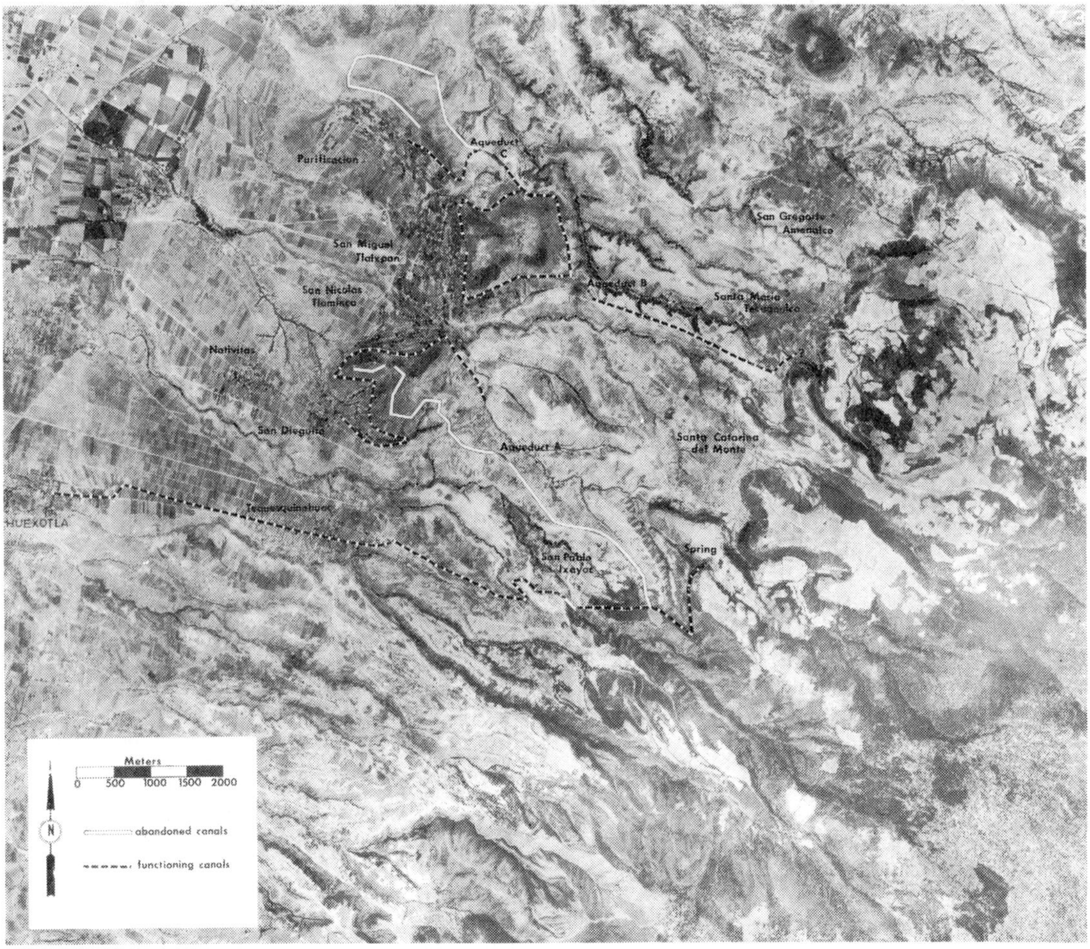

Fig. 32 — Major irrigation canals examined, functioning and abandoned. Vertical air-photo.

Classification: Small dispersed village; 175 to 250 people.

Prehispanic Waterworks

The east-central sector of our survey area is traversed by a series of canals and aqueducts—both operative and abandoned—which have served to carry water from permanent springs scattered along the western base of the main Sierra into residential communities and agricultural fields in the Upper and Lower Piedmont zones. Figs. 31 and 32 show those major segments of this hydraulic network that we examined in the course of our surveys. We did not map either the modern canals linking the villages of San Gregorio Amanalco, Santa María Tecuanulco, and Santa Catarina del Monte, nor the northernmost canal system leading down across the Lower Piedmont and onto the main Lakeshore Plain through San Juan Tezontla, Papalotla, and other communities. These and other functioning canals are shown on the sketch map accompanying Wolf and Palerm's discussion of irrigation in this region (1955: 270).

Although our principal concern is with prehispanic features, the still-functioning canals and aqueducts are so closely associated with those that are abandoned and more obviously prehispanic, that we must consider both together as a single system. As will become somewhat clearer below, much or all of this system (at least in its general outlines) clearly dates to pre-Conquest times, and only certain sections have been abandoned more recently. In the following discussion, we will describe only the main canals and aqueducts, and will make no attempt to deal with the numerous secondary canals feeding off the main supply routes.

There are two principal subunits of the waterworks system under consideration: (1) a northern network, supplied by one or several springs (not located by us) east of San Gregorio Amanalco and Santa María Tecuanulco, which runs westward to Purificación and San Miguel Tlaixpan; and (2) a southern network, supplied by a single permanent spring south of Santa Catarina del Monte, which runs westward through San Pablo Ixayoc and Tequesquinahuac to Huexotla, and also to the Aztec ruins (Tx-A-62) on Cerro Tetzcotzingo. A shorter canal system, supplied by the more-or-less permanent water flow through a large barranca, leads through San Nicolas Tlaminca, San Dieguito, and Natívitas.

The Northern Subunit

In the northern network, water runs through a complex series of major and secondary canals as it passes from the spring(s) through the villages of San Gregorio Amanalco, Santa María Tecuanulco, and Santa Catarina del Monte. A northern branch of this same network carries water to San Juan Tezontla, San Joaquin, and Santa Inés, beyond our present area of concern. At the western edge of Santa María Tecuanulco a pair of simple, parallel canals, each dug about 25 cm into the tepetate surface and measuring roughly 25 to 50 cm wide, carry water westward across the erosion-scarred surface of the Upper Piedmont.

About 3 km to the west of Santa María Tecuanulco this pair of canals angles off abruptly to the northwest across the top of a large aqueduct (Aqueduct B) of earth and rock-rubble construction (Pl. 55,*a*). This latter feature is 375 m in length, stands from 2 to 5 m high, and measures roughly 2 m wide across its upper surface. At the north end of Aqueduct B, water is stored in a large reservoir, and from this point is directed to the north and west around the midsection of Cerro San Miguel into the households and irrigated terraces of San Miguel Tlaixpan. In all cases, water canals are simply dug a few cm into tepetate, or are built up slightly above ground surface with earth and rock-rubble fill. Within the village of San Miguel Tlaixpan itself, canal walls are often stone-lined, but little construction of this nature was noted in other areas, and little stuccoing of canal walls or bases was seen.

Near the northeast corner of Cerro San Miguel a canal forks off to the northwest and carries water across a large earth and rock-rubble aqueduct (Aqueduct C) onto the southern flank of Cerro Purificación (Pl. 56,*b*). Aqueduct C, the largest of the four aqueducts in this area, measures roughly 400 m long, stands 13 m high at its midpoint, and is 2 to 3 m wide across its top. The modern canal, a simple affair a few cm deep, runs along the side of the aqueduct, about midway between its base and top. At least two superimposed levels of abandoned canals are discernable on the aqueduct's upper surface (Pl. 57,*a*). The uppermost canal rests upon a basal platform, 2 m wide and 50 cm high. This canal itself is a semicircular trough roughly 25 cm deep. Both the canal and its basal platform are constructed of a coarse gravel mortar, apparently of posthispanic construction. Faint traces of a stone-lined canal, running along the top of the aqueduct directly below the basal platform of the upper canal, can be seen at intervals along the aqueduct's length.

At the western end of Aqueduct C the canal system again bifurcates into two segments which encircle Cerro Purificación. Only one of these segments is still functioning. This supplies Purificación with water for household use and some terrace irrigation. The northern segment, encircling Cerro Purificación on the east, north, and west, is now abandoned, and apparently has been for some time. Over most of its 4 km length it exists as a clearly visible terrace of earth and rock rubble, often elaborately built up to heights of 1 to 3 m (Pl. 57,*b*). Along the steep western flanks of the hill there are several examples of two- or three-tiered butresses, totaling up to 10 m high, supporting the former canal bed. In at least two places the canal has been cut through solid rock.

Aztec settlement is abundant throughout the area traversed by the canal and aqueduct system we have described. Tx-A-69, -70, -71, -72, -76, -77, and -78 are all situated around, alongside, or near the functioning and abandoned canals. There are, however, no obvious or definite means of associating the construction and use of such waterworks with any of these Aztec communities.

Pre-Aztec settlement is scant or nonexistent within the area traversed by the canals: A Terminal Formative hamlet (Tx-TF-16), an Early Classic hamlet (Tx-EC-8), and a Late Classic hamlet (Tx-LC-8) are located just to the northeast of Aqueduct B; the westernmost edge of a Terminal Formative segregated elite district (Tx-TF-14) overlaps the abandoned canal near the eastern end of Cerro Purificación.

The Southern Subunit

This network is apparently supplied by a sin-

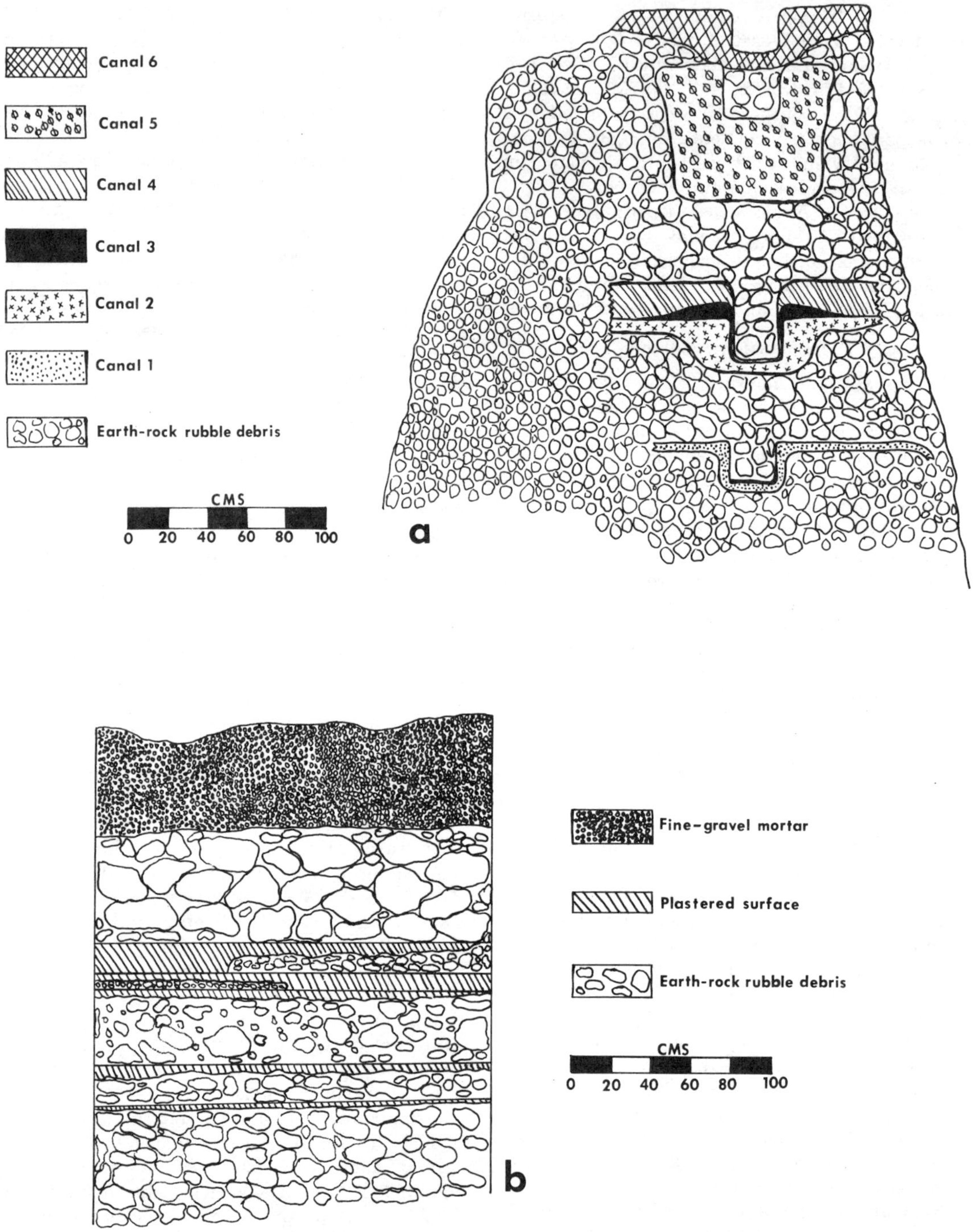

Fig. 33—*a*) Composite cross section of superimposed canals, Causeway A. *b*) Longitudinal section through superimposed canals, Causeway A.

gle spring situated at about 2650 m in the western foothills of the main Sierra, to the south of Santa Catarina del Monte. Today water flows from this point through a rock-lined canal into the villages of San Pablo Ixayoc, Tequesquinahuac, and finally to Huexotla, some 8.5 km to the west. This water is used almost exclusively for household purposes, and its utilization for purposes of irrigation is very minor or absent.

In the foothills east of San Pablo Ixayoc, faint traces of an abandoned canal can be traced from the functioning canal northwestwards to Aqueduct A. This latter feature is a massive earth and rock-rubble construction, about 250 m long and 10 m high at its center, measuring roughly 2 m wide across its upper surface (Pl. 56,*a*). At least six levels of canals are vertically superimposed atop the aqueduct (Fig. 33). This construction has produced a mass of rock-rubble fill and intervening canal floors standing somewhat over 2 m high along most of the aqueduct's top surface.

The uppermost three or four canal levels are constructed of a coarse mortar of red volcanic gravel, indistinguishable from that employed in the colonial and modern architecture in the area. The bottoms and side walls of the lowermost canals are stuccoed, and are quite distinct in appearance relative to the overlying upper levels. In all cases, the canals measure roughly 25 cm wide and 25 cm deep.

West of Aqueduct A traces of the abandoned canal are better preserved. On the western slopes of Cerro Metecatl the canal is clearly visible as an artificially built-up and levelled feature, standing up to 1 m high in several places.

This canal terminates in the Aztec ceremonial-civic complex on Cerro Tetzcotzingo (Tx-A-62), where, as our earlier description of that site indicated, the canal is clearly associated with the prehispanic remains. This clearly demonstrates the Aztec date of the abandoned canal system leading over Aqueduct A (although part or all of this system may have continued in use durduring post-Conquest times). This consideration strongly suggests, though it does not prove, that the main outlines of the remaining canal networks we have described in this section also date to Aztec times in terms of their construction and use.

The villages of San Nicolas Tlaminca, San Dieguito, and Natívitas are supplied with water (predominately for household use, but with some terrace irrigation in San Nicolas Tlaminca) by means of a shallow, stone-lined canal carrying water from the bed of a barranca north of Aqueduct A around the base of the Cerro Cocotl-Tetzcotzingo-Metecatl complex. The water flow of this barranca is apparently year-round, and its source is probably a spring similar to that which supplies the Huexotla canal further south.

The density of prehispanic occupation within the area traversed by the southern subunit of canal networks is substantially less than that of the northern subunit. Aside from the Tx-A-62 complex on Cerro Tetzcotzingo, and the Aztec urban center at Huexotla (Tx-A-87), there are only a handful of small Aztec villages that might have appropriated household or irrigation water from this canal system: Tx-A-59, Tx-A-60, and Tx-A-86. Significant pre-Aztec occupation is limited to the sizable Formative sites on the slopes of Cerro Tetzcotzingo-Metcatl (Tx-LF-12, Tx-TF-20, and Tx-TF-21).

Particularly relevant to the prehispanic construction and operation of this southern canal network is an early colonial text — "The Titles of Tetzcotzinco (Santa María Natívitas)"—published and translated by McAfee and Barlow (1946). This document begins with a plea by various subjects of Netzahualcoyotl to their ruler for water rights. Netzahualcoyotl stated in reply (ibid: 112-17):

'Do not worry, 15. because yonder's what you ask for, 16. the water you will drink. 17. Let the *Chichimeca* assemble 18. and go and take the springing water. 19, It rises in Yelloxochitlan, 20. in truth, it is there; 21. fetch it hither. 22. And by virtue of your blood 23. you will obtain it so as to bring it here 24. so as to guide it here, 25. by your toil you will fetch it 26. in order to work 27. in my town, Tetzcotzinco.

28. Then Nezahualcoyotl took them to Yelloxochitlan; 29. there he showed all the hills to Xochipantzin, 30. and said, 31: 'My son, know that they're full: 32. carry off the water for it's yours. 33. And know that while you live, 34. these are the hills I give you:

35. First, Mt. Quetzaltepec 36. (in truth Quetzalcoatl is there) 37. so that your town (Santa María Natívitas) may keep it, 38. so that Nezahualpilli may guide.'

39. Second, Mt. Otlatlitec. 40. All of it is borne through the woodland.

41. Third, Mt. Quauhyacac. 42. All of it is borne 43. around the back of the hills in an aqueduct.

And from Mt. Tzinacanoztoc it goes straight 45. to Tezontla and Ixayoc. 46. None shall take it from you, for it is my royal property. 47. In truth (these waters) will serve all of my children 48. who are there in the royal town of Tetzcoco.

49. The fourth is your royal town of Tetzcotzinco; 50. there it's all full of fine obsidian, of jade bracelets. 51. In truth, my home is your royal house, 52. Quetzalitzcalco; 53. this is full of gold, 54. for in truth [the town] will be your shield and your sword.

55. And the water, my children will drink it 56. there in my royal town, 57. put inside an aqueduct, it comes.

58. And the young men's water, 59. and the woodland, 60. they will be worked by the young ladies, 61. because they're (now) their property.

62. And the water that rises in Cuauhpechco 63. shall not be appropriated by anyone, 64. because it must always be flowing here in my royal retreat, 65. Tezoyuca, where Cuauhyacac forms a neck.

66. Here it will always work. 67. It will be following the aqueduct 68. which skirts the hill. 69. I leave it, I grant to Tlalopopcatzin [of?] Tezontla. 70. His children will drink it, and will be aided, be succored. 71. Absolutely no one shall take it from them, 72. for it is theirs, for through their efforts they brought it in.

73. And may you make your town strong, 74. and all the woodlands. 75. And the Quetzaltepec water, 76. perhaps Huexotla will ask Tlazolyahuitl and Maxiuitl for a little, 77. and when you want it you may have it, 78. because it is your water, your property.'

79. And then Nezahualcoyotl and Xochipantzin brought in the water 80. and their men came to tap it in Xoloteopan, 81. whereby it came alongside Chiconquiauitl, thence straight alongside Tetecatl (Metecatl), 82. thence by Tetzcotzinco; 83. and thence it came to enter the home town of Xochipantzin. 84. And then he [Nezahualcoyotl]said to them:

85. 'And this water of Zacaxohitlan comes from Yolloxochitlan, 86. on being steered through Tetzcotzingo; 87. it is the property of Xochipantzin's wife the lady Xiloxochitl Iquetzaltzin 88. and their son Quetzalmalmacuixe, the tlatocapilli.

89. Then he Nezahualcoyotl said to them, 90. 'And may you make your town strong. And Quauhtlatzacuilotzin wouldn't make any commitments, 92. and didn't want to come. 93. I called him, to see if he asked for anything, 94. and he replied that he was already satisfied. 95. And the Quetzaltepec water, 96. perhaps Huexotla, Tlazolyahuitl and Maxihuitl will ask for a little. 97. And when you want it you may have it, 98. because it is your water, your royal property. 99. It's your town; 100. all the woodlands are your royal fields, 101. and if the children of Maxihuitl and Tlazolyahuitl are good, 102. you will leave it to them, 103. And if they are unruly, 104. then only shall you take it away from them; 105. this is all I have to say; 106. it is my royal command.'

107. And on the side of the hill called Tetzcotzinco, 108. there they drew his picture, 109. as his face was; 110. and beside it on the stone, 111. something like a *quetzalcuetlachtli,* 112. his artificers drew, or sculptured, 113. by order of Nezahualcoyotzin, 114. whereby he was represented 115. so that there they should see it, 116. his children, his grandchildren and everybody.'

This suggests to us (as it did to Wolf and Palerm, 1955) that the canal and aqueduct system was constructed by the authority of Netzahualcoyotl in the 15th century. It is apparent that a part of the water carried by this canal system was intended for the "pleasure gardens" and royal retreats at Tetzcotzingo and elsewhere. It also appears that at least two Aztec communities (Santa María Natívitas and Huexotla are specifically mentioned) had certain hereditary rights to a part of this water. What use these communities made of this water is not made explicit, but there is no direct mention of applying it for agricultural purposes.

Writing in 1582, Pomar (1941: 53) offers a useful general statement regarding prehispanic irrigation and its uses in Late Aztec times:

> Río principal y caudaloso no hay ninguno en esta ciudad [Texcoco] ni cerca de ella, porque los arroyos de agua que corren por ella apenas pueden llegar á la laguna tiempo de seca. Aun para esto fué menester incorporar y reducir en uno muchas fuentes de sus propios nacimientos, quitándolos de sus cursos y corrientes naturales, recogiéndolos en caños y acequias que para ello hicieron Nezahualcoyotzin y Nezahualpitzintli, no tanto para beber, porque tenían agua de pozos para esto, cuanto para regar sus huertas y jardines y otras posesiones y casas de placer, aunque ahora se sirven de ella en muchas partes de sus riberas para regadíos de sementeras de maíz y trigo, y en que han hecho los españoles molinos y batanes; como es del río que viene á esta ciudad de las fuentes de Alatlhitia y de otras sus vecinas, de las montañas y serranía de esta ciudad, en los capítulos pasados referidas, con que antiguamente se regaban unas montañuelas y cerros pequeños que llaman *cuauhyacatl,* que quiere decir principio de monte, en donde los señores de esta ciudad [Texcoco] tenían muchas y diversas plantas de flores de muchas y varias colores y muy singulares olores, así de las pro-

pias y que naturalmente se dan y crían en esta tierra, como otras de tierras templadas y calientes, que criaban con mucho regalo y beneficio.

Pomar's description implies that irrigation works in prehispanic times were intended primarily for supporting a variety of exotic vegetation and recreational facilities contained in the pleasure gardens and rural retreats of Texcocan rulers. At the time Pomar wrote, however, in the late sixteenth century, these hydraulic resources had all been converted to agricultural and other utilitarian purposes.

Prehispanic Occupation of the Sierra

Shortage of time prevented intensive examination of the rugged slopes and high valleys of the Texcocan Sierra. Likewise, the beligerent and hostile attitude of many inhabitants of Santa Catarina del Monte, Santa María Tecuanulco, and San Gregorio Amanalco permitted only superficial surveys within the borders of these three villages at the western base of the Sierra. Our hurried reconnaissance in both these areas, however, indicates little or no prehispanic occupation of any significance. These impressions are reinforced by our failure to find any significant trace of prehispanic occupation in San Pablo Ixayoc, a village south of Santa Catarina del Monte where we had no difficulty in carrying out intensive surveys.

With a single exception, we noted only a few scattered Aztec sherds in those sections of these three villages and the slopes and valleys of the Sierra that we walked through. The exception consists of a unique ceremonial complex atop the treeless, windblown peak of Cerro Tlaloc at an elevation of over 13,000 feet along the crest of the main Sierra, about 22 km east of Chimalhuacan (well east of the limits of our survey maps). This site has previously been reported and described by Wicke and Horcasitas (1957). In addition to their observations of surface remains, these investigators excavated a one-meter-square pit in which Aztec and Late Toltec sherds occurred together to a depth of 15 inches (1957: 90, 93):

> In general the sherds were badly weathered. Judging from their shapes, many were from incense burners. Signs of Archaic [Formative] or Teotihuacan types were completely absent. The most significant feature of the sherds collected is the large proportion of black-on-red forms. . . .
>
> Fragments of pottery belonging to the Tula-Mazapan complex [Late Toltec] were also noted. Among them were parts of a dish with the characteristic parallel undulating red lines on a yellowish base. Part of a Tlaloc effigy vessel was also uncovered. It is similar, even in the detail of the twisted handle, to one found by Acosta at Tula.
>
> Sherds of the Aztec complex were also noted, but they lacked the characteristic thin-line decorations, probably as a result of weathering . . . .
>
> Two 'gingerbread' figures were uncovered as well as two animal heads and a Mazapan figurine head. . . .
>
> In addition to the ceramics, a number of minute bits of turquoise cut in quadrilaterals were discovered. It is probable that they once formed part of a mosaic.

Our own brief observations of surface pottery revealed only a very light scatter of Aztec sherds throughout the site area.

Wicke and Horcasitas (1957: 88) have described the architectural complex consisting of massive walls of rough lava blocks (Fig. 34):

> One enters the complex . . . from the north by means of a long wall-lined passageway. Here the rocks which originally made up the upper parts of the wall have fallen, covering the lower parts. In several places, however, the lower part of the wall is visible and here construction methods may be noted. The stones forming these walls, as well as those of the rest of the complex, are only roughly hewn. Care was taken, though, to face the walls with flat-surfaced stones. The source of the stone is a nearby quarry to the southeast of the ruins.
>
> On entering the pasageway formed by the walls described above, one walks over rock outcroppings which form four natural terraces. All that is visible here are two walls on either side, the rising incline in front and the sky above. . . .
>
> Just before arriving at the end of the passageway we encountered a circular arrangement of stones which almost blocked the way, as it left only a narrow space open on each side.
>
> Essentially the temple consisted of a double-walled enclosure containing the foundations of several structures. In some cases the stones are so tumbled that only the vaguest idea of the original ground plan can be determined. In three of the corners are concentrated large masses of fallen stones. These seem to indicate, by the depression in the center of each, that they formed the walls of corner structures.
>
> Among these foundations is a rectangular pit which has been cut out of the living rock and which measures one meter by two meters and 30 cm. Its actual depth could not be determined, as it has been partially filled with stones. One of the blocks at its mouth appears to have been used to cover part of the opening. As to the purpose of the pit, we can only guess. Water supply would have been a problem, especially in the dry season. . . . The closest stream was two hours away, though dry stream beds were seen closer by. Thus the cut could have been a means of supplying the temple with water. There is also the possibility that this was the chasm into which the bodies of the sacrificed victims were thrown.

The fragment of a crudely carved stone idol,

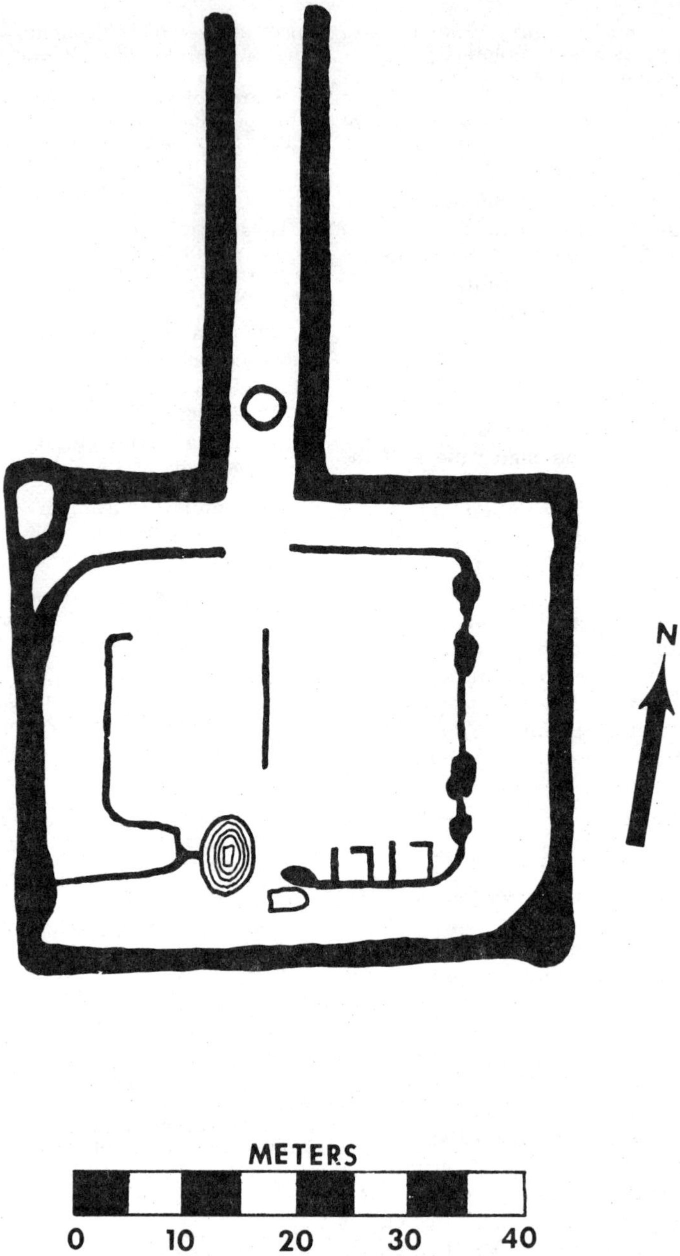

Fig. 34—Plan of large ceremonial structure atop Cerro Tlaloc. From Wicke and Horcasitas (1957), with minor modifications.

which Wicke and Horcasitas identify as a representation of Tlaloc, was found near the southwest corner of the complex.

In their collapsed condition, the walls of the architectural complex measure about 2 to 3 m thick and stand roughly 1 to 2 m high.

Wicke and Horsasitas cite several documentary sources referring to the ceremonial importance of Cerro Tlaloc in late prehispanic times, including Duran's description of a ceremonial center said to have been located at the top of this peak. They also give an account of the use of this locality as a place of ceremonial activity, involving the sacrifice of a human infant, as late as 1887.

SUMMARY

Middle Formative

The initial occupation of the Texcoco Region by fairly substantial communities occurred early in the first millennium B.C. There are no indications of such inhabitation prior to this time, and our survey did not recover recognizable traces of Early Formative or preceramic material.

Middle Formative occupation is largely restricted to small hamlets of under five hectares in surface area, with populations of fewer than 50 people. These communities are for the most part situated well up in the Lower Piedmont zone between elevations of 2300 and 2500 m, and very often lie along or near major or secondary barrancas. In most cases, Middle Formative sites continued to be occupied in Late and Terminal Formative times, and Middle Formative surface pottery is usually mixed with variable proportions of later material. Likewise, little or no Middle Formative architecture can be identified as such on the basis of surface examination. In nearly all cases we have assumed that where such architecture is preserved (not at all common on Formative sites), its superficial aspect dates to the latest period of significant occupation.

The single exception to this predominant Middle Formative settlement pattern is a large nucleated village (Tx-MF-13) covering some 45 hectares, with an estimated population of 600 to 1200 people. In marked contrast to the Lower Piedmont location of nearly all other Middle Formative sites, this large community is situated at 2240 m on the flat Lakeside Plain, at the edge of Lake Texcoco, just below the eastern base of Cerro Chimalhuacan (2520 m).

Late Formative

Two significant demographic trends become clearly apparent by Late Formative times in the middle first millennium B.C. First, there was a substantial population increase as evidenced by the greater abundance and larger size of sites. Second, the greater variety of site types, and indications of greater architectural complexity within some sites suggest a certain amount of increased socio-political differentiation within the Texcoco Region relative to Middle Formative times.

Small hamlets of fewer than 50 people are still the dominant settlement type, but several dispersed and nucleated villages, each measuring between 8 and 40 hectares and containing from 100 to 1800 people, are also present. A single large site of 86 hectares may have had a residential population as high as 3500 people.

Many Late Formative communities expanded directly from existing Middle Formative sites. A significant number, however, grew up in previously unoccupied areas, both adjacent to the same barranca systems along which Middle Formative communities had clustered in the Lower Piedmont, and beside watercourses not formerly utilized for residential purposes. The large Middle Formative village at the base of Cerro Chimalhuacan appears to have shrunk in size and occupational density. This is the only major exception to the general trend toward increase in size and density of existing Middle Formative communities in Late Formative times.

One of the most interesting aspects of Late Formative settlement is the appearance of a few sites on the Lakeshore Plain at localities far from any hill land, and apparently well below the Conquest-period shoreline of Lake Texcoco (e.g. Tx-LF-13, -14). This anticipates a trend that continues into Terminal Formative times on a somewhat more expanded basis.

Terminal Formative

The trends toward population expansion and socio-political differentiation established during Late Formative times continued into the Terminal Formative period at the end of the first millennium B.C. Although small hamlets of fewer than 100 people were still the most numerous single type of site, over 95 percent of the estimated population resided in much larger dispersed villages, nucleated villages, and secondary regional centers. A dozen sites measured over 15 hectares in surface area and contained nucleated populations of several hundred to a few thousand persons. Several of such sites show distinct ceremonial-civic precincts, with the first beginnings of truly monumental public architecture in the Texcoco Region.

A unique characteristic of Terminal Formative settlement, not found in any earlier or subsequent occupation of the Texcoco Region, was the sizable number of architecturally-complex hilltop or ridgetop sites (Tx-TF-4, -10, -13, -14, -36, and -51). None of these sites show evidence of significant reoccupation or use after Terminal Formative times.

Some Late Formative sites were largely or partially abandoned in Terminal Formative times. A more general trend, however, is toward an expansion in the size of Late Formative communities in the Terminal Formative period, and the founding of new residential loci in previously unoccupied areas. The Terminal Formative saw a general filling in of the Texcoco Region to an extent unmatched until Aztec times, well over a millennium later.

In Terminal Formative times the fairly distinct outlines of four principal demographic zones appear for the first time: (1) in the southwest, around the western base of Cerro Chimalhuacan (Tx-TF-44, -46, -50, -51); (2) in the south-central sector east of modern Coatlinchan (Tx-TF-25, -30, -31, -32, -33, -34, -35, and -36); (3) in the central sector along the western base of the arc of hills formed by the Cerro Purificación-San Miguel-Cocotl-Tetzcotzingo complex (Tx-TF-14, -17, -20), and (4) in the northern sector, along the southern base of the Patlachique Range (Tx-TF-1, Tx-TF-4).

Within each of these zones are to be found the full range of site types, including one or two communities sufficiently large, densely occupied, and architecturally complex to be considered as secondary regional centers. This type of demographic zoning may be faintly foreshadowed, on a somewhat different pattern, in Late Formative times.

Early Classic

With the beginning of Classic times early in the first millennium A.D. came a profound shift in settlement configuration, and an abrupt termination of the long-term trends towards population expansion, socio-political differentiation, and colonization of vacant lands which had characterized the preceeding millennium of the Formative era. Accompanying the substantial decrease in the absolute number of sites and the complete or partial abandonment of many Terminal Formative communities in Early Classic times, was the reversal to a pattern of predominately small hamlets, few of which exceeded five hectares in surface area or 100 people in population. Very few sites of this period reveal obvious architectural remnants, and, with one or two possible exceptions, there are no indications of the former presence of any structures other than small domestic household units. The only significant exception is a site (Tx-EC-32) covering roughly 60 hectares at the southern edge of the survey area where a heavy Early Toltec overlay has seriously obscured the character of Classic occupation. Even here there may be little or no architectural complexity or social differentiation, and surface remains are suggestive of dispersed occupation.

Early Classic communities occur both within the borders of largely-abandoned Terminal Formative sites, and in previously unoccupied areas. Most sites were situated within the Lower Piedmont zone throughout the survey area, with some settlement along the lakeshore and at the western base of the Sierra in the Upper Piedmont. The demographic zoning of Terminal Formative times is no longer obvious. Rather, there appears to be a relatively uniform scatter of sites throughout the region as a whole.

Late Classic

The features of settlement patterning established in Early Classic times persisted through the middle of the first millennium A.D., with one major innovation: the near-complete abandonment of the south-central sector of the Texcoco Region (the southern half of the central survey strip, the broad area between the central and southern survey strips, and much of the eastern third of the southern survey strip).

Early Toltec

The last centuries of the first millennium A.D. saw a shift in demography and settlement configuration fully as marked and dramatic as that which characterized the onset of the Classic period. There was a tremendous increase in the amount of occupied residential area, accompanied by a concentration of a great majority of the population into a few large, nucleated sites containing abundant monumental architecture. Furthermore, practically all settlement was restricted to the Lower Piedmont and lakeshore segments of the northern and southern margins of the survey area, with a nearly complete abandonment of the entire central part of the Texcoco Region (a pattern that had been anticipated in the antecedent Late Classic period). There were now two demographic foci, a northern and southern, separated by a practically empty band about 16 km wide.

Late Toltec

The beginning of the second millennium A.D. saw a substantial decrease in size and occupational density of the Early Toltec centers, and a scattering of population in numerous tiny hamlets and small dispersed villages. This ruralization process was accompanied by a partial filling in of the central area which had been virtually devoid of permanent settlement during Early Toltec times. Large segments of this latter region, however, continued to remain unoccupied.

A marked trend of Late Toltec settlement was the establishment of residential sites on the Lakeshore Plain zone, in many cases at or near the shoreline of Lake Texcoco. This apparent lacustrine orientation throughout the survey area is all the more impressive considering the scarcity of interior sites throughout the central and southern portions of the Texcoco Region in Late Toltec times.

Aztec

The configuration of Aztec settlement was structured by the combined processes of rapid population expansion and urbanization operating upon the basic pattern established in Late Toltec times. Except along the shoreline of Lake Texcoco, most small hamlets and dispersed villages founded in the Late Toltec period grew in size and increased in occupational density during Aztec times: more slowly, at first, then with increasing rapidity in the Late Aztec period. Small communities were established in unoccupied areas during Early Aztec times. These sites proliferated and expanded at an unprecedented rate in the Late Aztec period when there was a general filling in of available ecological niches. Only in the southeastern quadrant of the survey area, where a broad tongue of rugged high ground projects westward from the base of the Sierra to the edge of the Lakeshore Plain between Coatlinchan and Coatepec, was there a significant exception to this general trend. Interestingly enough, this same area continues to be very sparsely occupied today.

At least two large urban communities (Tx-A-87 and Tx-A-88) came into existence during Early Aztec times, and three additional major centers developed in the Late Aztec period (Tx-A-24, Tx-A-56, Tx-A-109). None of these Aztec centers had been important population foci in Toltec or Classic times, and the rapidity of their growth and development, which apparently occurred wholly within the Aztec period, is impressive.

By the time of the Spanish Conquest, population in the Texcoco Region had reached its maximum prehispanic peak. A majority (about 65 percent) of this population was concentrated in five urban centers. The remainder resided in dispersed villages and hamlets, distributed more or less evenly throughout most of the Texcoco Region apart from the southeastern corner. In marked contrast to all earlier periods, there were large concentrations of population in the Upper Piedmont zone and at the Lower Piedmont-Lakeshore Plain juncture.

General Conclusions

Four distinct demographic cycles are clearly apparent in the changing configuration of prehispanic settlement in the Texcoco Region:

1) A Formative cycle, beginning with the initial occupation of the area by relatively sedentary peoples early in the first millennium B.C., and continuing through nearly a thousand-year period of steady population growth, filling in of the landscape, and socio-political differentiation.

2) A Classic cycle, initiated early in the first millennium A.D. by a dramatic shift in settlement pattern and an abrupt termination of the long-term trends of the antecedent Formative cycle. Population declined drastically, and there was a reversal to a pattern of scattered hamlets and small villages as the dominant mode of occupation.

3) An Early Toltec cycle, in the last three centuries of the first millennium A.D., characterized by the abrupt appearance of several large, nucleated population centers along the northern and southern peripheries of the Texcoco Region. The great majority of the area's population was concentrated in these urban communities, and there was a near-complete abandonment of the broad central section of the survey area.

4) A Late Toltec-Aztec cycle between A.D. 1000 and the Spanish Conquest in 1520, initiated by a break up of the large Early Toltec urban centers. The first third of this period was an era of demographic decline and stagnation in which much of the population was widely scattered in small communities. The last three centuries of the prehispanic era saw a rapid population buildup from this base to unprecedented levels, accompanied by extensive urbanization.

TABLE 6
TABULAR PRESENTATION OF PREHISPANIC DEMOGRAPHIC DATA
(Middle Formative)

Site No.	Hectares	Population Min.	Population Max.	Classification	Other Occupations
1	1	10	50	Hamlet	LT, Az
2	1	10	50	Hamlet	LF, TF
3	5	10	50	Hamlet	LF, TF
4	1	10	50	Hamlet	LF
5	4	20	100	Hamlet	TF
6	1	10	50	Hamlet	TF, EC, LC
7	4	10	50	Hamlet	TF
8	2	10	50	Hamlet	LF, TF
9	1	10	50	Hamlet	LF
10	1	10	50	Hamlet	LF, TF
11	1	10	50	Hamlet	LF
12	1	10	50	Hamlet	LF, TF
13	45	600	1200	Large nucleated village	LF, TF, Az
14	1	10	50	Hamlet	TF
15	l.t. 1	10	50	Hamlet	LF, TF
16	1	10	50	Hamlet	LF, TF
17	1	10	50	Hamlet	LF
18	1	10	50	Hamlet	LF, TF
19	l.t. 1	10	50	Hamlet	LF, TF
TOTALS	74	790	2150	...	...
				(Late Formative)	
1	l.t. 1	...	None	Hilltop ceremonial precinct	ET
2	l.t. 1	10	50	Hamlet	TF, LT, Az
3	l.t. 1	10	50	Hamlet	TF
4	l.t. 1	10	50	Hamlet	MF, ET, LT
5	l.t. 1	10	50	Hamlet	MF, TF
6	l.t. 1	10	50	Hamlet	TF, EC, LC, ET, LT, Az
7	2	10	50	Hamlet	ET, LT
8	20	250	500	Small dispersed village	MF, TF
9	33	650	1300	Large nucleated village	MF
10	1	10	50	Hamlet	MF, TF
11	1	10	50	Hamlet	MF, TF
12	86	1700	3500	Secondary regional center	MF, TF
13	l.t. 1	10	50	Hamlet	LT
14	5	100	200	Small nucleated village	...
15	2	10	50	Hamlet	TF, LT
16	6	10	50	Hamlet	...
17	8	100	200	Small dispersed village	TF, EC
18	9	100	200	Small dispersed village	MF, TF
19	2	10	50	Hamlet	...
20	l.t. 1	10	50	Hamlet	TF
21	1	10	50	Hamlet	MF, TF
22	40	600	1800	Large nucleated village	Az
23	6	20	100	Hamlet	MF
24	3	10	50	Hamlet	...
25	3	10	50	Hamlet	MF, TF, EC, Az
26	1	10	50	Hamlet	TF
27	1	10	50	Hamlet	MF, Az
28	l.t. 1	10	50	Hamlet	TF, ET
29	12	150	250	Small dispersed village	MF, TF, Az
TOTALS	251	3860	9000	...	...
				(Terminal Formative)	
1	74	1200	2500	Secondary regional center	ET, Az
2	8	100	150	Small segregated elite district	...
3	1	...	None	Hilltop ceremonial precinct	ET, LT, Az
4	15	300	600	Large segregated elite district	...

TABLE 6 Cont.
Terminal Formative (cont.)

Site No.	Hectares	Population Min.	Population Max.	Classification	Other Occupations
5	l.t. 1	10	50	Hamlet	Az
6	2	50	100	Small segregated elite district	...
7	6	100	150	Small dispersed village	Az
8	l.t. 1	10	50	Hamlet	...
9	l.t. 1	10	50	Hamlet	...
10	l.t. 1	10	50	Small segregated elite district	...
11	25	400	800	Large nucleated village	LF, ET
12	l.t. 1	10	50	Hamlet	Az
13	10	150	300	Small nucleated village	...
14	18	300	500	Large segregated elite district	...
15	5	...	None	Hilltop ceremonial precinct	Az
16	6	100	150	Small nucleated village	...
17	118	1800	3500	Secondary regional center	MF, LF, EC, LC, Az
18	l.t. 1	10	50	Hamlet	Az
19	11	100	150	Small dispersed village	EC, Az
20	24	200	350	Small dispersed village	LF
21	40	100	200	Small dispersed village	LF, Az
22	1	10	50	Hamlet	LT, Az
23	4	10	50	Hamlet	LF, Az
24	1	10	50	Hamlet	Az
25	50	500	750	Large dispersed village	LF, Az
26	1	10	50	Hamlet	Az
27	1	10	50	Hamlet	EC, Az
28	1	10	50	Hamlet	LF, LT
29	1	10	50	Hamlet	LF, LT, Az
30	50	1000	2000	Secondary regional center	Az
31	19	200	400	Small dispersed village	EC
32	12	100	200	Small dispersed village	MF, LF
33	15	250	500	Small nucleated village	EC, Az
34	9	150	300	Small nucleated village	...
35	16	100	200	Small dispersed village	...
36	35	600	1200	Large segregated elite district	...
37	10	100	150	Small dispersed village	EC
38	4	10	50	Hamlet	Az
39	10	50	150	Hamlet	...
40	4	20	100	Hamlet	MF, LF
41	1	10	50	Hamlet	LF
42	1	10	50	Hamlet	MF, LF
43	1	10	50	Hamlet	MF, LF, Az
44	11	150	300	Small nucleated village	Az
45	1	10	50	Hamlet	Az
46	19	400	800	Large nucleated village	...
47	5	...	None?	Camp ? Quarry ?	ET ...
48	l.t. 1	...	None	Hilltop ceremonial precinct	LT, Az
49	l.t. 1	10	50	Hamlet	LF, ET
50	52	750	1500	Secondary regional center	MF, LF, EC, Az
51	40	600	1200	Large segregated elite district	...
52	1	10	50	Hamlet	EC. LC
TOTALS	747	10,070	20,200	...	...
				(Early Classic)	
1	l.t. 1	10	50	Hamlet	LC, LT, Az
2	l.t. 1	...	None	Hilltop ceremonial precinct	LF, ET
3	10	20	100	Hamlet	LC, ET, LT, Az

TABLE 6 Cont.
Early Classic (cont.)

Site No.	Hectares	Population Min.	Population Max.	Classification	Other Occupations
4	1	10	50	Hamlet	ET, Az
5	l.t. 1	10	50	Hamlet	LF, TF, LC, ET, LT
6	l.t. 1	10	50	Hamlet	LF, TF, LC, ET, LT, Az
7	4	10	50	Hamlet	LC, LT, Az
8	3	10	50	Hamlet	LC
9	9	100	150	Small dispersed village	LF, LC, Az
10	4	10	50	Hamlet	LC, Az
11	l.t. 1	10	50	Hamlet	TF, Az
12	5	20	100	Hamlet	MF, TF, LC, LT
13	6	20	100	Hamlet	LC, Az
14	6	100	200	Small nucleated village	LC, LT
15	l.t. 1	10	50	Hamlet	TF, Az
16	l.t. 1	10	50	Hamlet	LC
17	l.t. 1	10	50	Hamlet	TF, LC
18	25	250	500	Small dispersed village	LC, Az
19	6	100	200	Small nucleated village	Az
20	l.t. 1	10	50	Hamlet	TF, Az
21	5	20	100	Hamlet	TF
22	2	10	50	Hamlet	TF, Az
23	l.t. 1	10	50	Hamlet	...
24	13	125	250	Small dispersed village	TF
25	l.t. 1	10	50	Hamlet	...
26	4	20	100	Hamlet	...
27	3	10	50	Hamlet	...
28	1	10	50	Hamlet	MF, LF, TF, Az
29	l.t. 1	10	50	Hamlet	LT
30	l.t. 1	...	None	Hilltop ceremonial precinct	ET, Az
31	5	20	100	Hamlet	LC, ET
32	60	300	900	Secondary regional center?	LC, ET, LT, Az
33	1	10	50	Hamlet	LC
34	3	10	50	Hamlet	LC, ET, LT, Az
35	4	20	100	Hamlet	LC
36	3	10	50	Hamlet	LC
37	1	10	50	Hamlet	LC, ET
TOTALS	197	1335	4000	...	...
				(Late Classic)	
1	l.t. 1	10	50	Hamlet	EC, LT, Az
2	10	20	100	Hamlet	EC, ET, LT
3	l.t. 1	10	50	Hamlet	Az
4	3	10	50	Hamlet	ET
5	l.t. 1	10	50	Hamlet	LF, TF, EC, ET, LT, Az
6	l.t. 1	10	50	Hamlet	LF, TF, EC, ET, LT
7	4	10	50	Hamlet	EC, LT, Az
8	2	10	50	Hamlet	EC
9	9	125	175	Small dispersed village	LF, EC, Az
10	2	10	50	Hamlet	EC, Az
11	5	20	100	Hamlet	MF, TF, EC, LT
12	3	10	50	Hamlet	EC
13	6	100	150	Small dispersed village	EC, LT
14	l.t. 1	10	50	Hamlet	EC
15	l.t. 1	10	50	Hamlet	TF, EC
16	4	10	50	Hamlet	EC, Az
17	4	20	100	Hamlet	EC, ET
18	80	400	1200	Secondary regional center?	EC, ET, LT, Az
19	l.t. 1	10	50	Hamlet	EC
20	1	10	50	Hamlet	EC, ET, LT, Az
21	2	10	50	Hamlet	EC
22	1	10	50	Hamlet	EC
23	l.t. 1	10	50	Hamlet	EC, ET
TOTALS	144	855	2675	...	...

TABLE 6 Cont.
(Early Toltec)

Site No.	Hectares	Population Min.	Population Max.	Classification	Other Occupations
1	2	10	50	Hamlet	LT, Az
2	3	10	50	Hamlet	Az
3	2	10	50	Hamlet	...
4	180	3600	7200	Primary regional center	TF, EC, LC, LT, Az
5	2	...	None?	Hilltop ceremonial precinct	LF, EC
6	1	...	None?	Hilltop ceremonial precinct	TF, LT, Az
7	200	4000	8000	Primary regional center	EC, LC, Az
8	19	200	300	Small dispersed village	...
9	l.t. 1	10	50	Hamlet	TF, Az
10	9	20	100	Hamlet	Az
11	2	10	50	Hamlet	Az
12	3	10	50	Hamlet	...
13	80	800	1600	Large dispersed village	TF, LT, Az
14	1	10	50	Hamlet	EC, LC, LT, Az
15	23	200	300	Small dispersed village	Az
16	l.t. 1	...	None?	Camp ?	LT
17	35	350	700	Large dispersed village	EC, LC
18	400	6000	12,000	Primary regional center	EC, LC, LT, Az
19	30	300	600	Small dispersed village	EC, LC, LT, Az
20	1	10	50	Hamlet	...
21	20	100	200	Small dispersed village	TF, LT, Az
22	8	20	100	Hamlet	LT
23	35	150	400	Small dispersed village	EC, LC, LT
24	l.t. 1	...	None	Hilltop ceremonial precinct	EC, Az
TOTALS	1059	15,820	31,900	...	

(Late Toltec)

Site No.	Hectares	Population Min.	Population Max.	Classification	Other Occupations
1	3	10	50	Hamlet	Az
2	1	10	50	Hamlet	Az
3	l.t. 1	10	50	Hamlet	Az
4	2	10	50	Hamlet	Az
5	l.t. 1	10	50	Hamlet	EC, LC, Az
6	5	10	50	Hamlet	Az
7	7	50	100	Hamlet	Az
8	2	10	50	Hamlet	Az
9	1	10	50	Hamlet	...
10	6	20	100	Hamlet	Az
11	2	10	50	Hamlet	EC, LC, ET, Az
12	50	500	750	Large dispersed village	EC, LC, ET, Az
13	l.t. 1	5	15	Hamlet	Az
14	1	...	None	Hilltop ceremonial precinct	TF, ET, Az
15	1	10	50	Hamlet	TF, ET, Az
16	1	10	50	Hamlet	ET, Az
17	l.t. 1	10	50	Hamlet	Az
18	2	10	50	Hamlet	...
19	l.t. 1	10	50	Hamlet	Az
20	l.t. 1	10	50	Hamlet	ET, Az
21	l.t. 1	10	50	Hamlet	Az
22	2	10	50	Hamlet	ET, Az
23	l.t. 1	10	50	Hamlet	ET
24	3	10	50	Hamlet	Az
25	l.t. 1 (?)	...	None	Camp ?	ET, Az
26	3	10	50	Hamlet	ET, Az
27	l.t. 1	10	50	Hamlet	LF, TF, EC, LC, ET, Az
28	14	100	150	Small dispersed village	TF, ET
29	4	10	50	Hamlet	ET
30	2	10	50	Hamlet	Az
31	2	10	50	Hamlet	Az

TABLE 6 Cont.
Late Toltec (cont.)

Site No.	Hectares	Population Min.	Population Max.	Classification	Other Occupations
32	4	20	100	Hamlet	Az
33	5	20	100	Hamlet	...
34	12	50	100	Hamlet	Az
35	20	150	300	Small dispersed village	...
36	2	10	50	Hamlet	LF, TF, Az
37	l.t. 1	...	None?	Camp ?	ET, Az
38	3	20	100	Hamlet	LF, TF
39	3	10	50	Hamlet	Az
40	l.t. 1	10	50	Hamlet	Az
41	l.t. 1	10	50	Hamlet	...
42	1	10	50	Hamlet	EC, LC
43	1	10	50	Hamlet	MF, TF, EC, LC
44	1	10	50	Hamlet	TF, Az
45	1	10	50	Hamlet	Az
46	1	10	50	Hamlet	Az
47	1	10	50	Hamlet	Az
48	1	10	50	Hamlet	Az
49	1	10	50	Hamlet	Az
50	l.t. 1	10	50	Hamlet	...
51	1	10	50	Hamlet	EC
52	4	20	100	Hamlet	...
53	125	750	1500	Secondary regional center	EC, LC, ET, Az
54	25	125	150	Small dispersed village	EC, LC, ET, Az
55	l.t. 1	...	None?	Hilltop ceremonial precinct	TF, Az
56	40	200	400	Small dispersed village	TF, ET, Az
57	30	150	300	Small dispersed village	ET, Az
58	17	100	200	Small dispersed village	ET
59	15	100	150	Small dispersed village	EC, LC, ET
TOTALS	443	2760	6515	...	...
				(Aztec)	
1	4	10	50	Hamlet	LT
2	1	10	50	Hamlet	LT
3	8	20	100	Hamlet	...
4	l.t. 1	10	50	Hamlet	...
5	l.t. 1	...	None?	Camp ?	...
6	30	...	None?	Isolated ceremonial-civic precinct	LT
7	1	10	50	Hamlet	...
8	l.t. 1	10	50	Hamlet	...
9	1	10	50	Hamlet	...
10	36	150	300	Small dispersed village	LT
11	24	150	300	Small dispersed village	LT
12	12	100	150	Small dispersed village	LT
13	5	10	50	Hamlet	LT
14	15	75	150	Small dispersed village	EC, LC, ET, LT
15	2	10	50	Hamlet	...
16	6	100	200	Small dispersed village	ET
17	115	300	600	Large dispersed village	MF, TF, EC, LC, ET, LT
18	3	10	50	Hamlet	ET
19	l.t. 1	...	None	Hilltop ceremonial precinct	...
20	1	...	None	Hilltop ceremonial precinct	TF, ET, LT
21	55	250	500	Small dispersed village	...
22	13 (?)	75	150	Small dispersed village	...
23	18	100	150	Small dispersed village	...
24	450	6750	13,500	Primary regional center	ET, LT
25	115	600	1200	Large dispersed village	...
26	10	75	150	Small dispersed village	...
27	17	150	300	Small dispersed village	LT
28	75	600	1200	Large dispersed village (Incompletely mapped)	LT

TABLE 6 Cont.
Aztec (cont.)

Site No.	Hectares	Population Min.	Population Max.	Classification	Other Occupations
29	l.t. 1	...	None	Hilltop ceremonial precinct	...
30	100	1000	1500	Large dispersed village (Incompletely mapped)	...
31	50	350	700	Large dispersed village (Incompletely mapped)	...
32	4	20	100	Hamlet	...
33	l.t. 1	5	15	Hamlet	...
34	6	20	100	Hamlet	...
35	30	200	400	Small dispersed village	...
36	1	10	50	Hamlet (Incompletely mapped)	
37	5	20	100	Hamlet (Incompletely mapped)	ET
38	65	325	650	Large dispersed village (Incompletely mapped)	LF, TF
39	10	75	150	Small dispersed village	ET
40	100	1000	1500	Large dispersed village (Incompletely mapped)	ET, LT
41	3	10	50	Hamlet	LT
42	2	...	None?	Camp ?	...
43	3	...	None?	Camp ?	ET, LT
44	2	10	50	Hamlet	LF, TF, LT
45	5	10	50	Hamlet	LT
46	20	100	200	Small dispersed village	LT
47	5	20	100	Hamlet	LT
48	l.t. 1	10	15	Hamlet	...
49	25	150	300	Small dispersed village	...
50	3	10	50	Hamlet	...
51	l.t. 1	10	50	Hamlet	...
52	3	10	50	Hamlet	...
53	25	250	500	Small dispersed village	...
54	5	10	50	Hamlet	...
55	l.t. 1	10	15	Hamlet	...
56	450 ?	12,000	25,000	Primary regional center	ET, LT
57	50	200	400	Small dispersed village	EC
58	100	250	500	Small dispersed village	LF, TF
59	75	375	750	Large dispersed village	TF
60	20	100	200	Small dispersed village	...
61	5	...	None	Hilltop ceremonial precinct	TF, LT
62	15	...	None	Isolated ceremonial-civic precinct	...
63	l.t. 1	10	15	Hamlet	...
64	35	200	400	Small dispersed village	EC, LC
65	25	150	300	Small dispersed village	MF, LF, TF
66	50	200	400	Small dispersed village	TF, EC, LC
67	5	...	None	Hilltop ceremonial precinct	TF
68	5	10	50	Hamlet	...
69	30	200	400	Small dispersed village	...
70	7	20	100	Hamlet	...
71	9	20	100	Hamlet	...
72	400	4000	8000	Large dispersed village(s)	...
73	30	250	350	Dispersed village (Incompletely mapped)	...
74	3	20	40	Dispersed village (Incompletely mapped)	...
75	4	10	50	Hamlet	...
76	15	125	250	Small dispersed village	...
77	7	20	100	Hamlet	...
78	100	750	1500	Large dispersed village	...

TABLE 6 Cont.
Aztec (cont.)

Site No.	Hectares	Population Min.	Population Max.	Classification	Other Occupations
79	11	20	100	Hamlet	. . .
80	30	100	150	Small dispersed village	. . .
81	30	150	300	Small dispersed village	. . .
82	l.t. 1	. . .	None	Isolated ceremonial-civic precinct	. . .
83	l.t. 1	5	15	Hamlet	. . .
84	l.t. 1	5	15	Hamlet	. . .
85	l.t. 1	5	15	Hamlet	. . .
86	20	150	300	Small dispersed village	. . .
87	300	7500	15,000	Primary regional center (Urban core)	. . .
87	540	4000	8000	Primary regional center (Dispersed suburbs)	
88	*ca.* 210	5500	11,000	Primary regional center	. . .
89	4	10	50	Hamlet	. . .
90	4	10	50	Hamlet	. . .
91	15	20	100	Hamlet	. . .
92	7	10	50	Hamlet	. . .
93	2	10	50	Hamlet	. . .
94	7	10	50	Hamlet	. . .
95	10	20	100	Hamlet	. . .
96	4	10	50	Hamlet	. . .
97	4	10	50	Hamlet	. . .
98	4	10	50	Hamlet	. . .
99	85 ?	1250	2500	Secondary regional center	MF, LF, TF
100	2	. . .	None?	Isolated ceremonial-civic precinct	. . .
101	l.t. 1	. . .	None	Hilltop ceremonial precinct	EC, ET
102	12	20	100	Hamlet	EC, LC, ET
103	45	225	450	Small dispersed village	EC, LC, ET, LT
104	5	10	50	Hamlet	. . .
105	3	10	50	Hamlet	TF
106	1 ?	10	50 ?	Hamlet ?	LT
107	32	200	400	Small dispersed village	LT
108	l.t. 1	. . .	None	Hilltop ceremonial precinct	TF, LT
109	260 ?	6000	12,000	Primary regional center	
110	17	175	250	Small dispersed village	MF, LF, TF, EC, ET, LT
TOTALS	4609	57,585	116,395	. . .	. . .

l.t. = less than.
MF = Middle Formative, LF = Late Formative, TF = Terminal Formative, EC = Early Classic, LC = Late Classic, ET = Early Toltec, LT = Late Toltec, Az = Aztec.

TABLE 7
SUMMARY OF PREHISPANIC DEMOGRAPHIC DATA

Period	No. of Sites	Hectares	Population Min.	Population Max.
Middle Formative	19	74	790	2150
Late Formative	29	251	3860	9000
Terminal Formative	52	747	10,070	20,200
Early Classic	37	197	1335	4000
Late Classic	23	144	855	2675
Early Toltec	24	1059	15,820	31,900
Late Toltec	59	443	2760	6515
Aztec	110	4609	57,585	116,395
Modern (1960, for Texcoco Region as a whole)	70	3219	73,476	

TABLE 8
OCCUPATION OF MAJOR NATURAL ZONES
(Calculations Based on Maximal Estimates of Prehistoric Population)

Period	Upper Piedmont				Lower Piedmont				Lakeshore Plain			
	Population		Hectares		Population		Hectares		Population		Hectares	
	No.	Per cent	No.	Per cent	No.	Per cent	No.	Per cent	No.	Per cent	No.	Per cent
Modern (1960) Whole Texcoco Region	3684	5.0	430	13.3	39,134	53.2	2036	63.4	30,659	41.8	753	23.4
Late Aztec	15,635	13.5	994	21.6	73,230	62.9	2881	62.5	27,530	23.6	734	15.9
Late Toltec	250	3.8	6	1.4	4165	64.0	269	60.8	2100	32.2	168	37.9
Early Toltec	0	0	0	0	30,900	96.9	996	94.3	1000	3.1	62	5.7
Late Classic	0	0	0	0	2425	90.7	138	95.7	250	9.3	6	4.3
Early Classic	100	2.5	4	2.0	3600	90.0	181	91.9	300	7.5	12	6.1
Terminal Formative	1650	8.1	53	7.1	15,800	77.9	603	80.6	2800	13.9	91	12.2
Late Formative	50	0.6	1	0.4	8250	91.6	227	90.5	700	7.8	23	9.2
Middle Formative	50	2.3	1	1.4	900	41.8	28	37.8	1200	55.8	45	60.9

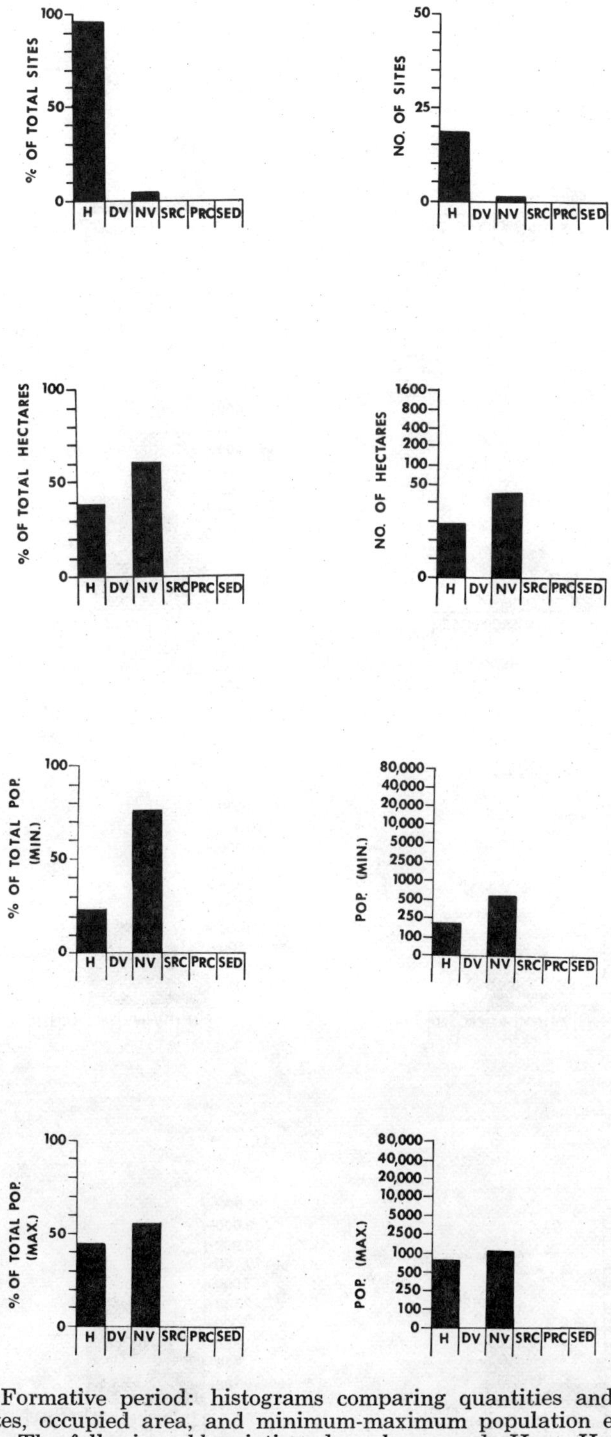

Fig. 35—Middle Formative period: histograms comparing quantities and proportions of numbers of sites, occupied area, and minimum-maximum population estimates, for various site types. The following abbreviations have been used: H = Hamlet; DV = Dispersed Village NV = Nucleated Village; SRC = Secondary Regional Center; PRC = Primary Regional Center; SED = Segregated Elite District; MF = Middle Formative; LF = Late Formative; TF = Terminal Formative; EC = Early Classic; LC = Late Classic; ET = Early Toltec; LT = Late Toltec; Az = Aztec.

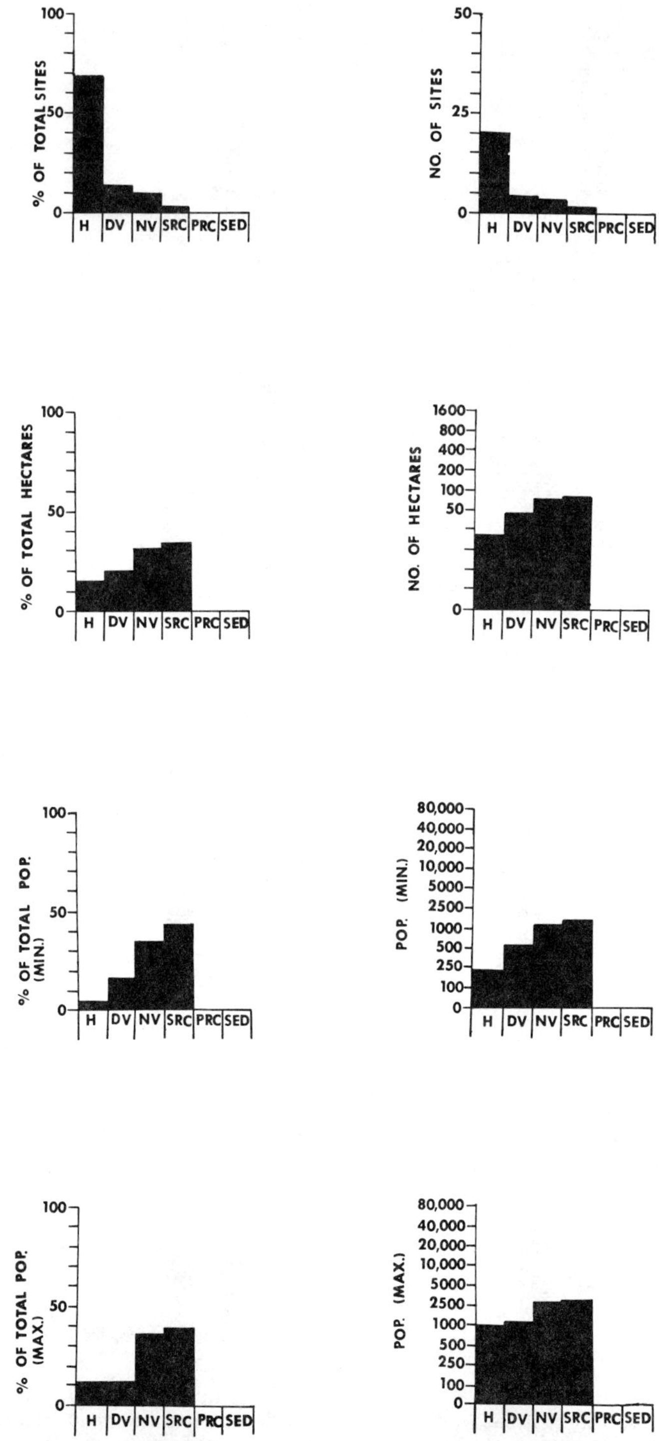

Fig. 36—Late Formative period: histograms comparing quantities and proportions of numbers of sites, occupied area, and minimum-maximum population estimates, for various site types. See note Fig. 35 p. 165.

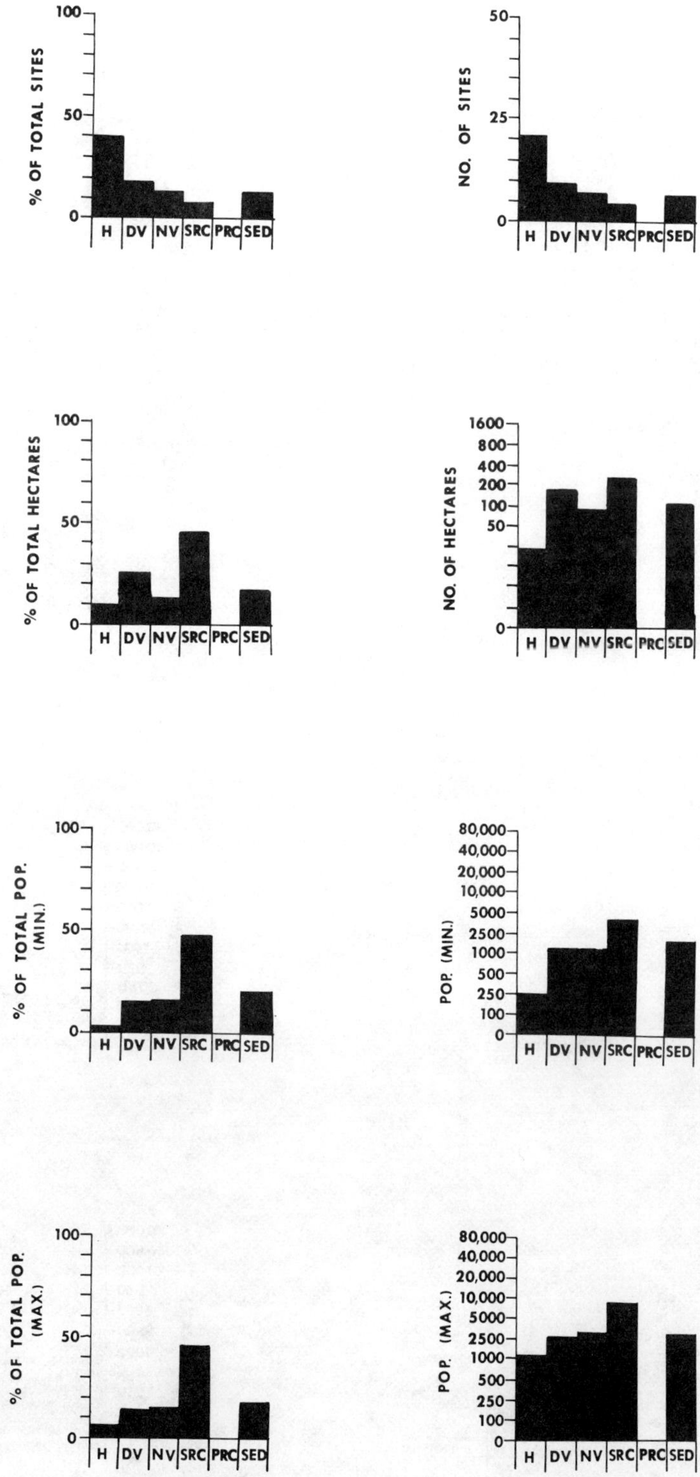

Fig. 37—Terminal Formative period: histograms comparing quantities and proportions of numbers of sites, occupied area, and minimum-maximum population estimates, for various site types. See note Fig. 35 p. 165.

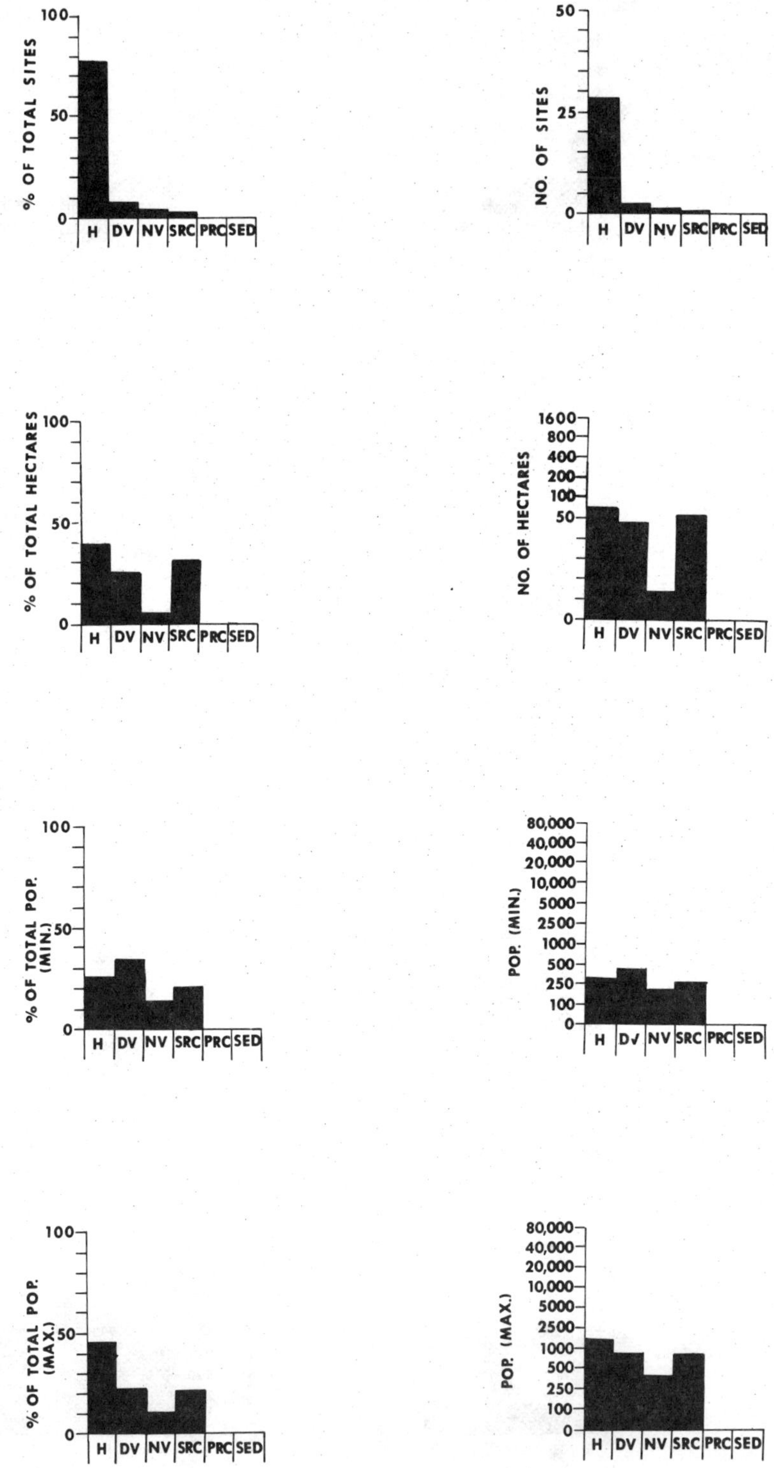

Fig. 38—Early Classic period: histograms comparing quantities and proportions of numbers of sites, occupied area, and minimum-maximum population estimates, for various site types. See note Fig. 35 p. 165.

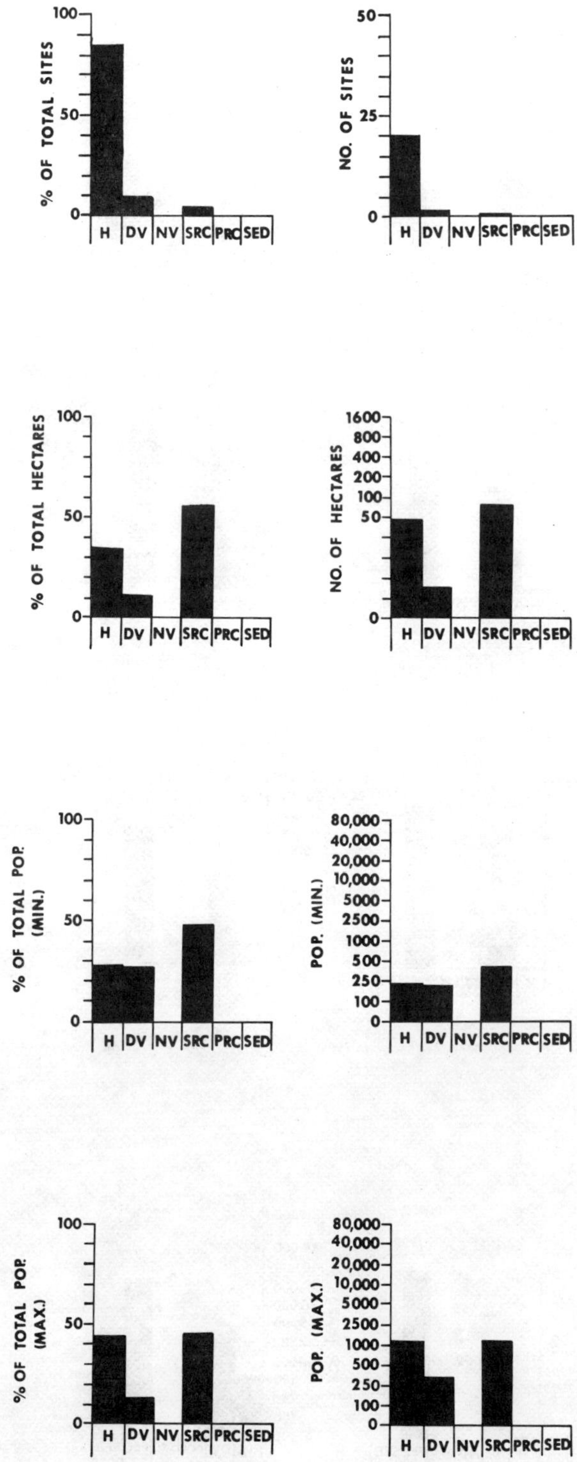

Fig, 39—Late Classic period: histograms comparing quantities and proportions of numbers of sites, occupied area, and minimum-maximum population estimates, for various site types. See note Fig. 35 p. 165.

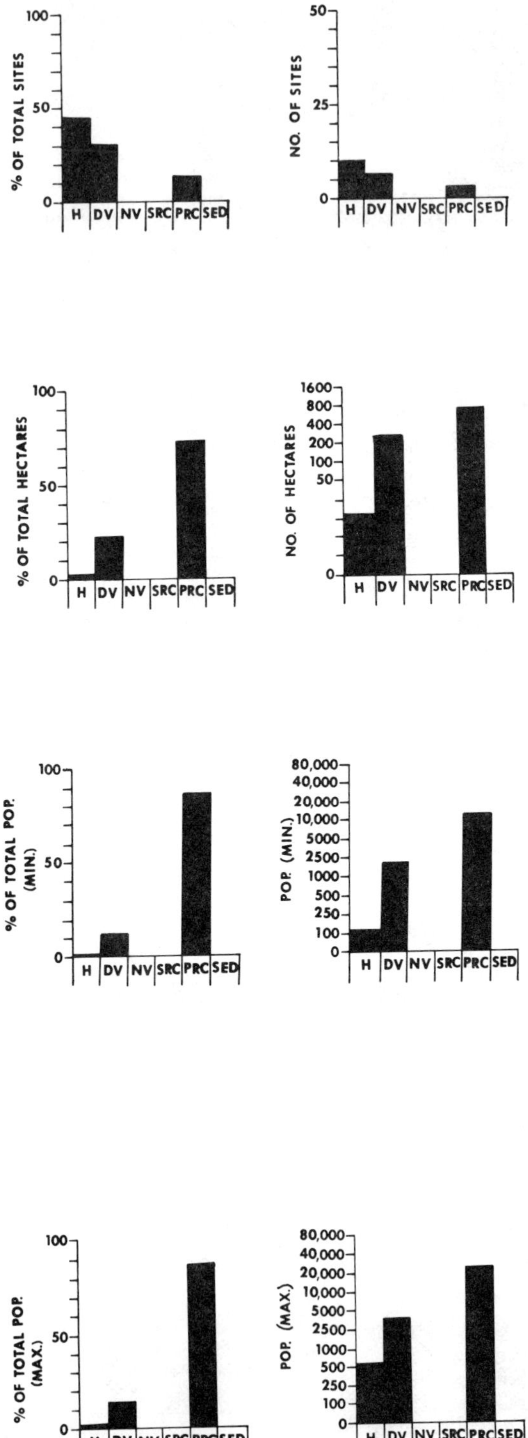

Fig. 40—Early Toltec period: histograms comparing quantities and proportions of numbers of sites, occupied area, and minimum-maximum population estimates, for various site types. See note Fig. 35 p. 165.

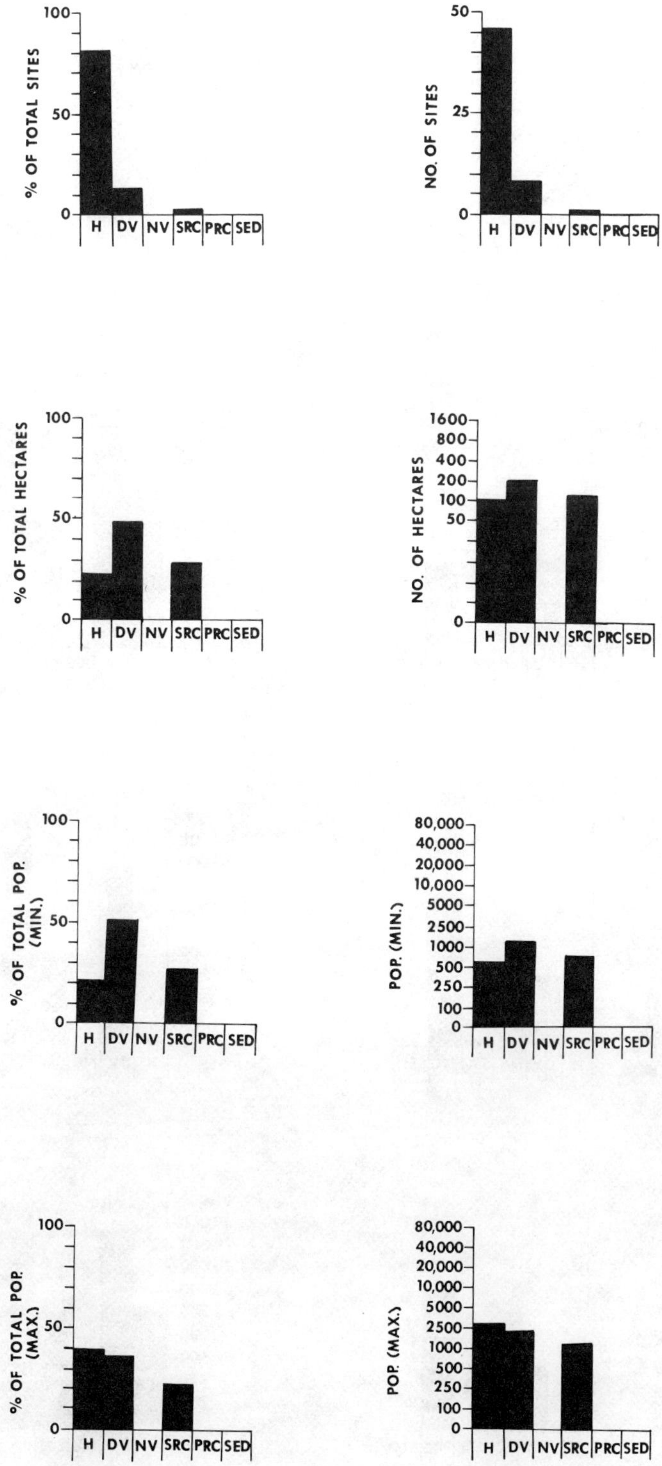

Fig. 41—Late Toltec period: histograms comparing quantities and proportions of numbers of sites, occupied area, and minimum-maximum population estimates, for various site types. See note Fig. 35 p. 165.

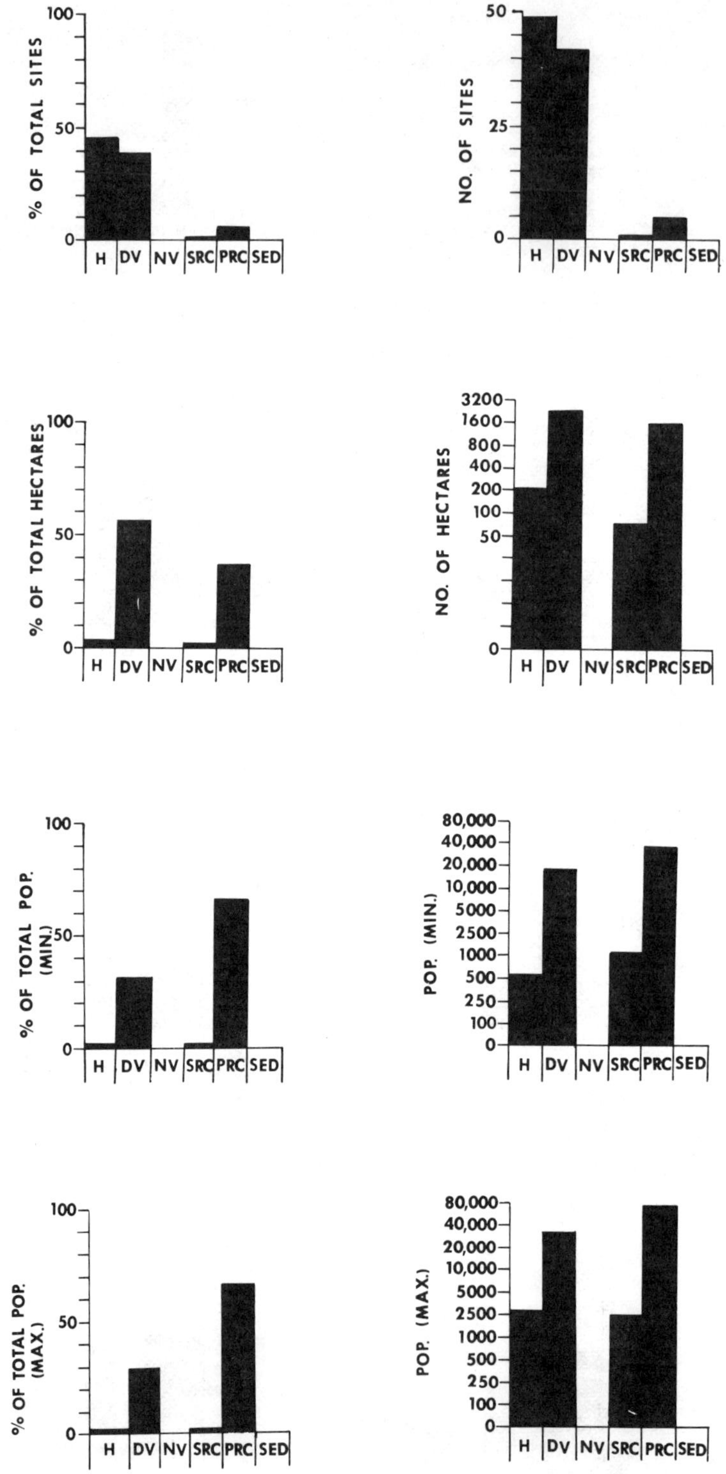

Fig. 42—Aztec period: histograms comparing quantities and proportions of numbers of sites, occupied area, and minimum-maximum population estimates, for various site types. See note Fig. 35 p. 165.

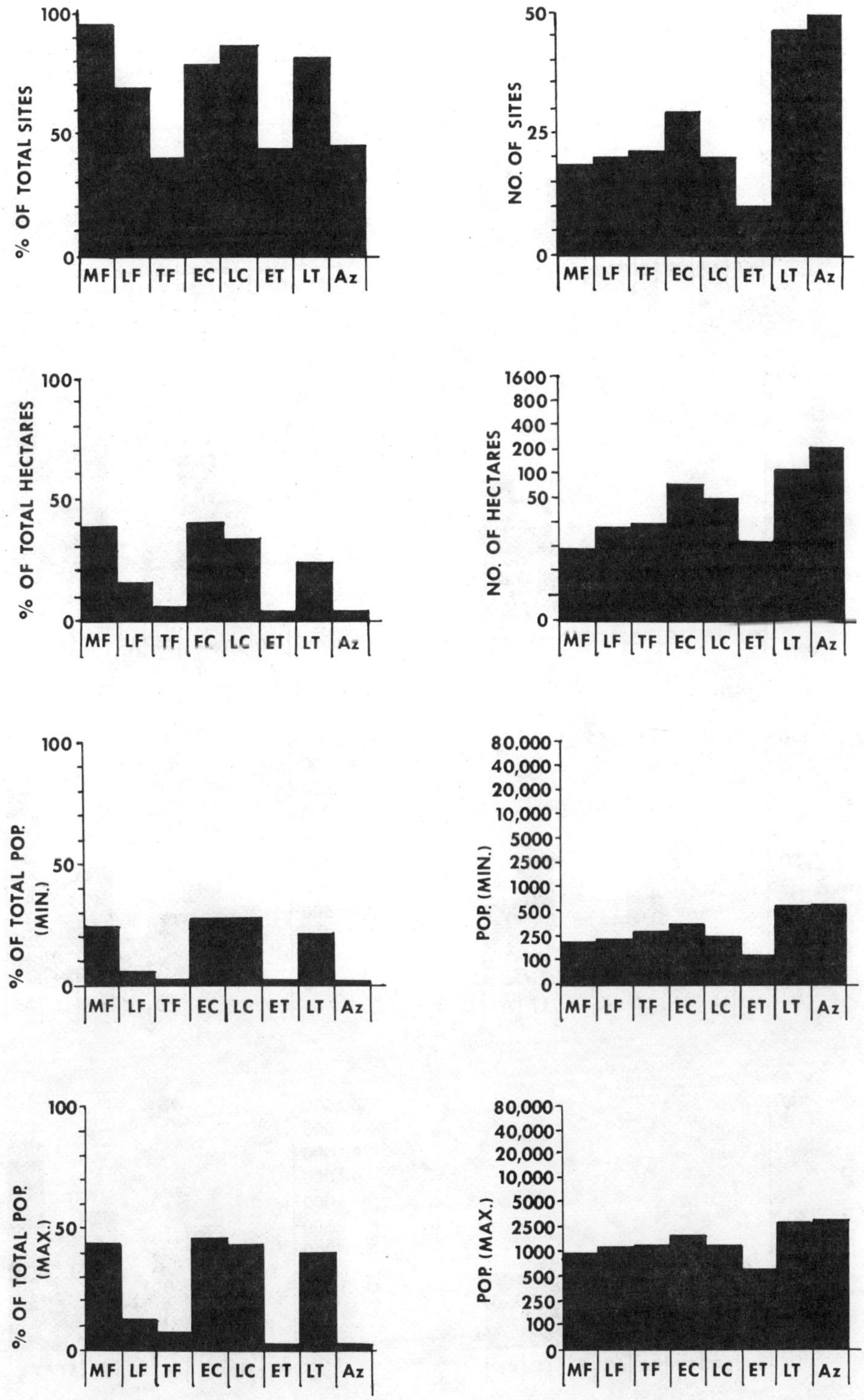

Fig. 43—Hamlet site type: histograms comparing quantities and proportions of numbers of sites, occupied area, and minimum-maximum population estimates, for the main time periods. See note Fig. 36 p. 165.

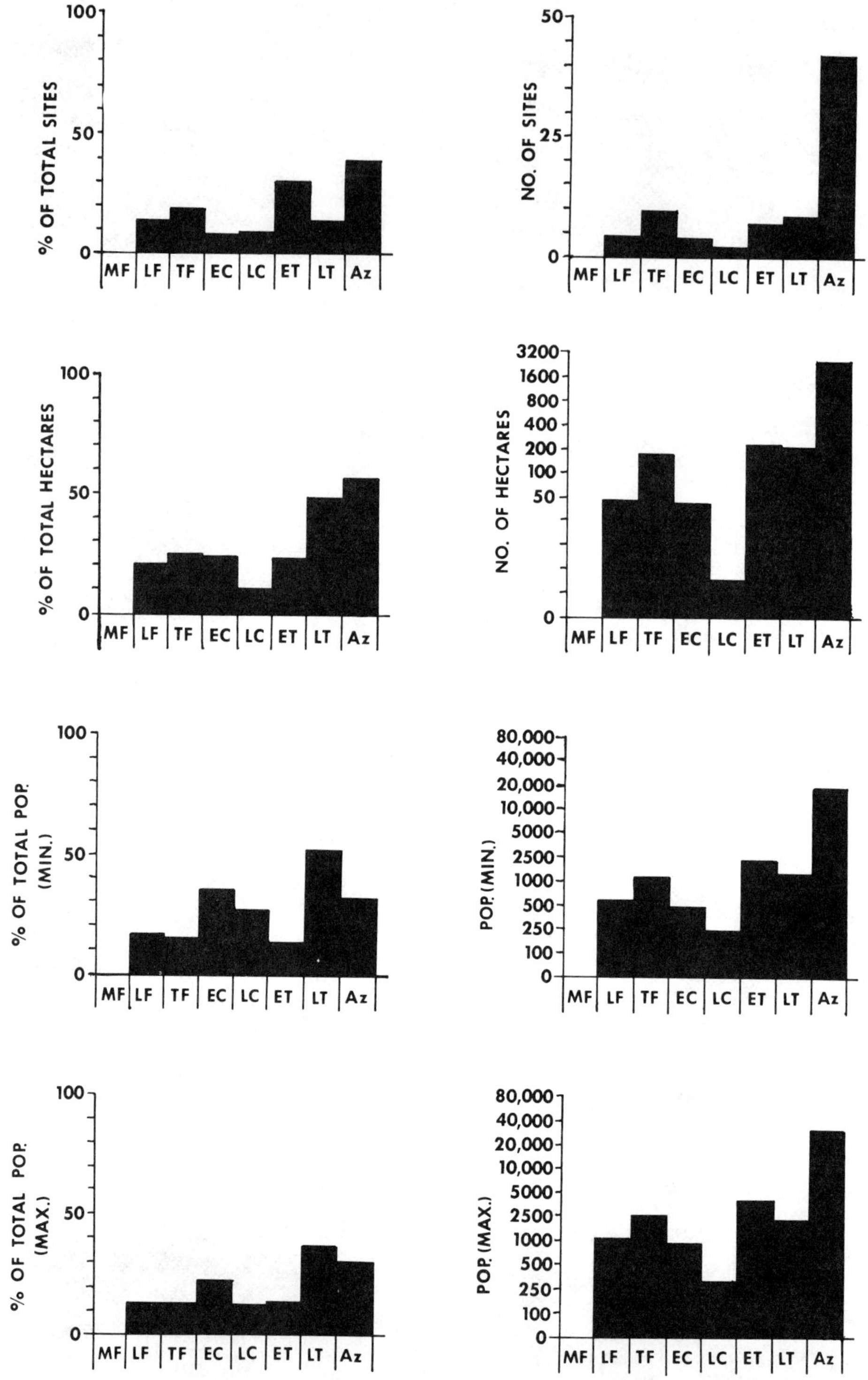

Fig. 44—Dispersed Village site type: histograms comparing quantities and proportions of numbers of sites, occupied area, and minimum-maximum population estimates, for the main time periods. See note Fig. 35 p. 165.

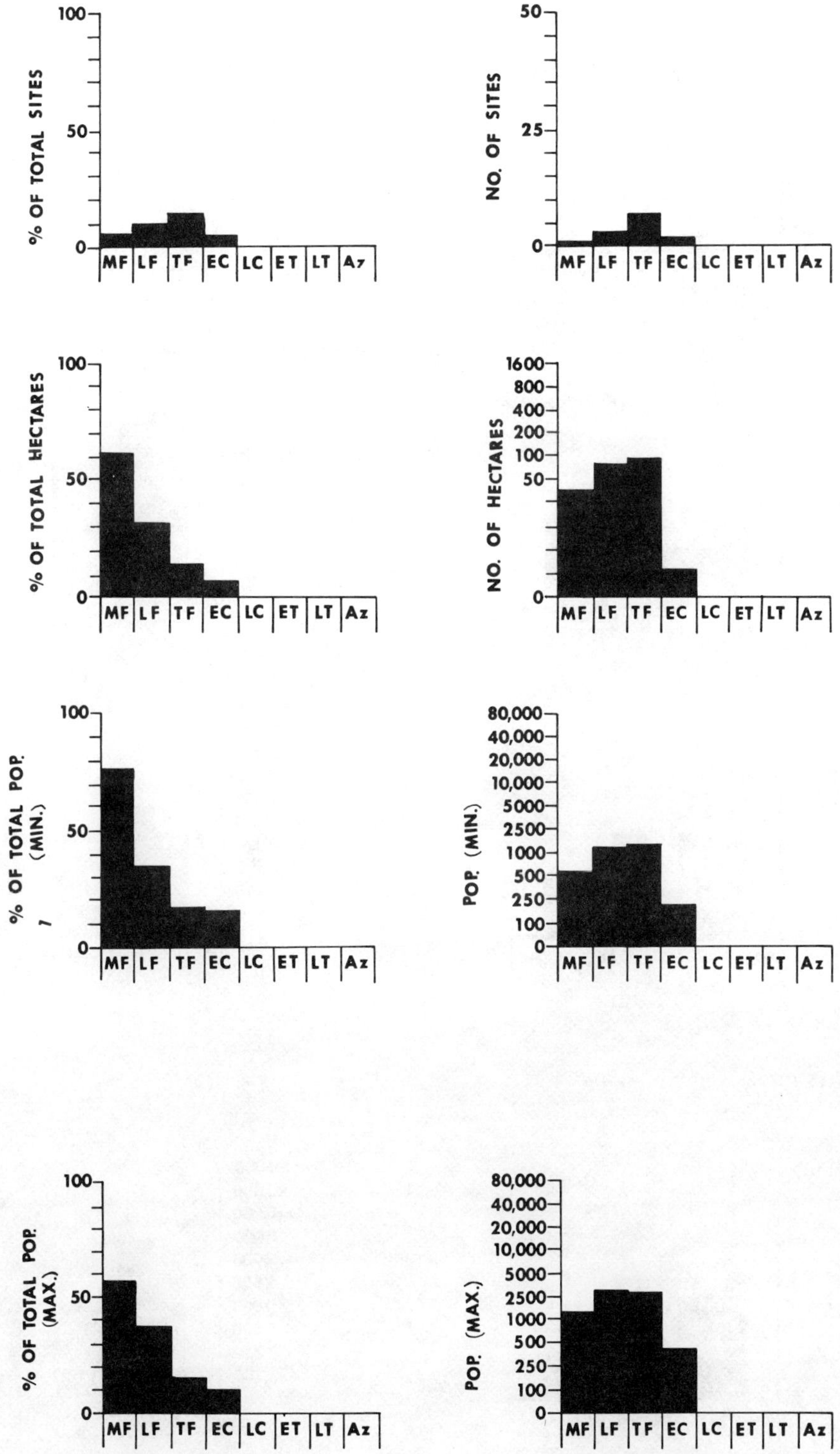

Fig. 45—Nucleated Village site type: histograms comparing quantities and proportions of numbers of sites, occupied area, and minimum-maximum population estimates, for the main time periods. See note Fig. 35 p. 165.

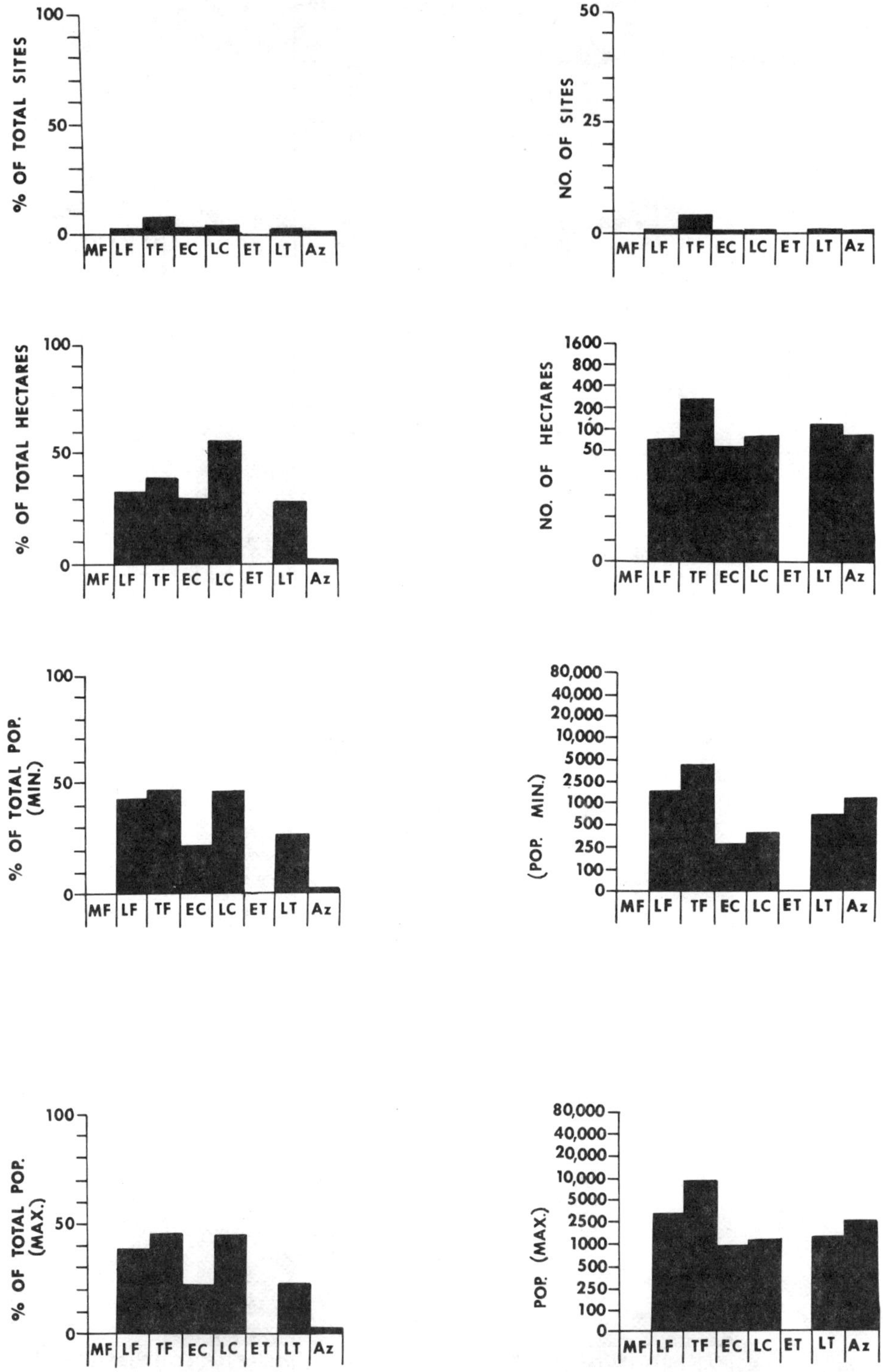

Fig. 46—Secondary Regional Center site type: histograms comparing quantities and proportions of numbers of sites, occupied area, and minimum-maximum population estimates, for the main time periods. See note Fig. 35 p. 165.

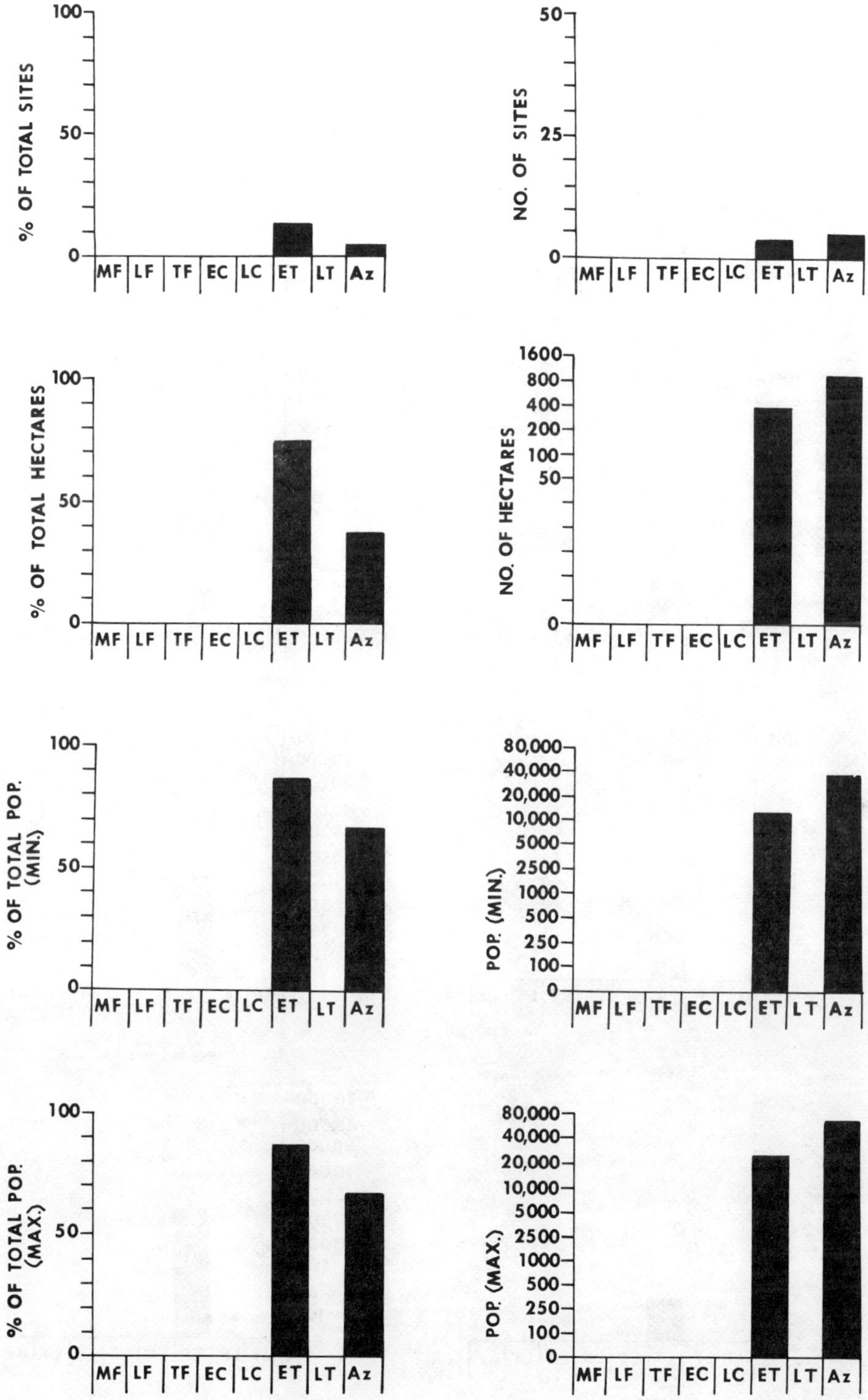

Fig. 47—Primary Regional Center site type: histograms comparing quantities and proportions of numbers of sites, occupied area, and minimum-maximum population estimates, for the main time periods. See note Fig. 35 p. 165.

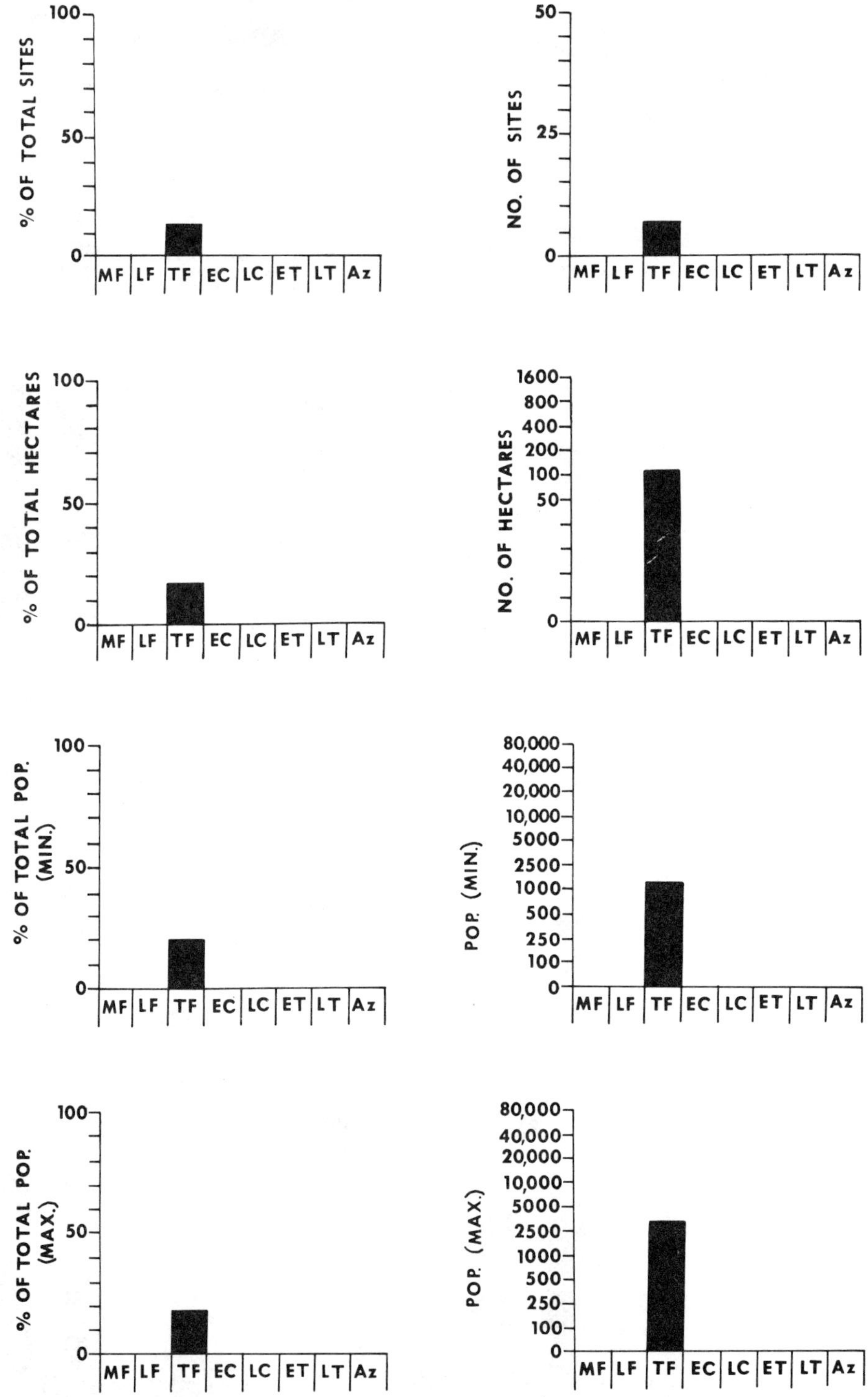

Fig. 48—Segregated Elite District site type: histograms comparing quantities and proportions of numbers of sites, occupied area, and minimum-maximum population estimates, for the main time periods. See note Fig. 35 p. 165.

III

THE TEXCOCO REGION IN VALLEY OF MEXICO PREHISTORY

INTRODUCTION

To this point we have presented a predominately descriptive analysis, and our attention has been wholly concentrated on the Texcoco Region itself, It will now be our purpose to compare our findings with data on settlement patterning from other areas of the Valley of Mexico in order to develop hypotheses and interpretations concerning the developmental processes and regional variability of cultural evolution in this key area.

The quantity and quality of settlement pattern data available to us for this purpose make our task both less complicated and more difficult: fully comparable data (at least in published form) are lacking for most of the Valley of Mexico, and we will have to be more speculative than would be desirable at many points. The only other full-scale settlement pattern study in the Valley of Mexico has been Sanders' (1965) investigation in the Teotihuacan Valley, immediately adjacent to the Texcoco Region on the north. Otherwise, we have only data (some of which is quite fragmentary) on individual site locations and characteristics. This latter information can be extremely useful, but is often difficult to evaluate in the absence of regional surveys.

It will become apparent to the reader that our ability to fully comprehend our data from the Texcoco Region will always depend upon information from other parts of Mesoamerica outside the Valley of Mexico. Our interpretations will thus remain more or less incomplete until the following chapter when we relate the Texcoco Region and the Valley of Mexico to the rest of Mesoamerica.

MIDDLE FORMATIVE
(*ca.* 850-550 B.C.)

General Valley of Mexico

Within the Valley of Mexico, with but two known exceptions, the earliest known significant occupation by ceramic-using peoples dates to Middle Formative times. Known sites of this general horizon outside the Texcoco Region are Tlatilco (Piña Chan, 1958), the lower levels at Zacatenco (Vaillant, 1931) and El Arbolillo (Vaillant, 1935), the lower levels at Tlapacoya (Barba de Piña Chan, 1956; Piña Chan, 1958), and the 18 hamlets and occupational traces in the Teotihuacan Valley (Sanders, 1965). Except for the Teotihuacan Valley hamlets, there is little or no specific information concerning the full extent and complexity of these sites and social communities.

Recent excavations on Tlapacoya island (Tolstoy and Paradis, 1970) have revealed substantial Early Formative material stratigraphically below ceramics of El Arbolillo I type. Since these Early Formative materials most strongly resemble those found in many of the grave lots at Tlatilco, it is now apparent that at least part of the latter site must also date to the Early Formative as well. Hints that this might be the case were already present after Tolstoy and Guénette (1965) re-excavated Tlatilco. Early Formative pottery is not known from elsewhere in the Valley of Mexico, but should undoubtedly appear as more surveys and excavations are carried out in the southern section of this region.

The Tlatilco site is situated at 2275 meters elevation on a broad alluvial floodplain between two arms of the Río Hondo at the western side of the Valley of Mexico (Piña Chan, 1958, Mapa 4). West of the site a long, wide tongue of high ground rises rapidly to a height of more than 50 meters above the zone of occupation. Intermittent excavations here over a 20-year period have revealed a large number of human burials and associated artifactual material. Early and Middle Formative was apparently substantial here, probably covering somewhat over 30 hectares, but little is known regarding architecture or site function.

Perhaps the most significant aspect of our present knowledge of the Tlatilco site is the substantial proportion of distinctly Olmec or Olmecoid pottery and figurines in the assemblages of recovered artifacts. This Early Formative material is known to occur in abundance elsewhere in the Valley of Mexico only on the island of Tlapacoya in the northeast corner of Lake Chalco. At this latter locality, Early and Middle Formative material appears below Late and Terminal Formative levels at about 2250 meters on gently sloping terrain at the base of a massive, steep-sided, extinct volcanic crater which stands more than 150 meters high. The size, complexity, and character of the Early and Middle Formative occupations at Tlapacoya is even less clear than at Tlatilco, although the Formative site apparently extends for several hundred meters along the shoreline (Kent Flannery, personal communication).

Middle Formative occupation at Zacatenco occurs over a series of low hills and intervening low ground, some 10 to 20 meters above the adjacent plain and shoreline of Lake Texcoco (Vaillant, 1930, Map III). A broad ridge of high ground rises steeply to the north of the site area. At El Arbolillo, Middle Formative refuse is distributed over the gently sloping lower flanks of a high ridge, at the edge of a narrow alluvial floodplain in a small sub-valley not far from the edge of Lake Texcoco. Occupation was apparently substantial at both Zacatenco and El Arbolillo, although, once again, there is little information regarding characteristics of size, architecture, or complexity.

The Teotihuacan Valley

In the Teotihuacan Valley, Middle Formative occupation is limited to 18 small sites distributed around the edges of the main alluvial floodplain and at considerably higher elevations in the small mountain valleys and hillslopes of the rugged Patlachique Range (Sanders, 1965: 92-93, Fig. 4). Traces of Middle Formative ceramics have also been found in the lower levels of excavations at Late Formative sites, and occasionally in surface collections from later sites (including the Classic urban center of Teotihuacan).

The Texcoco Region

In the Texcoco Region, a single nucleated site (Tx-MF-13) extends over about 45 hectares of level ground at the northeastern base of Cerro Chimalhuacan. Aside from this large community, all other Middle Formative sites in the Texcoco Region (totalling 18) are in the form of small, scattered hamlets, most of which are situated well up in the Lower Piedmont adjacent to barranca or river systems. At least two-thirds of the total Middle Formative population of the Texcoco Region was concentrated at Tx-MF-13, and perhaps a higher proportion was permanently based there if some of the small hamlets actually represent temporary residence.

It is clear that substantial Middle Formative communities in the Valley of Mexico — only one or two of which are possibly more complex than nucleated villages of under 50 hectares in area—are limited to very specific ecological niches: low-lying areas, often near rivers and always adjacent to lakes, with ready access to steep hillslope. Tlatilco, Tlapacoya, El Arbolillo, Zacatenco, and Tx-MF-13 in the Texcoco Region all occur in such a context. Where efforts have been made to look for sites in other types of localities, only small hamlets or occupational traces have been found. We still are not in a position to understand what these latter sites represent. It remains to be demonstrated whether they were merely temporary or seasonal camping locations, or whether they were permanent, sedentary residential loci.

It is clear that Middle Formative populations in the Valley of Mexico were very much involved in the exploitation of aquatic resources, and dependent upon them for a substantial portion of their subsistence. Only where such resources were abundantly available did Middle Formative populations build up and nucleate to any significant degree. Recent analysis of faunal remains from Tolstoy's excavations at Tlapacoya, Tlatilco, and El Arbolillo have been particularly revealing as regards the exploitation of aquatic resources (Kent Flannery, personal communication). Large quantities of waterfowl and mud turtle are represented at all three sites.

Proximity to lake resources, however, was not the only factor which structured the Middle Formative demographic pattern in the Valley of Mexico. For reasons outlined below, the accessibility to both low-lying, level land, and to steep hillslope appear to have been equally significant factors in the placement of large residential communities at this period.

It seems reasonable to suggest that the evident desirability of easy access to both these very distinct topographies can best be understood in the context of agricultural systems operative in Middle Formative times. It appears that canal irrigation, of any greater complexity than simple feeder ditches leading directly from stream beds into immediately adjacent fields, did not exist in Mesoamerica until some time after 500 B.C. (Sanders, 1965: 167; MacNeish, 1964). Thus, it appears that three cultivation systems would have provided the greatest subsistence security during Middle Formative times in semi-arid highland regions with severe winter frosts: (1) Rainfall cultivation on well-drained hillslopes in the Lower Piedmont zone where precipitation tends to be consistently higher relative to the Lakeshore Plain, and where frost severity is less than for the latter zone. (2) Simple floodwater irrigation, most practicable at or near the bases of hillslopes where runoff water was most readily available. (3) Cultivation in areas of high water table where subsurface water can easily be brought to the field surface by non-complex means. A modern example of this latter technique is the "pot irrigation" practiced today in restricted areas of alluvial floodplain in the Valley of Oaxaca (Flannery, *et al.*, 1967), in which water is hand-carried to individual plants from shallow wells dug at frequent intervals.

All large Middle Formative sites in the Valley of Mexico are situated in niches where hillside, high-water-table, and floodwater cultivation would all have been highly feasible. It should be kept in mind that although the latter two systems are practicable only in low-lying land, this land must have adequate drainage. Thus, the broad, flat expanses of the main lakeshore plain—in all probability permanent swamp land prior to the drainage of the lake in historic times—would have been largely unsuitable for agricultural purposes prior to the initiation of artificial drainage projects. Apparently such drainage was done on a significant basis only in Postclassic times when *chinampa* and *chinampa*- like agriculture greatly expanded the agricultural productivity of lands in and around the lake system for the first time. In Middle Formative times the only lakeside land with adequate natural drainage for agricultural purposes was almost certainly restricted to the lowest gentle slopes of steep hills elevated a few meters above the general level of the main lakeshore plain. Natural terraces of small rivers or streams would also provide suitable land for cultivation purposes, as would alluvial fans at the mouths of streams as they entered the lake from adjacent hillslopes.

The small, scattered Middle Formative settlements which are found outside the optimum environmental niche were probably involved in the exploitation of a resource constellation from which the lacustrine element was absent and where cultivable high-water table land was much more restricted. The close proximity to major barrancas of most Middle Formative hamlets in the Texcoco Region is suggestive of the importance of some form of barranca-oriented agriculture as the basic subsistence pattern. The deep, narrow barrancas of today, intrenched up to 20 meters into the erosion-scarred land surface, are generally unsuitable for any sort of stream-bank cultivation. Prior, however, to the extensive deforestation and overgrazing which initiated the process of severe erosion in the early colonial period (Gibson, 1964), these waterways were very likely shallow streams whose water flow could readily be tapped for small-scale, productive cultivation by means of hand-carrying and/or a simple network of short feeder ditches leading directly from the stream bed into nearby fields and gardens.

The distribution of Middle Formative settlement in the Texcoco Region and the Teotihuacan Valley suggests that there were no permanent residential foci involved in the full-time exploitation of lacustrine resources in this part of the Valley of Mexico. North of Cerro Chimalhuacan the broad Lakeshore Plain and the shoreline zone itself are devoid of any recognizable Middle Formative occupation. This pattern suggests that there was little structured specialization of basic exploitative activities on a community basis, except possibly within the large Tx-MF-13 settlement where both agricultural and lacustrine resources could be effectively utilized.

Flannery's (personal communication) recent analysis of faunal remains collected during Tolstoy's excavations at Tlatilco, Tlapacoya, and El Arbolillo have introduced a new dimension into our understanding of Early and Middle Formative subsistence patterns in the Valley of Mexico. This is the importance of the hunting of land mammals. At all three sites, large quantities of whitetail deer, jack rabbit, pocket gopher, and some mule deer indicate the dependence upon such hunting. In all cases, the largest single meat source would appear to have been white-tail deer. Bones of domestic dog are also abundant in Middle Formative levels at all three sites.

Deer, at least, would be expected to have been most abundant in the hilly areas away from the main settlements on the piedmont and lakeshore. This is even more predictable when we consider that the oak-pine woodland belt of Central Mexico is within the optimum zone of white-tail deer range in Mesoamerica (Leopold, 1959: 508). Thus, it might be reasonable to suggest that some of the less substantial Middle Formative occupations at higher elevations might represent remnants of hunting camps rather than permanent settlements of agriculturalists.

The role of hunting in Middle Formative subsistence in the Valley of Mexico takes on increased significance when we consider the limitations of agricultural productivity in the Mexican *altiplano* at this period. Formative maize was presumably best adapted to the relatively moist, frost-free zones of the Mesoamerican Tierra Templada and Tierra Caliente (Wellhausen, *et. al.*, 1952). Its productivity in the semi-arid Tierra Fria, with the added impediments of early fall frosts and erratic rainfall patterns, may have been relatively low.

LATE FORMATIVE (*ca.* 550-250 B.C.)

General Valley of Mexico

The general features of what little is known of Late Formative settlement in the Valley of Mexico outside the Texcoco Region and the Teotihuacan Valley appear to be in accord with the basic trends operating in these two latter areas: population growth and the elaboration and expansion of an existing cultural pattern. All the important Middle Formative sites (Zacatenco, El Arbolillo, Tlapacoya, Tlatilco, and Tx-MF-13) mentioned in the last section continue to be occupied through the Late Formative period. Except in the case of Tx-MF-13, where Late Formative occupation is somewhat reduced and dispersed relative to that of the Middle Formative, there is little or no information concerning the relationship between size, occupational density, or community complexity of Middle and Late Formative occupations at any of these localities.

New sites appeared in areas previously unoccupied in Middle Formative times. Piña Chan (1956-57) has mentioned several localities (including Coatepec, Xaloztoc, Lomas de Becerra, Copilco, Azcapotzalco, Tetelpan, Cuicuilco, Ecatepec, and a number of others), but only for Ticoman, midway between El Arbolillo and Zacatenco in the western Valley of Mexico, are there any useful published data concerning environmental context and characteristics of occupation (Vaillant, 1931).

Late Formative occupation at Ticoman extends over the lower slopes of a rocky peninsula jutting south into Lake Texcoco from a large block of higher ground to the north (Vaillant, 1931: 426). The site area is several meters above the old lake, and overlooks a broad saddle of low, relatively level ground at the base of the higher hills to the north. As in the case of El Arbolillo and Zacatenco, Late Formative occupational debris at Ticoman is apparently substantial, but there has never been a measurement of site area nor an appraisal of occupational complexity.

Late Formative occupation at Cuicuilco on the broad piedmont slopes (now lava covered) in the southwestern Valley of Mexico, may have been quite substantial (Wolf and Palerm, 1956). This locality takes on considerable significance at the beginning of the subsequent Terminal Formative era when Cuicuilco developed into a major regional center with truly monumental public architecture and a large nucleated population. The original environmental context and site characteristics of Cuicuilco are extremely difficult to evaluate as most of the area was covered with several meters of lava during a volcanic eruption at some point in the late first millennium B.C. As Sanders (1965: 168) has noted, however, the site area was apparently situated on the largest segment of low and relatively level piedmont plain in the southern Valley of Mexico.

The Teotihuacan Valley

Moving to the Teotihuacan Valley (Sanders, 1965: 93-94, Fig. 5), we find that the basic Middle Formative settlement pattern continued, in somewhat elaborated form, into Late Formative times. The majority of sites are still the small hamlets (21 sites) and occupational traces (at six localities) characteristic of the Middle Formative occupation of this area. Some Middle Formative hamlets continued to be used in Late Formative times, others were abandoned (especially in the dominant Middle Formative demographic focus in the Patlachique Range), and new sites appeared in previously unoccupied zones.

The most significant departure from the Middle Formative pattern during Late Formative times in the Teotihuacan Valley was the appearance of two small nucleated villages, each about six hectares in surface area and with estimated populations of 250 to 300 people. Both communities are situated in low, level areas at the edge of the main alluvial plain. Excavations at one site (Cuanalan, T-F-4) indicated a pattern of closely packed, simple adobe-walled houses, and no indication of architectural differentiation within the community. As will presently be made clear, the Late Formative settlement pattern of the Teotihuacan Valley is a simplified version of the somewhat more complex series of events in the Texcoco Region to the south. One factor in the marginal character of the Teotihuacan Valley at this point is very likely the consistently lower rainfall in this area relative to precipitation farther south in the Valley of Mexico.

The Texcoco Region

For the Texcoco Region we have previously mentioned the processes of population expansion, demographic nucleation, and cultural elaboration which are clearly operative on the basic Middle Formative pattern in Late Formative times. Relative to the Middle Formative period there are now more sites, more larger and densely-occupied sites, and more different kinds of sites. Tx-LF-9 and Tx-LF-22 are large nucleated villages of several hundred people, and Tx-LF-12, extending over 86 hectares, may have had a residential population as high as 3500 people. Roughly 70 per cent of the estimated Late Formative population in our survey area was concentrated in these three communities, and over 40 per cent at Tx-LF-12 alone.

It is in the Late Formative that we have the first impression of three or four discrete regional centers (Tx-LF-9, Tx-LF-12, Tx-LF-22, and perhaps Tx-LF-29) in the Texcoco Region, each with a hinterland of dependent, dispersed rural population. This contrasts with the Middle Formative situation where there was a single large community, in a prime ecological niche, with only scattered occupation over the rest of the area. This changing settlement configuration suggests the replication, in Late Formative times, of small, independent political entities—which can probably be conceptualized as related chiefdom units—from a Middle Formative base in which large areas (including the Teotihuacan Valley and most of the Texcoco Region) were very sparsely populated and outside the limits of any effective socio-political sphere.

We can thus visualize the Late Formative as a transitional era in the Valley of Mexico in which small, relatively independent regional centers were becoming established as foci of small political entities, each associated with a discrete territory. Such replication of an existing cultural pattern was possible only so long as there was adequate vacant land and access to strategic resources so that demographic pressure did not build up to, or beyond, the point where there would have been strong selection for a basic structural reorganization. As we will presently see, the culmination of this basic Formative pattern was attained during the subsequent Terminal Formative period.

The configuration of Late Formative settlement in the Texcoco Region clearly indicates a series of marked departures from the factors which structured the main outlines of Middle Formative occupation in this area. The only large, nucleated Middle Formative community (Tx-MF-13) was situated at the single location where lake, steep hillslope, high water table, and low-lying but well-drained land occur together in this area. The largest and most densely-occupied Late Formative sites, however, are up in the Lower Piedmont, far from the lakeshore, often situated at or near the base of steep foothills or ridges. Furthermore, occupation in the area of the large nucleated Middle Formative village at Tx-MF-13 declined in both size and population density (Tx-LF-26, -27, -28, -29).

An added complication is the existence of several small lakeside communities (most importantly, Tx-LF-13, -14, and -15). Both Tx-LF-13 and Tx-LF-14 are apparently situated well within the borders of Conquest-period Lake Texcoco, and Tx-LF-15 seems to be located at or near the shoreline of this body of water. The placement of these sites lends further support to the work of earlier investigators who have suggested a low lake level during Late Formative times (e.g., Sanders, 1965; Lorenzo, 1956) relative to that of the Postclassic. Whether or not this same relatively low lake level existed during the Middle Formative period is presently an open question.

Tx-LF-13 and Tx-LF-15 are both tiny hamlets, but Tx-LF-14 appears to have been a substantial community, with perhaps as many as 200 inhabitants. These sites would probably have been situated on marshy ground at the edge of a salt lake, far from any suitable agricultural land. We have no idea as to the permanency of these settlements, but it is clear that in Late Formative times significant numbers of people in the Texcoco Region were expending considerable effort in the specialized exploitation of lacustrine resources. Hunting water fowl, collecting lake plants, and salt-making would all have been potentially productive activities at these locations.

The overall configuration of Late Formative settlement in the Texcoco Region suggests two obvious shifts in subsistence base from Middle Formative times: (1) a greatly increased reliance upon agriculture on the slopes of the Lower Piedmont, together with an improvement and elaboration of the technology of water and soil control (floodwater and canal irrigation, and hillslope and barranca-bed terracing) upon which such increased reliance would presumably have been dependent (assuming that there was no significant increase in rainfall during the Late Formative); and (2) a much greater specialization in the exploitation of nonagricultural lacustrine resources, either by certain communities on a full-time basis, or segments of communities on a part-time basis.

We are somewhat at a loss to explain the substantial decline in Late Formative times of the size and occupational density of the large Middle Formative site (Tx-MF-13) at the base of Cerro Chimalhuacan. One possibility, if we are correct in assuming that high-water-table agriculture was of basic importance in the subsistence of this community, is that this cultivation system was becoming increasingly less productive in Late Formative times. If it can be adequately demonstrated that the Middle Formative lake level was significantly higher than it was in Late Formative times (when it was clearly low), this hypothesis will be strengthened. Conditions producing any significant drop in lake level would also have the effect of lowering water table level, thus rendering less practicable any cultivation system based on easy access to permanent subsurface water. Any reduction in productive potential of this strategic Middle Formative resource would also have provided strong selective value for the technological improvement and expansion of other forms of cultivation.

TERMINAL FORMATIVE
(*ca.* 250 B.C.—A.D. 100)

General Valley of Mexico

The Terminal Formative is one of the archaeologically least-known periods in the Valley of Mexico. Outside the Teotihuacan Valley and the Texcoco Region, only Cuicuilco and Tlapacoya in the southern Valley are known to have significant Terminal Formative occupations.

Cuicuilco, as noted above, is situated on the broad, gentle piedmont slope west of Lake Xochimilco. The site has been largely covered by several meters of lava, the product of a volcanic eruption which also destroyed the productive potential of this region sometime during the late first millennium B.C. In addition to the well-known principal structure at Cuicuilco—a massive, tiered, rock-rubble temple platform measuring about 120 meters in diameter and standing some 20 meters high (Cummings, 1933: 26)—later reconaissance (Wolf and Palerm, 1956) indicated the presence of at least three other large temple platforms. These monumental structures occurred within an area of at least 20 hectares, (and probably far larger) over which heavy sherd concentrations were found in areas not covered by the lava. During 1967 large-scale construction in this area exposed several additional temple platforms of smaller size, and a residential area of undetermined extent (personal observations, JRP).

It is now virutally impossible to reconstruct the specific environmental characteristics of the Cuicuilco region prior to its being covered by lava. Wolf and Palerm (1956) have noted traces of possible ancient canals extending from the adjacent hillslopes beneath the lava surrounding and covering the site. Sanders (1965: 169) has argued that canal irrigation was important in the subsistence base at Cuicuilco, and that intensive irrigation cultivation on the broad, gentle piedmont slopes played a significant role in the emergence of Cuicuilco as a regional center in Terminal Formative times.

As will become apparent when we consider the role of irrigation at Teotihuacan, the practical difficulties of establishing the existence of this agricultural technique at Cuicuilco are considerable (and perhaps insurmountable in view of the lava cover). The fact remains, however, that canal irrigation systems would very probably have been quite feasible and highly productive at both localities. As far as we know, the large concentration of permanent springs at Teotihuacan is a unique feature in the Valley of Mexico. This may well be the only important location in the Valley of Mexico where there is now such a close juxtaposition of a large, permanent water supply, and a large, low-lying alluvial plain which could be effectively irrigated over its entire extent. There may once have been such a juxtaposition in the Cuicuilco area prior to the destruction of this region by volcanic eruption.

Formative occupation at Tlapacoya island, in the northeastern corner of Lake Chalco, apparently reached its maximum extent and complexity in Terminal Formative times (Barba de Piña Chan, 1956). There is no information concerning the size of the Terminal Formative community there, but excavations have revealed a complex stone-faced temple platform, measuring about 30 meters square, and standing perhaps five meters high. This structure is situated within the borders of what appears to be a fairly substantial residential zone on gently sloping ground along the base of a steep volcanic crater.

The Teotihuacan Valley

Within the Teotihuacan Valley the distinctive settlement configurations of the two principal phases of the Terminal Formative (Tezoyuca-Patlachique and Tzacualli) have been delineated. In Tezoyuca-Patlachique times the principal demographic focus had shifted to near the large concentrations of permanent springs in the main alluvial plain (the site of a tremendous demographic and architectural build-up in subsequent Tzacualli and Classic times). Here Millon (1966: 60) has delineated two closely spaced, but physically detached, principal settlement zones totalling some 400 hectares in surface area, situated in the northern sector of the far larger Classic center. Ceremonial-civic architecture of moderate dimensions is apparently present at the Tezoyuca-Patlachique site, and a residential population of 5000 has been suggested (Millon, 1966: 71).

Tezoyuca-Patlachique occupation is widely distributed but much less concentrated elsewhere in the Teotihuacan Valley. Some 60 sites have been located throughout this area, most of which are hamlets and dispersed villages with little or no indication of ceremonial-civic architecture (Sanders, 1965: 94-98, Fig. 6). The piedmont slopes on the lower northern flanks of the Patlachique Range continued to be the relatively most densely occupied segment of the area (aside from the dense population focus near the springs) as it had been in Late Formative times. Although many small Late Formative sites continued to be occupied during Tezoyuca-Patlachique times, the two largest Late Formative communities at the edge of the alluvial plain were abandoned.

Five or six very distinctive settlements appeared in Tezoyuca-Patlachique times in the Teotihuacan Valley. These are densely nucleated sites, ranging in size from four to six hectares, situated at the tops of low, rounded hills extending off the north edge of the main Patlachique Range. Excavation at one such site revealed remains of ceremonial-civic architecture of moderate dimensions. These hilltop sites also had ceramic assemblages (the Tezoyuca complex) which could be consistently distinguished in several ways from those of other sites of this phase, (the Patlachique complex), although the two ceramic groups are closely related and apparently contemporaneous.

Sanders (1965: 94-98, 168-69) visualized the Tezoyuca-Patlachique situation in the Teotihuacan Valley in the following manner. The half-dozen hilltop sites represent centers of elite residence and exclusive foci of important ceremonial activity. Each of these centers stood at the head of a discrete political entity, and their hilltop location suggested a general context of inter-group competition over territory and access to strategic resources (most significantly, perhaps, to the alluvial plain below which was becoming increasingly significant with the expansion of canal irrigation). Hamlets and villages on the lower slopes were dependent rural populations oriented toward one or another of the hilltop centers.

Sanders' ideas were formulated before the large size and population of the Tezoyuca-Patlachique community at Teotihuacan was fully ascertained. The presence of this relatively huge demographic focus requires a reworking of his basic hypotheses regarding the socio-political structuring of the Teotihuacan Valley in Tezoyuca-Patlachique times. It now seems apparent that the urbanization process at Teotihuacan, which Sanders assigned to the subsequent Tzacualli phase, had clearly been initiated in the antecedent Tezoyuca-Patlachique. Even as early as this latter phase, Teotihuacan had very likely emerged as the dominant sociopolitical focus within the Teotihuacan Valley. The hilltop localities may represent foci of more or less independent socio-political entities, but we believe their relatively small size suggests quite strongly that they were far from being on an equal footing with Teotihuacan.

Thus, by Tezoyuca-Patlachique times

Teotihuacan had emerged as the dominant, if not yet the sole, power focus in the Teotihuacan Valley. Its power base very probably lay in control over the great hydraulic resource represented by the concentration of about 80 permanent springs at the edge of the archaeological site. Assuming the existence and significance of canal irrigation, this location obviously was the point from which to control the agricultural productivity of the alluvial plain below the springs. It is not really necessary, however, to postulate the presence of canal irrigation here in order to account for the development of a large demographic center at the head of these springs. The springs would have provided an abundant and permanent water source that could have been readily tapped for intensive cultivation within a relatively small radius by means of short feeder canals. It is entirely conceivable that adequate drainage was the key problem, and that local drainage projects in Tezoyuca-Patlachique times secured the tremendous productive potential of high-water-table agriculture in the area immediately around the springs (similar to the modified *chinampa* cultivation practiced in this very locality today). Canal irrigation may not have been significant in the lower alluvial plain until the subsequent Tzacualli phase, when, as will be made clear shortly, Teotihuacan very quickly developed into a major urban center.

The combined surveys of Sanders and Millon have clearly demonstrated the dramatic demographic changes which occurred during the Tzacualli phase in the Teotihuacan Valley. The population of the large Tezoyuca-Patlachique center above the springs at Teotihuacan grew to approximately 30,000 people distributed over an area of some 17 square km (Millon, 1966: 71-72). The main portion of the huge Sun Pyramid was constructed during this period, together with several other principal ceremonial-civic structures. The main outlines of the basic grid plan of the center were also established at this time, including the large central avenue (Calle de los Muertos) and the Avenida Este (Millon, 1966: 72).

Apart from the large center at Teotihuacan, some 90 additional Tzacualli-phase sites have been located throughout the Teotihuacan Valley (Sanders, 1965: 101, Fig. 7). These are principally dispersed villages, hamlets, and occupational traces distributed around the edges of the main alluvial plain and in the gently sloping terrain of the surrounding piedmont slopes. All the Tezoyuca-Patlachique phase hilltop centers along the base of the Patlachique Range were abandoned. Sanders (1965) estimated that roughly half the Tzacualli-phase population of the Teotihuacan Valley was concentrated in and immediately around the main center at Teotihuacan, with the remainder distributed in a much more dispersed fashion throughout scattered villages and hamlets. Since it now appears that Tzacualli Teotihuacan was substantially larger than Sanders thought, it is likely that a significantly larger proportion of the total Tzacualli population of the Teotihuacan Valley resided at the urban center than he originally estimated. The apparent lack of any significant ceremonial-civic architecture at all Tzacualli sites other than Teotihuacan led Sanders (1965) to regard the latter center as the single socio-political and ceremonial focus of a highly integrated polity which directly incorporated at least the entire Teotihuacan Valley, and whose influence very probably extended far beyond into other parts of the Valley of Mexico and Central Mexico.

Tzacualli, Teotihuacan's principal power base, in Sanders' (1965: 171) view, was a full-scale, integrated network of irrigation canals by means of which the maximum productive capacity of the entire alluvial plain below the springs (*ca.* 50 square km) could be realized. The complex organizational and coordinational requirements of such a full-scale system (principally, the scheduling of equitable water distribution to all localities, and the construction and continuous maintenance of many kilometers of inter-connected primary and secondary canals) would have provided strong selection for political centralization. Once such a productive system was in effective operation, a local demographic base and political structure capable of expanding symbiotic and extractive networks into other areas could be maintained and elaborated. Cuicuilco was apparently also in a position to achieve similar developmental and organizational breakthroughs, and at an even earlier period. As previously noted, however, the developmental potential of Cuicuilco was abruptly terminated in the late first millennium B.C.

In the continuing absence of any direct evidence of canal irrigation in the Teotihuacan Valley prior to Postclassic times, Sanders' arguments, however convincing, have remained hypothetical.

The Texcoco Region

As we have noted earlier, in our surveys of the Texcoco Region we found very little diagnostic Tzacualli pottery. Only at Tx-TF-7, -16, -17, -31, -39, and -42 are there significant concentrations of recognizable Tzacualli material. Tzacualli pottery seemed to be dominant at the small sites of Tx-TF-7, -16, and -42, and occurred elsewhere mixed with more abundant Tezoyuca-Patlachique material.

We are faced with two alternative possibilities in evaluating the apparent scarcity of Tzacualli pottery in the Texcoco Region: (1) the very limited presence of diagnostic Tzacualli material indicates a correspondingly limited occupation of the Texcoco Region during the time when Tzacualli ceramics were abundant in the Teotihuacan Valley to the north; (2) the Tzacualli complex represents a localized Teotihuacan Valley variant utilized in this relatively restricted area at the same time that the basic Tezoyuca-Patlachique complex continued to be the dominant assemblage elsewhere in the Valley of Mexico. At present we are not in a position to properly evaluate the merits of these two alternatives, although the characteristics of Early Classic occupation in the Texcoco Region leads us to favor the former. Our discussion of Terminal Formative settlement in the Texcoco Region will therefore be most meaningful relative to the Tezoyuca-Patlachique occupation of the Teotihucan Valley, and probably elsewhere in the Valley of Mexico.

In the Texcoco Region, Terminal Formative occupation represents the elaboration, expansion, and culmination of existing trends developed in Middle and Late Formative times, together with a few radical departures from these basic trends. Relative to the antecedent Late Formative, there are nearly twice as many sites, over three times as much occupied area, and a substantial population increase (Table 7). There are more large, nucleated sites, and a general filling in of large areas which had previously been vacant or very sparsely occupied. The appearance of a large, nucleated village (Tx-TF-46; Pl. 24, 25, 26) on flat, poorly drained land, at or very near the lowered shoreline of Lake Texcoco suggests that the specialized exploitation of lacustrine resources, apparently initiated in the Late Formative, was expanded and elaborated in Terminal Formative times.

The proliferation of sites on the gentle slopes of the Lower Piedmont strongly suggests that agriculture in this zone was further expanded and intensified relative to Late Formative times. As in the Late Formative, settlement configuration indicates no orientation toward the main alluvial plain east of the Lake Texcoco shoreline. This flat, poorly-drained zone undoubtedly continued to be agriculturally marginal. Furthermore, the lowered lake level at this period would have rendered most of this area equally unattractive for the residence of people engaged in the exploitation of lacustrine resources.

On the broad, gentle slopes of the Lower Piedmont we can predict an expansion and intensification of both small-scale floodwater irrigation systems and simple networks of ditches and canals leading water from streams and small rivers into nearby cultivation plots. It is conceivable that the permanent springs scattered along the base of the main Sierra at the eastern edge of our survey area were directly tapped for household use and irrigation water in Terminal Formative times; however, in marked contrast to the hydraulic resources of the Teotihuacan Valley, the individual springs in the Texcoco Region were widely scattered and far removed from prime agricultural land. Their direct exploitation would have required the construction of aqueduct and causeway systems extending for several kilometers across the rugged lower Sierra and Upper Piedmont. As will be made increasingly clear, archaeological and documentary evidence suggest that such hydraulic works did not appear prior to Late Aztec times. It is more likely that the main value of these springs in Terminal Formative times was their substantial contribution to the flow of water along natural watercourses across the Lower Piedmont where water was being diverted from streams and small rivers for agricultural purposes. As such, these springs would have constituted strategic resources of primary significance to Terminal Formative populations residing in the Lower Piedmont. Intercommunity competition for access to, and control of, the flow of water from these springs may well have been an important factor in structuring socio-political relationships within the Texcoco Region during this period.

Recent analysis (Wheeler, 1968) of faunal remains from Dixon's (1966) excavations at Temesco (Tx-TF-51) has revealed that white-tailed deer, peccary, pocket gopher, cottontail rabbit, duck, and domestic dog were all utilized at this community in Terminal Formative times.

Despite the general trends of population expansion and increase in site size, the three largest Late Formative sites (Tx-LF-9, Tx-LF-12, and Tx-LF-22) were largely or wholly abandoned by the Terminal Formative (as were the two largest Late Formative communities in the Teotihuacan Valley). We are presently at a loss to explain this site abandonment in both areas. The largest Terminal Formative sites grew up in areas of scanty Late Formative settlement (as was also the case in the Teotihuacan Valley). As in the Teotihuacan Valley, there are several substantial Terminal Formative sites situated on isolated hilltops or along ridge crests, at 50 to 100 meters above the level of the surrounding Lower Piedmont or Lakeshore Plain (Tx-TF-2, -4, -6, -14, -36, and -51). All these sites contain distinctive remnants of ceremonial-civic architecture, including temple platforms several meters high. Just as in the Teotihuacan Valley, these site locations were occupied only during the Terminal Formative (or, more precisely, Tezoyuca-Patlachique) era, and lack any sign of significant antecedent or subsequent usage.

In neither the Teotihuacan Valley nor the Texcoco Region are these hilltop sites the largest demographic foci in the local area. It also seems clear that these communities in both areas are architecturally more complex than most contemporary sites on the lower piedmont slopes and Lakeshore Plain. Although we did not detect any superficially apparent distinction between the ceramic assemblages of these hilltop sites and lower-lying communities in the Texcoco Region, there may well be such a ceramic differentiation equivalent to that noted above for the hilltop and low-lying sites in the Teotihuacan Valley during Tezoyuca-Patlachique times. Assuming that such hilltop and low-lying sites were contemporary, our suggestion is that the hilltop and ridge crest sites in both the Teotihuacan Valley and Texcoco Region can best be understood as segregated elite districts where certain high-ranking lineages and their retainers resided on a full-time or periodic basis. The relationships between such elite residential districts and other population centers may become somewhat clearer in the next few paragraphs.

We have previously noted our impression of three or four Late Formative demographic clusters in the Texcoco Region. By Terminal Formative times we can delineate four main demographic zones, on the basis of gross population distribution and site features, which are likely to have been significant socio-political entities as well:

1) In the southwestern sector of the Texcoco Region, with principal population foci at Tx-TF-51, Tx-TF-50, and Tx-TF-46. Each of these three principal communities is situated within a distinctive environmental context: (*a*) Tx-TF-51 occurs at the edge of a low bluff overlooking the main Lakeshore Plain, at the western edge of a broad expanse of gently sloping piedmont plain. Its location is particularly strategic as it controls the main pass leading into the Texcoco Region from the southwest. (*b*) Tx-TF-50 is found on the main floor of the Lakeshore Plain, at the juncture of steeply sloping and gently-sloping-to-level terrain. (*c*) Tx-TF-46 is located within the borders of Conquest-period Lake Texcoco, on flat ground apparently at or very near the Terminal Formative shoreline.

The bulk of the obvious ceremonial-civic architecture in this zone occurs at Tx-TF-51. Aztec and modern overlay at Tx-TF-50, however, is such that this site's Terminal Formative architectural complexity is probably badly obscured.

The total estimated population of this demographic zone ranges between 2600 and 4850, with over 90 per cent concentrated in the three main communities.

2) In the Lower Piedmont slopes over the northern half of the broad area between the central and southern survey strips. The principal population concentrations are sites Tx-TF-30 and Tx-TF-36. Although all sites are situated within the general Lower Piedmont zone, all major site types are represented: Tx-TF-36 is a nucleated ridge-crest center (Pl. 23,*a*) with definite ceremonial-civic architecture—presumably an elite residential sector; Tx-TF-30 is a large, nucleated regional center on the main piedmont slope, which may contain ceremonial-civic structures (severe erosion here makes it quite difficult to ascertain this point); other communities are nucleated and dispersed villages and hamlets, with no indication of significant ceremonial-civic architecture. The total estimated population for this demographic zone ranges between 2900 and 5500, with 50 to 60 per cent concentrated in the two main communities.

3) In that segment of the Lower Piedmont bordered on the east by the arc of high ground formed by the Cerro Purificación-Cerro San Miguel-Cerro Metecatl-Cerro Tetzcotzingo complex in the east-central portion of the central survey strip. Tx-TF-17 and Tx-TF-14 are the two principal communities. This area is very similar to the second demographic zone mentioned above, both in terms of its environmental context (predominately broad, gently sloping ground, cut by numerous watercourses), and the range of site types present. Tx-TF-14 is a typical ridge-crest

location (Pl. 22), with a nucleated residential zone of moderate proportions and indications of ceremonial-civic architecture of moderate dimensions. Tx-TF-17 is a large, nucleated, low-lying site—measuring 118 hectares in surface area, the largest Terminal Formative site in our survey area—with few indications of ceremonial-civic architecture (although this latter impression may be somewhat misleading as much of the Tx-TF-17 site area is intensively cultivated today) (Pl. 18,*b*). Other sites in this general area are dispersed villages and hamlets of variable size. The total estimated population of this third demographic zone ranges from 2550 to 5000, with over 80 per cent concentrated in the two principal communities.

4) Along the southern edge of the Patlachique Range in the central portion of the northern survey strip. There are two principal communities: (*a*) Tx-TF-1, a large, nucleated, low-lying site situated on gently sloping ground at the base of a steep ridge at the edge of the main alluvial plain (Pl. 17, 18); (*b*) Tx-TF-4, a typical nucleated hilltop site with distinct ceremonial-civic structures and significant architectural complexity (Pl. 19, 20, 21). Smaller sites, principally hamlets and dispersed villages, are found dispersed over the gentle slopes and hilltops around the edges of the alluvial floodplain of the Río Papalotla to the east. The total estimated population of this demographic zone ranges between 2300 and 4350, with about 90 per cent concentrated in the three major communities.

We suggest that these four principal demographic clusters represent separate socio-political entities—territorial statelets or perhaps chiefdoms. In each entity a major part of the population was concentrated in two or three principal communities. In general, these latter sites consisted of one or two segregated elite districts situated on hilltops or ridge crests, and a single large, nucleated community on the main gently sloping plain of the Lower Piedmont. Smaller numbers of people resided in hamlets and dispersed villages scattered throughout the Lower Piedmont plain and along the shoreline of Lake Texcoco. The only significant departure from this general picture was in the southwestern sector of our survey area where there was apparently a more intensive and elaborated specialization in the exploitation of lacustrine resources than elsewhere.

There is little in the Terminal Formative settlement configuration of the Texcoco Region which would suggest that any one of the four main political entities was relatively dominant. All major sites are of roughly similar size, and all major settlement types are found within each of the four demographic zones. We can predict the existence of a situation in which there was competition over territorial control and access to strategic resources within the Texcoco Region. However, in marked contrast to the Tezoyuca-Patlachique and Tzacualli phases in the Teotihuacan Valley (and probably in the Cuicuilco area as well), there is no indication that any single site was clearly a dominant power focus in the Texcoco Region during the Terminal Formative period. Tezoyuca-Patlachique phase Teotihuacan (400 hectares and approximately 5000 people) covered over three times as much surface area as the largest Terminal Formative site in the Texcoco Region (Tx-TF-17), and contained roughly twice as many people. The somewhat more dispersed settlement zone which we have designated as Tx-TF-25, -30, -31, -32, -33, -34, and -35 contained between 2300 and 4350 people in an occupied area of about 176 hectares (not including intervening areas where occupational density is absent or negligible). Only if this latter population cluster were to be regarded as a single great community (which would be difficult to justify) would there be any single site in the Texcoco Region comparable to Teotihuacan in Terminal Formative times.

Looking at the Valley of Mexico as a whole (and recalling that there remains considerable uncertainty regarding the character of occupation outside the Teotihuacan Valley during the Tzacualli phase), it would appear that two principal centers —Teotihuacan and Cuicuilco—developed rapidly during Tezoyuca-Patlachique times. A major factor in the development of large centers was undoubtedly the unusually high agricultural productivity feasible at both locations—i.e., some form of canal irrigation, and/or artificially improved and expanded high-water-table cultivation, over a large area of low-lying, yet relatively well drained land, easily accessible to a large, permanent water supply.

The Texcoco Region may be regarded as more typical of the remainder of the Valley of Mexico where such a highly desirable combination of land and water resources is not known to occur. Future investigations of unexplored segments of the Valley of Mexico are likely to reveal an additional 20 to 40 demographic clusters similar in size and settlement configuration to those we have noted for the Texcoco Region.

In view of their size, population, and architectural complexity, both Cuicuilco and Teotihuacan probably maintained some degree of political hegemony beyond their local regions during Tezoyuca-Patlachique times. In the future we may be able to demonstrate that Cuicuilco exercised supra-local control over much of the southern and western Valley of Mexico, while Teotihuacan functioned in a similar fashion in the east and north. We can further predict that there would have been some degree of competition between Cuicuilco and Teotihuacan as these centers confronted each other as foci of expanding symbiotic-extractive networks in which there was much to be gained by incorporating larger numbers of smaller socio-political entities on a dependent and subordinate basis.

We can delineate three hypothetical types or levels of competition at the Tezoyuca-Patlachique horizon: (1) at the highest level, between the major regional centers of Cuicuilco and Teotihuacan, in which the primary concern was over securing the allegiance of secondary political centers for purposes of trade, tribute, and military alliance; (2) at an intermediate level, between a major center (Cuicuilco or Teotihuacan) and any one of several secondary centers which might attempt to resist the efforts of the major center to incorporate it within its symbiotic-extractive network; and (3) at the lowest level, between individual secondary centers, over access to local resources.

The conceptualization of the Tezoyuca-Patlachique horizon as an era of intensive competition, at several levels, between separate political entities, seems particularly attractive as it lends itself well to understanding some of the socio-political implications of the rather abrupt and startling changes in regional settlement configuration which began to take place early in the first millennium A.D. We have previously noted the tremendous increase in size, population, and architectural complexity of Teotihuacan in the Tzacualli phase. This remarkable urbanization process apparently accelerated most rapidly shortly after the abrupt volcanic destruction of the Cuicuilco center late in the first millennium B.C. There has been at least one attempt (West, 1965) to link the Tzacualli florescense in the Teotihuacan Valley with the immigration of a large number of refugees from the destroyed center at Cuicuilco.

Whatever the effects on the Tzacualli-phase florescence of Teotihuacan of the rapid, violent termination of Cuicuilco's role as a competing major center, we are still in a poor position to evaluate the specifics of such a relationship. Indeed, as noted earlier, it is precisely at the Tzacualli horizon that we are most unclear as to the patterns of settlement configuration anywhere outside the Teotihuacan Valley. At this point, our best opportunity to illuminate the critical Tzacualli phase is to move immediately to a discussion of the Early Classic period.

EARLY CLASSIC
(*ca.* A.D. 100-450)

General Valley of Mexico

In a recent summary of Classic-period occupation in the Valley of Mexico outside the Teotihuacan Valley, Bernal (1966: 98) has noted the known existence of some 25 localities where architectural and/or ceramic remains of this era had been reported prior to our survey of the Texcoco Region. In Bernals opinion, all these sites were relatively small, and represented nothing more complex than villages and towns ("aldeas y pueblos"). In nearly all cases the only information available concerning these sites is the mere mention of the presence of Classic sherds or architecture, with no data concerning specific location, site size, or architectural complexity. To our knowledge, Tozzer's (1921) report on the 1913-14 excavations of a Classic residential compound at Santiago Ahuitzotla, near Atzcapotzalco on the main alluvial plain close to the western shore of Lake Texcoco, is the only significant published source relevant to the character of Classic occupation outside the Teotihuacan Valley. And, since Tozzer's excavations and observations were restricted to an area of about 40 by 20 meters, his remarks are of limited value for our purposes. Vaillant (1938: 539) noted an abundance of Classic pottery in his nearby excavations at El Corral, but gave no specifics regarding the character of occupation there. Armillas (personal communication) has noted the substantial deposits of Early Classic (Miccaotli phase) material in the Atzcapotzalco area.

Today the Atzcapotzalco area has been obliterated by the heavy overlay of modern Mexico City. It is therefore unlikely that we will ever be able to evaluate the character of Classic occupation there. The site was probably a substantial one, however, certainly not in the same class as Teotihuacan, but perhaps significantly larger than most other known Classic sites in the Valley of Mexico. It is probably highly significant that the Atzcapotzalco Classic community is situated on the largest expanse of potentially irrigable alluvial plain in the western Valley of Mexico. It is entirely conceivable that an important Terminal Formative-Early Classic center emerged at Atzcapotzalco following the volcanic destruction of the Cuicuilco center and the agricultural capacity of the Cuicuilco plain.

Thus, our comparative material for the Classic horizon is even more restricted than that of the preceeding Terminal Formative. Apart from the Teotihuacan Valley and Texcoco Region, we can say practically nothing regarding even the barest outlines of site locations and distribution of different types of settlements. As will shortly be made clear, the ability to adequately interpret the problems generated by the configuration of Classic settlement in the Teotihuacan Valley and Texcoco Region is dependent upon additional systematic regional surveys within the Valley of Mexico and around its borders.

The Teotihuacan Valley

Within the Teotihuacan Valley, Millon's surveys of the Teotihuacan urban zone have succeeded in delineating the surface extent, estimated population, and something of the architectural configurations for each of the four principal phases of the Classic period (Miccaotli, Tlamimilolpa, Xolalpan, and Metepec). Our principal interest at this point is with Miccaotli and Tlamimilolpa which we have defined as Early Classic for our purposes. From a surface area of 17 square kilometers and roughly 30,000 inhabitants in Tzacualli times, the Teotihuacan urban complex expanded to about 22.5 square kilometers and 45,000 people by Miccaotli, with an apparent rapid expansion to 65,000 inhabitants over a roughly similar area in the Tlamimilolpa phase (Millon, 1966: 72-73). The basic grid network of avenues laid down in Tzacualli times was filled in and expanded in the Early Classic, and a number of major ceremonial-civic complexes were added along the main central avenue (Calle de los Muertos) and elsewhere. Residential complexes have been uncovered, including large mazes of tightly packed small houses and apartment complexes cut through by narrow, twisting alleyways.

The configuration of Early Classic rural population in the Teotihuacan Valley represents a dramatic restructuring of population distribution relative to the antecedent Formative era. Although some 100 site locations were identified, the majority of these were very small villages, hamlets, or mere occupational traces. Most substantial communities—nucleated villages and small towns—were restricted to two very distinctive settings (Sanders, 1965: 107-21, Fig. 7):

1) On the piedmont slopes, well above the main alluvial plain, along extensions (in some cases imaginary, but often in the form of well-defined roadways) of the urban center's major north-south and east-west avenues. All communities in this category were nucleated villages, each with a few hundred inhabitants. One such community (T-C-8) a few kilometers west of the urban center, was partially excavated. This work revealed well-constructed, well-proportioned residential quarters, quite similar architecturally to living complexes known from Teotihuacan itself, with ceramic and artifact assemblages equivalent to those known from sections of the urban center. Of particular significance is the relatively high proportion of obsidian scrapers. These tools, almost identical in form to iron scrapers used today in highland Mexico for scraping the interior walls of the maguey plant to facilitate sap flow for the manufacture of pulque, suggest that pulque production was a major industry at this locality. This indication, combined with the characteristic piedmont-slope situation of most other rural Classic sites, led Sanders to believe that most rural settlements of this period were specialized in exploitative activities—such as maguey cultivation and pulque production—feasible in agriculturally marginal sections of the Teotihuacan Valley.

2) A second constellation of communities—including two sites classified as small towns, four large, nucleated villages, and a number of hamlets and small villages—are strung out along the lower northern and eastern flanks of Cerro Gordo several kilometers north of the main urban center. Most of these settlements are oriented along a single WNW-ESE axis about 17 kilometers long. Some of the larger communities in this region are miniature duplications of Teotihuacan itself—with a grid of small avenues and cross streets, and modest ceremonial-civic architecture concentrated along a central roadway.

The most remarkable feature of Early Classic settlement patterning in the Teotihuacan Valley is the all-pervasive impact of the main urban center in structuring the location and distribution of population. Perhaps 75 per cent of the total regional population was now concentrated within a single great community, and the placement of rural occupation was clearly determined by the needs and directives of Teotihuacan.

The Texcoco Region

In the Texcoco Region a drastically different demographic process was in operation. In marked contrast to the great Early Classic population expansion and nucleation in the Teotihuacan Valley, there was a substantial decrease in number of sites, occupational area, occupational density, and population in the Texcoco Region relative to Terminal Formative times (Table 7) Many Terminal Formative sites were wholly or largely abandoned, including all those hilltop and ridge-crest sites we classified as segregated elite districts. With a single exception (Tx-EC-32), all Early Classic communities were hamlets and small villages, with almost no indication of ceremonial-civic architecture of even very modest proportions. Most of these communities are situated on the gentle slopes of the Lower Piedmont, but several (Tx-EC-1, -33, -34, -35, and -36) are located along or near the Classic-period lakeshore, and one site (Tx-EC-23) is found in the steeper Upper Piedmont not far below the base of the main Sierra. Some of these settlements occupy small sections of old Terminal Formative sites (Tx-EC-5, -6, -9, -11, -12, -15, -17, -21, and -22); others are located in previously unoccupied areas. There is little or no suggestion of the demographic clustering we observed for Terminal Formative times. Early Classic sites appear to be scattered rather continuously throughout the Lower Piedmont sector of the Texcoco Region, with no indication of site orientation along real or imaginary axes.

Considered as a whole, the configuration of Early Classic settlement represents an abrupt and complete reversal of the long-established basic Formative trends of population expansion, community proliferation, demographic clustering, and replication of small, independent political entities in the Texcoco Region.

The single exception to this general pattern is a larger community (Tx-EC-32) near the southern edge of our survey area. This is the Portezuelo site, previously discussed by Hicks and Nicholson (1964). Here, Classic occupation is somewhat obscured by a heavy Early Toltec overlay (Tx-ET-18), but enough can be seen to indicate Classic settlement stretching over an area of roughly 60 hectares. The Portezuelo site has sometimes been viewed as a kind of provincial center dependent upon Teotihuacan (Sanders, 1961; Mayer-Oakes, 1959, 1960). Our present impression, however, is that, despite the total surface area over which Classic sherds are scattered, Classic occupation here was not substantial. Concentrations of Classic surface pottery are seldom greater than light, and never exceed the light-to-moderate range of our subjective scale of visual estimation. Unless the true character of Classic occupation is largely obscured by the much heavier Early Toltec overlay (a distinct possibility), we would tend to view Tx-EC-32 as little more than a larger variant of our standard Classic villages in the Texcoco Region. Almost certainly, Classic Portezuelo was not a population center of more than modest proportions.

In his prediction of where Classic sites would be found in the Texcoco Region, Sanders (1965: 176-77) suggested that the Lower Piedmont slope could be expected to show the greatest occupational density at this period. His reasoning was based upon (*a*) the greater productivity of simple neolithic agriculture in this area where drainage and access to runoff water from the Sierra were better, rainfall was higher, and danger from frosts lower relative to the main alluvium of the flat Lakeshore Plain; and (*b*) the assumption that population was lower and land pressure much less severe than in Aztec times when the main Lakeshore Plain was intensively cultivated and heavily populated.

Sanders' hypothesis has proved essentially valid. The bulk of Early Classic occupation in the Texcoco Region is concentrated precisely where he predicted. We would suggest that most Early Classic communities in our survey area were primarily engaged in the type of agricultural exploitation Sanders envisioned: that is, cultivation of the gentle slopes using techniques of floodwater irrigation and simple networks of feeder ditches channeling water from streams and river beds into nearby fields. There is no indication from the distributional pattern of Classic sites in the Texcoco Region that permanent springs at the base of the Sierra were now being utilized directly for irrigation agriculture. There is no obvious clustering of Classic communities in or around areas into which canals and aqueducts operative in Late Aztec and modern times have carried water from these springs for agricultural and household purposes. Furthermore, the placement of the largest Classic community in the Texcoco Region (Tx-EC-32, Tx-LC-18) is not at all suggestive that control of these Sierra springs, or utilization of their water supply for agricultural purposes, were significant factors in its location.

Sanders' 1965 concept of Classic settlement in the Texcoco Region and the Valley of Mexico as a whole, however, requires some modification as it does not allow for the tremendous impact of the Teotihuacan urban center in areas outside the Teotihuacan Valley. We have the impression that Sanders expected to find numerous Classic sites, of substantial size and population, distributed throughout the Valley of Mexico. He has suggested (e.g., n.d., 1965) that regional socio-political structure in the Valley of Mexico during Classic times may have been a modified form of the late Postclassic pattern. At this latter period there were a number of major secondary regional centers, of which one or two were relatively more powerful, but among which there was competition and even militaristic confrontation on a basis of relative equality. Sanders acknowledged the apparent greater regional political predominance of Classic Teotihuacan relative to that of any one of the late Postclassic centers, however, it is clear that he did not expect to encounter the extreme situation of a complete regional power monopoly by a single center that our data from the Texcoco Region suggest.

It seems apparent that Teotihuacan's direct influence pervaded the entire Texcoco Region from Tzacualli times through Early Classic. Furthermore, the drastic population decline at the Terminal Formative-Early Classic juncture in our survey area suggests that large segments of population were withdrawn (forcibly or otherwise) into the Teotihuacan urban zone at the time of its initial rapid demographic buildup. We are presently ignorant both of the organizational and integrative mechanisms by which this demographic restructuring was accomplished, and of the area over which Teotihuacan extended such tight and direct control.

The apparent scarcity, however, of known large Classic sites in the Valley of Mexico outside the Teotihuacan Valley leads us to believe that future surveys might reveal a Classic settlement pattern similar in general outline to that of the Texcoco Region in as yet unexplored areas in the Valley of Mexico.

Our previous discussion has raised two principal problem areas: (1) the transition from Formative to Classic; and (2) the regional socio-political structure of the Early Classic period. In commenting upon the former, we have the impression of a highly competitive situation in Terminal Formative times throughout the Valley of Mexico. This era saw two primary centers of roughly equivalent size and power (Tezoyuca-Patlachique Teotihuacan and Cuicuilco), together with numerous secondary centers, struggling among themselves, on various levels, for access to strategic productive resources and trade routes. A preceeding millennium of sedentary agricultural life and population expansion had laid the groundwork for such potentially hostile local and regional confrontations. The stage was then set for regional integration on a much broader scale if any one center could make the quantum jump in organizational capacity necessary for such a step. Tzacualli Teotihuacan obviously made such a quantum jump, and found it necessary, and/or advantageous, to concentrate the majority of a large regional population within a single great community.

Sanders has forcefully argued (1965, 1968) that a principal factor in Teotihuacan's organizational breakthrough at the end of the Terminal Formative period was the tremendous productive capacity offered by the unique feasibility of large-scale canal irrigation in the large Teotihuacan Valley alluvial plain, and the coordinational requirements for the effective operation of such a water-control system. We have clearly expressed our agreement with Sanders' basic hypothesis. Nowhere else in the Valley of Mexico—except probably in the Cuicuilco area prior to its volcanic destruction—was it possible to establish such a local demographic and political base from which to initiate the expansion of symbiotic-extractive networks. Furthermore, the abrupt removal of Cuicuilco as a political rival undoubtedly contributed significantly to Teotihuacan's meteoric rise to pan-Mesoamerican significance in Tzacualli and Early Classic times.

It will be made increasingly clear when we begin to discuss relevant developments in Mesoamerica outside the Valley of Mexico, that we should consider at least one additional element in the origin of Teotihuacan's political dominance. This is the matter of access routes to other important regions: the Teotihuacan Valley is the most direct and efficient route from the Valley of Mexico to the central Gulf Coast, and to the large highland basins of Tlaxcala-Puebla and Pachuca. Major highways have extended through the Teotihuacan Valley to these regions during colonial and modern times, as have principal railroad lines since the late nineteenth century.

Once Teotihuacan had become fully established in Early Classic times, its direct influence throughout the entire Valley of Mexico was apparently all-pervasive and complete. We can suggest that Early Classic communities throughout the Valley of Mexico—typified by those we have located in the Texcoco Region—represent small concentrations of people engaged in a variety of specialized, state-directed exploitative activities tied directly to the economic networks focused on Teotihuacan. Lakeshore sites were probably involved in salt-making, collecting lake plants and insects, hunting water fowl, and perhaps fishing. Sites on the lower hillslopes are likely to have been engaged in cultivating the wide expanse of gently-sloping ground rising above the lakeshore plain. Sites higher up in steeper portions of the Sierra foothills may have been oriented primarily toward collecting forest resources and hunting.

The apparent lack of any architectural remains of even modest proportions at most Classic sites in the Texcoco Region might suggest seasonal or temporary residence at some locations by people whose permanent homes were in secondary regional centers, or even in Teotihuacan itself. Somewhat larger and more elaborate sites, such as Tx-EC-32 in the Texcoco Region, can probably be viewed as small provincial administrative centers directly dependent upon Teotihuacan, which were charged with the regional coordination of local production and the delivery to Teotihuacan of raw materials and staple goods. All these hypothetical considerations should be readily amenable to archaeological testing.

LATE CLASSIC (*ca.* A.D. 450-700)

The Teotihuacan Valley

The basic demographic trends established in the Teotihuacan Valley and Texcoco Region during Early Classic times continued into the Late Classic period in both areas. Millon's survey (1966: 74) has revealed that in the Xolalpan phase Teotihuacan attained its maximum population size and density (conservatively estimated at 85,000 people in an area of about 20.5 square kilometers). It was at this time that the urban center achieved its fullest architectural complexity: practically all major ceremonial-civic structures along and around the principal avenues had been constructed and were in use; a series of residential complexes have been unearthed, ranging from large, spacious, well-constructed apartments to small, cramped, sloppily-erected quarters; and there is evidence of a systematic process of tearing down old residences and rebuilding which Millon (1966) has termed "urban renewal."

Millon's impression (1966: 77) of Metepec-phase Teotihuacan, at the end of the Late Classic, is that of a population reduction to roughly 70,000 inhabitants within an area of about 20 square kilometers.

Intensive surface surveys and excavations have recently located sections within the Teotihuacan urban zone where concentrations of distinctly Oaxacan, Gulf Coast, and Mayan ceramics and artifacts occur in unusually high proportion (Millon, 1967). These have tentatively been interpreted as wards of "foreigners" residing at Teotihuacan. The chronological placement of these foreign enclaves seems to be Late Classic (Xolalpan phase), with a probable beginning of such occupation in Tlamimilolpa times in the Early Classic period.

tinued on an even more extreme basis in the Late Classic. While a number of Early Classic communities continued to be occupied into the Late Classic, there was a very marked intensification of the movement of rural population into Teotihuacan (Sanders, 1965: 101-21). By the Metepec phase, at the end of the Late Classic period, as much as 90 per cent of the total Teotihuacan Valley population may have been permanently based at Teotihuacan (1965: 121).

The Texcoco Region

In the Texcoco Region, the configuration of Late Classic settlement is very similar to that of Early Classic. There was a significant decrease, however, in the number of sites, size of occupied area, and estimated population relative to Early Classic times. This was apparently accompanied by some increase in the size of the single large community at Tx-EC-32 (Portezuelo) which may have expanded to roughly 80 hectares in Late Classic times (Tx-LC-18). The bulk of the population decrease and site abandonment was restricted to a single section of the Texcoco Region: the southeastern quadrant, including the southern half of the central survey strip, the area lying between the central and southern survey strip, and the eastern third of the southern survey strip. If our temporal evaluations of the Classic ceramic assemblage are valid, this whole broad zone—where a dozen Early Classic villages and hamlets had been situated—was largely devoid of significant sedentary occupation in Late Classic times. As will shortly be made clear in our discussion of Early Toltec occupation of the Texcoco Region, this Late Classic phenomenon anticipates an even more extreme depopulation of the entire central portion of the Texcoco Region in the centuries following the collapse of Teotihuacan as a major center. For this reason, we will defer our interpretation of this re-

The trend toward increased concentration in the urban zone of the Teotihuacan Valley's rural population which was well established in Early Classic times was congional Late Classic-Early Toltec demographic vacuum until the following section of this chapter.

It is clear that the drying up of rural settlement and the increased concentration of population in fewer centers that characterize the Late Classic of the Teotihuacan Valley are also operative in the Texcoco Region. While the basic regional political and economic structure we suggested for the Early Classic Valley of Mexico is probably still valid for the Late Classic period, there is strong indication that new pressures were selecting for a reworking of established organizational patterns. When we look outside the Valley of Mexico into other areas of Mesoamerica we will see that new centers were beginning to emerge as focal points of political and economic power during the last third of the first millennium A.D. Teotihuacan very clearly was forced to adapt to a constantly changing pattern of events, and was strongly influenced by developments in other parts of Mesoamerica, particularly those in Central Mexico where new power centers were growing up around the peripheries of the Valley of Mexico. The Late Classic demographic dislocations and extreme population concentration in Teotihuacan's heartland reflect the urban center's efforts to cope with new problems and difficulties. By the end of the Classic era, however, sometime in the eighth century A.D., Teotihuacan's commitment to, and investment in, a set of long-established and well-intrenched archaic institutions rendered it ineffectual as a center of pan-Mesoamerican significance. The configuration of Early Toltec settlement in the Teotihuacan Valley and Texcoco Region offers significant insights into the critical Classic-Postclassic juncture in Central Mexico.

EARLY TOLTEC (A.D. 700-950)

General Valley of Mexico

We are here treating the Oxtotipac and Xometla phases established in the Teotihuacan Valley as a single period. The reader should be aware that once more refined ceramic chronologies are published, there may have to be a number of modifications made in our necessarily generalized interpretations of the Early Toltec era.

Early Toltec ceramics—most notably the distinctive Red-on-Buff material designated as Coyotlatelco from the original type site near Atzcapotzalco (Tozzer, 1921)—have been reported from a score of sites in the Valley of Mexico outside the Teotihuacan Valley and Texcoco Region (Rattray, 1966*a*). In practically all cases, however, information is limited to restricted excavations or limited surface collections, with very little or no specific data relevant to the size and complexities of communities or to environmental setting. From Rattray's (1966*a*: Map I) distributional map of known Coyotlatelco sites in the Valley of Mexico, one has the distinct impression that a major consideration in their location was the association of steeply-sloping ground, gently-sloping land, and lakeshore. Roughly half of these reported sites—including several apparent substantial communities—are concentrated on the narrow piedmont plain around the southern and eastern base of the Sierra de Guadalupe north of Tepeyac. However, this apparent distributional pattern of Coyotlatelco sites could very likely be primarily a function of differential intensity of investigation from area to area.

The single excavation known to us (outside the Teotihuacan Valley) of an Early Toltec site which was not limited to small pits or where Early Toltec pottery was not thoroughly mixed with earlier or later material, has been Rattray's (1966*b*) work at Pueblo Perdido near Atzcapotzalco close to the western shore of Lake Texcoco. Here Rattray uncovered a section of what she termed a "Coyotlatelco Palace" in an area measuring roughly 35 by 17 meters in surface area. This architectural feature consisted of a complex of rooms on the west side of a large sunken patio. The remaining sides of the patio were not excavated, and the limits of the complex could not be defined in any direction due to dense modern construction in the area. A series of multiple rectangular rooms, each measuring about five by three meters on a side, with adobe walls and stuccoed floors, occur around a larger (six by six meters) stone-walled, stuccoed room, which fronts on the main plaza at the head of a low stone stairway. Because of its large size and relatively elaborate construction, Rattray has assigned a ceremonial function to this latter room.

The Teotihuacan Valley

In the Teotihuacan Valley, Early Toltec settlement configuration represents a marked break with that of the Classic period (Sanders, 1965: 121-27, 179-87; Fig. 9). The huge Classic urban center at Teotihuacan was drastically reduced in size and occupational density, though it still continued to be the most important demographic focus in the Teotihuacan Valley. A half dozen nucleated towns, ranging between 20 and 50 hectares in surface area, a few with distinctive ceremonial-civic architecture of moderate dimensions, occur to the southwest of the old Classic center around the edges of the main alluvial plain. A number of nucleated villages and hamlets also occur in the same general area.

A striking feature of Early Toltec occupation in the Teotihuacan Valley is the marked concentration of settlement around the edges of the middle and lower segments of the main alluvial plain. The higher piedmont slopes are everywhere devoid of sites, and only a few small villages and hamlets are found around the edges of the upper section of the main alluvial plain east of the old Classic urban center. Interestingly enough, Oxtotipac-phase ceramics are limited to this latter niche, and to small sections of the Classic urban center.

Sanders has interpreted the Teotihuacan Valley Early Toltec settlement configuration as reflecting the continuation of basic Classic-period organizational and exploitative patterns at a much attenuated level following Teotihuacan's collapse as a major power center in the eighth century A.D. In the context of massive population loss, a large block of the remaining inhabitants of the Teotihuacan Valley remained concentrated in the general vicinity of the old center. Most of the remainder were distributed in nucleated towns and villages around the lower alluvial plain where intensive canal irrigation could be practiced. With the great reduction in population pressure, agriculturally marginal sections of the Teotihuacan Valley remained very sparsely occupied.

With the Teotihuacan Valley now reduced to marginal status in a regional political framework whose principal centers were elsewhere, access to prime agricultural land now became the primary determinant of settlement location. The conditions selecting for and requiring the extreme population nucleation and concentration within Teotihuacan which had been operative during Classic times abruptly terminated. Wards of highly skilled craftsmen, traders, retainers, and other segments of Classic population which had been dependent upon the symbiotic and extractive networks formerly focused on Teotihuacan presumably gravitated toward new power centers, or would have been forced to revert to local sources of livelihood. As in Terminal Formative times, control of the principal local water source continued to give Early Toltec Teotihuacan a basis for exerting its authority over the population dependent upon intensive canal irrigation in the alluvial plain below the springs. Furthermore, its situation on the principal access route from the Valley of Mexico to the Tlaxcala-Puebla Basin and the Gulf Coast probably meant that Early Toltec Teotihuacan retained some measure of importance as a coordinating center for interregional trade and tribute networks.

The Texcoco Region

The configuration of Early Toltec settlement in the Texcoco Region is clearly in line with the population dispersal outward from Teotihuacan noted above for the Teotihuacan Valley. Three main demographic trends are clearly operative in our survey area at this time: large population buildups at the northern and southern margins of the Texcoco Region; the concentration of a vast majority of the population in large, nucleated centers containing abundant ceremonial-civic architecture of impressive dimensions; and a virtual abandonment of the entire central two-thirds of the Texcoco Region. This latter phenomenon is the end point of a process of population decline and abandonment of this area initiated in Late Classic times.

In addition to these characteristics, Early Toltec settlements are situated in very diagnostic ecological settings within the Texcoco Region. With but few exceptions they occur at or near the base of steeply-sloping ground, with easy access both to low-lying, gently-sloping land and to principal drainage systems (Tx-ET-4, -7, -13, -17, and -18). The lacustrine resources of the shoreline of Lake Texcoco apparently also represented a niche of some secondary significance (Tx-ET-1, -16, -19, and -21). Except for the somewhat enigmatic Tx-ET-15, all other sites are small villages and hamlets.

Except for the problem of the deserted central zone, it is clear that, just as in the Teotihuacan Valley, a primary factor in the distribution of Early Toltec population of the Texcoco Region was ready access to prime agricultural land. The lower floodplain of the Río Papalotla (surrounded by the large Tx-ET-4, -7 and -13 communities) is today one of the lushest agricultural zones in the Texcoco Region. The broad piedmont slopes north and west of Tx-ET-17 and -18 are similarly highly productive at present. In addition to deep soil cover, good drainage, and relatively high water table, small networks of irrigation canals leading off main water courses would have been feasible in both areas. This clear orientation of Early Toltec occupation toward the best *naturally* productive agricultural land in the Texcoco Region is suggestive of the lack of land pressure in this area during this period.

The character of Early Toltec occupation in the Texcoco Region greatly clarifies the centrifugal process of population slough-off from Teotihuacan which was operative during the generations immediately following its collapse as a major power center. Large blocks of population moved with little difficulty into productive areas where Teotihuacan's policies of extreme nucleation had created demographic near-vacuums during the Classic period. The basic pattern of population nucleation so characteristic of the Classic period, was retained at the local level in Early Toltec times. As in the Teotihuacan Valley, the vast majority of the Texcoco Region's Early Toltec population was concentrated in a few large communities.

Once regional surveys have been extended to other parts of the Valley of Mexico, we can probably expect to find a widespread pattern of nucleated local centers containing a few thousand inhabitants, each dominating a small segment of the area once directly controlled by Teotihuacan. Several such centers undoubtedly existed along the southern flanks of the Sierra de Guadalupe and near Atzcapotzalco on the western shore of Lake Texcoco where abundant Coyotlatelco material has been found. Rattray's (1966*b*) "Coyotlatelco Palace" at Pueblo Perdido may represent an elite residence in one of these local centers.

Our impression of the regional sociopolitical structuring during Early Toltec times in the Valley of Mexico is similar in some respects to what we have previously suggested for the Terminal Formative period: that is, a sizable number of relatively small territorial entities of roughly equivalent size and power. There are, however, basic differences between these eras which far outweigh the outward similarities. Whereas the Terminal Formative pattern represented the culmination of a millennium of slow population growth and a gradual filling-in of available ecological niches, the Early Toltec configuration was produced by the collapse of the focal point of a long-established regional political structure. Furthermore, in Terminal Formative times the Valley of Mexico was on the threshold of emerging as the key, nuclear area within Mesoamerica—a position it was to hold firmly throughout much of the first millennium A.D. In marked contrast, the Early Toltec period was the first portion of a four-century era in which the Valley of Mexico was temporarily relegated to a marginal role in pan-Mesoamerican affairs. Principal power centers were now situated elsewhere—most importantly, at Cholula and Tula to the immediate southeast and northwest, respectively, of the Valley of Mexico.

The rather startling Early Toltec abandonment of the broad central section of the Texcoco Region can best be understood with reference to the emergence and development of these new power centers at the peripheries of the Valley of Mexico. Our interpretation of this phenomenon will therefore be deferred to the subsequent chapter.

LATE TOLTEC
(*ca.* A.D. 950-1150)

General Valley of Mexico

This is undoubtedly the least known period in Valley of Mexico prehistory. Aside from Vaillant's (1938: 544) brief comment that Mazapan sherds have been found in the Tlatelolco district and near Chapultepec in the west-central Valley of Mexico, there is virtually no published data relevant to occupation during this era outside the Teotihuacan Valley and Texcoco Region.

The Teotihuacan Valley

In the Teotihuacan Valley (Sanders, 1965: 127-31, 181-87, Fig. 10) two demographic processes were operative on the basic Early Toltec settlement configuration: (1) an acceleration of the ruralization and population dispersal initiated at the end of the Classic period; and (2) further decline in regional population size. The site of the old Classic city at Teotihuacan continued to function as the largest local community, but it is unlikely that more than 10 per cent of the Teotihuacan Valley's Late Toltec population was located there. Most of the Early Toltec sites around the edges of the prime agricultural land in the lower main alluvial plain continued to be occupied, although settlement was more dispersed than formerly. The lower piedmont slopes around the edges of the upper main alluvial plain—an area of very sparse Early Toltec settlement—were now occupied by clusters of dispersed villages, tiny hamlets, and small regional centers.

The overall Late Toltec pattern for the Teotihuacan Valley as a whole was one of about a dozen demographic clusters, each consisting of a central small town or large village, containing modest ceremonial-civic architecture, surrounded by a scattering of small, dispersed villages and tiny hamlets. In Sanders' view (1965), this dispersed, extensive pattern of occupation reflected the nadir of Postclassic decline in regional political significance in this area prior to the re-emergence of major power centers in the Valley of Mexico during the thirteenth century and later. The attenuated carry-overs from Classic times of population nucleation and presumably associated organizational and integrative mechanisms, which were apparent in the configuration of Early Toltec settlement in the Teotihuacan Valley, had completely died out by Late Toltec times. The dispersed Late Toltec pattern provided the framework upon which the remarkable demographic resurgence of the Aztec period was structured. The distinction between Early and Late Toltec settlement in the Teotihuacan Valley thus also marks the division between two basic socio-political patterns in Central Mexico: the Classic and the Postclassic.

The Texcoco Region

Late Toltec settlement in the Texcoco Region is characterized by much the same processes of ruralization, population dispersal, and population decline which were operative in the Teotihuacan Valley at the same time. Two of the four large, nucleated, and architecturally-complex Early Toltec sites in the Texcoco Region (Tx-ET-4, Tx-ET-18) continued to be occupied by fairly substantial populations in Late Toltec times (Tx-LT-12, Tx-LT-53). In both cases, however, occupational density and community size were greatly reduced relative to the Early Toltec period. Only Tx-LT-53 appears to have functioned as a regional center. All other communities were dispersed villages and hamlets, with no obvious ceremonial-civic architecture whose construction or use can clearly be assigned to Late Toltec times. Other large Early Toltec centers were not completely abandoned, but their Late Toltec population was reduced to several small villages or hamlets scattered through the general area of the formerly nucleated settlement zone.

A comparison of our general Early Toltec and Late Toltec settlement pattern maps makes it quite clear that the tightly nucleated occupation of Early Toltec times gave rise to a much larger number of much smaller and more dispersed communities, distributed much more widely throughout the same general area. Reduced numbers of people spread out thinly across the landscape. A few tiny communities—perhaps representing single household units—even moved into the broad central zone which had been practically devoid of sedentary occupation in the preceeding Early Toltec. Late Toltec populations were obviously exploiting much the same ecological niches as their Early Toltec forebearers. However, the completely different demographic structure suggests that the factors which, during Early Toltec times, had favored, required, or selected for tightly nucleated settlement were no longer operative during the Late Toltec period.

An additional feature which differentiates Late Toltec settlement from that of the Early Toltec is the greater orientation toward a lacustrine niche in the Late Toltec period. Only in the shoreline zone did the overall size and density of Late Toltec occupation increase relative to that of Early Toltec times. The fact that these Late Toltec lakeshore sites in our central and northern survey strips are situated in swampy, poorly drained areas, far from land where agriculture would have been feasible, suggests two alternative interpretations:

1) A significant number of people became involved in full-time exploitation of lacustrine resources during the Late Toltec period.

2) These lakeshore villages and hamlets

represent seasonally-occupied sites where segments of Late Toltec populations, that resided in agricultural communities during part of the annual cycle, resided on a temporary basis for the purpose of hunting waterfowl, collecting lake plants and insects, and fishing.

In view of the apparent breakdown or disintegration of inter-regional political and economic networks in the Valley of Mexico at this period, we now tend to favor the second line of reasoning. These considerations would not necessarily apply to lakeshore communities around the base of Cerro Chimalhuacan and Cerro Portezuelo in the southwestern corner of our survey area (Tx-LT-54, -56, -57, and -58) since agricultural land was readily available to the inhabitants of these settlements. Both agricultural and lacustrine exploitations could be carried out at these latter localities.

In contrast to the configuration of Late Toltec settlement in the Teotihuacan Valley, we can detect no small demographic clusters—each with a small regional center surrounded by a dispersed dependent population in small villages and hamlets—in the Texcoco Region. Throughout the northern third of our survey area, dispersed villages and hamlets appear to be scattered more or less continuously around the edges of the main floodplain of the Río Papalotla and the adjacent Lower Piedmont slopes. Similar communities are scattered relatively evenly over the Lakeshore Plain throughout the northern half of the survey area. A scattering of tiny hamlets (most of which probably represent single households, or even temporary camps) is the only type of occupation in the Lower Piedmont slopes of the broad central zone. In the southern part of the Texcoco Region a much different occupational pattern persists: long, continuous linear strips of dispersed settlement at four or five localities, with none of the widespread scatter of small villages and hamlets as in the northern half of the survey area.

There are indications of two distinct, contemporaneous ceramic traditions in existence in different parts of the Valley of Mexico during all or part of the Late Toltec period. One, the Mazapan, has previously been identified and described in the Teotihuacan Valley (Vaillant, 1938; Sanders, 1965) and at the large site of Tula (Acosta, 1940) just north of the Valley of Mexico. We have encountered this ceramic complex throughout the Texcoco Region. A second tradition, usually referred to as Aztec I (or Culhuacan variant) has been encountered throughout the southeastern quarter of the Valley of Mexico (Griffin and Espejo, 1947; 1950) and at Cholula beyond the southeastern borders of the Valley of Mexico (Noguera, 1954). This ceramic differentiation within the Valley of Mexico stands in marked contrast to most earlier and subsequent periods when relatively uniform ceramic traditions extended over the whole of this area. It may well be the case that the Late Toltec Mazapan and Early Toltec Coyotlatelco-Xometla ceramic assemblages may be partially coeval in the Texcoco Region. This may account for a part of the apparent drastic population drop-off between the Early and Late Toltec periods in our survey area. This population decline was far more pronounced in the Texcoco Region than in the adjacent Teotihuacan Valley.

The distribution of the Mazapan ceramic tradition is very poorly known, but it seems to be generally restricted to the central and northern sections of the Valley of Mexico and to the Tula area. The Aztec I tradition, on the other hand, is unknown in the Tula area, was represented by a mere handful of diagnostic sherds in the Teotihuacan Valley, and was only slightly more abundant in the Texcoco Region. This apparently mutually-exclusive spatial distribution of Mazapan and Aztec

I ceramic assemblages is highly suggestive of their association with separate socio-political entities—especially when one considers sixteenth century documentary evidence (e.g., Dibble, 1951; Alva Ixtlilxochitl, 1965*a* and *b*) which refer to northerly "Chichimec" groups and southerly "Toltec" groups confronting each other within the Valley of Mexico at the time of Xolotl (i.e., early second millennium A.D.).

We will develop our interpretation of the Mazapan-Aztec I, "Chichimec-Toltec" problem somewhat more fully in the following chapter when we extend our horizons outward from the Valley of Mexico. However, at this point it will prove enlightening and useful to formulate some preliminary discussion on this matter, fixing our attention on the Valley of Mexico alone. This discussion will center primarily around certain aspects of the Codice Xolotl (Dibble, 1951) which seems to be particularly significant regarding inter-regional socio-political structure within the Valley of Mexico during Early Postclassic times. The Texcoco Region is the section of the Valley of Mexico most fully depicted in the Codice Xolotl, and this document should be more relevant for our survey area than for other major geographic units.

Only the first third of the time period represented by Dibble's interpretation of the Codice Xolotl is relevant for our present purposes. This era begins with groups of nomadic "Chichimecs," under the general leadership of Xolotl and his son Nopaltzin, entering the Valley of Mexico from the north in the wake of regional population dispersals following the destruction of Tula. These two leaders proceeded to explore the Valley of Mexico. They encountered existing centers of sedentary agriculturalists ("Toltecs") throughout the southern Valley. Similar "Toltec" centers existed at Cholula and Huexotzingo in the adjacent Puebla Basin. Remaining sections of the Valley of Mexico were largely devoid of sedentary agriculturalists. Hunting and gathering "Chichimec" populations then moved into these latter areas, and Xolotl established a regional capital at Tenayuca in the west-central Valley.

At first "Chichimec" and "Toltec" populations remained aloof from one another, but as time passed elite Chichimec lineages intermarried with agricultural "Toltecs," and those "Chichimecs" residing in the Texcoco Region, Teotihuacan Valley, and the area around Tenayuca underwent a fairly rapid acculturation—that is, they were Toltecized, and adopted sedentary agriculture as their main economic base. Wars were prosecuted with northerly "Chichimec" groups, principally Otomi speakers, who wished to retain their traditional nomadic way of life. The subsequent series of events would appear to fall within the Aztec period, and will be mentioned later.

We are well aware of the inherent limitations in the use of such semi-legendary, quasi-historical sources as the Codice Xolotl. Too often these accounts have been accepted literally and without reservation in making interpretations of the prehispanic era in Central Mexico. However, the *general outlines* of the Codice Xolotl do seem to correspond with some of our archaeological data from the Texcoco Region, and appear to be potentially useful in clarifying certain aspects of Early Toltec and Late Toltec settlement configuration in our survey area. Conversely, a correlation of archaeological evidence with the Codice Xolotl indicates something of the interpretative value and practical limitations of such documentary data.

In utilizing the Codice Xolotl for our purposes, we will not be particularly rigorous in accepting the chronology which Dibble suggests is most suitable for the events depicted within the document (he begins Xolotl's activities shortly after A.D. 1200), nor will we be too much concerned with the specific correlation of archaeological sites and locations mentioned in Dibble's interpretation of the Codice. Any rigorous chronological scheme for data of this semi-legendary variety is highly suspect at best, and we will assume that the authors of the Codice were only concerned with (or aware of) principal site locations in a very generalized way. In other words, we are most interested in broad cultural patterns, not in specific events, individuals, or places.

The first item of importance from the Codice Xolotl account is the very clear indication that large sections of the central and northern Valley of Mexico were not exploited by sedentary agriculturalists in Early Postclassic times. Second, the southern Valley of Mexico and the Puebla Basin to the southeast were very clearly occupied by sedentary agriculturalists at this same period. These general patterns seem to be meaningful both with respect to the distinction we have noted above regarding the differential distribution of Mazapan and Aztec I ceramics, and to the general configurations of Early and Late Toltec settlement in the Texcoco Region.

The apposition of the Mazapan tradition in the north and the Aztec I tradition in the south, with little spatial overlap, is suggestive of the presence of separate cultural groups in these respective areas between which there was little social intercourse. Furthermore, the basic validity of the Codice Xolotl's depiction of the Toltecization of "Chichimec" groups following an initial period of cultural isolation is reinforced by the spread of the Aztec tradition throughout and beyond the Valley of Mexico in the Aztec period. More important, the extreme scarcity of substantial residential communities throughout the broad central sector of the Texcoco Region during Early Toltec and Late Toltec times lends some credence to the Codice Xolotl's claim that this specific area was exploited by nomadic hunters and gatherers prior to the acculturation process which led to a sedentary mode of life and primary dependence upon agriculture.

We do not necessarily have to accept in its entirety the Codice Xolotl's account of immigrations of northern nomands into the Valley of Mexico in order to account for either this settlement configuration or for the distribution of Mazapan and Aztec I ceramics. An equally acceptable (and perhaps theoretically more sound) alternative hypothesis is that the Texoco Region formed part of a buffer zone separating the spheres of influence of Tula (to the north) and Cholula (to the south) during the period of several centuries after A.D. 700 when these two sites replaced Teotihuacan as principal power centers in central Mexico. The placement of this hypothetical political frontier was probably in great measure conditioned by the demographic depression created in the Texcoco Region by Teotihuacan's policy of extreme population nucleation and concentration during the long Classic period.

Within this zone of political instability, permanent residence and a sedentary, agricultural mode of life would have been hazardous. The only feasible means of exploiting such a zone would have been a pattern involving short-term encampments and rapid movements by small groups of people engaged in hunting deer, rabbit, and other small mammals on the piedmont slopes and in the Sierra, or hunting waterfowl and fishing along the lakeshore. The small, temporary hunting and fishing camps produced by such an exploitative pattern would have left little or no obvious material remnants on the ground surface, particularly in badly eroded or heavily alluviated areas. Furthermore, it seems more likely that the populations engaged in such activity would have been inhabitants of the sedentary communities at the peripheries of this central zone of the Texcoco Region, rather than bands of wandering nomads immigrating from the north.

If our impressions and interpretations are basically correct, it would appear that the Late Toltec settlement configuration of both the Teotihuacan Valley and the Texcoco Region is to be understood in the context of the situation of these two areas at the southern margins of the major interregional symbiotic-extractive network focused on Tula, some 100 kilometers to the north. The relatively small and dispersed population, and the lack of large, architecturally-complex sites suggest that both the Teotihuacan Valley and Texcoco Region were peripheral participants in this network. The distribution of sites in both the Teotihuacan Valley and the Texcoco Region indicates that easy accessibility to prime agricultural land and lacustrine resources were principal factors in the determination of settlement location. The suggestion is that Late Toltec communities were largely oriented toward localized production and consumption of subsistence products, but there is a great need to clarify the character of their relationships with Tula and Cholula during this period.

AZTEC (EARLY, *ca.* A.D. 1150-1350; LATE, *ca.* A.D. 1350-1520)

In attempting to deal with this period in Valley of Mexico prehistory, we are faced with an almost overwhelming abundance of documentary material in both primary and secondary form. These written sources must be evaluated in the context of very limited archaeological data. Although some of the earliest systematic archaeological work done in the Valley of Mexico (e.g., Gamio, 1912; Boas, 1911-12) pertained to the Aztec period, only a trickle of published information from areas outside the Teotihuacan Valley and Texcoco Region has appeared since that time. Furthermore, the great majority of published reports have been concerned with ceramic sequences and ceremonial-civic architecture, and deal only with excavations of small pits or isolated features. The only full-scale excavation to be published, carried out by the Mexican government and Departmento de Monumentos Prehispánicos at Tenayuca (Noguera, 1935), was largely concerned with the monumental architecture and associated ceramics within a limited sector of this large site. Vaillant's substantial excavations at Chiconautla have been reported only superficially (Vaillant, 1941), and his work at Los Melones and Nonoalco has received only brief mention (Vaillant, 1938). Only a few aspects of the long program of excavation at Tlatelolco have been published, in the form of a series of short papers in the Mexican journal *Tlatelolco a Traves de los Tiempos*.

Since there is very little opportunity to make a general synthesis of the Aztec period in the Valley of Mexico on the basis of available archaeological data from outside the Teotihuacan Valley and Texcoco Region, we will begin our discussion of this era with a general summary of the documentary sources. Here we will only be concerned with the main outlines of political and economic structure which are most relevant to the interpretation of our settlement pattern data from the Texcoco Region. Following this, we will present a more detailed discussion of documentary material bearing specifically on the Texcoco Region. We will then move to a discussion of Aztec settlement patterns in Texcoco Region and the Teotihuacan Valley, and attempt to relate these data to the documentary sources.

General Valley of Mexico — Documentary Data

At the time of Spanish contact in 1519, there were three principal power centers in the Valley of Mexico: Tenochtitlan, Texcoco, and Tlacopan (Tacuba). Of these, Tenochtitlan was the largest and relatively most powerful, and appears to have been in the process of increasing and extending its local and inter-regional authority at the expense of Texcoco and Tlacopan. Estimates of Tenochtitlan's population in 1519 have ranged between 60,000 and 300,000 (Sanders and Price, 1968: 151). Estimates of the 1519 population of the entire Valley of Mexico have ranged from 1.5 million to over three million (Sanders, 1966).

Although these three centers were loosely allied (the so-called Triple Alliance) for purposes of extending military conquest and enforcing tribute payments from over a wide extractive network, each stood at the head of a territorial domain from which tribute was extracted for its exclusive benefit (with some overlap of tributary areas). These territorial domains extended well beyond the Valley of Mexico, particularly into the Gulf Coast area, the Tarascan frontier, Morelos, and northern Oaxaca (Barlow, 1949*a*). Strong, direct, and continuous ties between major centers and subordinate localities, however, were restricted to the Valley of Mexico and its immediately adjacent borders. Elsewhere there were only peripheral ties, generally consisting of little more than tributary demands sanctioned by the threat of military reprisal, with little or no attempt at further integration of the tribute-paying region into the realm of the dominant centers (Kelly and Palerm, 1953: Appendix B).

Below this highest level of political organization were a large number of secondary centers, each with a nucleated, urban population of several thousand people. Although these secondary centers were politically dependent upon one of the three principal powers, each controlled the internal affairs of its own territorial domain of subordinate towns and villages. Sanders and Price (1968: 151-52) have estimated a total of about 60 such semiautonomous, territorial units within the Valley of Mexico at the time of the Spanish Conquest, "each with a population range of between 12,000 and 50,000 and an average territory of approximately 130 km^2." Some of the more important of these secondary centers included Chalco, Ixtapalapa, Xochimilco, Tenayuca, Xaltocan, Otumba, Teotihuacan, Tepetlaoxtoc, Huexotla, and Coatlinchan, In contrast to the ephemeral character of sociopolitical integration at the highest levels, and the shifting alliances between major power centers, these smaller territorial units were apparently stable over long periods of time.

The ruling sectors of both major and secondary centers were comprised of members of a few elite kin groups or lineages. Many of these rulers were closely related, and often bonds of kinship and marriage linked even the ruling elite of centers engaged in active military conflict. The mention of such intercenter conflict and hostility is abundant throughout the documentary literature, and even at the time of the Spanish Conquest, Cortes readily obtained the assistance of Texcocan forces in the final overthrow of Tenochtitlan. Indeed, the organization of the Triple Alliance itself was very largely the product of a series of major military confrontations over the years between roughly 1427 and 1433, between the then-predominant center of Atzcapotzalco, on the one hand, and the allied forces of Texcoco, Tenochtitlan, and Huexotzingo, on the other (Barlow, 1949*b*).

The Valley of Mexico was economically integrated by a series of major and secondary markets. Major centers, as Tenochtitlan, had large, daily markets (e.g., Diaz del Castillo, 1960, Cortes, 1962). Markets were held at longer intervals at secondary centers—for example, the weekly market at Chimalhuacan operating in 1579 (Paso y Troncoso, 1905: 78). The detailed decriptions of the huge market at Tenochtitlan are particularly revealing: as Sanders (1952) has pointed out, the tremendous variety of goods and products redistributed through the market system, including large amounts of basic, staple materials, tools of production, etc., are indicative of the highly developed occupational specialization within Aztec society, and the non-food-producing character of large segments of the urban population.

The importance of the lake system in the operation of this market structure is very clear from documentary sources. Not only is there abundant mention of the large numbers of canoes carrying goods and people between various points, but a great majority of major Aztec communities were situated on or near the lakeshore. At no other period was this lacustrine orientation so pronounced.

There is somewhat more confusion with respect to levels of social organization below that of the semi-autonomous territorial unit we have mentioned above. This confusion stems largely from the imprecise usage of the term *calpulli* by the Spanish chroniclers, and the varied interpretations of this *calpulli* unit by modern scholars. Sanders (1965: 64) has delineated the most salient features of the Aztec *calpulli* as follows:

1) It was a communal land-holding unit.
2) Membership was by birth [i.e., it was a kin group].
3) In most cases it was the local community.
4) In the larger communities, such as towns, it comprised a ward division.

The *calpulli* was the basic structural unit of Aztec society. Everyone, except for a few low-status individuals, was a member of a particular *calpulli*. *Calpulli* were ranked, both internally, and relative to one another. An individual's social position depended both upon the relative ranking of his *calpulli*, and his lineage or sub-lineage membership within the *calpulli* unit. The basis for *calpulli* ranking is not entirely clear, but Kirchoff's (1959) concept of the conical clan, and Sahlins' (1958) definition of the ramage, have proved to be the most useful models for understanding the fundamental organizational principles of the *Calpulli* framework (e.g., Monzon, 1949). Authority within the *calpulli* was vested in the highest ranking lineage of the *calpulli*. These elite members had certain traditional rights to the labor and services of fellow *calpulli* members. In return, these elite members provided necessary administrative and judicial functions. Similarly, positions of authority at supra-*calpulli* levels of socio-political organization were monopolized by specific elite lineages of high ranking *calpulli*.

Theoretically, the highest positions of authority in Tenochtitlan, Texcoco, Tlacopan, and other major power centers would have been occupied by members of the highest ranking lineages of the highest ranking *calpulli*. The extent of inter-marriage and close kin ties between primary rulers of major centers even suggests that these very powerful positions were monopolized by a single *calpulli* or set of a few closely related lineages. The suggestion that *calpulli* tended to be endogamous units (Carrasco, 1961) is consistent with this general interpretation. Such a restriction of marital ties would have functioned to consolidate and enhance traditional rights, privileges, positions, and resources within a single group.

Most importantly for our purposes, however, is the status of the *calpulli* as an internally autonomous, territorial group of kinsmen, with traditional rights and duties in the Aztec social order. In all cases, the most important traditional right was equitable access to strategic resources. In the case of rural populations this was predominately agricultural land, although sections of lake, and certain mines or quarries may also have been involved. In large nucleated communities certain part-time or full-time craft, artisan, or mercantile specializations, traditionally reserved for members of a specific *calpulli*, probably supplemented or replaced access to agricultural or lacustrine resources. Important positions in the civil, religious, and mercantile hierarchy were, of course, reserved for members of certain high ranking *calpulli* and lineages.

The chief duty of the non-elite *calpulli* was the collective payment of tribute—in goods and/or services—levied by various authorities at higher organizational levels. This was generally realized by corvée labor groups who cultivated tracts of land set aside for support of various civil and religious functionaries, constructed public architecture, maintained the households of elite personages, and performed military service. Each *calpulli* maintained its own ceremonial precinct devoted to the worship and propitiation of its own patron deity. Military and religious training for its boys and young men was also a *calpulli* responsibility, and special schools were set up for this purpose. Thus, the distribution of ceremonial-civic complexes containing religous temples, young men's schools, and possibly the house of the *calpulli* headman, should permit the archaeological identification of *calpulli* units, even within large, nucleated centers.

The existence of one or more organizational levels immediately below the *calpulli* is suggested by the use of such terms as "barrio pequeño" by the Spanish chroniclers (Sanders, 1965: 66). However, the character and significance of these levels have remained obscure. The only such unit for which a meaningful summary discussion is feasible at this point is the household, at the very base of the Aztec social order. Sanders and Price (1968: 154) have described the general organization of this unit as one of "extended patrilocal families residing in multifamily houses and nuclear families occupying apartments in such structures."

Surprisingly few systematic studies bearing on the Aztec household have been published. In fact, we know of only one: Carrasco's (1964) analysis of detailed censuses from the Tlacatecpan ward of Tepoztlan, Morelos, made in about 1540. Here, Carrasco (1964: 187) found that "the basic social unit is the house (*calli*) or the people of one house (*cencaltin*). It is a residential, landholding and tribute-paying unit." In his analysis of some 549 such units, Carrasco has delineated two particularly significant characteristics of household organization: (1) the great variety in household size and composition; and (2) the general developmental cycle through which a typical household could be expected to pass through time. Because of their specific relevance to our own data from the Texcoco Region, we will discuss both these matters briefly at this point.

There were two dominant household types in Carrasco's sample: (*a*) nuclear family households, centered around a single married couple, but usually comprising additional dependent members in the form of children and/or miscellaneous relatives of the married couple; and (*b*) households centered around joint families—that is, "two or more married couples connected by consanguineal ties among members of the different couples" (1964: 190). Joint family households with two married couples were clearly predominant among units of this latter type (185 of a total of 235 such joint family households), but Carrasco recorded 41 three-couple households, eight four-couple households, and one five-couple unit. These nuclear-family and joint-family households together accounted for nearly 98 per cent of the total 3100 persons involved. The remaining 18 households were clearly unusual types: 14 "consanguineal" households "consisting of individuals related to each other consanguineally, conjugal and affinal ties being absent" (ibid); and four non-family households, "in which individuals live alone or with non-relatives" (ibid).

Some 201 households in one section of the Tlacatecpan ward were directly subject to the authority of the local *cacique*. The size and composition of these households differed significantly in two respects from the other 348 units not directly subject to the *cacique* (Carrasco, 1964: 190-91): "Among the *cacique's* subjects there is a much larger number of joint families; they form the largest type and include a majority (71.7 per cent) of that population. Among the ward people, not only are the nuclear families dominant, but they also account for the majority of that total population (52.6 per cent)." In addition, the average household size among the *cacique's* subjects was 6.2 persons (with a total range between 2 and 23 persons), while among the ward people it was 5.2 persons per household (with a total range between 1 and 18 persons). The *cacique's* own household contained five married couples and 23 persons, by far the largest unit in the sample.

Carrasco was able to discern a clear developmental cycle through which a typical household unit was likely to progress over the period of its existence. He saw this cycle (1964: 208) as "a change from nuclear toward joint families of the head-with-sons and later of the head-with-brothers types, only occasionally growing to larger types. All along the cycle split-offs could take place that produced more nuclear families subject to the same cycle. The original family from which a couple split off could go back to the nuclear type or remain joint but smaller; a younger couple, a married son or younger brother would move up to the family headship at the death of the head. The death of the household head in a nuclear family could result in a more normal type or their members joined other families."

There were, of course, definite possibilities for social dislocations as a result of two decades of Spanish rule in the population studied by Carrasco. As will presently be made clear, however, the excavation of a Late Aztec house in the Teotihuacan Valley, and the recovery of a large number of house floorplans of this period from the Texcoco Region, strongly suggest that many of Carrasco's main interpretations are valid for the prehispanic era.

The Texcoco Region—Documentary Data

With this general background in mind, we will now move to a specific discussion of documentary data relevant to political and economic organization within the Texcoco Region in Late Aztec times. For this purpose we will rely primarily upon a number of secondary sources, and only the most important and directly relevant of the sixteenth century chronicles (e.g., Alva Ixtlilxochitl, 1965*a* and *b*; Pomar, 1941; Dibble, 1951; Paso y Troncoso, 1905). As in our more general treatment of the Valley of Mexico as a whole, we will not be particularly concerned with events said to have occurred much over a century prior to the Spanish Conquest. Accounts of this shadowy era are filled with a myriad of migratory groups and their activities, together with the specific actions of many individuals. While we do not doubt the ultimate utility of such data when subjected to penetrating analysis and critical evaluation, such studies (where they have not already been performed) are beyond the scope of this present work.

Coatlinchan is said to have been the center which exercised principal authority within the Texcoco Region prior to the rise of Texcoco in the fifteenth century (Gibson, 1964: 17). Gibson's (1956) exhaustive analysis of relevant sixteenth century documentary sources has delineated the full extent of the area directly subject to Texcoco's authority in late prehispanic and early colonial times (sometimes referred to as the Acolhua domain). This region covered most of the eastern Valley of Mexico, and extended south into Morelos, and north and east into southern Hidalgo, northern Puebla, and western Tlaxcala. Some of the more important centers dependent upon Texcoco within the Valley of Mexico included Tizayuca, Xaltocan, Axapusco, Teotihuacan, Tequisistlan, Tezoyuca, Tepetlaoxtoc, Papalotla, Chiautla, Atenco, Huexotla, Coatlinchan, Chimalhuacan, Coatepec, Ixtapaluca, and Chalco.

Each of these centers, in turn, stood at the head of a smaller tributary province. Sanders (1965: 73-75) has already discussed the areas subject to Late Aztec centers in the Teotihuacan Valley (Tezoyuca, Chiconautla, Tepexpan, Acolman, Teotihuacan, and Otumba). We have been able to locate specific information on the communities dependent upon two secondary centers in the Texcoco Region in 1579 (and presumably also in Late Aztec times): Coatepec and Chimalhuacan (Paso y Troncoso, 1905). In 1579 Coatepec (Tx-A-99) was the principal *cabecera* within a zone containing four other smaller *cabeceras*: Sancta Ana Tetitlan, Sanct Francisco Aquauhtla, Sanct Miguel Tepetlapa, and Santiago Quatlapanca. Of these, only San Francisco Acuautla definitely exists as a modern community (south of our survey area).

There were five smaller communities (*barrios* and *estancias*) directly subject to Coatepec: Sanct Martyn Tlaylotlacan, Sanct Jhoan Tlachichco, Sanct Sebastian Xocoatlahco, Sancta María Magdalena Ameyalco, and Sancta Cathalina Ancapa. None of these communities definitely exist today. Subject to the smaller cabecera of Santa Ana Tetitlan were the *estancias* and *barrios* of Sancta Cruz Mathaluca, La Visitacion de Nuestra Señora Tlalalauhca, and Sanct Matheo Aztotlytic—none of which definitely exist as communities today. The communities of Sanct Andres Chiauhtla, Sancta Thomás Texcaltitlan, Santo Domyngo Tlalanoztoc, and Los Rreyes Suchitenco (all apparently nonexistent at present) were subject to the *cabecera* of Sanct Francisco Aquauhtla. Sanctistevan Macatlan, Sanct Clemente Amoltepec, and San Bartolome Huapalteupa (all presently nonexistent) were under the jurisdiction of Sanct Miguel Tepetlapa. Sanct Pedro Chalma (also extinct) was subject to Santiago Quatlapanca. Of these five *cabeceras* and their 17 dependent *estancias* and *barrios*, only two of the cabeceras (Coatepec and San Francisco Acuautla) definitely exist as functioning communities today. Some of these sixteenth century communities, of course, may still exist as *barrios* or wards within modern villages.

The cabecera of Chimalhuacan had 31 dependent *estancias* and *barrios* in 1579: Sancto Domyngo Huiznavac, Tlacuchcalco, Itzcotlan, Huexotitlan, Chinampa, Cihuatecpan, Ayacac, Tzocuyloc, Tequitcapa, Xochiyacac, Atlyquisca, Chimalpa, Atlapachiuhya, Culhuacan, Omaxac, Tocuyla, Viznahuac, Ixtlahuaca, Tzapotla, Iztapa, Xolticpac, Tlatlatecpan, Achichilacachpan, Mizquititlan San Lorenzo, Atlapulco Sanct Agustin, Chimalpan Sanct Sebastian, Acticpac Sancta María Magdalena, Tepotoniloya, Aticpactequitcapa, Ahuehuetitlan, Tennenecuylco Sanct Gregorio. Of these, only San Agustín Atlapulco, San Sebastian Chimalpa, and Santa María Magdalena Aticpac, in addition to Chimalhuacan itself, definitely exist as communities today.

Thus far, we have been unable to locate comparable information for other early colonial *cabeceras* within the Texcoco Region.

We have previously depicted the physical plant of the ruling establishment in Texcoco as described by Alva de Ixtlilxochitl. This establishment was the administrative hub of the Acolhua domain. It housed substantial numbers of retainers, civil and religious officials and dignitaries, and served as a storage deposit for weapons, food stuffs, and other products (Alva Ixtlilxochitl, 1965 *b*: 173-86). Here Texcocan rulers and their associates consulted with their principal advisors, dispensed justice, contemplated in luxurious surroundings, took part in religious ceremonies, attended to the arts and sciences, and oversaw the raising and education of elite young people.

Of particular significance with respect to the political organization of the Acolhua domain is the composition of the elite body of personages who systematically congregated around the Texcocan ruler and who presumably functioned as his principal advisors and councilors in affairs of state (ibid). This elite body comprised the rulers of the 14 dependent centers of Teotihuacan, Acolman, Tepetlaoxtoc, Huexutla (Huexotla), Coatlichan (Coatlinchan), Chimalhuacan, Otumpan (Otumba), Tolantzinco (Tulancingo, at the northwestern edge of the Valley of Mexico), Quauhchinanco (Huachinango?, in northern Puebla, well northeast of the Valley of Mexico), Xicotepec (in northern Puebla, far northeast of the Valley of Mexico), Tepechpan (Tepexpan), Teyoyocan (Tezoyuca), Chicunahtla, (Chiconautla), and Chiauhtla (Chiautla).

With few exceptions, these centers are those usually mentioned as being most closely and continuously allied with Netzahualcoyotl and his immediate forebearers and descendants throughout the trying period of the internicine wars with Atzcapotzalco (1427-1433) and the remainder of the Late Aztec era. The distribution of these 14 centers delineates the heartland of the Texcocan realm, which is clearly the Texcoco Region and the Teotihuacan Valley. Ties with other parts of the Acolhua domain were relatively more tenuous, and particularly so in the case of Chalco and the southeastern Valley of Mexico. Chalco had been allied with Atzcapotzalco against Texcoco in the early part of the fifteenth century (Alva Ixtlilxochitl, 1965*a*: 157, 158, 224, 303). The 1579 *Relaciones* of Coatepec and Chimalhuacan contain several references to warfare and animosity between these two centers and Chalco in prehispanic times (Paso y Troncoso, 1905: 55, 70, 75). The Codex Xolotl (Dibble, 1951: 91) indicates that the frontier with Chalco was guarded in the early fifteenth century.

The personnel and facilities of the Texcocan ruling establishment were maintained by tribute levies, in goods and services, upon the population of its domain. In contrast to the wealth of specific documentary information pertaining to the tribute collected by Tenochtitlan in Late Aztec times from a large segment of central and southern Mexico (Barlow, 1949*a*; Molins Fabrega, 1954-55), there is very little data of this sort available for Texcoco. We are now aware only of Alva Ixtlilxochitl's (1965*a* and *b*) references to goods and services owed to the Texcocan rulers.

This author (1965*b*: 168-70) describes a system in which the produce of certain lands within the territory of each subject community was reserved for local and regional authorities. The responsibility for supplying the subsistence requirements of the central ruling establishment in Texcoco itself was shifted from one administrative district to another on a 70-day basis. At this point Alva Ixtlilxochitl becomes quite specific, and lists eight tributary districts charged with supplying foodstuffs to Netzahualcoyotl's establishment in Texcoco: Tetzcuco (i.e., the population in the immediate vicinity of the capital center), Atenco, Tepepolco, Axapochco, Quauhtlatzingo, Ahuatepec, Tetitlan, and Tecpilpan.

Each of these districts supplied the following goods, each day for a period of 70 days:

> . . . en grano veinticinco tlacopintlis de maíz. para tomarlos, que era una medida que en aquel tiempo se usaba, y cada tlacopintli tenía tres almudes más de una fanega, que reducidos á fanegas montan treinta y una fanegas y tres almudes; otros tres tlacopintlis de frijoles, y tortillas hechas cuatrocientas mil, de cacao cuatro xiquipiles que montan treinta y dos mil ca-

caos, cien gallos, veinte panes de sal, veinte cestones de chile ancho y otros veinte de chile menudo, diez de tomates y diez de pepitas. . . .

Elsewhere, Alva de Ixtlilxochitl (1965*b*: 209-10) indicates that Netzahualcoyotl

> . . . tenía señsaldas cinco suertes de tierras, las más fértiles que había cerca de la ciudad, en donde por gusto y entretenimiento le hacían sementeras, hallándose al beneficio de ellas personalmente, como era en Atenco que está junto á la laguna en el pueblo de Papalotlan, y en los de Calpolanpan, Mazaapan y Yahualiuhcan. Para el adorno y servicio de estos palacios y jardines y bosques que el rey tenía, se ocupaban los pueblos que caían cerca de la corte por sus turnos y tandas; de los cuales para el servicio, adorno y limpieza de los palacios del rey, eran señalados los pueblos de Huexotla, Coatlinchan, Coatepec, Chimalhuacan, Iztapalocan, Tepetlaoztoc, Acolman, Tepechpan, Chicuhnauhtla, Teyoyocan, Chiauhtla, Papalotla, Xaltocan, y Chalco, que servían medio año: el otro medio año era á cargo de los pueblos de la campiña, que eran Otumpan, Teotihuacan, Zempoalan, Aztaquemecan, Ahuatepec, Axapochco, Oxtotipac, Tizayocan, Tlalanapan, Coyoac, Quatlatlauhcan, Quatlaeca y Quauhtlatzinco. Para le recámara del rey estaban señalados los pueblos de Calpolalpan, Mazaapan, Yahualiuhcan, Atenco y Tzihuinquilocan; y para los bosques y jardines las provincias de Tolantzinco, Quauhchinanco, Xicotepec, Pauhatla, Yauhtepec, Tepechco, Ahuacayocan y Quauhnahuac, con sus pueblos sujetos, acudiendo por su torno y tanda al dicho efecto, teniendo cada provincia y pueblo á su cargo el jardín, bosque ó labranza que el era señalado.

Once again (1965*b*: 266), with respect to the subsistence and clothing requirements of the ruling establishment,

> de ordinario en palacio se gastaban en cada un año (segun parece por los padrones reales), treinta y un mil y seiscientas fanegas de maíz, doscientas cuarenta y tres cargas de cacao, ocho mil gallos, cinco mil fanegas de chile ancho y delgado y pepitas, y dos mil medidas de sal; y para el vestuario, así para el rey como todos los demás caballeros que asistían en su casa y corte y para la demás gente referida, quinientas setenta y cuatro mil y diez mantas, que todas las más eran finísimas y de precio. Esto era de las rentas que el rey tenía en las provincias de su patrimonio, porque de las provincias conquistadas, los tributos de ellas se guardaban en los almacenes que tenía, así en la ciudad de Tetzcuco como de Mexico, en donde se hacían las reparticiones que atrás quedan referidas, para hacer mercedes el rey á sus hijos, deudos y á otros señores y capitanes beneméritos, así en guerras como en otras ocupaciones de valor y virtud. Por la parte que caía al Norte de las casas referidas y cerca de las cocinas, estaban unos graneros y trojes de admirable grandeza, en donde el rey tenía gran cantidad de maíz y otras semillas que se guardaban para los años estériles, y en cada una de ellas cabían cuatro ó cinco mil fanegas, y estaban con tanto orden y concierto, que por todas partes el aire las cogía, con que las semillas duraban muchos años.

From the aforegoing accounts, it is apparent that the Texcocan ruling establishment made numerous demands upon the labor and production of its subject population within the Acolhua domain. It is not wholly clear to what degree the Texcocan rulers exercised direct control of land and other strategic resources outside the heartland of their political domain. Within the Texcoco Region itself, however, and also in the Teotihuacan Valley, it appears that specific areas were reserved as recreational facilities and cultivation plots for the exclusive benefit of the central authority. It is probable that the tributary network focused on Texcoco represents an elaborated and expanded version of the smaller networks operating at lower organizational levels down to the *calpulli* unit.

Molins Fabrega (1954-55) has argued that Alva Ixtlilxochitl's figures for the quantities of foodstuffs entering Late Aztec Texcoco through tributary networks are consistent with his own interpretations of the quantities of similar materials flowing into Tenochtitlan by the same means. It is Molins' thesis that these great quantities of staple goods were required at both major centers for redistribution to the large segments of urban populations who were non-food-producers and largely dependent upon the central authority for their subsistence needs: administrative officials, court retainers, skilled craftsmen and artisans, as well as corvée laborers involved in the construction and maintenance of public architecture.

Molins calculates that Alva de Ixtlilxochitl's figures for the quantities of maize and beans annually absorbed by Texcoco through its tributary network (633,000 litres of maize; 76,000 litres of beans) would support a total dependent population of some 26,000 persons (ibid: 310). This would appear to be an absolute maximum figure, for Molins uses a minimal daily food requirement and does not consider the matters of food storage or the part-time support of certain laborers, servants, and retainers, etc. who may well have been self-supporting throughout much of an annual cycle. It is interesting to note that our own maximum estimate of Texcoco's Late Aztec population is 25,000 people.

Alva Ixtlilxochitl's numerous references (e.g. 1965*a*: 139, 140, 295, 296; 1965*b*: 69, 70, 158) to the large numbers of skilled craftsmen who were incorporated into the Texcocan urban center at various points in the fourteenth and fifteenth centuries, lend additional support to Molins' basic hypothesis. Some of these people are said to have come of their own accord, attracted by the reputation of Texcoco and reputed largess and generosity of its rulers. Others are reported to have been called in by the express wishes of the Texcocan rulers, for the purpose of increasing the renown of their capital. In most cases, the support of these skilled craftsmen by the ruling establishment is either explicity stated or implicitly suggested.

The exploitation of the resources of Lake Texcoco by the population of the Texcoco Region in Late Aztec times is succinctly described by Pomar (1941: 54-55):

> No cría ningún género de pescado, si no es á las bocas de los ríos, del agua de los que en ella entran, y esto es poco y pequeño y ruín. Tampoco cría ningún género de aves, porque los géneros de patos y ánsares y otras aves de agua que en ella hay, vienen, según dicen, de la Florida, y no duran más de cuanto dura el invierno; pero con toda su maldad todavía sacan de ella los indios sus vecinos muchos y muy ordinarios provechos. Lo primero es la mucha caza de aves que toman con redes, y el pescadillo que cogen, de que se mantienen casi todo el año, y un género de comida que llaman *tecuitlatl,* que hacen de unas lamas verdes que cría, lo cual hecho tortas y cocido, queda con un color verde oscuro, que llaman los españoles queso de la tierra, Cría otro género de comida que se llama *ezauhitli,* que hacen de unos gusanillos como lombrices, tan delgados y tan cuajados por su multitud y espesura, que apenas se puede juzgar si es casa viva ó no. Y otra que llaman *ahuauhtli,* que también comen ya los españoles los viernes, y que son unos huevecillos de unas mosquillas que se crían en ella; y otra que se llama *michpitlin* y *cocolin;* aunque las más de éstas no comían ni al presente comen personas principales, sino pobres y gente miserable. No se cría sal del agua de ella, ni aun salitre bueno, proque el que se da en sus riberas no sirve de más de para hacen jabón.

This same author (1941: 62) offers an additional comment on the extraction of salt: "No tienen salinas naturales, sino que la sal que gasten y de que usan es de panes, y sacada por artificio de cierta tierra salitral que se cría en algunas partes de la ribera de la laguna."

It appears that migratory water fowl were the most important food resource offered by Lake Texcoco during the Late Aztec period. This view is amply supported by a variety of additional documentary evidence compiled by Linne (1948). The existence of salt-making and the collection of lacustrine algae and insect eggs and larvae around the shores of the salt lake, are also documented. Some fishing was practiced, but this seems to have been a relatively secondary activity in Lake Texcoco.

The Teotihuacan Valley — Archaeological Data

Overall occupational density and population size in the Teotihuacan Valley attained their maximum prehispanic peaks in Aztec times (Sanders, 1965: 76-90, 187-92, Fig. 11). Five of the six principal Late Aztec centers in this area mentioned in documentary sources (Chiconautla, Tepexpan, Acolman, Teotihuacan, and Otumba) were identified archaeologically. These centers contained impressive ceremonial-civic architecture, and had nucleated populations estimated at between 1,000 and 10,000 people. Concentric zones of more dispersed occupation surrounded the central demographic core. This latter zone also contained a ceremonial-civic zone of impressive dimensions. These principal communities were situated on gently sloping ground at the edge of wide expanses of the main alluvial plain—except in the case of Chiconautla which was located at the edge of Lake Texcoco. The placement of this latter site was apparently chiefly conditioned by considerations of access to the regional trade network which was based on canoe transport on the lake system.

Surface collections from Aztec Otumba revealed that clay figurines and, more particularly, figurine molds, were highly concentrated in one particular section of the site. This indicated a *barrio* specialization in figurine production, and suggested that the existence of this and other kinds of craft and artisan specializations could be demonstrated by means of more intensive investigations at Aztec urban centers throughout the Valley of Mexico.

In contrast to preceeding periods, principal centers were now found throughout the length of the Teotihuacan Valley—including the agriculturally least productive Upper Valley. However, four of the six Aztec centers were located around the edges of the irrigable plain of the Middle and Lower Valley where Classic and Toltec occupation had also been concentrated.

Perhaps the most impressive aspect of Aztec demography in the Teotihuacan Valley was the expansion of substantial rural settlement into nearly all available environmental zones. All principal centers were surrounded or bordered by bands of more dispersed occupation which extended in practically continuous fashion over the lower piedmont slopes around the edges of the main alluvial plain. Even where large urban communities were absent, in more marginal areas, similar bands of linear settlement extended over gently sloping ground around the bases of steep hills, along low ridge crests, and into small tributary valleys.

Rural Aztec occupation within these broad linear strips was characteristically in the form of more-or-less discrete clusters of 10 to 40 house mounds. Occupational traces between such clusters decreased markedly in most instances, though they often persisted at lower intensities in intervening areas, making site delineation difficult in some cases. Obvious ceremonial-civic architecture of modest dimensions was consistently present in rural settlements, but did not occur at every occupational cluster. Sanders (1965: 87) reasoned that these discrete clusters of mounds represented a sub-*calpulli* level of organization (i.e., the *barrio pequeño* unit of the Spanish chroniclers), while the occurrence of distinct ceremonial-civic architecture marked the presence of the larger *calpulli* entity, comprised of several *barrio pequeño* units.

Excavation of a rural housemound produced evidence (1965: 88) of a domestic residential unit which, over a period of perhaps a half century at the end of the prehispanic era, ". . . began with one nuclear family, expanded to two, possibly three, and was reduced to one at the end." This sequence conforms directly to Carrasco's (1964) previously mentioned developmental cycle of household and family composition in his analysis of early colonial census material from Tepoztlan, Morelos.

The size and distribution of Aztec population in the Teotihuacan Valley strongly suggests that agricultural possibilities of all types were being fully exploited. The prime agricultural zone—the irrigated main alluvial plain below the springs of Teotihuacan—continued to support a major segment of the population, but large numbers of people were clearly dependent upon more marginal cultivation systems (i.e., rainfall farming, and floodwater irrigation).

More refined research may eventually demonstrate what preliminary reconaissance surveys have already suggested: that substantial numbers of people were engaged in a variety of full-time or part-time craft and artisan activities. We have previously mentioned the indications of *barrio* specialization in figurine manufacture at Otumba. Analysis of spindle whorl collections (M.H. Parsons, n.d.) has also indicated that spinning of maguey and cotton fiber, in both urban and rural communities, was important in the Teotihuacan Valley during Aztec times. Such specializations supplemented agriculture as a source of subsistence since the products of such activities were incorporated into regional and local trade networks, or were sponsored and consumed by the ruling elite of secondary or primary urban centers.

The Texcoco Region—Archaeological Data

Settlement Configuration

As in the Teotihuacan Valley, the major demographic processes operative in the Aztec occupation of the Texcoco Region were a great population expansion from a base established during Late Toltec times, together with rapid urbanization. And, even more so than in the Teotihuacan Valley, the maximum peak of prehispanic population size in the Texcoco Region was attained in the Aztec period. Large nucleated centers were established early in the Aztec period at Huexotla (Tx-A-87) and Coatlinchan (Tx-A-88) at the lower edge of the Lower Piedmont in the south-central sector of the Texcoco Region. A less impressive population focus was also established at Chimalhuacan (Tx-A-109). Elsewhere throughout the survey area the general Early Aztec occupational pattern was one of the proliferation and replication of the hamlet and small village sites established in Late Toltec times. There was a general filling in of the Lower and Upper Piedmont zones throughout the northern half of the Texcoco Region, with numerous small communities distributed in fairly continuous fashion. A substantial decline in the eastern half of the southern survey strip relative to the Late Toltec period can probably be attributed to the effects of population nucleation at Coatlinchan and Chimalhuacan. An analagous decline at the western end of the central survey strip may reflect a similar process of population concentration at Huexotla.

Particularly interesting features of Early Aztec occupation are (*a*) the close juxtaposition of the two principal centers (Huexotla and Coatlinchan), and (*b*) the fact that both these centers grew up in areas where occupation in all preceeding periods had been very sparse. The locations of the long-abandoned large communities of Terminal Formative and Early Toltec times were not reoccupied to any significant extent. As will become more apparent below, these unprecedented features of Early Aztec settlement clearly reflect the emergence of a new constellation of inter-regional sociopolitical and economic forces which conditioned the distribution of population after the late twelfth century.

At this point it is useful to refer to Wolf and Palerm's interpretation of documentary sources bearing on events in the Texcoco Region several centuries prior to the Spanish conquest. In their view (1955: 273-74)

> . . . the central political problem of the Texcocan state consisted in establishing the dominance of 'Toltec' economic, social, and political patterns over the purely predatory patterns of the 'Chichimecas.' The kings of the Chichimec dynasty [i.e., Xolotl and his descendants] made every effort to force the Chichimeca to adopt the ways of the resident Toltec population by forcing them to carry on agriculture, to change their diet to include more agricultural products, and to settle in nucleated villages. . . . We are probably dealing with an area [i.e., the Texcoco Region] which was colonized planfully from an already established political center, spurred and organized by the state under the aegis of the 'Toltecized' Chichimec kings.

Wolf and Palerm were more willing than we to accept, as essentially valid, references in documentary sources to specific events which reputedly took place several centuries before the Spanish conquest. Nonetheless, their analysis of this semi-legendary material does complement our impression, from a purely archaeological perspective, of a basic cultural change in the Texcoco Region during Early Aztec times. Viewed in larger perspective, these marked changes in the Texcoco Region reflect the re-emergence of the Valley of Mexico during Aztec times to a position of political dominance in Mesoamerica.

The population expansion and urbanization processes initiated in Early Aztec times accelerated througout the Late Aztec period. The Early Aztec urban centers all increased in size and population density, especially at Chimalhuacan (Tx-A-109). New major centers were established at Texcoco (Tx-A-56) and Tepetlaoxtoc (Tx-A-24). A somewhat smaller center developed at Coatepec (Tx-A-99). The expansion of rural occupation in the northern two-thirds of the Texcoco Region was equally impressive. The scattered hamlets and small villages characteristic of the Early Aztec period grew into substantial dispersed villages. Formerly empty areas between Early Aztec settlement clusters were very largely filled in with dispersed occupation to such an extent that the task of distinguishing individual villages or separate sociopolitical entities often becomes very difficult. This is particularly true of rural Late Aztec occupation in the Upper Piedmont at the eastern ends of the northern and central survey strips. Only in the southeastern quadrant of the Texcoco Region do these generalizations fail to apply. Except for the secondary demographic focus at Tx-A-99, this latter area remained very sparsely populated, as it had been since the end of Terminal Formative times.

With a few significant exceptions, impressive monumental architecture is largely restricted to the principal urban centers. The exceptions are a number of isolated or semi-isolated ceremonial-civic complexes scattered throughout the Texcoco Region (e.g., Tx-A-6, Tx-A-19, Tx-A-20, mound 103 at Tx-A-40, Tx-A-61, and Tx-A-100). Modest ceremonial-civic structures can occasionally be identified at rural sites, although erosion has been so severe in many sections of the Lower and Upper Piedmont that many architectural remnants have been reduced to amorphous masses of rock rubble whose original appearance is now totally obscured. For this reason, we have not been too concerned with the distribution of ceremonial-civic architecture on rural sites.

In looking somewhat more closely at the configuration of Late Aztec settlement in the Texcoco Region it is apparent that there are significant differences in population distribution and arrangement within our survey area. A majority of Late Aztec population was concentrated in the three large nucleated centers of Texcoco, Huexotla, and Coatlinchan at, or near, the juncture of the Lower Piedmont and Lakeshore Plain zones. Both Texcoco (Tx-A-56) and Huexotla (Tx-A-87) had substantial "suburbs" of dispersed population extending well to the east across the width of the Lower Piedmont along major barranca systems. It is even conceivable that the remarkable settlement concentration in the Upper Piedmont at the eastern end of the central survey strip (sites Tx-A-69 through -81) could be construed as a part of "suburban" Texcoco. Smaller satellite communities also existed to the west of both Texcoco and Huexotla, at or near the shoreline of Lake Texcoco.

Axtec Coatlinchan (Tx-A-88), in marked contrast to both Huexotla and Texcoco, lacked any substantial "suburban" outliers, as did the smaller Coatepec center (Tx-A-99). Chimalhuacan (Tx-A-109), another principal nucleated center, also lacked such a "suburban" zone, except possibly around the northern and western base of Cerro Chimalhuacan where heavy modern occupation has badly obscured the remains of prehispanic settlement.

The Tepetlaoxtoc site (Tx-A-24) presents a third type of Late Aztec principal center. In contrast to the Texcoco, Huexotla, Coatlinchan, Coatepec, and Chimalhuacan centers, Aztec Tepetlaoxtoc was a relatively dispersed community. We were also unable to identify a central ceremonial-civic zone such as those clearly present at both Huexotla and Chimalhuacan, and presumably at Coatlinchan, Texcoco, and Coatepec. In this respect, Aztec Tepetlaoxtoc is like the apparent situation at the Otumba center in the Teotihuacan Valley (Sanders, 1965: 82) where there was no obvious ceremonial-civic architecture. This lack of clear-cut monumental architecture at Otumba was likewise a unique feature among Late Aztec centers in the Teotihuacan Valley.

In addition to the relatively dispersed quality of Aztec Tepetlaoxtoc, the northern third of the Texcoco Region (i.e., our northern survey strip) is characterized by an overall Late Aztec settlement configuration which is basically different from that of the remainder of this area. The essential differentiating quality is the general pattern of dispersed settlement which typifies the whole of this northern zone. We have just seen that in the central and southern parts of the Texcoco Region the great majority of Late Aztec population is concentrated in a few large, nucleated centers, with a substantial minority residing in zones of dispersed occupation which can be considered "suburban" satellites of the two largest centers. The northern zone is more comparable to the general situation in the Teotihuacan Valley in that population was distributed somewhat more continuously and evenly in the form of intermittent occupational clusters within broad settlement bands on the Lower Piedmont, around the edges of a sizable alluvial floodplain crossed by a permanent stream (the Río Papalotla).

Agricultural Systems

The overall size and distribution of Aztec population in the Texcoco Region suggests that available strategic resources of all types were being fully maximized. We have just noted the orientation of Aztec settlement around the margins of the alluvial floodplain of the Río Papalotla in the northern part of the Texcoco Region. This orientation suggests that this plain and the gentle Lower Piedmont slopes at its peripheries were intensively cultivated during the Aztec period, as they are today and as they appear to have been in Early Toltec and Terminal Formative times. The Río Papalotla—today the only permanent stream of any size in the Texcoco Region—offers the best opportunity for canal irrigation (on a modest scale) in the survey area. Communities at the margins of the main plain would also have been in a position to take advantage of rainy-season runoff from the nearby slopes for floodwater irrigation. This northern zone thus offers the closest juxtaposition of two important cultivation systems in the Texcoco Region: modest canal irrigation on the main alluvial plain, and floodwater irrigation on the gentle slopes.

The tremendous concentration of Aztec population at the juncture of the Lakeshore Plain and Lower Piedmont in the central part of the Texcoco Region represents the first substantial occupation of this environmental niche in the prehispanic era. This pattern suggests that in the Aztec period, for the first time, the agricultural potential of substantial segments of the Lakeshore Plain was realized by means of large drainage projects. Without such drainage systems, the Lakeshore Plain would have remained agriculturally marginal or useless. The earlier-mentioned large canalized barrancas extending across the width of the Lakeshore Plain from the edge of the Lower Piedmont were very likely first constructed in Aztec times as a means of restricting the number of water channels and reducing the dangers of flooding of low-lying agricultural land during the rainy season (which was also the growing season).

It is equally apparent that rainfall and floodwater cultivation of the gentle slopes of the Lower Piedmont was expanded and intensified throughout the Aztec period. This general zone had been the demographic heartland of the Texcoco Region since Late Formative times, and its continuing importance in the Aztec period is expectable.

An especially impressive (and somewhat perplexing) feature of Aztec settlement is the extensive occupation of the Upper Piedmont zone along the eastern edge of our survey area in the central and northern survey strips. This zone represents another environmental niche newly appropriated for substantial residential purposes in Aztec times. The very evident demographic pressure in this section of the Upper Piedmont leads us to suspect that productive agriculture was achieved in this zone. Our perplexity derives from the relatively marginal quality of the Upper Piedmont with respect to dependable, intensive cultivation: not only is there a very limited supply of level land, but most of the natural water courses have long been so deeply intrenched as to seriously restrict the capabilities of effective irrigation of any kind. Furthermore, much of the potentially best agricultural land in the Upper Piedmont was utilized for residential purposes in Late Aztec times.

Hillside terracing would have provided one mechanism for intensifying the agricultural productivity of the rugged Upper Piedmont zone. The abundant remains of abandoned stone-faced terrace systems throughout this area are indicative of the great concern with creating and maintaining productive agricultural land. Although the chonological placement of these terraces remains a problem, their primary construction and use may be tentatively assigned to the Aztec period on the basis of two main considerations: the obviously maximal land pressure operative at that time; and the abundance of terrace remnants in the general vicinity of many Aztec sites, and their relative scarcity where Aztec occupation was sparse (i.e., the southeast quadrant of our survey area).

Maguey and nopal are two important crops which would have flourished under conditions of terrace agriculture wholly dependent upon rainfall. These hardy cultigens are highly resistant to aridity and cold, and would probably have been somewhat more productive and dependable than maize in the Upper Piedmont. We suggest that the population of the Upper Piedmont zone was specialized in maguey and nopal production during Late Aztec times.

We are now led into a consideration of the significance for prehispanic agriculture of the Aztec canal networks which carried water from scattered springs at the base of the Sierra across the Upper Piedmont and onto the lower ground to the west. We have already described the physical appearance and location of substantial portions of both functioning and abandoned canals and aqueducts. Today the canal and aqueduct systems through which water continues to flow function to supply water for household needs and some intensive irrigated terrace cultivation in a series of adjacent villages in the Lower Piedmont. Sixteenth century documentary sources (e.g. Pomar, 1941) bearing on this hydraulic system suggest that the bulk of the water involved was consumed for nonutilitarian purposes in a number of "pleasure gardens" and "royal retreats" of the Texcocan ruling elite. One source (McAfee and Barlow, 1946) does indicate that residents of the community of Santa María Natívitas (probably our Tx-A-59) did have access to some water from this system (for unspecified purposes). It does seem apparent, however, that a substantial portion of water supplied by this canal-aqueduct network did not serve to intensify agricultural production. Furthermore, as we have previously seen, at least a part of the water flowing through both the Río Papalotla drainage system, and from the springs at Teotihuacan, was appropriated by Netzahualcoyotl for nonutilitarian purposes in the fifteenth century.

Aztec occupation is abundant in that section of the Upper Piedmont crossed by the canal network leading from the Sierra springs. However, the severe erosion throughout this zone has so obliterated and obscured the original ground surface that we are unable to evaluate the possibilities of the former presence of secondary canals leading water from the main supply route into Aztec residential districts and/or agricultural fields in the Upper Piedmont. The main canals could conceivably have been tapped at numerous intervals along their length for household and agricultural uses. However, the relatively limited quantities of water available from the scattered springs would have placed severe restrictions on this kind of water utilization.

It is clearly apparent that the huge block of high, rugged ground in the southeastern quadrant of the Texcoco Region has been very sparsely occupied in both Aztec and modern times. The base of the Sierra at the eastern margin of this block is the only section of the foothills where water from springs is not appropriated for use by modern communities. In view of the great importance of such water sources for household uses and agricultural purposes today, it is probably safe to assume that there are no accessible springs in this section of the Sierra. A principal factor in the scanty Aztec and modern settlement in this area may be the scarcity of water for even essential household uses.

Another element which might have some bearing on the problem of the prehispanic functions of the canal networks we are considering is the near lack of Aztec occupation in the arc formed by the western slopes of the Cerros Purificación-San Miguel-Cocotl-Tetzcotzingo complex. Today much of this area is covered by the villages of Purificación, San Miguel Tlaixpan, and San Nicolás Tlaminca. These hillslopes are now intensively terraced, and the lower terraces are partially irrigated. Abandoned canals in the higher parts of the hillslopes may indicate that terraces in these sections were formerly irrigated as well. This area is now one of the most intensively cultivated sections of the Texcoco Region. The fact that it was not used for residential purposes in Aztec times indicates that it was reserved for other uses—perhaps agricultural, although we cannot rule out the possibility that the Tetzcotzingo "pleasure gardens" of the Texcocan rulers extended over much or all of this area. Another possibility (suggested to us by W. T. Sanders) is that much of this zone was intensively cultivated by means of irrigated terraces in Aztec times. In view of the obvious importance of the Cerro Tetzcotzingo ceremonial-civic complex to the Texcocan state, it seems reasonable to suggest that this same state created and reserved for itself the high productive capacity of irrigated terracing in the general vicinity of Tx-A-62.

Wolf and Palerm (1955) have argued that the construction of the Texcocan canal-aqueduct complex correlated with severe population pressure on existing resources in the mid-fifteenth century. They reasoned that the primary function of this hydraulic system was to increase agricultural productivity in the face of increasingly severe land pressure, and that the construction of this system was ". . . merely the culmination of a long-established trend" (1955: 274) toward the intensification of agriculture which had been operative in this area for a period of several centuries. They also attached major significance to the productive capacities of the irrigation system in maintaining the political dominance of the Texcocan domain (1955: 276): "... once the state had expanded, the very marginal location of the domain in the narrow corridor leading from north to south along the eastern shore of the lake would have tended to reduce the area to secondary importance, had irrigation not provided a permanent backbone of political cohesion."

We think that Wolf and Palerm's hypothesis regarding the role of canal irrigation agriculture in the Texcoco Region requires modification of two main points:

1) They have underestimated the productive potential of the Lakeshore Plain sector of the Texcoco Region. This was largely because of their belief that the prehispanic level of Lake Texcoco extended up to the base of the Lower Piedmont so that the principal centers of Texcoco, Huexotla, and Coatlinchan were situated directly on the shoreline. Our surveys have indicated that there were a number of residential sites, including several fairly substantial villages (e.g., Tx-A-46, Tx-A-53) well to the west of Texcoco and Huexotla. Furthermore, if the lake level had actually approached the western limits of these three centers, the entire large community of Chimalhuacan (Tx-A-109) would have been at least 10 meters below water level (Map 9).

There are at least two documentary sources which indicate that Texcoco itself (the lowest of the three main Aztec centers) was situated well inland from the edge of the lake (or, at least from where the lake water attained any appreciable depth). Diaz del Castillo (1960: 266) spoke of Cortes' order for the construction of a large canal from Texcoco to the lake, undertaken for the purpose of launching a series of ships (built in Texcoco) against Tenochtitlan in 1521. Diaz describes the large numbers of laborers required in order to

> . . . ensanchar y abrir más las acequías y zanjas por donde habíamos de sacar los bergantines a la laguna después que estuviesen acaba dos. . . .

Referring to the same incident, Alva Ixtlilxochitl (1965*b*: 416) relates that the ruler of Texcoco directed the construction of

> . . . una zanja profunda que tenía más de media legua de longitud, con la profundidad necesaria, que corría desde dentro los jardines y palacios del rey Nezahualcoyotl [in Texcoco] . . . hasta dentro de la laguna; y para esta obra mandó, que en cincuenta días que duró, trabajasen un xiquipil, que son ocho mil hombres cada día. . . .

It seems clear to us that the maximum Aztec lake level was somewhat below 2240 meters. This meant that there would have been a wide expanse of level, high-water-table land in the Lakeshore zone potentially available for agricultural purposes. We have already pointed out that in order to realize this agricultural potential, large-scale drainage programs would have been necessary. We have been arguing that such drainage projects were undertaken for the first time in the Aztec period, and that drainage, not canal irrigation, was the key to high agricultural productivity in the Texcoco Region. Full-scale drainage of the Lakeshore Plain zone would have opened up a vast area of prime, high-water-table agricultural land. Prior to such artificial drainage, comparable agricultural land would have been restricted to the naturally-drained gently-sloping ground east of Cerro Chimalhuacan. This latter area had been the focus of Middle Formative occupation.

The present rainy season water table in the Lakeshore Plain zone appears to lie two meters, or more, below ground level.

The level was undoubtedly substantially higher prior to the on-going drainage of the lake system initiated in the Colonial period Under proper drainage conditions, the natural high water table of the Lakeshore Plain would have offset the relatively greater frequency and severity of frost activity in this zone: crops could be planted soon after all possible danger from spring frosts was past in early May, and would have reached full maturity well before any possible danger from fall frosts in late September or October. In these respects, the productive capacity of the Texcocan Lakeshore Plain may have approached that of the *chinampa* area of Lakes Chalco and Xochimilco to the south.

Unfortunately we lack any archaeological or documentary data bearing on the artificial drainage of the Lakeshore Plain in Aztec times. Complex networks of drainage ditches are found in great abundance throughout this zone today, but as yet no attempt has been made to date their initial construction and use. An examination of the vertical airphoto (made in 1959) of the Texcoco Region (Plate 1) is particularly revealing from the point of view of the differences in field patterns between the Lakeshore Plain west of modern Texcoco, and the Lower Piedmont to the east of the town. In the former zone, fields characteristically take the form of long, narrow rectangles—much like chinampas in appearance—, whose appearance is structured by the drainage ditches surrounding each cultivation plot. In marked contrast, agricultural fields in the Lower Piedmont to the west are usually large, irregular squares or broad rectangles. Many of the fields in both zones are clearly the product of modern agricultural practices. However, the basic chinampa appearance of fields in large segments of the Lakeshore Plain may very well have its origin in the prehispanic period.

2) The second point at which we wish to criticize Wolf and Palerm's hypothesis is their overestimation of the role of canal irrigation in agricultural productivity of the Texcoco Region. We have already referred to the limited quantities of water available from these isolated springs, and to the great distances which separate these sources from the most productive agricultural land. Even today the water flowing through these canal networks is probably of greater significance for household purposes than for cultivation. Also, our impression from documentary sources is that large canal networks were primarily used for nonutilitarian purposes which had previously been available for agricultural uses. Our bases for this statement are Pomar's (1941: 54) previously cited account of Netzahualcoyotl's channeling of water from the Teotihuacan springs into his "royal retreat" at Acatetelco (Tx-A-6), and the mid-sixteenth century map showing large canals from the Teotihuacan Valley and the Río Papalotla leading water into this same site (Linne, 1948: Mapa X, XI) (Fig. 13).

If large-scale canal irrigation agriculture had indeed been a key factor underwriting Texcocan political dominance, then there is some problem in accounting for the relatively marginal position of the Teotihuacan Valley within the regional Aztec-period sociopolitical framework. As previously indicated, the Teotihuacan Valley is unusual within the Valley of Mexico in its great potential for highly productive cultivation based on large-scale networks of irrigation canals. We have supported arguments that this ecological factor was of primary significance in Terminal Formative times when Teotihuacan first attained its status as a major power center. In Aztec times, however, the Teotihuacan Valley centers were politically of little significance beyond the local level, and all were directly subordinate to Texcoco. Texcoco certainly relied significantly upon the productive capacity of irrigation agriculture for its subsistence requirements (i.e., all the Teotihuacan Valley centers delivered tribute in foodstuffs to Texcoco). We find it difficult to associate the productive potential of irrigation agriculture in the Texcoco Region with the rise and consolidation of Texcoco's political dominance in the Aztec period.

Occupational Specialization and Economic Symbiosis

The preceeding consideration of agricultural potentials has been of primary relevance to our interpretation of the configuration of Aztec settlement. It is quite apparent, however, that we shall also have to deal with a number of additional economic and sociopolitical factors in order to resolve some features of Aztec population distribution which are not clearly, or entirely, related to agricultural productivity. The most pressing demographic problems now facing us are (1) the extensive occupation of the Upper Piedmont in the central and northern survey strips, which does not seem to be wholly justified in view of the relatively limited agricultural possibilities of this zone; (2) the great population size and nucleation at the four main centers of Texcoco, Huexotla, Coatlinchan, and Chimalhuacan (if maximum accessibility to prime agricultural land in the Lakeshore Plain and the Lower Piedmont were the only principal factor involved in the distribution of population, we might rather expect to find a band of relatively more limited and dispersed occupation running the length of the Texcoco Region along the juncture of these two environmental zones); and (3) the occupation of the Lake Texcoco shoreline, which would appear to be unrelated to agricultural exploitation.

At this point we are interested in the relationships between settlement patterning, on the one hand, and economic symbiosis and extraction, on the other. Specifically, we wish to consider (*a*) the exploitation of nonagricultural resources; (*b*) the local and regional market system operating within the Valley of Mexico in Late Aztec times; and (*c*) the sponsorship of full-time and part-time bureaucrats, craftsmen, artisans, and laborers by ruling elites through tributary networks.

We have already discussed the documentary references to the exploitation of lacustrine resources in the Texcoco Region during Late Aztec times. Hunting waterfowl, fishing, collecting aquatic plants and insect larvae, and salt-making were all carried out in the lake or along the shoreline. Several of our sites are best (or better) understood with respect to these activities: Tx-A-1, -2, -3, -4, -5, -7, -8, -9, -10, -42, -43, -44, -45, -46, -47, -48, -49, -50, -51, -52, -53, -54, -55, -104, -105, -106, -107, and -110. Except for Tx-A-42 and -43, which may represent small hunting camps or collecting stations, most of these communities are hamlets. Tx-A-53, Tx-A-110, and Tx-A-46 have been classified as small dispersed villages. Tx-A-49 may represent a detached western barrio of the main Texcoco center.

The locations of the major urban centers of Chimalhuacan (Tx-A-109), Coatlinchan (Tx-A-88), Huexotla (Tx-A-87), and Texcoco (Tx-A-56) also suggest some lacustrine orientation of these large communities. This is most immediately apparent in the case of Chimalhuacan and Texcoco. It is also noteworthy that all four of these principal sites are situated at precisely those localities where the width of the Lakeshore Plain is most restricted—i.e., where there is the least distance between the Lake Texcoco shoreline and the edge of the Lower Piedmont. Thus, four of the five principal Late Aztec centers in the Texcoco Region are situated so as to have maximum accessibility to three major resource zones: (*a*) the lacustrine niche of Lake Texcoco and its shoreline; (*b*) the prime high-water-table agricultural land of the artificially drained Lakeshore Plain; and (*c*) the land best suited to rainfall agriculture and small-scale canal irrigation in the deep-soil ground of the lowermost Lower Piedmont zone.

The situation of Texcoco (Tx-A-56) is particularly strategic in this regard. This community lies at the southern edge of the widest expanse of alluvial plain where large-scale drainage projects would have opened up the greatest abundance of prime agricultural land. The fact that Texcoco emerged as a large urban site considerably later than did Huexotla (Tx-A-87) and Coatlinchan (Tx-A-88) may indicate that initial drainage of the Lakeshore Plain was carried out where this zone was least extensive. With increasing engineering competency and organizational capacity, massive drainage projects could then tap the much higher productive potential of the broad plain in the northwest quadrant of the Texcoco Region.

We may now be in a somewhat better position to understand some of the distinctions in the nature of Late Aztec occupation at the four principal centers just mentioned and the fifth large community, Tepetlaoxtoc (Tx-A-24). This latter site was unique by virtue of its relatively dispersed occupation and its lack of obvious monumental ceremonial-civic architecture. These unique qualities may partially reflect the less strategic location of Aztec Tepetlaoxtoc relative to Texcoco, Huexotla, Coatlinchan, and Chimalhuacan.

We have argued elsewhere (Parsons, in press) for the association of Texcoco Fabric Marked pottery with salt manufacture around the shoreline of Lake Texcoco in Aztec times. If this association is valid, there are at least nine sites within this niche in the Texcoco Region where salt production was an important activity: Tx-A-3, -5, -9, -10, -49, -50, -51, -107, and sections of Tx-A-109 (Chimalhuacan). Of these sites, the ceramic assemblages at Tx-A-5, -9, -50, and -51 consist almost exclusively of Texcoco Fabric Marked material. The surface pottery at Tx-A-3, -10, -49, -107, and -109 also contains standard Aztec ceramic types found at residential sites throughout the Texcoco Region. This differentiation indicates that the former group of sites (Tx-A-5, -9, -50, and -51) were localities where salt production was carried on apart from residence. The second group of sites appears to have combined salt manufacture and residential functions. Smaller percentages of Texcoco Fabric Marked pottery occurred at Tx-A-2, -6, -44, -47, and -48, suggesting that salt production may have been of some secondary importance at these sites.

The near lack of Texcoco Fabric Marked ceramics in our collections from 16 sites in the general vicinity of the Lake Texcoco shoreline (Tx-A-1, -4, -7, -8, -42, -43, -45, -46, -52, -53, -54, -55, -104, -105, -106, and -110) indicates that other types of exploitative activities were being pursued at these localities. We have no direct indication of what these activities were; however, the location of these sites suggests an orientation toward hunting water fowl, fishing, and collecting aquatic plants and insect larvae. Tx-A-42, and Tx-A-43 are so small that they almost certainly represent temporary hunting camps or collecting stations. The relatively substantial village communities of Tx-A-53 and Tx-A-110 were ideally situated with respect to both lacustrine resources to the west and high-water-table agriculture on the Lakeshore Plain to the east.

Excepting Tx-A-42 and Tx-A-43, the ceramic assemblages found on these shoreline sites contain the full range of standard pottery types and vessel forms found at Aztec residential sites throughout the Texcoco Region. This leads us to believe that these sites (including most of the very small ones) were lived in. We would predict that the exploitation of lacustrine resources provided a significant supplement to agriculture for a substantial segment of Aztec population. In view of the highly developed occupational specialization suggested by Spanish accounts of the large market at Tenochtitlan-Tlatelolco, the lacustrine niche in the Texcoco Region may have been the exclusive province of persons wholly divorced from other productive activities.

An equally acceptable alternative is that lakeshore resources were extracted by persons whose primary orientation was toward agriculture. This is perhaps most likely with respect to the hunting of water fowl during the winter season when many thousands of migratory birds nested around the edges of the lake system. Agriculture and the hunting of water fowl offer an especially complementary exploitative pattern since large quantities of water fowl were available only during the agricultural off-season of the winter months.

If we shift our attention to the exploitative possibilities of the Sierra zone at the eastern margin of the Texcoco Region, we find that deer and a variety of wood products (principally charcoal, firewood, and construction lumber) are the most obvious resources available to prehispanic populations. We have seen that this zone has remained essentially devoid of permanent occupation throughout the prehispanic period down to the present day. We suspect that the extensive Late Aztec population in the Upper Piedmont was somewhat involved in lumbering and charcoal burning in the adjacent Sierra. Deer hunting was probably not particularly significant, as documentary sources suggest that large game was reserved for the recreation of the ruling elite.

We would argue that lumbering and charcoal burning, together with maguey and nopal production, constituted the set of strategic resources exploited by the Aztec population of the Upper Piedmont. This same population may have also engaged in preparing a number of finished products from the basic raw materials: for example, charcoal, shaped wooden beams, roasted maguey hearts, maguey fiber for spinning and weaving, and pulque. The relative scarcity of spindle whorls on Upper Piedmont sites, and their particular abundance in Huexotla, Texcoco, and Chimalhuacan (surface collections were not made at Coatlinchan) (M.H. Parsons, n.d.), indicates that most of the final spinning and weaving of maguey fiber was performed by specialized craftsmen in the principal urban centers.

It is also conceivable that a portion of the Late Aztec occupation of the Upper Piedmont represents the part-time residence of laborers and engineers involved in the construction and maintenance of the canal-aqueduct system which carried water from the base of the Sierra down to the Lower Piedmont (this possibility was suggested to us by Dr. Angel Palerm). There is little doubt that large numbers of people were involved in the construction of this hydraulic system. After a relatively short construction period, however, the maintenance of the canals and aqueducts could presumably have been performed by a much smaller body of workers. Furthermore, the substantial character of all houses in this area which have escaped total obliteration through erosion (i.e., all preserved wall bases are stone, and measure between 30 and 50 cm thick; traces of well-made stuccoed floors are occasionally visible) suggests permanent residence throughout the occupied sector of the Upper Piedmont in Late Aztec times.

We are now led directly into a consideration of archaeological evidence for the existence of specialized non-food producers in the Lower Piedmont zone. The only concrete data we can offer at the present time is the distribution of spindle whorls mentioned above. The spinning of cotton and maguey fiber was apparently most important at large urban centers (perhaps excepting Tepetlaoxtoc, where whorls were not abundant), and at several village sites in the Lower Piedmont. Alva Ixtlilxochitl (1965*a*: 146-47) indicates that early in the fifteenth century the ruler of Texcoco was able to call upon his subjects in Huexotla, Coatlinchan, Ixtapaluca, and "otros muchos de otras provincias" to make a large quantity of cloth from raw cotton supplied by the ruler of Tenochtitlan. Apart from this we can only refer back to our earlier discussion of the documentary sources which indicated that substantial numbers of skilled craftsmen and artisans were incorporated into the Texcoco urban community where at least a part of their production was underwritten by the ruling elite.

The existence of mechanisms for the absorption and distribution of a wide variety of products has been implicit throughout our discussion of occupational specialization in Late Aztec times. One of these mechanisms was the market. The documentary sources have indicated the existence of a large number of local and regional markets which integrated the Valley of Mexico and possibly the adjacent *tierra templada* and *tierra caliente* of Morelos and Veracruz into a major symbiotic network in the late prehispanic period (e.g., Sanders, 1956). As one of the two or three principal power centers in the Valley of Mexico, Texcoco almost certainly had a daily market comparable in size and organizational complexity to that described by Diaz del Castillo and Cortes at Tenochtitlan-Tlatelolco in 1519. Smaller markets, held at less frequent intervals at Huexotla, Coatlinchan, Coatepec, Chimalhuacan, and Tepetlaoxtoc probably served the needs of small populations over more restricted areas.

At this point we are unable to offer any direct archaeological evidence for the existence of markets at these centers in the Aztec period. We are reasonably confident, however, that their presence can eventually be demonstrated archaeologically. We would argue that at least a part of the specialized production of agricultural and nonagricultural materials was generated by the existence of the market system and absorbed directly into this system at both regional and local levels.

Tribute networks were another mechanism which functioned to generate and absorb the production of agricultural and nonagricultural goods. Murra (1956) has cogently explicated this for the Inca of Peru. Tribute to the Inca state was rendered solely in services. Such services, for example, might be in the form of corvée labor, or might consist of spinning and weaving cloth using raw materials provided by the state. The Inca state had apparently taken over the function of markets, and had eliminated the market institution, at least at the regional level (Murra, 1956). In the Aztec state, the functions of tribute networks and market systems were probably complementary and overlapping.

Pottery was very probably one item absorbed into trade and tribute networks. By means of a systematic detailed study of the distributional patterns of decorative motifs and vessel forms over broad areas it may eventually be feasible to delineate the specific routes along which trade and tribute flowed in Aztec times.

The large-scale movements of goods and people throughout the Valley of Mexico in the Aztec period would presumably have exercised some effect on the placement of market centers and the distribution of population. In looking at the Valley of Mexico as a whole (Map 2) one is immediately impressed by the concentration of major Aztec centers at or near the edges of the lake system. We have already discussed the advantages of such a location with respect to maximizing accessibility to both lacustrine resources and artificially-drained, prime high-water-table agricultural land. An additional advantage, of equal or even greater significance, was the importance of access to the lake system as a transportation-communication artery. In an area of rugged terrain and very primitive overland transport, the lake network tremendously facilitated the flow of materials and people throughout the length of the Valley of Mexico. The heavy canoe traffic described by Spanish conquistadores in 1519 demonstrates that the lake's transportation-communication potential was fully utilized in Late Aztec times.

At no other period in the prehispanic era can we detect a lacustrine orientation of major centers in the Valley of Mexico which so obviously reflects the importance of this aspect of the lake system. The locations of large pre-Aztec communities are much more clearly related to local agricultural productivity. This is perhaps most apparent at Terminal Formative and Classic Teotihuacan. In Late Aztec times, however, there were many primary and secondary centers in the Valley of Mexico situated at or near the lakeshore in areas of limited agricultural potential, while many older centers in areas of high agricultural productivity had long been abandoned or were reduced to secondary status (e.g., Teotihuacan). Probably the most outstanding example was Tenochititlan itself, on an island in a salt lake. Tenochtitlan's greatest resource was its strategic location with respect to the trade and tribute networks which operated over the lake system. Tenochtitlan was ideally situated so as to control and coordinate the lake-borne flow of goods, and likewise to function as the main central market place in the Valley of Mexico. Its power derived from this base enabled Tenochtitlan to extend its tributary networks sufficiently so as to provide for its subsistence requirements from productive agricultural zones over a far-flung area (Barlow, 1949*a*).

The configuration of Aztec settlement in the Texcoco Region should thus be understood in the context of high population pressure, intensive exploitation of resources, and participation within a stratified series of market and tributary networks focused on secondary and primary centers in the Valley of Mexico. We have attempted to demonstrate that population and political power were most highly concentrated in strategic locations where accessibility to both prime agricultural land and the lacustrine transportation artery was maximized. The extent of population pressure required a substantial exploitation of less productive agricultural land by smaller numbers of people residing in dispersed villages and hamlets. We have argued that the populations of such marginal areas, rather than being oriented toward subsistence agriculture, specialized in a more restricted set of exploitative activities (e.g., maguey and nopal cultivation, as well as lumbering, in the Upper Piedmont and adjacent Sierra). Such specialization would require that all participants be fully integrated into the redistributional networks focused on the markets and ruling elite of principal urban centers. The concentration of population, markets, and ruling elite in large centers would have functioned to create and expand a variety of additional exploitative niches within these communities: among them craft and artisan specializations, bureaucratic and administrative functions.

The Texcoco-Chalco Frontier

It is obvious that the full complexity of the Aztec settlement configuration cannot be understood completely in terms of our aforegoing discussion. There will always remain a residue of variables, which, because of the nature of archaeological evidence, are likely to be inaccessible to even the most sophisticated techniques of prehistoric investigation. However, because of the availability of a certain amount of documentary information, we are able to better understand certain aspects of Late Aztec settlement distribution which do not appear to be related to the variables we have considered up to this point. The most significant problem which we can further elucidate is the paucity of Aztec occupation in the south-central and southeastern sectors of the Texcoco Region. We have previously suggested that the limited water supply and the marginal quality of the rugged peninsula of high ground extending westward from the main Sierra in this zone acted as deterrents to any extensive inhabitation of this area. These, however, are not adequate explanations when we consider (*a*) that maguey and nopal would have been productive throughout the area, (*b*) that even good agricultural land remained vacant, and (*c*) that the existing population centers in this region (Coatlinchan, Coatepec, and Chimalhuacan) lacked the "suburban" satellite communities so characteristic of Huexotla, Texcoco, and Tepetlaoxtoc. Another rather unusual feature is the concentration of large ceremonial-civic structures with very sparse occupational debris (Tx-A-100) in the low, gently sloping region along the main pass into the Chalco area. This is the only significant large concentration of isolated ceremonial-civic architecture within our survey area.

We believe these aberrant characteristics of occupation can be viewed as manifestations of the sociopolitical frontier between the domains of Texcoco (to the north) and Chalco (to the south). We have referred to the documentary evidence of this frontier, and of the hostility between Texcoco and Chalco during the Aztec period. The sparse occupation and paucity of dispersed settlement would appear to reflect the unsettled conditions prevailing in the borderland between these two domains. The ceremonial-civic architecture concentrated along the main route of communication between Chalco and Texcoco may represent an architectural expression of the frontier's political significance.

Local Organization

We now turn to the implications of our data for Aztec social organization at the local level. This discussion will revolve around two matters: the local community and the household.

The documentary sources have indicated that the *calpulli*, the *barrio pequeño*, and the household were the three most significant units of local organization. Sanders (1965, 1966) has argued that in rural settlements individual *calpulli* comprised separate communities of several hundred individuals, while *barrio pequeño* units formed discrete clusters of 20 to 40 houses within these *calpulli* communities. Because of the relatively continuous distribution of dispersed rural occupation in the Texcoco Region, we have had little success in delineating on the ground discrete zones of occupation which might be regarded as *calpulli* or *barrio pequeño* units. Similarly, the generally poor preservation of architectural features made it impossible for us to objectively delineate sociopolitical entities on the basis of the distribution of ceremonial-civic structures. There is only one discrete occupational unit which might be construed as a *calpulli* community: Tx-A-25, a large dispersed village with an estimated population of between 600 and 1200 people, extending over an area of about 115 hectares, with fairly definite modest ceremonial-civic architecture in the southeastern corner of the site. The characteristics of this site correspond reasonably well with Sanders' view of the rural Aztec *calpulli* as a physical community.

The few isolatable occupational clusters of a size which might indicate *barrio pequeño* (or other sub- *calpulli*) status include Tx-A-26, Tx-A-27, Tx-A-39, Tx-A-53 (this site might also be considered as a small *calpulli*), Tx-A-70 and -71 considered together as a single unit, Tx-A-76, and Tx-A-86. Population estimates of these units range between 75-to-150 and 250-to-500 people, with an overall average of 132 to 264. Settlement size measures from 10 to 25 hectares, with an average of about 16 hectares. Of this group, only Tx-A-70-71 and Tx-A-76 contain preserved architectural remnants which might represent small ceremonial-civic structures. These seven settlements are essentially equivalent to what Sanders has considered as *barrio pequeño* units in the Teotihuacan Valley.

We have located a sizable number of Aztec housemounds on rural sites (and at the large Tepetlaoxtoc center, Tx-A-24) in which bases of stone walls are sufficiently preserved so as to provide a reasonable impression of the arrangement and size of rooms in domestic residential quarters (Figs. 16-19, 22, 23, 25-27). At this point we are unable to specify the function of any particular room within a room complex, and we are additionally hampered by our inability to distinguish between residential structures and a variety of nonresidential outbuildings which might be associated with a residential unit. Room patterns were obtained from scattered localities throughout the Texcoco Region, and in no case do we have a good sample from any single site or area. We also lack any control over the chronology of room construction and abandonment. Even with these limitations, however, an examination of these room plans does suggest a number of preliminary interpretations relevant to household organization.

Perhaps our strongest impression is of the great variability in the size of house structures. There are at least two structures which apparently consist of a single room each (Fig. 19,*d*, *e*). The great majority of our sample is comprised of small complexes of between three and six rooms, which vary between two and five meters wide or long. There are several large units containing up to 10 or more rooms (Figs. 16,*g*; 17,*d*; 18,*a*,*b*; 22,*c*; 23,*d*).

Except for a few of the smallest structures (which might be considered residences of single nuclear families or as outbuildings), most of the houses in our sample would appear to be two or three nuclear family units, with separate small residential apartments of one or two rooms each. In some cases these apartments are clearly grouped around a central patio (e.g., Figs. 18,*b*; 26,*c*). A smaller number of structures would appear to have housed larger numbers of people. There are no clear-cut differences in room size, either among house complexes of roughly the same size, or between larger and smaller house units —that is, relatively small rooms and relatively large rooms occur in roughly equal proportions at all structures. In cases where unusually large walled enclosures are present (e.g., Fig. 17,*d*), we are not entirely sure that the walls of less-substantial internal partitions have not been obliterated from the ground surface. We tentatively conclude that the expression of status differentiation in nonurban Late Aztec residential architecture is more a matter of the number of rooms and overall household size than of absolute room size. However, we are seriously handicapped at this point by our lack of data from the principal urban centers where a high proportion of elite individuals presumably resided.

Our limited information on residential architecture seems to be in basic accord with Carrasco's (1964) general conclusions from his analysis of an early colonial census from Tepoztlan, Morelos. Our findings suggest considerable variation in household size, with a modal size of two or three nuclear family units. The limited numbers of very large households probably represent the residential complexes of the headmen of *calpulli* or *barrio pequeño* units.

IV

THE TEXCOCO REGION IN MESOAMERICAN PREHISTORY

INTRODUCTION

Although the Valley of Mexico is a distinct topographic unit whose internal cultural development can be meaningfully discussed in isolation, it is quite apparent that reference must be made to other parts of Mesoamerica in order to elucidate some aspects of our settlement pattern data. It will now be our purpose to examine the distribution and characteristics of archaeological sites and materials in central and southern Mesoamerica at points where this information is particularly relevant to the configuration of prehispanic settlement in the Texcoco Region.

EARLY AND MIDDLE FORMATIVE (*ca.* 1500-550 B.C.)

Although many areas remain virtually unknown archaeologically, recent investigations on the Pacific coast of Chiapas and Guatemala (Coe and Flannery, 1967; Shook, 1965; Lowe and Mason, 1965), in the Grijalva Depression of Chiapas (Lowe and Mason, 1965), and on the Gulf Coast of Veracruz and Tabasco (M. Coe, 1965, 1968; García Payón, 1966; M. Coe, *et al.*, 1967) have demonstrated that these zones were culturally nuclear in Mesoamerica throughout the Early and Middle Formative. Well-developed status differentiation, relatively dense and nucleated occupation, and the presence of numerous large, elaborate sites indicate a level of cultural sophistication in advance of that attained in the contemporary Valley of Mexico. In the Valley of Oaxaca Flannery and his associates (Flannery, *et al.*, 1967; Flannery, 1968) have revealed a substantial Early and Middle Formative population whose density and degree of societal evolution are apparently without parallel in the Valley of Mexico (perhaps excepting Tlatilco). Similarly, Grove's (1968) surveys in Morelos have suggested a level of cultural complexity in that region which probably cannot be duplicated in the Valley of Mexico during this period (once again excepting Tlatilco).

In terms of environmental and archaeological features, the Formative occupations mentioned above are similar in the following respects:

1) All are located in areas which are completely or relatively frost free, so that, except for some parts of the Valley of Oaxaca, crops can be planted and harvested year-round provided sufficient moisture is available.

2) Except for the Valley of Oaxaca and the Grijalva Depression, all are in humid or sub-humid zones.

3) All are situated near permanent rivers, whose beds are not deeply incised. This means that the water table is relatively high within the rivers' floodplains. The largest rivers and widest floodplains are found in the southern Gulf Coast, precisely where the largest and most elaborate sites are located.

4) Artifact assemblages, in at least the larger sites, share a common constellation of ceramic and artistic traits which are widely distributed throughout Mesoamer-

ica at this horizon, and which have come to be labelled Olmec or Olmecoid.

It seems reasonable to argue that the florescence of Early and Middle Formative culture in Mesoamerica was closely related to agricultural productivity under conditions which required a minimum of technological innovation and where there were few insecurities arising from frosts and inadequate or unpredictable water supply. Major sites of this period are clearly oriented toward the natural levees and floodplains of rivers where permanent high water table or periodic flooding would have permitted the successful harvesting of two or three crops per year. Without a considerable investment in the technology of water control and humidity conservation, such subsistence security could not have been achieved in the semi-arid highland basins subject to severe winter frosts in the Central Mexican *altiplano*. This would be particularly true prior to the evolution of rapid-maturing strains of maize which are as yet unknown in the Mesoamerican Formative (Wellhausen, *et al.*, 1952). Within the Valley of Mexico the only known Early Formative sites (Tlatilco and Tlapacoya) are situated in zones of natural high water table, with the added advantage of ready access to lacustrine and hillslope resources, All known Middle Formative settlements of any size in the Valley of Mexico are also found in this same environmental niche.

In addition, however, to the basic significance of agricultural productivity, there is another dimension of Early-Middle Formative cultural development which must be considered before the full complexity of the distribution of different kinds of sites and artifacts can be adequately understood. We refer here to the widespread distribution of Olmec and Olmecoid artifacts and stylistic tradition. This phenomenon has probably been the subject of more controversy and discussion than any other single topic in Mesoamerican archaeology. Over the past 20 years religious cults and missionaries, militaristic empires, and trade networks have all been advanced as mechanisms to account for the distribution of Olmec materials.

Flannery (1968) has recently proposed a model which seems to best account for what we now know about the distribution of Olmec materials and the characteristics of the Formative groups who participated most fully in this distribution. Stated very briefly, Flannery argues that the distribution of distinctive Olmec pottery and artistic tradition is to be understood as but a single aspect of inter-regional exchange networks in which a variety of exotic items, and perhaps even basic foodstuffs, were being passed between the elite members of sophisticated groups. Although such an exchange network functioned to enhance and reinforce the status of certain members of such groups, the exchange or "trade," as such, did not create social differentiation within populations. Rather, a basic prerequisite for the initiation and elaboration of inter-regional exchange networks was the existence of an elite sector which "sought to express its differential status" (1968: 106) through the continuous acquisition and consumption of exotic items, of restricted availability, which would serve to validate and enhance social standing. Therefore, the groups most intensely involved in exchanges of this type were those situated in areas where the productive capacity of local subsistence systems was sufficient to support relatively large, nucleated, differentiated populations.

Flannery also argues that, because of their high productive capacity, the Formative peoples of the southern Gulf Coast—the Olmec—were the most advanced and prestigious group in Mesoamerica at this horizon. He also assumes that the configuration of stylistic traits and artifacts popularly known as "Olmec" was indigenous to the Gulf Coast area. Referring to ethnographic accounts of inter-regional exchange systems from the northwest coast of North America, and from traditional Burma, he suggests that the spread of Olmec traits reflects the desire of elite individuals in other areas "to emulate the religion, symbolism, dress, and behavior of the Olmec elite, insofar as it would enhance their own status among their own people" (1968: 106).

Grove's (1968) investigations in Morelos emphasize an additional aspect of this Early-Middle Formative inter-regional exchange network which is implicit in Flannery's model, that is, the source areas of specific exotic materials were not the only features of interest to groups participating in inter-regional exchanges. The routes of access along which items and people moved were equally significant. All the six large sites in Morelos which Grove classified as "Olmec" on the basis of ceramic and stylistic traits were situated at strategic points along major river valleys. Thus, in addition to their accessibility to prime agricultural land in high-water-table floodplains of the frost-free *tierra templada,* these sites were also in a position to coordinate the movements of materials along principal routes of communication.

The presence of Olmec materials and the size and complexity of the Early-Middle Formative occupations at Tlatilco and Tlapacoya, together with the absence of such ceramic and stylistic traits and the relative cultural impoverishment elsewhere in the Valley of Mexico (including the Texcoco Region), can perhaps be best understood in the context of the preceeding discussion. Aside from obsidian and possibly salt, it is difficult to envision any specific items or products which might have justified the participation of these Valley of Mexico groups in inter-regional exchange networks of the type Flannery has suggested. However, in addition to their situation in the most productive niche available to Early-Middle Formative populations in the Valley of Mexico, both Tlapacoya and Tlatilco are strategically situated with respect to the flow of goods and people between Morelos, to the south, and the entire Valley of Mexico and Toluca-Michoacan region, to the north and west. Tlapacoya is located near the lower end of the main pass into Morelos across the southeastern corner of the Valley of Mexico, while Tlatilco lies near the base of a major pass into the Toluca Basin (Grove, 1968, has also noted the strategic aspect of these sites). Communication between Tlatilco and Tlapacoya would have been easy and rapid by means of canoes across the lake system.

García Payón (1941) has reported an Early-Middle Formative site in the archaeological zone of Tecaxic-Calixtlahuaca in the central Toluca Basin, directly west of the head of the main pass leading up from the Valley of Mexico. Formative occupation is concentrated at the edge of the Río Tejalpa floodplain, at the base of a massive section of steeply sloping ground. The bulk of ceramics and figurines are virtually identical to Middle Formative material from the Valley of Mexico, and there is definite Olmec material present (1941: 214). The Formative occupation of the Tecaxic-Calixtlahuaca site lies on a tributary of the upper Lerma River, and the main pass from the Valley of Mexico leads directly into the headwaters of the main Lerma River. The Lerma Valley, in turn, is the major route leading northwestward into northern Michoacan and Guanajuato. This latter area is archaeologically very hazy. An important Late Formative site—Chupícuaro—is located on the Lerma River some 130 km northwest of the Tecaxic-Calixtlahuaca area (Porter, 1956). Neither Early-Middle Formative ceramics nor Olmecoid material have been reported from Chupícuaro, and there is little known concerning this horizon elsewhere in the Michoacan-Guanajuato-Queretaro Region.

In contrast to Morelos, Oaxaca, and other highland areas in the frost free *tierra templada*, it is clear that Early-Middle Formative populations in the Valley of Mexico were participating peripherally in the inter-regional exchange networks which linked the Gulf Coast and much of southern Mesoamerica. The basis for this limited participation was probably the inability of Early-Middle Formative subsistence systems in the *tierra fria* to support the levels of population density and cultural sophistication which were prerequisite to full-scale involvement. Beyond assuring movement of goods through the Valley of Mexico (presumably from the west), and perhaps acquiring obsidian and salt, the more advanced peoples to the south would have had relatively little interest in establishing and maintaining ties with populations lacking both indigenous elites and desirable raw materials.

We suggest that one element in the initial emergence of some degree of social stratification in the Valley of Mexico during Early-Middle Formative times was the possibility for certain strategically-situated groups to facilitate and insure, or, to deny and hinder, the passage of products along a major route between central and western Mexico, on the one hand, and southern and eastern Mexico, on the other. Such a situation may have permitted certain individuals to maintain ties with more sophisticated peoples to the south and to the west who were the principals in long-distance exchange networks. The formation of such relationships with prestigious foreigners, and the accumulation of a variety of insignia (including Olmec ceramics and art) through these alliances, would have served to enhance and elevate the status of limited numbers of people in the Valley of Mexico.

An alternative—and perhaps more plausible—hypothesis would be to view the Early-Middle Formative occupations at Tlapacoya, Tlatilco, and Tecaxic-Calixtlahuaca as weakly stratified groups along the northern fringes of the major exchange networks centered on the Gulf Coast and Morelos. These highland groups, strategically located along major communication routes and within the most productive zones available in the *tierra fria* at this period, may have been capable of marginal participation in exchange relationships with demographically and organizationally superior populations in the southern highlands. In this manner, a few groups in the Valley of Mexico and Toluca Basin acquired the material insignia of Olmec type and style as they formulated alliances with prestigious trading partners to the south and attempted to enhance their own standing in an area where such outside contacts were otherwise lacking.

Tscholl (1966) has reported some Olmecoid material from Formative sites in the Puebla Basin. This latter region is ecologically similar to the Valley of Mexico, and is linked to the *tierra templada* of Morelos, southern Puebla, and Veracruz by means of several major river valleys. The Puebla Basin was probably related to more advanced Early-Middle Formative groups to the south and east in much the same manner as was the Valley of Mexico. In marked contrast to the situation in the Classic and Postclassic periods, contacts between the Valley of Mexico and the Puebla Basin in Early-Middle Formative times were apparently minimal: for example, the Teotihuacan Valley, the major access route between these two highland basins, was then devoid of large sites and Olmecoid artifacts. The symbiotic-extractive networks which closely linked much of the Central Mexican highland zone in Classic and Postclassic times were products of a full-scale organizational revolution in the last centuries B.C., and had no basis in the Early-Middle Formative regional exchange networks focused on the nuclear Gulf Coast.

THE TERMINAL FORMATIVE-CLASSIC TRANSITION

(*ca.* 200 B.C. to A.D. 200)

This era was perhaps the most critical juncture in Mesoamerican cultural development. It was during this period that the Valley of Mexico and the adjacent Central Highlands—which throughout most of the long Formative period had been developmentally marginal relative to the nuclear Gulf Coast and Southern Highlands — emerged as the key area in Mesoamerica. From this point onward the main power centers and highest population densities in prehispanic Mesoamerica were located in this central *altiplano*, and have remained there through the present day.

This critical juncture is very poorly documented archaeologically. This is particularly true with respect to most of the Valley of Mexico and the bordering highland areas (the Toluca Basin, Morelos, the Puebla-Tlaxcala Basin, and southern Hidalgo). We have previously noted the placement of the two major Terminal Formative centers in the Valley of Mexico—Cuicuilco and Teotihuacan—in areas of uniquely high agricultural productivity. We must here emphasize, though, another aspect of their location which was probably of equal significance in their emergence as principal power centers: both Teotihuacan and Cuicuilco are situated on principal natural routes of communication betwen the Valley of Mexico and adjacent areas of Central Mexico. Teotihuacan lies along the main avenue leading into the Tlaxcala-Puebla Basin, southeastern Hidalgo and north-central Veracruz to the east. Cuicuilco rests at the lower end of major passes into the Toluca Basin to the west and Morelos-Guerrero to the southwest.

The strategic placement of both Teotihuacan and Cuicuilco strongly suggests the importance in Terminal Formative times of coordinating and controlling the movement of products and people between different regions and across different ecological zones. Guerrero, Morelos, and the Toluca Basin remain virtually *tierra incognita* for this horizon, although García Payón (1941: 220, 223-25) has illustrated and discussed ceramic material from near Toluca which is clearly related (and perhaps identical) to the Tzacualli and Early Classic phases in the Valley of Mexico, and the Vaillants (1934: 53-4) reported a collection of Early Classic figurines from near Gualupita, Morelos which are identical to those in the Valley of Mexico.

In the Puebla-Tlaxcala Basin, both Tscholl (1966) and Snow (1969) have found substantial Formative occupation with strong affinities to the Late-Terminal Formative ceramic assemblages in the Valley of Mexico. Both Tscholl's and Snow's surveys indicate significant changes in settlement distribution at the Formative-Classic juncture. In Puebla and southern Tlaxcala, Tscholl has delineated a Classic pattern characterized by reduced rural population, with nucleated occupation at a few large sites. In northern Tlaxcala, Snow indicates that Classic occupation was largely confined to numerous small settlements, located on lower hillflanks which had not been occupied during the preceeding Formative.

These data from the Puebla-Tlaxcala Region suggest that this area was involved in the demographic dislocations produced by the organizational revolution at Teotihuacan in the first century A.D. Further investigations elsewhere around the peripheries of the Valley of Mexico are likely to reveal a similar pattern of demographic restructuring during Terminal Formative and Early Classic times in Morelos, the Toluca Basin, southern Hidalgo, and perhaps even parts of northeastern Guerrero, as Teotihuacan extended its authority and systematically arranged or influenced the distribution of population to suit its needs.

Settlement pattern surveys in the Toluca Basin, Morelos, and northeastern Guerrero might prove especially revealing since this region was presumably subject to Cuicuilco, rather than Teotihuacan, prior to the abrupt termination of Cuicuilco's existence late in the Formative era.

Looking somewhat further afield, there are a few suggestions of large-scale population dislocations and systematic rearrangement at the Formative-Classic juncture in several parts of Mesoamerica which might be ultimately related to the emergence of Teotihuacan as a power center of pan-Mesoamerican significance. In the Guatemala highlands, for example, Borhegyi (1965: 12-20) has noted that "many flourishing and important Preclassic sites on the Canchon plateau southeast of Kaminaljuyú in the Dept. of Guatemala were permanently abandoned by the beginning of the Early Classic period [*ca.* A.D. 300 in Borhegyi's chronology]. On the other hand, there was a mushrooming of new ceremonial sites in the Western Highlands and the Hilly Middle Country." Borhegyi also notes the substantial innovations in architecture and site planning which accompanied the Preclassic-Classic transition in the Guatemala highlands. Similarly, Shook (1965: 185-86) reports that "all the Preclassic sites examined in the Mexico-Guatemala border area seemingly were abandoned at some time at the end of the Preclassic period."

These poorly-understood demographic patterns may become more meaningful when we examine the tremendous impact of Classic Teotihuacan throughout much of Guatemala and in many other sections of Mesoamerica.

THE CLASSIC FLORESCENCE (*ca.* A.D. 200-550)

Artifact material of unmistakably Teotihuacan style is distributed widely over the central Mexican *altiplano*, although known sites are few. We have already noted the presence of Classic pottery and figurines of definite Teotihuacan style throughout the Puebla-Tlaxcala Basin. One of the few known Classic sites of any size in central Mexico is situated at Cholula, in the southern Puebla Basin, where sizable ceremonial-civic architecture in pure Teotihuacan style is buried beneath the much larger series of structures dating to Postclassic times. Ceramics and ceremonial-civic architecture of relatively modest scale have also been reported from southeastern Hidalgo near Tulancingo and Tepeapulco (Sanders, 1965: 175). In Morelos, indications of Classic occupation in the Teotihuacan stylistic tradition have also been noted at Chalcatzingo and from near Xochicalco (ibid).

From the apparent paucity of known Classic sites in the central Mexican *altiplano* bordering the Valley of Mexico, together with the indication of direct Teotihuacan influence throughout this area which the ceramic-artistic-architectural remains suggest, we can infer that much of central Mexico may have been directly incorporated into the urban system focused on Teotihuacan in much the same manner as was the Valley of Mexico itself. Looking beyond this core area we can detect very obvious evidence of the strong impact of Classic Teotihuacan throughout much of Mesoamerica. The two areas where this impact appears to have been most pronounced are highland Guatemala—most specifically at the large site of Kaminaljuyú—, and the southern Gulf Coast (M. Coe, 1965). In both these latter areas there was direct imitation of Teotihuacan architectural and ceramic styles on a scale far in excess of what might be expected on the basis of simple trade or tributary relationships alone. In some cases it appears that large quantities of pottery were imported into Kaminaljuyú directly from Teotihuacan itself (Kidder, Jennings, and Shook, 1946).

Teotihuacan artistic and architectural style and ceramics are known from many other parts of Mesoamerica—e.g., from major sites in the Peten (W. Coe, 1965; M. Coe, 1966), the Valley of Oaxaca (Bernal, 1965), central Veracruz (Medellín Zenil, 1960), and Michoacan (Corona Nuñez, 1966). In all these areas, however, distinctly Teotihuacan styles are not nearly so dominant as at Kaminaljuyú and the southern Gulf Coast, but are mixed and blended with preponderant local traditions, or occur in relatively low quantities as tradewares. Furthermore, in some areas—such as the Grijalva Depression of Chiapas (Lowe and Mason, 1965: 226)—there is only very limited evidence of any contact with Teotihuacan at all. It appears that Classic Teotihuacan was most specifically interested in maintaining strong, direct ties with some areas and not with others. Sanders and Price (1968: 168) have suggested that Kaminaljuyú's chief importance to Teotihuacan was its strategic placement with respect to controlling the rich cacao-producing area of coastal Chiapas and adjacent Guatemala (the Xoconusco province which later paid tribute to Aztec Tenochtitlan in the form of cacao—Barlow, 1949*a*). We would also note in this regard that another principal cacao-producing zone, the Gulf of Honduras area (Chapman, 1959: 60) is located to the northeast of Kaminaljuyú at the lower end of the Montagua Valley. Kaminaljuyú was thus situated midway between the two principal cacao zones of Mesoamerica, and could have controlled and coordinated the production and distribution of this important commodity for Teotihuacan's needs.

Likewise, the southern Gulf Coast was an important port-of-trade enclave in late Postclassic times from which major Aztec centers in the Valley of Mexico derived a wide variety of tropical products (Chapman, 1959). This region may have had a very similar significance for Classic Teotihuacan.

We can thus envision Classic Teotihuacan as the focal point in a pan-Mesoamerican socio-economic network which operated as two distinct subsystems: 1) A core area was restricted to the Valley of Mexico and adjacent areas in Puebla-Tlaxcala, and southern Hidalgo; and perhaps in the Toluca Basin, Morelos, and northeastern Guerrero—in which Teotihuacan exercised complete and direct authority. A large segment of the regional population of this core zone probably resided at Teotihuacan where they engaged in full-time nonagricultural specializations and intensive cultivation in the local area. Smaller groups resided throughout the rest of this core zone (in which the Texcoco Region was included), where they were engaged in specialized exploitations of agricultural, lacustrine, and Sierra resources. The coordination of such production was overseen by small regional centers directly dependent upon the central authority at Teotihuacan.

2) The second subsystem was Teotihuacan's relationship with areas which controlled the production of, and/or access to, critical goods and products required by Teotihuacan, but which were too far away from the main power center to permit direct administration. In these cases—principally the southern Gulf Coast and the Xoconusco-Kaminaljuyú-Gulf of Honduras zone— effective administration was apparently achieved by moving segments of the Teotihuacan community into certain strategic locations. The intervening areas between strategic localities were much less closely tied in with Teotihuacan.

As we examine what is known of the character of Classic occupation throughout Mesoamerica, we are increasingly impressed with the uniqueness of Teotihuacan. Other large Classic sites are known—for example, Monte Alban, Tajin, and the impressive Maya centers of the Peten and the Usumacinta drainage. Nowhere, however, can we detect another Classic community which came anywhere close to the size and complexity of Classic Teotihuacan. If this basic impression is essentially correct, then throughout its florescent era, Teotihuacan remained essentially unchallenged with respect to its manipulation of far-flung natural and demographic resources.

THE CLASSIC-POSTCLASSIC TRANSITION (*ca.* A.D. 600-900)

The decline of Classic Teotihuacan and the disintegration of the far-flung symbiotic-extractive networks centered on that community marks another critical juncture in Mesoamerican cultural development (e.g., Wolf, 1959). In the centuries surrounding Teotihuacan's final collapse at about A.D. 700, an organizational revolution was in progress whose scope and impact were fully comparable to the processes which had first brought Teotihuacan to power over 500 years earlier.

We may be able to elucidate the basis for the eclipse of Teotihuacan's power by considering some implications of the configuration of Classic and Aztec settlement in the Valley of Mexico. It seems likely that within Teotihuacan's core area in central Mexico, economic and political integration in Classic times were effected by means of an entirely different set of organizational mechanisms than those which structured Aztec society in the same region. During Late Aztec times in and around the Valley of Mexico, a large proportion of the varied products of specialized occupation was absorbed and distributed by means of a complex series of stratified markets in numerous population centers linked by canoe routes across the lake system. In the Classic period there was a single great center of consumption and production whose redistribution of materials was probably monopolized by the Teotihuacan state.

The scarcity, or even absence, of large Classic centers other than Teotihuacan, together with the clear lack of orientation of Classic communities toward the transportation-communication potential of the lake system, further reinforce our impression of the basic distinction between Classic and Aztec social organization in the central Mexican highlands. Late Aztec society was multi-centered, with principal centers, secondary centers, and rural communities ordered within a multi-level political hierarchy. Integration at local and regional levels was effected, in part, by means of the market system. In Classic times, centralized control over a substantially smaller regional population was achieved by concentrating a large segment of this population within a single great urban community whose location had been primarily determined by factors relating to its local agricultural productivity. The lop-sided distribution of Classic population probably meant that there was little place in the core area of Teotihuacan's sphere of influence for the complex system of local and regional markets which were so crucial to the movement of goods throughout this region in the Late Aztec period. The only place where redistribution of products was required on a large-scale basis would have been at Teotihuacan itself.

Herein, perhaps, lay one of the major flaws in Classic Teotihuacan's organizational structure that led to its massive collapse after A.D. 700. Teotihuacan's role as a pan-Mesoamerican power center was ultimately dependent upon its ability to effectively control and exploit the demographic and natural resources within its core area of the central Mexican highlands. Over a period of more than 500 years Teotihuacan had made a substantial investment in the political institutions which proved so effective in regulating and coordinating these resources. Wolf (1959: 106-09) has suggested that these institutions, which he viewed as essentially theocratic and ideological, proved increasingly ineffective as subordinate populations in outlying areas become acculturated and there was a growing disparity between the interests of "center and hinterland."

We would only like to suggest here that as the regional population expanded (as it obviously did, for whatever reason), Teotihuacan would have been increasingly less able to nucleate a large proportion of the population of its core area within the principal urban community. Since its organizational structure was apparently founded on a policy of extreme demographic nucleation, Teotihuacan could not readily cope with large populations in its immediate hinterland. Furthermore, with population size and density strained to the maximum limit at Teotihuacan itself, it was no longer possible to pull in increments of population from outside. Thus, a critical juncture was reached at which Teotihuacan's traditional organizational mechanisms became disfunctional. Incapable of making the basic structural reorganizations necessary to maintain control of the population and strategic natural resources of its core area, Teotihuacan's power base crumbled.

From all over Mesoamerica there is abundant evidence of the drastic realignment of regional political and economic affiliations during the period between A.D. 600 to 900. M. Coe (1965: 715) has noted that in the southern Gulf Coast, where Teotihuacan's influence had been so strong and direct for several centuries, the period after about A.D. 600 saw "an entirely different cultural alignment" in which local ceramic and architectural styles once again reasserted themselves, and strong ties were formed with Campeche and the Yucatan peninsula. In highland Guatemala, most important Classic sites (including Kaminaljuyú) were abandoned prior to A.D. 1000, and there was an abrupt termination of Teotihuacan influence in architectural style at Kaminaljuyú by A.D. 700. (Borhegyi, 1965: 31-32). There was a similar abandonment of Classic sites after about A.D. 600 in western and central Chiapas (Lowe and Mason, 1965: 229). Likewise, in the Valley of Oaxaca the large complex of Monte Albán was abandoned, except for burial purposes, after A.D. 700. Perhaps best known of all is the remarkable collapse of all the impressive Classic Maya centers in the Peten and its peripheries to the northwest and southeast at about A.D. 900. It is also interesting to note that there was a temporary disruption in the erection of dated stelae at about A.D. 600 over much of the Peten (Willey, Bullard, Glass, and Gifford, 1965: 570).

In the Central Highlands bordering the Valley of Mexico the most obvious development was the emergence of three new principal power centers (Sanders, 1965: 183-86): Cholula, in Puebla to the southeast; Xochicalco, in Morelos to the southwest: and Tula, in Hidalgo to the north. All three are poorly known archaeologically, but all appear to have existed as locally-important secondary centers during at least the latter part of Teotihuacan's florescence. With Teotihuacan's decline after A.D. 700, many of its functions were taken over by these new centers on a reduced scale. For a period of several centuries after this point, the Valley of Mexico existed as a politically-fragmented frontier, or buffer, zone between major power centers situated around its peripheries. Sanders (1965: 186) has noted that Tula's primary expansion appears to have been northward and westward, whereas Cholula was apparently dominant in the Mixteca-Puebla Region to the south.

We are now in a much better position to understand some aspects of Late Classic and Early Toltec settlement configuration in the Texcoco Region which were previously beyond our grasp. We refer principally to the withdrawal of population from the central part of the Texcoco Region which began in the Late Classic period and was fully implemented during Early Toltec times. On the Late Classic horizon this process can be viewed as a reflection of the initial crumbling of Teotihuacan's power monopoly as old organizational mechanisms proved inadequate to cope with a host of complications that included an emerging competitive center at Cholula. As we have seen, even at Teotihuacan itself, there is evidence of some degree of disruption and stress during the Metepec phase at the end of the Classic period as greater proportions of local populations were concentrated at the main urban center where overall population was declining (Sanders, 1965; Millon, 1966).

With the ultimate collapse of Teotihuacan, the broad occupational gap across the center of the Texcoco Region very probably reflects the status of this zone as a kind of disputed no-man's land lying midway between Tula's sphere of control to the north, and that of Cholula to the south. This hypothesis is strengthened when we consider that the Texcoco Region also appears to be a border zone separating the northern Tula (Mazapan) ceramic tradition from the southern Cholulan (Aztec I) tradition in Late Toltec times. Adequate testing of this hypothesis will require detailed comparison of ceramic assemblages and further sampling of settlement distributions in the intervening territory between Tula and Cholula.

V

GENERAL SUMMARY AND CONCLUSIONS

This investigation has attempted to utilize the changing configuration of regional settlement patterns as a means of reconstructing the broad outlines of culture history and inferring certain aspects of cultural process within one segment of the eastern Valley of Mexico. At certain points our data have also had implications for broader problems of Mesoamerican prehistory. It should be emphasized that our interpretations have been structured on a limited set of variables: (*a*) the location of sites with respect to major natural resources; (*b*) the placement of particular settlement types with respect to other contemporary communities; (*c*) the comparative variability of contemporary sites in terms of occupational density, surface area, and architectural complexity; and (*d*) the changes and continuities of these relationships through time. Aside from employing densities of surface pottery as an index of occupational density, we have utilized artifactual data only as a means of establishing a general chronology. A major contribution of our project has been the problems we have defined, and hypotheses we have proposed, which can be attacked and tested by means of refined analyses of artifact distribution and variability.

We have delineated four principal settlement cycles within our survey area.

1) A Formative cycle (*ca.* 800 B.C. to A.D. 0) beginning with the initial occupation by substantial, sedentary communities of ceramics-using people in Middle Formative times, and proceeding through almost a millennium of steady population expansion, elaboration of settlement types, and differentiation into well-defined territorial units. We visualized the end of this cycle in the Texcoco Region (the Terminal Formative period) as representative of the general situation within the Valley of Mexico, with Cuicuilco and Teotihuacan exercising some degree of supra-local dominance in the southwest and northeast sectors, respectively, by virtue of the unique productive capacities and strategic placement of their local environs.

2) A Classic cycle (*ca.* A.D. 0 to 600), initiated by a dramatic population depression within our survey area (possibly beginning as early as Tzacualli times). This marked reduction in both population size and number of sites correlated with the tremendous expansion in size, population, and architectural complexity at Teotihuacan itself. This has led us to suspect that the Texcoco Region, possibly together with much of the entire Valley of Mexico, was incorporated directly into the Teotihuacan state where extreme population nucleation was a primary organizational mechanism. The juncture between the Formative and Classic cycles is of primary significance for it probably witnessed the evolution from a "Chiefdom" to a "State" level of development.

3) A transitional Classic-Postclassic cycle (*ca.* A.D. 650-1150), composed of two very distinctive sub-cycles following in the wake of Teotihuacan's decline and collapse as a principal power center. (*a*) A period

(Early Toltec) of substantial demographic resurgence within the Texcoco Region as large groups of people abandoned the old urban center (now devoid of any political and economic significance beyond the local level), and occupied large, nucleated communities in certain parts of the sparsely populated heartland of Teotihuacan's former domain. A broad occupational gap in the center of the Texcoco Region is perhaps best understood in the context of the emergence of new major power centers at Tula and Cholula, and the creation of a frontier buffer zone in the central Valley of Mexico between their respective spheres of influence. (*b*) Another period (Late Toltec) of temporary severe population decline and extreme ruralization as small communities scattered widely throughout our survey area. We are presently unable to offer a completely satisfactory interpretation of this situation. It is probably relevant, however, that at this point in time the Valley of Mexico reached the nadir of its temporary relegation to secondary status in pan-Mesoamerican affairs in which Tula and Cholula had attained the zenith of their predominance. The sparse, dispersed character of Late Toltec occupation of the Texcoco Region may reflect the location of this area at a point about midway between these two competing principal power centers, in a political no-man's land where large, nucleated communities could not function.

4) A Late Postclassic cycle (*ca.* A.D. 1200 to 1520), characterized by a tremendous expansion of population and great increase in size and number of communities. This is undoubtedly reflective of the reemergence of major power centers within the Valley of Mexico that once again assumed the dominant role in pan-Mesoamerican affairs which had been temporarily lost after the collapse of Teotihuacan. All natural zones (below the Sierra) in our survey area were then heavily occupied. Both the Upper Piedmont and the Lakeshore Plain-Lower Piedmont juncture, that had supported only sparse residential populations in earlier periods, were densely settled. We have hypothesized that large-scale drainage projects secured the tremendous agricultural potential of the Lakeshore Plain for the first time. An elaborate market system, in which all parts of the Valley of Mexico were linked by means of canoe routes across the lake system, permitted an intensification and elaboration of occupational specialization. This would have made possible a relatively dense occupation of agriculturally-marginal zones where full-time attention was focused on a restricted set of resources and productive activities—for example, the cultivation and processing of maguey and nopal in the Upper Piedmont of the Texcoco Region.

PROBLEMS FOR FUTURE RESEARCH

This brief summary can be further amplified by means of outlining a series of problem areas which our survey has defined, and for which we have proposed a variety of hypotheses. Our main objective at this point is to suggest the guidelines and objectives for future research projects that can provide substantive data necessary for testing and elucidating the problems and hypotheses which now present themselves. We need to know considerably more regarding the functions of different kinds of sites and the range of activities that were performed within and between communities. We need specific data bearing on the differential statuses of population groups residing at different localities. We are woefully deficient in our understanding of the full range of exploitative possibilities available to prehispanic populations, and the regional and temporal variability of these possibilities within the Texcoco Region. We have very little data concerning modern land use, demography, and the social and political dimensions of water distribution throughout the modern irrigation systems operating in the survey area. Our information concerning the modification of the landscape during the Colonial and Republican periods is likewise very limited. This latter situation could be partially corrected through an intensive examination of published materials, but only a thorough archival study can provide fully adequate detail.

The research needs we have sketched above fall into four distinct categories: archaeological, environmental, ethnographic, and archival. In reality, all are aspects of a single general problem: the adaptation of human populations to the natural and cultural environment of the Texcoco Region. Ideally, maximal results could be achieved by a group of specialists from several different fields cooperating together, each aware of the interests of the others and of the potential contribution of his own skills to questions being asked by each member of the team. This type of interdisciplinary approach is rare in anthropological research, but can be, and has been, achieved. In concluding this report, we will present a specific set of problems and hypotheses which have developed from our pilot investigations. These should be amenable to clarification and testing through the cooperative efforts of archaeologists, ecologists, geographers, geomorphologists, historians, and ethnographers.

1) The occupation of the Texcoco Region and the Valley of Mexico by nonagricultural peoples, and the transition to economies dependent upon food production. We have contributed nothing to this problem, upon which primary attention has been focused in the Valleys of Tehuacan and Oaxaca to the south. Our survey methodology can only deal with ceramic-using populations, and a whole new body of techniques must be brought to bear on the preceramic era. The paucity of natural caves in this area, where surface formations are wholly volcanic in origin, or derived from volcanic deposits, probably means that there will be considerable difficulty in locating and testing cultural deposits (especially living sites) dating to this early period. The severe erosion on piedmont slopes, and intensive cultivation and residential occupation of much of the Texcoco Region for over two millennia have undoubtedly obscured or obliterated the bulk of preceramic open-air sites. The deep alluvial deposits in the Lakeshore Plain zone, where mammoth bones and associated stone tools have been located at Tepexpan and Ixtapan (e.g. Aveleyra Arroyo de Anda, 1956) probably offer the best opportunity for elucidating the preceramic era in the Texcoco Region. Here it is highly unlikely that standard surface surveys will be at all productive. A starting point might be made by conducting detailed examinations of the many deep drainage ditches throughout this zone for traces of stone tools and skeletal material.

2) The character of Early Formative occupation for the Valley of Mexico as a whole. At present, only two Early Formative sites are known for this entire area: Tlapacoya and Tlatilco. Both are apparently large, architecturally complex, socially differentiated, with abundant stone and ceramic material which is stylistically Olmec. Intensive surface surveys in the Teotihuacan Valley and the Texcoco Region have not located occupations dating to this period. We suspect, as Sanders (1965) has argued, that the southern Valley of Mexico, with its higher precipitation and greater security for rainfall agriculture, will prove to be the focus of Early Formative occupation in this area. We need to know how less-sophisticated Early Formative groups related both to Tlatilco and Tlapacoya, and to the Morelos-Guerrero Region across the main Sierra to the south. We also have very little idea of how Tlatilco

and Tlapacoya were related to one another. Did each stand at the head of a separate "chiefdom" unit involved in a separate set of exchange relationships with groups in Morelos-Guerrero to the south and Toluca-Michoacan-Hidalgo to the west and north? Or, did Tlatilco and Tlapacoya interact cooperatively along the same exchange axis as middlemen or suppliers of specific materials? Were both Tlatilco and Tlapacoya occupied by actual "Olmec" colonists whose main function was to facilitate and maintain the flow of exotic commodities between the western and northern fringes of the Valley of Mexico and the Morelos-Guerrero-Oaxaca area to the south? Or, were the residents of these sites composed of indigenous elites whose status was reinforced and enhanced by their participation in the exchange networks which passed through the Valley of Mexico?

3) The growth of the Tx-MF-13 site as a major population focus in Middle Formative times; the significance of this community in terms of socio-political and economic integration at local and regional levels; the variability in social status of the resident population at Tx-MF-13; and the relationships between the Tx-MF-13 community and the small settlements scattered throughout other parts of the Texcoco Region. The important Tx-MF-13 site should be carefully mapped, systematically surface sampled, and selectively excavated. These investigations should be oriented toward (*a*) precisely delineating the surface area of this site at various stages in its occupational history as a Formative population focus; (*b*) specifying the ranges and proportions of functions and activities carried out within the occupational zone; (*c*) defining the range, variability, and function of architectural types; (*d*) locating a substantial burial population as a means of dealing with the range and variability of rank, status, and social composition within the community; (*e*) recovering items derived from "foreign" areas; (*f*) obtaining remains of faunal and floral products utilized in Middle Formative times at this locality; and (*g*) securing representative pollen sequences from the deep alluvial deposits in this area.

Similarly, more limited programs of surface sampling and selected excavation should be carried out at a number of the small Middle Formative hamlets throughout the survey area. The major objective here would be to ascertain whether some or all of these sites represent small groups of permanent residents engaged in subsistence agriculture and hunting-gathering, or, if they are seasonally- or temporarily-occupied encampments occupied by people exploiting a more limited set of resources (e.g., hunting, collecting, cultivation of maguey-nopal).

4) The processes of accelerating population expansion into the Lower Piedmont zone and the increased differentiation of settlement types which characterize the Late and Terminal Formative periods in our survey area. Could palynological and geomorphological studies demonstrate whether or not there was any significant lowering of the water table in the Tx-MF-13 zone which would have reduced the agricultural productivity of this area after Middle Formative times? Was maize becoming increasingly frost-adapted in Late and Terminal Formative times relative to the Middle Formative period? Was there any marked increase or intensification of local occupational specialization on a community basis during the later part of the Formative era? Perhaps the best localities to attack this latter problem would be the lakeshore settlements at Tx-LF-14 and Tx-TF-46. We have suggested that these occupations represent a completely lacustrine orientation. Can this be demonstrated archaeologically? If so, what was the relationship between lakeshore settlements and agricultural communities in the Lower

Piedmont? Other representative settlement types should be systematically tested in hopes of elucidating the full range of intersite functional and status variability during the Late and Terminal Formative periods.

Important Lower Piedmont sites where Middle, Late, and Terminal Formative occupations are all present (e.g., Tx-LF-12, Tx-TF-17) should be carefully tested in order to (*a*) more accurately delineate the occupational history of these multicomponent sites; (*b*) define the range of functions and activities present at each time period, and their variability through time; and (*c*) reconstruct the evolution of ranking and stratification within the populations of these communities during the long Formative era. Could ceramic chronology and artifact typology be refined and standardized to the point where we could deal effectively with the specifics of the composition and origins of groups that moved from established communities into vacant areas and founded new settlements throughout the long period of demographic expansion in Late and Terminal Formative times?

Ceramic chronology also needs to be refined from the viewpoint of clarifying the status of the Tezoyuca pottery complex (West, 1965; Sanders, 1965). Following Sanders (1965) we have treated it as a contemporary elite facies of the Patlachique assemblage. It is not wholly clear, however, that this is a completely valid procedure. In the Teotihuacan Valley, Terminal Formative hilltop sites quite comparable to our Segregated Elite Districts in the Texcoco Region (Tx-TF-4, -14, -36, and -51) are characterized by ceramics of the Tezoyuca complex. We did not differentiate between the Tezoyuca and Patlachique ceramic complexes in our own surveys, and it is quite probable that the pottery in our Segregated Elite Districts is also of the Tezoyuca complex. If it can be adequately demonstrated that there is little or no temporal overlap between the Tezoyuca and Patlachique ceramic complexes, our interpretation of the Terminal Formative occupation of the Texcoco Region must be substantially modified.

5) Regional sociopolitical structure within the Valley of Mexico on the Tezoyuca-Patlachique horizon. This is a particularly critical problem area as this point in time probably represents the threshold of the first emergence of a true State polity in Mesoamerica. Can broad regional surveys and careful comparative studies of artifact assemblages delineate separate spheres of influence for Cuicuilco and Teotihuacan in the southwestern and northeastern Valley of Mexico, respectively? Also, what was the extent and nature of the relationships between Cuicuilco and Teotihuacan at this time? Can it be demonstrated that these two centers were actively competing for control over large blocks of demographic and natural resources as we have suggested? Is our impression of numerous small, competitive territorial units, of roughly equivalent size and influence, distributed rather evenly and continuously throughout the Valley of Mexico, essentially valid? Could a fine-scale comparative analysis of artifact assemblages from a series of settlement types in each of the four territorial units within our survey area be useful in understanding the extent and character of communication between these units?

6) The temporal and spatial distribution of the Tzacualli ceramic complex in the Valley of Mexico. This is a crucial problem as it was during the Tzacualli phase that Teotihuacan attained the status of a major urban center. It is not at all clear what was happening in other parts of the Valley of Mexico and adjacent parts of central Mexico at this time. We did not encounter much definite Tzacualli material in the Texcoco Region, but we are not particularly confident of our ability to distinguish Tzacualli from Tezoyuca-Patlachique cer-

amics in our badly weathered surface samples. Furthermore, we are uncertain of the significance of the limited quantities of definite Tzacualli pottery which we did locate. Intensified surface collecting and stratigraphic excavations at the several sites in the Texcoco Region (Tx-TF-7, -16, -17, -31, -39, and -42) where both Tezoyuca-Patlachique and Tzacualli ceramics were present might resolve the relationship between these two assemblages in the east-central Valley of Mexico. This relationship must be properly understood before we can be reasonably certain of when Teotihuacan initiated its program of full-scale population concentration, and how large an area was affected by its policies at the end of Terminal Formative times.

7) The integrational and organizational mechanisms by which Teotihuacan extended and sanctioned its influence throughout its 600-year history as a major power center of pan-Mesoamerican significance. This constitutes a problem of major significance for all students of Mesoamerican prehistory. Its satisfactory resolution is dependent upon a wide variety of data from the whole of Mesoamerica. Many interpretations have envisioned Teotihuacan as an essentially theocratic center, whose sanctions were ultimately based on ideological and religious concepts. There can be little doubt that religion was a powerful unifying force at all periods in prehispanic Mesoamerica. We are not entirely convinced, however, that ideological sanctions would have been wholly adequate to underwrite Teotihuacan's impact on Mesoamerica in Classic times.

In the Valley of Mexico we need to know whether the demographic depression in the Texcoco Region at the beginning of our Early Classic period was representative of a general pattern over a broad area, or merely a unique example of extreme population reduction. An attempt should be made to evaluate the possibilities of salvage archaeology in the Atzcapotzalco area. If this cannot be carried out, the status of the Classic center at Atzcapotzalco will remain poorly defined.

The Tx-EC-32, Tx-LC-18 community at Portezuelo along the southern margin of our survey area should be a prime target for intensified surface collecting and selected excavation. What was the density of Classic occupation here? How was this site related to Teotihuacan? What was the range and distribution of occupations, activities, and status positions at the site? Furthermore, can we clarify the relationships between Tx-EC-32 and the small villages and hamlets scattered throughout other parts of the Texcoco Region in Classic times? Were the inhabitants of these latter sites engaged in a variety of specialized exploitations of a restricted set of resources?

Those Terminal Formative sites in the Texcoco Region which continued to be partially occupied in Early Classic times (Tx-TF-11, -17, -19, -31, -33) should be tested in an attempt to elucidate the processes of population decline and displacement during the Terminal Formative-Classic juncture. Such a program might also be capable of detecting significant shifts or continuities in occupational specialization and other activities practiced at such sites from Terminal Formative to Classic levels. It might be demonstrated, for example, that there were marked changes in Terminal Formative and Early Classic architecture at these sites; or, that from a relatively generalized range of activities and occupations on the Terminal Formative level, one or two such activities were greatly elaborated and intensified during Early Classic times. This latter possibility would provide some confirmation of our hypothesis that Classic sites in the Texcoco Region were highly specialized in a particular activity, or set of activities, in line with their incorporation within a State-directed economic network centered on Teotihuacan. Similarly, a demonstration that the Early Classic inhabitants of such sites occupied dwellings of markedly inferior and insubstantial quality relative to that of their Terminal Formative forebearers, might lend some support to our impression (based on the dearth of definite Classic architectural remains on the ground surface) of temporary or seasonal occupation of many Classic sites in our survey area.

One of the most promising possibilities for dealing with the problem of innovations in social structure which occurred in central Mexico during the rise and consolidation of a State polity at Teotihuacan is the analysis of burial populations and their associated artifacts from a variety of sites throughout this region. Few other techniques are so potentially productive with regard to cliciting information on comparative ranking and stratification within contemporary populations and through time. If there were major innovations in status roles and new realignments of social ties accompanying the transition from Formative to Classic in our survey area, a comparison of burials from Terminal Formative and Early Classic occupations in the Texcoco Region should contribute significantly to an understanding of such processes. Classic Portezuelo (Tx-EC-32) and Teotihuacan itself constitute particularly critical sites for such analysis.

8) The decline and collapse of Teotihuacan as a major power center in the seventh and eighth centuries A.D. Can systematic archaeological testing clarify the processes involved in the progressive population decline during Late Classic and Early Toltec times in the broad central sectors of the Texcoco Region? Relative to Early Classic times, is there any indication of a shift in the relationships with Teotihuacan of Late Classic settlements in our survey area? Is there any indication that the influence of Cholula was markedly increasing within the southern end of the Texcoco Region during the Late Classic period? We have very little idea of the character of Cholula as a regional center during Classic times. Before we can really expect to objectively evaluate Cholula's role in central Mexico during the Classic period, we will have to know substantially more regarding its size, complexity, characteristic artifact assemblages, and relationship to Teotihuacan throughout the first millennium A.D. Some attention should also be focused on the character of Classic occupation at Xochicalco and Tula, for which there is presently very little information available. It is highly likely that both Tula and Xochicalco— in addition to the more obvious case of Cholula—had begun to emerge as centers of more than just local importance during the Late Classic period.

If our suggestion that regional population expansion posed a severe strain on Teotihuacan's organizational structure in Late Classic times is to be evaluated, it will be necessary to have relatively complete settlement pattern data from several additional areas in central Mexico. This would be most crucial for the remainder of the Valley of Mexico and adjacent areas in the Tlaxcala-Puebla Basin, the Valley of Morelos, the Toluca Basin, and southern Hidalgo.

9) The configuration of regional sociopolitical alignments in central Mexico during the Early Postclassic (our Early Toltec and Late Toltec periods), and the contrast between basic organizational and integrative mechanisms of Classic and Postclassic polities in nuclear Mesoamerica. This was an era which saw the emergence of principal pan-Mesoamerican power centers on the peripheries of the Valley of Mexico. For several centuries this latter area apparently existed as a politically-fragmented buffer zone lying between competing centers to the north (Tula), southeast (Cholula), and southwest (Xochical-

co). We know very little concerning the relationships between these three Postclassic centers. The patterns and processes of their growth and occupational history remain very obscure. There is very little published data relevant to their impact on settlement distribution in central Mexico. There is still only a minimal quantity of published information concerning the specific distribution and chronological sequence of artifact assemblages at Tula, Cholula, and Xochicalco. Until at least the general outlines of all these problems are made clear, the interpretation of Early and Late Toltec settlement patterns in the Texcoco Region can advance but little beyond the impressionistic and conjectural stage.

Within our survey area two problems stand out as particularly crucial to an understanding of the Early Postclassic period. First, how do the three primary centers of the Early Toltec period (Tx-ET-4, -7, and -18) relate to Teotihuacan, on the one hand, and to Tula and Cholula, on the other? Would it be possible to demonstrate, as we have suggested, that these centers were founded by large blocks of population which had emigrated from a declining Teotihuacan whose rapidly deteriorating power and influence no longer warranted a huge, densely nucleated demographic base after A.D. 700? Could the status of our hypothetical political frontier in the broad central sector of the Texcoco Region be clarified by showing that Tx-ET-4 and Tx-ET-7 were more closely linked to Tula, while Tx-ET-18 was similarly oriented toward Cholula?

Second, what processes were involved in the great demographic depression and population dispersal which occurred in Late Toltec times in the Texcoco Region? A clarification of the relationship between the Coyotlatelco and Mazapan ceramic complexes is critical in this regard. The large Early Toltec communities at Tx-ET-4, -7, and -18 should be carefully mapped and surface sampled to more accurately delineate the distribution of Early Toltec and Late Toltec ceramic complexes. Smaller sites of both periods should also be systematically tested to determine the range and variation of activities and occupational specializations through time and space. If characteristic Late Toltec pottery (i.e., the Mazapan complex) could be consistently associated with specific functions and activities which seldom or never appeared at the Early Toltec level (as defined by the presence of Coyotlatelco pottery), the argument for partial chronological overlap between the two ceramic assemblages would be somewhat strengthened. Stratigraphic excavations at Tx-ET-4, -7, and -18 should be especially productive with respect to the chronological relationships between Coyotlatelco and Mazapan pottery, and should also permit a considerable refining of Early Toltec ceramic chronology (principally the relationship between the Coyotlatelco and Oxtotipac complexes).

We have suggested that a marked population decline in Late Toltec times in the Texcoco Region was largely the product of (*a*) the continued presence and stabilization of a political frontier across this area between hostile major centers at Tula and Cholula, and (*b*) a further decline in the regional influence of Teotihuacan and other power centers in the Valley of Mexico relative to the Early Toltec period. The net effects of these processes would have been (*a*) continuation of the impossibility for sedentary agriculturalists living in large communities to exploit much of the Texcoco Region; and (*b*) an intensified outward flow of local populations toward the zones of greater security and improved economic possibilities within the direct spheres of influence of Tula, Cholula, and other major urban centers to the north and south. If these hypotheses are essentially valid, we might expect (*a*) to identify most of the small Late Toltec sites in the central sector of our survey area as temporarily-occupied hunting-gathering camps, and (*b*) to find evidence of substantial population expansion in and around the major urban centers at Tula and Cholula during Late Toltec times.

10) The implications of the tremendous demographic expansion which was initiated during Early Aztec times in our survey area, with rapid acceleration to a prehispanic (and probably an all-time) peak in the Late Aztec period. This process in the Texcoco Region parallels a very similar population spiral in the adjacent Teotihuacan Valley. It is quite apparent that this impressive demographic recovery in the eastern Valley of Mexico must be understood in the general framework of the reemergence of principal pan-Mesoamerican power centers in the Valley of Mexico after about A.D. 1200. At present we understand very little of the relationship between the rapid development of new Early Aztec centers in the Valley of Mexico at Huexotla (Tx-A-87), Coatlinchan (Tx-A-88), Culhuacan, Chalco, Xaltocan, Atzcapotzalco, Xochimilco, Tenayuca, etc., on the one hand, and the relative decline in regional influence of the major Early Postclassic centers at Tula, Cholula, and Xochicalco, on the other.

We regard this as a logical and expectable process whereby major power foci gravitated back to a key area of high ecological potential following an era of temporary political fragmentation which had been set in motion by the collapse of Teotihuacan and the disintegration of the political and economic alignments that structured Mesoamerican civilization during the Classic period. However, the specifics of this process remain in the realm of speculation. Full-scale research programs should be directed toward an analysis of the Late Toltec-Early Aztec juncture at Cholula, Tula, Xochicalco, and several Valley of Mexico centers (Tenayuca and Teotihuacan, both with substantial Toltec and Aztec components, offer ideal locations in this regard). Within the Texcoco Region itself there apparently was no Late Toltec settlement of any size that expanded into an important Aztec community in Early Aztec times. Huexotla (Tx-A-87)—with most of the prehispanic site situated in agricultural fields and pasture lands well south of the modern village—offers the best locality in the survey area at which to investigate the general problems of Aztec urbanization. Intensive mapping, and systematic surface collecting and excavation throughout the Tx-A-87 urban zone would be highly productive. By contrast, Coatlinchan (Tx-A-88) and Chimalhuacan (Tx-A-109) are now largely covered with dense modern settlement. Much of Texcoco (Tx-A-56) and Chiautla (lying between our northern and central survey strips) seem to lie buried beneath alluvium at the Lower Piedmont-Lakeshore Plain juncture, where modern occupation is likewise very heavy. Tepetlaoxtoc (Tx-A-24), together with representative rural communities should also be carefully tested in order to accurately characterize the growth of these settlements from small villages or scattered hamlets in Early Aztec times to large villages and (in the case of Tepetlaoxtoc) a primary regional center in the Late Aztec period.

We have suggested, or implied, that population within both the Texcoco Region and the entire Valley of Mexico had attained such high levels in the Lake Aztec period that all exploitative niches were being fully utilized. This undoubtedly entailed a maximization of agricultural and nonagricultural possibilities, together with an intensification of occupational specialization and symbiosis at local and regional levels. In this regard, we have put forth a series of specific hypotheses that should be further tested.

First, in the Aztec period the great agricultural potential of the lowlying Lakeshore Plain was secured for the first time by means of massive drainage projects. The distribution of Aztec population throughout our survey area strongly suggests this. It will be necessary to substantiate this impression through a demonstration that agricultural plots were actually present in this zone for the first time during the Aztec period. Intensive modern cultivation has apparently obliterated all traces of ancient field patterns on the ordinary airphotos available to us. These patterns, however, might emerge on color airphotos taken at several different points in an annual cycle. Infra-red photography might be even more productive in this regard. Would palynological and paleo-pedological studies be helpful in ascertaining when the Lakeshore Plain was first cultivated on a significant basis? What is the antiquity of the present system of drainage ditches which cover the Lakeshore Plain? Could an exhaustive survey along these ditch systems reveal structural remains or refuse deposits which could be associated with the earliest construction or use of the drainage system? Would resistivity techniques be at all useful in detecting regular patterns of subsurface differences in soil density and humidity which could be attributed to buried ditches and ridge fields?

Second, the substantial Late Aztec population in the Upper Piedmont zone of the Texcoco Region was specialized in the cultivation of maguey and nopal on terraced hillslopes. The manufacture of pulque, and processing of a variety of other products (e.g., preparing and spinning maguey fiber) from these important domestic plants probably constituted another major category of activities in this area. These same communities would also have had ready access to a variety of wood products from the heavily forested slopes of the Sierra immediately to the east. Representative sites in the Upper Piedmont zone should be carefully tested in an attempt to delineate the distribution and preponderance of these occupations. Heavy concentrations of obsidian scrapers on some sites, for example, would suggest that the manufacture of pulque was important, while large numbers of spindle whorls would be indicative of the importance of spinning. Some effort should also be made to determine whether the date of construction and primary utilization of the innumerable abandoned terrace systems throughout the Upper Piedmont could be adequately fixed in time?

Third, communities at and near the lakeshore were oriented toward the exploitation of lacustrine resources on at least a part-time or seasonal basis. Salt-making, hunting water fowl, collecting lake plants, and fishing could all have been profitable in this zone. Could a systematic testing program identify the range and distribution of activities within representative lakeshore settlements? Were these settlements occupied on a seasonal basis by people who engaged in other activities throughout the rest of an annual cycle? Or, was residence on a year-round basis by full-time lacustrine specialists?

Fourth, urban centers were the foci of two basic types of redistributive networks: (*a*) periodic markets, in which a wide variety of raw materials, staple foodstuffs, and finished products were exchanged; and (*b*) tributary obligations in goods and services which were channeled into public works and support of State-level ceremonial and civic apparatus. Large-scale excavations—now possible only at Huexotla (Tx-A-87) and Tepetlaoxtoc (Tx-A-24)—might be successful in revealing complexes identifiable as market places, secular palaces, and temple precincts where quantities of goods were stockpiled for exchange and redistribution. Such excavations might also enable us to delineate the full range and distribution of occupations, social status, and *barrio* or *calpulli* alignment within the Huexotla and Tepetlaoxtoc urban communities. Selective excavation and surface collecting should likewise be extended to representative rural communities for purposes of comparing the range and variability of occupations and social status in urban and rural settlements.

11) The full range and distribution of natural resources and microenvironmental niches throughout all periods of the prehispanic era in the Texcoco Region. What have been the salient characteristics and changes through time in annual precipitation, soil fertility, water table behavior, location and flow of springs, surface runoff, down-cutting and sheet erosion, and alluviation? Would it be possible, through palynological studies, to reconstruct the succession of floral regimes in this area? The ultimate objectives here, of course, are (*a*) to establish the correlation between settlement configuration and critical environmental characteristics at different points in time, and (*b*) to supplement archaeological evidence relative to resource utilization.

12) Modern land use and resource exploitation in all environmental niches throughout the Texcoco Region. Of paramount interest here are (*a*) the sociopolitical dimensions of water distribution through the still-functioning networks of irrigation canals; (*b*) the techniques of traditional cultivation systems; (*c*) the relative productivity of different kinds of agricultural lands and cultivation systems where relatively traditional technologies are still employed; and (*d*) the techniques and possibilities of traditional nonagricultural exploitations (e.g., wood-cutting in the Sierra, salt-making along the lakeshore, hunting and gathering in the Sierra and lakeshore zones). Such ethnographic data would be invaluable in understanding the configuration of prehispanic settlement with respect to both productive potentials and inter-community relationships.

13) The utilization of the Texcoco Region throughout the historic and late prehispanic periods as revealed through archival studies. What documentation can be brought to bear on the specific changes in exploitative patterns which became established after the Spanish Conquest? Was there a marked shift, as seems likely, from predominately intensive agriculture in late prehispanic times to a predominately extensive system of plow agriculture and herding in the Colonial period? Is there any documentary evidence bearing on the initiation and progress of severe sheet erosion and down cutting which has led to the extremely eroded condition of most sloping ground in the Texcoco Region at the present time? Is there any documentation bearing on the problem of terrace construction, modification of the irrigation networks, and drainage of the Lakeshore Plain in historic times?

APPENDIX I

CERAMIC MARKERS USED FOR PERIOD DESIGNATIONS

Richard E. Blanton
Jeffrey R. Parsons

INTRODUCTION

Our ceramic chronology is not intended to be as precise or specific as those recently presented by several investigators (e.g., Bennyhoff, 1966; Mueller, 1966; Sanders, 1965). This is primarily due to two considerations: (1) the fine-scale chronologies most recently defined have not yet been fully published; and (2) many of the phases and sub-phases that have been recognized are based on fine distinctions in form and decoration which have been obscured or totally obliterated in our badly weathered surface samples in which sherds are usually quite small. Therefore, at this stage, we have not attempted to refine our dating of sites below the level of 200- to 300-year periods. We feel this is realistic in view of the limitations of our surface samples, and adequate to permit the meaningful delineation of major patterns of settlement distribution through time. Our time periods are thus defined by constellations of ceramic types that consistently occur together and form distinctive stylistic units.

The reader should be aware of the limitations of our ceramic typology. Unless otherwise noted, all pottery described and illustrated is from type samples selected from our 1967 surface collections in the Texcoco Region. The only major exception is the Aztec-period material, for which the illustrations and descriptions have been adapted from previously prepared analyses of Teotihuacan Valley ceramics (Parsons, 1966). Our surface collecting in the Texcoco Region was oriented toward obtaining chronological information, and for this reason we selected only rim sherds and decorated body sherds. Several hundred collections were made, from which a few hundred type sherds (upon which our descriptions are based) were hastily selected at the end of the field season for shipment to the University of Michigan Museum of Anthropology. In selecting these type sherds, we attempted to include a full range of the most diagnostic vessel forms and decorative variants. It must be emphasized, however, that this was done quickly, with no systematic selection procedures beyond that of simple "eye-balling." Thus, we have little to contribute in the way of quantitative data beyond simple subjective impressions of those types that were more or less common, and to what extent certain categories of ceramics are differentially distributed.

We have made no attempt to describe the complete ceramic assemblages for each time period. Rather, we have restricted our attention to those ceramic types which proved most useful to us in evaluating site chronology from badly weathered surface collections of small sherds. Our most deficient category is Classic-period decorated pottery. Surface color has been related, as closely as possible, to color categories defined on the *Munsell Soil Color Charts* (1954). We have often used the term "sand and pumice" to characterize the general appearance of tempering material. In this context, "sand" refers to a combination of small, angular quartz (or quartzite) fragments, together with irregular pieces of pinkish and black material. "Pumice" refers to small chunks of soft, porous volcanic material, generally black, red, orange, or white in color. We have generally limited our comparisons to published descriptions of ceramic material from the Valley of Mexico and its immediate environs.

Explanatory note for illustrations of ceramic material which follow:

UMMA = University of Michigan Museum of Anthropology

PSUDA = Pennsylvania State University Department of Anthropology

Middle Formative

I. Plainware

A. Utilitarian Ware

1. Ollas (Fig. 49): Lips are bolstered, everted, or direct. Rim diameters vary from 12 to 42 cms. Wall thickness below the rim ranges between 0.4 and 0.9 cms.

Paste—Proportion of temper ranges from 30 to 50 per cent. Temper consists mainly of pumice and sand. Color is reddish-brown, or buff, often with a gray, gray-brown, or gray-black core. Texture is compact. Air bubbles are occasionally abundant.

Exterior surface—The most common color is a reddish-brown (5YR 4/3, 5/3, 5/4, and 2.5YR 5/4, 4/4); also noted were gray (5YR 5/1), pinkish gray (7.5YR 7/2), light brown (7.5YR 6/4), brown (7.5YR 5/4, 5/2), and dark brown (7.5YR 4/2). Most sherds are burnished, with rough horizontal burnish streaks common. Some vessels are apparently unburnished, with rough finish.

Interior surface—For the most part the interior and exterior surfaces of olla necks are identical. Occasionally a reddish slip or paint was noted on the neck interior or around the edge of the rim interior.

Comparisons—Vaillant's (1930) Bay Ware ollas of his Early and Middle Periods at Zacatenco are essentially identical to our ollas. In particular the rim forms illustrated on his Pl. I, *u, v, y,* and *z* and Pl. III, *l, t,* and *w* duplicate material illustrated in this report. Piña Chan (1958) illustrates material from Tlatilco which is similar to our Plainware ollas: his *Café Rojizo (Bayo)* ollas (1958: Fig. 8, *p, q,* and *u*); *Café Obscuro* ollas (ibid: Fig. 9, *a, b;* Fig. 22, *o, p;* Fig. 36, *a-f;* Fig. 45, *a, b, c, d, f*); *Café Claro* ollas (ibid: Fig. 10, *d;* Fig. 21, *x;* Fig. 22, *d;* Fig. 39, *a-d, f-j*); and *Café Negruzco* ollas (ibid: Fig. 33, *a, b, d, e*).

2. Basins (Fig. 50): Forms include shouldered basins, incurved basins, and everted-rim basins. Rim diameters range from 8 to 34 cms, with most measuring between 20 and 34 cms. Wall thickness below the rim varies between 0.4 and 1.1 cms.

Paste—Proportion of temper ranges between 30 and 50 per cent. Temper is comprised mainly of pumice and sand. Color is buff, gray-buff, orange-buff, or dark brown, often with a gray or gray-black medial area. Texture is compact.

Exterior surface—Some sherds may have a weak red (10R 4/3) or reddish brown (2.5YR 5/4, 4/4, and 5YR 5/4) paint or slip. Other colors noted include dark reddish-gray (5YR 4/2), brown (7.5YR 5/4), and dark brown (7.5YR 4/2). Finish ranges from rough horizontal burnish to fairly smooth horizontal burnish.

Interior surface—Predominant colors are reddish-brown (2.5YR 5/4 and 4/4.) light brown (7.5YR 6/4), brown (7.5YR 5/4), and dark gray (10YR 4/1). Forms with everted rims may show a red paint (10R 4/3) on the lip surface. Surface finish generally identical to the exterior.

Comparisons—Vaillant's Undecorated cajete from his Middle Period at Zacatenco (1930: Pl. III, *x*) corresponds to our material, as do Piña Chan's *Rojizo (Bayo)* (1958: Fig. 8, *h, k;* Fig. 20, *d, k, n, v;* Fig. 45, *n*), *Café Claro* (ibid: Fig. 21, *l, m;* Fig. 39, *p*), and *Café Obscuro* (ibid: Fig. 36, 9) cajetes from Tlatilco.

3. Tecomate (*Fig. 50*): Rim diameter ranges from 8 to 20 cms, and occasionally as large as 30 cms. Wall thickness below the rim varies between 0.6 and 1.5 cms.

Paste—Temper consists of sand and pumice, and its proportion is usually from 25

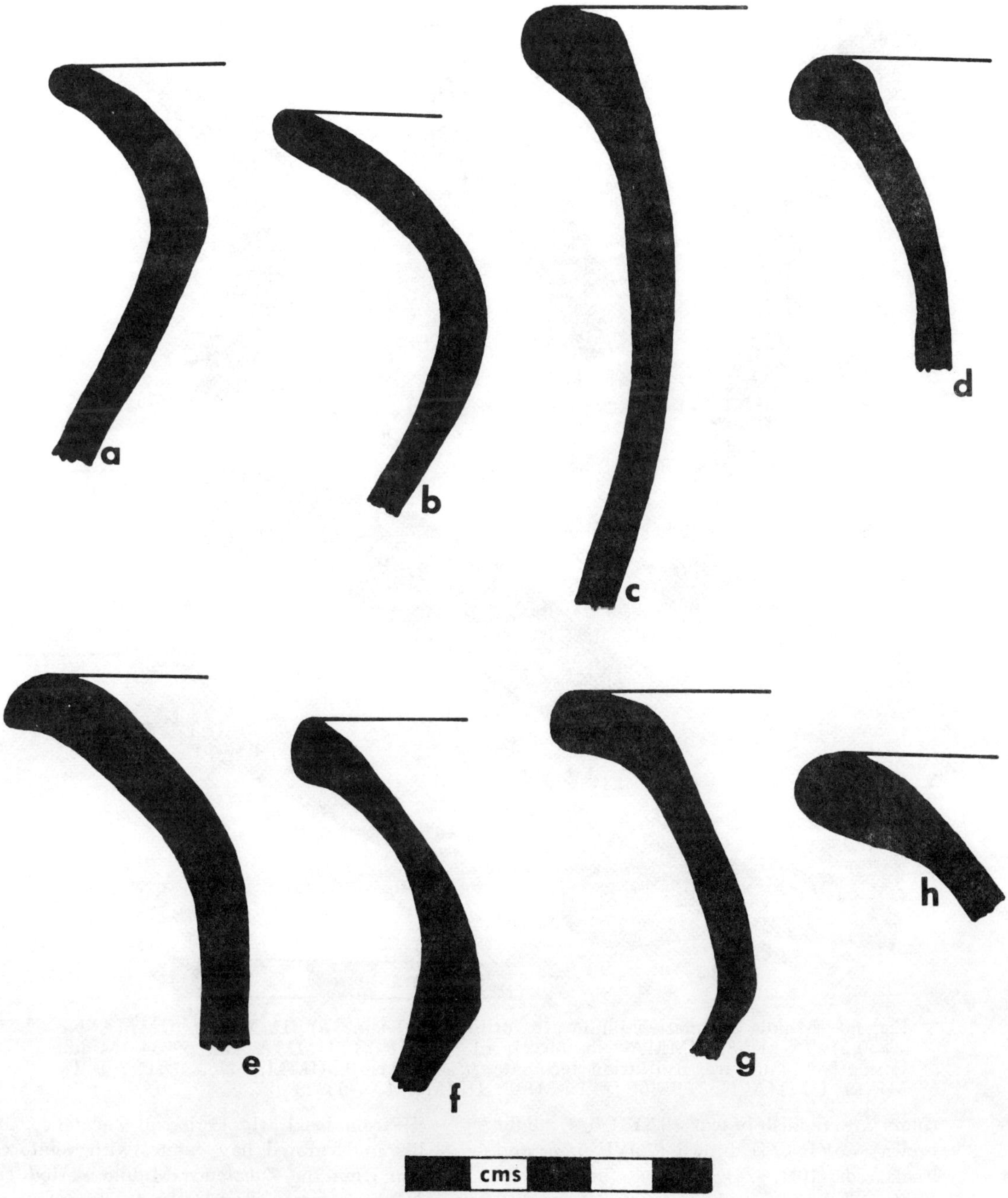

Fig. 49—Middle Formative plainware, utilitarian olla: *a*) Tx-MF-13, UMMA No. 59833; *b*) Tx-MF-13, UMMA No. 59836; *c*) Tx-MF-13, UMMA No. 59834; *d*) Tx-MF-8, UMMA No. 59827; *e*) Tx-MF-13, UMMA No. 59834; *f*) Tx-MF-13, UMMA No. 59836; *g*) Tx-MF-13, UMMA No. 59835; *h*) Tx-MF-13, UMMA No. 59826.

to 35 per cent. Some sherds contain elongated black crystalline material which may be hornblende. Color is usually orange-buff or gray, often with a gray medial area. Texture is compact.

Exterior surface—Vessels with exterior ledges may have a weak red paint or slip on the ledge surface (10R 4/4). Predominant

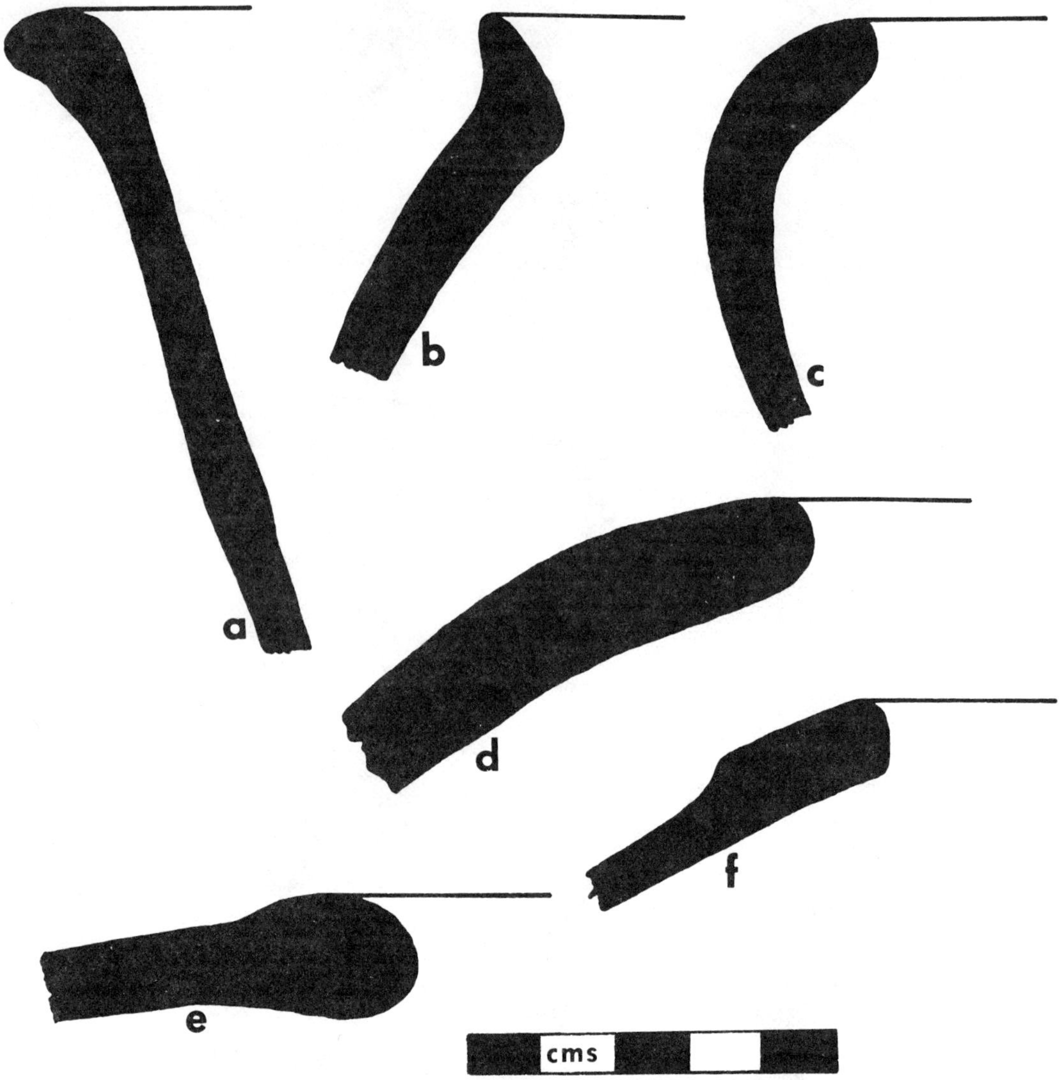

Fig. 50—Middle Formative plainware, utilitarian basin: *a*) Tx-MF-10, UMMA No. 59830;*b*) Tx-MF-8, UMMA No. 59827; *c*) Tx-MF-13, UMMA No. 59834. Middle Formative plainware, utilitarian tecomate: *d*) Tx-MF-9, UMMA No, 59841; *e*) Tx-MF-13, UMMA No. 59836; *f*) Tx-MF-7, UMMA No. 59828.

colors are reddish-brown (2.5YR 5/4), light brown (7.5YR 6/4), brown (7.5YR 5/2), and weak red (10R 5/4). Surface finish is by horizontal burnish, which ranges in quality from rough to fairly smooth.

Interior surface—No painted surfaces could be detected. Color ranges from reddish-brown to brown (as exterior). In general, interior surface finish tends to be rougher than that of exterior.

Comparisons—Vaillant's (1930) undecorated bay bowl, with restricted mouth (Pl. I, *n*) from his Early Period at Zacatenco, and his undecorated bay cajete, with reinforced rim from the Zacatenco Middle Period (Pl. III, *z*) correspond closely to our tecomate form. The tecomate forms illustrated by Piña Chan (1958: Fig. 8, *g;* Fig. 9, *a, b;* Fig. 33, *n, ñ;* Fig. 45, *o*) are also comparable to our material.

II. Decorated Ware

A. Service Ware

1. Cream Slipped Incised (*Figs. 51, 52*): Form variants include vessels with flaring,

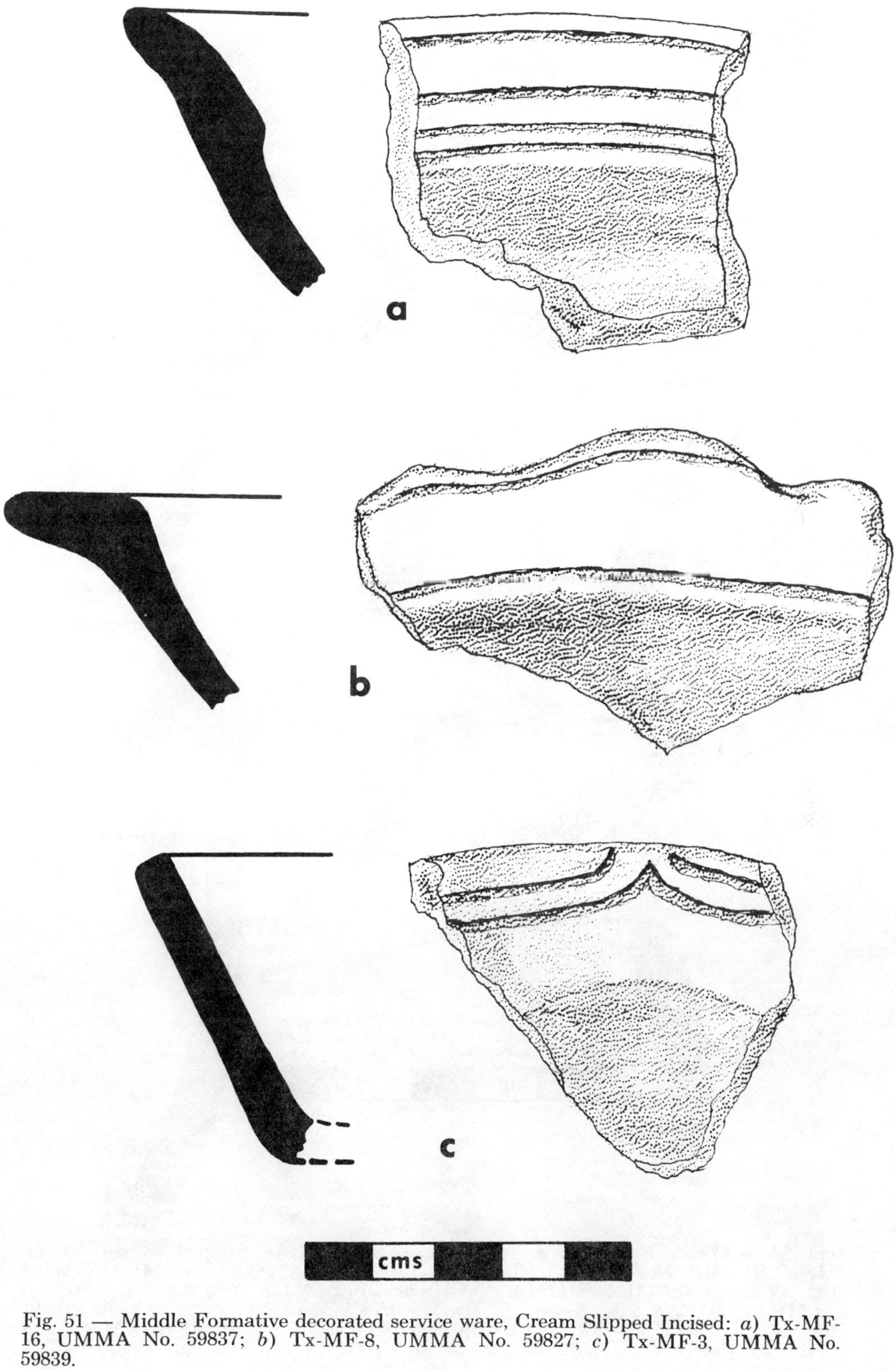

Fig. 51 — Middle Formative decorated service ware, Cream Slipped Incised: *a*) Tx-MF-16, UMMA No. 59837; *b*) Tx-MF-8, UMMA No. 59827; *c*) Tx-MF-3, UMMA No. 59839.

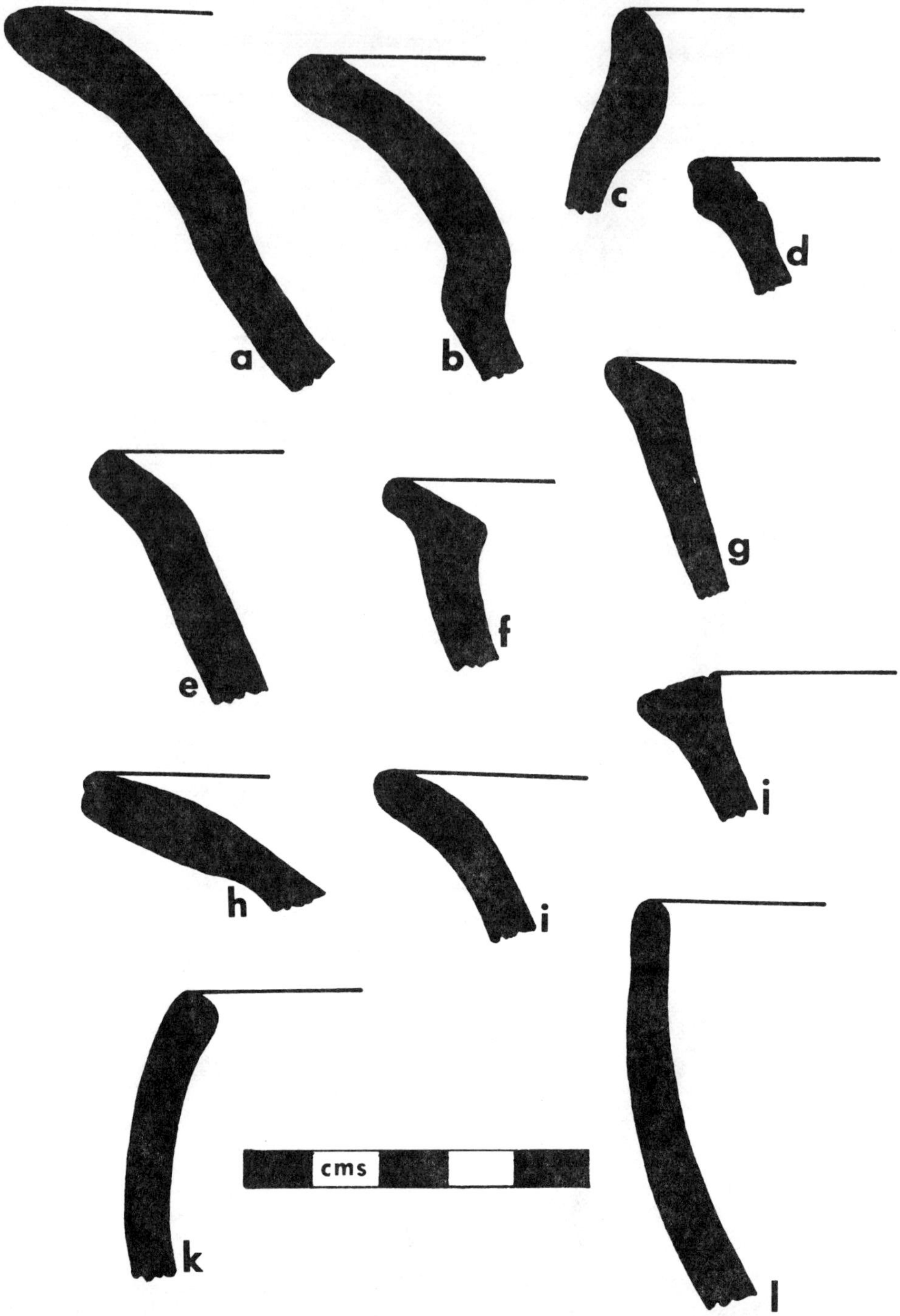

Fig. 52 — Middle Formative decorated service ware, Cream Slipped Incised: *a*) Tx-MF-13, UMMA No. 59831; *b*) Tx-MF-1, UMMA No. 59825;*c*) Tx-MF-1, UMMA No. 59825; *d*) Tx-MF-5, UMMA No, 59829; *e*) Tx-MF-8, UMMA No. 59827; *f*) Tx-MF-13, UMMA No. 59834; *g*) Tx-MF-3, UMMA No. 59839; *h*) Tx-MF-13, UMMA No. 59831; *i*) Tx-MF-13, UMMA No. 59831; *j*) Tx-MF-8, UMMA No. 59827; *k*) Tx-MF-13, UMMA No. 59834; *l*) Tx-MF-13, UMMA No. 59834.

incurved, and upright walls, which may occur with interior ledges, bevelled lips, wavy rims, and with widely spaced tabs around the edges of the rim. Most vessels have two parallel horizontal incised lines on or near the lip. Rim diameters range from 12 to 36 cms. Wall thickness below the rim varies between 0.4 and 1.3 cms. This type proved to be the single most useful ceramic marker for the Middle Formative period in our survey area.

Paste—Temper consists of pumice and sand, and its proportion ranges between 15 and 40 per cent. Color is buff, orange-buff, or dark brown, often with a darker medial area. Texture is compact.

Exterior surface—Where paint has been preserved the entire surface is usually white (10YR 8/2), although very pale brown (10YR 8/3, 8/4) and pinkish (7.5YR 8/4) also occur. Where paint has been worn off, colors of the natural clay surface include reddish-brown (2.5YR 5/4, 4/4, and 5YR 5/3, 5/4), dark reddish-gray (5YR 4/2), brown (7.5YR 5/4), and weak red (10R 4/4). The cream slip is usually thickly applied, and generally crackled. In most cases it has been applied to the entire exterior surface. Finish is by horizontal burnishing, which is usually of a smooth quality.

Interior surface—The entire surface has been slipped. Where the slip is preserved, the dominant color is white, with a few examples of pale brown and pinkish (as above). Where the slip has been worn away, color is like exterior surface. Finish is generally identical to that of the exterior or is somewhat smoother.

Comparisons—This ceramic type is found over a large part of Mesoamerica on the Middle Formative horizon. There are strong ties with the Incised White Ware Tradition of coastal Guatemala (Coe and Flannery, 1967: 42), and with similar types in the Tehuacan Valley, Grijalva Depression, Monte Alban, and the northern Gulf Coast (ibid). In the Valley of Mexico very similar, or identical, material has been illustrated by Piña Chan (1958: Fig. 12, *d, i, k;* Fig. 38, *b, g, h*) from Tlatilco, and by Vaillant (1930: Pl. II, *a, b, e, f*) from his Early Period at Zacatenco.

2. White-on-Red (*Fig.* 53): Decoration has been badly obscured by erosion, and generally little more can be seen apart from vestiges of white over red paint. Rim diameter averages about 20 cms. Wall thickess below the rim is about 0.7 cms. One annular base was noted in our type collection.

Paste—Temper consists mainly of pumice and sand, and its proportion is about 30 to 35 per cent. Color is buff. Texture is compact.

Exterior surface—Vestiges of red paint are generally in the 10R 4/3 category, while the overlying white paint usually corresponds to 10YR 8/2. Surfaces have been smoothly burnished.

Interior surface — Most of this area is red (10R 4/3), occasionally with a band of white paint (10YR 8/2) around the rim. Surface is smoothly burnished.

Comparisons—Vaillant's White Ware category (1930: Pl. II) includes White-on-Red vessels which are generally similar in appearance to our material, although his vessels have predominantly interior decoration, while ours have most of their painted decoration on the exterior wall. Some of the *Blanco sobre Rojo* material from Tlatilco illustrated by Piña Chan (1958: Fig. 13, *a, f;* Fig. 29, *a, b, g;* Fig. 42, *g*) is somewhat comparable to our Texcocan sherds.

3. Red-on-White (*Fig. 53*): All vessels are flaring bowls with interior ledges. Some may have parallel horizontal lines incised on the lip. One notched rim form was noted. Rim diameter ranges from 24 to 44 cms. Wall thickness varies between 0.4 and 1.1 cms. Character of decoration has been badly obscured by weathering.

Paste—Temper consists mostly of pumice and sand, and occurs in a proportion of roughly 25 to 30 per cent. Predominant colors include dark gray-brown, dark brown, buff, and reddish-buff, often with a gray core. Texture is compact.

Exterior surface—May be either slipped in white (10YR 8/2) or pale brown (10YR 8/3), or unslipped. In the latter case the predominant color is reddish-brown (5YR 5/3), and brown (7.5YR 5/4). No red decoration was observed. Surface finish is horizontal burnish, which varies from fairly rough to fairly smooth.

Interior surface—Entire surface has been slipped with white, over which red designs have been placed. Design motifs are now so badly weathered that the original patterns are not clear. Red designs usually seem to

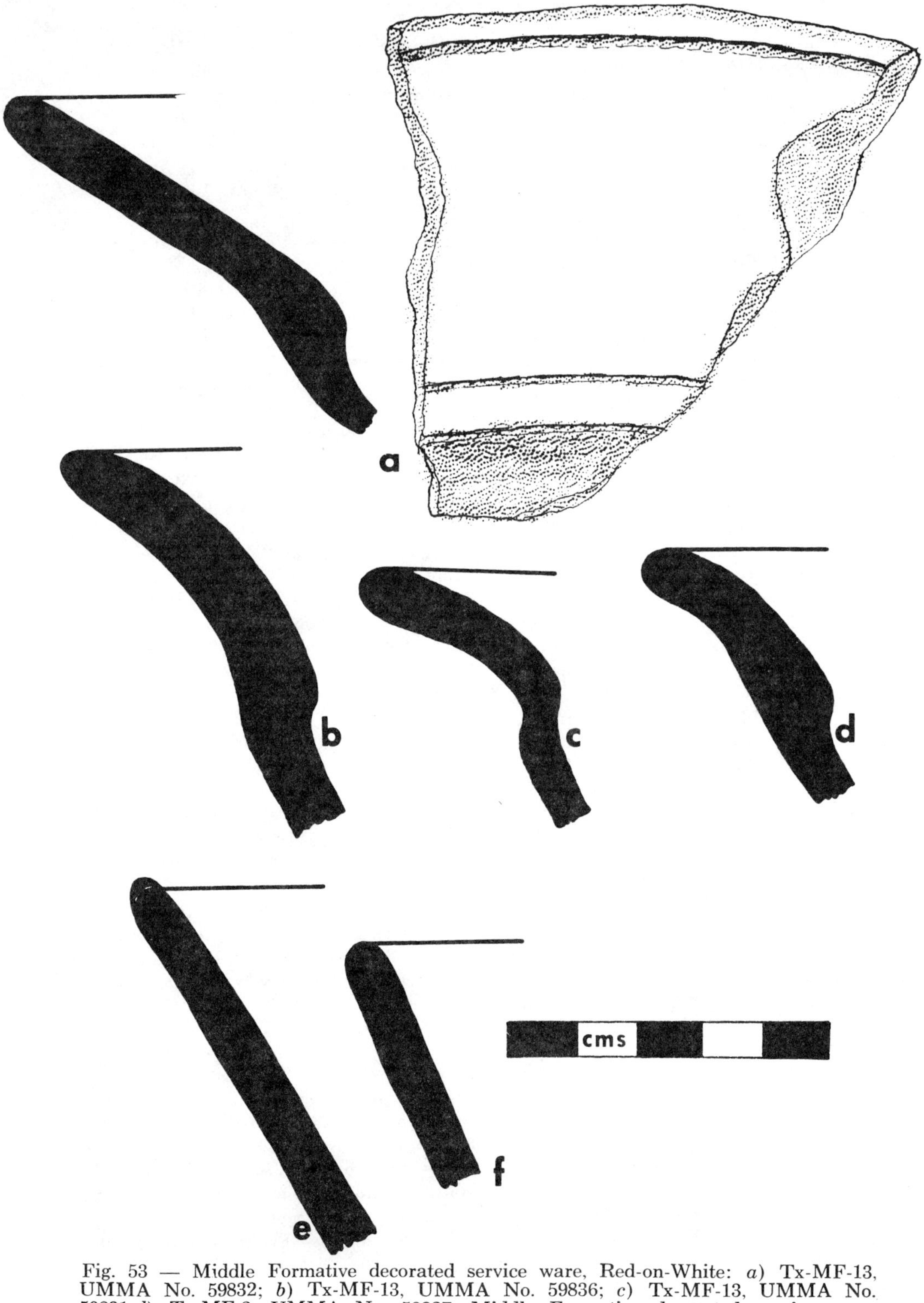

Fig. 53 — Middle Formative decorated service ware, Red-on-White: *a*) Tx-MF-13, UMMA No. 59832; *b*) Tx-MF-13, UMMA No. 59836; *c*) Tx-MF-13, UMMA No. 59831;*d*) Tx-MF-8, UMMA No. 59827. Middle Formative decorated service ware, White-on-Red: *e*) Tx-MF-7, UMMA No. 59828; *f*) Tx-MF-7, UMMA No. 59828.

occur on the upper part of the wall. Surface finish as on exterior.

Comparisons — Some of the *Rojo sobre Blanco* material from Tlatilco illustrated by Piña Chan (1958: Fig. 28, *a*) is quite similar. Vaillant's Red-on-White ware from his Middle Period at Zacatenco (1930: Pl. V, *a-e*) is generally comparable to our material, although his red designs are more geometric than ours appear to be.

Late Formative

I. Plainware

A. Utilitarian Ware

1. Ollas (*Fig. 54*): Rim diameter ranges from 10 to 40 cms. Wall thickness below the rim measures between 0.5 and 1.5 cms.

Paste—Temper comprised of pumice and sand, together with small chunks of obsidian or hornblende. Proportion of temper ranges from 15 to 35 per cent. Color is generally buff, gray-buff, orange-buff, gray, and occasionally brick red, often with a gray-black core. Large air bubbles are sometimes present. Texture is compact.

Exterior surface—A few sherds had traces of bands of red paint (10R 4/3, 4/4, 4/8)

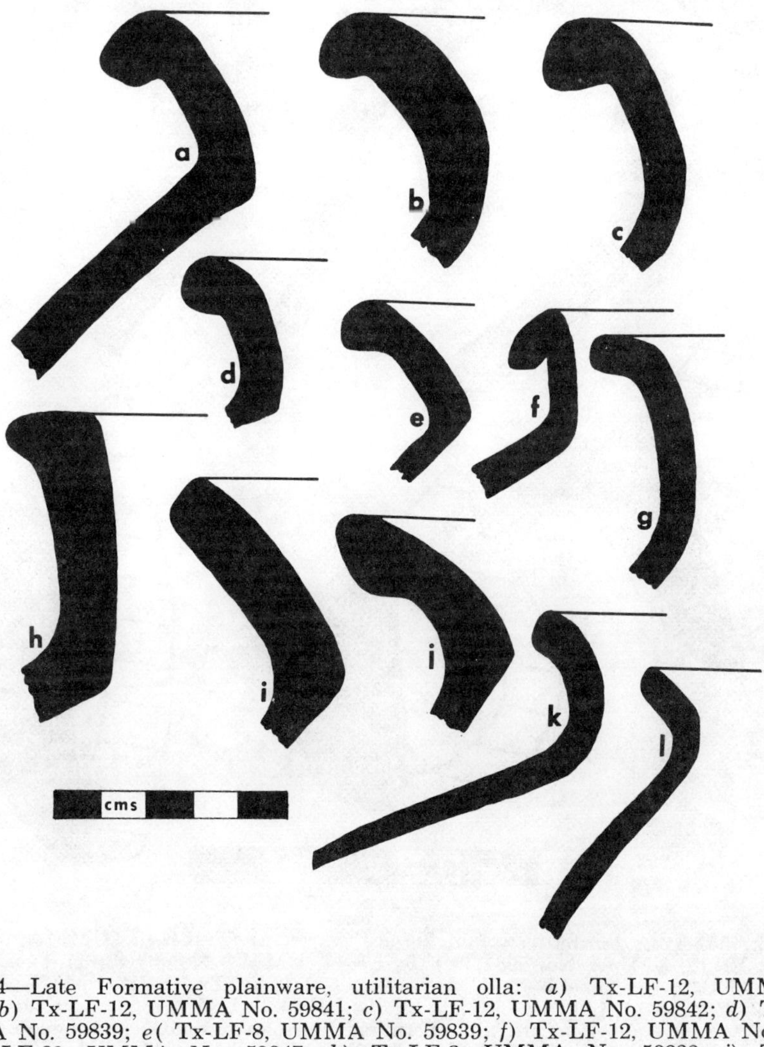

Fig. 54—Late Formative plainware, utilitarian olla: *a*) Tx-LF-12, UMMA No. 59841; *b*) Tx-LF-12, UMMA No. 59841; *c*) Tx-LF-12, UMMA No. 59842; *d*) Tx-LF-8, UMMA No. 59839; *e*(Tx-LF-8, UMMA No. 59839; *f*) Tx-LF-12, UMMA No. 59840; *g*) Tx-LF-23, UMMA No. 59847; *h*) Tx-LF-8, UMMA No. 59838; *i*) Tx-LF-8, UMMA No. 59838; *j*) Tx-LF-8, UMMA No. 59838; *k*) Tx-LF-23, UMMA No. 59847; *l*) Tx-LF-23, UMMA No. 59847.

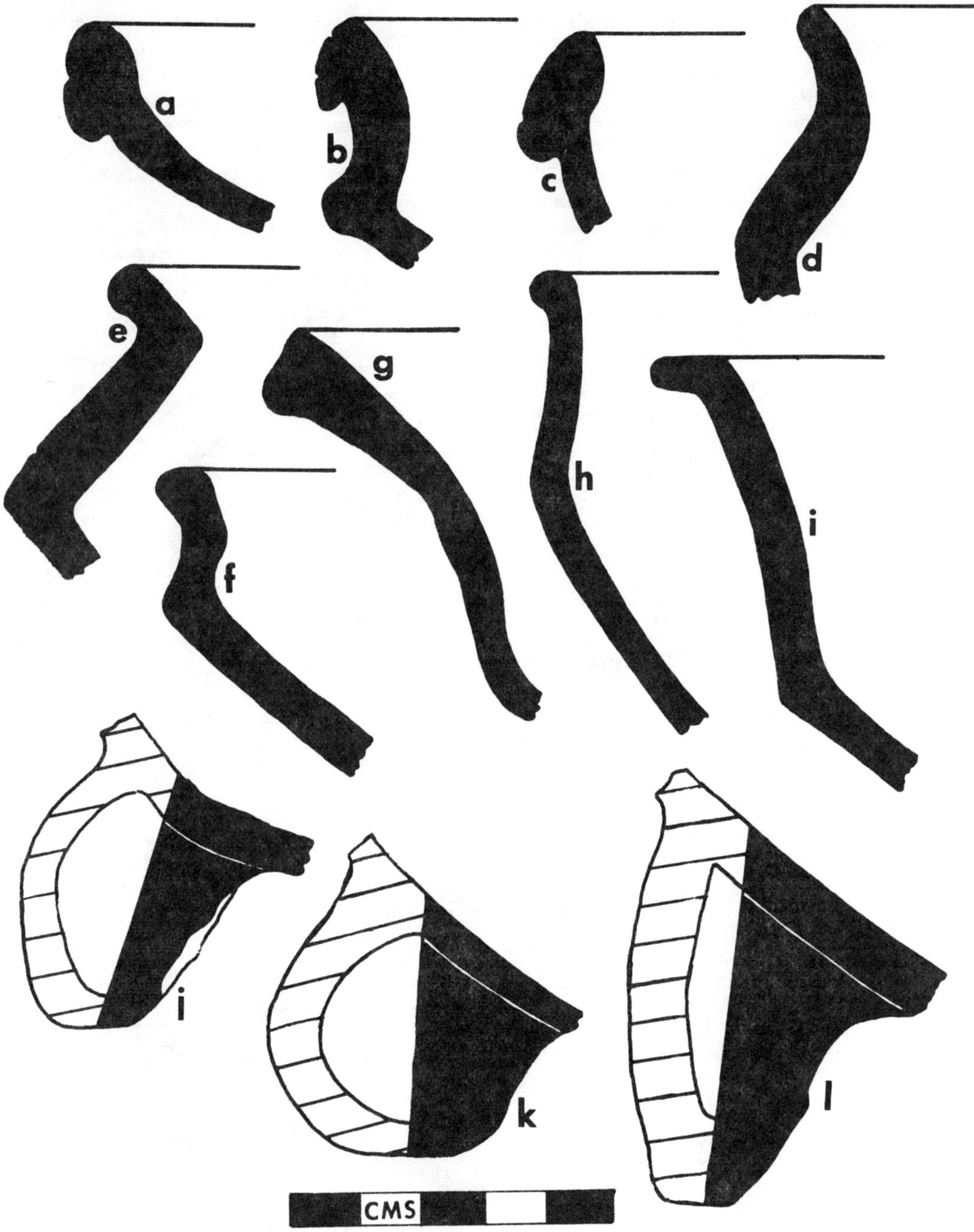

Fig. 55—Late Formative plain service ware: *a*) Tx-LF-12, UMMA No. 59841; *b*) Tx-LF-12, UMMA No. 59841; *c*) Tx-LF-12, UMMA No. 59842; *d*) Tx-LF-12, UMMA No. 59841; *e*) Tx-LF-12, UMMA No. 59841; *f*) Tx-LF-12, UMMA No. 59841; *g*) Tx-LF-12, UMMA No. 59841; *h*) Tx-LF-24, UMMA No. 59846; *i*) Tx-LF-12, UMMA No. 59841, Late and Terminal Formative unattached hollow bulbous supports: *j*) Tx-TF-51, UMMA No. 59845; *k*) Tx-LF-12, UMMA No. 59840; *l*) Tx-LF-12, UMMA No. 59842.

around the neck or rim. Unpainted sections of the sherds were generally reddish-brown (2.5YR 5/4, 4/4, and 5YR 5/3, 4/3, 5/4), red (2.5YR 5/6), reddish-yellow (5YR 6/6, and 7.5YR 7/6), light brown (7.5YR 6/4), pinkish-gray (7.5YR 6/2), brown (7.5YR 5/4, 5/2), pale brown (10YR 6/3), and light yellowish-brown (10YR 6/4). Color may be quite variable even on the surface of a single sherd. Finish is by horizontal burnish, which ranges from rough to fairly smooth. In some cases the area around the rim and neck are well burnished, while the remainder of the vessel is much rougher.

Interior surface—In some cases the area between the rim and the neck has been slipped or painted in a reddish-brown (2.5YR 4/4) or weak red (10R 4/4). Unpainted surfaces are red (2.5YR 4/6, 5/6), reddish-brown (2.5YR 5/4, 4/4,) and 5YR 4/3, 5/3, and 5/4), pink (5YR 7/4), light reddish-brown (5YR 6/3), reddish-yellow (5YR 6/6), light brown (7.5YR 6/4), brown (7.5YR 5/4, 5/2, and 10YR 5/3), pale brown (10YR 6/3), and dark yellowish-brown (10YR 4/4). The surface between the lip and the neck is normally smoothly burnished. Below this point the vessel walls are unburnished and quite rough.

Comparisons—Vaillant's Bay Ware ollas from his Late Zacatenco period (1930: Pl. VII, *g, m, r, v, b'*) and from Ticoman (1931: Pl. LXIX, *b, e, f, g, i, h, t*) correspond closely to our material.

B. Service Ware

1. Bowls (*Fig. 55*): Vessel form is variable. Walls may be simple, upright, or shouldered, or with an interior ledge. Rims can be bevelled, bolstered, or everted, occasionally with interior or exterior incision. Rim diameters range from 12 to 40 cm, with an average of about 28 cm. Wall thickness varies between 0.4 and 1.3 cm. Hollow, bulbous tripodal supports appear to be standard.

Paste—Temper consists of sand and pumice, with small fragments of what may be obsidian and hornblende crystals. Proportion of temper ranges between 15 and 30 per cent. Texture is compact. Some sherds have abundant air bubbles.

Exterior surface—The predominant colors are black and brown, with considerable variation. Often two or more colors are found on a single vessel or even a single sherd. Color does not appear to be the result of painting. Color variants noted are black (2.5YR 2/0, 7.5YR 2/0, and 10YR 2/1), red (2.5YR 5/8), reddish-brown (5YR 4/4, 5/3, and 5/4), light brown (7.5YR 6/4), brown (7.5YR 5/4, 5/2), and very dark gray (10YR 3/1). Finish is often fairly smooth to smooth horizontal burnish around the rim or over the whole vessel. Vessel bases are often roughly burnished.

Interior surface—Coloring is essentially identical to the exterior surface. Finish is typically smooth horizontal burnishing.

Comparisons—The most comparable published material is Vaillant's Black-Brown Ware from Ticoman (1931: Plate LXXIV, *e, f, h*). His vessel supports (ibid: Pl. LXXV, *h, m, g*) are also similar to our Late Formative material. Vaillant's Late Period Service Wares from Zacatenco (1930: Pl. VIII, *c, g*) are akin to our Texcoco Region material in form and decoration.

II. Decorated Ware

A. Service Ware

1. Red-on-Buff. Several form variants occur (Fig. 56), including hemispherical bowls with hollow supports, shouldered bowls with and without interior ledges, tecomates, shallow dishes, and nonshouldered bowls. For bowls, rim diameter ranges between 18 and 36 cms., and wall thickness between 0.5 and 1.3 cms. For the single plate form in our type collection, rim diameter measures 34 cm, and wall thickness between 0.9 and 1.2 cms. For the single shallow dish form in our type collection, rim diameter is 24 cms, and wall thickness between 0.5 and 0.9 cms. For tecomates, rim diameters range between 28 and 32 cms., and wall thickness varies from 0.9 to 1.6 cms.

Paste—Temper consists predominately of pumice and sand, occasionally including some long black crystals which may be hornblende. Proportion of temper ranges between 20 and 30 per cent. Color is buff, orange-buff, brown, grayish-buff, or reddish-brown, often with a gray to gray-black medial adea. Texture is compact. Air bubbles are often abundant.

Exterior surface—Red paint (10R 4/6, and 10R 4/4, 4/3) typically occurs in broad bands, often around the rim. Most shouldered bowls are painted red between the rim and the shoulder angle. Unpainted areas are reddish-brown (2.5YR 4/4, and 5YR 4/3, 5/3, and 5/4), light brown (7.5YR 6/4), brown (7.5YR 5/4), and pale brown (10YR

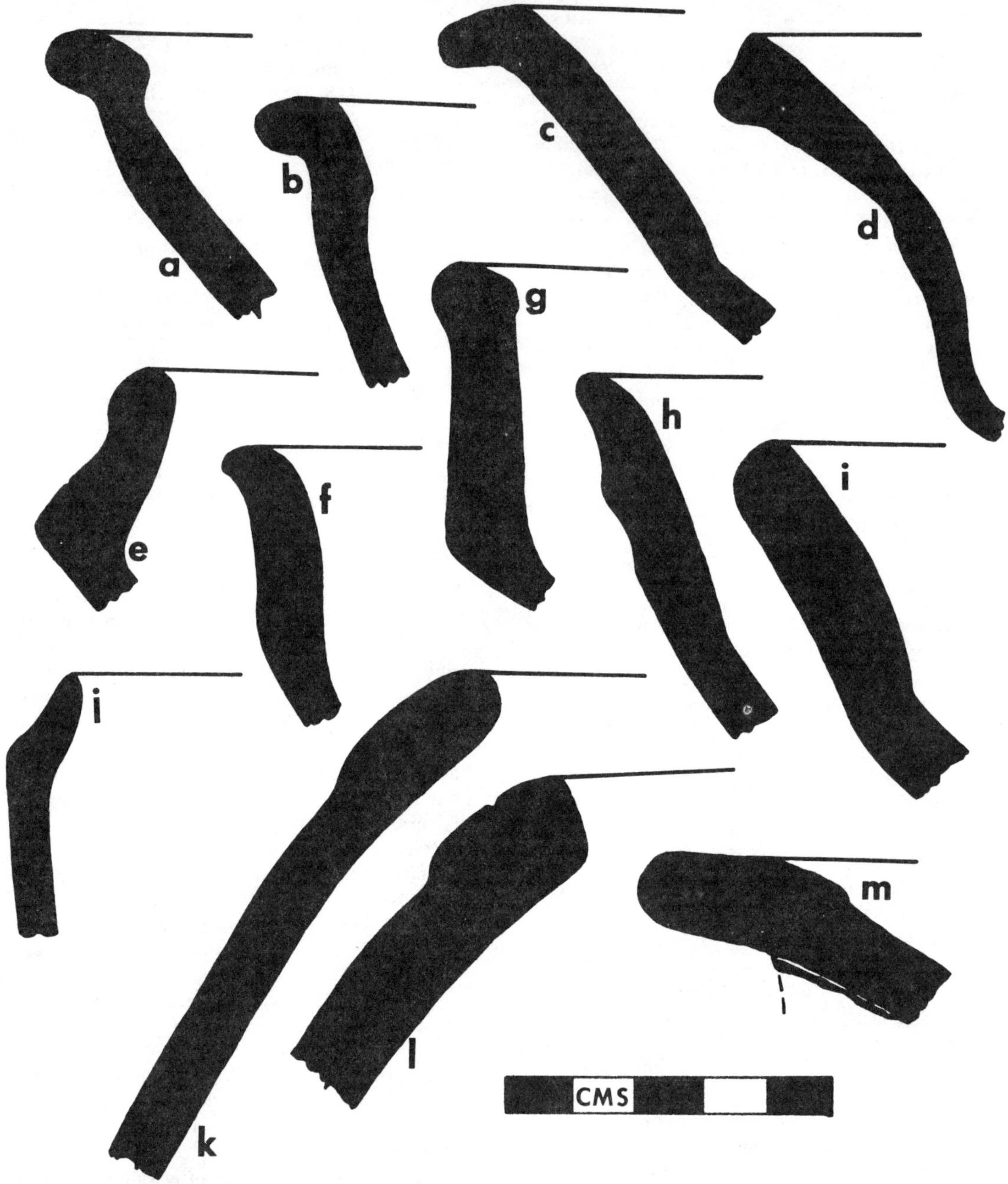

Fig. 56—Late Formative decorated service ware, Red-on-Buff: *a*) Tx-LF-12, UMMA No. 59842; *b*) Tx-LF-8, UMMA No. 59839; *c*) Tx-LF-12, UMMA No. 59840; *d*) Tx-LF-12, UMMA No. 59841; *e*) Tx-LF-8, UMMA No. 59838; *f*) Tx-LF-12, UMMA No. 59841; *g*) Tx-LF-8, UMMA No. 59838; *h*) Tx-LF-12, UMMA No. 59840; *i*) Tx-LF-8, UMMA No. 59838; *j*) Tx-LF-12, UMMA No. 59840; *k*) Tx-LF-8, UMMA No. 59838; *l*) Tx-LF-12, UMMA No. 59840; *m*) Tx-LF-8, UMMA No. 59838.

6/3). Red-painted areas are usually smoothly burnished. Unpainted sections of vessels are generally smoothly burnished, although occasionally the burnishing has been rough. Blackened areas, perhaps the result of firing or heating, were noted on some sherds.

Interior surface—Decoration and surface finish equivalent to the exterior surface.

Comparisons—Our material is quite comparable to Vaillant's Red-on-Yellow pottery from Ticoman (1931: Pl. LXX, *k, m, g, i, h*) and from his Late Period at Zacatenco (1930: Pl. VIII, *k;* Pl. IX, *b, m*). In general, our repertoire of Red-on-Buff design motifs from the Texcoco Region is somewhat less complex than Vaillant's ceramics of the same general type at Zacatenco and Ticoman.

Terminal Formative (Tezoyuca-Patlachique Phase)

I. Plainware

A. Utilitarian Ware

1. Ollas: Most are wedge-rim vessels (*Fig. 57*), but smaller quantities of everted-rim forms also occur. Rim diameters range from 18 to 42 cms. Wall thickness below the rim varies between 0.4 and 1.3 cm. In some cases there is distinctive thumb-impressed decoration around the edge of the lip. No vessel supports or external appendages were noted. Because of the small size of sherds in our collections, some vessels we are calling ollas may actually be basins.

Paste—Temper consists of pumice and sand for the most part, and occurs in proportions between 25 and 45 per cent. Color varies from orange-buff to buff or gray-buff, often with a darker gray or gray-black medial area. Texture is compact. Numerous air bubbles are occasionally present.

Exterior surface—With a very few exceptions, all our sherds appear to be unpainted. The most common color is reddish-brown (2.5YR 5/4), 4/4, and 5YR 5/3, 5/4). Other colors noted include light reddish-brown (5YR 6/4), yellowish-red (5YR 5/6), brown (7.5YR 5/4, light brown (7.5YR 6/4), and light yellowish-brown (10YR 6/4). Finish is usually fairly rough horizontal burnishing, although some vessels are relatively smoothly finished.

Interior surface—Color and surface finish generally similar to exterior surface, except for a tendency for smoother burnishing of the vessel interior.

Comparisons—Noguera's (1943) *Barro bayo, Cafe rojizo,* and *Barro gris aspero* categories from El Tepalcate (our Tx-TF-46) contain olla forms identical to our material from the Texcoco Region as a whole. West (1965: Fig. 2, *j, k*) illustrates material from Tezoyuca which is comparable to our ollas.

2. Shouldered Bowls and Basins (*Fig. 58*): Rim diameters measure between 22 and 44 cms. Wall thickness ranges from 0.6 to 1.6 cms. Small tab handles appear to be characteristic.

Paste—Temper consists predominately of sand and pumice, and occasionally contains small chunks of white material which may also be pumice. Proportion of temper ranges from 25 to 40 per cent. Color is usually buff or orange-buff, often with a gray or gray-black medial area. Texture is compact. Often a large number of air bubbles occur.

Exterior surface—No paint or slip could be detected. The most common color is light brown (7.5YR 6/4). Also present are brown (7.5YR 5/4), reddish-brown (5YR 5/4, 5/3, and 2.5YR 4/4, 5/4), and dark reddish-gray (5YR 4/2). Sometimes the color is variable over the surface of a single sherd. Finish is commonly fairly rough horizontal burnish, although burnishing is sometimes of a higher quality.

Interior surface—Color and finsh essentially identical to exterior surface.

Comparisons—Noguera's (1943) *Barro bayo, Cafe rojizo,* and *Barro gris aspero* categories from El Tepalcate (our Tx-TF-46) contain shouldered bowl forms identical to our material from the Texcoco Region as a whole.

B. Service Ware

1. Small Shouldered Bowls (*Fig. 58, j, l*): Rim diameters range from 18 to 22 cms. Wall thickness varies between 0.5 and 0.9 cms. Small lug handles are occasionally present.

Paste—Temper consists of sand and pumice for the most part. Proportion of temper ranges between 30 and 35 per cent. Color is buff or orange-buff, sometimes with a gray-black medial area. Texture is compact.

Exterior surface—Painting and slipping are apparently absent. The most frequent colors noted are reddish-brown (5YR 5/3), light brown (7.5YR 6/4), and very pale

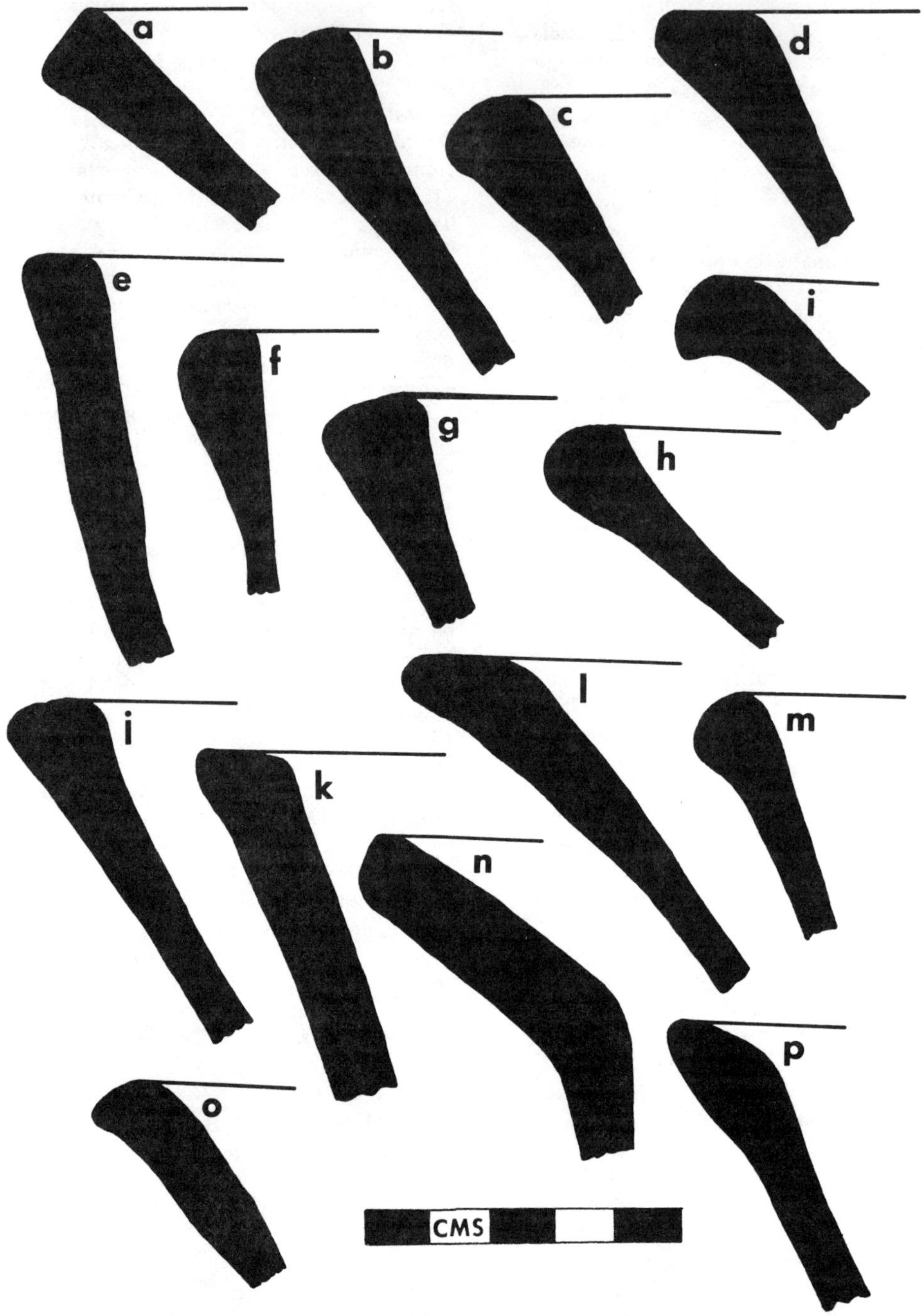

Fig. 57—Terminal Formative (Tezoyuca-Patlachique) plainware, utilitarian olla: *a*) Tx-TF-51, UMMA No. 59857; *b*) Tx-TF-51, UMMA No. 59857; *c*) Tx-TF-51, UMMA No. 59856; *d*) Tx-TF-51, UMMA No. 59858; *e*) Tx-TF-51, UMMA No. 59858; *f*) Tx-TF-51, UMMA No. 59857; *g*) Tx-TF-51, UMMA No. 59858; h) Tx-TF-50, UMMA No. 59854; *i*) Tx-TF-50, UMMA No. 59848; *j*) Tx-TF-51, UMMA No. 59858; *k*) Tx-TF-39, UMMA No. 59859; *l*) Tx-TF-51, UMMA No. 59858; *m*) Tx-TF-51, UMMA No. 59856; *n*) Tx-TF-51, UMMA No. 59860; *o*) Tx-TF-4, UMMA No, 59848; *p*) Tx-TF-51, UMMA No. 59858.

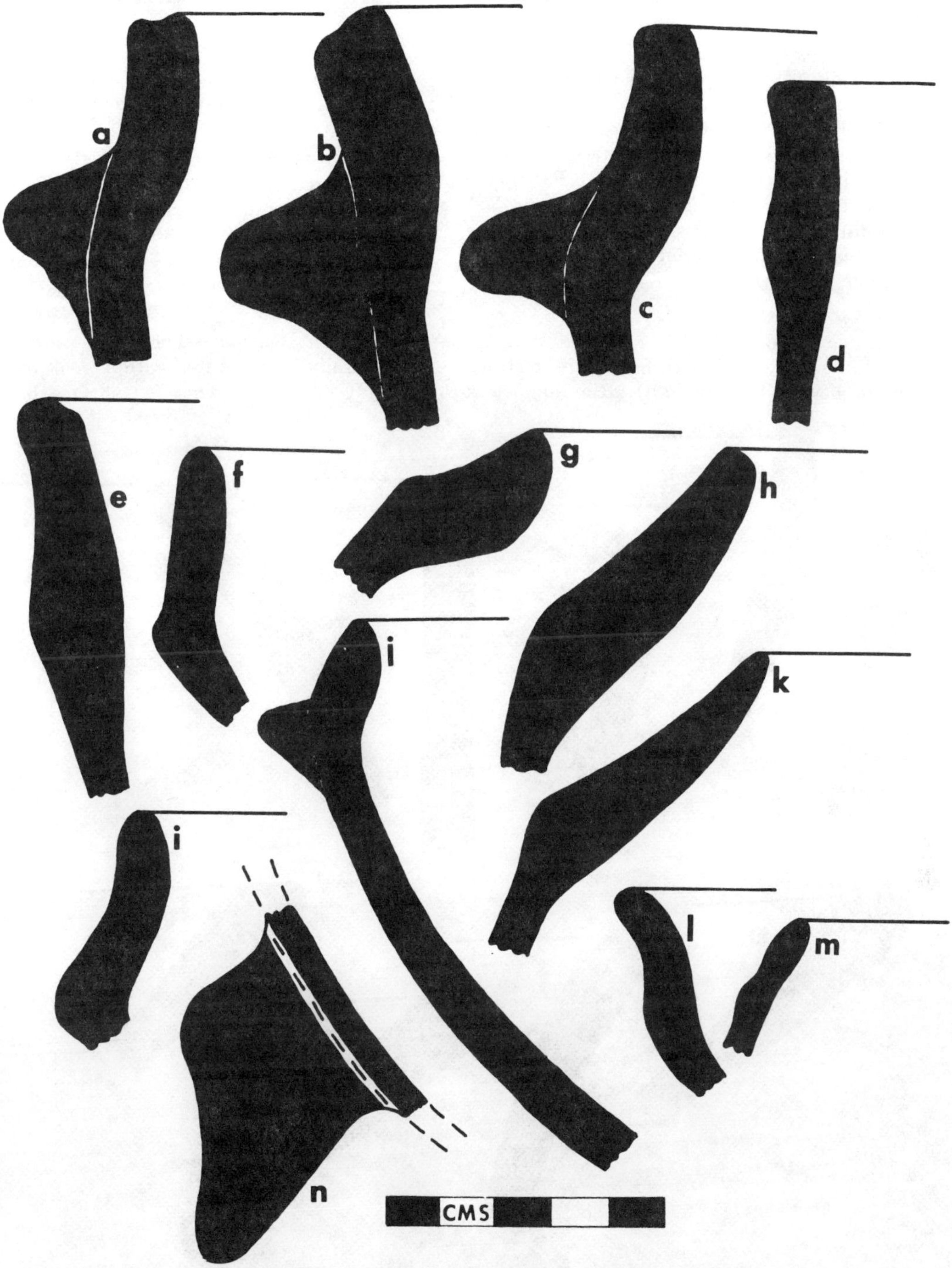

Fig. 58—Terminal Formative (Tezoyuca-Patláchique) plainware, shouldered bowls and basins: *a*) Tx-TF-51, UMMA No. 59857; *b*) Tx-TF-51, UMMA No. 59860; *c*) Tx-TF-51, UMMA No. 59860; *d*) Tx-TF-51, UMMA No. 59860; *e*) Tx-TF-51, UMMA No. 59858; *f*) Tx-TF-4, UMMA No. 59848; *g*) Tx-TF-51, UMMA No. 59858; *h*) Tx-TF-4, UMMA No. 598-48; *i*) Tx-TF-4, UMMA No. 59848; *j*) Tx-TF-51, UMMA No. 59858; *k*) Tx-TF-14, UMMA No. 59853; *l*) Tx-TF-51, UMMA No. 59856; *m*) Tx-TF-7, UMMA No. 59849 (Tzacualli); *n*) Tx-TF-20, UMMA No. 59850 (unattached support).

brown (10YR 7/4). Finish varies from fairly rough to fairly smooth horizontal burnish.

Interior surface—Color and finish essentially identical to exterior surface.

Comparisons—Noguera's (1943) *Barro cafe claro* category from El Tepalcate (our Tx-TF-46) contains small shouldered bowl forms identical to our material from the Texcoco Region as a whole.

II. Decorated Ware

A. Service Ware

1. White-on-Red: Vessel forms are restricted to bowls (*Fig. 59; a-d*). Rim diameters measure between 12 and 28 cms. Wall thickness ranges from 0.5 to 0.9 cms. Hollow supports (*Fig. 55, j*) are apparently characteristic.

Paste—Temper consists mostly of pumice and sand, occasionally with small tabular chunks of white material. Proportion of temper is about 30 to 35 per cent. Color is gray-buff, orange-buff, or buff, sometimes with a darker medial area. Texture is compact.

Exterior surface—The whole surface has generally been covered with a weak red paint (10R 4/3, 4/4). This red surface has been

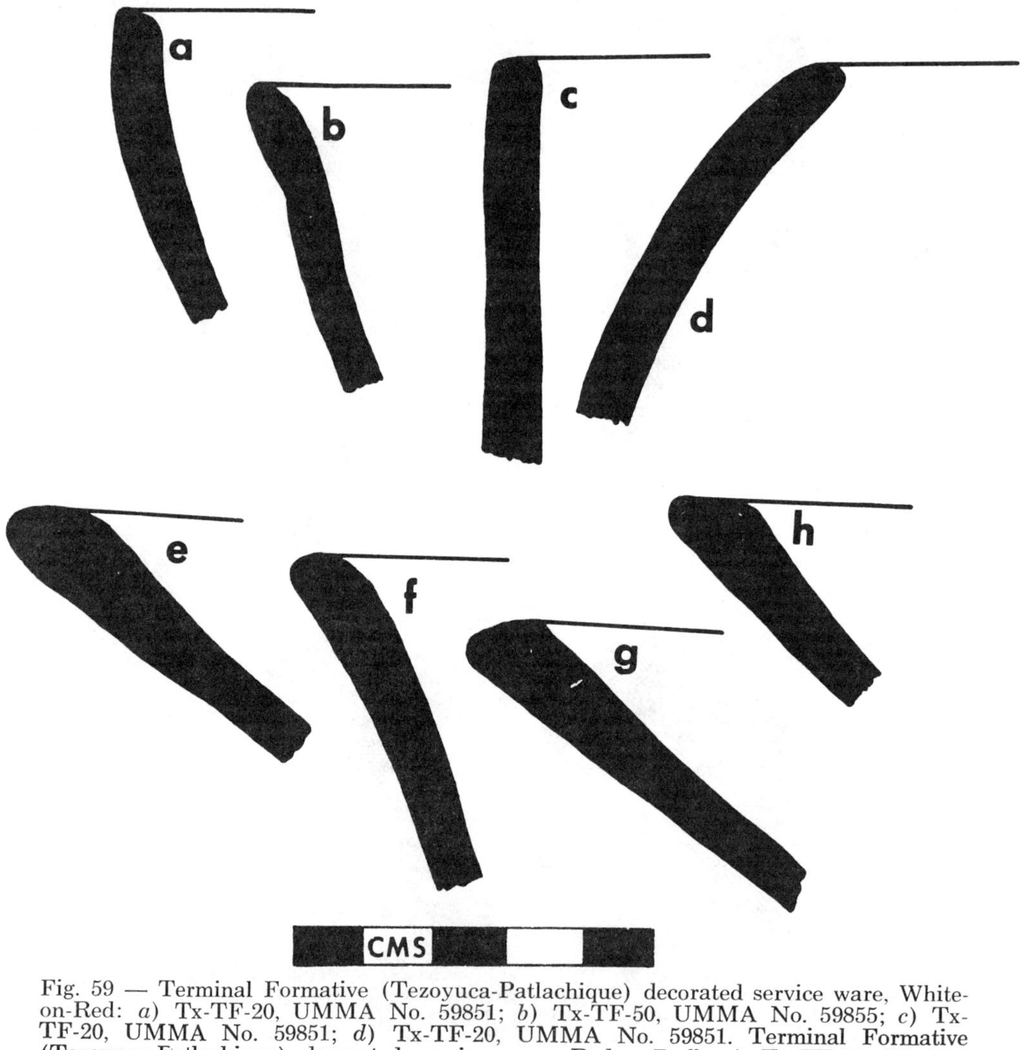

Fig. 59 — Terminal Formative (Tezoyuca-Patlachique) decorated service ware, White-on-Red: *a*) Tx-TF-20, UMMA No. 59851; *b*) Tx-TF-50, UMMA No. 59855; *c*) Tx-TF-20, UMMA No. 59851; *d*) Tx-TF-20, UMMA No. 59851. Terminal Formative (Tezoyuca-Patlachique) decorated service ware, Red-on-Buff: *e*) Tx-TF-51, UMMA No. 59858; *f*) Tx-TF-51, UMMA No. 59858; *g*) Tx-TF-50, UMMA No. 59855; *h*) Tx-TF-51, UMMA No. 59858.

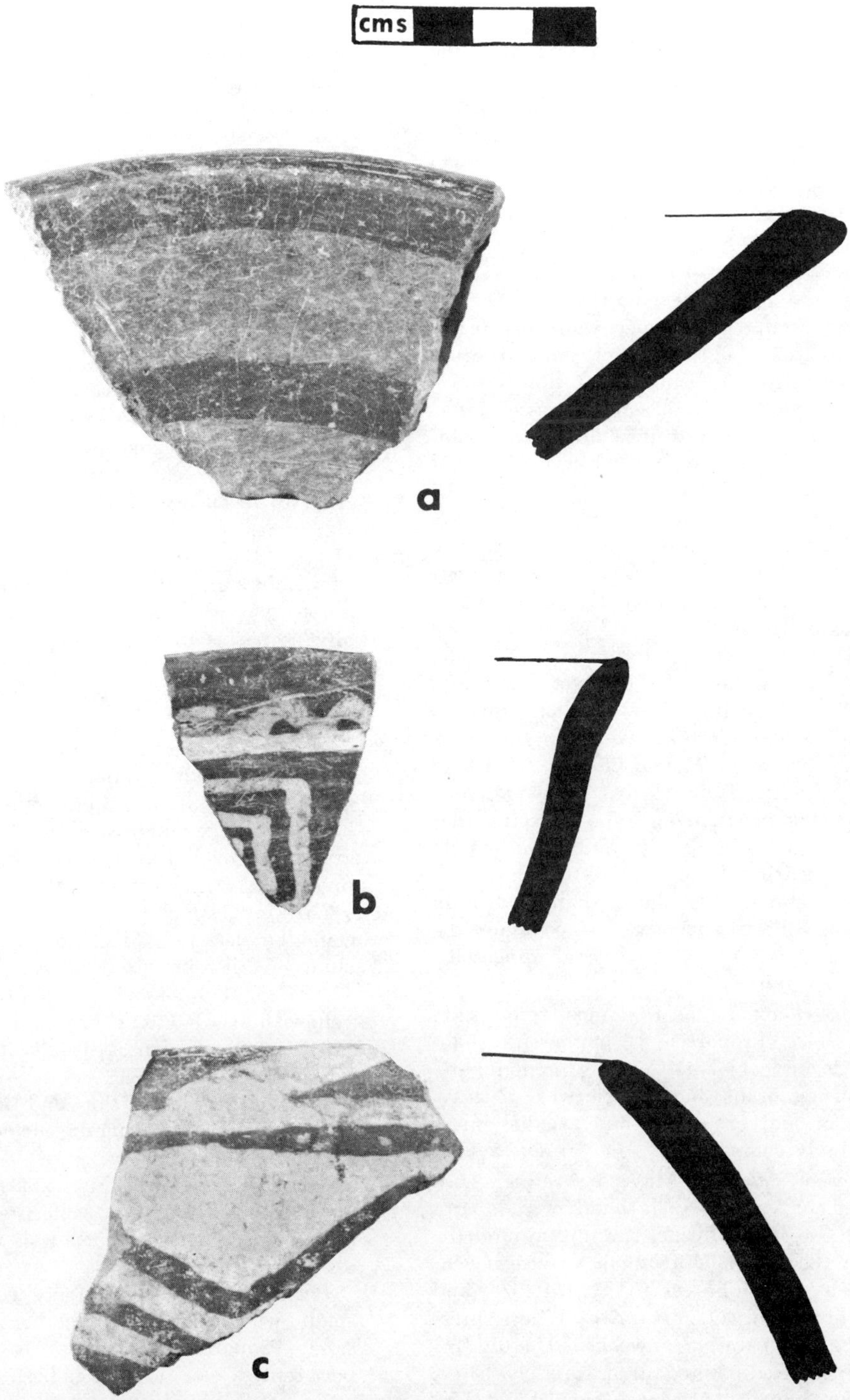

Fig. 60—Terminal Formative (Tezoyuca-Patlachique) decorated service ware: *a*) Red-on-Buff bowl, interior surface. Tx-TF-50, UMMA No. 59855; UMMA Neg. 119-2-2; *b*) White-on-Red bowl, exterior surface. Tx-TF-50, UMMA No. 59855; UMMA Neg, 119-2-2; *c*) White-on-Red bowl, exterior surface. Tx-TF-20, UMMA No. 59851. UMMA Neg. 119-2-2.

smoothly burnished. White (2.5Y 8/2, 10YR 8/2) designs have been applied to the burnished red surface. The white paint has been thickly applied, and is generally badly worn. Occasionally it has weathered to a pale yellowish-brown (10YR 8/3). Design motifs are commonly geometric, featuring solid triangles and interlocking chevron elements (*Fig. 60, b, c*).

Interior surface—Entire interior may be painted red, or only a band several cms wide running around the upper wall just below the lip. Color and finish of painted areas are generally identical to exterior surface. White decoration is absent on vessel interiors. Where interior wall is unpainted, color is commonly a natural reddish-brown (2.5YR 5/4).

Comparisons—Noguera (1943: Fig. 1, 24-28) illustrates material from El Tepalcate (our Tx-TF-46) which is identical to our White-on-Red pottery from the Texcoco Region as a whole.

2. Red-on-Buff: Vessel forms (*Fig. 59, e-h*) include flaring bowls, basal break bowls, and a shallow dish with hollow bulbous supports. In the case of flaring bowls, rim diameter measures between 22 and 26 cms., and wall thickness varies from 0.5 to 1.2 cms. The one basal break bowl in our type collection has a rim diameter of 18 cms, and a wall thickness measuring from 0.5 to 0.8 cms. The rim diameter of the single shallow dish in our type collection measures 18 cms, and the wall thickness of this same vessel ranges between 0.6 and 1.1 cms.

Paste—Temper consists mostly of sand and pumice. Proportion of temper is roughly 25 to 35 per cent. Color is predominately buff or orange-buff, often with a gray-black or darker orange-buff medial area. Texture is compact.

Exterior surface—May be either unpainted, or with a single band of red paint from 1.5 to 4 cms. wide, running around the rim of the vessel. Unpainted surface is generally a reddish-brown (5YR 4/4, 5/3, and 5/4) or brown (7.5YR 5/4). Where present the red paint is a weak red (10R 4/3 and 4/4). Red-painted areas are characterized by smooth horizontal burnishing. Unpainted surfaces are also horizontally burnished, but in a much less careful manner.

Interior surface—Color and surface treatment essentially like exterior surface. Decoration tends to be in the form of two or more parallel, concentric red bands around the upper part of the vessel wall (*Fig. 60,a*).

Comparisons—Noguera (1943) illustrates and describes material from El Tepalcate (our Tx-TF-46) which is identical to our Red-on-Buff pottery from the Texcoco Region as a whole.

Terminal Formative (Tzacualli Phase)

I. Plainware

A. Utilitarian Ware

1. Ollas: A variety of forms occur (Fig. 61) including bevelled-rim vessels, wedge-rim vessels, and everted-rim vessels. Thumb impressions around the edge of vessel rims are occasionally present. Rim diameters range from 16 to 40 cms. Wall thickness below the rim varies between 0.4 and 1.6 cms. Because of the typically small size of individual sherds in our type sample, some of the examples we are classifying as ollas may actually be basins or large bowls.

Paste—Temper is comprised mainly of sand and pumice, generally with small black chunks (obsidian or hornblende), and often with abundant small white particles scattered throughout. Proportion of temper ranges from 25 to 35 per cent. Color is typically buff or orange-buff, usually with a gray or gray-black medial area. Air bubbles are often present. Texture is compact.

Exterior surface—No painting or slipping could be detected. Most common colors include reddish-brown (2.5YR 5/4), brown (7.5YR 5/4), light brown (7.5YR 6/4), light yellowish-brown (10YR 6/4), and pale brown (10YR 6/3). Finish is usually fairly rough horizontal burnishing.

Interior surface—Color and finish essentially identical to exterior surface.

B. Service Ware

1. Shouldered Bowl (Fig. 58,*m*): The single example in our type collection has a rim diameter of 18 cms, and a wall thickness of about 0.6 cms.

Paste — Temper is largely comprised of small white particles, together with some sand. Proportion of temper is roughly 35 per cent. Color is orange-buff. Texture is compact.

Exterior surface—No painting or slipping could be detected. Color is reddish-brown (2.5YR 5/4). Finish is fairly smooth horizontal burnish.

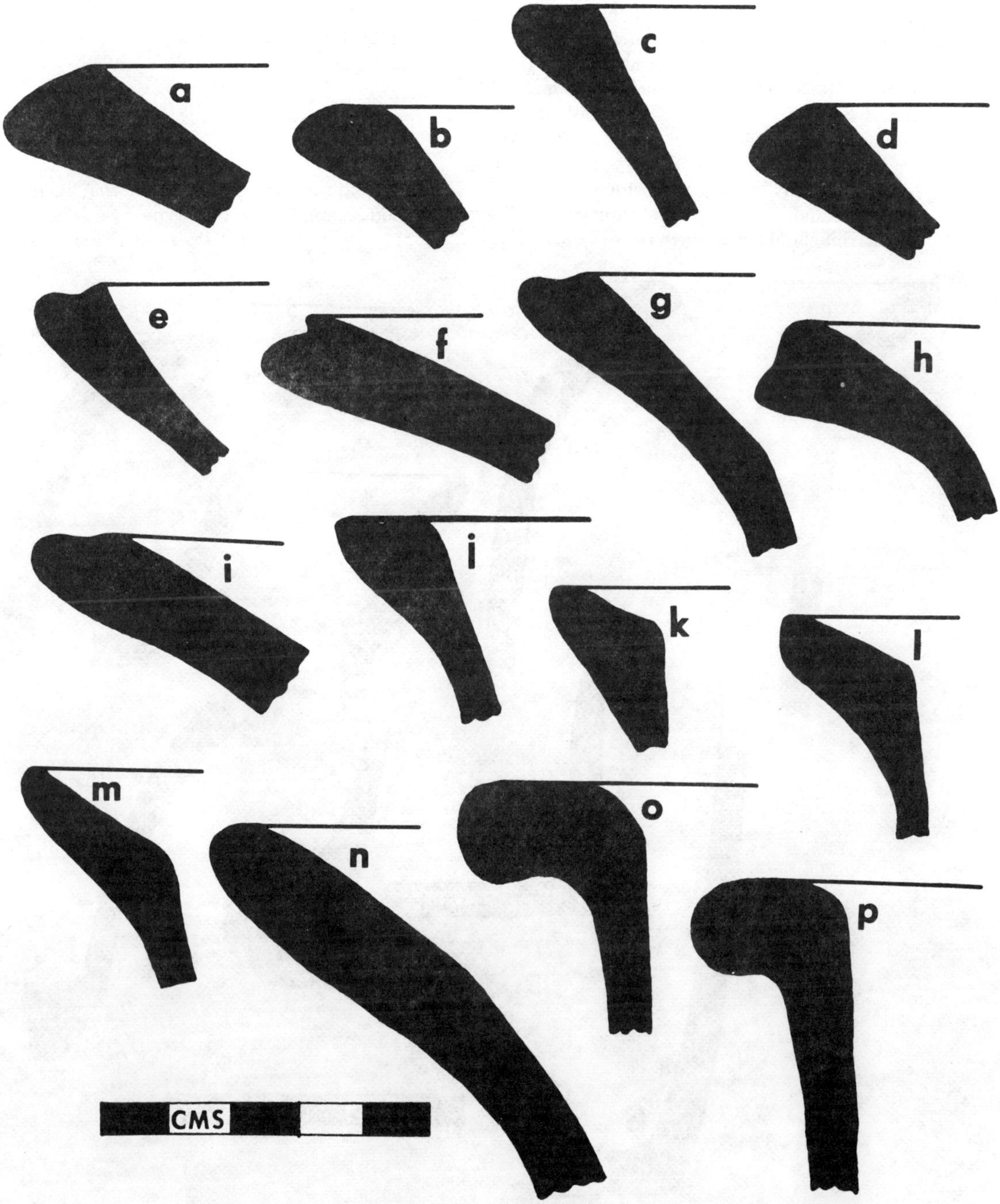

Fig. 61—Terminal Formative (Tzacualli) plainware, utilitarian olla: *a*) Tx-TF-17, UMMA No. 59849; *b*) Tx-TF-7, UMMA No. 59849; *c*) Tx-TF-7, UMMA No. 59849; *d*) Tx-TF-7, UMMA No. 59849; *e*) Tx-TF-7, UMMA No. 59849; *f*) Tx-TF-7, UMMA No. 59849; *g*) Tx-TF-7, UMMA No. 59849; *h*) Tx-TF-7, UMMA No. 59849; *i*) Tx-TF-7, UMMA No. 59849; *j*) Tx-TF-16, UMMA No. 59852; *k*) Tx-TF-16, UMMA No. 59852; *l*) Tx-TF-16, UMMA No. 59852; *m*) Tx-TF-16, UMMA No. 59852; *n*) Tx-TF-7, UMMA No. 59849; *o*) Tx-TF-7, UMMA No. 59849; *p*) Tx-TF-7, UMMA No. 59849.

Interior surface—Color and finsh essentially identical to the exterior surface.

Comparisons—Millon, Drewitt, and Bennyhoff (1965: Fig. 112) illustrate rim-shouldered bowls from the Sun Pyramid at Teotihuacan, which are very comparable to our material in form. Our pottery is so badly worn that any decoration which may once have existed is no longer apparent. The black rim-shouldered bowl from Pueblo Perdido in the western Valley of Mexico illustrated by Rattray (1968: 104) is comparable in form to our example from the Texcoco Region.

II. Decorated Ware

A. Service Ware

1. White-on-Red (*Fig. 62, a, b*): Our only good examples of this type are from a single vessel found at Tx-TF-7. This is a flar-

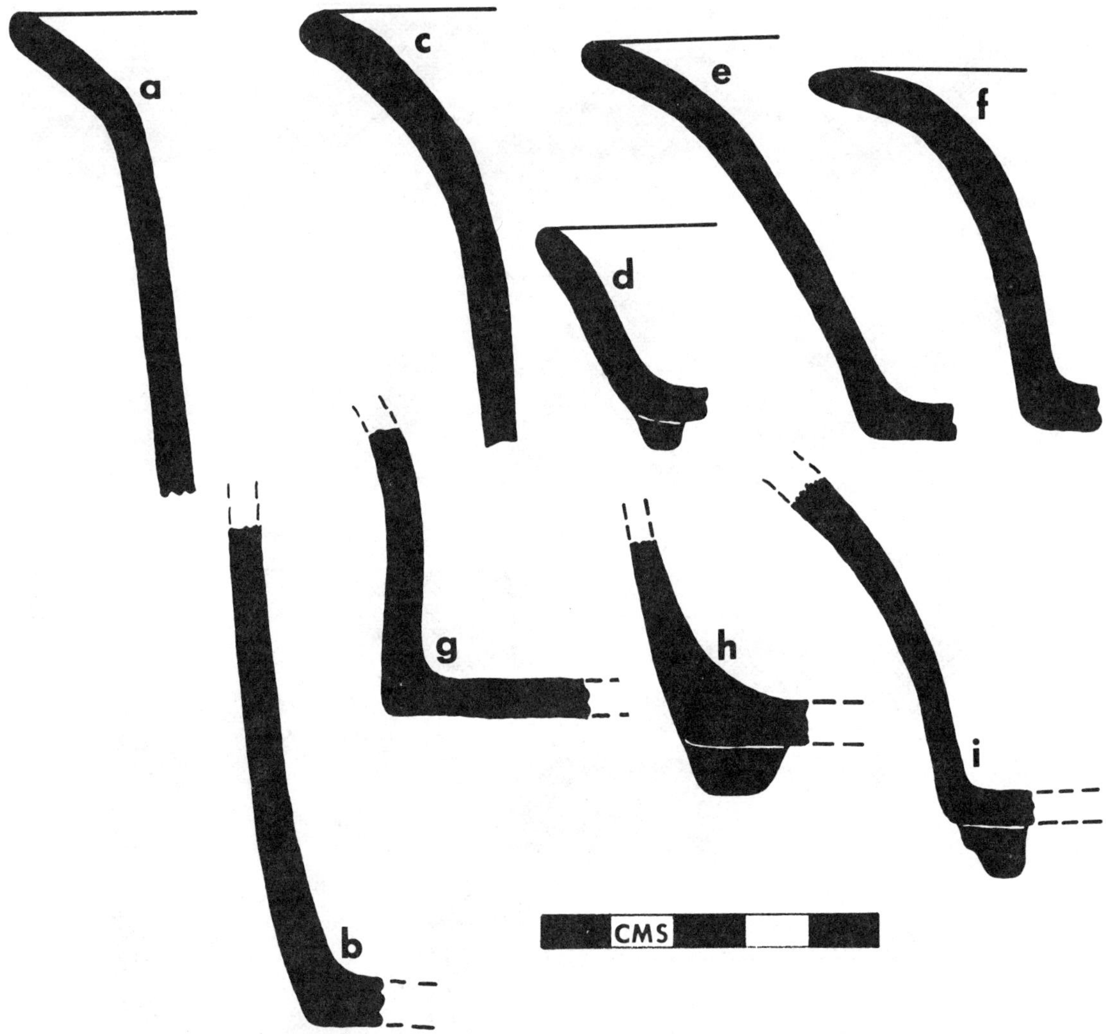

Fig. 62—Terminal Formative (Tzacualli) decorated service ware, White-on-Red: *a*) and *b*) Tx-TF-7, UMMA No. 59849. Early Classic plain and decorated service ware: *c*) Tx-EC-19, UMMA No. 59862 (Monochrome); *d*) Tx-EC-10, UMMA No. 59867 (Monochrome); *e*) Tx-EC-8, UMMA No. 59869 (Red-on-Buff; *f*) Tx-EC-36, UMMA No. 59870 (Monochrome); *g*) Tx-EC-10, UMMA No. 59867 (Red-on-Buff, basal fragment); *h*) Tx-EC-27, UMMA No. 59872 (Monochrome, basal fragment, with nubbin support); *i*) Tx-EC-26, UMMA No. 59873 (Monochrome, basal fragment, with nubbin support).

ing cylindrical vase with flat bottom. Rim diameter of this vessel is 18 cms. Average wall thickness is about 0.5 cms. No appendages of any kind can be detected.

Paste—Temper is predominately composed of abundant small white particles, together with some sand. Proportion of temper is roughly 30 per cent. Color is orange-buff. Texture is compact.

Exterior surface — Surface is badly weathered, but remnants of elaborate white design motifs can still be detected. These motifs are complex linear and geometric forms which are distinguishable from Tezoyuca-Patlachique phase White-on-Red decoration principally by greater fineness of line and much thinner paint. Prior to application of white designs, the entire exterior surface was painted red (10R 4/4). Finish is smooth horizontal burnishing.

Interior surface—Lacks white decoration. Red paint extends only a short distance below the rim. Remainder of vessel wall is a natural reddish-brown (2.5YR 5/4). Finish is fairly rough horizontal burnish, with little or no burnish on and around the base.

Comparisons—This vessel is identical in form and decoration to material illustrated by Armillas (1944: Lamina I, Fig. 3), Sejourné (1966: Fig. 197), and Millon, Drewitt, and Bennyhoff (1965: Fig. 110, *a-j*) from Teotihuacan.

Early Classic

I. Plainware

A. Utilitarian Ware

1. Ollas (Fig. 63): The most significant feature of this vessel form is the broad, flat, wide-everted rim. This proved to be the most useful single criterion for recognizing Early Classic occupation in our survey area. Rim diameter ranges between 20 and 42 cms. Wall thickness below the rim measures between 0.3 and 1.3 cms. Because of the typically small size of the individual sherds in our type collections, some of the specimens we classify as ollas may actually be basins or large bowl forms.

Paste — Temper consists mostly of sand and pumice, occasionally with small black and white chunks. Proportion of temper is roughly 25 to 35 per cent. Color is buff, orange-buff, or gray-buff, often with a grayish medial area. Occasionally either the exterior or interior half of the vessel will be darker in color than the lighter-colored opposite side. Texture is compact.

Exterior surface—No paint or slipping could be detected. The most common color is reddish-brown (5YR 5/3 and 5/4; 2.5YR 5/4). Red (2.5YR 5/6), light reddish-brown (5YR 6/3), reddish-gray (5YR 5/2), dark reddish-gray (5YR 4/2), reddish-yellow (5YR 6/6), light brown (7.5YR 6/4), brown (7.5YR 5/4), pale brown (10YR 6/3), light yellowish-brown (10YR 6/4), dark grayish-brown (10YR 4/2), and very dark gray (10YR 3/1) also occur. Occasionally the color is not consistent over a single sherd. Finish is mostly horizontal burnish, which varies from rough to fairly smooth. A few examples of vertical burnish were noted.

Interior surface—Color is generally identical to the exterior, but sometimes appears lighter due to better burnishing.

Comparisons—Ollas of this general form are apparently included within Tolstoy's (1958) categories of Burnished Ware Monochrome and Coarse Brown Ware from the northern Valley of Mexico. However, Tolstoy provides no illustrations of this material, and specific comparisons are not possible.

B. Service Ware

1. Monochrome Basal-Break Bowls (Fig. 62,*c-i*): This distinctive form features flaring wall, abrupt basal angle, flat bottom, and small, solid, tripodal nubbin supports. Rim diameters range from 14 to 24 cms. Wall thickness measures between 0.3 and 0.7 cms. Height of nubbin supports varies between 0.3 and 0.8 cms. In two cases total vessel height (above the nubbin support) could be determined: 3 cms. and 5.5 cms.

Paste—Temper consists mostly of sand and some pumice. Proportion of temper ranges between 20 and 35 per cent. Color is usually buff, with some grayish-buff and orange-buff paste. A gray medial area is often present. Texture is compact.

Exterior surface — The dominant color is brown (7.5YR 5/4, 5/2, 4/4; and 10YR 5/3). Light brown (7.5YR 6/4), dark grayish-brown (10YR 3/2), very dark gray (10YR 3/1), very dark grayish-brown (10YR 3/2), very dark brown (10YR 2/2), and black (10YR 2/1) also occur. Surfaces have been smoothly burnished, and traces of high polish can still be detected on many sherds. Some vessels have stick-trailed decoration in

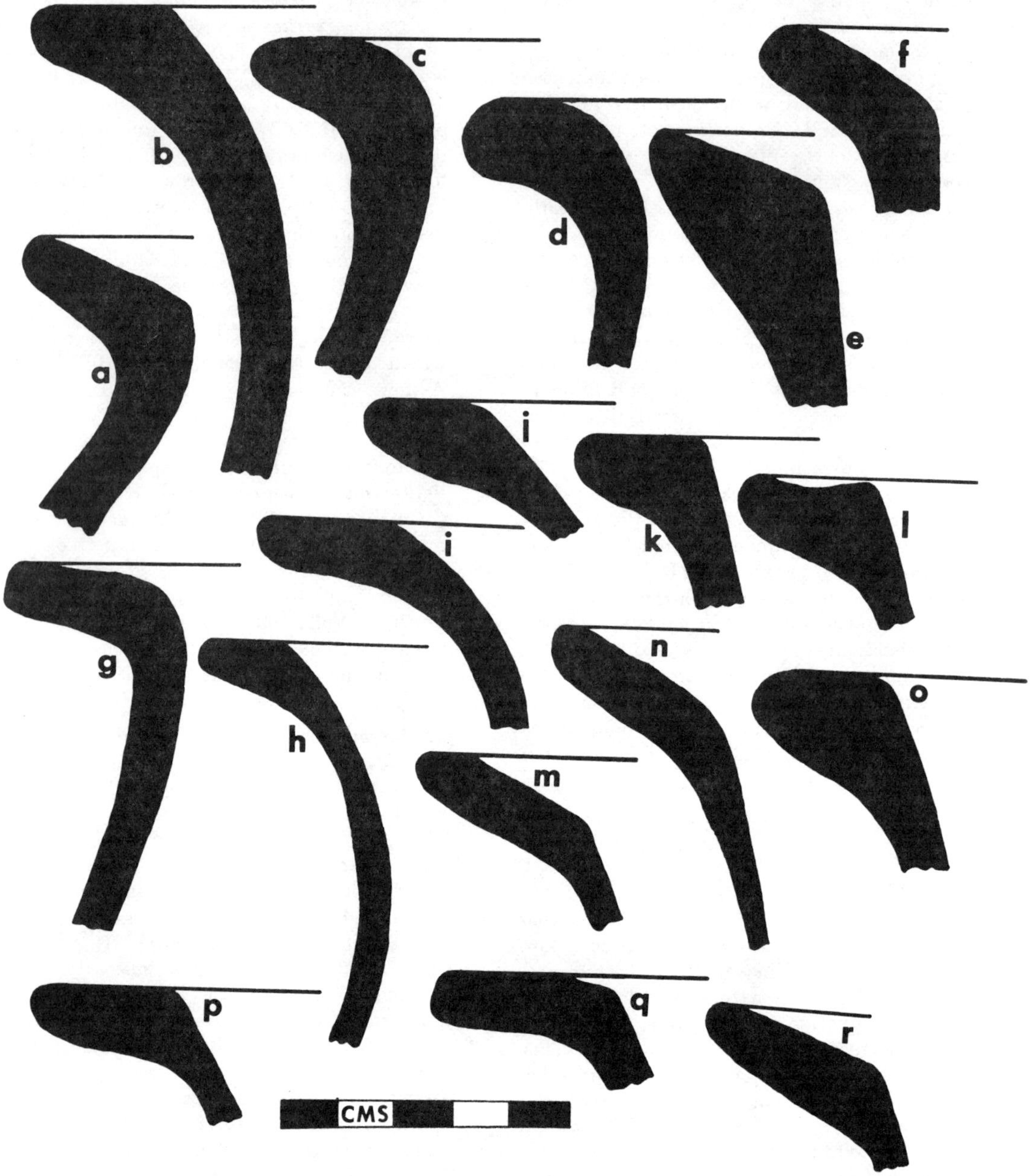

Fig. 63—Early Classic plainware, utilitarian olla: *a*) Tx-EC-19, UMMA No. 59862; *b*) Tx-EC-19, UMMA No. 69862; *c*) Tx-EC-14, UMMA No. 59865; *d*) Tx-EC-10, UMMA Uo. 59867; *e*) Tx-EC-10, UMMA No. 59867; *f*) Tx-EC-36, UMMA No. 59870; *g*) Tx-EC-14, UMMA No. 59865; *h*) Tx-EC-8, UMMA No. 59869; *i*) Tx-EC-27, UMMA No. 59872; *j*) Tx-EC-19, UMMA No. 59862; *k*) Tx-EC-19, UMMA No. 59862; *l*) Tx-EC-19, UMMA No. 59862; *m*) Tx-EC-8, UMMA No. 59869; *n*) Tx-EC-27, UMMA No. 59872; *o*) Tx-EC-19, UMMA No. 59862; *p*) Tx-EC-14, UMMA No. 59865; *q*) Tx-EC-36, UMMA No. 59870; *r*) Tx-EC-18, UMMA No. 59863,

the form of long, widely spaced vertical burnish marks. Occasionally simple linear incised designs are present.

Interior surface—Color and finish tend to be quite similar to the exterior surface. Burnish is occasionally of a more streaky quality relative to the exterior.

Comparisons—Tolstoy's (1958) category of Burnished Ware Monochrome includes vessel forms similar or identical to our Monochrome Basal-Break Bowls. Since Tolstoy, however, does not illustrate specific examples, comparisons are difficult. Hicks and Nicholson (1964) describe material from their Portezuelo excavations which is virtually identical to our examples from the Texcoco Region as a whole. Sejourné (1966: Fig. 77), Linne (1934: Figs. 50, 53; 1942: Fig. 203), and Armillas (1944: Lam. I, Fig. 4) illustrated identical material from Teotihuacan.

II. Decorated Ware

A. Service Ware

1. Red-on-Buff (Fig. *65,b*): Vessel form is difficult to ascertain due to small size of sherds. Apparently we are dealing with large cylindrical vases or basins, with flat bases and solid nubbin supports. The single large rim sherd in our type collection has a rim diameter of about 22 cms. Wall thickness measures between 0.5 and 0.7 cms. Two complete nubbin supports measured 2 and 4 cms. in height.

Paste — Temper is predominantly sand. Proportion of temper is about 25 to 35 per cent. Color is buff or gray-buff, often with a gray-black medial area. Texture is compact.

Exterior surface—Decoration is in the form of simple, large circular and wide linear motifs, often outlined with incised lines. The red paint is well burnished, often specular, and ranges in color from a weak (10R 4/4) to a darker shade (10R 3/6). The red designs are applied to a highly burnished, unpainted surface of natural reddish-brown (5YR 5/4), brown (7.5YR 5/4), and pale brown (10YR 6/3). In some cases stick-trailed decoration is present in the form of vertical streaks spaced about 0.5 cms. apart.

Interior surface—Decoration is absent on all sherds in our type collection. No painting or slipping could be detected. Colors are brown (7.5YR 5/4 and 10YR 5/3), grayish-brown (10YR 5/2), and pale brown (10YR 6/3). Finish is by smooth horizontal burnishing.

Comparisons—Tolstoy's (1958: 26) San Martin Red-on-Buff Burnished Ware from the northern Valley of Mexico seems to be partially similar or identical to our own material. Hicks and Nicholson (1964) describe identical material from their Early Classic phase at Portezuelo. Sejourné (1966: Figs. 164, 172, 189, and 190), Linne (1942: Fig, 205, 206, 209, 210), and Armillas (1944) describe similar and identical material from Teotihuacan.

III. Special Wares

A. Thin Orange (Fig. 64*a, b*): The only forms represented in our type sample are simple hemispherical bowls with annular bases. Rim diameter varies between 16 and 30 cms. Wall thickness measures from 0.3 to 0.4 cms. This pottery is an excellent Classic marker, but cannot be used (at least in the fragmented and badly worn state available to us) to distinguish between Early and Late Classic.

Paste—Temper consists of very distinctive small white fragments, of tabular and irregular form, together with some sand and pumice. Proportion of temper is about 35 to 50 per cent. Color is predominately orange, occasionally with a grayish medial area. Air bubbles are often abundant. Texture is compact.

Exterior surface—No traces of painting or slipping could be detected. Predominant color is reddish-yellow (5YR 6/6 and 7/6), occasionally with a slight greenish or greenish-gray tint. Finish is by smooth horizontal burnishing. A few sherds contain simple linear incised decoration.

Interior surface—Color and finish same as exterior. No incision was noted in our type sample.

Comparisons—This ceramic type has been widely reported from Mesoamerica on the Classic horizon. It is generally felt that Thin Orange pottery was produced within a restricted area of southeastern Puebla, and distributed throughout much of Mesoamerica through trade networks. Within the Valley of Mexico, Thin Orange pottery identical to our own (although often with greater variety of form and elaboration of decoration) has been described by Armillas (1944: Lam. I, Fig. 6), Sejourné (1966: Figs. 131,

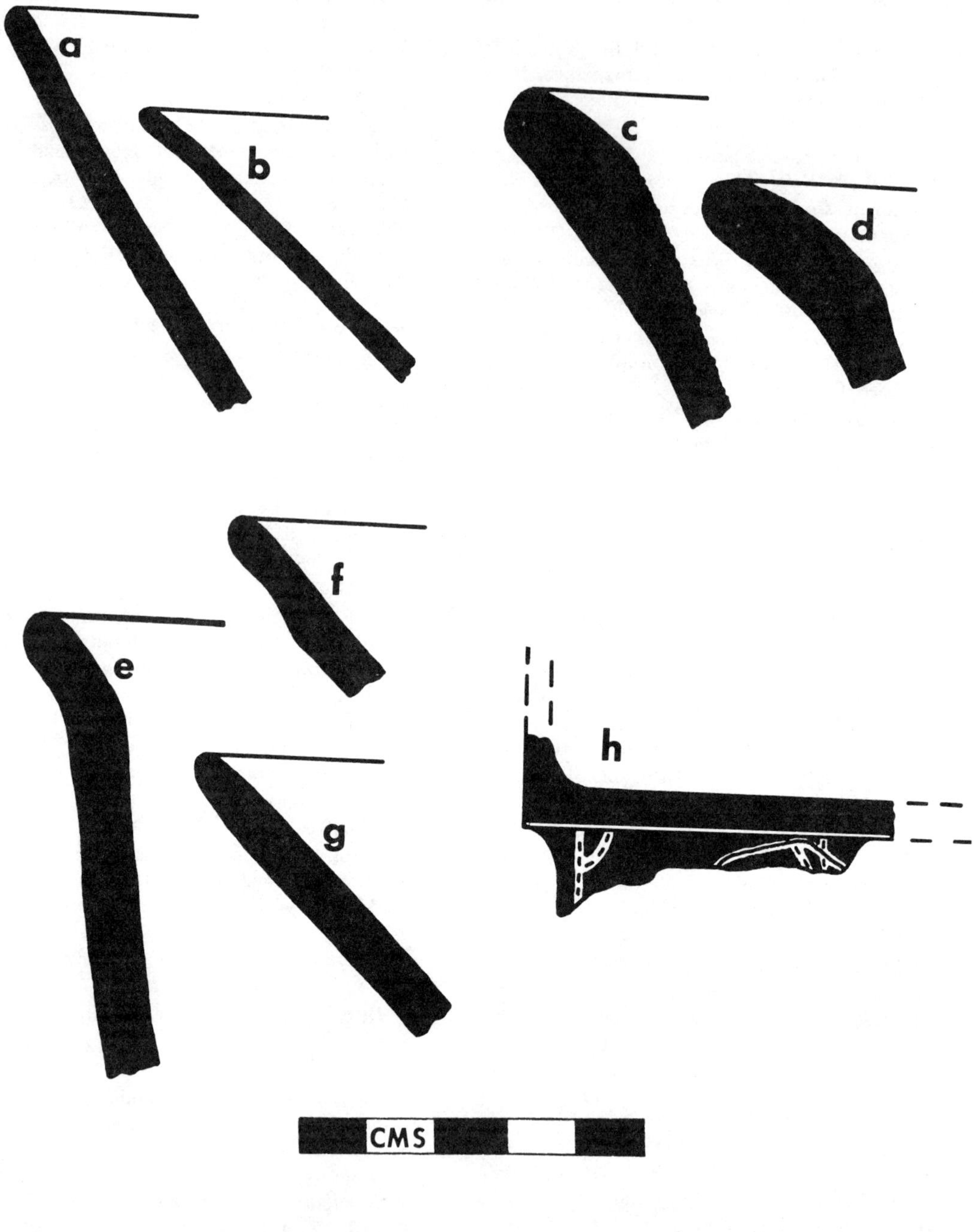

Fig. 64—Classic Thin Orange: *a)* Tx-EC-8, UMMA No. 59869; *b)* Tx-EC-9, UMMA No. 59868; Classic Granular Red-on-White: *c)* Tx-EC-17, UMMA No. 59864; *d)* Tx-EC-14, UMMA No. 59865; Late Classic Red-on-Buff: *e)* Tx-LC-9, UMMA No. 59868; *f)* Tx-LC-13, UMMA No. 59865; *g)* Tx-LC-18, UMMA No. 59871; Late Classic hollow cylindrical support: *h* Tx-LC-9, UMMA No. 59868.

Fig. 65—Classic decorated service ware: *a*) Granular Red-on-White, exterior surface. Tx-EC-36, UMMA No. 59870; UMMA Neg. 119-2-2; *b*) Early Classic incised Red-on-Buff, basin, exterior surface of body sherd. Tx-EC-9, UMMA No. 59870; UMMA Neg. 119-2-2; *c*) Late Classic Red-on-Buff, shallow dish or bowl, interior surface; Tx-LC-9, UMMA No. 59865; UMMA Neg. 119-2-2.

132, 135), and Linné (1934: Figs. 44, 52; 1942: Fig. 299) from Teotihuacan. Hicks and Nicholson (1964) have reported this material at Portezuelo, and Tolstoy (1958) recovered it throughout his survey area in the northern Valley of Mexico.

B. Granular Red-on-White (Fig 64,*c, d;* 65,*a*): Vessel form is difficult to ascertain because of typically small sherd size. Most vessels are probably either ollas or basins. Rim diameter ranges from 24 to 36 cms. Wall thickness measures between 0.6 and 1.2 cms. As in the case of Thin Orange, this ceramic type is an excellent Classic marker, but cannot be used to differentiate between Early and Late Classic as it seems to persist throughout the Classic period.

Paste—Temper consists of sand and gravel, together with some small dark fragments which may be obsidian or hornblende. Proportion of temper is about 50 per cent. Color is light buff to cream. Texture is compact.

Exterior surface—Entire surface has been covered with a thin whitish slip, which varies in color from white (2.5Y 8/2) to pinkish-white (7.4YR 8/2) to pink (7.5YR 8/2). Weak red (10R 4/4, designs have been applied over the underlying whitish slip. These designs are generally sloppily executed linear motifs, usually consisting of wide bands running around the vessel rim and zones of crosshatched lines below the lip. Surface is unburnished, with a rough, granular texture.

Interior surface—Color, finish, and decoration generally similar to the exterior.

Comparisons—Tolstoy (1958) describes a "Granular Red-on-Yellow" from his survey area in the northern Valley of Mexico which seems to be identical to our Granular Red-on-White. Hicks and Nicholson (1964) describe identical material from the Portezuelo site.

Late Classic

I. Plainware

A. Utilitarian Ware

1. Ollas (Fig. 66): In contrast to Early Classic ollas, Late Classic forms typically have shorter necks, narrower and less-everted rims, and with a marked rolling over and under of the rim at the very end of the Classic period (Metepec phase). Rim diameter ranges from 22 to 30 cms. Wall thickness below the rim varies between 0.5 and 1.3 cms. This form proved to be the single most useful ceramic criterion for identification of Late Classic occupation.

Paste—Temper consists mostly of sand and pumice. Proportion of temper ranges from 30 to 50 percent. Color is buff and orange-buff, often with a gray or gray-black medial area. Texture is compact.

Exterior surface—Paint and slip are generally absent, except in a few cases where the entire vessel (or at least the upper third) is covered with a specular red paint (10R 4/4). Colors include pale red (10R 6/4), reddish-brown (2.5YR 4/4 and 5YR 5/3), brown (7.5YR 5/4 and 10YR 5/3), light brown (7.5YR 6/4), grayish-brown (10YR 5/2), and pale brown (10YR 5/3). Surface finish tends to be relatively rough horizontal burnishing, although some smoothly burnished sherds were noted. Where surface has been painted, burnish is of a high quality.

Interior surface—Almost always unpainted and unslipped, except in a very few cases where the exterior wall has been painted and some of the red has been applied around the top of the inner rim as well. Otherwise color and finish correspond to exterior surface.

2. San Martin Orange Ollas (Fig. 66,*g-j*): This type is distinguished as a separate category because of its distinctive color, paste, and form. This pottery occurs throughout the Texcoco Region survey area, but in much lower proportion than the ollas described immediately above. Rim diameters ranged between 14 and 26 cms. Wall thickness measured from 0.7 to 1.3 cms.

Paste—Temper consists of sand and pumice. Proportion of temper is about 25 to 35 per cent. Color is deep orange to orange-buff, and occasionally gray, often with a dark medial area. Texture is compact.

Exterior surface—Painting and slipping are apparently absent. Most common color is reddish-brown (2.5YR 5/4). Reddish-yellow (5YR 6/6) also occurs. Finish on the neck and upper body is usually vertical burnishing, of fairly rough quality. Some sherds may be horizontally burnished in this area.

Interior surface—Color ranges from red (2.5YR 5/6), to reddish-yellow (5YR 6/6),

Fig. 66—Late Classic plainware, utilitarian olla: *a*) Tx-LC-10, UMMA No. 59867; *b*) Tx-LC-13, UMMA No. 59865; *c*) Tx-LC-9, UMMA No. 59868; *d*) Tx-LC-4, UMMA No. 59861; *e*) Tx-LC-4, UMMA No. 59861; *f*) Tx-LC-10, UMMA No. 59867; *g*) Tx-LC-4, UMMA No. 59861 (San Martin Orange); *h*) Tx-LC-4, UMMA No. 59861 (San Martin Orange); *i*) Tx-LC-13, UMMA No. 59865 (San Martin Orange); *j*) Tx-LC-4, UMMA No. 59861 (San Martin Orange).

to reddish-brown (5YR 5/3). One vessel in our type collection is reddish-brown (2.5YR 5/4) over part of the surface, and dark gray (2.5YR 4/0) on the remainder. Finish is by horizontal burnish, which is usually fairly rough in quality.

Comparisons—Our material is identical to Tolstoy's San Martin Orange Plain (1958: 32) from his survey area in the northern Valley of Mexico. Apparently this pottery is less common in the Texcoco Region than in the Teotihuacan Valley and other northern segments of the Valley of Mexico.

B. Service Ware

1. Basal-break bowls and/or vases, with large, hollow, cylindrical supports (Fig. 64,*h*): These occur in very low frequency in our survey area, and only one specimen (a body sherd) was included in our type collection. We describe it (i.e., the hollow cylindrical support) here simply because it appears to be quite diagnostic of Late Classic occupation. The single basal sherd in our collection has a wall thickness of about 0.4 cms., and its base measures 0.6 cms. thick. Basal diameter of this vessel is approximately 24 cms. Neither height of vessel nor of the hollow cylindrical support could be measured.

Paste—Temper is mostly sand and pumice. Proportion of temper is about 30 per cent. Color is buff, with a gray medial area. Texture is compact.

Exterior surface — Color is a light yellowish-brown (10YR 6/4). Finish is horizontal burnish, of smooth quality. Vestiges of polish can be detected on our badly weathered specimen.

Interior surface—Color and finish like exterior.

Comparisons—Hicks and Nicholson (1964) describe very similar or identical material from their Late Classic phase at Portezuelo. Linné (1942: Fig. 201) and Armillas (1944: Lamina I, Fig. 11) illustrate vessels from Teotihuacan which seem to be quite comparable to our material.

II. Decorated Ware

A. Service Ware

1. Red-on-Buff (Fig. 64,*e-g;* 65,*c*): This type occurs in very low frequency throughout our survey area. Vessel form is often quite difficult to evaluate because of small sherd size. All specimens in our type collection appear to be flaring bowls and shallow flaring dishes. Rim diameter ranges between 26 and 40 cms. Wall thickness measures from 0.5 to 0.7 cms.

Paste—Temper consists of pumice and sand. Proportion of temper is quite variable, from 15 to 50 per cent. Color is buff or gray-buff, sometimes with a gray medial area. Texture is compact.

Exterior surface—No decoration, painting, or slipping could be detected in our type collection. Color is generally pale brown (10YR 6/3) and light yellowish-brown (10YR 6/4), although black (10YR 2/1) was sometimes present. Surfaces are unburnished, or only roughly burnished around the rim.

Interior surface—Decoration consists of red designs—simple parallel lines or bands —applied over an unpainted surface. Red paint is sometimes specular, and ranges from a weak (10R 4/4) to dark (10R 3/6) shade. Unpainted areas range from light brown (7.5YR 6/4) to brown (7.5YR 5/4) and dark brown (7.5YR 3/2). Finish is by means of horizontal burnish, which varies in quality from smooth to fairly rough.

Comparisons—Tolstoy's (1958: 26) San Martin Red-on-Buff Burnished Ware from his survey area in the northern Valley of Mexico appears to be partially equivalent to our Late Classic material. Hicks and Nicholson (1964) mention Red-on-Buff bowls with interior decoration from their Late Classic phase at Portezuelo which may correspond to our own material.

Early Toltec

I. Plain Ware

A. Utilitarian Ware

1. Ollas (Fig. 67,*a-d*): Principal form variants are rolled-rim and everted-rim vessels. Rim diameters range between 22 and 32 cms. Wall thickness below the rim varies from 0.7 to 2 cms. No appendages of any kind were noted.

Paste—Temper is composed of sand and pumice. Proportion of temper ranges between 30 and 50 per cent. Color is generally buff, often with a gray-black medial area. Texture is compact.

Exterior surface—No paint or slip could be detected. Colors range from light yellowish-brown (10YR 6/4), to pale brown (10YR 6/3), to gray (7.5YR 5/0), to grayish-brown

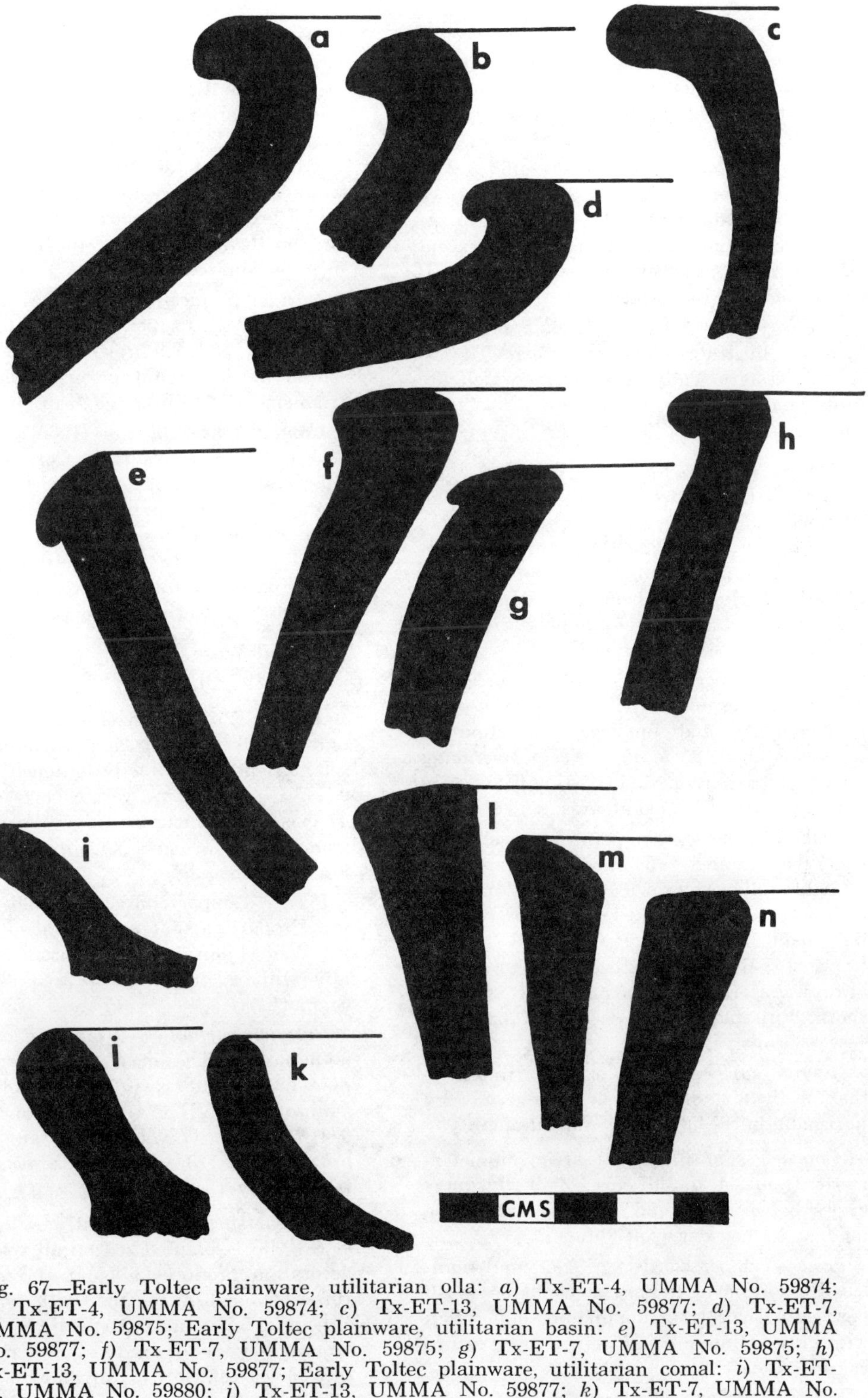

Fig. 67—Early Toltec plainware, utilitarian olla: *a*) Tx-ET-4, UMMA No. 59874; *b*) Tx-ET-4, UMMA No. 59874; *c*) Tx-ET-13, UMMA No. 59877; *d*) Tx-ET-7, UMMA No. 59875; Early Toltec plainware, utilitarian basin: *e*) Tx-ET-13, UMMA No. 59877; *f*) Tx-ET-7, UMMA No. 59875; *g*) Tx-ET-7, UMMA No. 59875; *h*) Tx-ET-13, UMMA No. 59877; Early Toltec plainware, utilitarian comal: *i*) Tx-ET-18, UMMA No. 59880; *j*) Tx-ET-13, UMMA No. 59877; *k*) Tx-ET-7, UMMA No. 59875; Early Toltec plainware, utilitarian basin: *l*) Tx-ET-7, UMMA No. 59875; *m*) Tx-ET-7, UMMA No. 59875; *n*) Tx-ET-7, UMMA No. 59875.

(2.5YR 5/2). Some fire blackening occurs. Sometimes color is not consistent over the surface of a single sherd. Finish is generally rough; burnishing is either absent or very sloppily performed.

Interior surface—The most common color is pale brown (10YR 6/3), but brown (7.5YR 5/4) and grayish-brown (2.5YR 5/2) also occur. Finish tends to be rough, except for the area just below the rim which is often smoothly burnished.

Comparisons—Rattray (1966*a*: 114, Fig. 1, *a, b*) illustrates ollas from Cerro Tenayo in the western Valley of Mexico which are quite similar to our everted-rim forms from the Texcoco Region.

2. Basins (Fig. 67,*e-h, l-n*): Principal form variants are everted-rim, wedge-rim, and bolstered-rim vessels, most of which have a distinctly bevelled edge. Rim diameters range between 24 and 48 cms, averaging about 40 cms. Wall thickness below the rim varies from 0.8 to 1.8 cms. No appendages were noted in our type collection.

Paste—Temper consists of sand (in which small particles of quartz or quartzite were predominant) and pumice. Proportion of temper is about 25 to 45 per cent, averaging about 30 per cent. Color is buff, usually with a gray-black medial area.

Exterior surface—No painting or slipping could be detected. The most common color is light yellowish-brown (10YR 6/4). Pale brown (10YR 6/3), light brown (7.5YR 6/4), light reddish-brown (5YR 6/4), and reddish-brown (5YR 5/4) also occur. Color is not always uniform on the surface of any one sherd. Fire blackening was noted on some vessels. Finish is rough.

Interior surface—Color is very similar to that of the exterior. Finish is generally by horizontal burnish, of fairly smooth quality.

3. Comales (Fig. 67,*i, j, k*): Rim diameters range from 44 to 46 cms. Wall thickness varies between 0.9 and 1.4 cms, with base tending to be somewhat thinner.

Paste—Temper consists of sand and pumice. Proportion of temper is about 35 to 40 per cent. Color is predominately buff, often with grayish interior and/or bottom. Texture is compact.

Exterior surface—No traces of painting or slipping could be detected. Color ranges from pale brown (10YR 6/3) to light brownish-gray (10YR 6/2). Fire blackening may be present. Basal surfaces are unfinished, and even appear to have been deliberately roughened. There is usually a distinct shoulder or ridge at the juncture of the base and wall. Wall surfaces are unburnished, with a rough texture, but appear to have been hastily smoothed by running the hand or finger over the unfired clay.

Interior surface—Color ranges from brown (7.5YR 5/4), to pale brown (10YR 6/3), and light yellowish-brown (10YR 6/4). Finish is by horizontal burnish, which varies from smooth to fairly rough in quality.

Comparisons—Rattray (1966 *a*: Fig. 1, *h, i*) illustrates vessels from Cerro Tenayo in the western Valley of Mexico which are quite similar to our comales from the Texcoco Region. Hicks and Nicholson (1964) describe comales from their Late Classic phase at Portezuelo which correspond in form to our Early Toltec comales.

II. Decorated Ware

A. Utilitarian Ware

1. Red-on-Buff Basins (Fig. 68): Form variants include everted- and bolstered-rim vessels, all with a distinctly flattened (bevelled) edge. Rim diameter varies between 22 and 47 cms. Wall thickness below the rim ranges from 0.5 to 1.2 cms. No appendages of any kind were noted.

Paste—Temper consists of sand and pumice. Proportion of temper is about 25 to 40 per cent. Color is buff to orange-buff, usually with a gray medial area. Texture is compact.

Exterior surface—No painting or slipping is apparent. The most common colors are pale brown (10YR 6/3) and light yellowish-brown (10YR 6/4). Light brown (7.5YR 6/4), brown (7.5YR 5/4), and reddish-brown (5YR 5/3 and 5/4) also occur. Finish is generally rough.

Interior surface—The flat, bevelled section of the rim is painted red on all vessels. This decoration produces a band of red (chiefly 10R 4/4 and 5/4, together with some 2.5YR 4/4 and 5/4, and 2.5YR 5/6) running around the top of the vessel. Remainder of the vessel interior is unpainted. Here the colors noted include reddish-brown (2.5YR 5/4 and 5YR 5/3), brown (7.5YR 5/4),

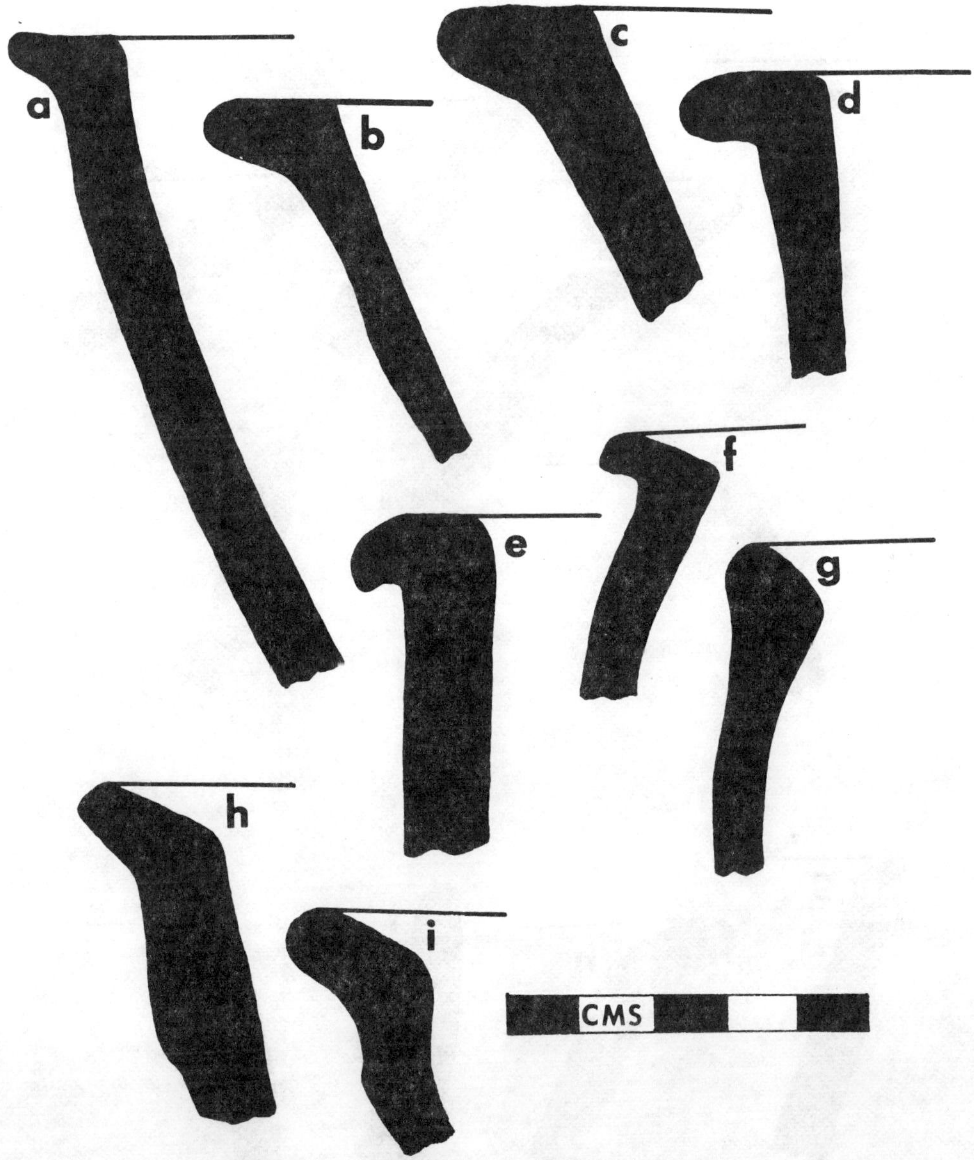

Fig. 68—Early Toltec decorated utilitarian ware, Red-on-Buff basin: *a*) Tx-ET-13, UMMA No. 59877; *b*) Tx-ET-18, UMMA No. 59877; *c*) Tx-ET-18, UMMA No. 59878; *d*) Tx-ET-18, UMMA No. 59878; *e*) Tx-ET-18. UMMA No. 59878; *f*) Tx-ET-18, UMMA No. 59879; *g*) Tx-ET-23, UMMA No. 59876; *h*) Tx-ET-4, UMMA No. 59874; *i*) Tx-ET-3, UMMA No. 59876.

light brown (7.5YR 6/4), dark yellowish-brown (10YR 4/4), and light yellowish-brown (10YR 6/4). Finish is by horizontal burnish, which is generally fairly smooth, but may occasionally be of rougher quality.

Comparisons—Our material appears to be identical or very similar to Rattray's (1966 *a*: 114, Fig. 1 *d*) *cazuela* vessels from Cerro Tenayo in the western Valley of Mexico.

B. Service Ware

1. Red-on-Buff Bowls (Figs. 69, 70): Form variants include both upright-wall and flaring-wall vessels, with the former predominant. Rim diameter ranges from 14 to 22

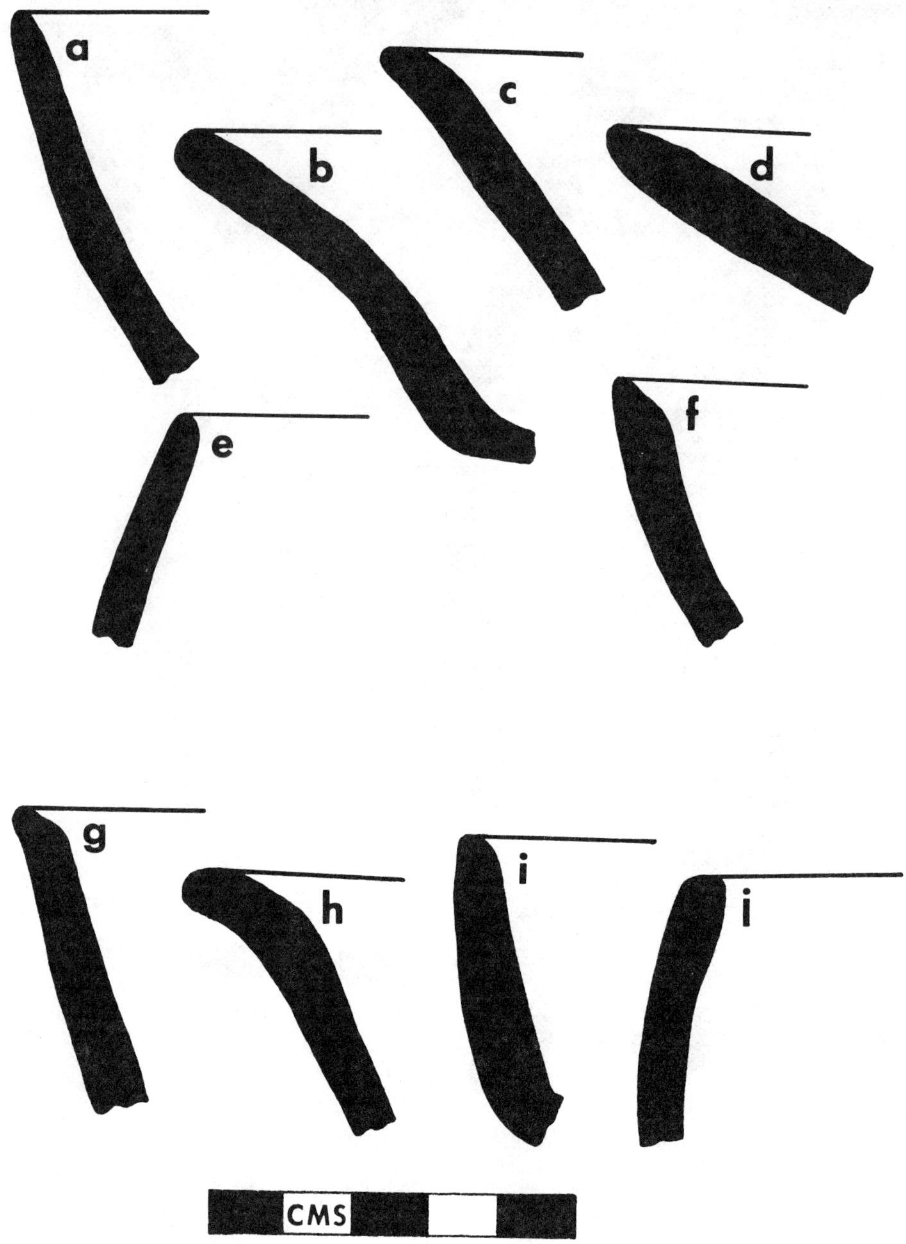

Fig. 69—Early Toltec decorated service ware, Red-on-Buff bowl: *a*) Tx-ET-13, UMMA No. 59877; *b*) Tx-ET-18, UMMA No. 59874; *c*) Tx-ET-13, UMMA No. 59877; *d*) Tx-ET-18, UMMA No. 59879; *e*) Tx-ET-13, UMMA No. 59877; *f*) Tx-ET-4, UMMA No. 59875; Early Toltec decorated service ware, Red-on-White bowl: *g*) Tx-ET-18, UMMA No. 59879; *h*) Tx-ET-18, UMMA No. 59879; *i*) Tx-ET-18, UMMA No. 59878; *j*) Tx-ET-13, UMMA No. 59877.

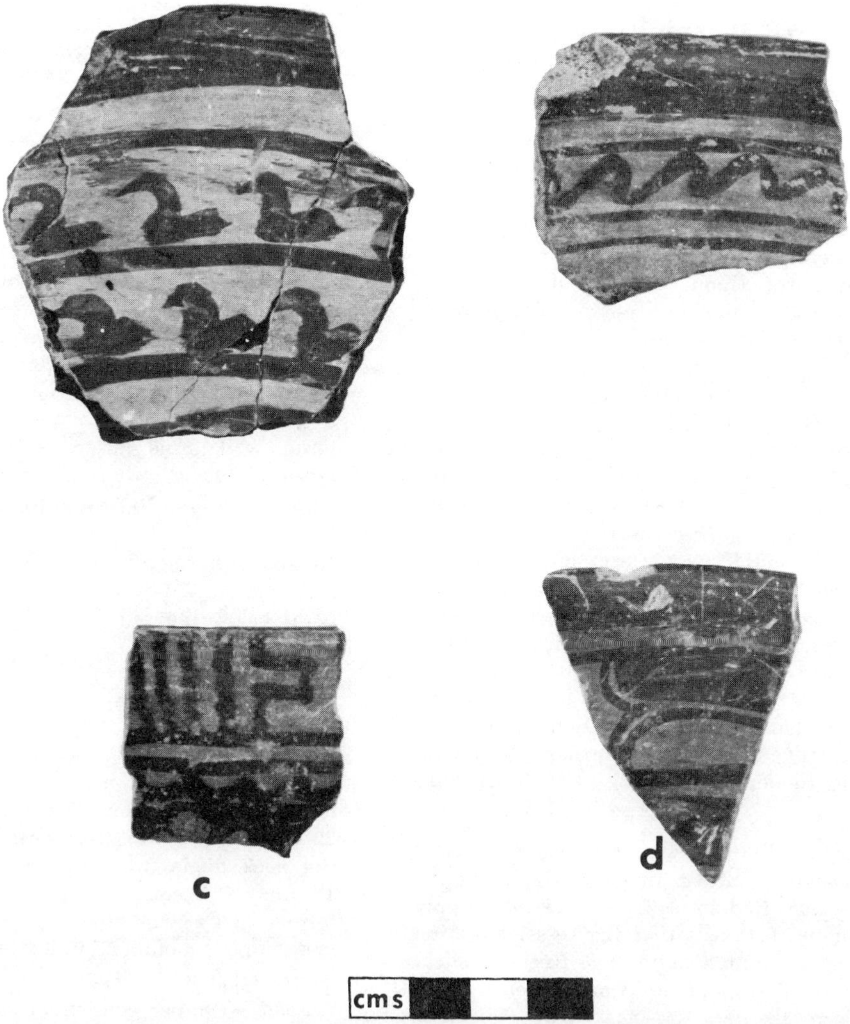

Fig. 70—Early Toltec decorated service ware, Red-on-Buff bowl: *a*) Tx-ET-13, UMMA No. 59877, UMMA Neg. 119-1-1; Interior surface; b) Tx-ET-13, UMMA No. 59877, UMMA Neg. 119-1-1, Interior surface; *c*) Tx-ET-18, UMMA No. 59879, UMMA Neg. 119-1-1, Exterior surface; *d*) Tx-ET-18, UMMA No. 59878, UMMA Neg. 119-1-1, Interior surface.

cms. Wall thickness varies between 0.5 and 0.7 cms. No appendages of any kind were noted.

Paste—Temper consists mainly of sand and pumice. The proportion of temper varies between 20 and 35 per cent. Color is orange or orange-buff, usually with a gray-black medial area. Texture is compact.

Exterior surface—Most vessels have exterior decoration, but some do not (a high proportion of the flaring-wall bowls lack exterior decoration). Decoration is typically in the form of fine-lined geometric red designs applied within the borders of an outlined panel running around the middle or upper part of the vessel wall. The red paint varies from weak (10R 4/4) to medium (10R 4/6) to dark (10R 3/6) shades. The red designs have been applied to an unpainted clay surface whose color varies from grayish-brown (10YR 5/2), to pale brown (10YR 6/3), to light yellowish-brown (10YR 6/4), to very pale brown (10YR 7/3), to brown (7.5YR 5/4), to light brown (7.5YR 6/4), to reddish-brown (5YR 5/4 and 5/3, and 2.5YR 5/4), to yellowish-red (5YR 5/6). In cases where there is red decoration on the exterior, the surface finish is by means of horizontal burnish of smooth quality. Where exterior decoration is absent, the surface is poorly burnished, and much rougher in texture.

Interior surface—Color and decoration essentially the same as the exterior, except for much lower frequency of red decoration. Finish is usually horizontal burnishing of smooth quality.

Comparisons—This ceramic type is the best known Early Toltec pottery in the Valley of Mexico. It was originally described by Tozzer (1921) from his excavations at Santiago Ahuitzotla near Atzcapotzalco in the western Valley of Mexico. Rattray (1966*a*) has exhaustively described a large quantity of this material from Cerro Tenayo in the western Valley. Hicks and Nicholson (1964) have included identical material in their Late Classic phase at Portezuelo. Sejourné (1966: Figs. 158, 159, 191) illustrates similar material from Teotihuacan. Tolstoy (1958: 43, Fig. 9) has described this same type from his survey area in the northern Valley of Mexico under the heading of Tula Red-on-Buff.

2. Red-on-White Bowls (Fig. 69,*g-j*): Vessel form and decoration are quite similar to the aforegoing Red-on-Buff category. The only major distinction is that the vessel has been slipped or painted white prior to the application of red decoration. Rim diameter varies between 18 and 20 cms. Wall thickness ranges from 0.5 to 0.9 cms.

Paste—Temper consists of sand (in which small quartz or quartzite particles are dominant) and some pumice. Color is generally buff, with a gray medial area. Texture is compact.

Exterior surface—Entire surface (or only a band around the upper part of the vessel has been covered with white paint (5Y 8/1, 2.5Y 8/2, and 10YR 8/2). On most vessels red (10R 4/3 and 4/4) designs, very similar to those employed in Red-on-Buff bowls, have been applied to the white surface. In our type collection the white paint has often been largely removed through weathering, and sometimes exists only as fragmentary vestiges. Where the white paint has been removed, or where it was never applied, the underlying natural clay color varies from reddish-brown (5YR 5/3 and 5/4), light brown (7.5YR 6/4), and light yellowish-brown (10YR 6/4).

Interior surface—Color is variable. Some vessels are unpainted and unslipped, with a natural clay color which varies from reddish-brown (5YR 5/4), to brown (7.5YR 5/4), to light yellowish-brown (10YR 6/4). On some vessels, a narrow red (10R 4/3) band extends around the top of the inner wall. In a few cases the entire vessel interior has been painted red. One sherd in our type collection had a pale yellow paint (2.4Y 8/4) over at least the upper part of the interior wall. This latter vessel has red interior similar to that of the exterior.

Comparisons—Rattray (1966*a*: 155) mentions that a small number of her Coyotlatelco Red-on-Buff sherds from Cerro Tenayo in the western Valley of Mexico have a cream paint below the red decoration.

Late Toltec

I. Plain Ware

A. Utilitarian Ware

1. Ollas (Fig. 71,*a-d*): All are flaring-mouth vessels, often with a sharply-defined interior neck angle. Rim diameter ranges from 22 to 30 cms. Wall thickness is greatest at the neck angle, where it measures between 1.2 and 2.4 cms, averaging closer to the former figure. On other sections of the neck and upper shoulder, wall thickness varies between 0.5 and 1.0 cm.

Paste—Temper consists of sand and pumice. Porportion of temper ranges from 25 to 45 per cent. Color is usually grayish-brown, often with a darker medial area. Texture is compact.

Exterior surface—Predominant colors are reddish-brown (2.5YR 5/4) and reddish (10R 4/4), which appear to be slips. Finish is by means of horizontal burnishing, which tends to be rough in quality.

Interior surface—Surface down to the neck angle has been slipped in reddish-brown or reddish, as the exterior. Below this point the natural clay color varies from brown (7.5YR 5/4), to light brown (7.5YR 6/4), to grayish brown (10YR 5/2), to pale brown (10YR 6/3). Finish as exterior surface.

Comparisons—Linné (1934: Figs. 96, 100, 106) illustrates identical or similar vessels from Teotihuacan.

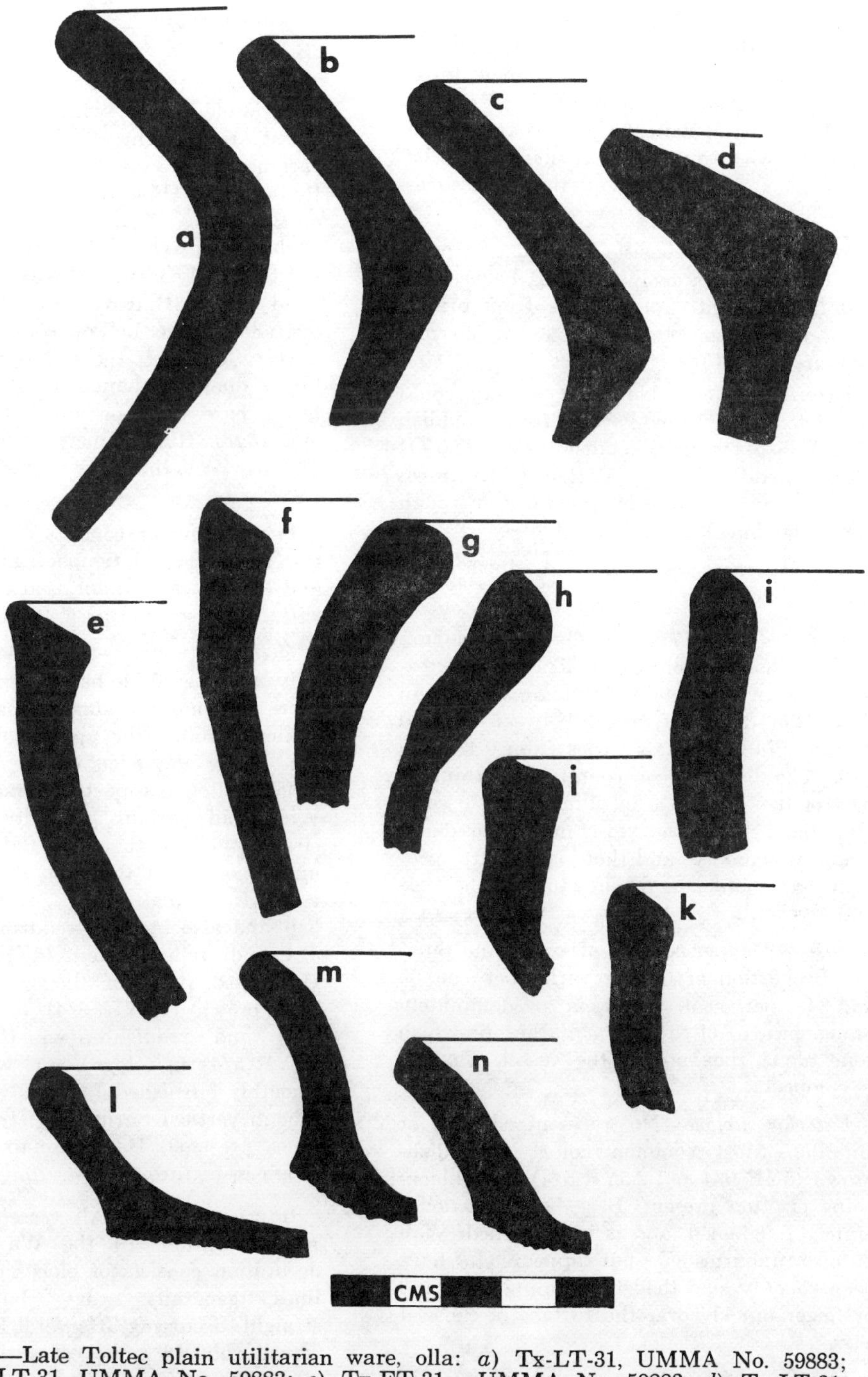

Fig. 71—Late Toltec plain utilitarian ware, olla: *a*) Tx-LT-31, UMMA No. 59883; *b*) Tx-LT-31, UMMA No. 59883; *c*) Tx-ET-31, UMMA No. 59883; *d*) Tx-LT-31, UMMA No. 59883; Late Toltec plain utilitarian ware, basin: *e*) Tx-LT-12, UMMA No. 59881; *f*) Tx-LT-57, UMMA No. 59886; g) Tx-LT-53, UMMA No. 59889; *h*) Tx-LT-31, UMMA No. 59883; *i*) Tx-LT-57, UMMA No. 59886; *j*) Tx-LT-57, UMMA No. 59886; *k*) Tx-LT-53, UMMA No. 59889; Late Toltec plain utilitarian ware, comal: *l*) Tx-LT-31, UMMA No. 59883; *m*) Tx-LT-57, UMMA No. 59886; *n*) Tx-LT-53, UMMA No. 59889.

2. Basins (Fig. 71,*e-k*): Vessels typically have a flattened, inward-slanted edge, or bevel. Some rims have a tendency to be slightly incurved. Some vessels are slightly shouldered. Rim diameter ranges from 22 to 44 cms, with most vessels measuring between 35 and 42 cms. Wall thickness varies from 0.6 to 1.6 cms.

Paste—Temper consists of sand and pumice. Proportion of temper ranges between 35 and 50 per cent. Color varies from orange to orange-brown, often with a grayish medial area. Texture is compact.

Exterior surface—No paint or slip could be detected. Color varies from reddish (2.5YR 5/6) to light reddish-brown (2.5YR 6/4) to reddish-brown (5YR 5/4) to brown (7.5YR 5/4). Finish is generally a rough horizontal burnish.

Interior surface—Color and finish very similar to exterior.

3. Comales (Fig. 71,*l-n*): These vessels are distinguishable from Early Toltec and Aztec comales principally by their high, thin wall. Rim diameter ranges between 30 and 38 cms. Wall thickness varies from 0.4 to 0.9 cms. The base is consistently the thinnest part of the vessel. As in all Postclassic comales, the base of the vessel has been deliberately roughened, and there is a sharp, pronounced shoulder at the juncture of the base and the wall.

Paste—Temper consists of gravel and pumice. Proportion of temper varies between 30 and 45 per cent. Color is predominately orange-brown, often with a darker brownish zone along the base of the vessel. Texture is compact.

Exterior surface—No traces of painting or slipping. Most common color is reddish-brown (5YR 6/4 and 2.5YR 5/4). Fire blackening is often present. Base has been deliberately roughened, and is unburnished. Wall is also unburnished, but appears to have been roughly smoothed by running the hand or finger quickly over the surface of the wet clay.

Interior surface—Painting and slipping absent. Colors noted are reddish-brown (5YR 6/4; 2.5YR 5/4), reddish (2.5YR 4/6, 5/6), and dark red (2.5YR 3/6). Finish is by means of horizontal burnish, which is usually of fairly rough quality.

II. Decorated Ware

A. Service Ware

1. Red-on-Buff Bowls (Fig. 72): All vessels are simple bowls, with upright walls and direct rims. Three distinctive decorative variants can be distinguished: (*a*) Wavy-line Red-on-Buff (Fig. 73,*b, c*), (*b*) Sloppy Red-on-Buff (Fig. 73,*a, d*), and (*c*) Wide-band Red-on-Buff (Fig. 74). Appendages could not be clearly identified except for the Wide-band Red-on-Buff variant which is characterized by large, hollow, conical tripodal supports. Some of these latter vessels have broad diamond-shaped striations on the interior base, and presumably functioned as *molcajetes*. Rim diameter ranges from 16 to 32 cms. Wall thickness varies between 0.5 to 0.8 cms.

Paste—Temper consists of sand and pumice. Proportion of temper ranges between 20 and 30 per cent. Color is usually buff, often with a gray medial area. Texture is compact.

Exterior surface—Red decoration occurs only on the Wide-band variant, in which there is usually a single broad band of red running around the upper part of the vessel just below the edge of the rim. Also, the large, hollow supports characteristic of the Wide-band variant generally have a large circular blob of the same red paint over the upper portion of the support. This red paint varies from weak (10R 4/4) to dark (2.5YR 3/6, and also includes reddish-brown (2.5YR 4/4, and yellowish-red (5YR 5/6) shades. Unpainted parts of the vessel range from light brown (7.5YR 6/4) to brown (7.5YR 5/4) and reddish-brown (5YR 5/4 and 2.5YR 5/4) in color. Vessel walls tend to be smoothly burnished (generally horizontal, although vertical burnishing streaks are sometimes present). Bases are unburnished, and rough in texture.

Interior surface—All vessels have interior red decoration. In the Wavy-line variant, decoration consists of blocks of thin parallel lines, generally wavy, but occasionally straight, occurring at several localities on the vessel wall. In some cases there may be a single large block of such lines. The Sloppy variant features red designs in the form of irregular splotches, crude concentric circles, irregular linear elements, and broad splashes of red color. In most cases, burnishing has occurred prior to the drying of these

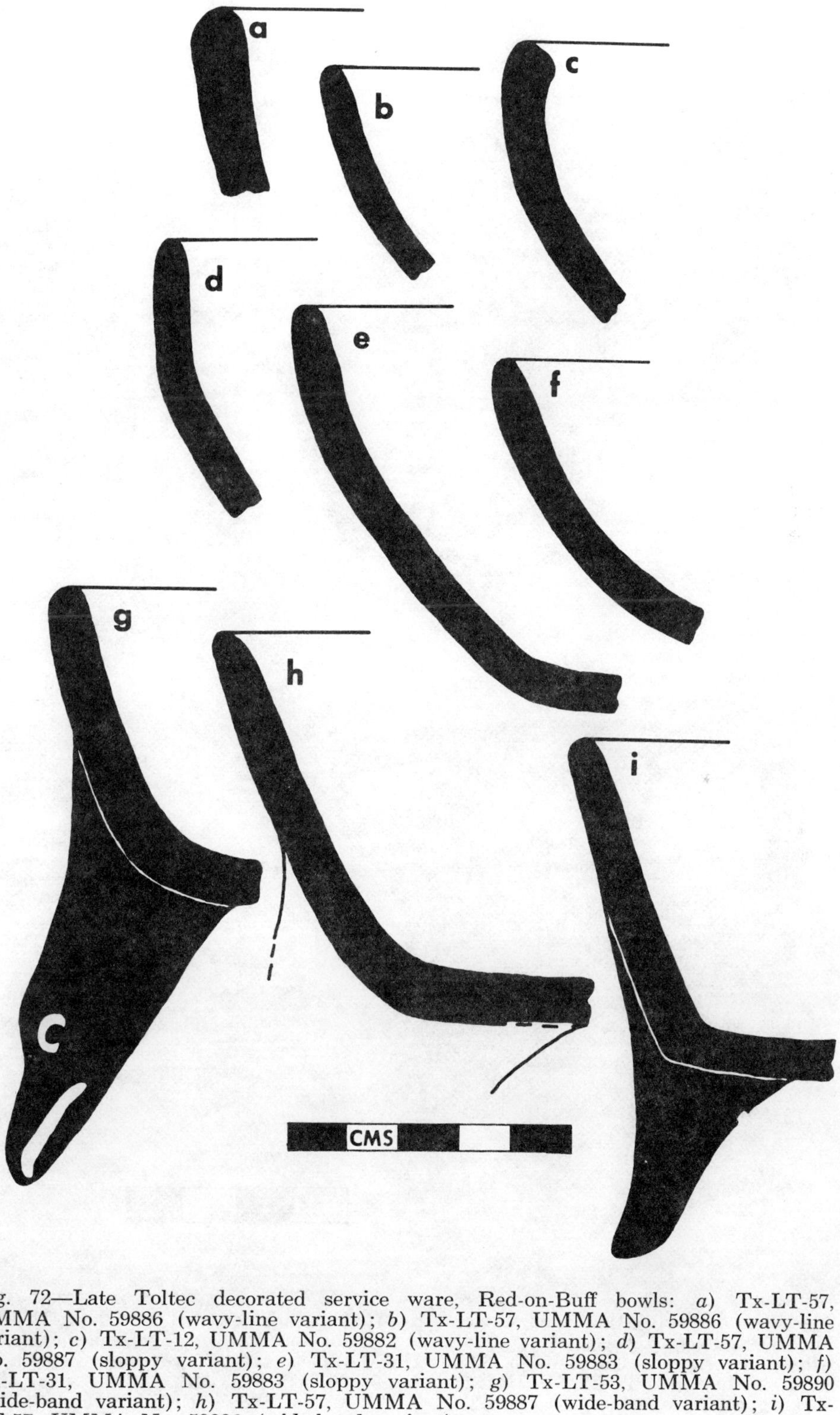

Fig. 72—Late Toltec decorated service ware, Red-on-Buff bowls: *a*) Tx-LT-57, UMMA No. 59886 (wavy-line variant); *b*) Tx-LT-57, UMMA No. 59886 (wavy-line variant); *c*) Tx-LT-12, UMMA No. 59882 (wavy-line variant); *d*) Tx-LT-57, UMMA No. 59887 (sloppy variant); *e*) Tx-LT-31, UMMA No. 59883 (sloppy variant); *f*) Tx-LT-31, UMMA No. 59883 (sloppy variant); *g*) Tx-LT-53, UMMA No. 59890 (wide-band variant); *h*) Tx-LT-57, UMMA No. 59887 (wide-band variant); *i*) Tx-LT-57, UMMA No. 59886 (wide-band variant).

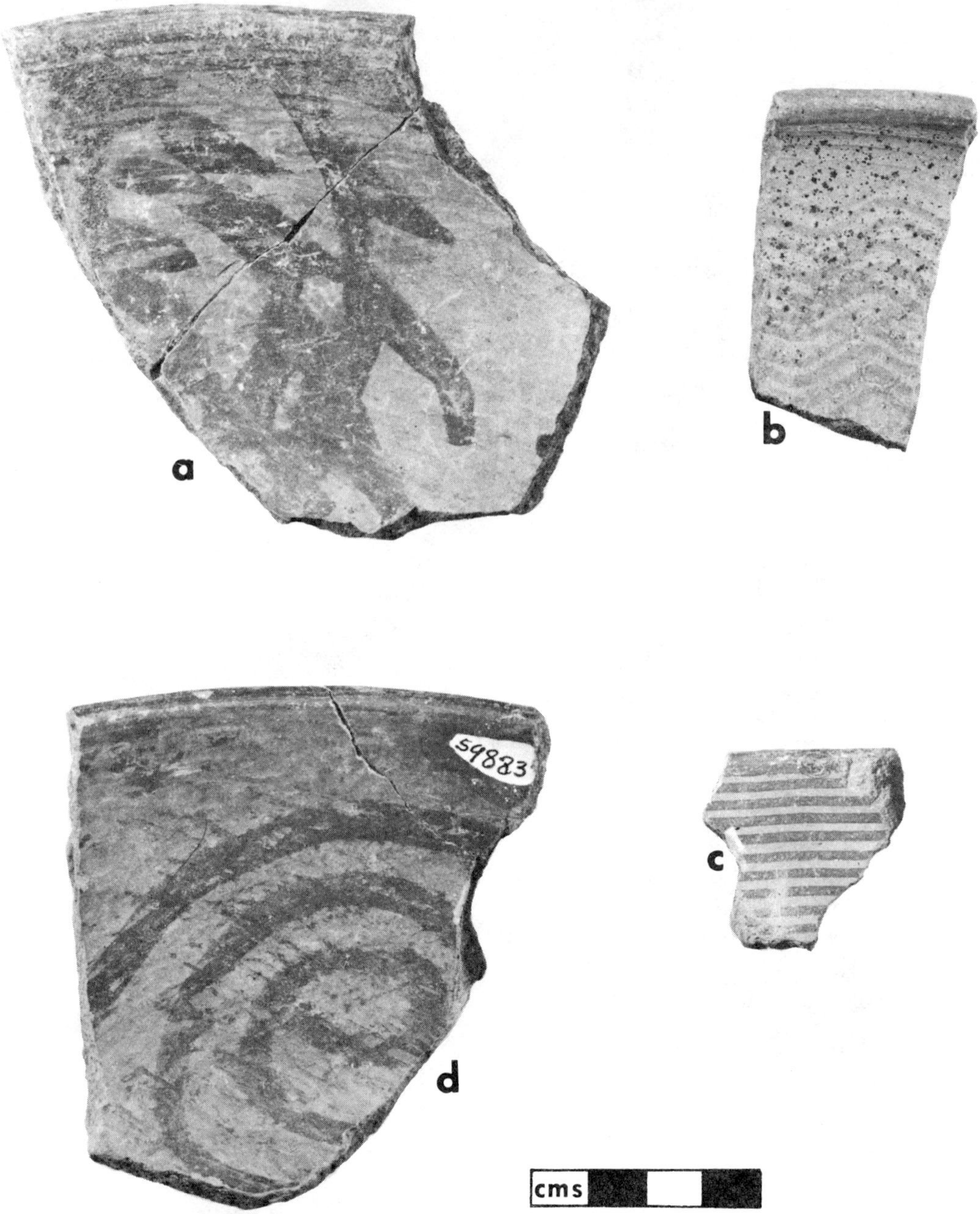

Fig. 73—Late Toltec decorated service ware, Red-on-Buff bowl: *a*) Tx-LT-31, UMMA No. 59883 Neg. 110-1-6, sloppy variant, interior surface; *b*) Teotihuacan Valley, Mazapan type site, UMMA No. 30617, UMMA Neg. 119-1-6, wavy-line variant, interior surface; *c*) Tx-LT-57, UMMA No. 59886, UMMA Neg. 119-1-6, wavy-line variant, interior surface; *d*) Tx-LT-31, UMMA No. 59883, UMMA Neg. 119-1-6, sloppy variant, interior surface.

Fig. 74—Late Toltec decorated service ware, Red-on-Buff bowl, wide-band variant, Tx-LT-53, UMMA No. 59890: *a*) Exterior surface from below, showing serpent-effigy support, UMMA Neg. 119-1-5; *b*) Interior surface of same vessel, UMMA Neg. 119-1-3.

latter designs since they are usually quite smeared. The Wide-band decorative variant features broad bands and zones of red, which often cover most of the vessel wall. Finish tends to be by means of horizontal burnish of smooth quality. Occasionally traces of high polish can still be detected. In a few cases burnishing has been rather irregular so that red paint has a very uneven appearance. Color of red decoration includes weak red (10R 4/4), deep red (10R 4/6 and 2.5YR 4/6), dark red (2.5YR 3/6), yellowish-red (5YR 5/6), reddish-brown (2.5YR 5/4 and 4/4), and dark reddish-brown (7.5YR 5/4). Unpainted sections are similar to the exterior wall.

Comparisons—This ceramic type is the best known and best described Late Toltec pottery in the Valley of Mexico. Linné (1934: Figs. 56A, 57, 59, 61, 63, 64, 68, 78, 82, 86, 87, 91, 92, 93 105, 108, and 111) illustrates material from Teotihuacan which is identical or very similar to our Wavy-line and Wide-band variants from the Texcoco Region. Hicks and Nicholson (1964) describe pottery from their Postclassic phase at Portezuelo which corresponds exactly to our Wavy-line and Wide-line variants. Tolstoy's (1958: 42) Mazapan Red-on-Buff is equivalent to our Wavy-line variant, and his Tula Red-on-Buff (ibid) partially cross-cuts our Wide-band category.

Early Aztec

Our Early Aztec period is defined predominately by the Culhuacan and Tenayuca (Aztec I and II) variants of Black-on-Orange pottery as described by Griffin and Espejo (1947, 1950). Since there proved to be very little Culhuacan (Aztec I) material in our survey area, Early Aztec occupation in the Texcoco Region was plotted primarily on the basis of the distribution of Tenayuca phase (Aztec II) Black-on-Orange (although small quantities of Aztec I material usually were also present wherever Aztec II ceramics occurred). Black-on-Red pottery also proved to be somewhat useful in defining Early Aztec occupation. We still have only a vague idea of the character of Early Aztec undecorated pottery. This is primarily because Early Aztec occupation so seldom occurs isolated from a much heavier admixture of Late Aztec. Thus, while undecorated pottery is very distinctive for defining Aztec occupation as a single, broad, undifferentiated period, we have been unable to employ it to differentiate Early and Late Aztec occupations. All undecorated material is here described in the Late Aztec section. We have had to treat the distinctive Black-and-White-on-Red in a similar manner for the identical reason.

Unless otherwise noted, all descriptions of Early and Late Aztec pottery have been abstracted from previously-analyzed material from the adjacent Teotihuacan Valley (Parsons, 1966). This appears to be justifiable in view of the essential similarity of Aztec pottery throughout the entire Valley of Mexico.

I. Decorated Ware

A. Service Ware

1. Black-on-Orange: The basic form variants are basins (Fig. 75,*a-f;* 77,*d*), dishes (Fig. 76,*a-c;* 77,*c*), *molcajetes* (Fig. 76,*d, e;* these vessels are dishes with striations on the interior base, used for grinding chile and other vegetable materials), plates (Fig. 76,*f, g;* 77,*a, b*), and bowls (Fig. 75,*g-j*). Basins typically have small horizontal loop handles or small solid lug handles. Dishes and molcajetes usually have thick, stubby, tripod conical supports. Bowls and plates lack appendages of any kind.

For basins, rim diameter ranges between 21 and 30 cms, and wall thickness between 0.6 and 1.2 cms. For dishes and molcajetes, rim diameter ranges between 10 and 30 cms, and wall thickness between 0.5 and 1.2 cms. For plates, rim diameter ranges between 20 and 25 cms, and wall thickness between 0.5 and 0.9 cms. For bowls, rim diameter ranges between 15 and 23 cms, and wall thickness between 0.5 and 0.8 cms.

Paste—Proportion of temper varies between 5 and 15 per cent. Larger and thicker-walled vessels generally are characterized by concentrations of tempering material at the upper end of this range, while smaller

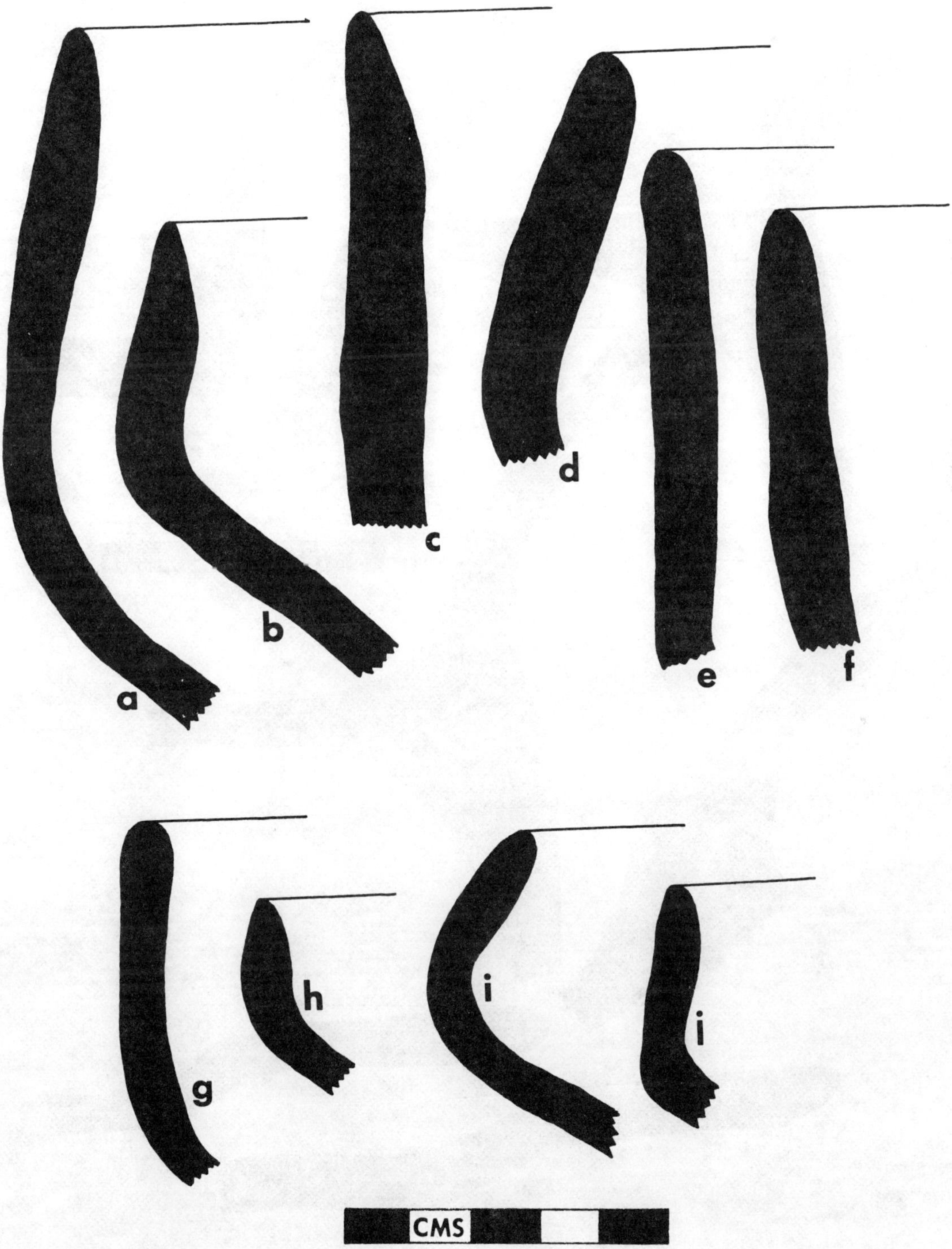

Fig. 75—Early Aztec decorated service ware, Black-on-Orange basin: *a*) through *f*), Teotihuacan Valley, PSUDA collection; Early Aztec decorated service ware, Black-on-Orange bowl: *g*) through *j*), Teotihuacan Valley, PSUDA collection.

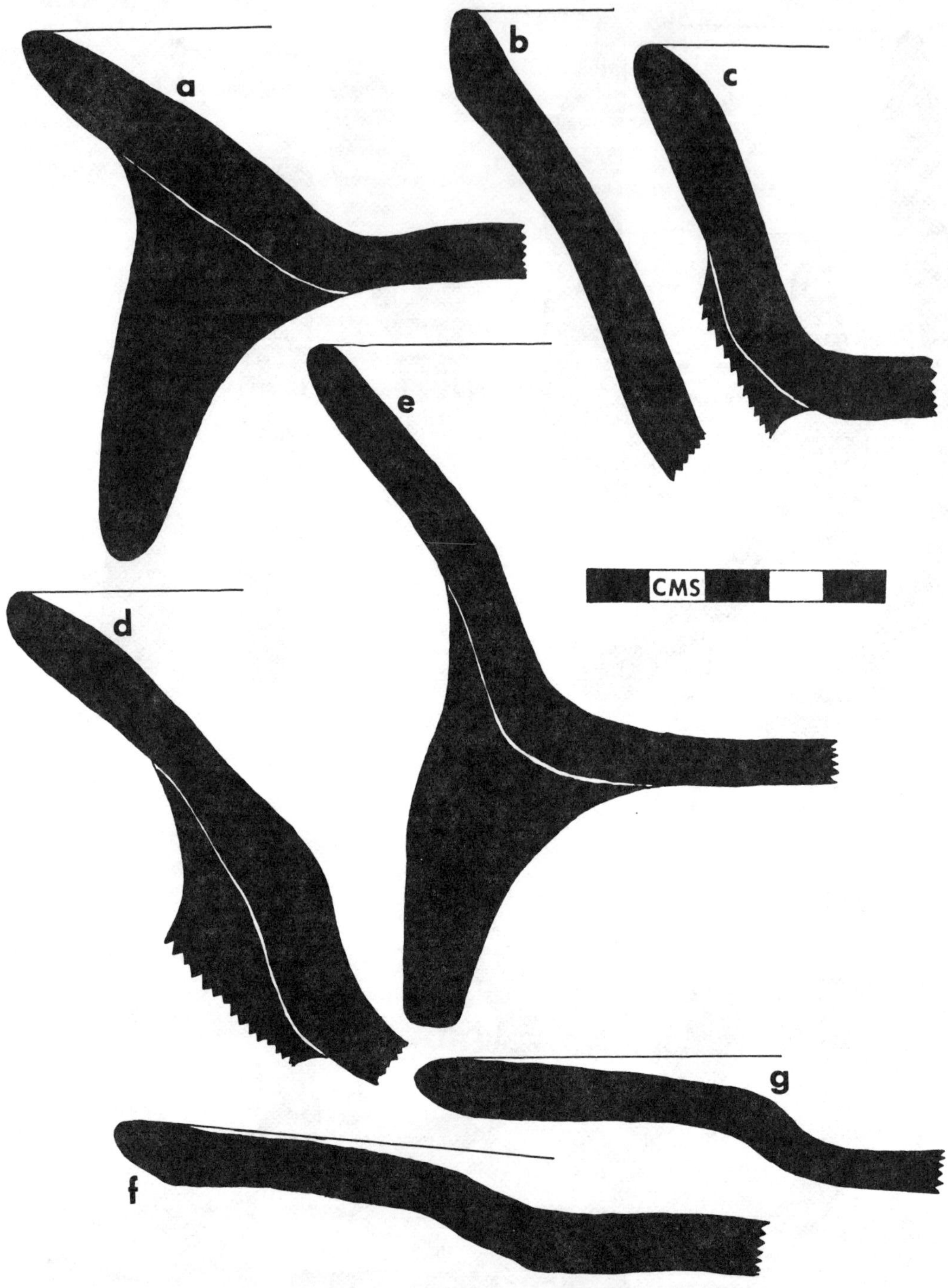

Fig. 76—Early Aztec decorated service ware, Black-on-Orange dish: *a*) through *c*), Teotihuacan Valley, PSUDA collection; Early Aztec decorated service ware, Black-on-Orange molcajete: *d*) and *e*), Teotihuacan Valley, PSUDA collection; Early Aztec decorated service ware, Black-on-Orange plate: *f*) and *g*), Teotihuacan Valley, PSUDA collection.

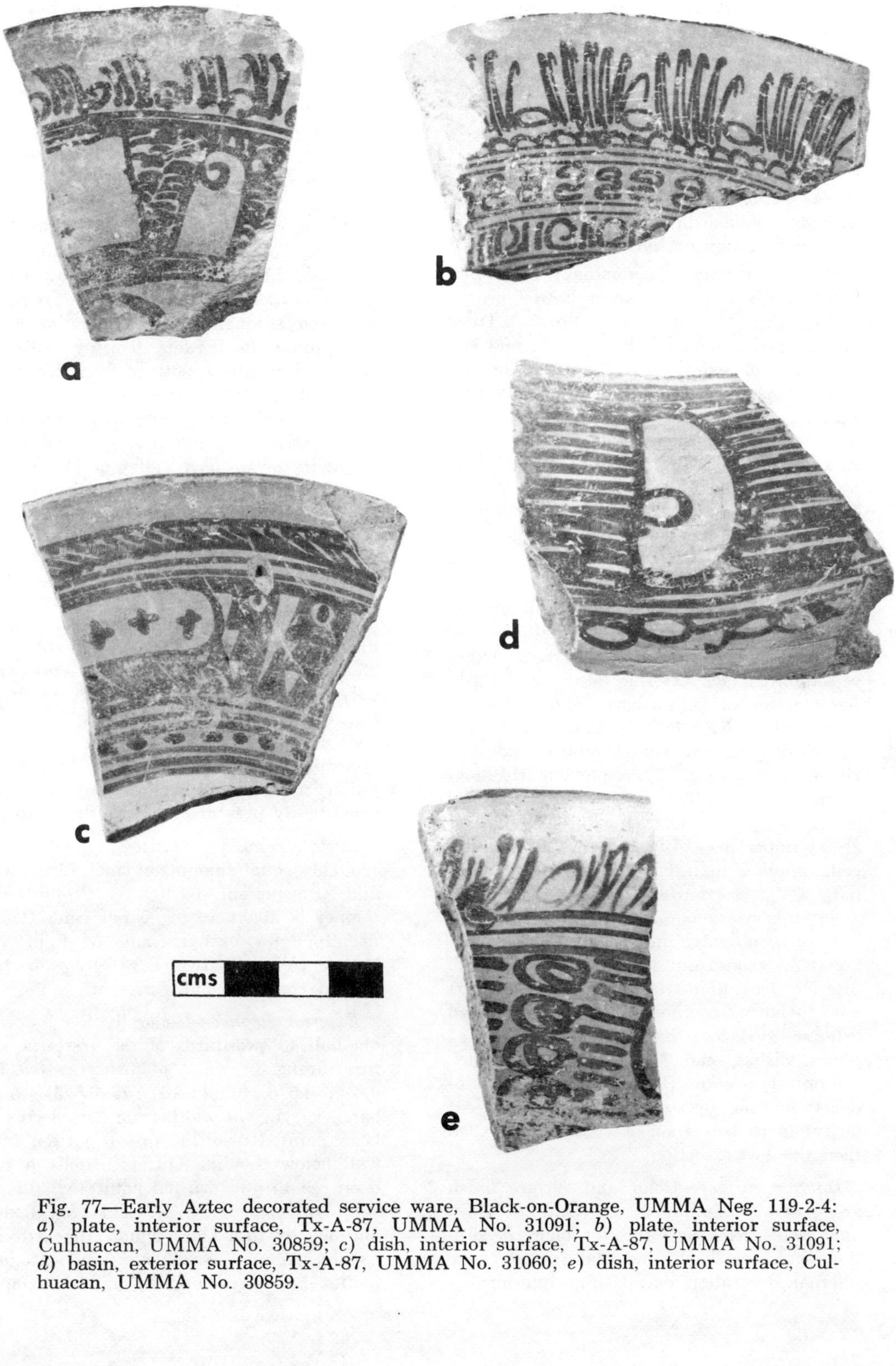

Fig. 77—Early Aztec decorated service ware, Black-on-Orange, UMMA Neg. 119-2-4: *a*) plate, interior surface, Tx-A-87, UMMA No. 31091; *b*) plate, interior surface, Culhuacan, UMMA No. 30859; *c*) dish, interior surface, Tx-A-87, UMMA No. 31091; *d*) basin, exterior surface, Tx-A-87, UMMA No. 31060; *e*) dish, interior surface, Culhuacan, UMMA No. 30859.

and thinner-walled vessels tend to fall toward the lower end. Temper is comprised of fine sand (about equal proportions of small black, transparent, and transluscent particles) and pumice (amorphous red-brown and yellowish grains). Color is generally orange to light brown, generally of a uniform shade, but sometimes with a grayish or brownish medial area. Paste is sometimes distinctly laminated in appearance, with thin pinkish layers alternating with the dominant orange or light brown.

Exterior surface—Predominant colors are light orange, orange-brown, yellowish-brown, reddish-orange, and reddish-brown. These appear to be natural clay colors, and not the result of painting or slipping. The following designations from the *Munsell Soil Color Charts* (1954) closely approximate the dominant color variations within this type: 2.5YR 4/4, 5/4, 4/5, 4/8, 5/6, 6/4, 6/6, 6/8; 5YR 4/2, 4/8, 6/8, 5/8, 5/6, 6/6, 4/2, 5/3, 6/3; 7.5YR 5.5/4, 5.5/5.5, 4/1, 6.5/7. Irregular dark gray and black splotching sometimes occurs, probably the result of blackening during firing.

Bowls and basins have exterior decoration in the form of black or brownish-black designs applied to the vessel surface. Other vessel forms lack exterior decoration. Early Aztec design motifs on bowls and basins are characterized by relatively thick lines, hastily applied in complex geometric and curvilinear forms (Fig. 77). A particularly diagnostic element is the *zacate* motif, comprised of one or more rows of thick, short lines of grassy appearance. Black decoration is typically applied in a band around the upper part of the vessel wall.

Surfaces are generally well smoothed and burnished, although quality of the burnishing is sometimes quite streaky. Vessels with exterior decoration (i.e., bowls and basins) tend to have smoother and better burnished exterior surfaces than those forms (i.e., plates, dishes, and *molcajetes*) which lack exterior decoration. There is a general tendency for the upper portion of vessel exteriors to be better smoothed and burnished then the lower section.

Interior surface—Color and surface finish are generally similar to the exterior. Bowl and basin forms lack interior black decoration; *molcajete,* dish, and plate vessels have internal decoration exclusively. Interior design motifs approximate those of the exterior. The interior surfaces of bowls and basins tend to be less carefully burnished than the exterior walls of these vessels. In general, the interior surfaces of plates, dishes, and *molcajetes* are more carefully smoothed and burnished than their exterior walls. The interior bases of *molcajetes* have often been badly worn through usage in grinding plant foods.

Comparisons—Franco (1945), and Griffin and Espejo (1947, 1950) have exhaustively described identical or very similar material from surface collections and excavations scattered throughout the Valley of Mexico and around its borders. Tolstoy (1958) has described identical pottery from his surface collections in the northern Valley of Mexico. Noguera (1935) excavated large quantities of essentially identical material at Tenayuca in the western Valley of Mexico. Vaillant (1938) has illustrated identical ceramics from his excavations at several localities in the Valley of Mexico.

2. Black-on-Red Incised: Vessels are all bowls, with two major form variants: (*a*) upright-wall bowls (Fig. 86,*a-d*), and (*b*) incurved-wall bowls (Fig. 86,*e*). Rim diameter ranges between 8 and 14 cms on incurved-wall bowls, and between 14 and 21 cms on the upright-wall vessels. Wall thickness measures between 0.5 and 0.8 cms. No appendages of any kind were noted. This pottery type occurs in low frequency, but is consistently present and quite diagnostic.

Paste—Temper consists of fine sand (roughly equal amounts of small black, white, and transluscent particles). Proportion of temper is about 10 to 20 per cent. Color is usually light orange, buff, or light gray-brown. A distinctive dark gray or black central core is usually present.

Exterior surface—Generally the lowermost one-half to two-thirds of the vessel is a natural orange-brown to reddish-gray (*ca.* 5YR 4/2.5, 4.5/6, 5.5/4; 10 YR 6.5/5). A red band, varying in width from 2 to 4 cms, has been painted over the upper portion of the wall below the lip. This is usually a thick, deep red to purplish-red paint (*ca.* 10R 3/2, 3/5, 3/4, 4/6, 4/7, 4/8). This red band is outlined by thin black bands. Black designs, usually simple curvilinear and geometric motifs, have been applied to the surface of the red band. These black designs have been roughly outlined by means of shallow, crude incision (Fig. 87,*c, d*). Surfaces have been well smoothed and burnished, especially the red-painted areas where traces of high polish are often present.

Interior surface—Usually undecorated and unpainted, with natural clay color as on lower part of the exterior wall. In some cases a broad black band has been painted on the vessel interior, occasionally with crude, curvilinear incised designs. Finish is generally smooth and well burnished.

Comparisons — Noguera (1935: Lamina XVI, 1, 2, 3) illustrates very similar material from his excavations at Tenayuca in the western Valley of Mexico.

3. Black-on-Red (Fig. 86,*a-e*): Vessels are simple bowls, with flat bottoms and upright or slightly recurved walls. No appendages of any kind were noted. Rim diameter ranges from 15 to 25 cms, and wall thickness from 0.6 to 0.8 cms.

Paste—As in Black-on-Red Incised (above).

Exterior surface—Color and finish as in Black-on-Red Incised (above), except that incision is absent, and black decoration is quite different. Vertical black lines, measuring between 0.3 and 1.0 cms wide, have been applied over the red paint, at intervals of 4 to 5 cms around the vessel exterior (Fig. 87,*a*).

Interior surface—Color is either black to black-brown (apparently a thick paint), or natural clay color (as exterior of Black-on-Red Incised, above). Surface has been well smoothed and burnished, particularly in cases of black interiors.

Late Aztec

I. Plainware

A. Utilitarian Ware

1. Ollas and Basins: These vessels are the same basic ware. Occasionally ollas can be clearly distinguished from basins, but often sherds are of such small size that it is quite difficult to objectively differentiate these two forms. For this reason, both are described here as a unit. On Aztec residential sites throughout the Texcoco Region, this material, together with the bowls described under Service Ware, below, comprise a dominant proportion of the surface sherds. A wide variety of form variants occur, of which only the most distinctive and diagnostic are described here:

a) High-necked vessels, with simple, direct rims, and large vertical loop handles (Fig. 78,*a-d*), which are clearly ollas. Rim diameter ranges from 8 to 18 cms, and modal wall thickness from 0.6 to 0.9 cms. Total neck height ranges between 5 and 11 cms on sherds which are large enough to show this dimension.

b) Flaring-mouth vessels, with short necks (Fig. 78,*e-i*), which are also clearly ollas. Rim diameter measures between about 10 and 20 cms, and modal wall thickness between 0.5 and 0.9 cms. No appendages were noted for these vessels.

c) Vessels with upright walls and flat, wide everted rims. Some are clearly ollas (Fig. 79,*a-e*), but in many cases we have been unable to differentiate ollas and basins. Rim diameter varies between about 10 and 35 cms (the larger rim diameters probably representing basins and the smaller indicating ollas). Modal wall thickness ranges between 0.6 and 0.9 cms, below the everted rim.

d) Flaring-mouth vessels, with bolstered rim, and a distinctly bevelled exterior edge, often with a marked overhang (Fig. 79,*f-j*). Both ollas and basins are probably about equally represented. Rim diameter ranges between about 12 and 40 cms (once again, the vessels with larger rim diameters are probably basins while the smaller-mouth vessels indicate ollas). Modal wall thickness measures between 0.6 and 1.0 cms, below the bolstered rim.

Paste—Temper consists primarily of sand (irregular small black, white, and translucent particles, some of which approach 0.1 cm in diameter). Proportion of temper ranges from 20 to 40 per cent in most vessels. Most common color is light brown to orange, usually uniform, but occasionally with a dark gray or brown medial area in thicker-walled vessels. Small irregular orifices are common. Texture is compact.

Exterior surface—The most common color is orange to reddish-brown (*ca.* 5YR 5.5/6 to 2.5YR 4.5/4). Next most common is light yellowish-brown to a dark grayish-brown (*ca.* 6.25YR 6.5/6 to 5YR 4/1.5). Varying shades of dark brown and black-brown also occur, but in very small quantities. Color is frequently variable over the

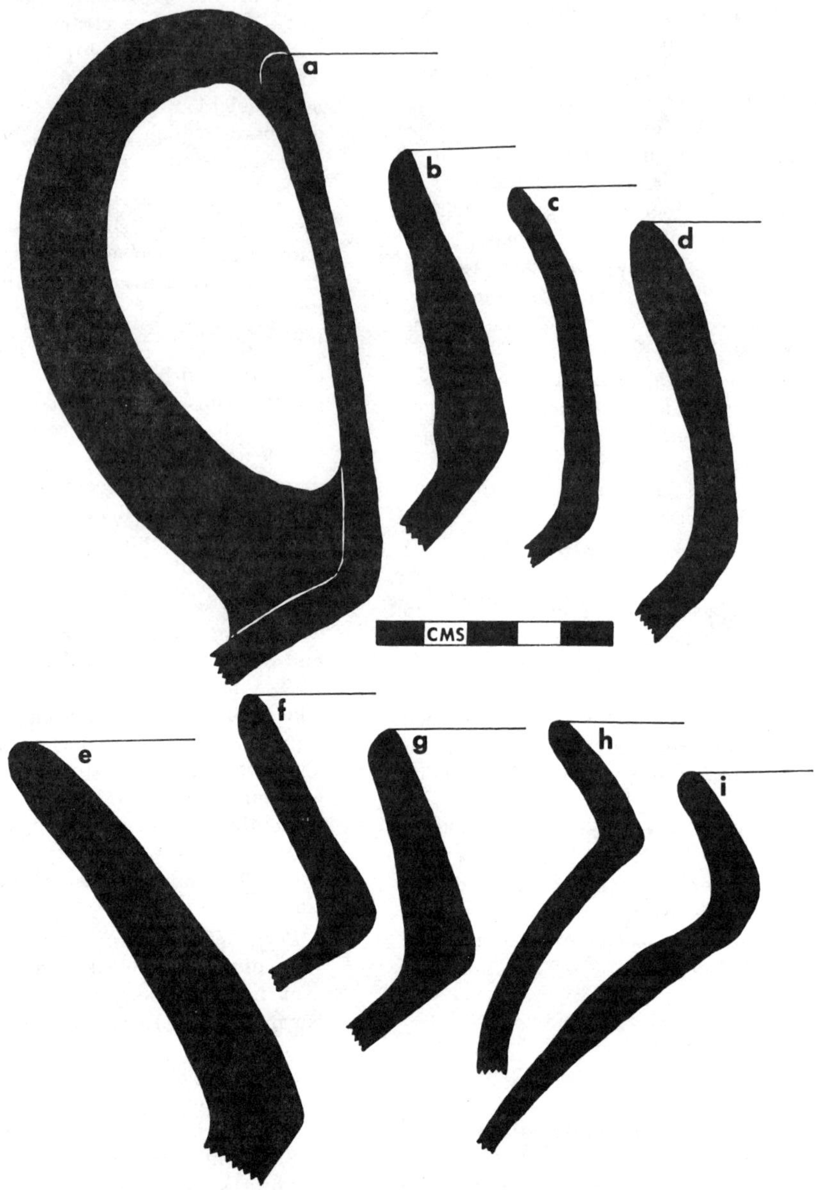

Fig. 78—Aztec plain utilitarian ware, olla with high, straight neck and direct rim: *a*) through *d*), Teotihuacan Valley, PSUDA collection; Late Aztec plain utilitarian ware, olla with flaring neck and direct rim: *e*) through *i*), Teotihuacan Valley, PSUDA collection.

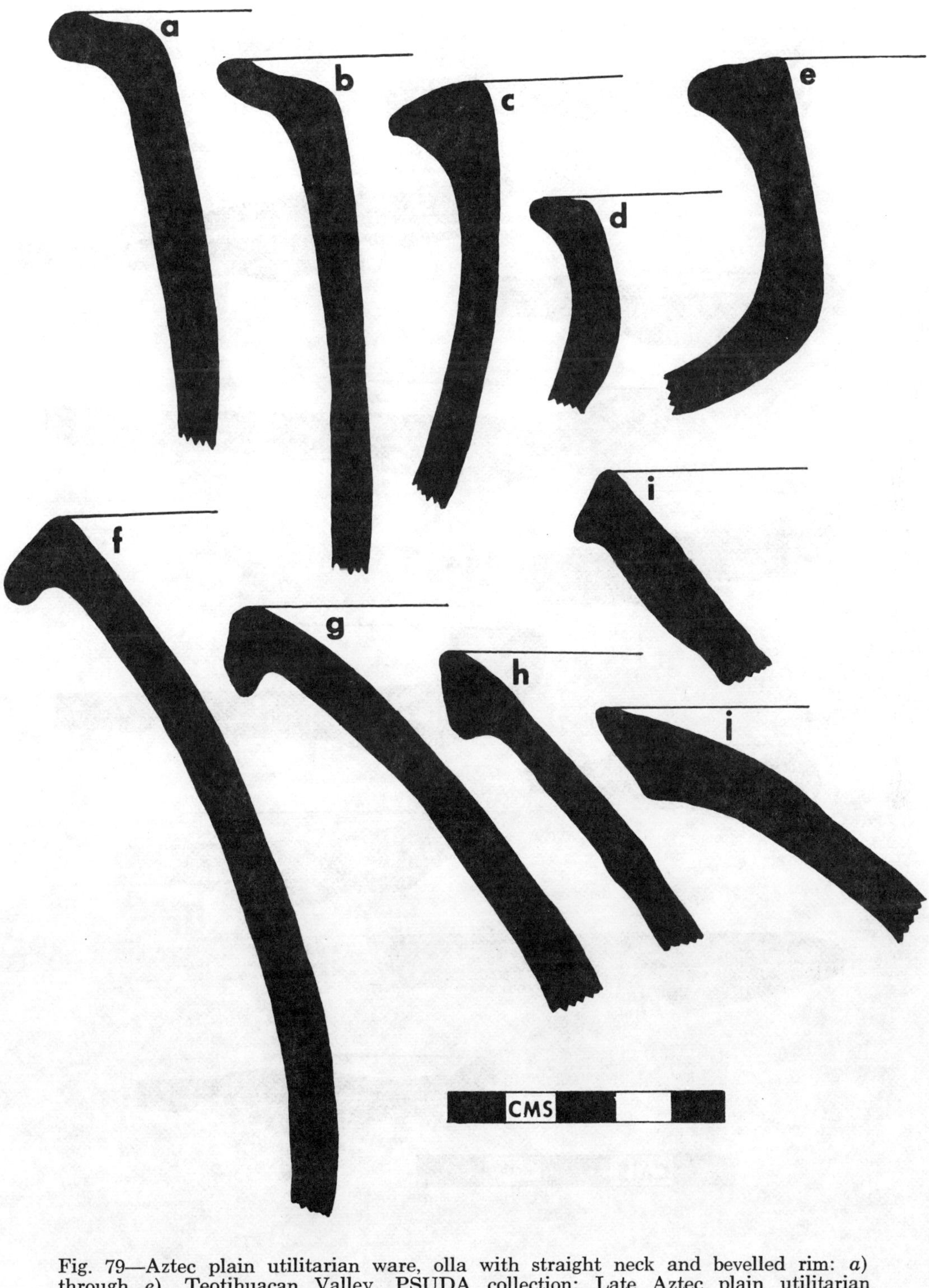

Fig. 79—Aztec plain utilitarian ware, olla with straight neck and bevelled rim: *a*) through *e*), Teotihuacan Valley, PSUDA collection; Late Aztec plain utilitarian ware, olla-basin with flaring neck and bevelled rim: *f*) through *j*), Teotihuacan Valley, PSUDA collection.

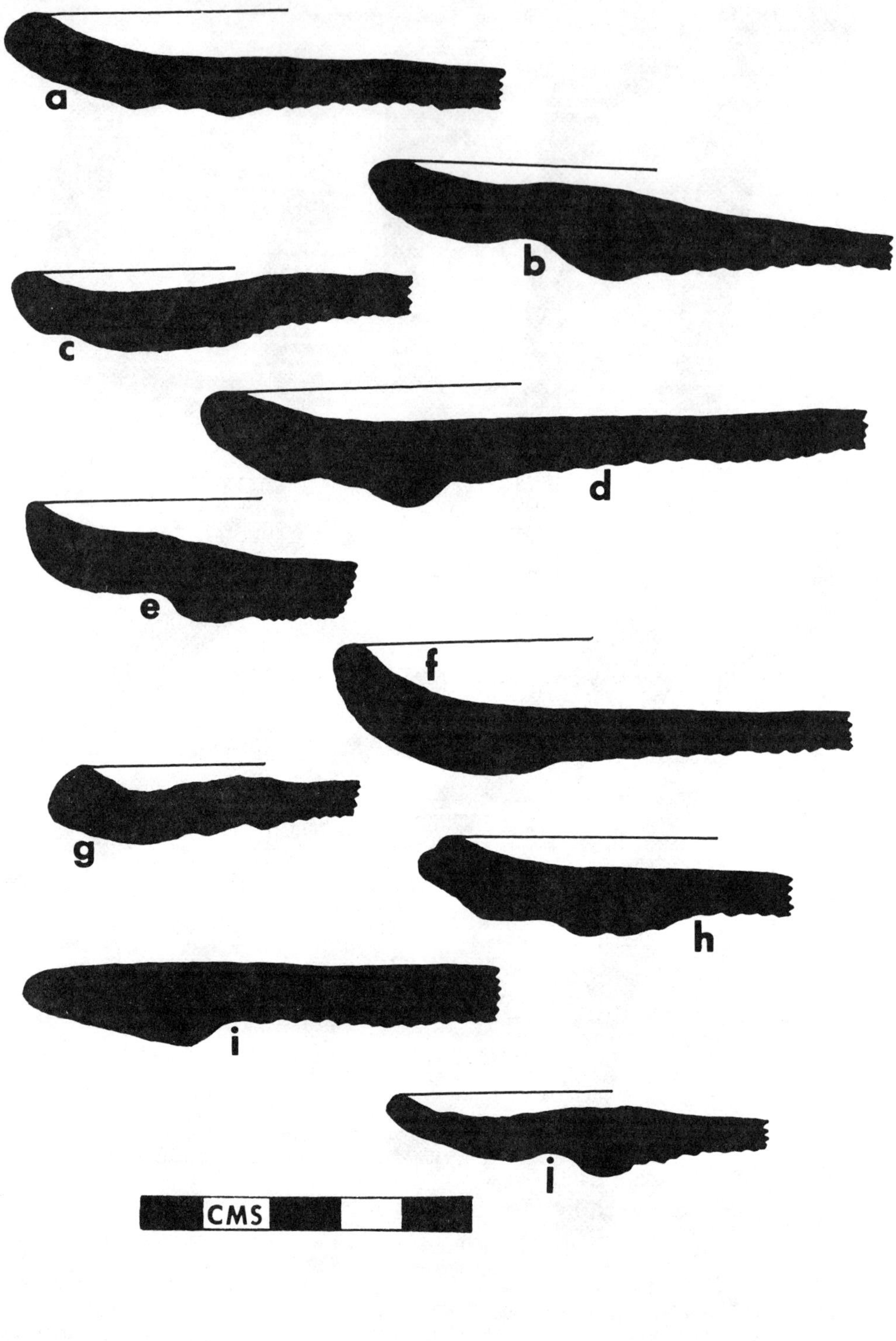

Fig. 80—Aztec plain utilitarian ware, comal: *a*) through *j*), Teotihuacan Valley, PSUDA collection.

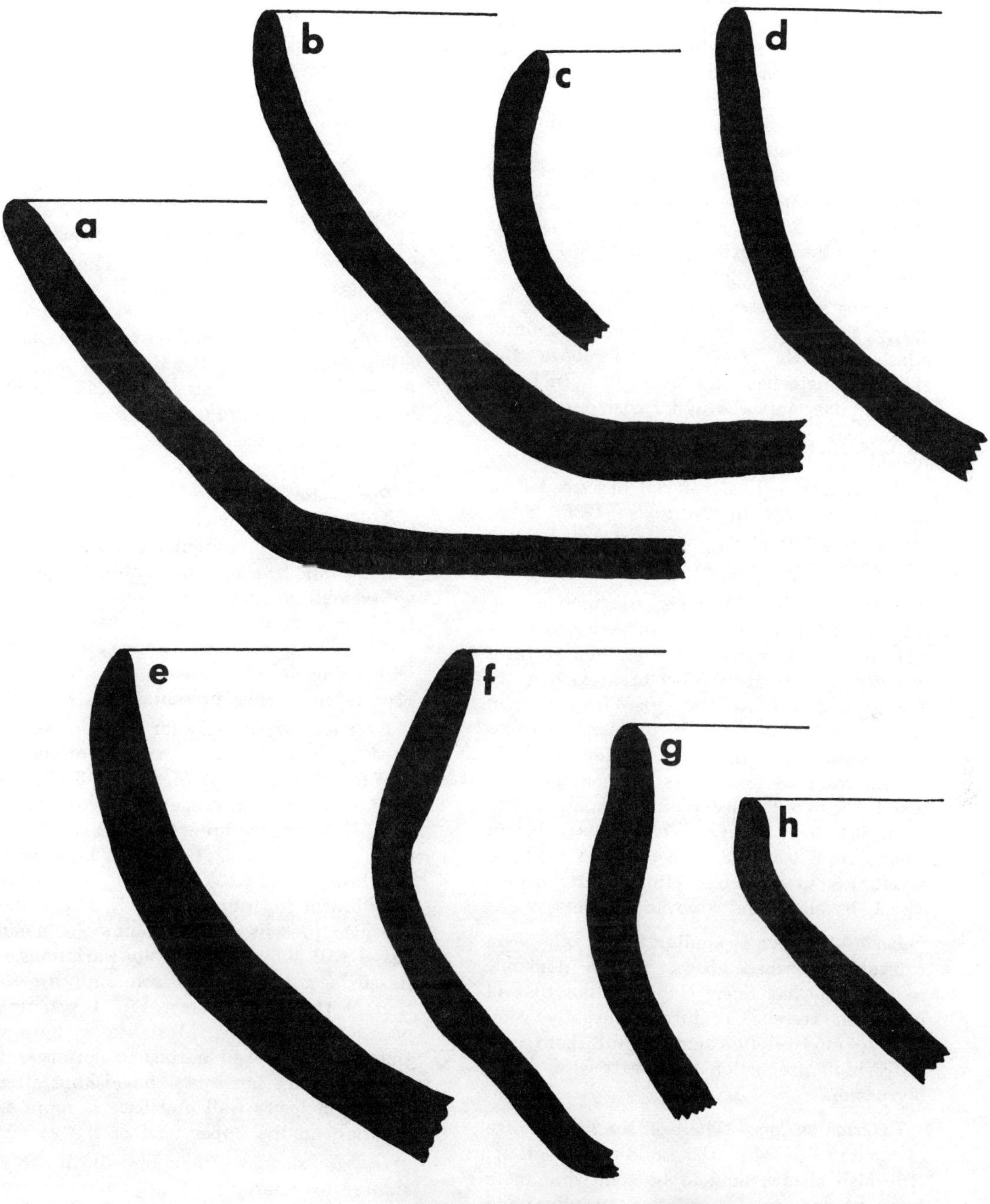

Fig. 81—Aztec plain service ware, Plain Orange Bowl: *a*) through *h*), Teotihuacan Valley, PSUDA collection.

surface of a single vessel, and some fire blackening occurs in the form of irregular splotches. In all cases surface color appears to be that of the natural fired clay, and clear traces of paint or slip are absent. Surfaces are generally moderately well smoothed and hastily burnished, with fairly distinct to distinct burnishing streaks visible. On necks of definite ollas, burnish is often vertical, particularly on high-necked vessels. Vessels of darker colors sometimes have a very distinctive pattern of irregular, fine-lined crackling.

Interior surface—Color and finish are generally similar to the exterior. On definite ollas, only the neck surface above the shoulder angle has been burnished. In high-necked ollas, only the uppermost part of the neck, just below the rim, has been burnished.

Comparisons—The material described here appears to cross-cut Tolstoy's (1958) Post-classic categories of Texcoco Dark Brown, Texcoco Orange, and Texcoco Brown.

2. Comales (Fig. 80): This distinctive vessel form is abundant on most Aztec residential sites. Clay vessels of very similar form are still used in the Valley of Mexico today for heating tortillas over open fires and on stoves. The comal's use in prehispanic times was presumably the same. Rim diameter ranges from 28 to 45 cms, with a mode of about 35 to 40 cms. Wall thickness varies from 0.4 to 1.3 cms. Total vessel height ranges from 0.8 to 3.5 cms, with a mode of about 1.5 to 2.5 cms. Rim forms include direct, bevelled, and grooved variants.

Paste—Temper is similar to the olla-basin category described above, with a tendency to be somewhat finer. Color is like that of olla-basin vessels. Texture is usually compact to moderately compact, but there is a fairly high proportion of vessels with crumbly paste.

Exterior surface—There is the same range of colors as in the olla-basin group. Brownish shades tend to be somewhat more frequent in comales relative to ollas and basins. Bases and walls are often blackened through usage. Base is unfinished, and appears to have been deliberately roughened. Walls are unburnished, but have been roughly smoothed by means of running the hand or finger along the surface of the wet clay.

Interior surface—Color as in olla-basin vessels. Interior color generally tends to be deeper and brighter than on the exterior. Irregular black and dark gray splotches are fairly common. Surfaces are usually well smoothed and burnished, except at the top of the wall.

B. Service Ware

1. Bowls: Dominant form variants are flaring-or upright-wall vessels with direct rims (Fig. 81,*a,e*). Incurved-wall bowls (Fig. 81,*f*) and shouldered vessels (Fig. 81,*g, h*) are also fairly common. All vessels have flat bottoms. Appendages of any kind are usually absent, although small tab handles occasionally occur. Rim diameter varies between 10 and 25 cms., and wall thickness between 0.5 and 1.0 cms. Sherds of this category comprise a large proportion of the surface pottery at all Aztec residential sites.

Paste—Proportion of temper ranges between 2 and 10 per cent. Temper consists of fine sand (small, irregular particles of black, white, and transluscent material), together with small amounts of pumice (amorphous red-brown grains). Color is usually a uniform light-to-medium orange, occasionally with pinkish laminations. A gray medial area is sometimes present.

Exterior surface—By far the dominant color is yellow-orange to reddish-orange (*ca.* 7.5YR 6.5/5, 5YR 6.5/6, 2.5YR 5/6). Much less common is a range of browns, varying from light orange-brown (*ca.* 5YR 5.5/6), to dark brown (*ca.* 5YR 4.5/4), light yellowish brown (*ca.* 10YR 6.5/4). A few dark gray-brown to gray (*ca.* 10YR 3.5/1) sherds are also present. Not uncommonly, a single vessel will show several color variations over its surface. In all cases, color appears to be that of the natural clay. Fire blackening is occasionally present. Most vessels have well smoothed, and well burnished surfaces, with fairly distinct horizontal burnishing streaks. Finish on lower wall and base is more sloppy than on the upper part of the vessel.

Interior surface—Color and finish are very similar to exterior.

Comparisons — This material partially cross-cuts Tolstoy's (1958) Texcoco Orange, Texcoco Brown, and Texcoco Dark Brown.

II. Decorated Ware

A. Service Ware

1. Black-on-Orange: As in Early Aztec, the

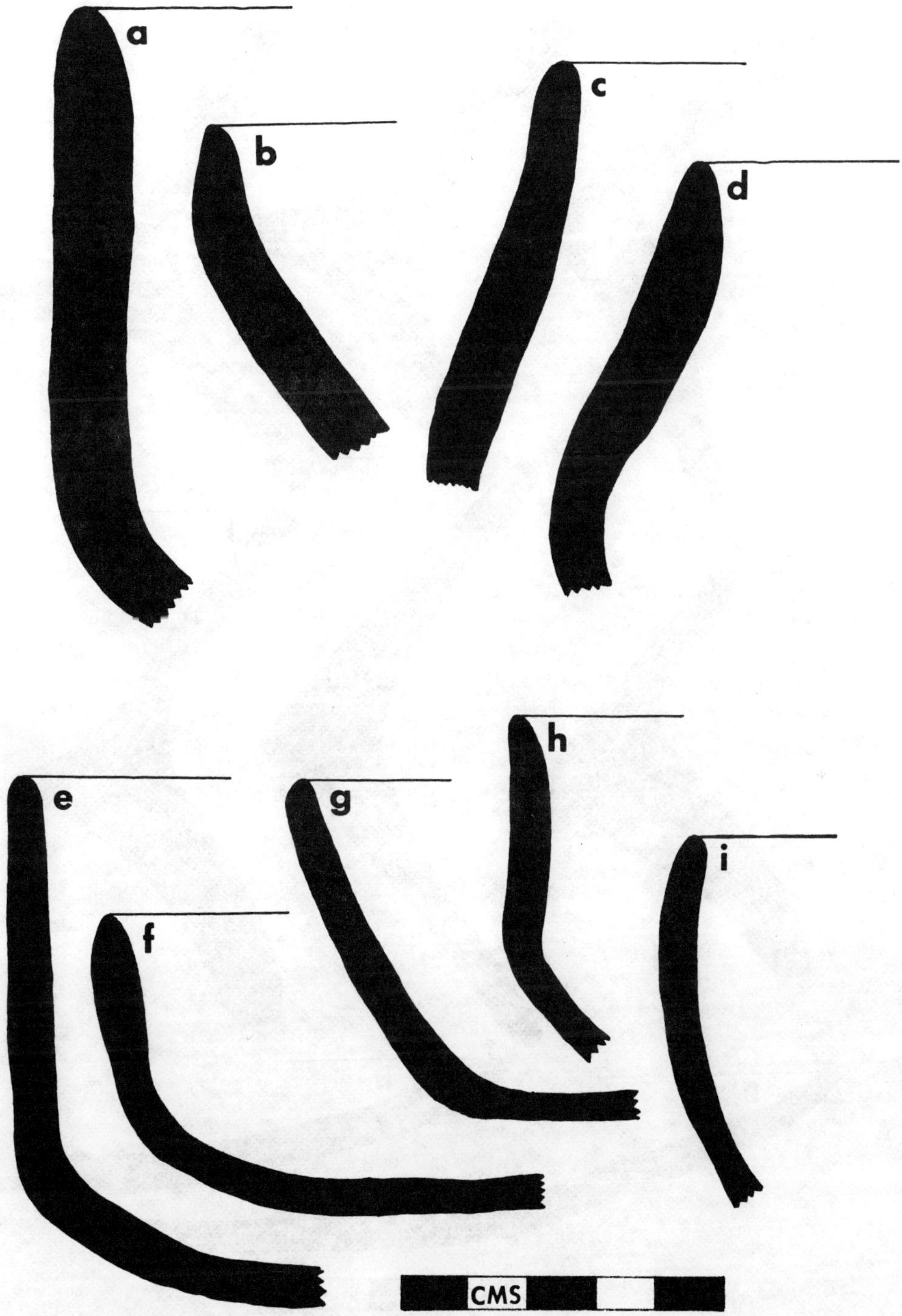

Fig. 82—Late Aztec decorated service ware, Black-on-Orange basin: *a*) through *d*), Teotihuacan Valley, PSUDA collection; Late Aztec decorated service ware, Black-on-Orange bowl: *e*) through *i*), Teotihuacan Valley, PSUDA collection.

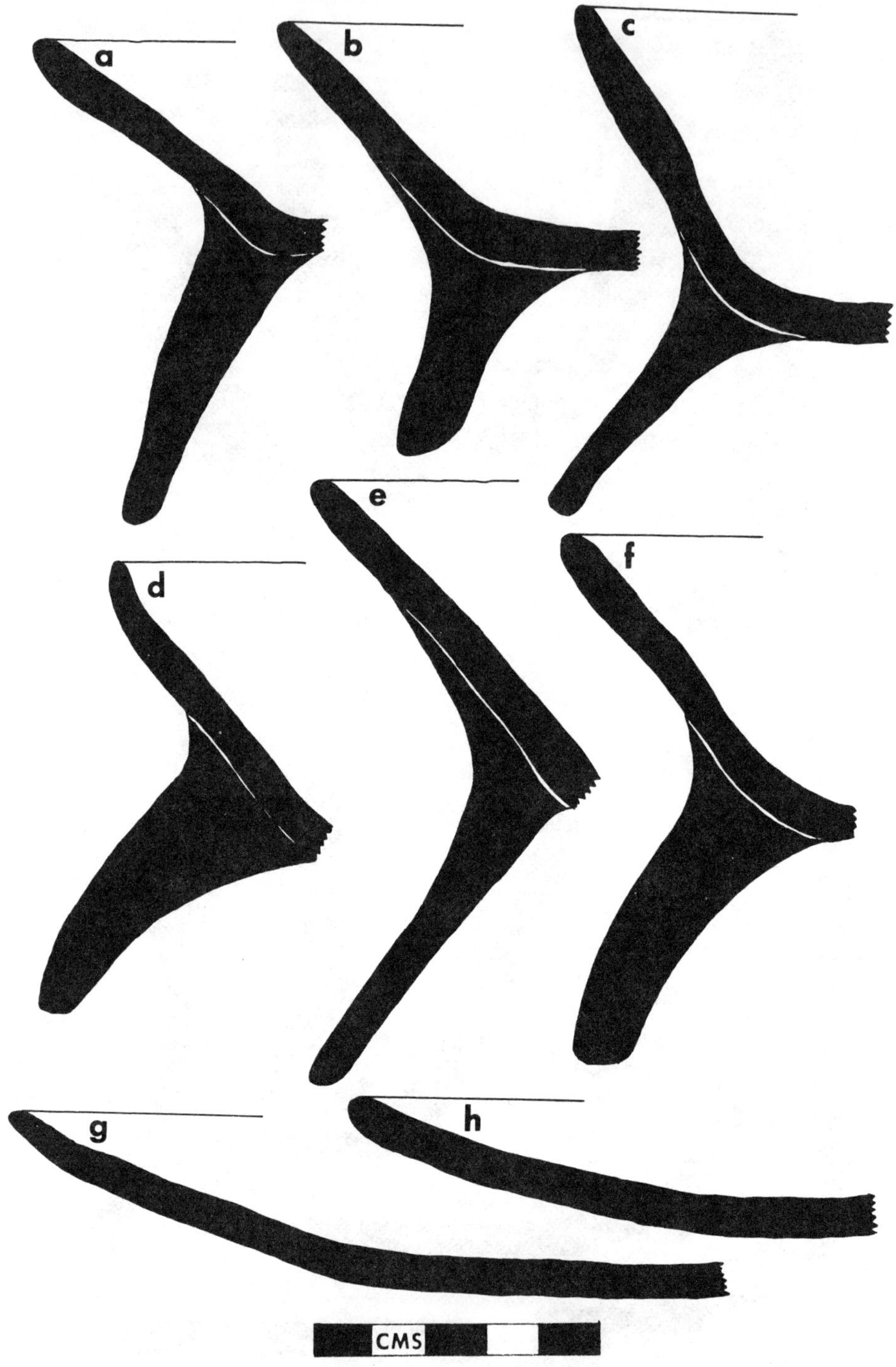

Fig. 83—Late Aztec decorated service ware, Black-on-Orange dish: *a*) through *c*), Teotihuacan Valley, PSUDA collection; Late Aztec decorated service ware, Black-on-Orange molcajete: *d*) through *f*), Teotihuacan Valley, PSUDA collection; Late Aztec decorated service ware, Black-on-Orange plate: *g*) through *h*), Teotihuacan Valley, PSUDA collection.

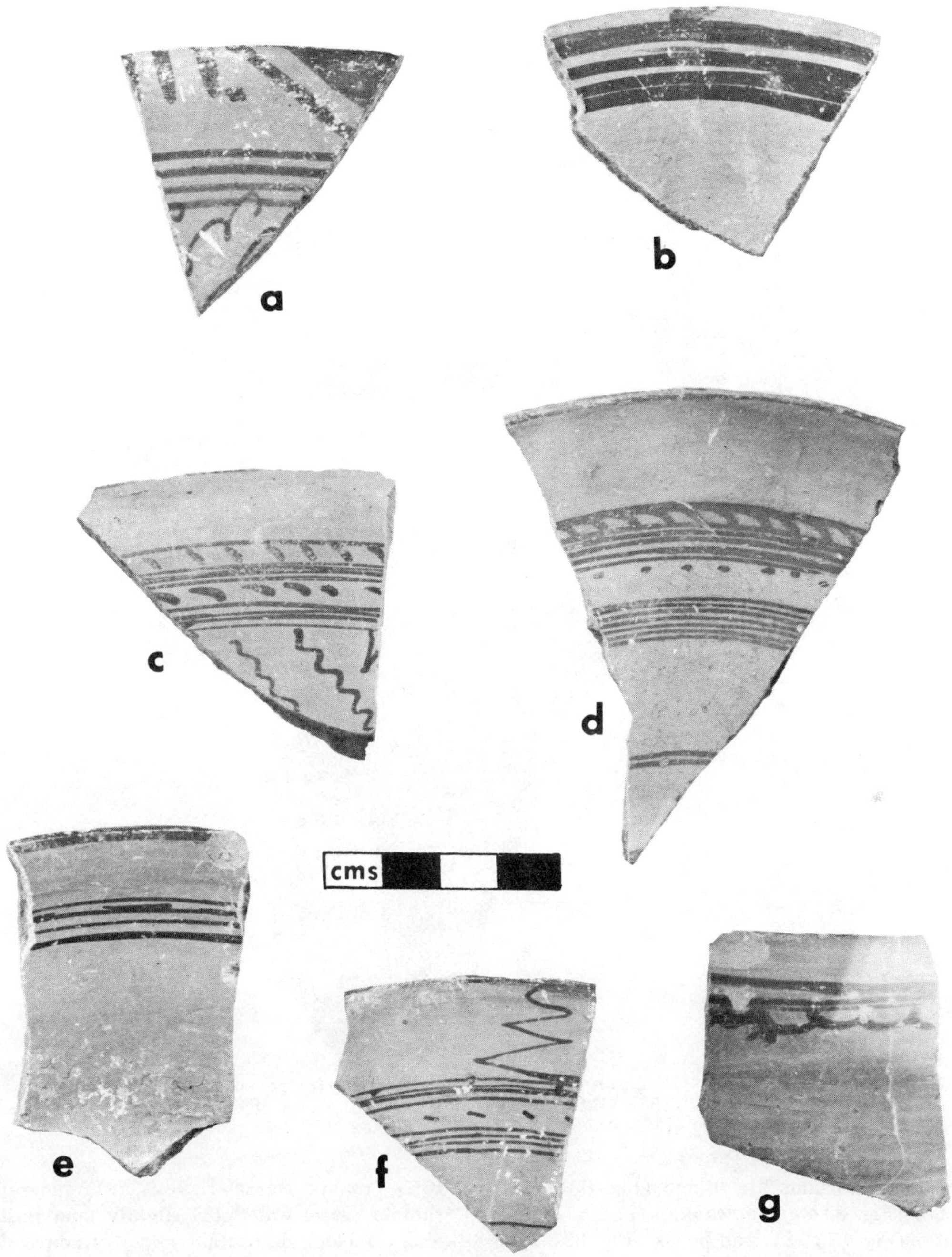

Fig. 84—Late Aztec decorated service ware, Black-on-Orange, UMMA Neg. 119-2-6: *a*) dish, interior surface, Peñon del Marques, UMMA No. 31155; *b*) dish, interior surface; Peñon del Marques, UMMA No. 31155; *c*) dish, interior surface, Tx-A-56, UMMA No. 31173; *d*) plate, interior surface, Culhuacan, UMMA No. 30861; *e*) dish, interior surface, Tx-A-87, UMMA No. 31060; *f*) plate, interior surface, Peñon del Marques, UMMA No. 31155; *g*) bowl, exterior surface, Culhuacan, UMMA No. 30861.

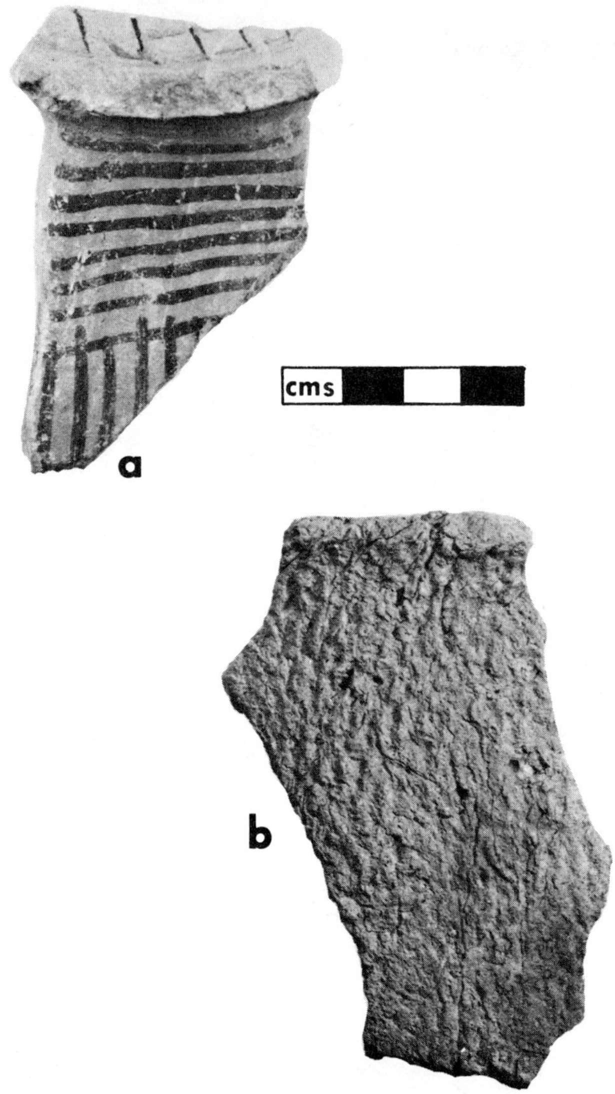

Fig. 85—*a*) Late Aztec Black-on-Orange slab support, exterior surface, Peñon del Marques, UMMA No. 31155, UMMA Neg. 119-3-2; *b*) Aztec Fabric Marked, exterior surfaces, Ecatepec, UMMA No. 30924, UMMA Neg. 119-3-4.

basic form variants are basins (Fig. 82,*a-d*), dishes (Fig. 83,*a-c*), *molcajetes* (Fig. 83,*d-f*), plates (Fig. 83,*g, h*), and bowls (Fig. 82,*e-i*). Basins occur with small horizontal loop handles and small solid lug handles. Dishes and molcajetes have either long, spindly, slightly arched, solid conical tripod supports, or wide, thin slab supports (Fig. 85,*a*). Bowls and plates lack appendages of any kind.

Late Aztec Black-on-Orange differs from Early Aztec pottery of this same type in three main characteristics: (*a*) generally thinner vessel walls; (*b*) slightly finer paste; and (*c*) black decoration whose principal design elements are groups of thin parallel lines, simple combinations of dashes, circles, and dots, and simple, fine-lined curvilinear motifs (Fig. 84).

For basins, rim diameter ranges between 20 and 33 cms, and wall thickness between 0.5 and 1.0 cms. For dishes and *molcajetes,* rim diameter ranges between 12 and 28 cms, and wall thickness between 0.3 and 0.7 cms. For plates, rim diameter ranges between 15 and 20 cms, and wall thickness between 0.3 and 0.7 cms. For bowls, rim diameter ranges between 10 and 28 cms, and wall thickness between 0.3 and 0.7 cms.

Paste—As in Late Aztec Service Ware, Bowls (above).

Exterior surface—Color and surface finish as in Late Aztec Service Ware, Bowls (above). Bowls and basins have exterior decoration only. Dishes, molcajetes, and plates lack exterior decoration. On bowls and basins, black decoration generally occurs in a thin band on the upper part of the vessel wall (Fig. 84,*g*). Standard design is a simple series of thin parallel lines, often incorporating lines of dashes, dots, or circles (Fig. 84). Solid conical supports lack black decoration, but slab supports are generally decorated with a variety of linear motifs (Fig. 85,*a*).

Interior surface—Color and surface finish as in Late Aztec Service Ware, Bowls (above). Basins and bowls lack interior decoration. Dishes, *molcajetes,* and plates have interior decoration exclusively. Designs are typically simple combinations of thin parallel lines and dot-dash-circle motifs, extending around the upper part of the interior wall (Fig. 84,*a-f*). Occasionally more complex curvilinear designs are present. On plates, decoration commonly extends over whole of the vessel interior.

Comparisons—The Tenochtitlan decorative variant described by Griffin and Espejo (1947, 1950) from excavations and surface collections throughout the Valley of Mexico, is largely equivalent to our material. Noguera (1935) has illustrated a considerable quantity of identical material from his excavations at Tenayuca in the western Valley of Mexico. Much of Franco's (1957) Aztec III material from the Valley of Mexico and its environs is equivalent to our Black-on-Orange pottery. Tolstoy (1958: 47, Fig. 9) describes and illustrates identical material from surface collections in the northern Valley of Mexico.

2. Black-on-Red (Fig. 86,*a-c*): All vessels are simple bowls, with upright walls, direct rims, and flat bottoms. Appendages of any kind are lacking. This is the same basic ware as Early Aztec Black-on-Red described above. Late Aztec Black-on-Red is characterized by thinner-walled vessels, and finer decoration relative to Early Aztec. Rim diameter ranges between 12 and 25 cms, and wall thickness between 0.4 and 0.7 cms. Black-on-Red pottery generally occurs in about the same proportion as Black-on-Orange ceramics on the surface of Late Aztec residential sites.

Paste—Temper is comprised of fine sand (roughly equal amounts of small, irregular black, white, and transluscent particles). Proportion of temper varies between 5 and 15 per cent. Color is generally light orange to light gray-brown, almost always with a very distinctive black medial area.

Exterior surface—Color and finish as in Early Aztec Black-on-Red (above). Character of black decoration is much different from Early Aztec Black-on-Red. Dominant motif is a cluster of from 2 to 10 thin, black, vertical, parallel lines. These units are usually repeated at intervals of several cms around the circumference of the vessel exterior, or may sometimes be applied continuously around the vessel wall (Fig. 87,*b*). A thin black line is often applied around the top of the rim. Other design variants occur, but always in very minor proportion.

Interior surface—Dominant color is a natural orange-brown, gray-brown, or light red-brown. In this case, interior decoration is absent. In a few cases, the entire interior surface has been painted a deep, bright red, and elaborate black designs have been applied to this surface. A few vessels have dark gray to gray-brown interiors. Surfaces are well smoothed and burnished. Red interiors have been highly polished.

Comparisons—As in the case of Black-on-Orange pottery, Black-on-Red ceramics have been described from many localities in the Valley of Mexico and around its borders: e.g., Tolstoy (1958: 45-47, Fig. 10), Noguera (1935: Fig. 4), Franco (1949), Piña Chan (1950). See Tolstoy (1958: 47) for a more complete bibliography of this ceramic type, which he refers to as Texcoco Black/Red.

3. Black-and-White-on-Red: Vessel form and range of vessel size are identical to Late Aztec Black-on-Red (above). This type occurs in somewhat lower proportions than Black-on-Orange, and Black-on-Red, but is common at all Aztec residential sites in the

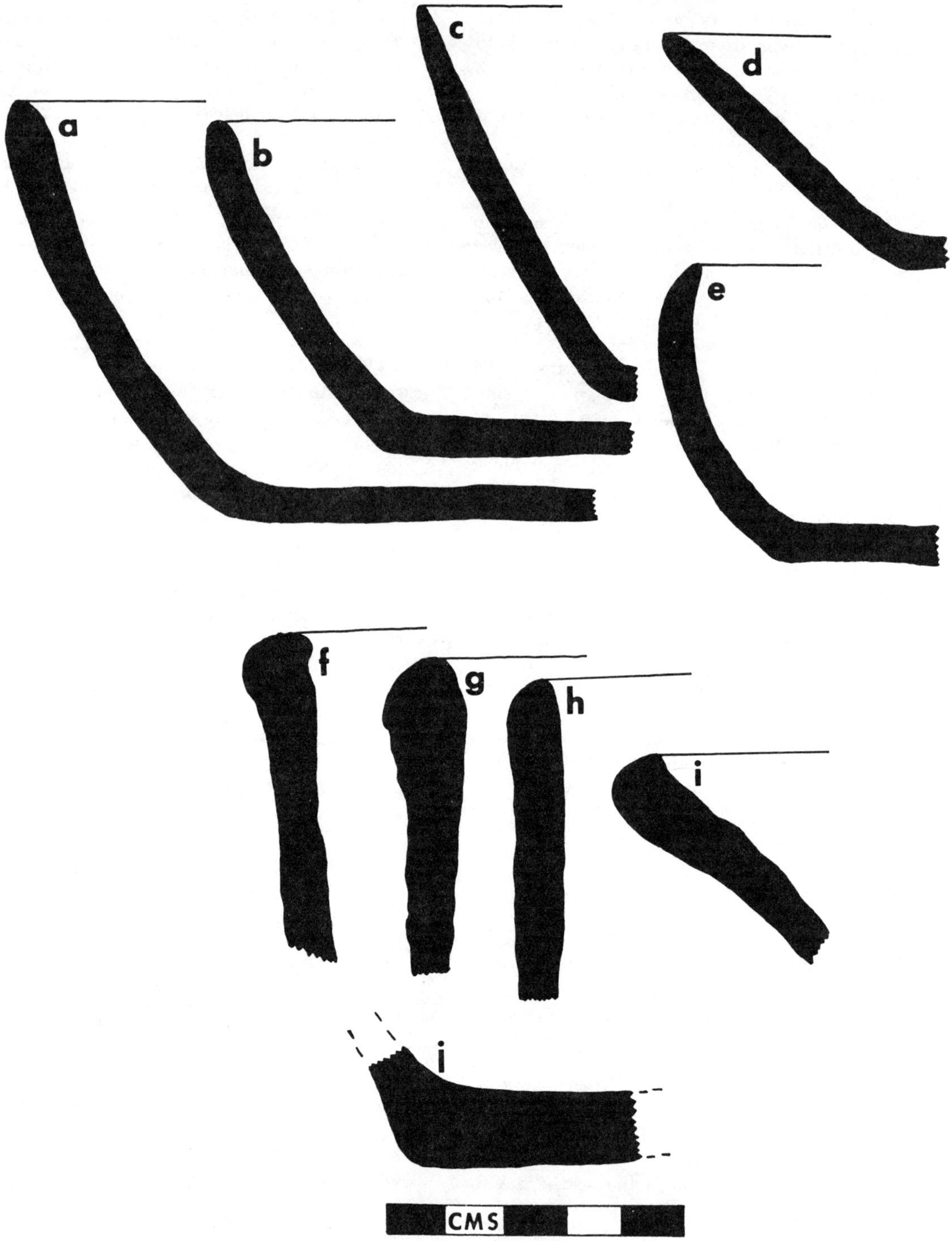

Fig. 86—Aztec decorated service ware, Black-on-Red and Black-and-White-on-Red bowls: *a*) through *e*), Teotihuacan Valley, PSUDA collection; Aztec Fabric Marked ware: *f*) through *i*), Teotihuacan Valley, PSUDA collection, rim sherds; *j*) Teotihuacan Valley, PSUDA collection, basal sherd.

Fig. 87—Aztec decorated service ware, Black-on-Red bowl; UMMA Neg. 119-3-2: *a*) Early Aztec, exterior surface, Chalco, UMMA No. 30633; *b*) Late Aztec, exterior surface, Tx-A-87, UMMA No. 31079; *c*) Early Aztec Black-on-Red Incised, exterior surface, Tx-A-87, UMMA No. 31055; *d*) Early Aztec Black-on-Red Incised, exterior surface, Tx-A-87, UMMA No. 31055.

Texcoco Region. Black-and-White-on-Red pottery clearly occurs in the Early Aztec period, but we have thus far been unable to differentiate the Early and Late Aztec variants of this type.

Paste—As in Late Aztec Black-on-Red (above).

Exterior surface—Surface finish, and color of black and red paint are the same as for Late Aztec Black-on-Red (above). Decoration is exclusively exterior, and very distinctive. White and black designs have usually been painted over a red-painted surface, although occasionally these designs are placed directly upon the light brown unpainted surface. Black paint occurs as thick lines, usually outlining rectilinear (Fig. 88,*b*, *c*) or triangular (Fig. 88,*a*) areas, which, in turn, are filled in with a thick, fugitive white paint. Vessels with more com-

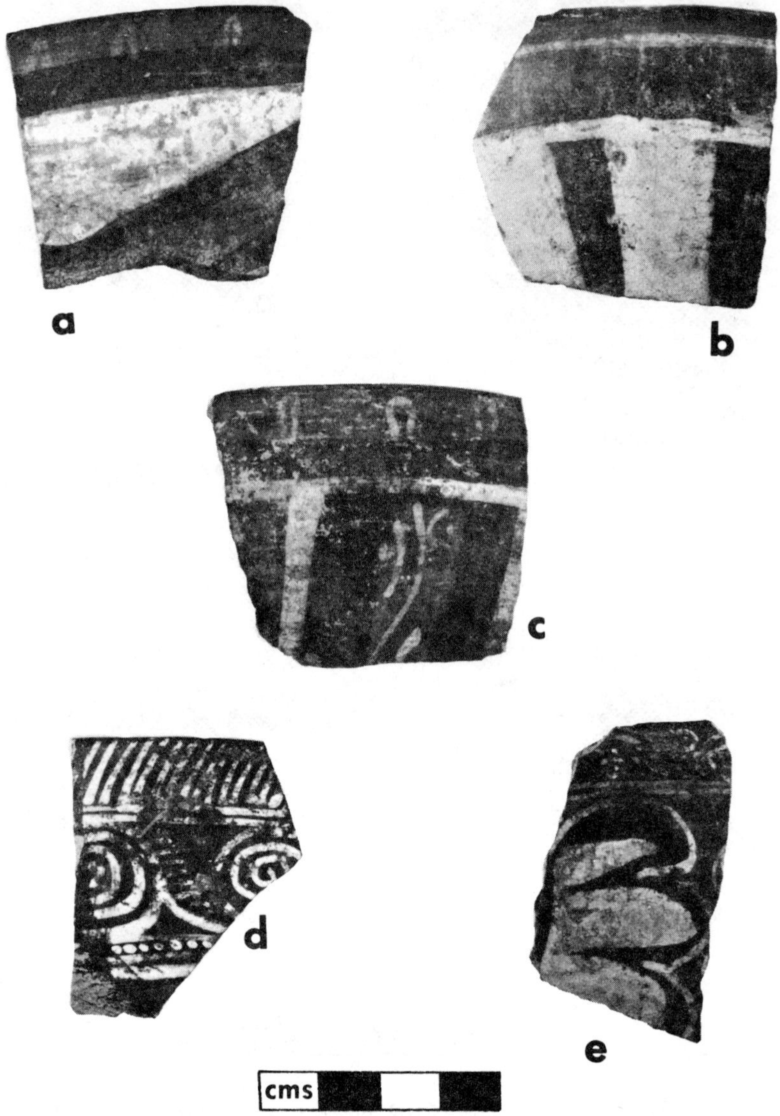

Fig. 88—Aztec Black-and-White-on-Red bowl; UMMA Neg. 119-4-1: *a*) Exterior surface, Tx-A-87, UMMA No. 31111; *b*) exterior surface, Tx-A-87, UMMA No. 31057; *c*) exterior surface, Tx-A-87, UMMA No. 31057; *d*) exterior surface, Culhuacan, UMMA No. 30866; *e*) exterior surface, Culhuacan, UMMA No. 30866.

plex decoration, emhasizing large curvilinear black designs and very intricate white motifs (e.g., Fig. 88,*d, e*), also occur in smaller quantities.

Interior surface—Decoration is lacking. Color and finish as in Late Aztec Black-on-Red (above).

Comparisons—This type has been described from several localities in the Valley of Mexico and its environs: e.g., Tolstoy (1958: 45-47, Fig. 10), Noguera (1935, Fig. 26), Franco (1949), Piña Chan (1950). For a more complete bibliography of this type, see Tolstoy (1958: 47).

III. Special Ware

A. Salt-making Pottery

1. Fabric-Marked (Fig. 85,*b*; 86,*f-j*): Vessel

form is somewhat difficult to ascertain because of the typically small size of surface sherds. Most vessels are apparently basins with bolstered and bevelled rims and flat bottoms. We have no information on vessel height. Walls are generally upright or flaring. Rim diameter ranges from 10 to 40 cms, with a mode of about 15 to 24 cms. Wall thickness measures between 0.5 and 1.6 cms, with a modal thickness of about 0.6 to 1.0 cms. This pottery is found in very high proportions at certain Aztec sites along the lakeshore, but occurs in very limited quantities elsewhere. A few sherds can usually be found on the surface at all Late Aztec sites. We have argued elsewhere (Parsons, In Press) that this pottery was associated with the manufacture of salt around the edge of Lake Texcoco.

Paste—Fiber tempering is very abundant, and in some cases the paste consists largely of fibrous material. Also present are small quantities of tiny black and white particles of irregular shape. Air bubbles are usually abundant. Color is light to medium orange, or tan, usually with a dark gray to black, or dark orange-brown medial area. In a few cases, all paste is a dark gray to black. Texture is usually quite crumbly and friable.

Exterior surface—Color ranges from light orange-brown, to red-orange, and gray-brown (*ca.* 7.5YR 6.5/6, to 2.5YR 5.5/4, to 10YR 7.5/4). No traces of paint or slip could be detected. The whole of the exterior surface is very rough, with no attempt at smoothing or burnishing. Rough texture apparently derives from the impression of fabric or basketry on the wet clay surface.

Interior surface—Color is similar to the exterior. Fabric impression is absent. Most of the upper part of the interior wall lacks any surface treatment beyond a cursory smoothing with the hand. The lower part of the vessel interior tends to be better smoothed, and often has been hastily burnished.

Comparisons—This distinctive ware was first systematically discussed by Griffin and Krieger (1947), although it had been described and illustrated by Holmes (1885) many years before. Tolstoy (1958: 35) and Mayer-Oakes (1959) describe identical material from the north-central Valley of Mexico.

APPENDIX II

TLATEL DESCRIPTIONS

EXPLANATORY NOTES

Tlatel numbers are those assigned in the field. They do not run continuously throughout this report, and are repeated (in some cases) several times from one site to another.

All preserved mounds not specifically described in Chapter 2, are listed in this section. Estimates of tlatel diameter are based upon total scatter of rock rubble and surface pottery. The reader should keep in mind that many mounds have been severely eroded, plowed down, or otherwise disturbed.

SITE: TX-TF-1

Tlatel Number	Height	Surface Area	Surface Pottery	Rock Rubble	Probable Function	Comments
43	3 m	5 m diam.	Light-to-moderate Terminal Formative (some Tzacualli), very light Aztec	Heavy	Ceremonial?	Three tiers of narrow terraces on down-slope side
44	1-1.5 m	12 m diam.	Moderate Terminal Formative, light Toltec	Heavy	Domestic residence	Situated on one of ancient terraces
51	50 cm	5 m diam.	Light Terminal Formative	Heavy	Domestic residence	
52	50 cm	7 m diam.	Light Terminal Formative, trace of Early Toltec	Heavy	Domestic residence	On lower terrace near barranca
57	8 m	20 m diam.	Moderate Terminal Formative, trace of Early Toltec	Heavy	Ceremonial-civic	Down-slope side is tiered in two 3 m terraces with a series of 9-10 steps leading to the top of the mound
58	2 m	25 m diam.	Very light Terminal Formative on mound and moderate around it, some Early Toltec and Aztec	Moderate	Civic-ceremonial?	Small plaza-like depression in center
67	1-4 m	15 m diam.	Moderate Terminal Formative, trace of Early Toltec and Aztec	Moderate	Domestic residence	
69	2 m	11 m diam.	Heavy Terminal Formative, trace of Late Formative, light Early Toltec	Heavy	Domestic residence	
70	50 cm-1 m	30 m diam.	Light-to-moderate Terminal Formative, Light Aztec and Toltec	Very heavy	Domestic residence	

SITE: TX-TF-2

Tlatel Number	Height	Surface Area	Surface Pottery	Rock Rubble	Probable Function	Comments
866	2 m	15x8 m	Light Terminal Formative (light-to-moderate on front terrace,	Heavy	Ceremonial ?	On terrace 15 m wide and 20 m long (spanning ridge top), terrace 2 m high on south and blends into slope on north
867	1.5 m	12x10 m	Light-to-moderate Terminal Formative	Moderate-to-heavy	Ceremonial ?	See Fig. 1
868	2-2.5 m	15 m diam.	Light Terminal Formative	Heavy	Ceremonial ?	Built on high bedrock prominence at south end of ridge

SITE: TX-TF-4

Tlatel Number	Height	Surface Area	Surface Pottery	Rock Rubble	Probable Function	Comments
139	1-1.5 m	12 m diam.	Light Terminal Formative, trace of Aztec and Early Toltec	Heavy	Domestic residence	Built on ancient terrace; well-preserved stone walls, 3.5 m E-W and 2 m N-S
140	1-2 m	30-35 m diam.	Light Terminal Formative, very light Aztec	Heavy	Domestic residence	
141	50 cm	3.5 m diam.	Light Terminal Formative	Moderate	Domestic residence	
142	1-2 m	25 m diam.	Light Terminal Formative, light Late Aztec	Moderate	Domestic residence	
143	1-2 m	40 m diam.	Light-to-moderate Terminal Formative	Heavy	Domestic residence ?	Located on ancient terrace. Down-slope side of mound is built up in four or five small tiers
144	None	20 m diam.	Moderate Terminal Formative, trace of Aztec	Heavy	Domestic residence	Series of exposed walls; several rooms *ca.* 3x4 m (Fig. 2,*b*)
145	3 m	10 m diam.	Moderate Terminal Formative, trace of Aztec and Early Toltec	Heavy	Ceremonial-civic ?	On steep slope; built on terrace 30 m wide and 6 m high; possible steps on the mound
146	1 m	5 m diam.	Moderate Terminal Formative, very light Toltec	Heavy	Domestic residence	On terrace below tlatel 145
147	50 cm	6 m diam.	Moderate Terminal Formative	Heavy	Domestic residence	Exposed wall sections
148	1 m	20x15 m	Very light Terminal Formative	Heavy	Domestic residence	Large sections of exposed stone wall bases (20 m long with cross walls, (Fig. 2,*a*)
149	1.5 m	7 m diam.	Moderate Terminal Formative	Heavy	Domestic residence	
150	1 m	12 m diam.	Light Terminal Formative, Aztec trace	Heavy	Domestic residence	Several exposed walls
151	1 m	15 m diam.	Moderate Terminal Formative	Heavy	Domestic residence	
153	50 cm	10 m diam.	Very light Terminal Formative, Aztec trace	Heavy	Domestic residence	
154	2 m	20 m diam.	No data	Heavy	Domestic residence	Three visable rooms, averaging 4 m square

Tlatel Number	Height	Surface Area	Surface Pottery	Rock Rubble	Probable Function	Comments
185	25 cm	12x6 m	Very light Terminal Formative	Moderate	Ceremonial-civic	On hilltop, at least 10 m above tlatels mentioned above; exposed walls well preserved (See Fig. 3)
186	2.5 m	16x16 m	Very light Terminal Formative	Heavy	Ceremonial-civic	Structure has at least 3 terraced tiers—first one is 1 m high, second is 1.3 m high, third is *ca.* 6 inches high; first tier (lowest) is 16x16 m, second is 11x11 m, third is *ca.* 8x4 m; sections of wall exposed in areas (See Fig. 3)
187	2 m	*ca.* 17x8 m	Very light Terminal Formative	Heavy	Ceremonial-civic	3 or 4 tiered structures (3 are clear); each is *ca.* 60 cm high; lowest tier is 17x18 m, second is *ca.* 11x9 m, third is *ca.* 4x3 m, located 23 m across the plaza from tlatel 186 (See Fig. 3)
188	2.3 m	28x28 m	Very light Terminal Formative	Heavy	Ceremonial-civic	Two definite tiers; lower one is 28 m square and 1.5 m high, upper tier is 16x12 m and 1 m high; most walls on upper tier are well exposed; structure has been potted in the center, pothole 1.5 m deep; appears to be a rubble-filled structure; also located on plaza (See Fig. 3)
191	1.5 m	30 m diam.	Very light Terminal Formative, very light Aztec	Heavy	Ceremonial-civic	Built on bedrock promontory, highest spot in the area; badly pitted; possible terrace 20 m west of mound
317	Very slight	64x48 m	Very light Terminal Formative, very light Aztec	Moderate	Ceremonial-civic ? Fortress ?	Located on very highest spot on hilltop; is 6-7 m higher than Tlatels 185-191; large thick walls and room complexes; walls 72-80 cm wide and up to 64 m long; very complex structure; extensive terracing of slopes north and east of the tlatel (see Fig. 4)
			SITE: TX-TF-10			
119	2 m	25 m diam.	Light-to-moderate Terminal Formative (some may be Tzacualli), very	Heavy	Ceremonial-civic	Well-preserved walls exposed on several sides; located on east side of a plaza (see Fig. 6)

Tlatel Number	Height	Surface Area	Surface Pottery	Rock Rubble	Probable Function	Comments
			light-to-light Middle Formative and Late Formative			
120	1 m	15x10 m	Very light Terminal Formative	Heavy	Ceremonial-civic ?	Exposed wall on south side; located on south side of plaza (see Fig. 6)
121	1 m	10 m diam.	Very light Terminal Formative	Heavy	Ceremonial-civic ?	Located on north side of plaza (see Fig. 6)
122	2 m	20 m diam.	Light Terminal Formative	Heavy	Ceremonial-civic ?	Located on north side of plaza (see Fig. 6)
123	3 m	22x20 m	Light Terminal Formative, trace of Aztec	Heavy	Ceremonial-civic	Located on highest part of hilltop; built on platform 3 m above plaza; on west side of plaza (see Fig. 6)
SITE: TX-TF-14						
404	10-50 cm	10 m diam.	Moderate Terminal Formative	Moderate	Domestic residence	Badly destroyed
408	1-2 m	20x 20 m	Light Terminal Formative, trace of Aztec	Moderate	Domestic residence	Has stone wall bases outlining edges of feature
410	25-50 cm	15 m diam.	Light Terminal Formative, trace of Aztec	Heavy	Domestic residence	Some traces of stone wall bases, *ca.* 50 cm thick
412	50-75 cm	20 m diam.	Light Terminal Formative	Moderate	Domestic residence	Has several preserved wall bases, one outlines a room 13x15 m, walls are about 50 cm thick
413	3 m	20x20 m	Light Terminal Formative, trace of Aztec	Moderate	Ceremonial-civic	A well-defined structure, fronting on plaza *ca.* 25x15 m (Pl. 22,*a*)
SITE: TX-TF-15						
414	25-75 cm	10 m diam.	Very light Terminal Formative	Heavy	Ceremonial-civic ?	A vague structure
415	1 m	25 m diam.	Light Terminal Formative, very light Aztec	Heavy	Ceremonial-civic ?	Separated from Tlatel 416 by a flat, narrow, clear area about 15 m wide

Tlatel Number	Height	Surface Area	Surface Pottery	Rock Rubble	Probable Function	Comments
416	2 m	15 m diam.	Very light Terminal Formative, light Aztec, trace of Early Toltec	Heavy	Ceremonial-civic ?	Capped by modern rock pile and wooden cross
417	25-50 m	8x10 m	Very light undiagnostic	Heavy	Ceremonial-civic ?	Outer edges defined by stone wall bases
			SITE: TX-TF-51			
102	3.5 m	30 m diam.	Moderate Terminal Formative	Heavy	Ceremonial-civic	Dixon's Mound 4, has a small pit inside
103	2.5 m	25 m diam.	Moderate-to-heavy Terminal Formative at base; light on upper surface	Heavy	Ceremonial	Dixon's Mound 3, has a large pit in center (Pl. 27,*a*)
104	4 m	25 m diam.	Moderate Terminal Formative at base; light on upper surface	Heavy	Ceremonial-civic	Dixon's Mound 2, has a small pit on top
105	7.5 m	35 m diam.	Moderate-to-heavy Terminal Formative at base; light on upper surface	Heavy	Ceremonial-civic	Dixon's Mound 1; some pitting on top (Pl. 27,*b*)
106	2 m	20 m diam.	Moderate-to-heavy Terminal Formative and light-to-moderate Aztec at base; light on upper surface	Moderate	Ceremonial-civic ?	Dixon refers to this as a possible agricultural terrace; only Aztec pottery on site found in vicinity of this feature
			SITE: TX-ET-4			
30	1.5-2 m	L-shaped 81 m E-W 116 m N-S 4 m wide	Light-to-moderate Early Toltec, light-to-moderate Late Toltec, very light-to-light Aztec, very light-to-light Late Classic	Very heavy	Domestic residence	Heavy obsidian—both chippage and finished artifacts, also quartz flakes; this tlatel may include a number of different domestic residences; road cuts through mound exposing plastered floor
31	4 m	15 m diam.	Light Early Toltec on mound and light-to-moderate around base of mound, Late Toltec trace, Light Early Classic	Heavy	Ceremonial-civic ?	

Tlatel Number	Height	Surface Area	Surface Pottery	Rock Rubble	Probable Function	Comments
32	*ca.* 2 m	4-5 m diam.	Light Early Toltec	Very heavy	Domestic residence	Rubble from surrounding field has been placed up on this tlatel, making it difficult to see the mound's real height
33	*ca.* 2 m	3-4 m diam.	Very light	Heavy	Ceremonial-civic ?	
34	*ca.* 2 m	6 m diam.	Light Early Toltec	Heavy	Domestic residence?	Consists of two distinct parallel moundings each about 10 m long by 4 m wide; rubble from the surrounding fields has been piled on this tlatel
35	1.5 m	6 m diam.	Moderate Early Toltec, Late Toltec trace, light Late Classic and Aztec	Heavy	Domestic residence	Rock rubble from surrounding field has been piled on this tlatel increasing its height (Pl. 28,*b*)
36	1.3 m	20x3.5 m	Very light on tlatel, light-to-moderate Early Toltec around base of mound	Heavy	Domestic residence	Much like tlatel 30 in outward appearance
37	1.5 m	30 m diam.	Moderate Early Toltec, light Late Toltec and Aztec	Moderate	Domestic residence	Area shows up as a lighter grayish area in contrast to the surrounding brown soil
38	1.5-2 m	6-8 m diam.	Very light Early Toltec, Late Toltec, and Aztec on the tlatel, light-to-moderate Early Toltec and some Late Toltec around tlatel	Heavy	Domestic residence	
39	3-4 m	15 m diam.	Moderate Early Toltec, light Early Classic, very light Aztec	Heavy	Ceremonial-civic	Topped by a modern shrine; modern graveyard just to the east
40	1 m	15x4 m	Light-to-moderate Early Toltec on south side of tlatel	Heavy	Domestic residence	Modern road cuts through mound in area where rock rubble is heavy but ceramics are light
41	0.5-1 m	3x10 m	Very light	Heavy	Domestic residence	Road cuts through it
63	None	40x20 m	Moderate Early Toltec, light Late Toltec and Aztec	Moderate	Domestic residence	Shows up as a light area in an otherwise dark field
64	None	20x25 m	Light-to-moderate Early Toltec, some Aztec	Moderate	Domestic residence	Shows up as a lighter area than the soil around it

Tlatel Number	Height	Surface Area	Surface Pottery	Rock Rubble	Probable Function	Comments
71	None	20 m diam.	Light-to-moderate Early Toltec, Late Toltec trace, Terminal Formative trace, light Aztec	Moderate	Domestic residence	In an area where pottery is very light except on the tlatel
72	None	25 m diam.	Moderate Early Toltec, light Late Toltec, very light Aztec	Heavy	Domestic residence	Rocks from surrounding area piled on east end of site by farmers; area has a lighter soil color
73	None	20 m diam.	Moderate Early Toltec	Heavy	Domestic residence	Shows up as a lighter area than surrounding field
74	None	20 m diam.	Light Early Toltec	Light	Domestic residence	Shows up as an area of lighter soil
75	None	20 m diam.	Very light-to-light Early Toltec	Light-to-moderate	Domestic residence	Shows up as an area of lighter soil
76	None	20 m diam.	Light Early Toltec	Light	Domestic residence	Shows up as an area of lighter soil
55	2 m	16x14 m	Light-to-moderate Early Toltec, light Late Toltec, light Aztec	Heavy	Ceremonial-civic ?	Built against hill slope; appears to be a terraced pyramid with 3 tiers, lowest is 1 m high, second is 0.5 m, third is 0.5 m
59	None	30 m diam.	Light-to-moderate Early Toltec, light Aztec	Light-to-moderate	Domestic residence	Shows up as an area of lighter soil
SITE: TX-ET-5						
45	10 m	20 m diam.	Light-to-moderate Early Toltec, Early Classic and Late Formative trace	Heavy	Ceremonial-civic	The largest mound on this ridgetop site; built on second of three terraces on ridgetop
46	2 m	14x4 m	Very light	Very heavy	Ceremonial-civic	Consists of two adjoining oval-shaped rock rubble basins with a 2 m deep depression in the center of each; located about 20 m south of Tlatel 45; built on the first (lowermost terrace on the ridgetop) terrace and into the second terrace
47	2 m	6 m diam.	Very light	Heavy	Ceremonial-civic	Just southeast of Tlatel 45, also on second terrace
48	1.5 m	4 m diam.	Very light	Heavy	Ceremonial-civic	Built on third (highest) terrace

SITE: TX-ET-7

Tlatel Number	Height	Surface Area	Surface Pottery	Rock Rubble	Probable Function	Comments
126	5 m	35x35 m	Moderate Early Toltec, very light-to-light Aztec	Heavy	Ceremonial-civic ?	Composed of two platforms, both 2 m high
127	4 m	20x30 m	Light-to-moderate Early Toltec	Heavy	Ceremonial-civic ?	Several exposed walls; possible Colonial feature on top of mound; plaster exposed in several places
129	8 m	15 m diam.	Very light on tlatel, moderate Early Toltec around tlatel, very light Late Toltec	Heavy	Ceremonial-civic ?	Has been potted in two places; possibly two steps leading up to the mound
159	10 m	36x36 m	Light Early Toltec, very light Classic, very light Aztec	Heavy	Ceremonial-civic	Largest of three pyramids built on a plaza; plaza is built 2.5 m above the surrounding fields (Fig. 10, Pl. 34,*a*)
160	6 m	30x30 m	Very light Early Toltec	Heavy	Ceremonial-civic	Mound is potted exposing adobe brick and rubble construction; located on east end of plaza (Fig. 10)
161	5 m	30x30 m	Light Early Toltec, Light Aztec	Heavy	Ceremonial-civic	Pyramid with several platforms; first is 2 m high and 30 m square; second is 3 m high and 10 m square; top of mound is very flat and 5 m square; pitting has exposed an interior structure of stone masonry covered by an overburden of 45 cm of debris; fragments of both blue and red plaster were found around the mound; is located on west side of plaza (Fig. 10; see Pl. 29)
162	3 m	24x24 m	Light Early Toltec	Heavy	Ceremonial-civic	Pyramid located south of the plaza (Fig. 10)
164	9 m	45 m diam.	Light-to-moderate Early Toltec, light Classic	Heavy	Ceremonial-civic	Rock boulder fill; largest pyramid in the area; has been badly potted; located west of plaza at base of Cerro Teponaxtle where the steep slopes start
165	2.5 m	24x15 m	Very light Early Toltec, very light Classic	Heavy	Ceremonial-civic ?	Possible pyramid; rock from surrounding fields has been

Tlatel Number	Height	Surface Area	Surface Pottery	Rock Rubble	Probable Function	Comments
						piled on it adding an additional half meter to its height; top has been fenced into two plots—one a garden and the other a coral
166	11 m	40x40 m	Moderate Early Toltec, Formative trace	Heavy	Ceremonial-civic	Pyramid, probably stepped; built up against the hillslope
170	2 m	12 m diam.	Light Early Toltec, very light Aztec	Heavy	Ceremonial-civic	Pyramid, cut into by modern terracing; badly disturbed by potting, cultivation, and construction
171	1 m	35 m diam.	Light-to-moderate Early Toltec, very light Aztec	Heavy	Domestic residence	Located on maguey terrace
			SITE: TX-ET-8			
176	0.5-1 m	*ca.* 8 m diam.	Light-to-moderate Early Toltec, Early Classic trace, Late Toltec trace, very light Aztec	Moderate	Domestic residence	Located on very edge of barranca channel, east side of barranca
402	1 m	10 m diam.	Moderate Early Toltec, light Aztec	Light-to-moderate	Domestic residence	Located on west edge of barranca about 6 m below fields of maize and beans that come close to barranca bank
			SITE: TX-ET-12			
483	60 cm	12 m diam.	Moderate Early Toltec, light Aztec	Light-to-moderate	Domestic residence	Has one preserved wall with a tepetate core
487	30 cm	12 m diam.	Light Early Toltec, very light Aztec	Moderate	Domestic residence	Two poorly preserved walls
497	30 cm	12 m diam.	Moderate Early Toltec, very light Aztec	Moderate	Domestic residence	
498	30 cm	12 m diam.	Moderate Early Toltec, very light Aztec	Moderate	Domestic residence	Two exposed walls composed of tepetate blocks
			SITE: TX-ET-17			
159	3 m	30 m diam.	Moderate Early Toltec and light Classic around base	Moderate	Ceremonial-civic	

Tlatel Number	Height	Surface Area	Surface Pottery	Rock Rubble	Probable Function	Comments
160	4 m	25 m diam.	Very light	Heavy	Ceremonial-civic	Several stone-wall bases on top of tlatel
164	3 m	30 m diam.	Light Early Toltec and Classic	Light-to-moderate	Ceremonial-civic	
165	7 m	40 m diam.	Light Early Toltec and Classic around base, nothing on structure itself	Light-to-moderate	Ceremonial-civic	Section of exterior plastered wall present
			SITE: TX-ET-18			
75	2 m	50 m diam.	Light Early Toltec	Heavy	Ceremonial-civic ?	Plastered floor exposed in several spots on eroded surface
112	1 to 4 m (built into hill slope)	25 m diam.	Light-to-moderate Early Toltec, mixed with lighter Classic and Aztec	Moderate	Ceremonial-civic	
117	3 m	40 m diam.	Light Early Toltec	Moderate	Ceremonial-civic	Grouped with Tlatels 116, 118, 119, and 120 around a small plaza
118	4 m	40x40 m	Light-to-moderate Early Toltec, light Classic	Moderate	Ceremonial-civic	Largest of small group of pyramids around a small plaza
119	4 m	40 m diam.	Light Early Toltec	Moderate	Ceremonial-civic	Grouped with Tlatel 116, etc. around a small plaza
122	4.5 m	20x25 m	Moderate Early Toltec, light Classic, light Late Toltec	Moderate	Ceremonial-civic	Grouped with Tlatel 123 and 124 around a small plaza
123	3.5 m	30x35 m	Moderate Early Toltec, light Classic	Moderate	Ceremonial-civic	Grouped with Tlatel 122 and 124 around a small plaza (Pl. 31,*a*)
124	5 m	40 m diam.	Moderate Early Toltec, light Late Toltec, light Classic	Heavy	Ceremonial-civic	Grouped with Tlatel 122 and 123 around a small plaza
126	2 m	25 m diam.	Moderate Early Toltec, light Classic	Moderate	Ceremonial-civic	
128	2 m	15x25 m	Very light	Light	Ceremonial-civic	Isolated and cut into by 2 barrancas
129	2 m	40 m diam.	Light-to-moderate Early Toltec, light Classic	Light-to-moderate	Ceremonial-civic	

Tlatel Number	Height	Surface Area	Surface Pottery	Rock Rubble	Probable Function	Comments
130	3 m	30 m diam.	Light Early Toltec, light Classic	Moderate	Ceremonial-civic	Grouped with Tlatel 131 around a small plaza (Pl. 32,*a*)
131	2 m	35 m diam.	Light Early Toltec	Moderate	Ceremonial-civic	Grouped with Tlatel 130 around a small plaza (Pl. 32,*b*)
133	6 m	40 m diam.	Very light	Light	Ceremonial-civic	Pl. 33,*a*
135	10 m	50 m diam.	Light-to-moderate Early Toltec and light Classic around base	Moderate	Ceremonial-civic	Grouped with Tlatels 136-138 around a small plaza, largest pyramid on site (Pl. 33,*b*)
145	3.5 m	25x35 m	Very light	Moderate	Ceremonial-civic	Grouped with Tlatel 146 around a small plaza
146	2 m	25x30 m	Very light	Moderate	Ceremonial-civic	Grouped with Tlatel 145 around a small plaza
148	5 m	25x35 m	Light Early Toltec	Moderate	Ceremonial-civic	Grouped with Tlatel 149 on a small plaza (Pl. 31,*b*)
149	3.5 m	25x40 m	Light Early Toltec	Moderate	Ceremonial-civic	Grouped with Tlatel 148 on a small plaza
151	3 m	35 m diam.	Light-to-moderate Early Toltec and light Classic around base only	Moderate	Ceremonial-civic	
152	3.5 m	35 m diam.	Light-to-moderate Early Toltec and Late Toltec; light Classic around base	Moderate	Ceremonial-civic	
			SITE: TX-ET-23			
107	2.2 m	20 m diam.	Light Early Toltec, Classic trace, Aztec trace	Heavy	Ceremonial-civic	Pitted in center (Fig. 12)
108	1.7 m	20x25 m	Light Early Toltec, Classic trace, Aztec trace	Heavy	Ceremonial-civic	Remnants of several interior walls faced with finished stone (Fig. 12)
109	1.7 m	8 m diam.	Very light	Heavy	Ceremonial-civic	Pitted in center (Fig. 12)
110	1.7 m	8 m diam.	Light Early Toltec, Classic trace, Aztec trace	Heavy	Ceremonial-civic	Pitted in center (Fig. 12)

Tlatel Number	Height	Surface Area	Surface Pottery	Rock Rubble	Probable Function	Comments
SITE: TX-LT-6						
6	None	40 m diam.	Light-to-moderate Late Toltec, light-to-moderate Aztec	Moderate	Domestic residence	Toltec ceramics are heavier on S.E. side of site, and Aztec ceramics heavier on N.W. side. Tlatel shows up as a white-gray area in an otherwise brown field; parts of a burial had been plowed up; drainage ditch cuts through area showing a layer of pottery a meter thick
10	0.3 m	50 m diam.	Moderate Late Toltec, light-to-moderate Aztec	Light-to-moderate	Domestic residence	Shows up as a white-gray discoloration of the soil
11	None	*ca.* 50 m diam.	Light-to-moderate Late Toltec, light-to-moderate Aztec	Light-to-moderate	Domestic residence	Shows up as a white-gray discoloration of the soil; drainage ditch dug through the area exposed a ceramic layer 30 cm thick
SITE: TX-LT-31						
562	35 cm	8 m diam.	Light-to-moderate Late Toltec, moderate Aztec	Moderate	Domestic residence	Possible exposed wall
569	1 m	6 m diam.	Moderate-to-heavy Late Toltec, very light-to-light Aztec	Moderate	Domestic residence	
570	0.5 m	4 m diam.	Light-to-moderate Late Toltec, light Aztec	Moderate	Domestic residence	Wall corner fragment
577	Slight	11-12 m diam.	Light-to-moderate Late Toltec, light-to-moderate Aztec	Light-to-moderate	Domestic residence	Several possible walls
SITE: TX-A-6						
78	3 m	35 m diam.	Light-to-moderate Aztec	Moderate	Ceremonial-civic	Numerous large chunks of plaster have been plowed up; plow cut has exposed plaster wall and floor on southern edge of mound about 60 cm below ground surface
79	3.5 m	140x140 m	Light-to-moderate Aztec, trace of Late Toltec	Very light	Ceremonial-civic	Located 25 m directly south of Tlatel 78; built on two large stepped platforms; at least 3 layers of plaster floor superimposed

Tlatel Number	Height	Surface Area	Surface Pottery	Rock Rubble	Probable Function	Comments
80	70 cm	18x15 m	None noted	Light	Ceremonial-civic ?	Exposed adobe wall
82	2 m	15 m diam.	Light Aztec	None	Domestic residence?	Exposed adobe wall
			SITE: TX-A-10			
6	None	40 m diam.	Light Aztec, light-to-moderate Late Toltec	Light	Domestic residence	Pitting has exposed fragments of human bone, and abundant sherd refuse
10	30 cm	50 m diam.	Light-to-moderate Aztec, moderate Late Toltec	None	Domestic residence	Aztec ceramics heavier on one side of tlatel and Toltec on the other
11	None	50 m diam.	Light-to-moderate Aztec, light-to-moderate Late Toltec	Light	Domestic residence	
			SITE: TX-A-17			
53	50 cm	10 m diam.	Light Aztec, light Late Toltec	Heavy	Domestic residence	Several remnants of stone wall bases
54	1 m	10 m diam.	Light-to-moderate Aztec, light Late Toltec	Heavy	Domestic residence	Remnants of a stone wall base
56	1.5 m	8 m diam.	Light-to-moderate Aztec, light Late Toltec	Moderate	Domestic residence	
			SITE: TX-A-24			
98	1 m	8 m diam.	Light Aztec	Heavy	Domestic residence	
177	1 m	7 m diam.	Light Aztec, trace of Early Toltec	Heavy	Domestic residence	
183	None	20 m diam.	Light-to-moderate Aztec	Heavy	Domestic residence	Remnant of stone wall base 2 m long and 20 cm wide, resting on layer of soil *ca.* 30 cm deep, which in turn rests on tepetate
184	50 cm	15 m diam.	Light Aztec, light-to-moderate Toltec	Moderate	Domestic residence	Situated on edge of large barranca; wall remnant 50 cm high exposed in barranca cut

Tlatel Number	Height	Surface Area	Surface Pottery	Rock Rubble	Probable Function	Comments
192	1 m	30 m diam.	Moderate Aztec, Toltec trace	Heavy	Domestic residence	
195	1 m	20 m diam.	Moderate Aztec, both Early and Late, trace of Toltec	Heavy	Domestic residence	
198	30 cm	15 m diam.	Moderate Aztec, both Early and Late, light Toltec	Heavy	Domestic residence	
201	50 cm	30 m diam.	Moderate Aztec, very light Toltec	Moderate	Domestic residence	
205	1.5 m	25 m diam.	Light-to-moderate Aztec	Heavy	Domestic residence	
206	1 m	30 m diam.	Light-to-moderate Aztec	Heavy	Domestic residence	
207	1 m	40 m diam.	Light Aztec	Light	Domestic residence	
209	30 cm	6 m diam.	Moderate Aztec	Moderate	Domestic residence	Remnants of stone wall bases define a 3x5 m room, with no trace of interior partitions
212	30 cm	6 m diam.	Moderate Aztec	Moderate	Domestic residence	
213	3 m on downslope side	10x10 m	Light Aztec	Heavy	Ceremonial-civic ?	Built into the side of hill slope, the back of the tlatel level with the grade of the hill, a possible stairway on downslope
214	40 cm	20 m diam.	Moderate Aztec	Heavy	Domestic residence	Small remnant of stone wall base
216	None	16 m diam.	Moderate Aztec	Heavy	Domestic residence	Remnants of stone wall bases define one room, 5x3 m, and another 2 m wide and probably 2 or 3 other rooms (Fig. 16,*a*)
217	30 cm	15 m diam.	Light Aztec	Heavy	Domestic residence	Remnants of stone wall bases define at least two rooms, one 5x1.5 m, and the other 3x3 m (Fig. 16,*b*)
218	Slight	15 m diam.	Moderate Aztec	Heavy	Domestic residence	Remnants of stone wall bases define at least 3 rooms with no visable interior partitions, rooms are 3 by at least 3 m, 5 by at least 3 m, and 2 by at least 2 m (Fig. 16,*c*)

Tlatel Number	Height	Surface Area	Surface Pottery	Rock Rubble	Probable Function	Comments
219	2 m	30 m diam.	Light-to-moderate Aztec	Heavy	Domestic residence	
220	1 m	10 m diam.	Light Aztec, Light Toltec	Moderate	Domestic residence	
224	50 cm	15 m diam.	Light Aztec	Heavy	Domestic residence	Remnants of stone wall bases define the corner of at least one room
227	50 cm	15x5 m	Moderate Aztec	Moderate	Domestic residence	Remnants of stone wall bases define at least four rooms, 1.5x 1.5 m, 3x3 m, 3x3 m, and 3x4.5 m or more (Fig. 16,*d*)
228	None	30 m diam.	Light-to-moderate Aztec	Moderate	Domestic residence	Remnants of stone wall bases define 9 or 10 rooms (Fig. 16,*g*)
229	50 cm	10 m diam.	Light-to-moderate Aztec	Moderate	Domestic residence	Remnants of stone wall bases (Pl. 36,*a*)
230	1.5 m	20 m diam.	Moderate Aztec	Heavy	Domestic residence	Remnants of stone wall bases
231	1 m	25 m diam.	Moderate Aztec	Heavy	Domestic residence	Remnants of stone wall bases
232	50 cm	15 m diam.	Light-to-moderate Aztec	Moderate	Domestic residence	Remnants of stone wall bases define one room 4x2 m, and two other probable rooms
234	1 m	10 m diam.	Light-to-moderate Aztec	Heavy	Domestic residence	
235	Slight	13 m diam.	Light-to-moderate Aztec	Heavy	Domestic residence	Remnants of stone wall bases
237	50 cm	30 m diam.	Moderate Aztec	Heavy	Domestic residence	Remnants of stone wall bases
238	1 m	20 m diam.	Moderate Aztec	Heavy	Domestic residence	
239	1 m	20 m diam.	Moderate Aztec	Heavy	Domestic residence	
240	1 m	10 m diam.	Moderate Aztec	Heavy	Domestic residence	
241	1 m	8 m diam.	Moderate Aztec	Heavy	Domestic residence	

Tlatel Number	Height	Surface Area	Surface Pottery	Rock Rubble	Probable Function	Comments
243	50 cm	10 m diam.	Moderate Aztec	Heavy	Domestic residence	
245	20 cm	5 m diam.	Light Aztec	Moderate	Domestic residence	
246	50 cm	25 x10 m	Moderate Aztec	Heavy	Domestic residence	
248	50 cm	10 m diam.	Light Aztec	Moderate	Domestic residence	
249	1 m	7 m diam.	Moderate Aztec	Heavy	Domestic residence	
250	50 cm	5 m diam.	Moderate Aztec	Heavy	Domestic residence	Remnants of stone wall bases define at least 2 rooms of indeterminate size
253	30 cm	5 m diam.	Light-to-moderate Aztec	Heavy	Domestic residence	At center is a circular stone-lined pit (1 m in diameter), in this pit were fragments of human bone—perhaps a sub-floor burial
254	30 cm	5 m diam.	Moderate Aztec	Heavy	Domestic residence	Remnants of stone wall bases define a room 3x4 m
255	Slight	12 m diam.	Light Aztec	Moderate	Domestic residence	Remnants of stone wall bases
257	Slight	8 m diam.	Light-to-moderate Late Aztec	Moderate	Domestic residence	
258	None	27 m diam.	Moderate Aztec	Heavy	Domestic residence	Remnants of stone wall bases
259	Slight	5 m diam.	Light Aztec	Moderate	Domestic residence	Remnants of stone wall bases
260	75 cm	20x24 m	Light Aztec	Moderate	Domestic residence	
261	Slight	7x4 m	Moderate Aztec	Moderate	Domestic residence	
263	50 cm	14x7 m	Moderate Aztec	Heavy	Domestic residence	Remnants of stone wall bases define a room 3x2.5 m, and at least 3 others 3 m wide but of indeterminate size

Tlatel Number	Height	Surface Area	Surface Pottery	Rock Rubble	Probable Function	Comments
266	50 cm	7 m diam.	Moderate Aztec, Toltec trace	Moderate	Domestic residence	
269	Slight	18 m diam.	Moderate Aztec, Toltec trace	Heavy	Domestic residence	Remnants of stone wall bases define one room 2x2.5 m and a second of about the same size
270	None	4x6 m	Light Aztec	Light	Domestic residence	Remnants of stone wall bases of at least two rooms of indeterminate size
272	Slight	5 m diam.	Moderate Aztec, light Toltec	Heavy	Domestic residence	Remnant of stone wall bases
273	Slight	10 m diam.	Moderate Aztec	Heavy	Domestic residence	Remnant of stone wall bases
277	1 m	10 m diam.	Moderate Aztec	Heavy	Domestic residence	Remnant of stone wall bases
278	Slight	10 m diam.	Moderate Aztec, light Toltec	Heavy	Domestic residence	Remnant of stone wall bases
279	20 cm	5 m diam.	Moderate Aztec	Heavy	Domestic residence	Remnant of stone wall bases define one room, 3.5x3.5 m
280	20 cm	10x10 m	Moderate Aztec, light Toltec	Heavy	Domestic residence	Remnants of stone wall bases define 6 rooms, four are 3.5x2 m, one is 3x4 m, and the other is 3x3.5 m (Fig. 16,*f*)
282	1 m	5 m diam.	Light Aztec	Light	Domestic residence	Remnants of stone wall bases define at least 2 rooms, each 2 m square
286	20 cm	10 m diam.	Moderate Aztec	Heavy	Domestic residence	Remnants of stone wall bases
287	40 cm	8x4 m	Moderate Aztec	Moderate	Domestic residence	Fragments of 2 stone wall bases
288	1 m	20 m diam.	Moderate Aztec	Heavy	Domestic residence	A large amount of dressed stone
289	50 cm	13 m diam.	Light-to-moderate Aztec	Heavy	Domestic residence	
290	1 m	12 m diam.	Light Aztec	Heavy	Domestic residence	One stone wall base remnant 12 m long
299	Slight	8 m diam.	Moderate Aztec	Moderate	Domestic residence	Remnant of stone wall base 1 m long

Tlatel Number	Height	Surface Area	Surface Pottery	Rock Rubble	Probable Function	Comments
302	25 cm	14 m diam.	Light Aztec	Heavy	Domestic residence	Remnant of stone wall base, about 5 m long
305	50 cm	9 m diam.	Moderate Aztec, both Early and Late, trace of Late Toltec	Heavy	Domestic residence	One remnant of stone wall base, 2 m long
309	30 cm	12 m diam.	Moderate Aztec	Light-to-moderate	Domestic residence	Remnant of stone wall bases define at least two rooms of indeterminate size
310	None	20 m diam.	Light Aztec	Heavy	Domestic residence	One remnant of stone wall base, 2 m long
313	None	13 m diam.	Light Aztec	Light-to-moderate	Domestic residence	One remnant of stone wall base 2 m long
314	Slight	11 m diam.	Light-to-moderate Aztec	Light	Domestic residence	
315	None	8 m diam.	Light-to-moderate Aztec	Light	Domestic residence	
318	50 cm	10 m diam.	Moderate Aztec	Moderate	Domestic residence	
323	Slight	20 m diam.	Moderate Aztec	Moderate	Domestic residence	Remnants of stone wall bases define one room 2x2 m and parts of at least four other rooms
325	50 cm	10 m diam.	Moderate Aztec	Moderate	Domestic residence	
326	50 cm	12 m diam.	Moderate Aztec	Moderate	Domestic residence	Remnants of stone wall bases define several rooms (Fig. 16,*e*)
327	50 cm	15 m diam.	Moderate Aztec	Heavy	Domestic residence	
333	50 cm	18 m diam.	Moderate Aztec	Heavy	Domestic residence	Remnants of stone wall bases indicate at least 2 rooms, one 3 m long by more than 1 m wide
335	50 cm	10 m diam.	Moderate Aztec	Heavy	Domestic residence	Remnants of stone wall bases
336	1 m	20x8 m	Moderate Aztec	Heavy	Domestic residence	Remnants of at least one stone wall base

Tlatel Number	Height	Surface Area	Surface Pottery	Rock Rubble	Probable Function	Comments
338	50 cm	15 m diam.	Moderate Aztec	Heavy	Domestic residence	Remnants of stone wall bases define a room 2.5 m by more than 2 m
339	1 m	7 m diam.	Moderate Aztec	Heavy	Domestic residence	Remnant of one wall base of dressed stone on a tepetate block foundation
342	1 m	8 m diam.	Light Aztec	Heavy	Domestic residence	Remnant of a stone wall base, 1.5 m long
343	25 cm	15 m diam.	Moderate Aztec	Moderate	Domestic residence	Remnants of 2 parallel stone wall bases, 2.5 m apart, each 3 m long
345	1.5 m	20 m diam.	Moderate Aztec, both Early and Late, trace of Late Toltec	Heavy	Domestic residence	Remnants of several discontinuous stone wall bases
346	1 m	20 m diam.	Moderate Aztec, both Early and Late, trace of Toltec	Moderate	Domestic residence	Remnants of several stone wall bases
348	50 cm	5 m diam.	Moderate Aztec, both Early and Late	Moderate	Domestic residence	Remnants of 2 stone wall bases
349	None	15 m diam.	Light Aztec	Moderate	Domestic residence	
350	50 cm	15 m diam.	Moderate Aztec	Heavy	Domestic residence	
355	50 cm	20 m diam.	Moderate Aztec, both Early and Late	Heavy	Domestic residence	Remnant of 1 stone wall base
357	2 m	30 m diam.	Light-to-moderate Aztec	Heavy	Domestic residence ?	Remnants of 2 stone wall bases and 1 corner
358	2 m	30 m diam.	Light Aztec	Heavy	Domestic residence ?	Remnants of several stone wall bases and corners
398	3.5 m	25x15 m	Light-to-moderate Aztec, trace of Toltec	Heavy	Ceremonial-civic ?	Probable post-Conquest superstructure 2 m high with plastered walls, on top of tlatel
400	2 m	20 m diam.	Light Aztec, light Early Toltec	Heavy	Ceremonial-civic ?	
412	30 cm	9 m diam.	Moderate Aztec, both Early and Late, trace of Late Toltec	Heavy	Domestic residence	Remnant of 1 stone wall base, 5 m long

Tlatel Number	Height	Surface Area	Surface Pottery	Rock Rubble	Probable Function	Comments
424	50 cm	20 m diam.	Moderate Aztec, both Early and Late	Heavy	Domestic residence	
426	1 m	6 m diam.	Light Aztec, both Early and Late	Heavy	Domestic residence	
427	1 m	12 x 8 m	Moderate Aztec, both Early and Late	Heavy	Domestic residence	Remnants of 2 stone wall bases
429	Slight	5 m diam.	Moderate Aztec, both Early and Late	Moderate	Domestic residence	Remnant of 1 definite stone wall corner
430	1 m	15 m diam.	Moderate Aztec	Moderate	Domestic residence	
431	50 cm	5 m diam.	Light Aztec	Moderate	Domestic residence	
432	50 cm	6 m diam.	Moderate Aztec	Light	Domestic residence	
433	50 cm	25 m diam.	Moderate Aztec	Heavy	Domestic residence	
435	None	5 m diam.	Moderate Aztec, both Early and Late	Moderate	Domestic residence	Remnants of stone wall bases define 1 room 2.5x1.8 m and part of a second. Both have stone-faced, adobe core walls
438	1 m	30 m diam.	Moderate Aztec, both Early and Late, trace of Toltec	Moderate	Domestic residence	Remnants of 3 stone wall bases
445	1 m	20 m diam.	Moderate Aztec, both Early and Late	Moderate	Domestic residence	Remnant of 1 stone wall base
446	1.5 m	10 m diam.	Light Aztec, light Toltec	Heavy	Domestic residence	
448	None	18 m diam.	Light-to-moderate Aztec	Heavy	Domestic residence	Remnants of stone wall bases define 1 room 3x2.5 m, and at least 1 other room
451	None	6 m diam.	Light-to-moderate Aztec, both Early and Late	Heavy	Domestic residence	Remnant of 1 stone wall base 8 m long
452	1.5 m	5 m diam.	Light Aztec, both Early and Late	Heavy	Domestic residence	Has been incorporated into a modern stone wall; structure is very well preserved with stone wall bases standing at least 1 m high and defining 1 room 3x3 m

Tlatel Number	Height	Surface Area	Surface Pottery	Rock Rubble	Probable Function	Comments
453	50 cm	13 m diam.	Light Aztec	Heavy	Domestic residence	Remnants of several stone wall bases
454	1 m	5 m diam.	Moderate Aztec, both Early and Late, trace of Toltec	Light	Domestic residence	
455	Slight	6 m diam.	Light Aztec	Moderate	Domestic residence	Remnants of stone wall bases
456	Slight	5 m diam.	Light-to-moderate Aztec	Moderate	Domestic residence	Remnant of stone wall base 1 m long
457	Slight	20 m diam.	Moderate Aztec, both Early and Late	Moderate	Domestic residence	Small remnants of stone wall bases
460	Slight	No data	Light Aztec	Moderate	Domestic residence	Several remnants of stone wall bases
462	1 m	12 m diam.	Moderate Aztec, both Early and Late	Heavy	Domestic residence	Remnant of stone wall base corner
SITE: TX-A-25						
464	10 cm	12 m diam.	Moderate Aztec, both Early and Late	Moderate	Domestic residence	Resting on a layer of soil 5-6 cm thick
465	30 cm	10 m diam.	Light-to-moderate Aztec	Moderate	Domestic residence	
466	50 cm	4 m diam.	Light-to-moderate Aztec	Heavy	Domestic residence	
467	1 m	20 m diam.	Moderate Aztec	Light-to-moderate	Domestic residence	
468	30 cm	8 m diam.	Moderate Aztec	Light-to-moderate	Domestic residence	
470	1.5 m	17 m diam.	Moderate Aztec	Moderate	Domestic residence	
472	20 cm	10 m diam.	Moderate Aztec	Moderate	Domestic residence	Remnants of stone wall bases define a complex of at least 3 rooms (Fig. 17,*a*), walls are of adobe core construction, with stone exterior
473	50 cm	20 m diam.	Moderate Aztec, both Early and Late, trace of Terminal Formative	Moderate	Domestic residence	

Tlatel Number	Height	Surface Area	Surface Pottery	Rock Rubble	Probable Function	Comments
475	3 m	13 m diam.	Light Aztec	Heavy	Ceremonial-civic	Badly pitted with a trench dug through the center; interior fill of rock rubble and tepetate blocks
476	1.5 m	4x10 m	Light Aztec	Heavy	?	Badly distorted by cultivation and the piling of rocks from the surrounding fields on the tlatel
477	1.5 m	4x10 m	Light Aztec	Heavy	?	Badly distorted by cultivation and the piling of rocks from the surrounding fields on the tlatel
478	None	12 m diam.	Moderate Aztec, both Early and Late, trace of Terminal Formative	Moderate	Domestic residence	
479	4 m	25 m diam.	Light-to-moderate Aztec, both Early and Late	Heavy	Ceremonial-civic	Badly potted with a trench through the center, revealing an internal construction of solid stone and tepetate blocks
541	50 cm	8 m diam.	Moderate Aztec	Moderate	Domestic residence	Located on eastern slopes of the site; remnants of stone wall bases define a complex of at least 3 rooms
542	50 cm	6 m diam.	Moderate Aztec	Moderate	Domestic residence	Remnants of stone wall bases define a complex of at least 2 rooms; wall construction is tepetate core with stone facing
543	2 m	10 m diam.	Moderate Aztec, both Early and Late	Moderate	Domestic residence	Remnants of stone wall bases define a complex of at least 2 rooms, one of which is 3x2 m
544	1.5 m	8 m diam.	Moderate Aztec	Heavy	Domestic residence	Remnants of stone wall bases define a complex of at least 3 rooms of indeterminate size
SITE: TX-A-26						
611	*ca.* 1 m	10 m diam.	Light-to-moderate Aztec	Moderate	Domestic residence	Remnants of stone wall bases define 1 room 3x3 m, and part of a second
613	*ca.* 1 m	20 m diam.	Moderate Aztec, both Early and Late	Heavy	Domestic residence	Remnants of stone wall bases define a complex of at least 4 rooms (Pl. 37,*b*)

Tlatel Number	Height	Surface Area	Surface Pottery	Rock Rubble	Probable Function	Comments
614	*ca.* 1 m	18 m diam.	Moderate Aztec	Moderate	Domestic residence	Remnants of stone wall bases define a complex of at least two rooms
615	50 cm	10x10 m	Moderate Aztec, both Early and Late	Heavy	Domestic residence	Remnants of stone wall bases define a complex of at least four rooms (Fig. 17,*b*)
616	50 cm	6 m diam.	Light-to-moderate Aztec	Moderate	Domestic residence	Remnant of a stone wall base, 1 m long
617	50 cm	8-10 m diam.	Light Aztec	Heavy	Domestic residence	Remnants of stone wall bases define a complex of at least 3 rooms (Fig. 17,*c*)
618	50 cm	8 m diam.	Light-to-moderate Aztec	Heavy	Domestic residence	Remnants of stone wall bases define one room 5x5 m, with a possible interior partition
619	1 m	20 m diam.	Light-to-moderate Aztec	Heavy	Domestic residence	Remnants of stone wall bases define a complex of at least 3 rooms; one is 4x4 m
620	*ca.* 1 m	5 m diam.	Light Aztec	Moderate-to-heavy	Domestic residence	Remnants of stone wall bases define 1 room, 4x4 m
622	1.4 m	21 m diam.	Light-to-moderate Aztec	Moderate-to-heavy	Domestic residence	Remnants of stone wall bases define a complex of at least 2 rooms, probably with interior partitions
623	1.5 m on downslope side; none on up-slope side	10 m diam.	Light Aztec	Moderate-to-heavy	Domestic residence	Remnants of stone wall bases define 1 room 3.5 m x 5 m; stone and tepetate blocks used in construction
624	*ca.* 2 m on downslope side; 1 m on upslope side	9 m diam.	Light Aztec	Heavy	Domestic residence	Remnants of stone wall bases define 3 rooms, each 1.5x3 or 3.5 m
625	1 m on downslope side; none on upslope side	8 m diam.	Light-to-moderate Aztec	Moderate	Domestic residence	Remnants of stone wall bases define a complex of at least 2 rooms of indeterminate size

Tlatel Number	Height	Surface Area	Surface Pottery	Rock Rubble	Probable Function	Comments
626	1.5 m on downslope side; none on up-slope side	25x15 m	Light Aztec	Heavy	Domestic residence	Remnant of 1 stone wall base, 3 m long
			SITE: TX-A-27			
545	75 cm	8 m diam.	Moderate Aztec	Heavy	Domestic residence	Several remnants of stone wall bases
546	50 cm	5 m diam.	Moderate Aztec, trace of Late Toltec	Heavy	Domestic residence	
547	40 cm	6 m diam.	Moderate Aztec	Moderate	Domestic residence	
548	40 cm	6 m diam.	Moderate Aztec, predominately Early, trace of Late Toltec	Heavy	Domestic residence	Remnant of 1 stone wall base, tepetate core construction
549	1.5 m	5 m diam.	Moderate Aztec, predominately Early	Heavy	Domestic residence	Remnants of several stone wall bases
550	1 m	11 m diam.	Moderate Aztec	Heavy	Domestic residence	Remnants of 2 stone wall bases; of tepetate core construction
551	50 cm	7 m diam.	Moderate Aztec	Heavy	Domestic residence	Remnants of stone wall bases define at least 2 rooms of indeterminate size
554	1 m	55x30 m	Moderate Aztec, both Early and Late	Heavy	Domestic residence	Remnants of stone wall bases define a large complex of at least 8 rooms (Fig. 18,*a*)
555	40 cm	5 m diam.	Light Aztec	Moderate	Domestic residence	
556	2 m	12 m diam.	Moderate Aztec	Heavy	Domestic residence	Remnants of several stone wall bases
557	1.5 m	10x5 m	Moderate Aztec	Heavy	Domestic residence	Remnant of one stone wall base; tepetate core construction
558	30 cm	7 m diam.	Light-to-moderate Aztec	Heavy	Domestic residence	

Tlatel Number	Height	Surface Area	Surface Pottery	Rock Rubble	Probable Function	Comments
559	50 cm	8x8 m	Moderate Aztec	Heavy	Domestic residence	Remnants of 2 stone wall bases; tepetate core construction
560	20 cm	8 m diam.	Moderate Aztec	Moderate	Domestic residence	
561	2 m	12x12 m	Moderate Aztec, both Early and Late, trace of Late Toltec	Heavy	Domestic residence	Remnants of stone wall bases define a complex of at least seven rooms (Fig. 17,*e*)
562	35 cm	8 m diam.	Moderate Aztec, both Early and Late, light-to-moderate Late Toltec	Moderate	Domestic residence	
563	30 cm	9x5 m	Moderate Aztec, light Late Toltec	Moderate	Domestic residence	
564	2 m	10x4 m	Moderate Aztec, both Early and Late	Moderate	Domestic residence	Remnant of one stone wall base
565	1.5 m	6 m diam.	Moderate Aztec, trace of Late Toltec	Heavy	Domestic residence	Remnant of one stone wall base
566	2 m	28x15 m	Moderate Aztec	Heavy	Domestic residence	Remnants of stone wall bases define a complex of at least 10 rooms (Fig. 17,*d*)
567	3 m	35 m diam.	Moderate Aztec, light Late Toltec	Moderate	Domestic residence	Remnants of stone wall bases define a complex of several rooms of indeterminate size
568	2.5 m	8 m diam.	Light-to-moderate Aztec	Heavy	Domestic residence	Remnants of stone wall bases define a complex of several rooms of indeterminate size
571	1 m	6 m diam.	Light-to-moderate Aztec, light Late Toltec	Heavy	Domestic residence	
572	1.5 m	16 m diam.	Moderate Aztec, both Early and Late	Heavy	Domestic residence	Remnants of several stone wall bases
574	1 m	8 m diam.	Light Aztec, both Early and Late	Heavy	Domestic residence	
575	None	10 m diam.	Light-to-moderate Aztec, both Early and Late, trace of Late Toltec	Light	Domestic residence	Remnant of 1 stone wall base
612	50 cm	24 m diam.	Light-to-moderate Aztec	Heavy	Domestic residence	Remnants of stone wall bases define a complex of at least 16 rooms (Fig. 18,*b*)

SITE: TX-A-28

Tlatel Number	Height	Surface Area	Surface Pottery	Rock Rubble	Probable Function	Comments
578	1.5 m	9 m diam.	Light-to-moderate Aztec	Heavy	Domestic residence	
579	50 cm	5 m diam.	Moderate Aztec, both Early and Late, trace of Late Toltec	Moderate	Domestic residence	Remnants of stone wall bases define one room 5x2 m
580	1 m	16 m diam.	Light-to-moderate Aztec, both Early and Late	Heavy	Ceremonial-civic ?	Pitting has revealed an interior of solid rock rubble and tepetate fill
581	1 m	15 m diam.	Light Aztec	Heavy	Ceremonial-civic ?	Pitting reveals solid rock rubble and tepetate fill. The mounding of rock rubble suggests perhaps 2 rooms, one 2 m square, the other 3 m square
582	50 cm	12 m diam.	Light-to-moderate Aztec	Heavy	Domestic residence	Remnants of stone wall bases define a complex of at least 7 rooms (Fig. 19,*a*)
583	25 cm	25 m diam.	Light Aztec, trace of Late Toltec	Moderate	?	Remnants of stone wall bases, 60-70 cm wide (Fig. 19,*c*)
587	1.5 m	14 m diam.	Moderate Aztec, both Early and Late	Heavy	Domestic residence	Remnants of stone wall bases define a complex of at least 5 rooms (Fig. 19,*b*)
588	1.5 m	15 m diam.	Light-to-moderate Aztec, both Early and Late, trace of Late Toltec	Heavy	Domestic residence	Remnant of one stone wall base 1 m long and 30 cm wide
589	50 cm	10 m diam.	Moderate Aztec, both Early and Late	Moderate	Domestic residence	Remnants of two stone wall bases, each 1 m long and 40 cm wide
590	1 m	12 m diam.	Moderate Aztec, both Early and Late	Heavy	Domestic residence	Remnants of stone wall bases define a complex of at least 3 rooms of indeterminate size
591	1.5 m	20 m diam.	Moderate Aztec, both Early and Late, trace of Late Toltec	Heavy	Domestic residence?	Remnants of stone wall bases define a complex of at least 3 rooms of indeterminate size
592	1 m	9 m diam.	Moderate Aztec, both Early and Late	Heavy	Ceremonial-civic ?	Pitting reveals solid rock rubble interior; some dressed stone
593	1 m	*ca.* 8 m diam.	Light-to-moderate Aztec	Heavy	Domestic residence	Remnants of stone wall bases define a complex of at least 3 rooms; two are 5x6 m rooms

Tlatel Number	Height	Surface Area	Surface Pottery	Rock Rubble	Probable Function	Comments
594	1 m	18x5 m	Moderate Aztec, both Early and Late	Heavy	Domestic residence	
595	50 cm	10 m diam.	Light Aztec	Heavy	Domestic residence	Remnant of one stone wall base, about 60 cm wide
596	1 m	8 m diam.	Light-to-moderate Aztec, both Early and Late	Heavy	Domestic residence	Remnants of stone wall bases define one room 4x2 m (Fig. 19,*d*)
597	1 m	8 m diam.	Light Aztec	Heavy	Domestic residence	Remnants of stone wall bases define one room 4x3 m (Fig. 19,*e*)
598	1 m	14 m diam.	Light Aztec, trace of Late Toltec	Heavy	Domestic residence	Remnants of 2 stone wall bases
599	50 cm	8 m diam.	Light Aztec	Heavy	Domestic residence	
600	30 cm	5 m diam.	Light Aztec	Moderate	Domestic residence	
601	None	5 m diam.	Moderate Aztec	Moderate	Domestic residence	
603	None	8 m diam.	Light-to-moderate Aztec, both Early and Late	Moderate	Domestic residence	
604	None	10 m diam.	Light Aztec	Moderate	Domestic residence	
605	1 m	7 m diam.	Light Aztec	Heavy	Domestic residence	Remnant of one stone wall base, 4 m long and 30 cm wide
608	None	5 m diam.	Light Aztec	Moderate	Domestic residence	
609	None	12 m diam.	Light-to-moderate Aztec	Moderate	Domestic residence	
610	1.7 m	8 m diam.	Very light Aztec	Heavy	?	
797	30 cm	5 m diam.	Light Aztec	Heavy	Domestic residence	
798	40 cm	12 m diam.	Light Aztec	Heavy	Domestic residence	Remnants of stone wall bases define a complex of at least 2 rooms, one is 3 m square

Tlatel Number	Height	Surface Area	Surface Pottery	Rock Rubble	Probable Function	Comments
799	50 cm	5-7 m diam.	Light Aztec	Moderate	Domestic residence	
804	50 cm	5 m diam.	Moderate Aztec	Light	Domestic residence	Remnant of 1 stone wall base, 2 m long and 20 cm wide
805	30 cm	5 m diam.	Light-to-moderate Aztec, both Early and Late	Moderate	Domestic residence	Remnants of one stone wall base, 3 m long
807	1 m	7 m diam.	Light-to-moderate Aztec, both Early and Late	Moderate	Domestic residence	Remnants of stone wall bases define a complex of at least 3 rooms of indeterminate size
809	60 cm	5 m diam.	Light-to-moderate Aztec	Light	Domestic residence	
810	50 cm	5 m diam.	Light-to-moderate Aztec,	Moderate	Domestic residence	Remnant of 2 stone wall bases
812	50 cm	5 m diam.	Moderate Aztec	Moderate	Domestic residence	
814	50 cm	5 m diam.	Light Aztec	Moderate	Domestic residence	
817	30 cm	6-7 m diam.	Light-to-moderate Aztec, both Early and Late	Moderate	Domestic residence	
818	70 cm	5 m diam.	Moderate Aztec	Heavy	Domestic residence	
822	50 cm	10-13 m diam.	Moderate Aztec, predominately Early	Moderate	Domestic residence	
827	35 cm	7 m diam.	Moderate Aztec	Heavy	Domestic residence	
829	50 cm	12 m diam.	Light Aztec	Heavy	Domestic residence	
834	50 cm	5 m diam.	Light Aztec	Heavy	Domestic residence	
835	30 cm	7 m diam.	Moderate Aztec	Moderate	Domestic residence	
836	30 cm	5 m diam.	Very light Aztec	Moderate	Domestic residence	Remnants of 2 stone wall bases 30-35 cm wide
837	50 cm	5 m diam.	Light-to-moderate Aztec, predominately Early	Heavy	Domestic residence	

Tlatel Number	Height	Surface Area	Surface Pottery	Rock Rubble	Probable Function	Comments
838	50 cm	12 m diam.	Moderate Aztec, predominately Early	Heavy	Domestic residence	Remnants of stone wall bases define 1 room at least 3x2 m
839	30 cm	8 m diam.	Light Aztec	Heavy	Domestic residence	Remnant of 1 stone wall base, 2 m long
840	30 cm	6 m diam.	Light-to-moderate Aztec	Heavy	Domestic residence	
841	50 cm	12 m diam.	Moderate Aztec	Heavy	Domestic residence	
842	1.5 m	9 m diam.	Light-to-moderate Aztec	Heavy	Domestic residence	
843	50 cm	8 m diam.	Moderate Aztec, both Early and Late	Heavy	Domestic residence	Remnants of stone wall bases
845	1 m	10x5 m	Moderate Aztec, both Early and Late	Moderate	Domestic residence	On ridgetop in a grass-covered area; part of a complex of tlatels oriented around a plaza (Fig. 20)
846	2 m	8 m diam.	None	Heavy	Ceremonial-civic	Pitting reveals a solid rock rubble interior (Fig. 20)
847	50 cm	2.5x2.5 m	None	Heavy	Ceremonial-civic ?	3 m directly south of Tlatel 846 (Fig. 20)
848	1 m	6 m diam.	None on mound, Moderate Aztec in surrounding area	Heavy	?	See Fig. 20
849	1 m	6 m diam.	Moderate Aztec, both Early and Late	Moderate	Domestic residence	
850	None	8 m diam.	Light Aztec, predominately Early	Heavy	Domestic residence	Remnants of stone wall bases
852	None	5 m diam.	Moderate Aztec, both Early and Late	Moderate	Domestic residence	
853	25 cm	5 m diam.	Light Aztec, predominately Early	Moderate	Domestic residence	
855	None	8 m diam.	Light Aztec	Heavy	Domestic residence	Remnants of 2 stone wall bases, 3 m long, 30 cm wide, and 4 m apart
856	35 cm	8 m diam.	Moderate Aztec	Moderate	Domestic residence	Remnants of several wall bases

Tlatel Number	Height	Surface Area	Surface Pottery	Rock Rubble	Probable Function	Comments
857	20 cm	1 m diam.	Very light Aztec	Heavy	?	Remnants of stone wall bases define a very small structure
858	50 cm	15 m diam.	Moderate Aztec, both Early and Late	Moderate	Domestic residence	
860	50 cm	5 m diam.	Moderate Aztec	Heavy	Domestic residence	
861	50 cm	6 m diam.	Moderate Aztec	Moderate	Domestic residence	
862	50 cm	6 m diam.	Moderate Aztec	Heavy	Domestic residence	Remnants of stone wall bases define one room, 5x3 m
864	25 cm	8 m diam.	Moderate Aztec, both Early and Late	Moderate	Domestic residence	
865	None	5 m diam.	Light Aztec	Moderate	Domestic residence	Remnant of one stone wall base, 2 m long and 40 cm wide
SITE: TX-A-30						
682	80 cm	7-8 m diam.	Light Aztec	Moderate	Domestic residence	Remnants of stone wall bases define a complex of at least 2 rooms; one is about 2x4 m, the other is 2x2 m
683	1 m	5 m diam.	Light-to-moderate Aztec, both Early and Late	Heavy	Domestic residence	Remnant of one stone wall base
684	40 cm	6-7 m diam.	Light Aztec	Moderate	Domestic residence	Remnants of several stone wall bases in an area dotted with old terrace remnants
686	None	5 m diam.	Very light Aztec	Heavy	Domestic residence?	Remnants of stone wall bases define a room 1.5x2 m with walls of large unfinished rocks
687	40 cm	5 m diam.	Light Aztec	Heavy	Domestic residence	Remnant of 1 stone wall base
688	60 cm	4x5 m diam.	Light Aztec	Heavy	Domestic residence	Remnants of stone wall bases define 1 room 4x4.5 m, with terrace fragments in front of the structure
689	1 m	5 m diam.	Very light Aztec	Heavy	Domestic residence?	Built on same terrace as Tlatel 688

Tlatel Number	Height	Surface Area	Surface Pottery	Rock Rubble	Probable Function	Comments
690	60 cm	5 m diam.	Light Aztec	Heavy	Domestic residence	Remnants of stone wall bases define a room 3.5x4 m
691	30 cm	5 m diam.	Very light Aztec	Heavy	Domestic residence?	Remnants of stone wall bases define a small room 3x2.5 m with walls 30 cm thick
692	35 cm	5 m diam.	Light Aztec	Heavy	Domestic residence	
693	40 cm	8 m diam.	Light Aztec	Heavy	Domestic residence	Remnants of stone wall bases define one room 3.5x3.7 m with a possible interior partition
694	30 cm	7x8 m	Light Aztec	Heavy	Domestic residence	Remnants of several stone wall bases
695	60 cm	8x8 m	Moderate Aztec, both Early and Late, trace of Late Toltec	Heavy	Domestic residence	Remnants of several stone wall bases
696	1 m	5 m diam.	Moderate Aztec, both Early and Late	Heavy	Domestic residence	
697	1.5 m	26 m diam.	Moderate Aztec, both Early and Late	Moderate	Domestic residence	Remnants of stone wall bases define a complex of several rooms of indeterminate size
698	Slight	5 m diam.	Moderate Aztec	Moderate	Domestic residence	
699	30 cm	5 m diam.	Light-to-moderate Aztec	Light	Domestic residence	
700	50 cm	8 m diam.	Light-to-moderate Aztec	Moderate	Domestic residence	Remnants of several stone wall bases
701	1 m	10 m diam.	Light Aztec	Heavy	Domestic residence	Remnants of stone wall bases define one room, 4x3 m
703	50 cm	10 m diam.	Light-to-moderate Aztec	Moderate	Domestic residence	
704	75 cm	10 m diam.	Light-to-moderate Aztec	Moderate	Domestic residence	Remnants of several stone wall bases
705	1 m	9 m diam.	Light Aztec	Heavy	Domestic residence	
706	50 cm	5 m diam.	Light-to-moderate Aztec	Moderate	Domestic residence	

Tlatel Number	Height	Surface Area	Surface Pottery	Rock Rubble	Probable Function	Comments
708	1 m	7 m diam.	Light-to-moderate Aztec	Heavy	Domestic residence	
710	None	10 m diam.	Light-to-moderate Aztec	Moderate	Domestic residence	Remnant of one stone wall base
711	1 m	8 m diam.	Light Aztec, both Early and Late	Light	Domestic residence	Remnants of several stone wall bases define a room at least 1.5x2.5 m
712	1 m	13 m diam.	Moderate Aztec	Moderate	Domestic residence	Remnants of several stone wall bases
713	1 m	12 m diam.	Moderate Aztec, both Early and Late	Moderate	Domestic residence	
714	1 m	10 m diam.	Moderate Aztec, both Early and Late	Moderate	Domestic residence	Remnant of one stone wall base
715	50 cm	7 m diam.	Moderate Aztec, both Early and Late	Moderate	Domestic residence	
716	30 cm	7 m diam.	Light-to-moderate Aztec	Moderate	Domestic residence	Remnants of stone wall bases define one room, at least 6x2 m
718	1.5 m	9 m diam.	Light-to-moderate Aztec	Heavy	Domestic residence	Remnants of several stone wall bases
719	1 m	8 m diam.	Light-to-moderate Aztec	Heavy	Domestic residence	
721	1 m	8 m diam.	Light-to-moderate Aztec	Heavy	Domestic residence	
722	2 m	15 m diam.	Very light Aztec	Heavy	Ceremonial-civic	A pyramid with at least 2 major tiers, and several remnants of stone wall bases on top of the mound
723	2 m	14 m diam.	Light Aztec	Heavy	Ceremonial-civic	Located 8 m west and down slope from Tlatel 722. A 2-tiered pyramid—lower platform is 14 m in diameter and 1 m high, upper platform is 6 m in diameter and 2 m high
724	50 cm	7 m diam.	Light Aztec, both Early and Late	Moderate	Domestic residence	Remnants of stone wall bases define at least 4 rooms
725	30 cm	7 m diam.	Light-to-moderate Aztec	Moderate	Domestic residence	

Tlatel Number	Height	Surface Area	Surface Pottery	Rock Rubble	Probable Function	Comments
726	1 m	12 m diam.	Moderate Aztec, both Early and Late	Moderate	Domestic residence	Remnant of one stone wall base, 2 m long
727	70 cm	15 m diam.	Moderate Aztec, both Early and Late	Heavy	Domestic residence	
728	90 cm	8 m diam.	Moderate Aztec, both Early and Late	Heavy	Domestic residence	
729	1 m	7 m diam.	Light Aztec	Moderate	Domestic residence	Remnant of one stone wall base
730	1.5 m	8 m diam.	Light Aztec	Heavy	Domestic residence	
731	1.5 m	12 m diam.	Moderate Aztec	Heavy	Domestic residence	Remnants of several stone wall bases about 30 cm thick
732	1 m	30 m diam.	Moderate Aztec, both Early and Late	Moderate	Domestic residence	Remnants of stone wall bases define a complex of at least 4 rooms of indeterminate size
733	30 cm	8 m diam.	Light-to-moderate Aztec, both Early and Late	Moderate	Domestic residence	Remnants of stone wall bases define a room about 3x2 m
734	1 m	5 m diam.	Light Aztec	Moderate	Domestic residence	
735	1 m	17 m diam.	Moderate Aztec	Moderate	Domestic residence	Much dressed stone debris
736	Slight	10 m diam.	Moderate Aztec, both Early and Late	Light	Domestic residence	
737	1 m	5 m diam.	Light-to-moderate Aztec, both Early and Late	Heavy	Domestic residence	Portions of the tlatel have eroded off of the erosional remnant into the wash 2 m below
738	20 cm	5 m diam.	Light-to-moderate Aztec, both Early and Late	Moderate	Domestic residence	Remnant of one stone wall base, 1 m long and 30 cm wide
739	1 m	5 m diam.	Light-to-moderate Aztec, both Early and Late	Light	Domestic residence	
740	1 m	30 m diam.	Light Aztec	Heavy	?	Several remnants of stone wall bases
742	50 cm	5 m diam.	Light-to-moderate Aztec	Moderate	Domestic residence	Remnant of one stone wall base
743	30 cm	10 m diam.	Light Aztec	Light	Domestic residence	

Tlatel Number	Height	Surface Area	Surface Pottery	Rock Rubble	Probable Function	Comments
744	30 cm	5 m diam.	Light Aztec	Light	Domestic residence	Remnant of one stone wall base
745	None	7 m diam.	Light-to-moderate Aztec, both Early and Late	Light	Domestic residence	Remnant of one stone wall base, 1 m long
747	Slight	10 m diam.	Light-to-moderate Aztec, both Early and Late	Moderate	Domestic residence	
748	50 cm	7 m diam.	Light-to-moderate Aztec	Moderate	Domestic residence	
749	None	10 m diam.	Light-to-moderate Aztec	Heavy	Domestic residence	
750	Slight	5 m diam.	Light Aztec	Moderate	Domestic residence	
751	None	5 m diam.	Light Aztec, both Early and Late	Light	Domestic residence	Remnant of stone wall base, 2 m long
752	1.5 m	15 m diam.	Light Aztec	Heavy	Ceremonial-civic ?	Remnants of several stone wall bases. Topped by a post-Conquest stone structure
753	4 m on down-slope 2 m on up-slope side	8 m diam.	Moderate Aztec	Moderate	Domestic residence	
754	50 cm	10 m diam.	Moderate Aztec	Light	Domestic residence	Remnant of one stone wall base, 1.5 m long
755	1 m	5 m diam.	Light Aztec	Heavy	Domestic residence	
756	1 m	8 m diam.	Moderate Aztec, both Early and Late	Moderate	Domestic residence	Remnants of 2 stone wall bases, 2 m long
757	30 cm	5 m diam.	Moderate Aztec, both Early and Late	Moderate	Domestic residence	
758	1 m	5 m diam.	Light-to-moderate Aztec, both Early and Late	Moderate	Domestic residence	
760	50 cm	9 m diam.	Moderate Aztec, both Early and Late	Moderate	Domestic residence	
761	40 cm	8 m diam.	Light-to-moderate Aztec	Moderate	Domestic residence	

Tlatel Number	Height	Surface Area	Surface Pottery	Rock Rubble	Probable Function	Comments
762	None	5 m diam.	Light-to-moderate Aztec	Moderate	Domestic residence	Remnants of stone wall bases, define one room, 4x3 m
763	1 m	5 m diam.	Light Aztec	Heavy	Domestic residence	
764	75 cm	5 m diam.	Light Aztec	Heavy	Domestic residence	
765	30 cm	9 m diam.	Moderate Aztec	Heavy	Domestic residence	
766	1 m	5 m diam.	Light-to-moderate Aztec	Heavy	Domestic residence	
767	1 m	5 m diam.	Light Aztec	Heavy	Domestic residence	
768	35 cm	5 m diam.	Light Aztec	Heavy	Domestic residence	
769	35 cm	8 m diam.	Light-to-moderate Aztec	Moderate	Domestic residence	Remnants of stone wall bases define one room, 4x6 m
770	50 cm	5 m diam.	Light Aztec, both Early and Late	Moderate	Domestic residence	
780	1 m	5 m diam.	Light Aztec	Heavy	Domestic residence	In area with much ancient terracing
781	1 m	5 m diam.	Moderate Aztec, both Early and Late	Heavy	Domestic residence	
782	30 cm	5 m diam.	Moderate Aztec	Moderate	Domestic residence	
783	1 m	8 m diam.	Moderate Aztec	Heavy	Domestic residence	
784	20 cm	6 m diam.	Light-to-moderate Aztec	Moderate	Domestic residence	
786	30 cm	5 m diam.	Light Aztec	Moderate	Domestic residence	Remnants of one stone wall base, 2 m long
787	30 cm	20 m diam.	Moderate Aztec	Moderate	Domestic residence	
789	None	5 m diam.	Moderate Aztec, both Early and Late	Light	Domestic residence	Remnants of one stone wall base, 2 m long and 35 cm wide
790	None	5 m diam.	Moderate Aztec	Moderate	Domestic residence	

Number Tlatel	Height	Surface Area	Surface Pottery	Rock Rubble	Probable Function	Comments
791	None	5 m diam.	Moderate Aztec, both Early and Late, trace of Late Toltec	Light	Domestic residence	Remnants of one stone wall base 1.5 m long
792	50 cm	5 m diam.	Light-to-moderate Aztec	Heavy	Domestic residence	
793	50 cm	5 m diam.	Light-to-moderate Aztec	Heavy	Domestic residence	
794	50 cm	5 m diam.	Light Aztec	Heavy	Domestic residence	
796	None	10 m diam.	Moderate Aztec, both Early and Late	Moderate	Domestic residence	Remnants of one stone wall base, 2.5 m long
			SITE: TX-A-31			
628	50 cm	5 m diam.	Light Aztec	Moderate	Domestic residence	
629	1 m	5 m diam.	Light-to-moderate Aztec	Moderate	Domestic residence	
630*a*	1 m	5 m diam.	Light Aztec	Moderate	Domestic residence	Remnants of stone wall bases define 1 room 4.5x4 m or more. Walls are 30 cm thick and 70 cm high
630*b*	30 cm	5 m diam.	Light Aztec	Moderate	Domestic residence	Located 8 m east of Tlatel 630; remnants of stone wall bases define a complex of 2 rooms, one 3x4.5 m, the other 2x4.5 m, walls are 30-45 cm wide and 10-25 cm high
631	None	8 m diam.	Light Aztec	Light	Domestic residence	Remnants of stone wall bases define a complex of at least 3 rooms of indeterminate size
632	1 m	8 m diam.	Light-to-moderate Aztec	Heavy	Domestic residence	
633	75 cm	6 m diam.	Moderate Aztec, both Early and Late	Heavy	Domestic residence	Remnant of one stone wall base, 2.5 m long
634	1 m	15 m diam.	Light Aztec, both Early and Late	Heavy	Domestic residence	

Tlatel Number	Height	Surface Area	Surface Pottery	Rock Rubble	Probable Function	Comments
635	2 m	15x25 m	Light-to-moderate Aztec, both Early and Late, trace of Late Toltec	Heavy	Domestic residence	Remnants of stone wall bases enclose an area 10x20 m, with several vague interior divisions
636	1.5 m	12 m diam.	Light Aztec	Heavy	Domestic residence	Remnants of stone wall bases define a complex of at least 5 rooms of indeterminate size
637	1 m	11 m diam.	Light-to-moderate Aztec	Moderate	Domestic residence	Several worked tepetate blocks
638	2 m	10 m diam.	Very light Aztec	Heavy	Ceremonial-civic	Extensive pitting has revealed a solid rock-rubble interior, and numerous plaster fragments
639	75 cm	15 m diam.	Light-to-moderate Aztec	Heavy	Domestic residence	
640	90 cm	12 m diam.	Light Aztec	Heavy	Domestic residence	
641	1 m	10 m diam.	Moderate Aztec	Heavy	Domestic residence	
642	35 cm	5 m diam.	Moderate Aztec, both Early and Late	Heavy	Domestic residence	
643	1 m	6 m diam.	Moderate Aztec, both Early and Late	Moderate-to-heavy	Domestic residence	Remnants of 2 stone wall bases
644	1.5 m	5 m diam.	Light Aztec	Heavy	Domestic residence	
645	1 m	5 m diam.	Light Aztec	Heavy	Domestic residence	
646	75 cm	10 m diam.	Moderate Aztec	Moderate	Domestic residence	
647	75 cm	8 m diam.	Moderate Aztec, both Early and Late	Heavy	Domestic residence	
648	35 cm	5 m diam.	Moderate Aztec	Moderate	Domestic residence	Remnant of one stone wall base
649	1 m	10 m diam.	Light Aztec	Moderate	Domestic residence	
650	70 cm	5 m diam.	Light Aztec	Moderate	Domestic residence	Remnant of one stone wall base
651	50 cm	5 m diam.	Light Aztec	Moderate	Domestic residence	Remnants of stone wall bases define one room, 4x4 m

Tlatel Number	Height	Surface Area	Surface Pottery	Rock Rubble	Probable Function	Comments
652	75 cm	15 m diam.	Moderate Aztec	Heavy	Domestic residence	
653	1.5 m	7 m diam.	Light Aztec	Heavy	Domestic residence	
654	50 cm	10 m diam.	Very light Aztec	Moderate	Domestic residence?	Remnants of stone wall bases define a complex of at least 4 rooms (Fig. 22,*a*)
655	40 cm	10 m diam.	Very light Aztec	Moderate	Domestic residence ?	Remnants of 2 stone wall bases
656	1.5 m	8 m diam.	Light Aztec, trace Late Toltec	Heavy	Domestic residence	Remnants of 2 stone wall bases
657	30 cm	5 m diam.	Light-to-moderate Aztec	Moderate	Domestic residence	
658	50 cm	5 m diam.	Light Aztec, both Early and Late	Moderate	Domestic residence	
659	50 cm	5 m diam.	Light Aztec, both Early and Late	Moderate	Domestic residence	
660	40 cm	10 m diam.	Light-to-moderate Aztec	Heavy	Domestic residence	
661	50 cm	15 m diam.	Moderate Aztec	Moderate	Domestic residence	
662	30 cm	10 m diam.	Light Aztec	Moderate	Domestic residence	
663	30 cm	10 m diam.	Light Aztec	Moderate	Domestic residence	
664	30 cm	10 m diam.	Light Aztec, both Early and Late	Moderate	Domestic residence	
665	2 m	14 m diam.	Moderate Aztec, both Early and Late	Heavy	Domestic residence	Remnant of one stone wall base, 2 m long
666	20 cm	7 m diam.	Light-to-moderate Aztec, both Early and Late	Moderate	Domestic residence	
667	20 cm	9 m diam.	Light-to-moderate Aztec	Moderate-to-heavy	Domestic residence	
668	50 cm	5 m diam.	Light-to-moderate Aztec	Heavy	Domestic residence	

Tlatel Number	Height	Surface Area	Surface Pottery	Rock Rubble	Probable Function	Comments
669	1 m	5 m diam.	Moderate Aztec	Heavy	Domestic residence	
670	Slight	14 m diam.	Moderate Aztec, both Early and Late	Moderate	Domestic residence	Remnants of stone wall bases define one room, 1.5 m wide by at least 3 m long
671	Slight	15 m diam.	Light Aztec	Moderate	Domestic residence	
673	Slight	15 m diam.	Moderate Aztec, both Early and Late	Moderate	Domestic residence	Obsidian is much heavier here than elsewhere on the site
674	1.3 m	7 m diam.	Light-to-moderate Aztec	Heavy	Domestic residence	
675	2 m	15 m diam.	Moderate Aztec	Heavy	Domestic residence	Remnants of stone wall bases define a complex of at least 6 rooms (Fig. 22,*b*)
676	30 cm	5 m diam.	Moderate Aztec, trace of Late Toltec	Moderate	Domestic residence	
677	40 cm	5 m diam.	Light Aztec, both Early and Late	Moderate	Domestic residence	
679	1 m	8x9 m	Very light Aztec	Heavy	Domestic residence ?	
680	1.5 m	13 m diam.	Light-to-moderate Aztec	Moderate	Domestic residence	Remnants of stone wall bases
SITE: TX-A-32						
531	50 cm	35 m diam.	Moderate Aztec, both Early and Late, trace of Late Toltec	Heavy	Domestic residence	
532	1 m on down-slope side, 40 cm on up-slope side	18 m diam.	Moderate Aztec	Heavy	Domestic residence	
533	1 m	5 m diam.	Light Aztec	Heavy	Domestic residence	
534	1 m	25 m diam.	Light-to-moderate Aztec	Heavy	Domestic residence	

Tlatel Number	Height	Surface Area	Surface Pottery	Rock Rubble	Probable Function	Comments
535	1 m	10 m diam.	Light Aztec	Heavy	Ceremonial-civic ?	Pitting suggests this is a solid rock-rubble platform
536	30 cm	5 m diam.	Light Aztec	Heavy	Domestic residence	
537	50 cm	8 m diam.	Light Aztec, trace of Late Toltec	Heavy	Domestic residence	Remnants of stone wall bases define at least 2 rooms of indeterminate size
538	1 m	7 m diam.	Light Aztec	Heavy	Domestic residence	Remnants of several stone wall bases
SITE: TX-A-34						
771	1 m	25 m diam.	Moderate Aztec, both Early and Late	Moderate	Domestic residence	
772	1 m	20 m diam.	Moderate Aztec, both Early and Late	Moderate	Domestic residence	
773	50 cm	6 m diam.	Light-to-moderate Aztec, both Early and Late	Moderate	Domestic residence	Remnants of 2 stone wall bases
774	1 m	5 m diam.	Moderate Aztec, both Early and Late	Moderate	Domestic residence	
775	50 cm	5 m diam.	Moderate Aztec	Moderate	Domestic residence	
776	1 m	6x6 m	Light Aztec	Heavy	Domestic residence	Remnants of 2 stone wall bases define a room about 5 m square
777	1 m	5 m diam.	Moderate Aztec	Moderate	Domestic residence	
778	1 m	15 m diam.	Moderate Aztec	Heavy	Domestic residence	Remnants of several stone wall bases define 2 rooms, one about 4x3 m, and the other about 3x3 m
779	2 m	24 m diam.	Moderate Aztec, both Early and Late	Heavy	Domestic residence	

SITE: TX-A-38

Tlatel Number	Height	Surface Area	Surface Pottery	Rock Rubble	Probable Function	Comments
383	30 cm	10 m diam.	Moderate Aztec, trace of Late Toltec	Moderate	Domestic residence	
384	30 cm	18 m diam.	Light Aztec	Moderate	Domestic residence	
389	50 cm	7 m diam.	Moderate Aztec, trace of Late Toltec	Moderate	Domestic residence	Remnants of several stone wall bases
491	1 m	20 m diam.	Moderate Aztec, trace of Late Toltec	Moderate	Domestic residence	
492	1 m	15 m diam.	Moderate Aztec	Moderate	Domestic residence	
493	50 cm	10 m diam.	Moderate Aztec, both Early and Late	Moderate	Domestic residence	
494	50 cm	15 m diam.	Moderate Aztec	Moderate	Domestic residence	
495	20 cm	8 m diam.	Moderate Aztec	Moderate	Domestic residence	
510	1 m	11 m diam.	Moderate Aztec	Moderate	Domestic residence	Remnants of stone wall bases define a complex of at least 6 rooms (Fig. 23,*a*). Masonry of undressed river cobbles and tepetate blocks
511	70 cm	9 m diam.	Light Aztec, both Early and Late, moderate Late Formative, light Terminal Formative	Moderate	?	Remnants of stone wall bases define a complex of 6 rooms (Fig. 23,*b*).
512	1.5 m	6 m diam.	Light Aztec, both Early and Late, moderate Terminal Formative	Moderate	Domestic residence	Remnants of stone wall bases define a complex of at least 7 rooms (Fig. 23,*c*), river cobble masonry
513	Slight	8 m diam.	Light-to-moderate Aztec	Moderate	Domestic residence	Remnants of stone wall bases
514	2 m	7 m diam.	Light-to-moderate Aztec, both Early and Late, light-to-moderate Terminal Formative	Heavy	Ceremonial-civic	Pitting has revealed a solid rock-rubble interior

Tlatel Number	Height	Surface Area	Surface Pottery	Rock Rubble	Probable Function	Comments
515	1.5 m	25x25 m	Moderate Aztec, both Early and Late, light Late Formative, light Terminal Formative	Moderate	?	The mound slopes gradually up to a platform 15 m in diameter. Remnants of stone wall bases define a complex of 10 or more rooms (Fig. 23,*d*). Walls are 30-50 cm wide and made of river cobbles. Possible steps on the southern side facing the river. Mound built in 2 tiers, each about 1 m high
516	1.5 m	15 m diam.	Moderate Aztec, both Early and Late	Moderate	Domestic residence	Remnants of stone wall bases define a complex of at least 10 rooms (Fig. 23,*e*)
518	70 cm	12 m diam.	Moderate Aztec, both Early and Late	Heavy	Domestic residence	Remnants of stone wall bases define a complex of 2 rooms, each 3x5 m
519	30 cm	8 m diam.	Light Aztec	Moderate	Domestic residence	Remnants of stone wall bases define 1 room 3x5 m, and possibly other rooms
520	30 cm	20 m diam.	Moderate Aztec	Moderate	Domestic residence	Remnants of stone wall bases define 1 room, 1.5x3 m, and possibly others
521	1 m	13 m diam.	Light-to-moderate Aztec	Heavy	Domestic residence	
522	70 cm	5 m diam.	Moderate Aztec	Heavy	Domestic residence	
523	80 cm	12 m diam.	Light Aztec	Heavy	Domestic residence	Remnants of several stone wall bases
524	1 m	11 m diam.	Light-to-moderate Aztec	Moderate	Domestic residence	Remnants of 2 stone wall bases
525	50 cm	8 m diam.	Light-to-moderate Aztec	Moderate	Domestic residence	
526	50 cm	6 m diam.	Light Aztec	Heavy	Domestic residence	
527	50 cm	6 m diam.	Moderate Aztec, both Early and Late	Moderate	Domestic residence	
528	30 cm	5 m diam.	Moderate Aztec	Light	Domestic residence	

Tlatel Number	Height	Surface Area	Surface Pottery	Rock Rubble	Probable Function	Comments
529	70 cm	8 m diam.	Moderate Aztec	Moderate	Domestic residence	
530	1 m	7 m diam.	Moderate Aztec, both Early and Late, trace of Late Toltec	Moderate	Domestic residence	
			SITE: TX-A-39			
480	20 cm	15 m diam.	Moderate Aztec	Moderate	Domestic residence	
481	50 cm	10 m diam.	Moderate Aztec	Moderate	Domestic residence	Remnants of 1 stone wall base
482	20 cm	10 m diam.	Moderate Aztec, both Early and Late	Light	Domestic residence	
484	50 cm	10 m diam.	Moderate Aztec, very light Early Toltec	Light	Domestic residence	
485	60 cm	6 m diam.	Moderate Aztec, trace of Early Toltec	Moderate	Domestic residence	Remnant of 1 stone wall base
486	50 cm	11 m diam.	Moderate Aztec, both Early and Late	Moderate	Domestic residence	Remnants of stone wall bases define a complex of at least 10 rooms (Fig. 22,*c*). The walls are 30 cm wide, and built of dressed stone with a tepetate core
488	50 cm	13 m diam.	Moderate Aztec	Moderate	Domestic residence	Remnants of stone wall bases define a complex of at least 5 rooms. One room is 2x5 m; size of the others is indeterminate
489	30 cm	8 m diam.	Moderate Aztec	Moderate	Domestic residence	
499	50 cm	10 m diam.	Moderate Aztec, both Early and Late, light-to-moderate Early Toltec	Moderate	Domestic residence	
500	30 cm	20 m diam.	Moderate Aztec, very light Early Toltec	Moderate	Domestic residence	
501	25 cm	15 m diam.	Moderate Aztec, both Early and Late	Moderate	Domestic residence	Remnants of several stone wall bases

Tlatel Number	Height	Surface Area	Surface Pottery	Rock Rubble	Probable Function	Comments
502	30 cm	5 m diam.	Moderate Aztec, very light Early Toltec	Heavy	Domestic residence	
503	25 cm	3 m diam.	Moderate Aztec, very light Early Toltec	Heavy	Domestic residence	Remnant of 1 stone wall base
504	40 cm	12 m diam.	Moderate Aztec, light-to-moderate Early Toltec	Heavy	Domestic residence	
505	20 cm	4 m diam.	Moderate Aztec	Moderate	Domestic residence	
SITE: TX-A-40						
101	1.5 m	19 m diam.	Light Aztec	Light	Domestic residence	
103	10 m	60 m diam.	Light Aztec on the tlatel, moderate Aztec around tlatel both Early and Late, light Early Toltec and Late Toltec	Heavy	Ceremonial-civic	The walls, where exposed, are of adobe, mud, and tepetate; pyramid is locally known as El Gavilan
104	1 m	8 m diam.	Light Aztec	Moderate	Domestic residence	
106	1.3 m	10 m diam.	Light-to-moderate Aztec, light Early Toltec	Light	Domestic residence	
110	5 m	15 m diam.	Light Aztec on the tlatel, moderate just north of the tlatel, light Early Toltec	Light	Ceremonial-civic ?	
114	None	15 m diam.	Light Aztec	Heavy	Domestic residence ?	Extensive pitting has exposed 2 levels of plastered floors, a plastered basin, stairs, and walls; cuts in the walls and stairs expose the inner fill which consists of an adobe surrounded by small stones packed in mud
115	1 m	15 m diam.	Light Aztec, light Early and Late Toltec	Moderate-to-heavy	Domestic residence	
117	1 m	20 m diam.	Light-to-moderate Aztec, both Early and Late	Moderate	Domestic residence	

Tlatel Number	Height	Surface Area	Surface Pottery	Rock Rubble	Probable Function	Comments
367	1 m	12x5 m	Light Aztec	Heavy	Domestic residence	
368	1.5 m	20 m diam.	Light-to-moderate Aztec and Early Toltec	Heavy	Domestic residence	
369	7 m	40 m diam.	Very light	Heavy	Ceremonial-civic	Badly potted in several places exposing a fill of rock and mud, loosely consolidated. One step is discernable on the north side of the mound 3 m from the top and 7 m wide joining Tlatel 369 to Tlatel 371. Four steps on the west side all about 1.5 m high and 1.5 m wide (Pl. 37,*a*)
370	2 m	20x10 m	Very light	Heavy	Ceremonial-civic	Located 18 m east of Tlatel 369
371	2 m	10 m diam.	Very light	Heavy	Ceremonial-civic	Several remnants of stone wall bases
372	3 m	15x10 m	Very light	Heavy	Ceremonial-civic	Two steps, one 1 m high and 3 m wide; the other 2 m high and 3 m wide
373	4 m	20 m diam.	Very light	Heavy	Ceremonial-civic	Located 60 m S-SW of Tlatel 372
374	50 cm	20x10 m	Light Aztec	Heavy	Domestic residence ?	A trench has been cut through the tlatel exposing stucco walls painted red, blue, and white. One wall 25 cm thick is painted on both sides. This mound is located about 150 m away from the ceremonial complex
378	8 m	55x75 m	Light-to-moderate Aztec, mostly Late with a little Early, light Early Toltec	Heavy	Ceremonial-civic	Holes dug on the tlatel for planting maguey have exposed at least 2 layers of plaster floors. Remnants of stone wall bases form a corner in the northern part of the mound.
379	1 m	25x10 m	Light-to-moderate Aztec	Heavy	Domestic residence	Located on the bank of the Rio Papalotla, several possible stone wall bases

SITE: TX-A-49

Tlatel Number	Height	Surface Area	Surface Pottery	Rock Rubble	Probable Function	Comments
1	2.5 m	80x80 m	Light-to-moderate Aztec, about 1/3 Texcoco Fabric Marked, unusually high proportion of Chalco Cholula Polychrome	Light	Ceremonial-civic	Constructed in 2 broad platforms, the basal one standing 1.5 m high; the upper structure measures about 30 m on a side and 1 m high
2	1 m	20x40 m	Light-to-moderate Aztec, very little Texcoco Fabric Marked noted	Light	Domestic residence ?	
3	1.5 m	35 m diam.	Moderate Aztec, substantial Texcoco Fabric Marked ware	Light	Domestic residence ?	Considerably destroyed by plowing
4	1.8 m	80 m diam.	Moderate Aztec, high proportion of Texcoco Fabric Marked ware	Light	Domestic residence ?	Considerably destroyed by plowing

SITE: TX-A-56

Tlatel Number	Height	Surface Area	Surface Pottery	Rock Rubble	Probable Function	Comments
17	3.5 m	25x40 m	Light-to-moderate Aztec, light Late Toltec	Light	Ceremonial-civic	Several levels of stucco flooring or surfacing can be seen. Erosion on all sides, plus a deep looter's pit, show that the basic construction is of solid rock rubble and adobe brick (Pl. 38,*a*)
18	7 m	50x50 m	Moderate Aztec	Light	Ceremonial-civic	Structure consists of a stuccoed basal platform about 2 m high, and a plastered upper pyramidal mound 30x25 m in area and 5 m tall, at the eastern side of the supporting construction. Basic construction is of solid adobe brick throughout, with some outer stone-faced walls (Pl. 38,*b*)
57	20 cm	25 m diam.	Light-to-moderate Aztec	Light	Domestic residence	
58	1 m	25 m diam.	Light-to-moderate Aztec	Light	Domestic residence	

Tlatel Number	Height	Surface Area	Surface Pottery	Rock Rubble	Probable Function	Comments
59	25 cm	25 m diam.	Moderate Aztec, with Early somewhat predominate	Light	Domestic residence	
65	3 m	50x30 m	Light Aztec, light Early Toltec	Light	Ceremonial-civic	Solid adobe brick construction, with at least 3 levels of plastered floors
89	5 m	50x35 m	Moderate Aztec	Moderate	Ceremonial-civic	These 3 conjoined mounds form the Los Melones complex in the heart of modern Texcoco. Basic construction is adobe brick and rock rubble, with exterior walls of stuccoed finished stone. Several layers of stuccoed horizontal surfaces can be seen in the mounds' eroded wall profiles. Lower area eroded wall profiles. Lower area between and around these principal mounds apparently contains room complexes (Pl. 39,*a*)
90	5 m	50x35 m	Moderate Aztec	Moderate	Ceremonial-civic	
91	2 m	25x25 m	Light Aztec	Moderate	Ceremonial-civic	
92	4-6 m	150x80 m	Moderate Aztec	Moderate	Ceremonial-civic	
						Badly pitted, basic construction is solid adobe brick. Much of upper surface was originally stuccoed. Eastern third forms a high, broad platform, about 2 m above the level of the western section (Pl. 39,*b*)
93	2 m	50 m diam.	Moderate Aztec	Moderate	Ceremonial-civic	Much of upper surface originally stuccoed
SITE: TX-A-59						
6	50 cm	25x10 m	Moderate Aztec, both Early and Late, trace of Terminal Formative	Moderate	Domestic residence	Some preserved stone wall bases
8	20 cm	8 m diam.	Moderate Aztec	Moderate	Domestic residence	Several stone wall bases are preserved; these are resting on tepetate surface

Tlatel Number	Height	Surface Area	Surface Pottery	Rock Rubble	Probable Function	Comments
9	50 cm	20x20 m	Moderate Aztec	Moderate	Domestic residence	Remnant of stone wall base along east edge
10	20 cm	8 m diam.	Moderate Aztec	Moderate	Domestic residence	Remnants of stone wall bases define a single room 5 m on a side
11	20 cm	8 m diam.	Light Aztec	Moderate	Domestic residence	Remnants of stone wall bases define a single room 5 m on a side, with an internal partition wall dividing it into halves
12	10 cm	8x13 m	Moderate Aztec	Moderate	Domestic residence	Remnants of stone wall bases define an L-shaped structure, 8x13 m, with no trace of internal partitions
14	20 cm	8x8 m	Light-to-moderate Aztec	Heavy	Domestic residence	Remnants of stone wall bases define a single L-shaped room, 8x8 m, with no trace of interior partitions
16	10 cm	20x14 m	Light-to-moderate Aztec	Moderate	Domestic residence	Remnants of stone wall bases define a single rectangular room, 20x14 m with no traces of interior partitions
17	50 cm	9x10 m	Moderate Aztec	Moderate	Domestic residence	Remnants of stone wall bases define a single L-shaped room, 9x10 m, with no traces of interior partitions
19	50 cm	10x13 m	Moderate Aztec	Moderate	Domestic residence	Remnants of stone wall bases define a large room 10x10 m, no traces of interior partitions. Vague suggestion of 3 steps or terraces on one side
23	30 cm	10x10 m	Light Aztec	Moderate	Domestic residence	A few remnants of stone wall bases
24	50 cm	10x8 m	Light Aztec	Heavy	Domestic residence	A few remnants of stone wall bases
25	10 cm	8 m diam.	Light-to-moderate Aztec	Heavy	Domestic residence	Remnants of stone wall bases define a single room, 5x6 m, with no traces of interior partitions

Tlatel Number	Height	Surface Area	Surface Pottery	Rock Rubble	Probable Function	Comments
26	30 cm	10x6 m	Moderate Aztec	Heavy	Domestic residence	Remnants of stone wall bases define a single large room, 10 m long, with no traces of internal partitions
27	10 cm	8 m diam.	Light-to-moderate Aztec	Heavy	Domestic residence	Remnants of stone wall bases define a single room, 5x5 m, with no traces of internal partitions
SITE: TX-A-60						
42	30 cm	25x10 m	Moderate Aztec	Moderate	Domestic residence	Several remnants of stone wall bases. At least one room, 4x6 m, is defined
43	50 cm	10x5 m	Light-to-moderate Aztec	Moderate	Domestic residence	Remnants of stone wall bases define at least 2 rooms of uncertain dimensions
44	23 cm	12 m diam.	Light-to-moderate Aztec	Moderate	Domestic residence	Remnants of stone wall bases define at least 2 rooms of uncertain dimensions
45	30 cm	25x10 m	Moderate Aztec	Moderate	Domestic residence	Small remnant of stone wall base
46	50 cm	10 m diam.	Light Aztec	Moderate	Domestic residence	Several remnants of stone wall bases
SITE: TX-A-64						
75	15 cm	20 m diam.	Light-to-moderate Late Aztec	Heavy	Domestic residence	Badly destroyed by plowing, but outlines are fairly distinct
76	15 cm	20 m diam.	Light-to-moderate Late Aztec	Heavy	Domestic residence	Badly destroyed, but outlines are fairly distinct
77	10 cm	20 m diam.	Moderate Aztec, both Early and Late	Heavy	Domestic residence	Badly destroyed by plowing, but outlines are fairly distinct
80	1 m	20 m diam.	Light-to-moderate Aztec (mostly Late, with light Early); light Classic	Moderate	Ceremonial-civic ?	These 4 mounds are apparently joined together, probably built up on a single large basal platform. Mounds 80 and 81 define the east side of a level area which may be a plaza. Mounds 81, 82, and 83 delineate the

Tlatel Number	Height	Surface Area	Surface Pottery	Rock Rubble	Probable Function	Comments
						north side of the same level area which measures about 100 m long and 30 m wide
81	1 m	20 m diam.	Light-to-moderate Aztec (mostly Late, with light Early); light Classic	Moderate	Ceremonial-civic ?	
82	1 m	20 m diam.	Light-to-moderate Aztec (mostly Late, with light Early); light Classic	Moderate	Ceremonial-civic ?	
83	1 m	20 m diam.	Light-to-moderate Aztec	Moderate	Ceremonial-civic ?	

SITE: TX-A-69

Tlatel Number	Height	Surface Area	Surface Pottery	Rock Rubble	Probable Function	Comments
245	10 cm	15 m diam.	Light-to-moderate Aztec, very light decorated ware	Heavy	Domestic residence	Several distinct wall bases
246	75 cm	8 m diam.	Light Aztec, very little decorated ware	Moderate	?	Appears to be a solid platform mound
248	20 cm	15 m diam.	Light-to-moderate Aztec, very little decorated ware	Moderate	Domestic residence	Remnants of several stone wall bases define a complex of at least 5 rooms
249	15 cm	15 m diam.	Light-to-moderate Aztec, very little decorated ware	Heavy	Domestic residence	Remnants of stone wall bases define a complex of at least 4 rooms (Fig. 22,*e*)
251	35 cm	10 m diam.	Light-to-moderate Aztec	Heavy	Domestic residence	Has been cut by modern maguey terraces
252	1 m	10x15 m	Light-to-moderate Aztec, very little decorated ware	Moderate	Domestic residence	Several remnants of stone wall bases
253	1 m	15x15 m	Light-to-moderate Aztec	Moderate	Domestic residence	
254	1.5 m	10 m diam.	Light-to-moderate Aztec	Moderate	?	Remnants of stone wall bases define a single room, 5x5 m, atop a solid rock rubble platform
257	35 cm	15 m diam.	Moderate Aztec	Heavy	Domestic residence	Several stone wall bases define a complex of rooms (Fig. 22,*d*)

Tlatel Number	Height	Surface Area	Surface Pottery	Rock Rubble	Probable Function	Comments
259	35 cm	10 m diam.	Light-to-moderate Aztec	Moderate	Domestic residence	Remnants of several stone wall bases
260	50 cm	15 m diam.	Light-to-moderate Aztec	Moderate	Domestic residence	Remnants of several stone wall bases
262	10 cm	10 m diam.	Light-to-moderate Aztec	Moderate	Domestic residence	Remnants of several stone wall bases
263	25 cm	10 m diam.	Light-to-moderate Aztec	Moderate	Domestic residence	Remnants of stone wall bases define at least 1 room, 5x5 m
SITE: TX-A-70						
233	5 m	35x20 m	Light Aztec, light Modern	Moderate	Ceremonial-civic	Situated at north end of Causeway, a modern tlatel is located just north of this mound. Tlatel 233 could be partly modern
235	25 cm	10 m diam.	Moderate Aztec	Heavy	Domestic residence	Badly eroded
236	25 cm	10 m diam.	Moderate Aztec	Heavy	Domestic residence	Badly eroded; there are traces of a stone terrace face on the downslope side of the mound
SITE: TX-A-72						
183	25 cm	12 m diam.	Light-to-moderate Aztec	Heavy	Domestic residence	Remnants of stone wall bases define a complex of at least 6 rooms (Fig. 25,*a*)
188	25 cm	8 m diam.	Moderate Aztec, both Early and Late	Heavy	Domestic residence	Remnants of several stone wall bases
189	25 cm	8 m diam.	Moderate Aztec, both Early and Late	Heavy	Domestic residence	Remnant of stone wall base
190	50 cm	12 m diam.	Moderate Aztec	Light-to-moderate	Domestic residence	Remnants of several stone wall bases
191	50 cm	10 m diam.	Light-to-moderate Aztec	Moderate	Domestic residence	Remnants of several stone wall bases
193	15 cm	10 m diam.	Light-to-moderate Aztec	Moderate	Domestic residence	Remnants of several stone wall bases

Tlatel Number	Height	Surface Area	Surface Pottery	Rock Rubble	Probable Function	Comments
194	35 cm	15 m diam.	Light-to-moderate Aztec	Heavy	Domestic residence	Remnants of stone wall bases define a complex of at least 4 rooms (Fig. 25,*b*)
196	25 cm	15 m diam.	Light-to-moderate Aztec	Moderate	Domestic residence	Remnants of several stone wall bases
197	15 cm	10 m diam.	Light-to-moderate Aztec	Light	Domestic residence	Small remnant of stone wall base
198	50 cm	10x15 m	Moderate Aztec	Heavy	Domestic residence	
201	15 cm	10 m diam.	Moderate Aztec	Heavy	Domestic residence	
205	15 cm	10 m diam.	Moderate Aztec	Moderate	Domestic residence	A few remnants of stone wall bases
206	50 cm	15 m diam.	Light-to-moderate Aztec; mostly Late, but a little Early	Heavy	Domestic residence	
207	1 m	15 m diam.	Moderate Aztec, both Early and Late	Heavy	Domestic residence	
209	25 cm	15 m diam.	Moderate Aztec	Heavy	Domestic residence	Remnants of stone wall bases define a complex of 6-8 rooms (Fig. 25,*e*); (Pl. 40,*b*)
214	1 m	20 m diam.	Moderate Aztec	Heavy	Domestic residence	Remnants of several stone wall bases
215	75 cm	15 m diam.	Moderate Aztec	Heavy	Domestic residence	
218	25 cm	15 m diam.	Moderate Aztec, both Early and Late	Heavy	Domestic residence	
220	50 cm	15 m diam.	Moderate Aztec	Heavy	Domestic residence	Small remnants of stone wall bases
222	50 cm	12 m diam.	Moderate Aztec	Heavy	Domestic residence	
224	25 cm	10 m diam.	Light-to-moderate Aztec	Moderate	Domestic residence	
226	1 m	15 m diam.	Moderate Aztec, both Early and Late	Heavy	Domestic residence	Several remnants of stone wall bases

Tlatel Number	Height	Surface Area	Surface Pottery	Rock Rubble	Probable Function	Comments
227	20 cm	8 m diam.	Moderate Aztec, both Early and Late	Moderate	Domestic residence	Several remnants of stone wall bases
228	20 cm	8 m diam.	Moderate Aztec, both Early and Late	Heavy	Domestic residence	Several remnants of stone wall bases
229	30 cm	10 m diam.	Moderate Aztec, both Early and Late	Light	Domestic residence	Several remnants of stone wall bases
230	20 cm	8 m diam.	Light-to-moderate Aztec	Moderate	Domestic residence	
231	50 cm	8 m diam.	Light-to-moderate Aztec	Light-to-moderate	Domestic residence	Small remnant of stone wall base
232	1 m	10x15 m	Moderate Aztec	Light	Domestic residence	
240	20 cm	10 m .diam.	Light-to-moderate Aztec	Moderate	Domestic residence	Small remnant of stone wall base
241	15 cm	10 m .diam.	Light-to-moderate Aztec	Heavy	Domestic residence	
242	15 cm	15 m diam.	Light-to-moderate Aztec	Heavy	Domestic residence	Several remnants of stone wall bases (Fig. 25,*c*)
243	35 cm	15 m diam.	Moderate Aztec	Moderate	Domestic residence	Relatively high proportion of decorated ware
266	15 cm	10 m .diam.	Light-to-moderate Aztec	Moderate	Domestic residence	Small remnant of stone wall base
268	50 cm	8 m diam.	Light-to-moderate Aztec	Heavy	Domestic residence	Small remnant of stone wall base
270	35 cm	10x15 m	Moderate Aztec	Moderate	Domestic residence	Remnants of stone wall bases define a complex of at least 5 rooms (Fig. 25,*d*)
272	15 cm	15 m diam.	Moderate Aztec	Moderate	Domestic residence	Several remnants of stone wall bases
273	15 cm	10 m diam.	Moderate Aztec	Heavy	Domestic residence	
274	15 cm	10x15 m	Light-to-moderate Aztec, mostly Late, but a little Early	Heavy	Domestic residence	Remnants of stone wall bases define a complex of at least 3 or 4 rooms (Fig. 25,*f*)

Tlatel Number	Height	Surface Area	Surface Pottery	Rock Rubble	Probable Function	Comments
277	50 cm	10x15 m	Light-to-moderate Aztec	Moderate	Domestic residence	Several remnants of stone wall bases
283	50 cm	10x15 m	Moderate Aztec	Moderate	Domestic residence	Remnants of stone wall bases define a complex of at least 2 rooms (Fig. 25,*g*)
286	50 cm	10 m diam.	Moderate Aztec	Heavy	Domestic residence	Several remnants of stone wall bases
287	10 cm	10 m diam.	Moderate Aztec	Heavy	Domestic residence	
292	50 cm	15 m diam.	Light-to-moderate Aztec	Heavy	Domestic residence	
293	75 cm	15 m diam.	Moderate Aztec	Moderate	Domestic residence	
294	50 cm	15x10 m	Light-to-moderate Aztec	Moderate	Domestic residence	Remnants of stone wall bases define a single room, 5 m square
295	35 cm	15 m diam.	Light-to-moderate Aztec	Heavy	Domestic residence	
296	35 cm	10x8 m	Light-to-moderate Aztec	Moderate	Domestic residence	Remnants of stone wall bases define a complex of at least 2 rooms, one of which is 3.5 m square
297	50 cm	8x8 m	Light-to-moderate Aztec	Heavy	Domestic residence	
298	10 cm	15 m diam.	Light-to-moderate Aztec	Heavy	Domestic residence	
303	50 cm	15 m diam.	Moderate Aztec	Moderate	Domestic residence	Small remnant of stone wall base
304	25 cm	10x15 m	Moderate Aztec	Heavy	Domestic residence	
305	15 cm	10 m diam.	Light-to-moderate Aztec	Heavy	Domestic residence	
306	50 cm	10 m diam.	Light-to-moderate Aztec	Heavy	Domestic residence	Small remnants of stone wall bases
307	15 cm	10 m diam.	Moderate Aztec	Heavy	Domestic residence	
309	25 cm	15 m diam.	Light-to-moderate Aztec	Heavy	Domestic residence	

Tlatel Number	Height	Surface Area	Surface Pottery	Rock Rubble	Probable Function	Comments
311	1 m	15 m diam.	Light-to-moderate Aztec	Moderate	Domestic residence	Several remnants of stone wall bases
314	75 cm	15x15 m	Moderate Aztec	Heavy	Domestic residence	
316	50 cm	10x15 m	Light-to-moderate Aztec	Moderate	Domestic residence	
320	35 cm	12x10 m	Light-to-moderate Aztec	Moderate	Domestic residence	
321	20 cm	10x15 m	Light-to-moderate Aztec	Moderate	Domestic residence	Several remnants of stone wall bases, including 1 well-defined room 4 m square
322	25 cm	15 m diam.	Light-to-moderate Aztec	Moderate	Domestic residence	Remnant of stone wall base
327	35 cm	15 m diam.	Light-to-moderate Aztec	Heavy	Domestic residence	
328	35 cm	15 m diam.	Light Aztec	Moderate	Domestic residence	Remnant of stone wall base
333	50 cm	15 m diam.	Light-to-moderate Aztec	Moderate	Domestic residence	
335	50 cm	15x15 m	Light-to-moderate Aztec	Moderate	Domestic residence	Several remnants of stone wall bases
336	50 cm	15 m diam.	Light-to-moderate Aztec	Heavy	Domestic residence	Several remnants of stone wall bases
339	50 cm	10 m diam.	Light-to-moderate Aztec	Moderate	Domestic residence	
345	25 cm	10 m diam.	Moderate Aztec	Moderate	Domestic residence	Several remnants of stone wall bases
348	25 cm	20 m diam.	Moderate Aztec, mostly Late, but some Early	Moderate	Domestic residence	Small remnant of stone wall base
349	25 cm	15 m diam.	Moderate Aztec	Moderate	Domestic residence	Several remnants of stone wall bases
351	75 cm	20 m diam.	Light Aztec	Moderate	Domestic residence	
356	1 m	15x15 m	Moderate Aztec	Moderate	Domestic residence	Several remnants of stone wall bases

Tlatel Number	Height	Surface Area	Surface Pottery	Rock Rubble	Probable Function	Comments
358	1 m	12 m diam.	Light-to-moderate Aztec	Heavy	Domestic residence	Remnant of stone wall base
360	35 cm	15 m diam.	Light-to-moderate Aztec	Moderate	Domestic residence	Several remnants of stone wall bases
363	35 cm	15 m diam.	Moderate Aztec	Moderate	Domestic residence	Remnant of tepetate-block wall base; relatively high proportion of decorated pottery
364	10 cm	20 m diam.	Moderate Aztec	Moderate	Domestic residence	Remnants of stone wall bases define at least 4 rooms
365	25 cm	15 m diam.	Light-to-moderate Aztec	Moderate	Domestic residence	Remnant of stone wall base
366	20 cm	20 m diam.	Moderate Aztec	Moderate	Domestic residence	
370	15 cm	10 m diam.	Moderate Aztec	Heavy	Domestic residence	Remnants of stone wall bases define at least 2 rooms
371	50 cm	15 m diam.	Moderate Aztec	Moderate	Domestic residence	Several remnants of stone wall bases
372	20 cm	10 m diam.	Light-to-moderate Aztec	Light-to-moderate	Domestic residence	
374	10 cm	15 m diam.	Light-to-moderate Aztec	Moderate	Domestic residence	Remnant of stone wall base
376	25 cm	15 m diam.	Moderate Aztec	Moderate	Domestic residence	Several remnants of stone wall bases
377	50 cm	8 m diam.	Light-to-moderate Aztec	Heavy	Domestic residence	
378	25 cm	15 m diam.	Light-to-moderate Aztec	Heavy	Domestic residence	Remnants of stone wall bases define a single room, 4 m square
379	1 m	20 m diam.	Moderate Aztec	Heavy	Domestic residence	
384	10 cm	10x10 m	Light-to-moderate Aztec	Heavy	Domestic residence	Remnants of stone wall bases define at least 1 room 4x5 m
385	25 cm	8x10 m	Light-to-moderate Aztec	Moderate	Domestic residence	Remnant of stone wall base

SITE: TX-A-73

Tlatel Number	Height	Surface Area	Surface Pottery	Rock Rubble	Probable Function	Comments
391	50 cm	15 m diam.	Moderate Aztec	Heavy	Domestic residence	
393	1 m	15 m diam.	Moderate Aztec, both Early and Late	Heavy	Domestic residence	Remnants of stone wall bases define a complex of several rooms (Fig. 26,*a*)
397	75 cm	20 m diam.	Moderate Aztec, both Early and Late	Moderate	Domestic residence	Remnants of several stone wall bases
398	75 cm	15 m diam.	Moderate Aztec, both Early and Late	Heavy	Domestic residence	
399	30 cm	20 m diam.	Moderate Aztec	Light	Domestic residence	Remnants of stone wall bases define a complex of several rooms, including 1 room 3 m square (Fig. 26,*b*)
401	1 m	20 m diam.	Moderate Aztec, both Early and Late	Moderate	Domestic residence	Remnants of stone wall bases define at least 1 room, 4 m square
402	50 cm	20 m diam.	Moderate Aztec	Moderate	Domestic residence	Several remnants of stone wall bases
403	40 cm	15x15 m	Moderate Aztec, both Early and Late	Moderate	Domestic residence	Several remnants of stone wall bases

SITE: TX-A-76

Tlatel Number	Height	Surface Area	Surface Pottery	Rock Rubble	Probable Function	Comments
131	35 cm	10 m diam.	Light-to-moderate Aztec	Heavy	Domestic residence	
133	75 cm	15 m diam.	Light-to-moderate Aztec	Heavy	Domestic residence	Remnants of stone wall bases define at least 1 room, 5x7 m
134	1 m	15 m diam.	Moderate Aztec	Heavy	Domestic residence	Remnants of stone wall bases define a complex of at least 7 rooms situated around a small patio (Fig. 26,*c*)
135	20 cm	10x8 m	Light-to-moderate Aztec	Moderate	Domestic residence	Several remnants of stone wall bases
136	1 m	15 m diam.	Light-to-moderate Aztec	Heavy	Domestic residence	

Tlatel Number	Height	Surface Area	Surface Pottery	Rock Rubble	Probable Function	Comments
140	75 cm	15 m diam.	Moderate Aztec	Heavy	Domestic residence	
142	1 m on downhill slope; 30 cm on up-hill slope	20x15 m	Light-to-moderate Aztec	Heavy	Ceremonial-civic ?	Consists of a solid rock rubble platform (5x5 m), resting on the uppermost terrace of a 3-terrace complex
143	2 m on downhill side; 35 cm on up-hill hill side	15 m diam.	Light-to-moderate Aztec	Heavy	?	Several remnants of stone wall bases
144	1.5 m on downhill side; 35 cm on up-hill side	15 m diam.	Moderate Aztec	Heavy	?	
145	1 m	10 m diam.	Light-to-moderate Aztec	Heavy	Domestic residence	Remnants of several stone wall bases
146	1 m	10 m diam.	Moderate Aztec	Heavy	Domestic residence	
148	50 cm	15 m diam.	Moderate Aztec	Heavy	Domestic residence	Several remnants of stone wall bases
149	1 m	20 m diam.	Moderate Aztec	Heavy	Domestic residence	Remnants of stone wall bases define a complex of at least 5 rooms (Fig. 26,*d*)

SITE: TX-A-77

Tlatel Number	Height	Surface Area	Surface Pottery	Rock Rubble	Probable Function	Comments
126	15 cm	10 m diam.	Moderate Aztec	Moderate	Domestic residence	Several remnants of stone wall bases
130	1 m	15 m diam	Moderate Aztec	Moderate	Domestic residence	Remnant of stone wall base

SITE: TX-A-78

Tlatel Number	Height	Surface Area	Surface Pottery	Rock Rubble	Probable Function	Comments
119	50 cm	15 m diam.	Moderate Aztec	Heavy	Domestic residence	
121	20 cm	20 m diam.	Moderate Aztec	Heavy	Domestic residence	Remnants of stone wall bases define at least 1 room, 5.5x5 m
124	1.5 m	20 m diam.	Moderate Aztec	Heavy	Domestic residence	Several remnants of stone wall bases
152	15 cm	10 m diam.	Light-to-moderate Aztec	Moderate	Domestic residence	Remnant of stone wall base
157	50 cm	10 m diam.	Light-to-moderate Aztec	Heavy	Domestic residence	Remnants of stone wall bases define a complex of at least 5 rooms (Fig. 26,*f*)
158	50 cm	15 m diam.	Light-to-moderate Aztec	Heavy	Domestic residence	
159	50 cm	15 m diam.	Light-to-moderate Aztec	Heavy	Domestic residence	
160	50 cm	15 m diam.	Light-to-moderate Aztec, both Early and Late	Heavy	Domestic residence	
161	15 cm	15 m diam.	Moderate Aztec	Heavy	Domestic residence	Several remnants of stone wall bases
163	15 cm	15 m diam.	Moderate Aztec	Heavy	Domestic residence	
167	50 cm	15 m diam.	Moderate Aztec	Heavy	Domestic residence	
168	25 cm	15 m diam.	Light Aztec	Heavy	Domestic residence	Remnants of stone wall bases
170	25 cm	10 m diam.	Moderate Aztec	Heavy	Domestic residence	Remnants of stone wall bases define a single room, 4x4 m, this seems to be the only room on the structure
173	50 cm	15 m diam.	Moderate Aztec, both Early and Late	Moderate	Domestic residence	Several remnants of stone wall bases
178	25 cm	10 m diam.	Light-to-moderate Aztec	Moderate	Domestic residence	Situated on a stone-faced terrace, 20 m long and *ca.* 50 cm high

Tlatel Number	Height	Surface Area	Surface Pottery	Rock Rubble	Probable Function	Comments
179	35 cm	10 m diam.	Light-to-moderate Aztec	Moderate	Domestic residence	Remnants of stone wall bases define a complex of at least 3 rooms (Fig. 26,*e*)
180	50 cm	15 m diam.	Moderate Aztec, both Early and Late	Moderate	Domestic residence	
181	25 cm	10 m diam.	Light-to-moderate Aztec	Heavy	Domestic residence	Several remnants of stone wall bases
185	35 cm	15 m diam.	Light-to-moderate Aztec	Heavy	Domestic residence	Remnants of stone wall bases define at least 1 room, 4 m wide by more than 3.5 m long
186	25 cm	15 m diam.	Light Aztec	Moderate	Domestic residence	Several remnants of stone wall bases
			SITE: TX-A-79			
62	50 cm	20 m diam.	Light-to-moderate Aztec	Moderate	Domestic residence	Remnants of stone wall bases define a complex of at least 5 rooms of indeterminate size
71	20 cm	10 m diam.	Moderate Aztec	Moderate	Domestic residence	Several remnants of stone wall bases
			SITE: TX-A-80			
59	25 cm	10 m diam.	Light-to-moderate Aztec	Moderate	Domestic residence	Remnants of stone wall bases
60	50 cm	20 m diam.	Light Aztec	Moderate	Domestic residence	Remnants of stone wall bases define a complex of at least 3 rooms (Fig. 27,*a*)
61	50 cm	8 m diam.	Light-to-moderate Aztec	Moderate	Domestic residence	Remnants of stone wall bases define a complex of at least 3 rooms of indeterminate size
63	35 cm	10 m diam.	Light-to-moderate Aztec, both Early and Late	Moderate	Domestic residence	Remnants of stone wall bases
64	35 cm	12 m diam.	Light Aztec	Moderate	Domestic residence	Remnants of stone wall bases define a complex of several rooms (Fig. 27,*b*)

Tlatel Number	Height	Surface Area	Surface Pottery	Rock Rubble	Probable Function	Comments
65	15 cm	20 m diam.	Light-to-moderate Aztec	Moderate	Domestic residence	Several remnants of stone wall bases
67	1 m	13x8 m	Light Aztec	Moderate	Domestic residence	Several remnants of stone wall bases
68	25 cm	8 m diam.	Light Aztec	Moderate	Domestic residence	Remnants of stone wall bases define a single room, *ca.* 2 m square
			SITE: TX-A-81			
115	50 cm	15 m diam.	Moderate Aztec	Moderate	Domestic residence	
116	50 cm	15 m diam.	Light-to-moderate Aztec, both Early and Late	Moderate	Domestic residence	Several remnants of stone wall bases
118	35 cm	10 m diam.	Moderate Aztec	Moderate	Domestic residence	Several remnants of stone wall bases
			SITE: TX-A-87			
19	7 m	45x55 m	Light-to-moderate Aztec	Heavy	Ceremonial-civic	This is a large, solid rock rubble platform, composed of 2 parts: a basal platform with a stuccoed upper surface some 1.5 m high, which is most pronounced at the west face where it extends as an apron some 10 m beyond the main mound; and the main mound, a flat-topped structure which has been badly pitted, built up some 5.5 m above the level of the basal platform. Tlatels 19, 20, and 21 form a single large ceremonial-civic complex at the south edge of modern Huexoltla. (Pl. 48,*a*)
20	4 m	30x40 m	Light-to-moderate Aztec	Heavy	Ceremonial-civic	Built on a low platform which is most apparent at the east face where it is about 1.5 m

Tlatel Number	Height	Surface Area	Surface Pottery	Rock Rubble	Probable Function	Comments
						high. The main bulk of the mound is a solid rock rubble platform whose flat upper surface is covered with a complex of small rooms, with stuccoed floors and walls (Fig. 29; Pl. 48,*b*)
21	1.5 m	25 m diam.	Light-to-moderate Aztec	Moderate	Ceremonial-civic	Located just west of Tlatel 20, in a zone of dense occupation
26	1.5 m	30 m diam.	Light-to-moderate Aztec around the sides; light Aztec on top	Heavy	Ceremonial-civic	A solid rock rubble platform with a flat, stuccoed upper surface with remnants of stone wall bases
27	1.5 m	25 m diam.	Light-to-moderate Aztec	Moderate	Ceremonial-civic	A solid rock rubble platform with a flat, stuccoed upper surface (at least 2 superimposed floor levels), with traces of a stone stairway on the north face
31	2.5 m	10x30 m	Light Aztec	Heavy	Ceremonial-civic	The main structure rests atop a basal platform about 50 m square. These remains have been partially restored to produce a stone-walled enclosure with internal rooms and other features (Fig. 30; Pl. 49,*b*)
33	1.5 m	20 m diam.	Light-to-moderate around the sides; very light Aztec on top	Heavy	Ceremonial-civic	A solid rock rubble platform with a flat, stuccoed upper surface
34	2.5 m	25x20 m	Light Aztec	Heavy	Ceremonial-civic	Has been partially cleared and restored. Consists of 2 superimposed solid rock rubble platforms, both with stuccoed outer walls. The inner platform is about 15 m square, with a steep stairway on its west face (Pl. 49,*a*)
35	2 m	20 m diam.	Light Aztec	Heavy	Ceremonial-civic	
36	4 m	15 m diam.	Light-to-moderate Aztec	Moderate	Ceremonial-civic	Extensive pitting reveals solid adobe brick and rock rubble construction (Fig. 27,*c*)

Tlatel Number	Height	Surface Area	Surface Pottery	Rock Rubble	Probable Function	Comments
37	1.5-4 m	25 m diam.	Moderate Aztec	Heavy	Ceremonial-civic	Has been partially cleared and reconstructed. The structure consists of a basal platform of rock rubble with stuccoed exterior walls, upon which rests a complex of at least 4 small rooms with stuccoed floors and walls
40	50 cm	15 m diam.	Light-to-moderate Aztec	Heavy	Domestic residence	An isolated housemound at the south edge of the urban core
43	6 m	40 m diam.	Light Aztec, plus traces of Terminal Formative and Classic	Moderate	Ceremonial-civic	Partly restored, this is a round structure, built in 2 parts: 1) a basal platform, about 40 m in diameter and 1.5-2 m high; and 2) a main platform of solid rock rubble construction, about 25 m in diameter and 4 m high, with the remnants of an adobe-brick stairway on its east face (Pl. 50,*a*)
44	25 cm	30 m diam.	Light-to-moderate Aztec	Moderate	Domestic residence	
49	1 m	25 m diam.	Moderate Aztec	Heavy	Domestic residence	
52	1.5 m	15 m diam.	Light Aztec	Heavy	Ceremonial-civic	Apparently a solid rock rubble platform
53	4 m	20 m diam.	Very light Aztec	Moderate	Ceremonial-civic	Pitting reveals a solid rock rubble construction
64	1 m	15 m diam.	Light Aztec	Heavy	Ceremonial-civic ?	
85	40 cm	10 m diam.	Moderate Aztec	Heavy	Domestic residence	Several remnants of stone wall bases
29-C	1 m	20x12 m	Light-to-moderate Aztec	Heavy	Domestic residence	
31-C	1 m	8 m diam.	Moderate Aztec	Moderate	Domestic residence	Remnants of stone wall bases define a single room, 5 m square
32-C	1 m	12x5 m	Moderate Aztec	Heavy	Domestic residence	

Tlatel Number	Height	Surface Area	Surface Pottery	Rock Rubble	Probable Function	Comments
34-C	1 m	25 m diam.	Light-to-moderate Aztec	Moderate	Domestic residence	Remnants of stone wall bases define at least 1 room, 5 m square
35-C	1 m	8 m diam.	Light-to-moderate Aztec	Moderate	Domestic residence	Remnants of stone wall bases
36-C	50 cm	8 m diam.	Light-to-moderate Aztec	Moderate	Domestic residence	Remnants of stone wall bases define a complex of at least 4 rooms (Fig. 27,*c*)
39-C	15 cm	10x7 m	Moderate Aztec	Heavy	Domestic residence	Remnants of stone wall bases define a single enclosure, 10x7 m, with no indications of internal partitions
40-C	25 cm	10x10 m	Moderate Aztec	Moderate	Domestic residence	Remnants of stone wall bases
41-C	50 cm	8 m diam.	Light Aztec	Moderate	Domestic residence	Remnants of stone wall bases
50-C	1 m	10 m diam.	Light Aztec	Heavy	Domestic residence	Remnants of stone wall bases
52-C	1 m	10 m diam.	Moderate Aztec	Heavy	Domestic residence	Remnants of stone wall bases define a complex of at least 3 rooms (Fig. 27,*d*)
53-C	50 cm	8 m diam.	Moderate Aztec	Heavy	Domestic residence	Remnants of stone wall bases define a single room, 5x3 m
54-C	50 cm	10 m diam.	Moderate Aztec	Heavy	Domestic residence	
55-C	2.5 m	15 m diam.	Very light Aztec	Heavy	Ceremonial-civic ?	Pitting indicates solid rock rubble construction
56-C	30 cm	12 m diam.	Very light	Light	?	Remnants of stone wall bases
57-C	1.5 m	8 m diam.	Light-to-moderate Aztec	Heavy	Domestic residence	Remnants of stone wall bases

SITE: TX-A-100

154	3.5 m	30 m diam.	Very light Aztec	Heavy	Ceremonial-civic	Pl. 53,*a*

Tlatel Number	Height	Surface Area	Surface Pottery	Rock Rubble	Probable Function	Comments
158	3 m	15x40 m	Light Aztec	Heavy	Ceremonial-civic	
166	5 m	35 m diam.	Very light on the structure; light Aztec around the base	Heavy	Ceremonial-civic	
167	4 m	35x35 m	Very light on the structure; light Aztec around the base	Light	Ceremonial-civic	Extensive pitting has revealed that the main mound is constructed of solid adobe brick, with stuccoed exterior surface. The upper surface of the mound is also stuccoed, and remnants of stone wall bases and plaster floors indicate the former presence here of a small complex of rooms. A section of a stuccoed stairway is preserved on the east side of the mound (Pl. 54)
168	4 m	35x35 m	Very light	Heavy	Ceremonial-civic	Remnants of stone-adobe walls on top suggest the former existence of a small room complex
169	10 m	50 m diam.	Very light	Light	Ceremonial-civic	Pl. 53,*b*
170	2 m	10x20 m	Very light Aztec	Moderate	Ceremonial-civic	
			SITE: TX-A-109			
1	75 cm	15 m diam.	Moderate Aztec, Early and Late, with a predominance of Texcoco Fabric Marked	Moderate	Domestic residence	The mound has been cut on 2 sides by large drainage ditches; construction is solid earth fill, with no traces of internal construction
2	2 m	50 m diam.	Moderate Aztec	Moderate	Domestic residence ?	
7	2 m	80x90 m	Moderate-to-heavy Aztec; light Middle, Late, and Terminal Formative, Abundant Texcoco Fabric Marked	Light	Domestic residence ? associated with salt-making	Bisected by dirt road leading into Chimalhuacan from the main highway, appears to be a solid mass of earth, with no traces of internal construction

Tlatel Number	Height	Surface Area	Surface Pottery	Rock Rubble	Probable Function	Comments
8	2.5 m	85x70 m	Moderate-to-heavy Aztec; abundant Texcoco Fabric Marked, moderate Middle Formative	Light	Domestic residence ? associated with salt-making	Irregular upper surface
11	2.5 m	90x70 m	Light-to-moderate Aztec, abundant Texcoco Fabric Marked pottery, moderate-to-heavy Middle Formative	Generally light; heavy in S.W. corner	Domestic residence ? associated with salt-making	Irregular upper surface
17	2 m	50 m diam.	Moderate Aztec, light Middle, Late, and Terminal Formative	Heavy	Domestic residence	In heart of heavily occupied zone of modern Chimalhuacan

BIBLIOGRAPHY

Acosta, J.
1940 Exploraciones en Tula, Hgo. Revista Mexicana de Estudios Antropologicos, 4: 172-95. México, D.F.

Alva Ixtlilxochitl, Fernando de
1965*a* Obras Históricas, Tomo I. Edited by A Chavero. Pp. 508. Editora Nacional. México, D.F.
1965*b* Obras Históricas, Tomo II. Edited by A. Chavero. Pp. 455. Editora Nacional. México, D.F.

Anglerius, Petrus Martyr
1628 The Decades of the New World or West India, 2nd edition. Pp. 637. London.

Apenes, O.
1943 The "Tlateles" of Lake Texcoco. American Antiquity, 9(1): 29-32. Salt Lake City.
1944 The Primitive Salt Production of Lake Texcoco. Ethnos, 9(1): 25-40. Stockholm.

Armillas, P.
1944 Exploraciones Recientes en Teotihuacán, México. Cuadernos Americanos, 4: 1-16. México, D.F.

Aveleyra Arroyo de Anda, L.
1956 The Second Mammoth and Associated Artifacts at Santa Isabel Iztapan, Mexico. American Antiquity, 22(1): 12-28. Salt Lake City.

Barba de Piña Chan, B.
1956 "Tlapacoya", un Sitio Preclásico de Transición. Acta Antropológica, Epoca 2, 1(1), pp. 205. México, D.F.

Barlow, R.
1949*a* The Extent of the Empire of the Culhua Mexica. Ibero Americana, No. 28, pp. 141. University of California Press. Berkeley and Los Angeles.
1949*b* La Fundación de la Triple Alianza (1427-1433). Anales, Instituto Nacional de Antropología e Historia, 3: 147-55. México, D.F.

Batres, L.
1904 Exploraciones en Huexotla, Texcoco, y "El Gavilan." Pp. 15. México, D.F.

Bennyhoff, J.
1966 Chronology and Periodization: Continuity and Change in the Teotihuacan Ceramic Tradition. *In*: Sociedad Mexicana de Antropología, Teotihuacan Onceava Mesa Redonda, pp. 19-30. México, D.F.

Bernal, I.
1965 Archaeological Synthesis of Oaxaca. *In*: R. Wauchope (general editor), Handbook of Middle American Indians, 3(2): 788-813. University of Texas Press. Austin.
1966 Teotihuacan Capital de Imperio? Revista Mexicana de Estudios Antropológicos, 20: 95-110. México, D.F.

Blom, F. and O. LaFarge
1926 Tribes and Temples. Vol. 1, pp. 237. Tulane University. New Orleans.

Boas, F.
1911-12 Album de Colecciones Arqueológicas y Etnológicas Americana. Escuela Internacional de Arqueología, y Etnología. México, D.F.

Borhegyi, S.
1965 Archaeological Synthesis of the Guatemalan Highlands. *In*: R. Wauchope (general editor), Handbook of Middle American Indians, 2(1): 3-58, University of Texas Press. Austin.

Carrasco, P.
1961 El Barrio y la Regulación del Matrimonio en un Pueblo del Valle de México en el Siglo XVI. Revista Mexicana de Estudios Antropológicos, 17: 7-26. México, D.F.

1964 Family Structure of Sixteenth Century Tepoztlan. *In*: R. Manners (editor), Process and Pattern in Culture, pp. 185-210. Aldine Publishing Co. Chicago.

Chapman, A.
1959 Puertos de Intercambio en Mesoamerica Prehispánica. Instituto Nacional de Antropologiá e Historia, Serie Historia III. Pp. 77. México, D.F.

Coe, M. D.
1964 The Chinampas of Mexico. Scientific American, 211(1): 90-98. New York.
1965 Archaeological Synthesis of Southern Veracruz and Tabasco. *In*: R. Wauchope (general editor), Handbook of Middle American Indians, 3(2): 679-715. University of Texas Press. Austin.
1966 The Maya. Pp. 252. Frederick A. Praeger. New York and Washington.
1968 Map of San Lorenzo, An Olmec Site in Veracruz, Mexico. Dept. of Anthropology, Yale University. Pp. 15, plus map. New Haven.

Coe, M.D., R. Diehl and M. Stuiver
1967 Olmec Civilization, Veracruz, Mexico: Dating of the San Lorenzo Phase. Science, 155(3768): 1399-401. Washington, D. C.

Coe, M.D. and K. Flannery
1967 Early Cultures and Human Ecology in South Coastal Guatemala. Smithsonian Contributions to Anthropology, Vol. 3, pp. 136 plus 30 plates. Smithsonian Press. Washington, D.C.

Coe, W. R.
1965 Tikal, Guatemala, and Emergent Maya Civilization. Science, 147(3664): 1401-19, Washington, D.C.

Cook de Leonard, C.
1955 Una "Maqueta" Prehispánica. El México Antiguo, 8: 169-91. México, D.F.

Corona Nuñez, J.
1966 Los Teotihuacanos en el Occidente de México. Revista Mexicana de Estudios Antropológicos, 20: 111-16. México, D.F.

Cortes, H.
1962 Five letters of Cortes to the Emperor. Translated and with an introduction by J. B. Morris. Pp. 388. W. W. Norton & Co. New York.

Coy, P.
1966 Tetzcotzinco: Usurped and Neglected. Man, 1(4): 543-49. London.

Cummings, B.
1933 Cuicuilco and the Archaic Culture of Mexico. University of Arizona, Social Science Bulletin, Vol. 4, No. 8, pp. 56. Tuscon.

Diaz del Castillo, Bernal
1960 Historia Verdadera de la Conquista de la Nueva España. Pp. 648. Editorial Porrua. México, D.F.

Dibble, C.
1951 Códice Xolotl. Instituto de Historia, Primera Serie, No. 22. Pp. 166. México, D.F.

Dixon, K.
1963 Progress Report on Archaeological Excavations at Temesco, Edo. de Mexico (Summer, 1963). Pp. 11. Mimeographed. Long Beach State College. Long Beach.
1966 Progress Report on Excavations of Terminal Late Preclassic Ceremonial Architecture, Temesco, Valley of Mexico (Summer, 1965). Pp. 45. Mimeographed. California State College. Long Beach.

Flannery, K.
1968 The Olmec and the Valley of Oaxaca: A Model for Inter-Regional Interaction in Formative Times. *In*: E. P. Benson (editor), Dumbarton Oaks Conference on the Olmec, pp. 79-110. Washington, D.C.

Flannery, K., A. Kirkby, M. Kirkby and A. Williams
1967 Farming Systems and Political Growth in Ancient Oaxaca. Science, 158(3800): 445-54. Washington, D.C.

Franco, J.
1945 Comentarios Sobre Tipología y Filogenía de la Decoración Negra Sobre Color Natural del Barro en la Cerámica "Azteca II." Revista Mexicana de Estudios Antropológicos, 7: 163-86. México, D.F.

1949 Algunos Problemas Relativos a la Cerámica Azteca. El México Antiguo, 7: 162-208. México, D.F.

1957 Cenefas en la Cerámica Azteca. *In*: Motivos Decorativos en la Cerámica Azteca. Museo Nacional de Antropología, Serie Científica, No. 5: 7-36, plus 16 figures. México, D.F.

Gamio, M.
1912 Arqueología de Atzcapotzalco, México, D.F. Proceedings of the 18th International Congress of Americanists, pp. 180-87. London.

Garcia Payon, J.
1941 La Cerámica del Valle de Toluca. Revista Mexicana de Estudios Antropológicos, 5: 209-38. México, D.F.

1966 Prehistória de Mesoamérica. Universidad Veracruzana, Cuadernos de la Facultad de Filosofía, Letras, y Ciencias, pp. 204. Xalapa.

Gibson, C.
1956 Llamiento General, Repartimiento, and the Empire of Acolhuacan. The Hispanic American Historical Review, 36: 1-27.

1964 The Aztecs Under Spanish Rule. Pp. 655. Stanford Univ. Press. Stanford.

Griffin J. and A. Espejo
1947 La Alfarería Correspondiente al Ultimo Período de Ocupación Nahua del Valle de México, I. Tlatelolco a Través de los Tiempos, 6: 3-20. México, D.F.

1950 La Alfarería Correspondiente al Ultimo Período de Ocupación Nahua del Valle de Mexico, II. Tlatelolco a Través de los Tiempos, 9: 3-54. México, D.F.

Griffin, J. and A. Krieger
1947 Notes on Some Ceramic Techniques and Intrusions in Central Mexico. American Antiquity, 12: 156-68. Salt Lake City.

Grove, D.
1968 The Pre-Classic Olmec in Central Mexico: Site Distribution and Inferences. *In*: E. P. Benson (editor), Dumbarton Oaks Conference on the Olmec, pp. 179-85. Washington, D.C.

Hicks, F. and H. Nicholson
1964 The Transition from Classic to Postclassic at Cerro Portezuelo, Valley of Mexico. Actas, 25th International Congress of Americanists, pp. 493-505. México, D.F.

Holmes, W.
1885 Evidences of the Antiquity of Man on the Site of the City of Mexico. Transactions of the Anthropological Society of Washington, 3: 68-81. Washington, D.C.

1900 The Obsidian Mines of Hidalgo, Mexico. American Anthropologist, n.s., 2(3): 405-16. New York.

Kelly, I. and A. Palerm
1953 The Tajin Totonac, Part I. Smithsonian Institution, Institute of Social Anthropology, Vol. 14, pp. 384. Washington, D.C.

Kidder, A., J. Jennings and E. Shook
1946 Excavations at Kaminaljuyu, Guatemala. Carnegie Institute of Washington, Pub. 561, pp. 284. Washington, D.C.

Kirchoff, P.
1959 The Principles of Clanship in Human Society. *In*: M. Fried (editor), Readings in Anthropology, 2: 259-70. New York.

Leopold, A.
1959 Wildlife of Mexico: The Game Birds and Mammals. The University of California Press, pp. 568. Berkeley and Los Angeles.

Linne, S.
1934 Archaeological Researches at Teotihuacan, Mexico. The Ethnographical Museum of Sweden, Stockholm, n.s., Pub. 1, pp. 236. Stockholm.

1942 Mexican Highland Cultures. The Ethnographical Museum of Sweden, Stockholm, n.s., Pub. 7, pp. 223. Stockholm.

1948 El Valle y la Ciudad de México en 1550. The Ethnographical Museum of Sweden, Stockholm, n.s., Pub. 9, pp. 220. Stockholm.

Lorenzo, J. L.
1956 Notas Sobre Arqueología y Cambios Climáticos en la Cuenca de México. *In*: F. Mooser, S. White and J. Lorenzo, La Cuenca de Mexico, Consideraciones Geológicas y Arqueológicas, pp. 29-46. Instituto Nacional de Antropología de História, Dirección de Prehistória. México, D.F.

Lowe, G. and J. Mason
1965 Archaeological Survey of the Chiapas Coast, Highlands, and Upper Grijalva Basin. *In*: R. Wauchope (general editor), Handbook of Middle American Indians, 2(1): 195-236. University of Texas Press. Austin.

MacNeish, R.
1964 Ancient Mesoamerican Civilization. Science, 143(3606): 531-37. Washington, D.C.

Mayer-Oakes, W.
1959 A Stratigraphic Excavation at El Risco, Mexico. Proceedings of the American Philosophical Society, 103(3): 332-73. Philadelphia.
1960 A Developmental Concept of Pre-Spanish Urbanization in the Valley of Mexico. Middle American Research Institute, Middle American Records, 2: 165-76. Tulane University. New Orleans.

McAfee, B, and R. Barlow
1946 The Titles of Tetzcotzingo. Tlalocan, 2: 110-27. México, D.F.

Medellín Zenil, A.
1960 Cerámicas del Totonacapan. Universidad Veracruzana, Instituto de Antropología. Pp. 217. Xalapa.

Mendizabal, M.
1946 Influência de la Sal en la Distribución Geográfica de los Grupos Indígenas de México. *In*: Obras Completas, 2: 181-344. México, D.F.

Millon, R.
1966 Extensión y Población de la Ciudad de Teotihuacan en sus diferentes Períodos: un Cálculo Provisional. *In*: Sociedad Mexicana de Antropología, Teotihuacan, Onceava Mesa Redonda, pp. 57-78. México, D.F.
1967 Urna de Monte Albán IIIA encontrada en Teotihuacan. Instituto Nacional de Antropología e Historia, Boletín, 29: 42-44. México, D.F.

Millon, R., B. Drewitt and J. Bennyhoff
1965 The Pyramid of the Sun at Teotihuacan: 1959 Investigations. Transactions of the American Philosophical Society, n.s., Vol. 55, Pt. 6, pp. 93. Philadelphia.

Molins Fabrega, N.
1954-55 El Códice Mendocino y la Economía. Revista Mexicana de Estudios Antropológicos, 14(1): 303-37. México, D.F.

Monzon, A.
1949 El Calpulli en la Organización Social de los Tenocha. Universidad Nacional Autónoma de México, Instituto de História, Pub. 14, pp. 108. México, D.F.

Mueller, F.
1966 Secuencia Cerámica de Teotihuacan. *In*: Sociedad Mexicana de Antropología, Teotihuacan, Onceava Mesa Redonda, pp. 31-44. México, D.F.

Munsell Color Company
1954 Munsell Soil Color Charts. Baltimore.

Murra, J.
1956 The Economic Organization of the Inca State. Doctoral Dissertation, University of Chicago, Department of Anthropology, pp. 320.

Noguera, E.
1935 La Ceramica de Tenayuca y las Excavaciones Estratigráficas. *In*: Tenayuca, Publication de la Secretaria de Educación Publica, Departamento de Monumentos, pp. 141-201. México, D.F.
1943 Excavaciones en El Tepalcate, Chimalhuacan, México. American Antiquity, 9: 33-43. Salt Lake City.
1954 La Cerámica Arqueológica de Cholula. Pp. 315. México, D.F.

Palerm, A.
1960 The Agricultural Bases of Urban Civilization in Mesoamerica. *In*: Irrigation Civilizations: A Comparative Study, pp. 28-42. Pan American Union. Washington, D.C.

Palerm, A and E. Wolf
1954-55 El Desarrollo del Area Clave del Imperio Texcocano. Revista Mexicana de Estudios Antropológicos, 14(1): 337-50. México, D.F.
1960 Ecological Potential and Cultural Development in Mesoamerica. Studies in Human Ecology, Social Science Monographs, 3: 1-37. Pan American Union. Washington, D.C.

Parsons, J. R.
1966 The Aztec Ceramic Sequence in the Teotihuacan Valley, Mexico. Doctoral Dissertation, Department of Anthropology, University of Michigan, pp. 473.
1968 Teotihuacan, Mexico, and its Impact on Regional Demography. Science, 162(3856): 872-77. Washington, D.C.
In Press The Function of Texcoco Fabric Marked Pottery. Revista Mexicana de Estudios Antropológicos, 22. México, D.F.

Parsons, M.
n.d. Spindle Whorls from the Teotihuacan Valley, Mexico. Pp. 15. Mimeographed.

Paso y Troncoso, F. del (editor)
1905 Relación de Coatepec-Chalco, 1579, and Relación de Chimalhuacan-Atenco, 1579. *In*: Papales de la Nueva España, 6: 39-79. Madrid.

Piña Chan, R.
1950 Estratigrafía en los Terrenos Adjacentes a la Catedral Metropolitana. Tlatelco a traves de los Tiempos, 11: 67-92. México, D.F.
1956-57 Excavaciones Arqueológicas en Algunas Cuevas de la Región Texcocana. Revista Mexicana de Estudios Antropológicos, 14(2): 53-66. México, D.F.
1958 Tlatilco. Instituto Nacional de Antropología e Historia, 2 vols., pp. 126 plus 56. México, D.F.

Pomar, J.
1941 Relación de Tezcoco. *In*: J. Garcia Icazbalceta (editor), Nueva Colección de Documentos para la Historia de México, pp. 1-64. Editorial Chavez Hayhoe. México, D.F.

Porter, M.
1956 Excavations at Chupícuaro, Guanajuato, Mexico. Transactions, American Philosophical Society, 45: 515-637. Philadelphia.

Rattray, E.
1966*a* An Archaeological and Stylistic Study of Coyotlatelco Pottery. Mesoamerican Notes, 7-8: 87-193. Universidad de las Americas, México, D.F.
1966*b* El Complejo Cultural Coyotlatelco. Pp. 10. Mimeographed.
1968 A Tzacualli Burial from Pueblo Perdido. American Antiquity, 33(1): 103-05. Salt Lake City.

Sahlins, M.
1958 Social Stratification in Polynesia. Pp. 306. University of Washington Press. Seattle.

Sanders, W. T.
1952 El Mercado de Tlatelolco, un Estudio de Economía Urbana. Tlatoani, 1(1): 14-16. Instituto Nacional de Antropología e História. México, D.F.
1956 The Central Mexican Symbiotic Region, A Study in Pre-Historic Settlement Patterns. *In*: G. R. Willey (editor), Prehistoric Settlement Patterns in the New World, Viking Fund Publications in Anthropology, 23: 115-27. New York.
n.d. Prehispanic Demography, Land Use and Settlement Patterns of the Teotihuacan Valley, Mexico. 1961 Research Proposal submitted to the National Science Foundation. Pp. 16. Mimeographed.
1961 Review of Mayer-Oakes (1960). American Antiquity, 27(2): 259-60. Salt Lake City.
1965 The Cultural Ecology of the Teotihuacan Valley, pp. 209. Mimeographed. Department of Sociology and Anthropology, The Pennsylvania State University. University Park.
1966 Review of W. Borah and S. Cook, The Aboriginal Population of Central Mexico on the Eve of the Spanish Conquest (Ibero Americana 45). American Anthropologist, 68(5): 1298-99. Menasha.
1968 Hydraulic Agriculture, Economic Symbiosis and the Evolution of States in Central Mexico. Anthropological Archaeology in the Americas, pp. 88-107. The Anthropological Society of Washington. Washington, D.C.

Sanders, W. and B. Price
1968 Mesoamerica. Pp. 264. Random House Studies in Anthropology. New York.

Sejourné, L.
1966 Arqueología de Teotihuacan—La Ceramica. Pp. 262. Fondo de Cultura Económica. México, D.F.

Shook, E.
1965 Archaeological Survey of the Pacific Coast of Guatemala. *In*: R. Wauchope (general editor), Handbook of Middle American Indians, 2(1): 180-94. University of Texas Press. Austin.

Smith, C. E.
1965 Agriculture, Tehuacan Valley. Fieldiana: Botany, 31(3): 51-100. Chicago Natural History Museum. Chicago.

Snow, D.
1969 Ceramic Sequence and Settlement Location in Pre-Hispanic Tlaxcala. American Antiquity, 34(2): 131-45. Salt Lake City.

Spence, M. and J. Parsons
1967 Prehispanic Obsidian Mines in Southern Hidalgo. American Antiquity, 32(4): 542-43. Salt Lake City.

Tolstoy, P.
1958 Surface Survey of the Northern Valley of Mexico: The Classic and Post-Classic Periods. Transactions, American Philosophical Society, Vol. 48, No. 5, pp. 101. Philadelphia.

Tolstoy, P. and N. Guénette
1965 Le Placement de Tlatilco dans le Cadre du Pré-Classique du Bassin de Mexico. Journal de la Societé des Americanistes, 54(1): 47-91. Paris.

Tolstoy, Paul, and L. I. Paradis
1970 Early and Middle Preclassic Culture in the Basin of Mexico. Science, 167: 344-51. Washington, D.C.

Tozzer, A.
1921 Excavations at a Site at Santiago Ahuitzotla, D.F., Mexico. Bureau of American Ethnology, Bulletin 74, pp. 56. Washington, D.C.

Tscholl, P.
1966 Informe sobre el Estado de los Trabajos Arquelógicos. Pp. 6 plus map. Mimeographed.

Vaillant, G.
1930 Excavations at Zacatenco. American Museum of Natural History, Anthropological Papers 32(1): 1-197. New York.
1931 Excavations at Ticoman. American Museum of Natural History, Anthropological Papers 32(2): 198-439. New York.
1935 Excavations at El Arbolillo. American Museum of Natural History, Anthropological Papers 35(2): 136-279. New York.
1938 Correlation of Archaeological and Historical Sequences in the Valley of Mexico. American Anthropologist, 40: 535-73. Menasha.
1941 The Aztecs of Mexico. Pp. 340. New York.

Vaillant, G. and S. Vaillant
1934 Excavations at Gualupita. American Museum of Natural History, Anthropological Papers, 35(1): 1-135. New York.

Wellhausen, E., L. Roberts, E. Hernandez and P. Mangelsdorf
1952 Races of Maize in Mexico. Bussey Institute, Harvard University. Cambridge.

West, M.
1965 Transition from Preclassic to Classic at Teotihuacan. American Antiquity, 31(2): 193-202. Salt Lake City.

West, R. and P. Armillas
1950 Las Chinampas de México. Cuadernos Americanos, 2(2): 165-82. México, D.F.

Wheeler, J.
1968 An Analysis of Faunal Remains from the Site of Temesco, Valley of Mexico. Pp. 9. Mimeographed.

Wicke, C. and F. Horcasitas
1957 Archaeological Investigations on Monte Tlaloc, Mexico. Mesoamerican Notes, 5: 83-95. Mexico City College, Department of Anthropology. México, D.F.

Willey, G., W. Bullard, J. Glass and J. Gifford
1965 Prehistoric Maya Settlements in the Belize Valley. Peabody Museum of American Ethnology and Archaeology, Harvard University, Papers, Vol. 54, pp. 589. Cambridge.

Wolf, E.
1959 Sons of the Shaking Earth. Pp. 303. Univ. of Chicago Press. Chicago.

Wolf, E. and A. Palerm
1955 Irrigation in the Old Acolhua Domain, Mexico. Southwestern Journal of Anthropology, 11: 265-81. Albuquerque.
1956 New Light on the Archaic in the Valley of Mexico. Pp. 6. Paper presented at the 1956 Annual Meeting of the American Anthropological Association, Los Angeles. Mimeographed.

GLOSSARY

bancal—low earth embankment (*ca.* 50 cm high), used for boundary markers and erosion control.

barranca—arroyo or gully, generally with seasonal water flow.

barrio—territorial subdivision of a village or town.

comal—flat clay griddle used for heating tortillas.

jaguey—an artificial, open catchment basin, which collects surface drainage from a wide area for watering livestock and for household uses.

maguey—type of cactus, whose sap is used for making pulque, and fibers for a variety of textiles.

molcajete—pottery vessel with striated interior bottom, used for grinding certain vegetables and fruits.

nopal—type of cactus, with edible leaves and fruit.

olla—pottery jar.

pulque—alcoholic beverage produced from fermented sap of the maguey cactus.

soil cover
- shallow—less than 50 cm deep
- moderate—50 cm to 1 m deep
- deep—greater than 1 m deep

tepetate—hard, caliche-like subsoil.

tezontle—volcanic rock, quarried for construction uses.

tlatel—mound produced by the deterioration of a structure.

PLATES 1-57

PLATE 1

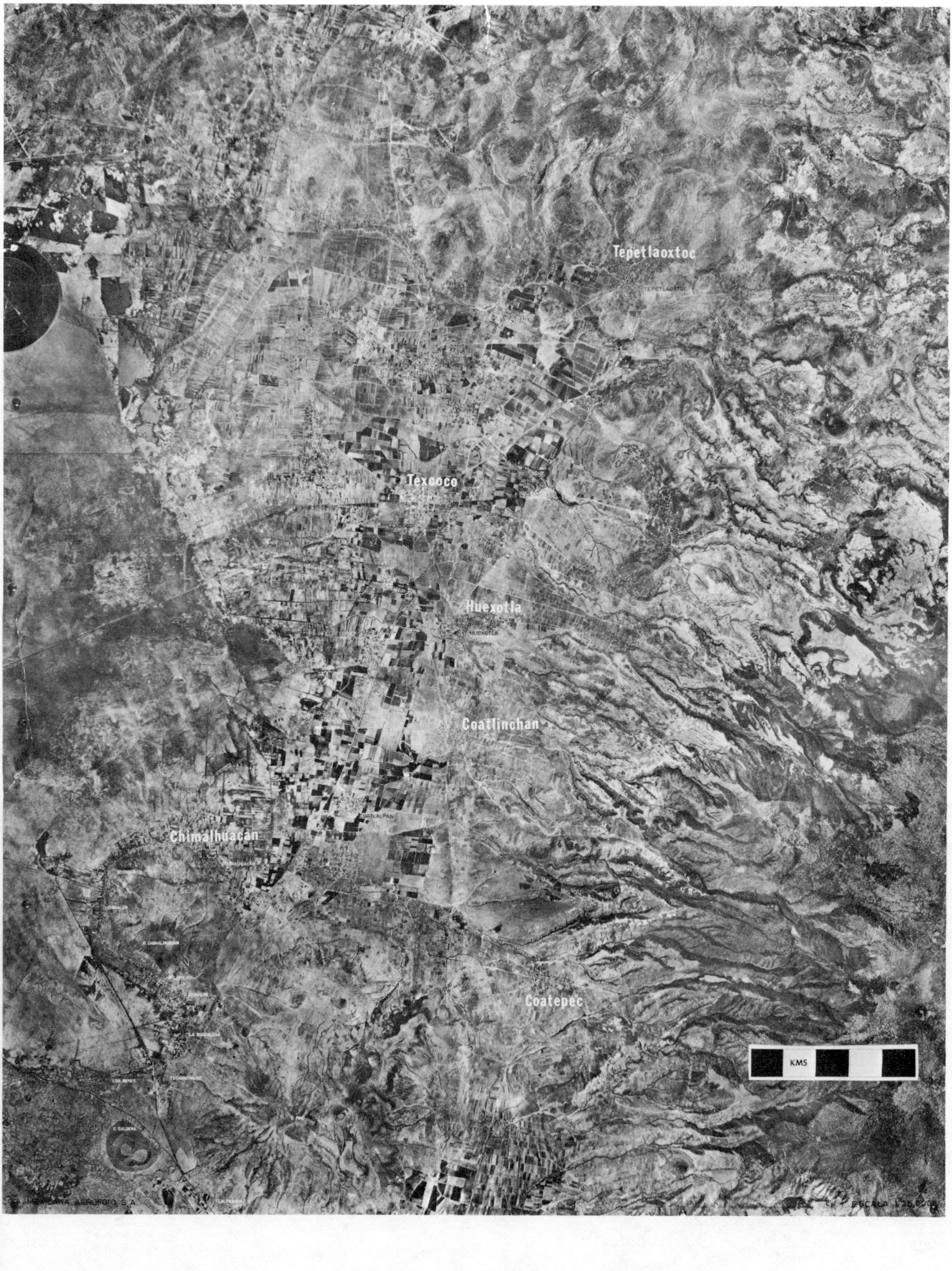

Plate 1—Vertical airphoto of the Texcoco Region. Courtesy Companía Mexicana de Aerofoto, México, D.F.

PLATE 2

a

b

Plate 2—*a*) Facing SSE across Lower Piedmont at base of Cerro Azteca in northwest section of survey area. UMMA Neg. 120-6-3. *b*) Facing SE toward modern village of Coatepec across uneroded section of Lower Piedmont in southeast section of survey area. UMMA Neg. 120-111-4.

a

b

Plate 3—*a*) Example of deeply-intrenched barranca in Upper Piedmont zone, east-central section of survey area. UMMA Neg. 120-72-4. *b*) Example of severe sheet erosion in Upper Piedmon't zone, east-central section of survey area. UMMA Neg. 120-110-1.

a

b

Plate 5—*a*) Modern salt-making near Nezquipaya, northwestern corner of survey area. UMMA Neg. 120-5-3. *b*) Main mound at Tx-A-51, probably representing salt manufacture in Aztec times. UMMA Neg. 120-10-2.

PLATE 4

a

b

Plate 4—*a*) Example of severe sheet erosion in Upper Piedmont zone, east-central section of survey area. UMMA Neg. 120-74-2. *b*) Typical barranca cutting through Lower Piedmont zone, southwestern section of survey area. UMMA Neg. 120-30-5.

PLATE 6

a

b

Plate 6—*a*) Facing SW across Lower Piedmont and Lakeshore Plain zones, with village of Natívitas in foreground, central section of survey area. UMMA Neg. 120-51-2, 120-51-3. *b*) Facing SE across upper of Río Papalotla floodplain and into Upper Piedmont zone in northeast section of survey area. UMMA Neg. 120-38-3.

a

b

Plate 7—*a*) Facing SSW across section of terraced slopes in San Miguel Tlaixpan. UMMA Neg. 120-57-6. *b*) Facing north across main section of intensively terraced land in villages of San Nicolás Tlaminca and San Miguel Tlaixpan. UMMA Neg. 120-49-4.

PLATE 8

Plate 8—Facing south across southern two-thirds of survey area. Western base of Sierra is at left; eastern edge of Lake Texcoco lies at the right edge of the photo. Village of San Miguel Tlaixpan is situated at left foreground. UMMA Neg. 120-88-1, 120-88-2, 120-88-3.

PLATE 9

Plate 9—Facing north across western half of northern third of survey area. The line of low hills running across the length of the photo is the Patlachique Range. Eastern edge of Lake Texcoco lies just to the right of this view. Cerro Azteca is highest peak at left. UMMA Neg. 120-90-1, 120-90-2, 120-90-3.

PLATE 10

Plate 10—Facing north across eastern half of northern third of survey area. Western base of Sierra is at right edge of photo. UMMA Neg. 120-90-4, 120-90-5, 120-90-6.

PLATE 11

Plate 11—Facing ESE along juncture of Upper Piedmont and Sierra in central section of survey area. Village of Santa María Tecuanulco at left. UMMA Neg. 120-84-3, 120-84-4, 120-84-5.

PLATE 12

Plate 12—Facing west across Upper Piedmont zone in central section of survey area. Western edge of village of Santa María Tecuanulco is at left. UMMA Neg. 120-84-6, 120-85-1, 120-85-2.

PLATE 13

Plate 13—Facing WNW across section of Upper Piedmont in central part of survey area. UMMA Neg. 120-85-3, 120-85-4, 120-85-5.

PLATE 14

a

b

Plate 14—*a*) General area of Tx-MF-13 site. UMMA Neg. 120-22-2. *b*) General area of Tx-MF-5 site. UMMA Neg. 120-109-1.

PLATE 15

a

b

Plate 15—*a*) Facing WNW across general area of Tx-MF-9 and western end of Tx-LF-12. UMMA Neg. 120-45-3. *b*) Facing WNW across main part of Tx-LF-12 site area. UMMA Neg. 120-48-2.

PLATE 16

a

b

Plate 16—*a*) Facing NNE over general area of Tx-LF-14. UMMA Neg. 120-2-1. *b*) Facing west over general area of Tx-LF-15. UMMA Neg. 120-4-3.

PLATE 17

a

b

Plate 17—*a*) Facing east across general area of Tx-TF-1. UMMA Neg. 120-108-6. *b*) Tlatel 57, Tx-TF-1. UMMA Neg. 120-20-5.

PLATE 18

a

b

Plate 18—*a*) Facing east across upper end of Tx-TF-1, and western edge of Tx-TF-2 along ridge crest. UMMA Neg. 120-108-5. *b*) Facing east across general area of Tx-TF-17. UMMA Neg. 120-40-6.

a

b

Plate 19—*a*) Section of Tlatel 317, Tx-TF-4. UMMA Neg. 120-54-3. *b*) Stone wall base, Tlatel 317, Tx-TF-4. UMMA Neg. 120-54-1.

a

b

Plate 20—*a*) Tlatel 119, Tx-TF-4. UMMA Neg. 120-34-4. *b*) Tlatel 145, Tx-TF-4. UMMA Neg. 120-41-4.

PLATE 21

a

b

Plate 21—*a*) and *b*) Ancient terracing in Tx-TF-4 site area. UMMA Neg. 120-37-2 and 120-54-6.

a

b

Plate 22—*a*) Tlatel 413, Tx-TF-14. UMMA Neg. 120-1-7-4. *b*) Looking north over general area of Tx-TF-14 site. UMMA Neg. 120-91-1, 120-91-2.

a

b

Plate 23—*a*) Facing WSW across general area of Tx-TF-36. UMMA Neg. 120-100-1. *b*) Abandoned terracing and old rock quarry below Tx-TF-51 site. UMMA Neg. 120-31-4.

a

b

Plate 24—*a*) General view of Tx-TF-46 site area, facing NNE. UMMA Neg. 120-7-4. *b*) Facing south from south edge of Tx-TF-46 site, toward village of Chimalhuacan. UMMA Neg. 120-3-2.

a

b

Plate 25—*a*) and *b*) Outlines of large walled compounds at Tx-TF-46. UMMA Neg. 120-98-1 and 120-97-3.

PLATE 26

a

b

Plate 26—*a*) and *b*) Stone wall bases at Tx-TF-46. UMMA Neg. 120-9-4 and 120-8-5.

a

b

Plate 27—*a*) Facing WNW across Tlatel 103, Tx-TF-51. UMMA Neg. 120-32-2. *b*) Tlatel 105, Tx-TF-51, UMMA Neg. 120-32-3.

a

b

Plate 28—*a*) Facing west across general area of Tx-ET-4. Tx-ET-5 is situated near left end of high ridge in background. UMMA Neg. 120-19-2. *b*) Tlatel 35, Tx-ET-4. UMMA Neg. 120-12-4.

a

b

Plate 29—*a*) Tlatel 161, Tx-ET-7, upper surface. UMMA Neg. 120-44-4. *b*) Tlatel 161, Tx-ET-7, profile of pit in center of mound showing contact between superimposed structures. UMMA Neg, 120-43-3.

a

b

Plate 30—*a*) Facing SE across general area of Tx-ET-18. UMMA Neg. 120-64-2. *b*) Facing west across general area of Tx-ET-18. UMMA Neg. 120-61-3.

PLATE 31

a

b

Plate 31—*a*) Tlatel 123, Tx-ET-18. UMMA Neg. 120-62-5. *b*) Tlatel 148, Tx-ET-18. UMMA Neg. 120-66-2.

a

b

Plate 32—*a*) Tlatel 130, Tx-ET-18. UMMA Neg. 120-63-4. *b*) Tlatel 131, Tx-ET-18. UMMA Neg. 120-63-5.

a

b

Plate 33—*a*) Tlatel 133, Tx-ET-18. UMMA Neg. 120-65-3. *b*) Tlatel 135, Tx-ET-18. UMMA Neg. 120-65-5.

a

b

Plate 34—*a*) Tlatel 159, Tx-ET-7. UMMA Neg. 120-42-3. *b*) Facing west across general area of Tx-ET-23. UMMA Neg. 120-33-4.

a

b

Plate 35—*a*) Lens of refuse at Tx-LT-25. UMMA Neg. 120-35-5. *b*) Tlatel 1, Tx-A-4, facing east. UMMA Neg. 120-1-2.

PLATE 36

a

b

Plate 36—*a*) Tlatel 229, Tx-A-24, showing typical example of badly eroded structure resting directly on tepetate sub soil. UMMA Neg. 120-52-3. *b*) Elaborate rock carving, along margin of Tx-A-24.

a

b

Plate 37—*a*) Tlatel 369, Tx-A-40. UMMA Neg. 120-55-2. *b*) Tlatel 613, Tx-A-26. UMMA Neg. 120-87-3.

a

b

Plate 38—*a*) Facing NW across Tlatel 17, Tx-A-56. UMMA Neg. 120-11-5. *b*) Facing south across Tlatel 18, Tx-A-56. UMMA Neg. 120-13-5.

a

b

Plate 39—*a*) Section of Tlatel 90, Tx-A-56 (Los Melones section). UMMA Neg. 120-36-4. *b*) Facing south across Tlatel 92, Tx-A-56. UMMA Neg. 120-39-1.

a

b

Plate 40—*a*) Facing west across Tx-A-43 site area. UMMA Neg. 120-27-4. *b*) Surface appearance of small room outlined by stone wall bases, Tlatel 209, Tx-A-72. UMMA Neg. 120-83-5.

PLATE 41

a

b

Plate 41—*a*) Stone canal leading into Reservoir at eastern end of Tyler's Causeway, Tx-A-62. UMMA Neg. 120-50-4. *b*) Facing west along stone canal which carried water from Reservoir onto Tyler's Causeway, Tx-A-62. Area D lies at western end of Tyler,s Causeway, at base of steep hill in background. UMMA Neg. 120-58-6.

PLATE 42

a

b

Plate 42—*a*) Facing NW across Tyler's Causeway, Tx-A-62. UMMA Neg. 120-49-2. *b*) Section of main canal and small lead-off canal, between Area D and Queen's Bath, Tx-A-62. UMMA Neg. 120-60-2.

a

b

Plate 43—*a*) Section of main canal, Tx-A-62, cut through rock near Queen's Bath. UMMA Neg. 120-68-4. *b*) Area C, Tx-A-62. UMMA Neg. 120-67-1.

a

b

Plate 44—*a*) King's Bath, Area B, Tx-A-62. UMMA Neg. 120-59-1. *b*) Queen's Bath, Tx-A-62. UMMA Neg. 120-68-5.

a

b

Plate 45—*a*) Area D, Tx-A-62. UMMA Neg. 120-69-5. *b*) Area E, Tx-A-62. UMMA Neg. 120-70-2.

PLATE 46

a

b

Plate 46—*a*) Area G, Tx-A-62. Ruler near feet of statue on left is six inches long. UMMA Neg. 120-71-2. *b*) Temple model, Tx-A-61. Ruler is six inches long. UMMA Neg. 120-51-5.

a

b

Plate 47—*a*) Facing ESE across area of abandoned terracing in Upper Piedmont zone, east-central section of survey area. UMMA Neg. 120-73-3. *b*) Section of recently uncovered stone face, possibly an ancient terrace. In Upper Piedmont zone, east-central section of survey area. UMMA Neg. 120-56-6.

a

b

Plate 48—*a*) Tlatel 19, Tx-A-87, showing plastered patio and stairway. UMMA Neg. 120-14-4. *b*) Section of room complex atop Tlatel 20, Tx-A-87. UMMA Neg. 120-16-4.

a

b

Plate 49—*a*) Tlatel 34, Tx-A-87, partially reconstructed. UMMA Neg. 120-24-1. *b*) Tlatel 31, Tx-A-87, partially reconstructed. UMMA Neg. 120-23-4.

a

b

Plate 50—*a*) Tlatel 43, Tx-A-87. UMMA Neg. 120-25-3. *b*) Reconstructed wall in northern section of Tx-A-87. UMMA Neg. 120-17-6.

a

b

Plate 51—*a*) Tlatel 171, Tx-A-99. UMMA Neg. 120-79-4. *b*) Section of Tx-A-109, lying beneath heavy modern occupation. UMMA Neg. 120-21-5.

a

b

Plate 52—*a*) Section of main pyramid at Tx-A-109, partially reconstructed. UMMA Neg. 120-28-5. *b*) Principal mound at Tx-A-88. UMMA Neg. 120-99-2.

a

b

Plate 53—*a*) Tlatel 154, Tx-A-100. UMMA Neg. 120-76-6. *b*) Tlatel 169, Tx-A-100. UMMA Neg. 120-78-5.

a

b

Plate 54—*a*) East face of Tlatel 167, Tx-A-100. UMMA Neg. 120-78-1. *b*) Section of stuccoed stairway on Tlatel 167, Tx-A-100. UMMA Neg. 120-77-2.

PLATE 55

a

b

c

Plate 55—*a*) Facing ENE across general area of Causeway B and modern water canal leading into San Miguel Tlaixpan. UMMA Neg. 120-81-6. *b*) Modern canal atop Causeway B. UMMA Neg. 120-82-3. *c*) Modern canal leading into Coatepec, near southeastern edge of survey area. UMMA Neg. 120-80-2.

PLATE 56

a

b

Plate 56—*a*) Facing north across length of Causeway A. UMMA Neg. 120-53-3. *b*) Facing north across Causeway C. UMMA Neg. 120-75-4.

a

b

Plate 57—*a*) Section of ancient canal atop Causeway C. Ruler is six inches long. UMMA Neg. 120-86-2. *b*) Section of ancient canal system above village of Purificación. UMMA Neg. 120-101-2.

No. 37. Obsidian Analyses and Prehistoric Near Eastern Trade: 7500 to 3500 B.C., by Gary A. Wright. Pages 92, 11 tables and 7 figures. Price $2.00.

No. 38. The Administration of Rural Production in an Early Mesopotamian Town, by Henry T. Wright, Contributions by Sandor Bokonyi, Kent V. Flannery and John Mayhall. Pages 162, 29 figures, 15 tables. Price $3.00.

No. 39. Rules of Descent: Studies in the Sociology of Parentage, by Guy E. Swanson. Pages 108, 4 figures, 7 tables. Price $2.00.

No. 40. Early Puebloan Occupations at Tesuque By-Pass and the Upper Rio Grande Valley, by Charles H. McNutt. Pages 140, 13 figures, 11 plates. Price $3.00.

No. 41. The Archaeology of Summer Island: Changing Settlement Systems in Northern Lake Michigan, by David S. Brose. 1970. Pages 236, 31 tables, 17 figures, 35 plates. Price $3.00.

No. 42. The Occupations of Migrants in Ghana, by Polly Hill. 1970. Pages 84, 11 tables. Price $2.00.

No. 43. Prehistoric Biological Relationships in the Great Lakes Region, by Richard Guy Wilkinson. 1971. Pages 168, 40 tables, 33 figures, 2 plates. Price $3.50.

MEMOIRS

No. 1. Prehistory and Human Ecology of the Deh Luran Plain. An Early Village Sequence from Khuzistan, Iran, by Frank Hole, Kent V. Flannery, and James A. Neely. Pages 504, 144 figures, 42 plates. Price $8.00.

No. 2. The Burial Complexes of the Knight and Norton Mounds in Illinois and Michigan by James B. Griffin, Richard E. Flanders and Paul F. Titterington. Pages 216, 177 plates. Price $7.00.

No. 3. Prehistoric Settlement Patterns in the Texcoco Region, Mexico, by Jeffrey R. Parsons. Pages 447, 8 tables, 14 maps, 88 figures. Price $8.00.

Primitive Man in Michigan, by W. B. Hinsdale, 1925. (Unbound) Michigan Handbook Series No. 1. Price $1.50.

Prehistoric Pottery of the Eastern United Stated, 3 parts. Price, $2.50. Each sold separately—$1.00.

MICHIGAN ARCHAEOLOGICAL SOCIETY MEMBERS RECEIVE A 25% DISCOUNT ABOVE BOOKS.